Iranian Weapons of
Mass Destruction

Iranian Weapons of Mass Destruction

The Birth of a Regional Nuclear Arms Race?

Anthony H. Cordesman and Adam C. Seitz

Published in Cooperation with the Center for Strategic and International Studies, Washington, D.C.

PRAEGER SECURITY INTERNATIONAL
An Imprint of ABC-CLIO, LLC

A B C   C L I O

Santa Barbara, California • Denver, Colorado • Oxford, England

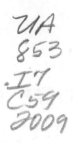
Copyright © 2009 by Center for Strategic and International Studies

All rights reserved. No portion of this book may be reproduced, stored in a
retrieval system, or transmitted, in any form or by any means, electronic, mechanical,
photocopying, recording, or otherwise, except for the inclusion of brief quotations in a
review, without prior permission in writing from the publisher.

Library of Congress Cataloging-in-Publication Data

Cordesman, Anthony H.
    Iranian weapons of mass destruction : the birth of a regional nuclear arms race? /
Anthony H. Cordesman and Adam C. Seitz.
        p. cm.
    Includes bibliographical references.
    ISBN 978–0–313–38088–4 (hard copy : alk. paper) — ISBN 978–0–313–38089–1 (ebook)
1. Nuclear weapons—Iran. 2. Weapons of mass destruction—Iran. 3. Iran—Military policy. 4.
Nuclear arms control—Iran. 5. Arms race—Middle East. 6. National security—Middle East. 7.
Middle East—Strategic aspects. I. Seitz, Adam C. II. Title.
UA853.I7C59   2009
358'.30955—dc22   2009018923

13 12 11 10 9   1 2 3 4 5

This book is also available on the World Wide Web as an eBook.
Visit www.abc-clio.com for details.

ABC-CLIO, LLC
130 Cremona Drive, P.O. Box 1911
Santa Barbara, California 93116-1911

This book is printed on acid-free paper ∞

Manufactured in the United States of America

Contents

Figures

1

Introduction

Iran presents the most serious single security challenge in the Middle East. Its actions pose a critical potential threat to a region that dominates the world's export of oil, gas, and petroleum products and help shape the ideological struggles within Islam. Its capabilities for asymmetric and proxy warfare have steadily expanded its power and influence in Iraq, Lebanon, Syria, and Afghanistan. Iran has also succeeded in building ties to hard-line Palestinian movements such as Hamas.

While Iran remains a relatively weak conventional military power, it has already compensated by building up power capabilities for asymmetric warfare in the Gulf region and by creating special elements in its Islamic Revolutionary Guards Corps to train and encourage the forces of groups such as Hezbollah. It has exploited its ability to export light weapons—including antitank and antiaircraft guided missiles —and artillery rockets, and even antiship missiles. The shaped-charge components and technology it provided to insurgents in Iraq were the single most lethal weapons technology in that fighting. The same was true of the Russian antitank guided weapons it supplied to Hezbollah before its war with Israel in 2006.

Iran can become a major regional military power, however, only if it can deploy long-range strike forces and equip them with weapons of mass destruction. Iran already has long-range missiles that can hit targets in much of the region and has systems with much greater range-payload in development. There are strong indications that Iran is reaching the breakout point in being able to build nuclear weapons and could be only years away from arming its missiles with nuclear warheads. The very risk of such actions may already have triggered changes in how Israel plans to structure and use its nuclear forces and is forcing the United States to choose between prevention, preemption, containment, and deterrence.

The pace of these developments has increased significantly in the last few years. At the same time, so has the complexity of Iranian actions. It is not possible to meaningfully address these actions and the risks they pose simply by focusing on Iran's nuclear programs. It is necessary to consider Iran's policies and politics, its command structure, how its search for weapons of mass destruction interacts with its missile and weapons delivery programs, and its options in developing and using other weapons of mass destruction such as chemical and biological warfare.

Iran's actions and capabilities to acquire and use weapons of mass destruction are also being shaped by at least four other major factors. One is the priority Iran is giving to medium- and long-range missiles. Another is the priority Iran is giving to irregular or asymmetric warfighting capabilities. A third is the slow pace of Iran's conventional military modernization and the decline in its conventional military strength relative to its neighbors and the United States. The fourth is its perception of its overall strategic posture relative to those neighbors and the United States.

This means it is necessary to take a net assessment approach to analyzing where these developments may lead. Iran's actions already are producing major U.S. and Israeli reactions and are beginning to trigger new military programs in its neighbor's forces such as missile defense. There are many kinds of arms races that can evolve out of Iran's actions, and each step forward that Iran takes will change the strategic map of the region and perhaps the world.

This analysis takes such an approach. In the process, it focuses on the details of what is and is not known about developments in Iran. These details matter when the stakes are this high, and so does a clear understanding of the level of uncertainty shaping virtually all of the key reporting on Iran's actions. It is easy to downplay or exaggerate, or to act as if it was possible to read the minds of Iran's leaders, have access to sensitive intelligence data, or translate suspicions and probabilities into facts. As this analysis makes clear, however, the unknowns or uncertainties are often the most important aspect of any valid analysis. Moreover, there is considerable evidence that Iran's actions will be opportunistic and driven by future events, rather than part of any fixed or coherent master plan. Accordingly, much of this study is a risk analysis, not a prophecy.

It should also be stressed that its content is heavily dependent on the work of other analysts and think tanks, which are referenced in the footnotes throughout this book. It also draws on the often uncertain work of Iranian opposition groups whose motives are obvious and whose credibility is not. In some cases, intelligence experts were kind enough to provide informal comments, as did other officials and military officers. None of this work, however, reflects any access to intelligence per se or to classified information of any kind. The reader should keep this firmly in mind. It simply is not practical to endlessly qualify every statement or repetitively flag the nature of every uncertainty.

Finally, the last chapter of this book may not be a prophecy, but it is a warning. Far too much of the current literature on the possibility that Iran may acquire nuclear weapons focuses only on proliferation and Iran's possession or nonpossession of a bomb. If Iran does go nuclear, however, it will trigger a massive series of changes in the regional military balance and may well push the Middle East and the United States into a new form of serious nuclear arms race. It is time to examine the potential warfighting impact of Iran's actions. It is also time to remember that history is not always a history of rational actors taking rational actions. The risks are so great that they can be existential for both Iran and Israel and threaten the entire global economy.

IRAN'S STEADILY LESS CONVINCING EFFORTS AT DENIAL

Iran's first efforts to acquire nuclear weapons technology were detected in the early 1970s, while the Shah (Mohammad Reza Pahlavi) was still in power. While Iran seems to have halted such efforts during the initial period of the Ruhollah Khomeini regime in the early 1980s, it changed its policies after Iraq began to use chemical weapons and long-range missiles during the Iran-Iraq War (1980–1988). By the mid-1980s, Iran was actively developing chemical weapons, acquiring ballistic missiles, and resumed its efforts to acquire nuclear technology with nuclear weapons applications.

Iran continues to deny that it has a nuclear weapons program, but has declared that it has chemical weapons as part of its obligations as a signatory to the Chemical Weapons Convention. Iran has never made a secret of its development of steadily larger and longer-range ballistic missiles, and for nearly a decade it has failed to fully comply with the efforts of the United Nations (UN) and the International Atomic Energy Agency (IAEA) to determine the true nature of its nuclear programs.

It has never been possible to prove that Iran has an active nuclear weapons program using material available in open sources, although a U.S. National Intelligence Estimate issued in 2007 declared that there was classified evidence that Iran had had an organized program and had suspended that program in 2003. Year after year, however, the IAEA has found new indicators of Iranian activities that Iran had not declared and has created a steadily longer list of incidents and weapons-related activities that Iran has failed to fully explain.

In terms of its missile capability, Iran is the only country not in possession of nuclear weapons to have produced or flight-tested missiles with ranges exceeding 1,000 kilometers.[1] Iran's continued expansion of the range of its ballistic missile programs further supports international concerns about Iran's nuclear ambitions and intentions.

IRAN'S PROGRESS TOWARD NUCLEAR-ARMED MISSILE CAPABILITY

At the same time, Iran has moved steadily closer to the ability to produce fissile material—the only thing it lacks to make nuclear weapons. While Iran has always managed to find some explanation for most of the activities the IAEA has challenged, the cumulative weight of evidence has grown so large that it is difficult not to believe that Iran is seeking to develop, manufacture, and deploy nuclear weapons and nuclear-armed missiles.

Iran has admitted it has chemical weapons, but has never properly declared its holdings of chemical weapons, and the status of its biological weapons program is unknown. Iran has, however, managed to conceal enough of its military activities and create enough ambiguity, so that there is no reliable way to characterize its ability to acquire weapons of mass destruction and improved means to deliver them or to estimate the current and future warfighting capabilities of Iran's chemical, biological, radiological, and nuclear weapons.

The situation is somewhat clearer in terms of delivery systems. Iran has long had long-range strike aircraft that can be used to deliver weapons of mass destruction, and its force development efforts since the end of the Iran-Iraq War have put a heavy and public emphasis on missiles. Iran already has ballistic missile forces capable of reaching targets throughout the Gulf region, its Shahab missiles have ranges in excess of 1,000 kilometers, and it is developing a range of new ballistic and cruise missile systems that can reach targets in Israel, Egypt, and Turkey, and deep into Europe. Iran has not, however, provided a public picture of whether it will arm its missiles with chemical, biological, radiological, and/or nuclear warheads.

In balance, Iran seems to be developing all of the capabilities necessary to deploy a significant number of nuclear weapons no later than 2020 and to mount them on missile systems capable of striking at targets throughout the region and beyond. It has reached a level of progress where it is conceivable that Iran could build its own nuclear device as early as 2009, although a time frame of 2011–2015 seems more likely for the deployment of actual weapons and nuclear-armed missile forces. Similarly, while Iran may not have a biological weapons program, it is already acquiring all of the equipment and core technology necessary to develop and manufacture them.

IRAN'S IMPACT ON THE REGIONAL MILITARY BALANCE

Iran's actions have already made major changes in the military balance in the Gulf and the Middle East. Iran may still be several years to half a decade away from becoming a meaningful nuclear power, but even the potential of Iranian nuclear weapons has led Iran's neighbors, the United States, and Israel to focus on an Iranian nuclear threat.

For the United States and Israel, this focus has led to the serious consideration of preventive war. The United States, however, is also examining options for defense and extended deterrence. So is Israel, with the fundamental difference that it sees Iran as a potential existential threat to its very existence.

For the Gulf States, and nations such as Turkey, the prospect of a nuclear Iran has led to consideration of the acquisition of nuclear weapons and missile defenses. All have sought to find diplomatic solutions to halting Iran's program and creating inspection regimes that can ensure that Iran does not covertly develop nuclear weapons or a breakout capability.

At the same time, none of the states involved can count on diplomacy succeeding, and the odds of success have slowly declined as Iran's nuclear and missile capabilities have moved forward. Neither "carrots," such as security and economic incentives, nor "sticks," such as UN sanctions and economic constraints, have so far had much success. The end result is that military options such as preventive war, deterrence, defense, and the ability to actually fight a nuclear exchange in ways that would cripple or destroy Iran receive steadily greater attention.

IRREGULAR WARS AND "WARS OF INTIMIDATION"

Iran's progress toward a nuclear weapons capability has had additional effects. Every state dealing with Iran must decide whether some form of accommodation is possible and consider its relations with Iran in the context of dealing with a future nuclear power. While a state such as Israel may focus on warfighting, other states—particularly Iran's neighbors—must increasingly deal with an Iran that can use nuclear weapons as a tacit or overt threat to bring pressure upon them. Even the future prospect of an Iranian weapon gives Iran added leverage in the wars of intimidation that shape much of the real-world behavior of nations in the region.

Iran's progress toward nuclear weapons capability also interacts with its growing capability for irregular or asymmetric warfare. It is one thing to deal with Iran's use of its Islamic Revolutionary Guards Corps when Iran is a relatively weak conventional power. It is another thing to risk taking decisive action, or retaliating in force against Iran's use of irregular warfare, when this risks creating lasting tension with a future nuclear power—or the risk of escalation if Iran actually deploys a nuclear capability. Furthermore, Iran's ties to Syria, influence in Iraq, links to Hezbollah, and relations with Hamas raise the specter that Iran not only can use proxies to help it fight irregular wars, but also to help it in some future covert delivery of nuclear weapons.

Unlike the Cold War, the shifts in the regional balance caused by Iran's potential nuclear weapons capabilities cannot be simplified into some form of "zero sum game." There is a wide range of different players with different interests both inside and outside the region. There are no clear rules to the game, or even knowledge of when and whether the game will exist. The playing field also includes critical additional areas such as the Afghan and Iraqi wars, the security of energy exports that are critical to the global economy, and the emerging role of China and Russia. Wild cards such as North Korea and Pakistan, the internal politics of the UN, and the weakening of the U.S. structure of global influence and alliance add still further complications.

THE PROBLEM OF TIME AND COMPLEXITY

Finally, any realistic examination of Iran's nuclear options must look beyond the issue of whether or not Iran crosses the nuclear threshold. It is dangerous to focus on arms control, diplomatic prevention, and preventive war; Iran in 2008 is not Iraq in 1981. Iran has had decades to build up a technology base. Iran has demonstrated that it has at least three different centrifuge designs and that it can now build every element of the production cycle needed to develop weapons-grade U-235 and the components of fission weapons from a highly dispersed industrial base scattered throughout the country.

There is no way to be certain of Iran's progress or the ability of various intelligence agencies to analyze it. There has been a flood of unclassified analysis, much of it contradictory and with extremely dubious sources, if any. Yet, there have been few meaningful official reports on Iran's efforts. The closest thing to unclassified intelligence has been a few summary statements by senior U.S. intelligence officials and a few pages of declassified summary judgments from the National Intelligence Estimate issued in 2007—judgments so ambiguous and badly written that their meaning has been a subject of continuing debate.

As a result, it is impossible to know how well the intelligence community can analyze and predict Iran's capabilities and how well it can target Iran's forces and facilities. It is equally impossible to determine how lethal any preventive or preemptive strikes can be, how large an attack force might be required, what level of battle damage assessment is really possible, how many restrikes might be required, and what level of persistent surveillance and restrike activity might be needed to achieve a given level of destruction or suppression of Iran's capabilities.

These uncertainties do not mean that there are not workable military options. It may well be possible to seriously delay Iran's efforts and make them more costly and inefficient. At the same time, it is far from clear that prevention is really possible through either diplomatic or military means.

Even successful diplomatic negotiations might lead Iran to dismantle its known facilities while creating, or strengthening, a covert program that any negotiable IAEA inspection regime might fail to detect or verify convincingly enough to lead to decisive international action. Even relatively successful Israeli or U.S. preventive strikes might also end in failure. Iran may have advanced to the point where a determined Iranian government can carry out an indigenous nuclear program in three to five years that supplies at least a few nuclear weapons.

Iran has already shown it has mobile long-range ballistic missiles and is working on cruise missiles. Iran is already deploying an active missile force that could be rapidly turned into a nuclear-armed force, which could then be used in the launch-on-warning or launch-under attack mode—greatly increasing the risks of any preventive or preemptive strike on Iran. The same would be true of arming aircraft and putting them into the same kind of quick reaction mode—one NATO (North Atlantic Treaty Organization) has used through most of its existence.

It is also possible that if Iran is prevented from creating an effective nuclear force, it might be willing to take the risk of planning for covert nuclear strikes, or turning nuclear weapons over to proxies such as Hezbollah. Furthermore, Iran will increasingly have the option of creating an even more covert and unpredictable biological weapons program at a time when technology and equipment for far more advanced and lethal weapons is now becoming available. Nuclear weapons may be the most lethal technology of the twentieth century, but it is far from clear that they will be the most lethal option in the first decades of the twenty-first century.

None of these possibilities are reasons to reject diplomatic options or assume that preventive military action will fail. They are convincing reasons to assume that such options will not necessarily succeed and to show great reservation about simplistic media reports or war plans or speculation by analysts who have no access to intelligence or expertise in real-world war planning.

They also are reasons to consider a future in which Iran at a minimum develops a serious degree of nuclear ambiguity, where no one can be certain whether it has a rapid nuclear breakout capability or a few hidden nuclear devices or "bombs in the basement." Even apparent success in negotiating with Iran, or in executing preventive military options, could also lead to a future where Iran slowly moves toward an actual test, deployment of weapons, and a steadily improving and less vulnerable nuclear weapons delivery capability.

The situation has already evolved beyond the point where the key question for policy making is whether Iran's neighbors, the United States and Israel, and the world can live with a nuclear-armed Iran. It is far from clear that Iran's neighbors, the United States and Israel, and the world have a choice. Iran has already created the equivalent of a game of three-dimensional chess in which there are far more than two players, where no player can see the full situation on the board, and each player has the latitude to make up at least some of the rules without bothering to communicate them to the other players. The fact that no one likes complexity or nuclear threats does not make war avoidable, and the same is true of games that have no predictable rules or end.

———————————————————————————————————

2

Policy, Doctrine, and Command

Iran presents many challenges in analyzing its efforts to acquire weapons of mass destruction. One is that a nation that denies it is acquiring such weapons does not have a public strategy or doctrine for using them, much less clear plans to acquire them. A second is that Iran has an extremely complex national command authority, where many key elements virtually bypass its president—as well as other national decision-making apparatuses—and report to its Supreme Leader.

Iran also seems to place its missile systems, and much of its military industry under its Islamic Revolutionary Guards Corps (IRGC), and it is this force that seems to be responsible for the development and control of any programs to develop, manufacture, and deploy weapons of mass destruction. Making this situation all the more complex and volatile is the growing influence of the IRGC—especial hard-line members—in the Iranian political arena.

IRAN'S POLICY AND DOCTRINE

Iran's public policy toward weapons of mass destruction is one that claims Iran is pursuing the path toward arms control and does not intend to deploy such weapons. Unlike its capabilities in asymmetric warfare, where Iran's political and military leaders make many public statements about Iran's intentions and policies, Iran consistently denies it has nuclear weapons, states that it no longer has chemical weapons, and states that it has rejected the option of developing biological weapons. In case after case affecting Iran's efforts to develop weapons of mass destruction, there is no clear data on its intentions as well as no reliable or unambiguous data on its actions and capabilities.

At the same time, Iran's leaders do make extreme statements about many security issues. If these statements are taken at face value, they can be interpreted to show that Iran may be hard or impossible to deter, might be reckless in escalating in a crisis, and might use weapons of mass destruction against Israel. It is more likely that such statements are designed to deter or intimidate outside powers, to reassure Iranians, and are for domestic political consumption, but this is no certainty. The fact that leaders use extreme language is no historical guarantee that they do not mean what they say.

Iran's Rhetoric of Denial

As will be discussed in detail in later chapters, Iranian leaders have been so consistent in denying that Iran has or would use weapons of mass destruction since the end of the Iran-Iraq War that it is almost redundant to present a range of such statements. At the same time, it is equally possible to trade an almost endless list of extreme statements regarding what Iran would do in war, and a list of threats to Israel and the United States.

Nuclear Weapons

Ayatollah Ali Khamenei, President Mahmoud Ahmadinejad, and other ranking Iranian decision makers continue to deny that Iran has, or intends to create, a nuclear weapons program. At the same time, they advocate the destruction of Israel and its supporters—and make other extreme and threatening statements—making it difficult to decipher what Iran's true intentions and policy are in regard to its nuclear ambitions.

Some of the efforts by Iranian officials to clarify their public religious and political views on nuclear weapons have, however, been issued in ways that create confusion about Tehran's actual intentions. In an August 10, 2005, statement to an emergency International Atomic Energy Agency (IAEA) meeting, then Iranian nuclear negotiator Sirus Naseri read a statement to the IAEA Board of Governors from the Islamic Republic, which asserted the following:

> The Leader of the Islamic Republic of Iran, Ayatollah Ali Khamenei has issued a fatwa that the production, stockpiling, and use of nuclear weapons are forbidden under Islam and that the Islamic Republic of Iran shall never acquire these weapons. President Mahmud Ahmadinejad, who took office just recently, in his inaugural address, reiterated that his government is against weapons of mass destruction and will only pursue nuclear activities in the peaceful domain.[1]

The reported fatwa seems to have been issued by Ayatollah Khamenei in September 2004 at Friday prayers. Yet, one month later, Iranian legislator Hojatoleslam Mohammad Taqi Rahbar asserted that the bill to ban nuclear weapons was "not expedient," because Iran is in a region of proliferators. He went on to say that "there are no Shari'a or legal restrictions on having such [nuclear] weapons as a deterrent."[2]

More recently, Iran's Supreme Leader Ayatollah Ali Khamenei asserted on June 3, 2008, that "no wise nation" would pursue nuclear weapons, but also stated that Iran would continue to develop a nuclear program for peaceful purposes.[3]

Chemical and Biological Weapons

Statements and actions by ranking Iranian officials have made it equally difficult to assess Iran's intentions regarding its chemical weapons programs, and any analysis of Iran's biological weapons effort must be even more speculative than an analysis of its chemical and nuclear weapons efforts and the details of its missile programs.

As might be expected, Iran has continually denied that it has active chemical or biological weapons programs, and it is a party to the Chemical Weapons Convention (CWC) and Biological Weapons Convention.

Iranian decision makers have often made statements that condemn the use of chemical weapons, while at the same time advocating the strategic and tactical advantages of possessing such weapons, as well as Iran's right to possess this "defensive" capability—to an extent echoing their public stance on nuclear weapons policy.

In 1988, Ayatollah Ali Akbar Rafsanjani was quoted as saying that "chemical and biological weapons are a poor man's atomic bombs and can easily be produced. We should at least consider them at least for our defense; although the use of such weapons is inhumane, the [Iran-Iraq] war taught us that international laws are only scraps of paper."[4]

Ayatollah Rafsanjani has made many statements to this effect. Another such statement that gets at the heart of the Iranian perspective of the need for a chemical and biological weapons program follows:

> With regard to chemical, bacteriological, and radiological weapons training, it was made very clear perhaps during the [Iran-Iraq] war that these weapons are very decisive. It was also made clear that the moral teachings of the world are not very effective when war reaches a serious stage and the world does not respect its own resolutions and closes its eyes to the violations and the aggressions which are committed on the battlefield. We should fully equip ourselves both in the offensive and defensive use of chemical, bacteriological, and radiological weapons. From now on you should make use of the opportunity and perform the task.[5]

Iran's Ambassador to the 3rd Conference of States Parties (CSP) to the CWC, which was held in the Hague in November 1998, stated that Iran had worked on chemical weapons during the Iran-Iraq War, but that "following the establishment of the cease fire (in July 1998), the decision to develop chemical weapons capabilities was reversed and the process was terminated."

H.E. Dr. G. Ali Khoshro, then Iranian Deputy Foreign Minister of Legal and International Affairs, made a similar statement to a CWC Review Conference held in April and May 2003:

> I have to recall the fact that due to the lack of reaction by the international community against Iraqi chemical weapons attack during the 8 year imposed war, in the last phase we got the chemical capabilities, but we did not use it, and following the cease fire we decided to dismantle. We did destroy the facilities under the supervision of the OPCW

[Organisation for the Prohibition of Chemical Weapons] inspectors and we got the certificate of the destruction of CWPF [chemical weapons production facility].[6]

Some official statements have contradicted their previous statements or other official's statements, regarding Iran's CW program. One such example of this is comments made by Iranian nuclear negotiator Saeed Jalil to the United Nations (UN), which contradict statements made by Ambassador Mohammad R. Alborzi, director general of the Iranian Foreign Ministry, to the OPCW regarding Iran's chemical weapons history.

On 23 January 2008, speaking in Brussels Iranian nuclear negotiator Saeed Jalil states that: "I assure you that the (chemical) weapons have no place in our defense doctrine." The context is made in the context of a discussion about Iranian actions during the Iran-Iraq war of 1980–1988 and is intended to support the proposition that Iran made no use of chemical weapons during that conflict. [This assertion may contradict a statement made at the OPCW in 1998 that Iran possessed CW in the latter stages of the war.][7]

But previously, on 18 November 1998, Ambassador Mohammad R. Alborzi, director general of the Iranian Foreign Ministry, delivered Iran's CW declaration during a session of the Conference of the States Parties (CSP) to the CWC in The Hague, Netherlands. In his statement, he admitted for the first time that Iran had once possessed CW, in the waning years of the Iran-Iraq War. But he claims that, "... following the establishment of cease fire, the decision to develop chemical weapons capabilities was reversed and the process was terminated."[8]

Iran's Rhetoric of Extremism

One can find many examples of extreme rhetoric from Iran's leaders and senior officers. It should be noted, however, that they do not make explicit threats to use weapons of mass destruction and that much of its most extreme rhetoric is issued in a context where it has little operational meaning and poses little risk to Iran. Nevertheless, this extreme and threatening rhetoric amid Iran's progressing nuclear and missiles programs creates further insecurity in a region plagued by ongoing violent conflicts. The most extreme of these statements have been directed toward Israel and its supporters.

Over the past several years, Iranian leaders—most prominently Iranian President Mahmoud Ahmadinejad—have made numerous statements calling for the destruction of Israel and the Jewish people. Some examples of such extreme rhetoric follow:

In a Friday sermon on December 15, 2000 (shown on Iranian TV), Ahmadinejad declared, "Iran's position, which was first expressed by the Imam [Khomeini] and stated several times by those responsible, is that the cancerous tumor called Israel must be uprooted from the region."[9]

A little over a year later on January 15, 2001, at a meeting with organizers of the International Conference for Support of the Intifada, Ahmadinejad stated, "The foundation of the Islamic regime is opposition to Israel and the perpetual subject of Iran is the elimination of Israel from the region."[10] Iranian journalist Kasra Naji translated this sentence from the original Farsi as follows: "It is the mission of the Islamic Republic of Iran to erase Israel from the map of the region."[11]

It is important to note that these statements were made prior to Ahmadinejad's election to the second highest office behind the Supreme Leader—and the highest democratically elected office—in the Islamic Republic of Iran. The election of such a hard-line candidate, whose extremist rhetoric was widely known throughout Iran, can thus be seen as having similar extremist opinions as the electorate of Iran.

In an address to the "World without Zionism" Conference held in Tehran on October 26, 2005, Iranian President Mahmoud Ahmadinejad stated that "our dear Imam [Khomeini] ordered that this Jerusalem occupying regime [Israel] must be erased from the page of time. This was a very wise statement."[12]

In a February 2008 message to Hassan Nasrallah, Secretary General of Hezbollah, the Commander of the Islamic Revolutionary Guard Corps, General Mohammad-Ali Jafari, wrote, "In the near future, we will witness the destruction of the cancerous microbe Israel by the strong and capable hands of the nation of Hezbollah."[13]

Ayatollah Ahmad Janati, a member of President Ahmadinejad's inner circle and Chairman of the Guardian Council of the Constitution, told reporters during the 22 of Bahman parade (marking the anniversary of the 1979 Islamic Revolution of Iran) that "every year there is a bigger crowd, the slogans are more enthusiastic, and the Islamic regime's situation is getting better and better." He then added that "the blind enemies should see that the wish of these people is the death of America and Israel."[14]

Yahya Rahim Safavi, one of the "hard-core" founders of the IRGC and its former commander in chief, is now senior advisor to Supreme Leader Khamenei. In a speech in February 2008, he declared that "with God's help the time has come for the Zionist regime's death sentence."[15]

Safavi has also continually referred to Israel as impure, unhygienic, and contaminated. In remarks at a memorial ceremony for assassinated terrorist Imad Mughniyeh held in the city of Hamadan on February 23, 2008, he stated that the "death of this unclean regime [Israel] will arrive soon following the revolt of Muslims."[16]

There is, however, another side to Iranian rhetoric that is more cautious and balanced, if sometimes self-contradictory. In 2005, Khamenei began a concerted effort to limit the damage done to Iran by Ahmedinejad's rhetoric by insisting that Iran did not seek the military destruction of Israel, and a senior adviser to Iranian Supreme Leader Ayatollah Ali Khamenei warned that provocative Iranian statements could hurt the country's cause in its nuclear dispute.[17]

But this did not stop Hossein Shariatmadari, a close confidant of Khamenei who serves as one of his major mouthpieces, who wrote an editorial in the Iranian daily Kayhan on October 30, 2005, in which he argued, "We declare explicitly that we will not be satisfied with anything less than the complete obliteration of the Zionist regime from the political map of the world."[18] On October 4, 2007, Shariatmadari stated, " 'Death to America' and 'Death to Israel' are not only words written on paper but rather a symbolic approach that reflects the desire of all the Muslim nations."[19]

It may be that Khamenei toned down his own rhetoric, but allowed his hand-picked editor-in-chief of *Kayhan* to maintain his original ideological position on the destruction of Israel to the Iranian public, or Khamenei may be leaving the possibility of improving relations with the West while simultaneously preaching against the state of Israel and its allies including the "morally corrupt" United States.

In a January 3, 2008, address to students in Yazd, Ayatollah Khamenei said,

> Cutting ties with America is among our basic policies. However, we have never said that the relations will remain severed forever . . . the conditions of the American government are such that any relations would prove harmful to the nation and thereby we are not pursuing them . . . any relations would provide the possibility to the Americans to infiltrate Iran and would pave the way for their intelligence and spy agents . . . relations with America has no benefit for the Iranian nation for now. Undoubtedly, the day the relations with America prove beneficial for the Iranian nation I will be the first one to approve of that.[20]

Former president Khatami has also presented more moderate views. In a speech at the University of Gilan on May 3, 2008, Khatami addressed how the Islamic Republic should export revolution. He asked,

> What did the Imam [Khomeini] want, and what was his purpose of exporting the revolution? [Did he wish that] we should export revolution by means of gunpowder or groups sabotaging other countries? . . . He [Khomeini] meant to establish a role model here, which means people should see that in this society, the economy, science, and dignity of man are respected . . . This was the most important way of exporting the revolution."[21]

By proposing that Tehran should expand its influence more by soft power than by insurgency, Khatami tacitly acknowledged that the sponsorship of militias, insurgency, and terrorism enjoys state sanction and does not constitute rogue behavior.

Iranian officials disapproved of Khatami's acknowledgment of these activities, and 77 members of the Majlis called for the Ministry of Intelligence and Security to investigate Khatami, in an attempt to maintain plausible deniability.[22]

In balance, the actions of Iran's leaders have also implied that they are more cautious than some of their words imply. Most seem to be aware of the risks of hard-line rhetoric, and their actions generally seem cautious and pragmatic. It also seems clear that lower-ranking actors within the Iranian national security system rarely dare to conduct operations without at least tacit approval of the senior leadership. In fact, individuals hesitate to make decisions without authorization from above.

This emphasis on consensus makes "rogue operations" by security officials unlikely. This scarcely means, however, that it is possible to predict how Iran's leaders will behave once they have significant numbers of nuclear weapons and missiles, or how their subordinates would behave if the leadership was lost, became divided, or could not communicate.

THE IMPACT OF IRAN'S NATIONAL COMMAND STRUCTURE

It is equally difficult to be certain of the way Iran's leaders approach the development of missiles and weapons of mass destruction, and Iran's national command structure presents significant uncertainties. Much depends on interpersonal dynamics, and access to the Supreme Leader. More formally, Iran's command-and-control structure is one of overlapping and parallel structures that confuse Iranians and foreign observers alike.

Decision Making in Iran

Identifying the key decision makers in Iran is desirable in assessing risks, in trying to establish lines of accountability, and in seeking to ensure that any Western diplomatic outreach is targeted at those who have the power to affect regime behavior. Unfortunately, it often is not clear where power really resides and the exact role of hard-line elements is hard to determine. So is how Iran's leadership structure actually functions, how it views any specific approach to acquiring weapons of mass destruction, and how various elements compete for power.

Major policies—such as confrontation with the United States and Israel, or support for radicals abroad—seem to require consensus among the regime's leadership, but the implementations of agreed policies may vary widely due to the intertwining of Iran's formal and informal decision-making processes, as well as the disconnect this creates in the implementation of policies.

The names of officials who hold formal positions in Iran's power structure are clear. In early 2009, for example, the names of the senior officials in overt decision-making positions were the figures listed in Figure 2.1.

Figure 2.1   Key Iranian Decision-Making Figures

Chief of State: Supreme Leader (Faqih) Ayatollah Ali Hoseini Khamenei
Head of Government: President Mahmoud Ahmedinejad[23]
Speaker of the Majlis (Parliament): Ali Larijani[24]
Head of the Expediency Council: Hashemi Rafsanjani[25]
First Vice President: Parviz Davudi
Chairman of the Guardian Council of the Constitution: Ayatollah Ahmad Janati
Iran's Chief Nuclear Negotiator: Saeed Jalili[26]
Spokesman for Iran's Supreme National Security Council (SNSC): Ahmad Khademolmelleh
Supreme Leader's Representative to the IRGC: Mullah Saeedi (dep. Mullah Mojtaba Zolnouri)
Head of the IRGC's Political Bureau: Brigadier General Yadollah Javani
Iranian Foreign Minister: Manouchehr Mottaki
Deputy Interior Minister: Mohammad-Baqer Zolqadr[27]
Chief of Staff of the Armed Forces: Major General Hassan Firouzabadi
Special Military Advisor to Khamenei: Yahya Rahim Safavi[28]

The National Command Authority and Formal Decision-Making Institutions

At least on paper, Iran has a coherent formal structure for security decision making. Iran's institutional structure also reinforces oversight, or at least knowledge, of security operations. The Iranian constitution endows the Supreme Leader with tremendous authority over all major state institutions, and Khamenei has found many other ways to further increase his influence.

In practice, the executive, legislative, and judicial branches of government all operate under the authority of the Supreme Leader. He seems to be the final decision maker in all major national security decisions, and this seems to include the acquisition of weapons of mass destruction, doctrine and plans for using them, and the authorization of their use in war.

Khamenei's Growing Authority

Khamenei is the head of state, the commander in chief, and the Islamic Republic's top cleric. Indeed Article 57 of the Iranian constitution grants the Supreme Leader absolute power, stating that the "powers of government in the Islamic Republic are vested in the legislature, the judiciary, and the executive powers, functioning under the supervision of the absolute religious leader." Moreover, the Council of Guardians, the constitution's official interpreter, has ruled that this clause defines only the Supreme Leader's minimum prerogatives.[29]

Despite the theocratic basis of the state of Iran, it does have some democratic characteristics. At the same time, elections have little meaning if the opposition is not allowed to run, and the elected have little power. Iranian democracy is severely constrained by the authoritarian aspects of Islamic rule. Under the constitution of the Islamic Republic of Iran and the system of Velayat-e-Faqih on which it is based, the ultimate power in Iran resides in the religious authority, the Faqih and his office; which rely on the IRGC to enforce their will.[30] This relationship between Iran's clerical leadership and the IRGC has become increasingly important to help it stave off internal pressure for political and economic reform as well as external pressure resulting from international concern over Iran's nuclear program.

Khamenei has used his broad mandate to exercise control not only over all three branches of government but also economic, religious, and cultural affairs through a range of government councils and representatives, such as the IRGC—whose commander in chief is appointed by the Supreme Leader—and the political guides he imbeds in the IRGC headquarters.[31] Also Khamenei has made anti-Americanism the cornerstone of his Islamic ideology to fall back on and rally the Muslim world behind him and retain his legitimacy as the Supreme Leader.

Although many Iranians may disapprove of Khamenei as a leader, he has succeeded in expanding his power and his influence in the Islamic world. According to a study by Karim Sadjadpour at Carnegie Endowment for International Peace, several factors have helped Khamenei consolidate power domestically:[32]

- A vast network of commissars stationed in strategic posts throughout government bureaucracies, dedicated to enforcing his authority

- The weak, conservative-dominated parliament, headed by Khamenei loyalist GholamAli Haddad-Adel (whose daughter is married to the Leader's son)

- The rapidly rising political and economic influence of the Revolutionary Guards, whose top leaders are directly appointed by Khamenei and have always been publicly deferential to him

- The political disengagement of Iran's young population, prompted by the unfulfilled expectations of the reformist era

- Most significant, the 2005 presidential election, which saw hard-liner Ahmadinejad trounce Khamenei's chief rival Hashemi Rafsanjani in a second round run-off

The Relative Roles of the President and the Supreme Leader

The Supreme Leader has influence in both the formal governmental security organizations as well as in the IRGC and its subordinate entities. The president exercises only indirect influence over the IRGC and its subordinate entities through the Ministry of Defense.

The president of Iran does exercise considerable day-to-day authority and has formal control of budget planning, but the Supreme Leader's power makes him a far more important official in shaping both Iran's security policies and its civil society. Under article 110 of the 1979 constitution, the Supreme Leader retains the constitutional right to declare war and call for general troop mobilization. He is also the supreme commander of both the IRGC and the regular army (Artesh).[33]

The Supreme Leader has the power to override any decision that the elected government makes, including the president. The religious authority also vets all candidates for any public office, and those deemed insufficiently Islamic or insufficiently supportive of the regime are barred from running.[34]

Presidential and parliamentary candidates must pledge in writing that they are committed, in theory and in practice, to the Iranian constitution, Islam, the absolute sovereignty of the Supreme Leader, and the late Khomeini.[35] This process gives the Supreme Leader control over who is selected to run for office, while still giving legitimacy to the governing bodies through an electoral process. A major lever of power is the Supreme Leader's ability to appoint and dismiss senior government officials.

The Iranian president appoints the cabinets, but they remain subservient to the Council of Guardians and the Expediency Discernment Council. The Council of Guardians also has the authority to veto any law approved by the Majlis—a power that the president does not even possess. But despite these authoritarian characteristics, most Iranians perceive the regime as legitimate.[36]

The Supreme Leader receives advice on national security and defense matters from two military officers in his office, and he receives reports on foreign affairs from a foreign affairs advisor. Although the Faqih is the commander in chief of the armed forces, he disposes of his responsibilities toward the defense establishment not through any direct chain of command. According to the formal system, the Faqih works through other bodies in exercising his control.

The SCNS, which is chaired by the president, is the key national defense and security assessment body. Representatives of the Artesh, the IRGC, other security agencies, and the Faqih sit on the council.

In short, the president's role in policy making is limited compared to those of the Supreme Leader. Major policy issues, such as Iran's nuclear program, are largely in the hands of the Supreme Leader and not the president. Other shifts in policy, such as Iran improving relationship with the West—namely, the United States and Israel, are also left largely to the Supreme Leader. Furthermore, any major policy shift by Iran would not come from a change in the Iranian presidency, but from a change in policy instituted by the Supreme Leader.

Informal Decision-Making Mechanisms

More broadly, almost every aspect of Iran's formal decision-making process can be ignored or bypassed in favor of personal relationships and interactions. Family, kinship, educational affiliations, and support from various clerical personalities and factions play a central role in military politics in general, for both the IRGC and the Artesh. Personal networks are almost always stronger than institutional power.[37]

Revolutionary organizations, which together may control more than half the state budget, operate outside the purview of Iran's executive structure.[38] The judiciary is also a power center, able to wield immense influence beyond even the confines of the court system.

Iran may develop better structured approaches to defining its national command authority if it acquires significant nuclear forces. Today, however, Iran's institutions overlap both on paper and in reality. The IRGC and the Artesh have duplicate services, further confused by overlap with Iran's intelligence and clerical bodies.

It is hard to tell whether the advantages of this system outweigh the liabilities. Multiple security institutions do make a successful coup or takeover far more difficult. The problem is that the overlapping nature of the security institutions also makes a coherent security policy far more difficult and can create serious problems in a crisis or war.[39]

The Growing Role of the IRGC

Iran's security organizations are numerous, often overlapping and have an uncertain command-and-control structure. Iranian decision making is misleading and confusing on paper and the reality is far more complex. The many informal mechanisms, and the importance of individual ties, make it difficult to give transparency to Iranian command, control, and decision-making apparatuses.

It is the IRGC, however, that seems to control the critical aspects of Iran's efforts to develop and deploy weapons of mass destruction, and which seems likely to establish the chain of command to the Supreme Leader for control over the storage, use, and release of such weapons. The IRGC has always had an informal role in Iran's decision-making apparatus, but the IRGC has become a leading political force with influence over Tehran's policy-making bodies.

The IRGC routinely exploits its access to the Supreme Leader's office, volunteers advice on national and foreign policy matters to the Leader and his key staff, and actively aims to influence policy and debate on security issues. The IRGC also exercises its influence through contact with conservative-leaning clergy in Qom, who have considerable influence in the judiciary, the Interior Ministry, the Expediency Council, and the Council of Guardians.[40]

The White House and the Department of State, under the Clinton and Bush administrations, have sometimes treated the IRGC as if it were a rogue element of the Iranian system. However, the IRGC's evolution and role suggest that the group has seldom engaged in activities not sanctioned by the Iranian leadership. In reality, the IRGC represents the core of the Iranian state, and Iran's reformists are those who, by acting on their own without either state support or any ability to deliver on promises are, in the Iranian context, the true rogue elements.

A Broadening Role in Politics and Government

The IRGC became a major political force in the 2004 parliamentary elections, when a number of ex-servicemen were allowed to run for elections by the conservative Guardian Council. Ahmadinejad's victory in the 2005 presidential elections seems to have expanded this political role, although there often seem to be tensions between the president and the Supreme Leader.

Ahmadinejad is an ex-member of the IRGC and has surrounded himself with a number of other ex-IRGC officers as well as has developed ties to some active IRGC commanders. The IRGC further expanded its political role in the 2008 parliamentary, and the subsequent appointment of active and retired IRGC elites into key decision-making positions and bodies has strengthened the formal and active role of the IRGC in Iranian politics.

A look at the structure and personnel of the Iranian government and its history of involvement in terrorism and insurgency demonstrates that the IRGC and the Qods Force are, in fact, the opposite of rogues—they are deliberate creations of the Islamic Republic's government, are tightly controlled by the government, and exist to serve the government's policy objectives in Iran and abroad.

Many in the Islamic Republic's current leadership—at least the nonclerical portion—spent their formative years at the front serving with the Revolutionary Guards.[41] As they enter politics, these IRGC members operate not only according to the official hierarchy, but also according to the extensive networks they developed during their IRGC service.

Khamenei's Control over the IRGC

Supreme Leader Khamenei uses several kinds of leverage to control the IRGC. First, as the commander in chief of the armed forces, he appoints the IRGC's commander in chief and chief officers. Second, as the Islamic Republic's Supreme Leader, he controls a vast web of representative offices imbedded in the IRGC provincial commands.

This network of Khamenei's representatives in offices at the various IRGC headquarters operates parallel to the IRGC's command structure. These representative offices form an extensive organization with tens of thousands of members, who control the IRGC and align it to Khamenei's guidelines. These appointed representatives report directly to Khamenei.

The purpose of these "political guides" is to maintain high-level control over and oversight of the IRGC's more senior officers and commanders. Their task is to control and ensure adherence among IRGC ranks to the political and ideological guidelines of the regime's Supreme Leader. They are also responsible for selecting and training suicide bombers and overseeing IRGC personnel in order to ensure that they comply with Khamenei's guidelines and policies.

According to reports by the National Council of Resistance of Iran (NCRI)—an organization that the U.S. Department of State reports has strong ties to a terrorist group called the Mujahadin-e Khalq Organization (MEK), Khamenei's chief representative at the IRGC in 2008 was Mullah Saeedi.[42]

Saeedi appointed Mullah Mojtaba Zolnouri as his deputy. He also created a commanding unit for the Supreme Leader division. During the restructuring of the IRGC, Mullah Saeedi appointed a provincial "political guide" for each province of the 31 provinces to work alongside the provincial IRGC commander.

These provincial representatives report to the Supreme Leader's office in Tehran. Each of the representatives stationed at a provincial brigade has a distinct headquarters, which includes the departments of "supervision," "political and ideological guidance," "public relations," "administrative and finance," along with a "political bureau." The political bureau is responsible for fundamentalist ideological training and reviewing the files of IRGC personnel to evaluate their credentials for promotion.[43]

Mullah Saeedi told Iran's official IRNA news agency that "the purpose of creating these political guides in the Passdaran was to perform an effective role in increasing the participation of the public in the elections."[44] These political guides are comprised of mullahs and IRGC personnel at the political bureau. They can also be seen as lying on the already blurred line of Iran's formal and informal decision-making apparatuses within the IRGC and the Iranian government.

The relationship between the IRGC and the Supreme Leader gives the IRGC more influence in the Iranian government and the policy-making process, while at the same time it helps the Supreme Leader to retain a tight grip on the political and military entities in Iran.

The IRGC Command Structure

The growing influence of the IRGC in nearly all aspects of Iranian society has made the IRGC's command structure a key to understanding Iran's posture and

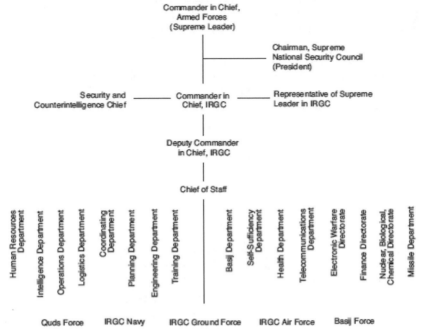

American Enterprise Institute (AEI) for Public Policy Research paper No 7, Ali Alfoneh, "What Do Structural Changes in the Revolutionary Guards Mean?," AEI, September 2008.

Figure 2.2   IRGC Organizational Chart (August 2008)

decision-making process. An illustrative picture of the IRGC decision-making apparatus is shown in Figure 2.2—but it should be noted that Iranian reporting does not provide accurate data and sources are somewhat contradictory.

New Face of the IRGC

On September 1, 2007, Khamenei promoted Mohammad Ali Jafari, then co-ordinator of the IRGC Research and Command Center, to the rank of major general and the post of commander in chief of the IRGC. Jafari is only the seventh in the organization's history. A list of IRGC commanders is shown in Figure 2.3.

An article published in *Rooz* on September 3, 2007, stated that Jafari is not as close to the political centers of power as his predecessor Safavi and that he focuses on military, rather than political, affairs. However, he is closely associated with Expediency Council Secretary-General and former IRGC commander Mohsen Rezai.[45]

In his first official speech as the IRGC commander in chief on October 20, 2007, Jafari talked about the new strategy and stated,

> Based on the guidelines issued by the Leader of the Islamic Republic, the strategy of the IRGC has been modified. Its main task now is to confront internal threats ...

Figure 2.3   IRGC Leaders (IRGC Commander in Chief)

Name	Year of Birth	Place of Birth	Educational Background	Tenure
Zamani, Abbas-Agha (Abou-Sharif)	1939	Tehran	Bachelor's degree in Islamic law	1979
Mansouri, Javad	1945	Kashan	N/A	April 22, 1979–?
Douz-Douzani, Abbas	1942	Tabriz	Introductory theology; unfinished studies in Arabic literature	1980–1981
Rezai, Morteza	N/A	N/A	N/A	1981
Rezai, Mohsen	1954	Masjed Soleiman	High school diploma	1981–1997
Safavi, Yahya Rahim	1958	N/A	High school diploma	1997–2007
Jafari, Mohammad Ali	1957	Yazd	IRGC War College	2007–present

Note: N/A = not available.

Source: Adapted from American Enterprise Institute (AEI) for Public Policy Research Paper No. 7, Ali Alfoneh, "What Do Structural Changes in the Revolutionary Guards Mean?," AEI, September 2008.

Maintaining internal security normally lies within the purview of the State Security Forces and other security organs. However, if the magnitude of security challenges were to cross a certain threshold, with the permission of the Leader and the Supreme National Security Council, the IRGC would have to take overall charge of the situation.[46]

Jafari set vital objectives for his forces: first, having up-to-date intelligence about the perceived enemy's movements and activities, and second, increasing the regime's missile capabilities. On November 1, 2007, Jafari characterized the 33-day war in Lebanon as the embodiment of the IRGC's new strategy and claimed,

Since the enemy's material and technological capabilities are superior to ours, we must move towards appropriate policies and means, enabling us to fulfill our requirements and ultimately force the enemy to experience defeat as it did during the 33-day war . . . One of the Americans' vulnerabilities in the region is that they have established a presence all around Iran. Thus, they cannot keep themselves out of our firing range.[47]

IRGC Restructuring

Upon his appointment to commander in chief, Jafari immediately implemented a major restructuring to move the IRGC's primary focus from external defense to internal security. The changes are more cosmetic than actual, but they do signal a renewed crackdown on reformism and civil society.

The IRGC has five branches consisting of a grounds force, an air force, a navy, the paramilitary Bassij Force, and the extraterritorial Qods Force. According to the NCRI (an organization that the U.S. Department of State reports has strong ties to the terrorist group Mujahadin-e Khalq Organization (MEK), some of the changes these branches have undergone in the course of the new strategic shift include the following:[48]

1. Although the Qods Force takes its ongoing and daily operational orders from the IRGC, its strategic policies and executive orders come directly from Khamenei, who is the regime's commander in chief of the armed forces.

2. During Jafari's tenure, the IRGC relieved the conventional navy of its control over the Persian Gulf operations and took direct charge of those operations itself.

3. The capabilities of the IRGC's air force, which controls the regime's missile development program, has been considerably bolstered. This is because, according to Jafari, the missile program is one the fundamental tenets of both the regime's defensive and also offensive strategies in the current circumstances.

4. The Bassij Force has been the focal point of the changes currently being implemented by Jafari. He set the stage with the slogan of "The IRGC's duties now have an internal focus" (to safeguard the regime's hold on power). Jafari began by removing then Bassij Force commander Mohammad-Hossein Hejazi from his post, appointing him instead as chief of the IRGC headquarters. He personally took over the command of the Bassij Force and chose a cleric, Hassan Taeb, as his deputy. Then in June 2008, in the course of the new round of changes, Jafari promoted Taeb to take over the Bassij command, with Hejazi appointed as his deputy.

5. The IRGC's ground forces have been restructured into 31 provincial brigades, with the Bassij Force units also reorganized in all provinces and reporting to IRGC provincial command.

This reorganization represents the most significant and unprecedented changes since the 1985 order by Rohallah Khomeini to equip the IRGC with an air force and a navy in addition to its ground forces. In the course of these extensive changes, the IRGC will shift focus from being a centralized force to having 31 distinct provincial brigades, the commanders of which will be given wide-ranging discretions.

When the restructuring is complete, each of the 30 provinces in Iran will have an IRGC brigade. Tehran will be the only province with two brigades (31 brigades in total across the country). The representation of the regime's Supreme Leader at the IRGC has also been given a higher profile. Supreme Leader representation now includes a deputy, a coordinator, and a headquarters in Tehran, as well as representatives—or political guides—embedded in each provincial brigade, each with his own headquarters established in the province. Figure 2.4 illustrates the IRGC organizational structure at the provincial level as of July 2008.

Soon after his appointment of Jafari to IRGC commander in chief, Ayatollah Khamenei ordered a massive purge of IRGC commanders whose services to the regime dated back to the eight-year war with Iraq. Most have been replaced by a next

Figure 2.4 IRGC Organizational Structure at the Provincial Level (July 2008)

Province	IRGC Unit	IRGC Commander	Previous Position	IGGC Deputy	Previous Position
Ardebil	Harzrat-e Abbas	Col. Jalil Baba-Zadeh	Ardebil Hazrat-e Abbas BDE chief	Col. Ghanbar Karim-Nezhad	Ardebil Basij chief
Azerbaijan, East	Ashoura	Cmdr. Mohammad-Taghi Ossanlou	31st Armored 'Ashoura Div. chief	N/A	N/A
Azerbaijan, West	Shohada	Brigadier General Mehdi Mo'ini	West Azerbaijan Shohada IRGC	Cmdr. Said Ghorban-Nezhad	West Azerbaijan Basij chief
Bushehr	Imam Sadegh	Col. Fath-Allah Jamiri	Bushehr Basij chief	Col. Abdol-Reza Mataf	Bushehr Basij deputy
Chahar-Mahal and Bakhtiari	Ghamar Bani-Hashem	Brigadier General Mohammad-Soleymani	Fars senior IRGC commander	Cmdr. Mehdi Jamshidi	N/A
Esfahan	Saheb al-Zaman	Brigadier General Gholam-Reza Soleymani	Senior Esfahan IRGC commander, 14th Imam Hossein Div. chief	N/A	N/A
Fars	Fajr	Brigadier General Gholam-Hossein Gheib-Parvar	25th Karbala Div. chief	Cmdr. Mohammad-Reza Mehdian-Far	Fars Basij chief
Gilan	Qods	Cmdr. Hamoun Mohammadi	Iran-Iraq War veteran	Cmd. Nazar Alizadeh	Gilan Basij chief
Golestan	Neynava	Brigadier General Naser Razaghian	Gorgan-based 1st Brigade of 25th Karbala Div. chief	N/A	N/A
Hamedan	Ansar al-Hossein	Cmd. Abdol-Reza Azadi	Hamedan IRGC chief	Cmdr. Mehdi Sedighi	Ansar BDE deputy, Quds training camp chief, Mottahari training

				camp chief, Ansar al-Hossein Div. deputy
Hormozgan	Imam Sajjad	N/A	N/A	N/A
Ilam	Amir al'emenin	Brigadier General Seyyed Sadeq Kaki	Hamedan IRGC senior commander, 3rd Ansar al-Hossein Brigade of the 4th Be'sat Div. chief	N/A	N/A
Kerman	Sar-Allah	Cmdr. Rouhollah Nouri	Hamzeh Seyyed al-Shohada base chief	Cmdr. Gholam-Ali Abou-Hamzeh	Kerman Basij chief
Kermanshah	Kermanshah IRGC	Cmdr. Mohammad-Nazar Azimi	4th Be'sat Inf. Div. chief	Cmdr. Bahman Reyhani	N/A
Khorasan, North	Javad al-A'emeh	Cmdr. Ali Mirza-Pour	N/A	Cmdr. Hossein-Ali Yousef-Ali-Zadeh	Khorasan North Basij chief
Khorasan, Razavi	Imam Reza	Cmdr. Ghodrat-Allah Mansouril	5th Nasr Div. chief	Cmdr. Hashem Ghiasi	Khorasan Razavi Basij chief
Khorasan, South	Ansar al-Reza	Brigadier General Gholam-Reza Ahmadi	Khorasan South Basij chief	N/A	N/A
Khuzestan	Vali-ye Asr	Cmdr. Mohammad Kazemeini	7th Vali Asr Div. chief	Cmdr. Mehdi Sa'adati	Khuzestan Basij chief
Kohkilou-yeh/ Boyer-Ahmad	Fath	Cmdr. 'Avaz Shahabi-Far	48th Independent BDE chief	Col. Ali-Asghar Habibi	N/A
Kordestan	Beit al-Moghaddas	Allah-Nour Nour-Allahi	Kordestan Basij chief	N/A	N/A
Lorestan	Abol-Fazl al-Abbas	Cmdr. Shahrokh	Independent 57th Hazrat-e Abolfazl BDE chief	Col. Teymour Sepahvand	Lorestan Basij chief

Markazi	Rouh-Allah	Cmdr. Mohammad-Taghi Shah-Cheraghi	Golestan Basij chief	Cmdr. Nour-Khoda Ghasemi	Chief of 1st Rouhollah Inf. BDE of Arak 17th Ali Ibn Abi-Taleb Div.
Mazandaran	Karbala	Brigadier General Ali Shalikar	25th Karbala Div. chief	Cmdr. Ali-Garmeh-i	Mazandaran Basij chief
Qazvin	Saheb al-Amr	Brigadier General Salar Abnoush	12th Hazrat-e Qa'em BDE chief	N/A	N/A
Qom	Ali Ibn-e Abi-Taleb	Brigadier General Akbar Nouri	17th Qom Ali-Ibn-e Abi-Taleb Inf. Div. chief	N/A	N/A
Semnan	Hazrat-e Gham'em al-Mohammad	Col. Mohammad-Hossein Babayi	Kerman Basij chief	N/A	N/A
Sistan and Baluchistan	Salman	Brigadier General Rejab-Ali Mohammad-Zadeh	N/A	Col. Habib Lak-Zayi	Sistan and Baluchistan Basij deputy
Tehran	Seyyed al-Shohada	Cmdr. Ali Zazli	Deputy operations chief of IRGC Central Command	Cmdr. Morteza Shaneh-Saz	Tehran Basij chief
Tehran, Greater	Mohammad Rasoul-Allah	Brigadier General Abdollah Eragh	Greater Tehran Basij chief	N/A	N/A
Yazd	Al-Ghadir	Brigadier General Mohammad-Ali Allah Dadi	Independent Al-Ghadir BDE chief	N/A	N/A
Zanjan	N/A	Cmdr. Seyyed Mehdi Mousavi	N/A	N/A	N/A

Note: "Cmdr." is used when the exact rank is unknown. N/A = not available.

Source: Adapted from American Enterprise Institute (AEI) for Public Policy Research Paper No. 7, Ali Alfoneh, "What Do Structural Changes in the Revolutionary Guards Mean?," AEI, September 2008.

generation of lower ranking "second-tier" commanders (i.e., those who held subordinate posts during the eight-year war with Iraq).

The most important IRGC posts have been filled with prominent hard-line figures such as Mohammad Hejazi, head of Saraallah—a powerful military unit in the IRGC; Jafar Assadi, commander of ground forces; and Hojjatoleslam Hussain Teab, chief of the Bassij force.[49]

Militarily, the changes should be viewed as reflecting a tactical shift toward centralization of power in order to reinforce and enhance the control of hard-liner IRGC elites over Iran's military forces. This shift also carries with it the advantage of eliminating the possibility of espionage within the organization of the military.

Politically, the appointment and promotion of hard-liners can be viewed as a way to send a message to the opposition within the Iranian civil society and lower/mid-ranking officers in the IRGC who are pro-reform.

IRGC and Iranian Nuclear Program

Jafari's rise to power has been accompanied by shifts in the IRGC that seem likely to have strengthened its role of shaping and controlling Iran's missiles and weapons of mass destruction. On August 21, 2005, Khamenei issued an order for the creation of an IRGC Research and Command Center, with Mohammad Ali Jafari as its coordinator. This was done in the course of crafting the desired strategy effectively conforming to the regime's new strategy. In accordance with Khamenei's orders, Jafari warned, "If the enemy were to wage an attack against us, we would threaten its interests all over the world."[50]

The IRGC's Growing Role in Weapons Programs

The elections and appointments of current and past members of the IRGC to ranking political decision-making positions have given the Guard Corps even greater influence over Iran's overall defense and nuclear strategy and policy.

The IRGC has several functions, including operating most of Iran's surface-to-surface missiles and is believed to have custody over potentially deployed nuclear weapons, most or all other chemical, biological, radiological, and nuclear weapons, and to operate Iran's nuclear-armed missile forces if they are deployed. It operates or controls much of Iran's military industries as well as dual-use and "civil" operations. As a result, the links between the IRGC and Iran's nuclear program have been so close that its leaders were singled out under the UN Security Council Resolutions passed on December 23, 2006, and March 24, 2007, and had their assets frozen.[51]

In a presentation before the National Press Club in Washington, D.C., on March 20, 2006, Alireza Jafarzadeh—a longtime spokesman for NCRI, a hard-line opposition group affiliated with the MEK (designated as a terrorist organization by the U.S. Department of State)—stated that "one institution that plays a pivotal role in the regime's nuclear program is Imam Hossein University, which is operated by the IRGC."[52]

He went on to say that "a number of nuclear experts have been transferred to the Imam Hossein University following reorganization in the regime's center for nuclear research. One of the high-level experts in the IRGC by the name of Mohammad Tavalaei is working at the Imam Hossein University's research center."[53]

"The Defense Ministry's nuclear program is also under the control of the IRGC. The highest ranking nuclear officials within the Defense Ministry are commanders and officers of IRGC." The details of some of these individuals, as presented by Alireza Jafarzadeh, are as follows:

> Mohsen Fakhrizadeh, has been a member of Scientific Board of the physics college at Imam Hossein University since 1991. He teaches a class, one day per week at this college. He is the director of the nuclear program at the Center for Readiness and New Defense Technology.
>
> Mansour Asgari, is a member of the IRCG. He graduated in 1990 and is a member of Scientific Board at the physics college in IRGC's Imam Hossein University and he teaches at the university 1 day[s] per week. Currently, he is one of the laser experts at the Center for Readiness and New Defense Technology, and works under the supervision of Fakhrizadeh.
>
> Mohamad Amin Bassam is a member of the IRGC. Currently he is one of the laser experts in the nuclear division of the Defense Ministry. He works under the supervision of Mohsen Fakhrizadeh. He is based and works at Parchin military complex in Tehran, where he conducts research on laser tests.[54]

Below is a list of the 21 top nuclear physicists of Imam Hossein University who are commanders and cadres of the IRGC, as presented by Alireza Jafarzadeh:[55]

1. Fereydoon Abbasi	Chair, Physics group
2. Mohsen Fakhrizadeh	Member, Scientific Board
3. Abolfazl Behjat-Panah	Member, Scientific Board
4. Mohsen Shayesteh	Member, Scientific Board
5. Ardeshir Bagheri	Member, Scientific Board
6. Amir-Reza Madani	Member, Scientific Board
7. Mohsen Torkaman-Sarabi	Member, Scientific Board
8. Yousef Hatefi	Member, Scientific Board
9. Javad Ahmadi	Member, Scientific Board
10. Massoud Abdollahzadeh	Member, Scientific Board
11. Seyyed Ali Aghajani	Member, Scientific Board
12. Mohammad Ali Torkaman-Motlagh	Member, Scientific Board
13. Tayeb Madani	Member, Scientific Board
14. Ibrahim Hajali	Member, Scientific Board
15. Mahmoud Abbassi	Member, Scientific Board
16. Mansour Asgari	Member, Scientific Board
17. Javad Khalilzadeh	Member, Scientific Board
18. Ismail Ahmadi Azar	Member, Scientific Board
19. Parviz Hossein-Khani	Member, Scientific Board
20. Hamid Kharazmi	Member, Scientific Board
21. Parviz Parvin	Member, Scientific Board

The growing IRGC control and influence over the defense industry, economy, and special weapons programs creates growing concern as to what the world can expect from a nuclear Iran controlled by military hard-liners. This also creates concern as to not only the international security implications of continued conventional weapons proliferation, but also the possibility of unconventional weapons proliferation.

As is described in the next chapter, the IRGC is also deeply involved in the country's nuclear, missile, and other weapons proliferation activities, and it maintains a special branch—the Qods Force—responsible for providing funds, weapons, improvised-explosive-device technology, and training to terrorist groups such as Hezbollah and Hamas and insurgents attacking Coalition and Iraqi forces in Iraq.[56]

A Nuclear Iran and Proliferation Issues

This raises the issue of whether the IRGC might play a future role in providing aid to other proliferators. Much of the nuclear material and technology that Iran now possesses came from outside assistance, whether it be from state actors—such as equipment, training, and technical expertise from North Korea, Russia, and China —or nonstate actors—such as the blueprints and technical expertise provided through the A. Q. Kahn network.

If and when Iran attains self-sufficiency, it might provide this same type of assistance to states and nonstate actors seeking nuclear technology or material, either through formal or informal networks, knowingly or unknowingly. In fact, Iran has already professed an interest in supplying some kind of aid to nations seeking this type of technology once it reaches self-sufficiency in its program.

On August 28, 2008, Iran indicated that it would be willing to share its nuclear technology with Nigeria to boost electricity production. A deal was signed at the end of three days of talks between the nations.[57] Both countries stressed that the nuclear program was for peaceful purposes only, but this display of Tehran's willingness to share nuclear technology and know-how just exacerbates international fears of nuclear proliferation to nations with inadequate and unproven nuclear safeguard programs and procedures.

A few months later on October 5, 2008, Iranian Foreign Minister Manouchehr Mottaki indicated that Iran is willing to supply other countries with nuclear fuel after it has reached self-sufficiency.[58] If these statements do represent Iran's policy on nuclear proliferation once it goes nuclear, this creates serious international security issues that current nonproliferation institutions are ill-prepared to deal with.

Another concern is that Iran could supply nuclear, biological, or chemical materials or weapons to extremist or terrorist organizations, such as Hezbollah or Hamas entities. Iran, or entities within Iran, currently supports a number of extremist, insurgent, and terrorist movements both regionally and globally with funding, weapons, and training. Certain key political figures within the Iranian government have acknowledged support for some of these groups on occasion, but are cautious about doing so on other occasions.

Prospects for Negotiating with Tehran

It is difficult to know what the future prospects are for negotiating with the Iranian government over any given aspect of Iran's search for weapons of mass destruction. Once again, Iran's leaders have made many conflicting statements. The key, however, almost certainly lies in the attitudes of Iran's Supreme Leader, Ayatollah Khamenei. So far, he seems to have blocked attempts to develop a serious and meaningful dialogue between Tehran and the rest of the international community regarding Iran's steadily progressing nuclear programs when senior decision-making officials have leaned toward, and at times advocated for, dialogue with its neighbors and the West.

He has been supported in such actions by many ranking decision makers in the Iranian government. As Iran has progressed in its nuclear program, defense industry, and overall self-reliance in the face of international threats, pressure, and sanctions, their actions and statements have become more defiant and the prospects for meaningful negotiations seem to have eroded. Statements that illustrate Tehran's determination to become a nuclear state include the following:

- On May 4, 2008, Iran's Supreme Leader Ayatollah Ali Khamenei asserted that Iran will continue with its nuclear program despite Western pressure to halt enrichment saying that "no threat can hinder the Iranian nation from its path. We will forcefully continue on our path and will not allow the oppressors to step on our rights."[59]

- On June 3, 2008, Iran's Supreme Leader Ayatollah Ali Khamenei asserted that "no wise nation" would pursue nuclear weapons, but his country will continue to develop its nuclear program for peaceful purposes.[60]

- On July 1, 2008, Iran's top diplomat indicated a readiness to negotiate a U.S.-backed proposal to end the nuclear standoff. Iranian Foreign Minister Manouchehr Mottaki stated that Iran was "seriously and carefully examining it." Referring to the offer made by the world's P5+1 (permanent UN Security Council members plus one—China, France, Russian Federation, the United Kingdom, the United States plus Germany), Mottaki went on to say that "we believe that talks are a good foundation for continuing our conversation in this field . . . We view the position taken by the five-plus-one as a constructive one." In June, Javier Solana delivered the incentives package and proposed a six-week "freeze-for-freeze," where Iran would suspend enrichment and the sanctions would be lifted. Tehran initially rejected the incentives offer but did not do so in face-to-face meetings with Solana.[61]

- On July 5, 2008, Iran formally responded to the P5+1 incentives package without specifically addressing the core issue of uranium enrichment. Instead, the letter indicated that Iran is willing to have comprehensive negotiations with Javier Solana, but insists that it will not suspend enrichment during negotiations. According to Iranian officials, "Iran's stand regarding its peaceful nuclear program has not changed." Some Western officials involved in the negotiations expressed disappointment. "There is nothing new in the response," one stated. Western officials contended that Iran was prolonging the diplomatic back-and-forth negotiations to continue its nuclear activities.[62]

- On July 27, 2008, President Mahmoud Ahmedinejad claimed that Iran now possesses 6,000 centrifuges at the Natanz enrichment plant and stated that "the West wanted us to stop. We resisted, and now they want to resume negotiations."[63]

- On July 31, 2008, speaking just days before a deadline set by world powers for Iran to reply to proposals to curb its nuclear ambitions, Ayatollah Khamenei asserted that Iran will "continue with its path" of nuclear development, signaling that Tehran did not intend to meet the deadline to respond to the U.S.-backed incentives package, aimed at achieving a temporary freeze-for-freeze.[64]

- On October 5, 2008, Iran stated that it will not halt enrichment in exchange for a guaranteed supply of nuclear fuel. Iranian Foreign Minister Manouchehr Mottaki said, "Iran's uranium enrichment policy remains unchanged. Enrichment will continue until Iran becomes self-sufficient in fuel production for nuclear plants."[65]

- On June 8, 2009, Iran's ambassador to the IAEA, Ali Asghar Soltanieh, said, "It is crystal clear and we have repeatedly said that we will not give up nuclear work and particularly enrichment activities."[66]

It is possible to take these statements for granted as a mark of growing Iranian defiance of the international community and the United States. Some experts have suggested that the Iranian nuclear program is quickly approaching the point of no return, a breakout capability, and certain "red lines."[67] Others have asserted that negotiations and sanctions are no longer viable options for dealing with Tehran and that a shift in policy and strategy toward one of military deterrence and containment of a nuclear Iran is needed.[68] These policy options are discussed in detail in Chapter 6.

As negotiations with nations such as North Korea have shown, however, such judgments may be premature. The only way to know the limits of diplomacy—and Iranian flexibility—is to keep negotiating. The leadership structure of Iran may not be promising, but there is little reason to give up on diplomacy and dialog as long as these do not become an end in themselves and prevent Iran's neighbors, the West, and other states from taking the necessary steps to ensure their security.

3

The Broader Strategic Context

The fact that Iran denies it is seeking nuclear weapons means that it has never articulated reasons for acquiring such weapons or how such efforts fit into the broader context of its national strategy. It is easy to speculate about Iran's reasons, and various experts have concluded that they are a mix of the following causes:

The heritage of the Shah's (Mohammad Reza Shah Pahlavi, 1941–1979) ambitions, nuclear program, and search for nuclear weapons

The status and influence awarded to declared and undeclared members of the nuclear club

The need for contingency capabilities that Iran may never translate into the actual production and deployment of nuclear weapons

Iran's fear of the United States, Israel, and "encirclement" by its neighbors

The fact that Israel, India, and Pakistan are regional nuclear powers

Its ambition for regional hegemony

Fear of U.S. and/or Israeli attacks and invasion

The leverage it can gain in putting political or military influence on its neighbors

The fact that Iran suffered from Iraqi chemical weapons attacks during much of the Iran-Iraq War from 1980–1988 without any meaningful protest or action by the international community, and it was found after the Gulf War in 1991 that Iraq had made a massive effort to develop biological and nuclear weapons

Its inability to match its neighbors' access to advanced conventional military weapons and technology from the United States, Europe, and Russia

An aggressive, religion-driven political system that is searching to find ways to export its religious revolution and influence in the region, particularly in a "Shi'ite crescent" involving Iraq, Syria, and Lebanon

The threat posed by Sunni religious extremism and denial of the Islamic legitimacy of Sh'ite beliefs

The fact that acquiring nuclear weapons and ballistic missiles, while expensive, is cheaper than a conventional arms race and will be partly paid for by the dual-use capabilities it obtains through paying for nuclear power

A mixed and uncertain opportunistic strategy that is both defensive and seeks to find ways to expand Iran's power and influence

All of the motives listed above are possible, and any expert can find aspects of Iran's statements, security policy, military doctrine, and history and actions that can be used to justify a given interpretation. The fact remains, however, that no one outside Iran's senior leaders can be certain of their motives, and their actions may be driven as much by events and future opportunities, and the success of any Iranian program, as by their current plans. No one can totally discount the possibility that Iran will not pursue the development of nuclear forces or simply halt at developing the ability to rapidly deploy weapons in the future: the so-called breakout or "bomb in the basement" scenario.

An examination of Iran's overall military efforts does, however, put Iran's *possible* programs in a broader strategic context. Such an examination makes it clear that Iran faces major problems in modernizing its conventional military forces, and the acquisition of nuclear forces would make it much harder for any Gulf or outside power to challenge its emerging strengths in asymmetric warfare or to attack or invade Iran.

IRAN'S CONVENTIONAL AND ASYMMETRIC FORCES

Iran has far weaker conventional forces in comparative terms than it had during the time of the Shah or the Iran-Iraq War. Nevertheless, it is slowly improving its conventional forces, is seeking to modernize its air fleet and air defenses, and is now the only regional military power that poses a serious conventional military threat to Saudi Arabia and Gulf stability. Iranian forces also conduct extensive military exercises and have sometimes confronted U.S. and British naval and air forces in the Gulf.

Iran has growing capabilities for asymmetric warfare, including a large Naval Guards force, submarines, antiship missiles, and mine warfare capabilities. Iran's Quds Force and intelligence services have supported insurgent movements in Iraq with training, weapons, and key components for improvised explosive devices (IEDs). Iran deals with outside terrorist groups and violent nonstate actors. It actively supports Hezbollah in Lebanon and hard-line groups such as Hamas and the Palestinian Islamic Jihad in attacking Israel. Iran is also well aware that Sunni and Shi'ite tensions are at an all-time high in the Islamic world, driven in part by neo-Salafist extremist and terrorist groups such as Al Qa'ida.

Iran can pose a mixture of conventional and asymmetric threats. Iran's options include the following:[1]

- Direct and indirect threats of using force (i.e., Iranian efforts at proliferation)
- Use of irregular forces and asymmetric attacks
- Proxy conflicts using terrorist or extremist movements or exploiting internal sectarian, ethnic, tribal, dynastic, and regional tensions
- Arms transfers, training in host country, and use of covert elements such as the Quds Force
- Harassment and attrition through low-level attacks, clashes, and incidents
- Limited, demonstrative attacks to increase risk and intimidation
- Strikes at a critical node or infrastructure

These threats are also anything but theoretical; Iran and other powers have already posed them in tangible form:

- Iranian Tanker War with Iraq
- Oil spills and floating mines in Gulf
- Libyan "stealth" mining of the Red Sea
- Use of the Quds Force in Iraq
- "Incidents" during the pilgrimage in Mecca
- Support of Shi'ite groups in Bahrain
- Missile and space tests (future nuclear test?)
- The Naval Guard's seizure of a British boat, confrontation with the U.S Navy, and exercises in the Gulf
- Development of limited "close the Gulf" capability
- Flow of illegals and smuggling across the Yemeni border

Iran has also greatly strengthened the asymmetric elements in its force structure, especially in the Islamic Revolutionary Guards Corps (IRGC). The IRGC now has the following elements:[2]

- 125,000+ men and the ability to draw upon a manpower pool with an additional 1,000,000 Basij paramilitary members
- A 20,000-man Naval Guards force, including 5,000 marines
- This naval branch and other IRGC elements are armed with HY-3 CSS-C-3 Seersucker (6–12 launchers, 100 missiles, 95–100 kilometers), and 10 Houdong missile patrol boats with C-802s (120 kilometers), and 40+ Boghammers with antitank guided missiles (ATGMs), recoilless rifles, and machine guns.
- Large-scale mine warfare capability using small craft and commercial boats
- Bases in areas that pose an immediate threat to all shipping through the Gulf, including Bandar e-Abbas, Khorramshar, Larak, Abu Musa, Al Farsiyah, Halul, and Sirri
- An air branch that is reported to fly unmanned aerial vehicles (UAVs) and unmanned combat air vehicles (UCAVs) and controls Iran's strategic missile force. These forces

include one Shahab short-range ballistic missile brigade (300–500–700 kilometers) with 12–18 launchers, and one Shahab-3 intermediate-range ballistic missile (IRBM) battalion (1,200–1,280 kilometers) with 6 launchers and 4 missiles each.

While there are very real limits to Iran's asymmetric capabilities, it also has built up forces designed to attack shipping and other targets in the Gulf and has repeatedly claimed that it has the capability to close the Gulf. The key Iranian assets and capabilities involved include the following:

- Kilo (Type 877) and an unknown number of midget (Qadr-SS-3) submarines; smart torpedoes, (antiship missiles?) and smart mine capability
- Use of 5 minelayers, amphibious ships, small craft, and commercial boats
- Attacks on tankers, shipping, and offshore facilities by the Naval Guards
- Raids with 8 P-3MP/P-3F Orion maritime patrol aircraft (MPA) and combat aircraft with antiship missiles [C-801K (8–42 km), CSS-N-4, and others]
- Free-floating mines, smart and dumb mines, and oil spills
- Land-based, long-range antiship missiles based on land, islands (Seersucker HY-2, CSS-C-3), and ships (CSS-N-4, and others. Sunburn?)
- Forces whose exercises demonstrate the capability to raid or attack key export and infrastructure facilities

Iran is developing a long-range missile force and seems to be developing a range of weapons of mass destruction. Iran has never properly declared its holdings of chemical weapons, and the status of its biological weapons programs is unknown. Most important, the disclosures by the International Atomic Energy Agency (IAEA) indicate that Iran will continue to covertly seek nuclear weapons.

If Iran deploys chemical, biological, or nuclear weapons, it could deliver them using missile, fighter-bombers, or covert means of delivery means. It could use its Scuds and some types of antiship missiles to deliver such warheads relatively short distances. Its Shahab-3 missiles already can reach most all of the key targets in the Gulf countries, including many Saudi cities on the Red Sea coast and in western Saudi Arabia, and Iran is developing liquid and solid-fueled missiles with substantially greater range-payloads than the Shahab.

Iran's missile developments also have value as deterrents, weapons of intimidation, or warfighting systems—even if they are not armed with weapons of mass destruction. Missile systems such as Iran's Shahab-3s are probably too inaccurate, and have too limited a payload capacity, to be effective in delivering conventional weapons against critical targets. They could have only a major military impact—even against area targets—if they were armed with warheads carrying weapons of mass destruction. This does not mean, however, that conventionally armed missiles could not be used as terror weapons against area targets, or as weapons of intimidation.

THE IMPACT OF WEAK AND AGING CONVENTIONAL FORCES

Iran is still heavily dependent on major conventional weapons systems that it acquired before the fall of the Shah, and which have never been fully updated since Iran lost access to U.S. and European arms during 1979–1980. It has never had free access to Russia's modern arms, and much of its inventory consists of Chinese and North Korean systems or designs of limited effectiveness.

The Lingering Impact of Past Defeats

As Figure 3.1 shows, Iran could not compete with Iraq in either the quality or volume of its arms imports during the Iran-Iraq War. Eight years of combat ended in 1988 with massive Iraqi victories that deprived Iran of some 40–60 percent of its inventory of land force weapons and made Iraq the Gulf's preeminent military power. The Iraqi victories in the spring and summer of 1988 destroyed or captured between 40 and 60 percent of the Iranian armor inventory and up to 50 percent of Iran's armored personnel carrier (APC) artillery.[3]

Since 1990, Saudi Arabia and the other southern Gulf States—Bahrain, Kuwait, Oman, Qatar, Saudi Arabia, and the United Arab Emirates—have each built up their military and security forces by making a massive collective military investment. Unlike Iran and Iraq, the military efforts of the southern Gulf States have also been carried out with the knowledge that the United States and its allies could provide power projection forces and that such protection would almost certainly be

Figure 3.1   The Iranian-Iraqi Arms Race during the Iran-Iraq War, 1981–1988
(In Millions of Current US Dollars)

Supplier	New Arms Agreements		Actual Deliveries	
	Iran	Iraq	Iran	Iraq
Soviet Union	240	20,650	370	21,370
China	3,970	5,520	2,750	4,380
All Other Communist	5,740	6,030	4,550	6,300
Total Communist	9,950	32,200	7,670	32,050
European Non-Communist	5,340	9,790	4,170	10,710
United States	*	**	*	**
All Other Non-Communist	1,410	5,260	1,970	3,900
Total Non-Communist	6,750	14,960	6,140	14,610
TOTAL	**17,480**	**47,250**	**13,810**	**46,660**

*   Does not include covert U.S. arms sales during Iran Contra.
**   Value less than $50 million.
Source: Richard F. Grimmett, *Trends in Conventional Arms Transfers to the Third World by Major Supplier,* Washington, D.C., Congressional Research Service (CRS), CRS 89-434F, July 31, 1989.

forthcoming because of the role the Gulf plays in the world's oil exports and the fact it has more than 60 percent of the world proven oil reserves.

Resources: The Causes of Iranian Weakness

An examination of regional military expenditure and arms import data since the Iran-Iraq War show that Iran cannot hope to keep pace with the southern Gulf States in modernizing its conventional forces, much less with the even more advanced conventional forces the United States, Britain, and France can deploy to the region. Saudi Arabia and the southern Gulf States are spending far more on their military budgets and arms imports than Iran:

- Figure 3.2 shows the nature of the shift in the resources devoted to the regional military buildup that began to emerge before Iran's defeat in the Iran-Iraq War, and Iraq's defeat in the Gulf War, but which has accelerated ever since. The southern Gulf leads the regional arms race that the northern Gulf States began. Saudi Arabia has by far been the largest spender in the Gulf, although several small southern Gulf States—notably the United Arab Emirates (UAE), Kuwait, and Oman—have been very large spenders in proportion to their sizes.

- Figure 3.3 shows the comparison between Iran's military expenditures and those of its neighbors in more detail.

- Figure 3.4 shows that the Gulf Cooperation Council (GCC) lead in military spending has only imposed either a consistent or smaller burden as a percentage of gross national product (GNP).

- Figure 3.5 shows comparative Gulf arms agreements and deliveries from 1988 to 2008. The GCC states have a massive collective lead over Iran and any credible combination of neighboring states. For Iran, this was partly a matter of choice and partly a matter of economic weakness. For Iraq, it has been forced upon Iraq by a United Nations (UN) arms embargo from September 1990 to the fall of Saddam Hussein in March 2003 and by its massive defeat in the U.S.-led invasion that drove Hussein from power.

- Figure 3.6 shows just how large a lead the GCC states have over Iran, a lead compounded by the failure of many Iranian military manufacturing efforts and far better GCC country access to the most advanced U.S. and European weapons and military technology.

- Figure 3.7 shows that the United States is the major arms supplier for most of the Gulf States, although major Western European suppliers have recently begun to plan an increasing role in supplying Saudi, Emirati, and Omani armed forces. As mentioned earlier, Iraq is now mainly dependent upon U.S. support to increase its force capabilities, and Iran is the sole primary recipient of arms supplies from Russia. Other Gulf States have chosen to include Russian arms imports as part of a broader force mix of systems from the United States and Europe.

Iran and the Regional Conventional Balance

The impact of decades of the inability to import the most advanced conventional weapons, the Iran-Iraq War, Iran's economic problems, and a lack of spending

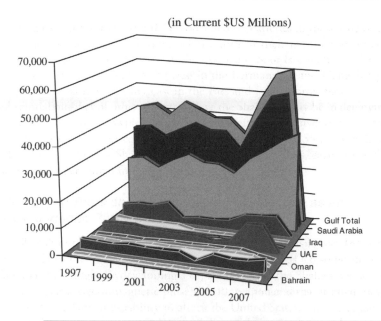

(in Current $US Millions)

	1997	1998	1999	2000	2001	2002	2003	2004 *	2005	2006	2007	2008
Bahrain	387	427	472	342	355	352	350	191	559	498	550	552
Kuwait	3,827	3,614	3,401	3,933	3,614	3,720	3,720	1,275	4,539	3,640	3,750	4,930
Oman	2,126	1,913	1,701	2,232	2,551	2,445	2,657	2,764	3,210	3,410	3,230	?
Qatar	1,382	1,382	1,488	1,275	1,807	2,020	2,020	2,232	2,327	2,430	1,090	?
UAE	3,614	3,933	4,039	3,189	2,976	2,976	2,976	1,701	2,817	9,888	10,292	?
Yemen	437	421	456	529	570	547	596	940	1,001	858	927	?
Iraq	1,982	1,382	1,488	1,488	1,488	?	?	?	?	?	?	?
Iran	4,996	6,165	6,060	7,972	2,232	3,189	3,189	3,720	6,590	6,759	7,450	?
Saudi Arabia	22,323	23,386	19,878	23,386	26,256	23,599	23,599	20,515	27,000	30,810	35,400	38,200
GCC Total	33,659	34,655	30,979	34,357	37,559	35,112	35,322	28,678	40,452	50,676	52,142	?
Gulf Total	41,074	42,623	38,983	44,346	41,849	38,848	39,107	33,338	48,043	58,290	60,379	?

Source: International Institute of Strategic Studies, Military Balance, various editions.
* The IISS did not report military expenditures for 2004. The number for 2004 represents the military budget, which does not include procurement costs.

Figure 3.2   Southern Gulf Military Expenditures by Country: 1997–2007

on military forces and arms imports is also clear from an examination of the current military balance in the Gulf. This is true even if one considers only the balance in terms of regional forces and ignores U.S., British, and French power projection capabilities.

(In Millions of Current US Dollars)

Gulf Military Spending by Country

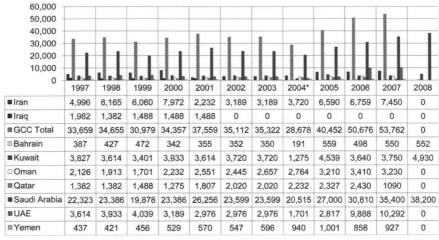

	1997	1998	1999	2000	2001	2002	2003	2004*	2005	2006	2007	2008
■Iran	4,996	6,165	6,060	7,972	2,232	3,189	3,189	3,720	6,590	6,759	7,450	0
■Iraq	1,982	1,382	1,488	1,488	1,488	0	0	0	0	0	0	0
■GCC Total	33,659	34,655	30,979	34,357	37,559	35,112	35,322	28,678	40,452	50,676	53,762	0
▨Bahrain	387	427	472	342	355	352	350	191	559	498	550	552
■Kuwait	3,827	3,614	3,401	3,933	3,614	3,720	3,720	1,275	4,539	3,640	3,750	4,930
▢Oman	2,126	1,913	1,701	2,232	2,551	2,445	2,657	2,764	3,210	3,410	3,230	0
■Qatar	1,382	1,382	1,488	1,275	1,807	2,020	2,020	2,232	2,327	2,430	1090	0
■Saudi Arabia	22,323	23,386	19,878	23,386	26,256	23,599	23,599	20,515	27,000	30,810	35,400	38,200
■UAE	3,614	3,933	4,039	3,189	2,976	2,976	2,976	1,701	2,817	9,888	10,292	0
▨Yemen	437	421	456	529	570	547	596	940	1,001	858	927	0

Iranian Spending versus Total Gulf Spending

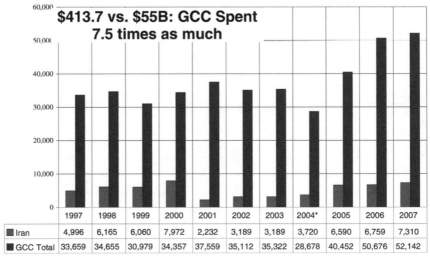

	1997	1998	1999	2000	2001	2002	2003	2004*	2005	2006	2007
■Iran	4,996	6,165	6,060	7,972	2,232	3,189	3,189	3,720	6,590	6,759	7,310
■GCC Total	33,659	34,655	30,979	34,357	37,559	35,112	35,322	28,678	40,452	50,676	52,142

Source: IISS, Military Balance, various editions.

Figure 3.3   Gulf Military Spending, 1997–2008

Iran has sought to create its own military industries, with some success. It has obtained some advanced weapons such as the TOR-M short-range surface-to-air missile and modern antitank guided weapons from Russia and antiship missiles from China. Nevertheless, its efforts still do not offset the decay of much of its aging inventory of conventional weapons, or the wear of wartime operations and constant exercises. Iran is not an emerging hegemon. It is falling steadily behind.

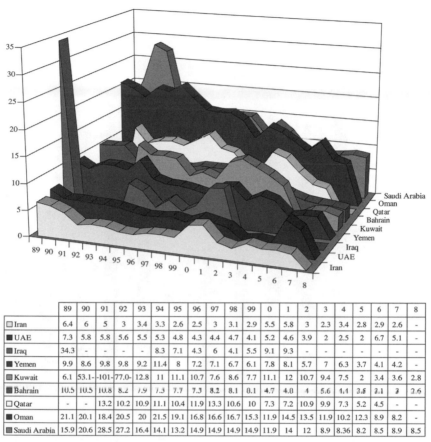

	89	90	91	92	93	94	95	96	97	98	99	0	1	2	3	4	5	6	7	8
☐ Iran	6.4	6	5	3	3.4	3.3	2.6	2.5	3	3.1	2.9	5.5	5.8	3	2.3	3.4	2.8	2.9	2.6	-
■ UAE	7.3	5.8	5.8	5.6	5.5	5.3	4.8	4.3	4.4	4.7	4.1	5.2	4.6	3.9	2	2.5	2	6.7	5.1	-
■ Iraq	34.3	-	-	-	-	8.3	7.1	4.3	6	4.1	5.5	9.1	9.3	-	-	-	-	-	-	-
■ Yemen	9.9	8.6	9.8	9.8	9.2	11.4	8	7.2	7.1	6.7	6.1	7.8	8.1	5.7	7	6.3	3.7	4.1	4.2	-
■ Kuwait	6.1	53.1-	-101-	77.0-	12.8	11	11.1	10.7	7.6	8.6	7.7	11.1	12	10.7	9.4	7.5	2	3.4	3.6	2.8
■ Bahrain	10.5	10.5	10.8	8.2	7.9	7.3	7.7	7.3	8.2	8.1	8.1	4.7	4.0	4	5.6	4.4	3.6	3.1	3	2.6
☐ Qatar	-	-	13.2	10.2	10.9	11.1	10.4	11.9	13.3	10.6	10	7.3	7.2	10.9	9.9	7.3	5.2	4.5	-	-
■ Oman	21.1	20.1	18.4	20.5	20	21.5	19.1	16.8	16.6	16.7	15.3	11.9	14.5	13.5	11.9	10.2	12.3	8.9	8.2	-
■ Saudi Arabia	15.9	20.6	28.5	27.2	16.4	14.1	13.2	14.9	14.9	14.9	14.9	11.9	14	12	8.9	8.36	8.2	8.5	8.9	8.5

Source: Adapted by Anthony H. Cordesman from the IISS, Military Balance, various editions, ACDA, World Military Expenditures and Arms Transfers, 1995, ACDA/GPO, Washington, 1996 and US State Department, World Military Expenditures and Arms Transfers, 1999-2000, Bureau of Arms Control, Washington, 2001.

Figure 3.4 Comparative Military Expenditures of the Gulf Powers as a Percent of GNP, 1989–2007

- Figure 3.8 shows that Iran's military strength is limited in comparative terms, even if one ignores the operational readiness of much of its inventory and force quality.

- Figure 3.9 shows the limits to Iran's total strength in armor, the key measure of land force conventional military strength.

- Figure 3.10 focuses on the total number of main battle tanks, perhaps the most important single measure of maneuver warfare strength.

- Figure 3.11 shows that Iran has even less strength if tank quality is considered, even including export versions of the T-72.

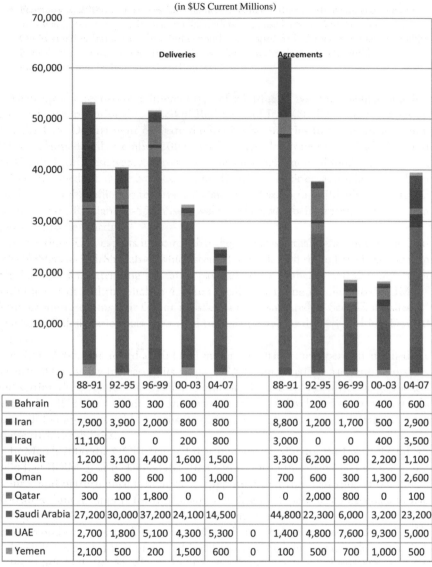

	Deliveries					Agreements				
	88-91	92-95	96-99	00-03	04-07	88-91	92-95	96-99	00-03	04-07
■ Bahrain	500	300	300	600	400	300	200	600	400	600
■ Iran	7,900	3,900	2,000	800	800	8,800	1,200	1,700	500	2,900
■ Iraq	11,100	0	0	200	800	3,000	0	0	400	3,500
■ Kuwait	1,200	3,100	4,400	1,600	1,500	3,300	6,200	900	2,200	1,100
■ Oman	200	800	600	100	1,000	700	600	300	1,300	2,600
■ Qatar	300	100	1,800	0	0	0	2,000	800	0	100
■ Saudi Arabia	27,200	30,000	37,200	24,100	14,500	44,800	22,300	6,000	3,200	23,200
■ UAE	2,700	1,800	5,100	4,300	5,300	1,400	4,800	7,600	9,300	5,000
■ Yemen	2,100	500	200	1,500	600	100	500	700	1,000	500

0 ＊ Data less than $50 million or nil. All data rounded to the nearest $100 million.
Source: Richard F. Grimmett, Conventional Arms Transfers to the Developing Nations, Congressional Research Service, various editions.

Figure 3.5   Gulf Arms Agreements and Deliveries by Country, 1988–2007

- Figure 3.12 shows Iran's limited total air strength even if U.S. aid capabilities are ignored and all partially operational Iranian aircraft are counted.
- Figure 3.13 provides a similar snapshot comparison of both fixed- and rotary-wing aircraft.

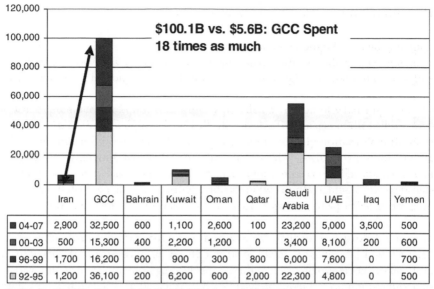

	Iran	GCC	Bahrain	Kuwait	Oman	Qatar	Saudi Arabia	UAE	Iraq	Yemen
■ 04-07	2,900	32,500	600	1,100	2,600	100	23,200	5,000	3,500	500
■ 00-03	500	15,300	400	2,200	1,200	0	3,400	8,100	200	600
■ 96-99	1,700	16,200	600	900	300	800	6,000	7,600	0	700
□ 92-95	1,200	36,100	200	6,200	600	2,000	22,300	4,800	0	500

0 = Data less than $50 million or nil. All data rounded to the nearest $100 million.
Source: Richard F. Grimmett, <u>Conventional Arms Transfers to the Developing Nations</u>, Congressional Research Service, various editions.

Figure 3.6   GCC vs. Iranian New Arms Agreements

(Arms Agreements in $US Current Millions)

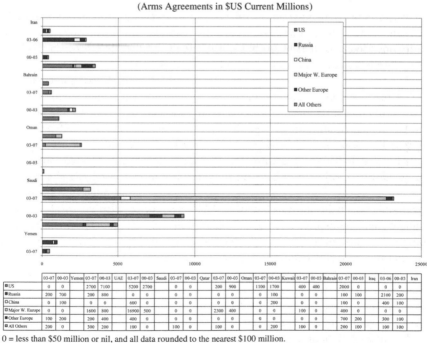

	03-07	00-03	Yemen	03-07	00-03	UAE	03-07	00-03	Saudi	03-07	00-03	Qatar	03-07	00-03	Oman	03-07	00-03	Kuwait	03-07	00-03	Bahrain	03-07	00-03	Iraq	03-06	00-03	Iran
■ US	0	0		2700	7100		5200	2700		0	0		200	900		1100	1700		400	400		2000	0		0	0	
■ Russia	200	700		200	800		0	0		0	0		0	100		0	0		100	100		2100	200	
□ China	0	100		0	0		600	0		0	0		0	200		0	0		100	0		400	100	
□ Major W. Europe	0	0		1600	800		16900	500		0	0		2300	400		0	0		100	0		400	0		0	0	
■ Other Europe	100	200		200	400		400	0		0	0		0	0		0	0		0	0		700	200		300	100	
▣ All Others	200	0		300	200		100	0		100	0		100	0		0	200		100	0		200	100		100	100	

0 = less than $50 million or nil, and all data rounded to the nearest $100 million.
Source: Adapted by Anthony H. Cordesman, CSIS, from Richard F. Grimmett, <u>Conventional Arms Transfers to the Developing Nations</u>, Congressional Research Service, various editions.

Figure 3.7   Gulf New Arms Orders by Supplier Country, 1988–2006

Figure 3.8 Gulf Military Forces, 2009

	Iran	Iraq*	Bahrain	Kuwait	Oman	Qatar	Saudi Arabia†	UAE	Yemen
Manpower									
Total Active	523,000	591,319	8,200	15,500	42,600	11,800	332,500	51,000	66,700
Regular	398,000	184,055	8,200	15,500	34,200	11,800	230,500	51,000	66,700
National Guard & Other‡	125,000	25,758	0	0	6,400	0	109,000	0	0
Reserve	350,000	–	0	23,700	0	0	–	0	0
Paramilitary	40,000	381,606	11,260	7,100	4,400	0	15,500	0	71,200
Army									
Total Manpower	450,000§	180,296	6,000	11,000	25,000	8,500	227,000	44,000	60,000
Active Army Manpower	350,000	180,296	6,000	11,000	25,000	8,500	125,000	44,000	60,000
IRGC/Saudi National Guard	125,000	–	–	–	–	–	102,000	–	–
Reserve	350,000	–	0	0	0	0	–	0	0
Total Main Battle Tanks**	1,613+	149+	180	368	117	30	1,016	471	790
Active Main Battle Tanks	1,613+	149+	180	293	117	30	861	471	790
Active AIFV/RECCE, Lt. Tanks	610	35	30	450	174	108	1,788	619(40)	345
Total APCs	640	1,415	235+	321	206	226	2,532	880	710
Active APCs	640	1,415	235+	281	206	226	2,532	880	240
ATGM Launchers	75	–	15	118+	58	148	2,040+	305+	71
Self-Propelled Artillery	310+	–	13	113	24	28	129	181	25
Towed Artillery	2,010+	–	26	0	108	12	131	93	310
MRLs	876+	–	9	27	?	4	81	72+	294
Mortars	5,000	–	21	78	101	45	400	155	502
SSM Launchers	48	–	0	0	0	0	10+	6	28

Light SAM Launchers	Some	–	85	60+	54+	0	1,000+	40+	800
AA Guns	1,700	–	27	12+	26	0	0	62	530
Air Force and Air Defense									
Air Force Manpower	30,000	1,887	1,500	2,500	5,000	2,100	60,000	4,500	3,000
Air Defense Manpower	12,000	–	0	0	0	0	23,000	0	2,000
Total Combat Capable Aircraft††	319	–	33	50	64	18	269–278	184	79
Bombers	0	–	0	0	0	0	0	0	0
Fighter Ground Attack	168	–	21	39	52	12	155	155	30
Fighter/Interceptor	118	–	12	0	0	0	121	0	43
RECCE/FGA RECCE	6+	16	0	0	0	0	10	7	0
AEW C^{4}I/BM	–	–	0	0	0	0	5	0	0
MR/MPA**	5	–	0	0	0	0	0	0	0
OCU/COIN	0	–	0	0	0	0	14	5	0
Combat Capable Trainers	27	–	6	11	12	6	57	17	6
Transport Aircraft‡‡	104+	4	4	5	16	6	45	23	18
Tanker Aircraft	0	–	0	0	0	0	15	0	0
Total Helicopters‡‡	287+	47	47	29	47	25	195	125+	20
Armed Helicopters‡‡	60+	–	24-	16	0	19	39	54+	8
Other Helicopters‡‡	227	47	23	13	47	6	156	71	12
Major SAM Launchers	279+	–	8	40	6+	–	224	Some	Some
Light SAM Launchers	Some	–	–	Some	40	75	1,649	–	Some

AA Guns	Some	—	—	Some	Some	—	1,220	—	—
Navy									
Total Naval Manpower	38,000$	1,872	700	2,000	4,200	1,800	22,500	2,500	1,700
Regular Navy	18,000	1,872	700	2,000	4,200	1,800	12,500	2,500	1,700
Naval Guards	20,000	0	—	500	0	0	0	0	0
Marines	5,000	0	—	—	—	—	10,000	—	0
Major Surface Combattants									
Missile	3	0	3	0	2	0	11	4	0
Other	3	—	0	0	0	0	0	0	0
Patrol Craft									
Missile	64	0	4	10	4	7	9	8	4
(Revolutionary Guards)	10	0	—	—	—	—	—	—	—
Other	82	16	4	0	7	14	56	6	16
Revolutionary Guards (Boats)	40+	0	—	—	—	—	—	—	—
Submarines	9+	0	0	0	0	0	0	0	0
Mine Vessels	5	0	0	0	0	0	3	2	6
Amphibious Ships	13	0	0	0	1	0	0	0	1
Landing Craft	8	0	5	2	4	0	4	28	5
Support Ships	26	0	1	1	7	—	5	3	0
Naval Air	2,600	0	—	—	—	—	—	—	—

Naval Aircraft						
Fixed-Wing Combat	0	0	0	0	0	2	0
MR/MPA	3	0	0	0	0	0	0
Armed Helicopters	10	0	0	0	27	14	0
SAR Helicopters	–	0	0	0	–	4	0
Mine Warfare Helicopters	3	0	0	0	0	0	0
Other Helicopters	17	0	–	–	19	–	–

Notes: Equipment in storage is shown in parentheses. Air force totals include all helicopters, including army-operated weapons, and all heavy surface-to-air missile launchers.

RECCE = reconnaissance; MLRs = multiple rocket launchers; SSM = surface-to-surface missile; SAM = surface-to-air missile; AA = antiaircraft; FGA = fighter ground attack; AEW = aircraft early warning; C^4I = command, control, communications, computers, and intelligence; BM = battlespace management; MR = maritime reconnaissance; MPA = maritime patrol aircraft; OCU = operational control unit; COIN = counterinsurgency; SAR = search and rescue.

* The figures for Iraq are from Multi-National Security Transition Command—Iraq (MNSTC-I), September 2008, and show assigned levels of manning. Iraqi paramilitary forces include police and border forces.

† Saudi totals for reserve include National Guard Tribal Levies. The equipment totals for land forces include the Saudi National Guard equipment. These additions total 1,139 AIFVs, 48 LAV, 136 LAVs with 90-mm guns, and 77 towed artillery weapons.

‡ "National Guard & Other" for Iraq includes support forces and Special Operations forces.

§ Iranian total includes roughly 120,000 Revolutionary Guard actives in land forces and 20,000 in naval forces.

** Total tanks include tanks in storage or conversion.

†† Totals do not include RECCE, FGA RECCE, AEW C^4I/BM, MR/MPA and OCU/COIN units.

‡‡ Includes navy, army, National Guard, and royal flights, but not paramilitary.

Source: Adapted from interviews with Saudi and U.S. experts, International Institute of Strategic Studies (IISS), *The Military Balance, 2008, Jane's Sentinel Security Assessment, Periscope;* MNSTC-I, September 2008, and Jaffee Center for Strategic Studies, *The Military Balance in the Middle East.*

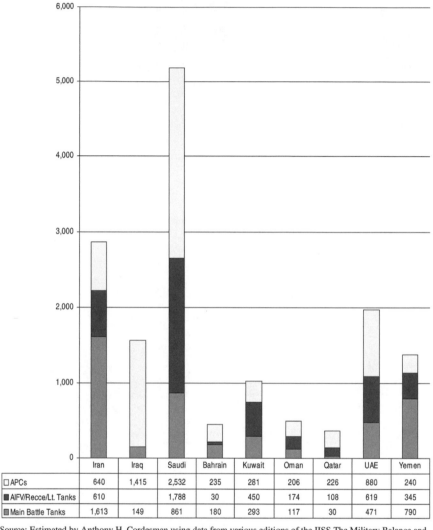

	Iran	Iraq	Saudi	Bahrain	Kuwait	Oman	Qatar	UAE	Yemen
☐ APCs	640	1,415	2,532	235	281	206	226	880	240
■ AIFV/Recce/Lt. Tanks	610		1,788	30	450	174	108	619	345
▨ Main Battle Tanks	1,613	149	861	180	293	117	30	471	790

Source: Estimated by Anthony H. Cordesman using data from various editions of the IISS The Military Balance and Jane's Sentinel.

Figure 3.9   Total Gulf Operational Armored Fighting Vehicles in 2009

- Figure 3.14 shows the lead nations such as Saudi Arabia and the United Arab Emirates have in advanced types of combat aircraft even if one ignores the power projection capabilities of U.S., British, and French air forces.

- Figures 3.15 and 3.16 show the lead other states have in reconnaissance (RECCE), air control and warning, and intelligence and other surveillance aircraft—again ignoring the power projection capabilities of U.S., British, and French air forces and their national satellite capabilities.

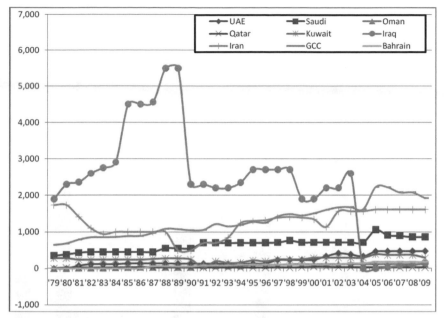

Note: Iranian totals include Revolutionary Guards, and Iraqi totals include Republican Guards and Special Republican Guards.
Source: Estimated using data from the International Institute of Strategic Studies (IISS), *Military Balance*, various editions, and Saudi and US experts.

Figure 3.10   Total Operational Main Battle Tanks in All Gulf Forces, 1979–2009

- Figure 3.17 shows comparative land-based air defense assets. Iran's principal systems are all obsolete or obsolescent, and this table ignores U.S. ability to deploy ship-borne air defense assets and land-based systems such as the Patriot and Theater High-Altitude Area Defense.

- Figure 3.18 shows total naval strength. The Iranian Navy is large, but virtually all of its large surface ships are worn and obsolete. Its strength lies largely in submarines, and smaller missile, mine warfare, and other craft best suited for asymmetric warfare.

- Figure 3.19 shows that Iran's strength in antiship missile forces exists largely in smaller vessels.

- Figure 3.20 shows Iran's strength in mine-laying capability, which is supplemented by the ability to lay mines with many small craft and fishing vessels and which is not matched by Gulf, U.S., or British minesweeping capability.

- Figure 3.21 shows comparative strength in naval helicopters and attack helicopters that could be used in missions in the Gulf. Large numbers of Iran's inventory are obsolescent and/or are not operational.

- Figure 3.22 shows Iran's limited amphibious lift. It would have to rely on ferries and ships operating in a passive environment and with full access to ports for any large-scale operation.

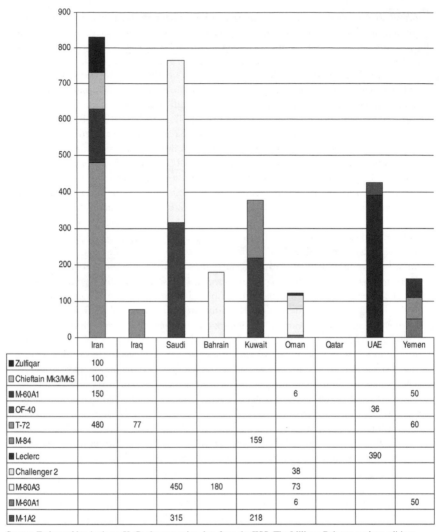

	Iran	Iraq	Saudi	Bahrain	Kuwait	Oman	Qatar	UAE	Yemen
■ Zulfiqar	100								
▨ Chieftain Mk3/Mk5	100								
■ M-60A1	150					6			50
■ OF-40								36	
▨ T-72	480	77							60
■ M-84					159				
■ Leclerc								390	
☐ Challenger 2						38			
☐ M-60A3			450	180		73			
■ M-60A1						6			50
■ M-1A2			315		218				

Source: Estimated by Anthony H. Cordesman using data from the IISS, The Military Balance, various editions.

Figure 3.11   Medium- to High-Quality Main Battle Tanks by Type in 2009

A summary quantitative overview cannot measure or portray all of the qualitative factors shaping the regional balance of conventional forces. Work by Jane's and others shows that Iran's regular army, air force, and navy will become more technologically advanced over time.[4] Figures 3.8 to 3.22 also do not mean that Iran is not a significant conventional power by Gulf standards or that it does not have the ability to defend its own territory in depth. At the same time, these figures do provide further evidence that Iran is not a regional hegemon and show that its weak conventional forces leave it highly vulnerable to naval and air attack.

(Does not include stored or unarmed electronic warfare, recce or trainer aircraft)

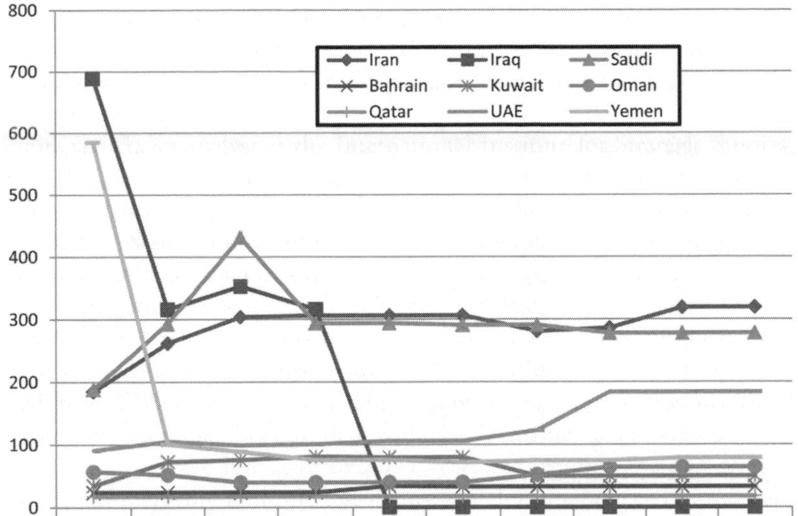

	1990	1993	2000	2003	2004	2005	2006	2007	2008	2009
Iran	185	262	304	306	306	306	281	286	319	319
Iraq	689	316	353	316	0	0	0	0	0	0
Saudi	189	293	432	294	294	291	291	278	278	278
Bahrain	24	24	24	24	34	33	33	33	33	33
Kuwait	35	73	76	81	80	80	50	50	50	50
Oman	57	52	40	40	40	40	52	64	64	64
Qatar	18	18	18	18	18	18	18	18	18	18
UAE	91	105	99	101	106	106	123	184	184	184
Yemen	585	101	89	76	76	72	75	75	79	79

Source: Adapted by Anthony H. Cordesman from various sources and IISS, The Military Balance, various editions.

Figure 3.12   Total Operational Combat Aircraft in All Gulf Forces, 1993–2009

IRAN'S OPTIONS FOR ASYMMETRIC WARFARE

These trends and weaknesses in Iran's conventional forces help explain why Iranian military doctrine has put greater emphasis on the use of asymmetric warfare strategies as a means of a deterrent and defensive posture against its neighbors and its Western adversaries since the end of the Iran-Iraq War in 1989. They also illustrate the danger, however, of relying on such options without a decisive deterrent to U.S. or Gulf escalation to the use of conventional air and missile attacks on Iran, or outright invasion.

Iran has found that asymmetrical tactics and strategy, including its nuclear, biological, and chemical weapons programs, would be most beneficial to maintaining balance of power, and expanding its power and influence in the Middle East region. This strategy has also enabled the Iranian government and military to operate more

Fixed Wing Combat Aircraft

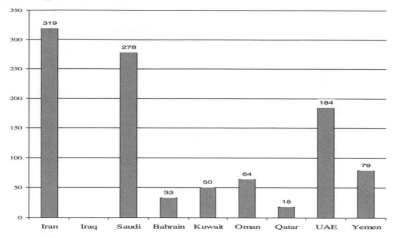

Armed and Attack Helicopters

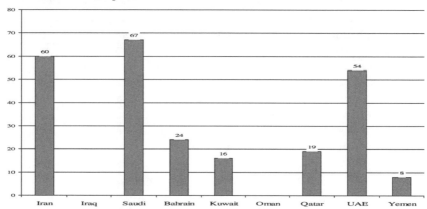

Note: Only armed or combat-capable fixed wing combat aircraft are counted, not other trainers or aircraft.
Note: Yemen has an additional 5 MiG-29S/UB on order. Iraq totals are for March 2003, before the Iraq War.
Source: Adapted by Anthony H. Cordesman from IISS, The Military Balance, various editions. Note that the actual RSAF total may be closer to 260-270 fixed wing combat aircraft.

Figure 3.13   Total Operational Combat Aircraft in 2009

covertly, both in terms of building capabilities for covert, proxy, and indirect warfare and in developing a possible nuclear weapons program.

Mere possession of better weapons has never been the only key to success, and perception of potential capabilities can have a great impact on success as well, both militarily and politically. The most likely "conflicts" in the Middle East are not formal or conventional conflicts, but rather asymmetric wars and/or "wars of intimidation." Iran is currently in an advantageous position to fight these types of war. Iran has maintained its conventional forces since the end of the Iran-Iraq War, but at the same time it has been pursuing a new strategy for fighting present and future foes.

(Totals do not include combat-capable recce but does include OCUs and Hawk combat-capable trainers)

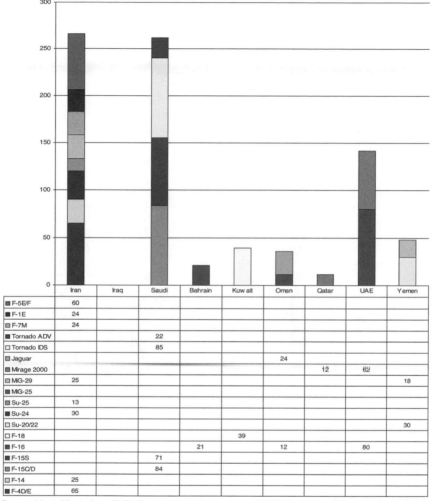

	Iran	Iraq	Saudi	Bahrain	Kuwait	Oman	Qatar	UAE	Yemen
■ F-5E/F	60								
■ F-1E	24								
▨ F-7M	24								
■ Tornado ADV			22						
□ Tornado IDS			85						
▨ Jaguar						24			
■ Mirage 2000							12	82	
□ MiG-29	25								18
■ MiG-25									
▨ Su-25	13								
■ Su-24	30								
□ Su-20/22									30
□ F-18					39				
■ F-16					21		12	80	
■ F-15S			71						
▨ F-15C/D			84						
□ F-14	25								
■ F-4D/E	65								

Source: Adapted by Anthony H. Cordesman from various sources and IISS, The Military Balance, various editions.

Figure 3.14   Gulf High- and Medium-Quality Fixed-Wing Fighter, Fighter Attack, Attack, Strike, and Multirole Combat Aircraft by Type in 2009

Tehran focused its defense efforts on creating a force structure to pursue an asymmetric strategy that focuses more on the use of proxies to create greater regional instability and export its revolution, while at the same time it has pushed the limits in its missile programs and pursued the research and development of chemical and biological agents as well as a suspect nuclear program, which together have the makings of a very dangerous and threatening weapons of mass destruction (WMDs) program.

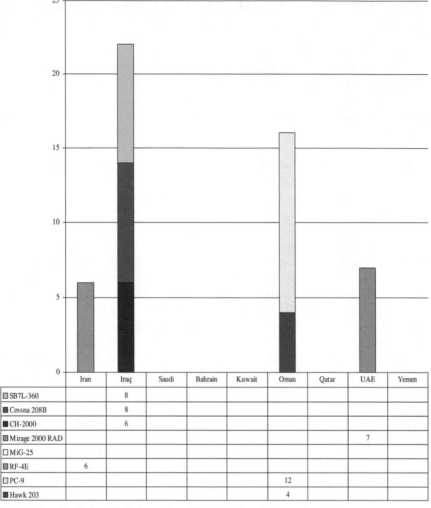

	Iran	Iraq	Saudi	Bahrain	Kuwait	Oman	Qatar	UAE	Yemen
▨ SB7L-360		8							
▤ Cessna 208B		8							
▪ CH-2000		6							
▨ Mirage 2000 RAD								7	
☐ MiG-25									
▨ RF-4E	6								
☐ PC-9						12			
▪ Hawk 203						4			

Source: Adapted by Anthony H. Cordesman from IISS, <u>The Military Balance</u>, various editions.

Figure 3.15   Gulf Reconnaissance Aircraft in 2009

This focus on asymmetric uses of force helps explain the context of why the U.S. Department of State has labeled Iran as the "most active" sponsor of terrorism—and much of what the Department of State describes as terrorism is actually asymmetric warfare:

Iran remained the most active state sponsor of terrorism. Elements of its Islamic Revolutionary Guard Corps (IRGC) were directly involved in the planning and support of terrorist acts throughout the region and continued to support a variety of groups in their use of terrorism to advance their common regional goals. Iran provides aid to

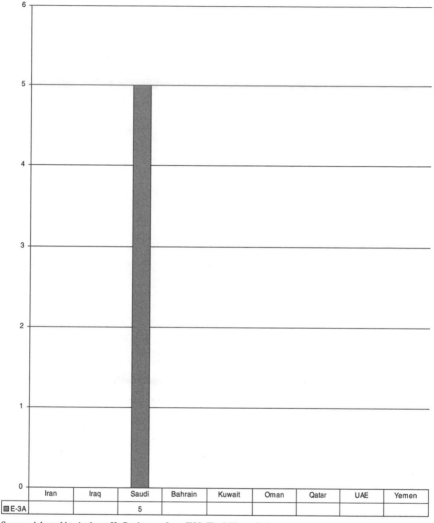

Source: Adapted by Anthony H. Cordesman from IISS, The Military Balance, various editions.

Figure 3.16 Sensor, Airborne Warning and Control System, Command, Control, Communications, Computer, and Intelligence (C⁴I), Early Warning (EW), and Electronic Intelligence Aircraft in 2009

Palestinian terrorist groups, Lebanese Hizballah, Iraq-based militants, and Taliban fighters in Afghanistan.

Iran remains a threat to regional stability and U.S. interests in the Middle East because of its continued support for violent groups, such as Hamas and Hizballah, and its efforts to undercut the democratic process in Lebanon, where it seeks to build Iran's and Hizballah's influence to the detriment of other Lebanese communities.

Figure 3.17   Gulf Land-Based Air Defense Systems in 2009

Country	Major SAM	Light SAM	AA Guns
Bahrain	8 I-Hawks	60 RBS-70s 18 FIM-92A Stingers 7 Crotales	27 guns 15 Oerlikons 35 mm 12 L/70s 40 mm
Iran	16/150+ I-Hawks 3/10 SA-5s 45 SA-2 Guidelines	SA-7/14/16, HQ-7 29 SA-15s Some QW-1 Misaqs 29 TOR-M1s Some HN-5s 30 Rapiers Some FM-80s (Ch Crotale) 15 Tigercats Some FIM-92A Stingers	1,700 guns ZSU-23-4 23 mm ZPU-2/4 23 mm ZU-23 23 mm M-1939 37 mm S-60 57 mm
Iraq	SA-2? SA-3? SA-6?	Roland 1,500 SA-7s 850 SA-8s Some SA-9s Some SA-13s Some SA-14s, SA-16s	6,000 guns ZSU-23-4 23 mm, M-1939 37 mm, ZSU-57-2 SP, 57 mm 85 mm, 100 mm, 130 mm
Kuwait	4/24 I-Hawks Phase III 5 Patriot PAC-2s	6/12 Aspides 48 Starbursts	12+ Oerlikons 35 mm
Oman	None	Blowpipe 2 Mistral SPs 34 SA-7s 6 Blindfires 20 Javelins 40 Rapiers S713 Martellos	26 guns 4 ZU-23-2s 23 mm 10 GDF-005 Skyguards 35 mm 12 L-60s 40 mm
Qatar	None	10 Blowpipes 12 FIM-92A Stingesr 9 Roland IIs 24 Mistrals 20 SA-7s	?
Saudi Arabia	16/128 I-Hawks 16/96 PAC-2 launchers 372 PAC-2 & 432 GEM missiles 141 Shahines	40 Crotales 400 Stinger/Avenger FIM 92-As 500 Mistrals	1,220 guns 92 M-163 Vulcans 20 mm 850 AMX-30SAs 30 mm 128 GDF Oerlikons 35 mm

	73 Crotales/Shahines (static defense) 17 ANA/FPS-117 radar		150 L-70s 40 mm (in store) 150 L-70s 40 mm (in store)
UAE	2/3 I-Hawks	20+ Blowpipes 20 Mistrals Some Rapiers Some Crotales Some RB-70s Some Javelins Some SA-18s	62 guns 42 M-3VDAs 20 mm SP 20 GCF-BM2s 30 mm
Yemen	Some SA-2s, 3s, 6s	Some 800 SA-7s, 9s, 13s, 14s	50 M-167s 20 mm 20 M-163 Vulcan SPs 20 mm 50 ZSU-23-4 SPs 23 mm 100 ZSU-23-2s 23 mm 150 M-1939s 37 mm 120 S-60s 57 mm 40 M-1939 KS-12s 85 mm

Note: ZSU = Zbroyni Syly Ukrayiny (Russian Weapons System); FIM = nomenclature for U.S. man-launched SAM.

Source: Adapted by Anthony H. Cordesman from the IISS, *The Military Balance*, *Periscope*, Jaffee Center for Strategic Studies, *Middle East Military Balance*, *Jane's Sentinel* and *Jane's Defence Weekly*. Some data were adjusted or estimated by the author.

Iran is a principal supporter of groups that are implacably opposed to the Middle East Peace Process, and continues to maintain a high-profile role in encouraging anti-Israel terrorist activity—rhetorically, operationally, and financially. Supreme Leader Khamenei and President Ahmadinejad praised Palestinian terrorist operations, and Iran provided Lebanese Hizballah and Palestinian terrorist groups, notably HAMAS, Palestinian Islamic Jihad, the al-Aqsa Martyrs Brigades, and the Popular Front for the Liberation of Palestine-General Command, with extensive funding, training, and weapons.

Despite its pledge to support the stabilization of Iraq, Iranian authorities continued to provide lethal support, including weapons, training, funding, and guidance, to some Iraqi militant groups that target Coalition and Iraqi security forces and Iraqi civilians. In this way, Iranian government forces have been responsible for attacks on Coalition forces. The Islamic Revolutionary Guard Corps (IRGC)-Qods Force, continued to provide Iraqi militants with Iranian-produced advanced rockets, sniper rifles, automatic weapons, mortars that have killed thousands of Coalition and Iraqi Forces, and explosively formed projectiles (EFPs) that have a higher lethality rate than other types of improvised explosive devices (IEDs), and are specially designed to defeat armored vehicles used by Coalition Forces. The Qods Force, in concert with Lebanese Hizballah, provided training outside Iraq for Iraqi militants in the construction and use of sophisticated IED technology and other advanced weaponry. These individuals then passed on this training to additional militants inside Iraq, a "train-the-trainer" program. In

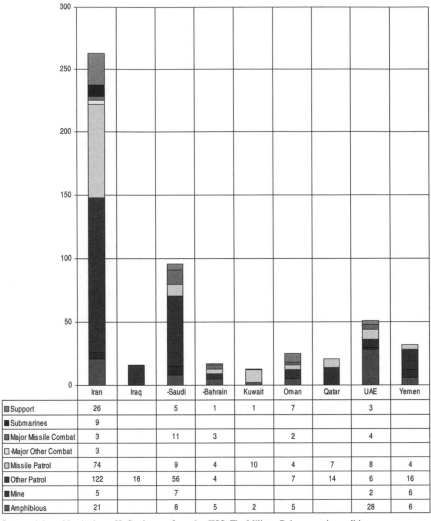

	Iran	Iraq	-Saudi	-Bahrain	Kuwait	Oman	Qatar	UAE	Yemen
■ Support	26		5	1	1	7		3	
■ Submarines	9								
■ Major Missile Combat	3		11	3		2		4	
□ -Major Other Combat	3								
□ Missile Patrol	74		9	4	10	4	7	8	4
■ Other Patrol	122	16	56	4		7	14	6	16
■ Mine	5		7					2	6
■ Amphibious	21		8	5	2	5		28	6

Source: Adapted by Anthony H. Cordesman from the IISS, The Military Balance, various editions.

Figure 3.18   Gulf Naval Ships by Category in 2009

addition, the Qods Force and Hizballah have also provided training inside Iraq. In fact, Coalition Forces captured a Lebanese Hizballah operative in Iraq in 2007.

Iran's IRGC-Qods Force continued to provide weapons and financial aid to the Taliban to support anti-U.S. and anti-Coalition activity in Afghanistan. Since 2006, Iran has arranged a number of shipments of small arms and associated ammunition, rocket propelled grenades, mortar rounds, 107mm rockets, and plastic explosives, possibly including man-portable air defense systems (MANPADs), to the Taliban.

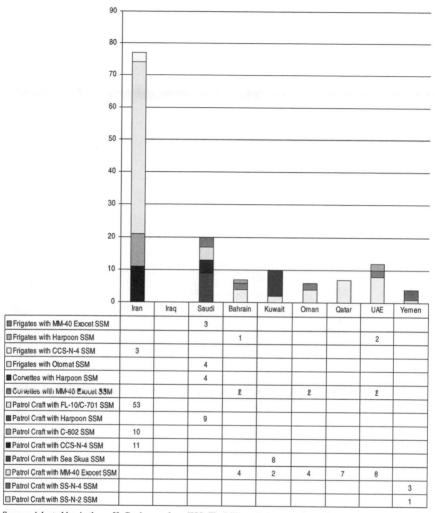

	Iran	Iraq	Saudi	Bahrain	Kuwait	Oman	Qatar	UAE	Yemen
■ Frigates with MM-40 Exocet SSM			3						
■ Frigates with Harpoon SSM				1				2	
☐ Frigates with CCS-N-4 SSM	3								
☐ Frigates with Otomat SSM			4						
■ Corvettes with Harpoon SSM			4						
■ Corvettes with MM-40 Exocet SSM				2			2	2	
☐ Patrol Craft with FL-10/C-701 SSM	53								
■ Patrol Craft with Harpoon SSM			9						
☐ Patrol Craft with C-802 SSM	10								
■ Patrol Craft with CCS-N-4 SSM	11								
■ Patrol Craft with Sea Skua SSM					8				
☐ Patrol Craft with MM-40 Exocet SSM				4	2	4	7	8	
■ Patrol Craft with SS-N-4 SSM									3
☐ Patrol Craft with SS-N-2 SSM									1

Source: Adapted by Anthony H. Cordesman from IISS, The Military Balance, various editions and material provided by US experts.

Figure 3.19   Gulf Warships with Antiship Missiles in 2009

Iran remained unwilling to bring to justice senior al-Qa'ida (AQ) members it has detained, and has refused to publicly identify those senior members in its custody. Iran has repeatedly resisted numerous calls to transfer custody of its AQ detainees to their countries of origin or third countries for interrogation or trial. Iran also continued to fail to control the activities of some AQ members who fled to Iran following the fall of the Taliban regime in Afghanistan.[5]

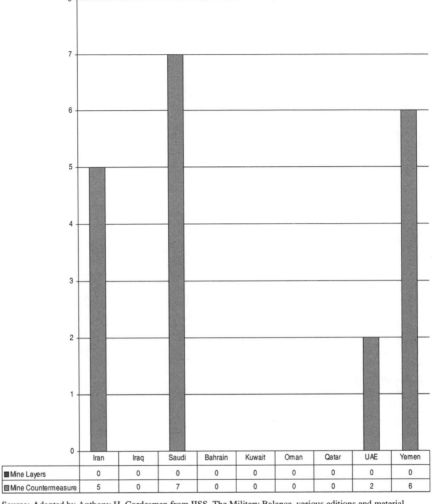

	Iran	Iraq	Saudi	Bahrain	Kuwait	Oman	Qatar	UAE	Yemen
■ Mine Layers	0	0	0	0	0	0	0	0	0
▣ Mine Countermeasure	5	0	7	0	0	0	0	2	6

Source: Adapted by Anthony H. Cordesman from IISS, The Military Balance, various editions and material provided by US experts.

Figure 3.20   Gulf Mine Warfare Ships in 2009

THE INTERACTION BETWEEN WMDS, CONVENTIONAL FORCES, AND FORCES FOR ASYMMETRICAL WARFARE

Whatever the actual motives of Iran's leaders may be, a combination of its emerging strengths in asymmetric warfare and nuclear-armed missile forces that can deter or limit conventional reprisals can do much to compensate for its lack of modern conventional forces.[6]

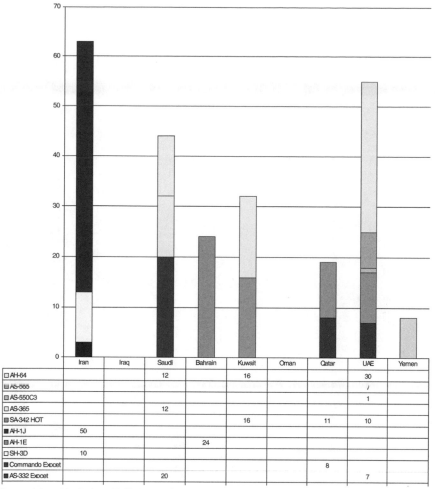

Source: Adapted by Anthony H. Cordesman from IISS, <u>The Military Balance</u>, various editions.

Figure 3.21   Gulf Attack, Antiship, and ASW Helicopters in 2009

	Iran	Iraq	Saudi	Bahrain	Kuwait	Oman	Qatar	UAE	Yemen
☐ AH-64			12		16			30	
▦ AS-565								7	
▨ AS-550C3								1	
☐ AS-365			12						
▣ SA-342 HOT					16		11	10	
■ AH-1J	50								
▩ AH-1E				24					
☐ SH-3D	10								
■ Commando Exocet							8		
■ AS-332 Exocet			20					7	

Iran can exploit a combination of carefully selected precision-guided munitions systems, weapons of mass destruction, and the widening use of asymmetrical warfare strategies to make up for shortcomings in conventional warfighting capabilities. Its long-range missiles and WMD programs can both provide a powerful deterrent and support its asymmetric strategies.

Asymmetric strategy is not based upon inflicting casualties on enemies, but rather on gaining support due to the casualties inflicted by your adversary. Jacques Baud writes that "despite every indication to the contrary, asymmetric strategies do not set themselves the objective to maximize violence, but to deliver a pain 'just sufficient' to provoke an 'over-reaction,' by playing on image and emotional impact."[7]

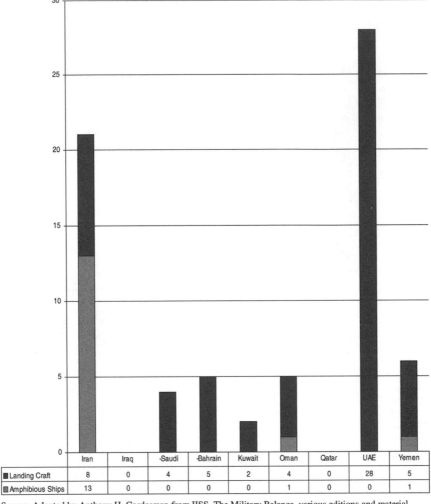

	Iran	Iraq	-Saudi	-Bahrain	Kuwait	Oman	Qatar	UAE	Yemen
■ Landing Craft	8	0	4	5	2	4	0	28	5
■ Amphibious Ships	13	0	0	0	0	1	0	0	1

Source: Adapted by Anthony H. Cordesman from IISS, The Military Balance, various editions and material provided by US and Saudi experts. Estimates differ on Saudi landing craft, because of different ways to count operational status. Some experts put the figure at 6 LCMs and 2 LCUs.

Figure 3.22   Gulf Amphibious Warfare Ships in 2009

Asymmetric warfare can also involve conflicts in which the resources of two belligerents differ in essence and, in the struggle, interact and attempt to exploit each other's characteristic weaknesses. Such struggles often involve strategies and tactics of unconventional warfare, the "weaker" combatants attempting to use a strategy to offset deficiencies in quantity or quality.[8]

For example, work by Michael Connell of the Center for Naval Analyses notes that the IRGC is developing such tactics in ways that could form a layered or "mosaic" defense with the army and air forces, where the IRGC would keep up constant pressure on any advancing U.S. forces. He indicates that the IRGC has developed special stay-behind units or "cells" that would include some 1,800 to 3,000 teams of three to four soldiers whose main mission would be to attack U.S. lines of supply and communication, strike at elements in rear areas, and conduct ambushes of combat troops. This could include sending units forward into countries such as Iraq and Afghanistan to attack U.S. forces there, or encourage local forces to do so, and sending teams to raid or infiltrate the southern Gulf States friendly to the United States.[9]

At the same time, Connell notes that if the Iranian Army was defeated and an attacker such as the United States moved into Iran's major cities, the IRGC, the Iranian Army, and the Basij are now organized and trained to fight a much more dispersed war of attrition in which force elements would disperse and scatter, carrying out a constant series of attacks on U.S. forces wherever they deployed as well as against U.S. lines of communication and supply. Such elements would have great independence of action rather than relying on centralized command. The IRGC and the Iranian Army have clearly paid close attention to both the limited successes that Saddam's Fedayeen had against the U.S. advance on Baghdad, and the far more successful efforts of Iraqi insurgents and militias in attacking U.S. and other Coalition forces following the fall of Baghdad.

One technique such forces practice is using cities and built-up areas as defensive areas that provide concealment and opportunities for ambushes and for the use of swarming tactics, which forces an attacker to disperse large numbers of forces to try to clear and secure given neighborhoods. Connell indicates that some 2,500 Basij staged such an exercise in the Western suburbs of Tehran in February 2007. Once again, Iran can draw on the lessons of the fighting in Iraq. It also, however, employed such tactics with great success against Iraqi forces during the Iran-Iraq War, and it has closely studied the lessons of urban and built-up area fighting in Somalia and Lebanon.

IRAN'S ASYMMETRIC WARFIGHTING CAPABILITIES (REAL AND POTENTIAL)

Iran's military development efforts changed drastically after the UN-sponsored cease-fire agreement went into effect on August 20, 1988, ending the eight-year-long Iran-Iraq War. Iran focused its efforts on chemical, biological, radiological, and nuclear (CBRN) research and development (R&D) programs, counterintelligence, and supporting fundamentalist and terrorist groups throughout the region. It pursued a different strategy for projecting power and influencing the regional balance. It also sought to influence and control nonstate actors and movements, potential, and the security forces and militias in Lebanon and Iraq. It also sought to exert power through the use of the IRGC in implementing a variety of strategies for asymmetric warfare.

The IRGC in Iran's Asymmetric Strategy

Iran's foreign policy is a product of the ideology of Iran's Islamic Revolution, blended with long-standing national interests, and is intended largely to overturn the "status quo" in the Middle East that Iran believes favors the United States, Israel, and Sunni Muslim regimes. The Iranian Revolutionary Guard Corps, its Quds Force, and the various proxies that they support are integral tools in the implementation of Iran's foreign policy aims.

The U.S. Department of State report on international terrorism for 2008, released April 30, 2009, again stated (as it has for more than a decade) that Iran "remained the most active state sponsor of terrorism" in 2008, and it again attributed the terrorist activity primarily to the IRGC.[10] The IRGC is not only involved in suspected terrorist and insurgent activities, it is also involved in Iran's asymmetric strategy in a number of other ways.

The IRGC operates most of Iran's surface-to-surface missiles and is believed to have custody over potentially deployed nuclear weapons, most or all other CBRN weapons, and to operate Iran's nuclear-armed missile forces if they are deployed. It operates or controls much of Iran's military industries as well as dual-use and "civil" operations. As a result, the links between the IRGC and Iran's nuclear program have been so close that its leaders were singled out under the UN Security Council Resolutions passed on December 23, 2006, and March 24, 2007, and had their assets frozen.[11]

At the same time, the IRGC has large paramilitary forces that can be used for both conventional and asymmetric warfare. The IRGC (Pasdaran) has some 125,000 men in its force structure and also has substantial capabilities for covert operations. This includes the Quds Force and other elements that operate covertly or openly overseas, working with Hezbollah of Lebanon, Shi'ite militias in Iraq, and Shi'ites in Afghanistan. It was members of the IRGC that seized 15 British sailors and marines, who seem to still have been in Iraqi waters, in March 2007.[12]

The IRGC has small elements equipped with armor and has the equivalent of conventional army units, and some units are trained for covert missions and asymmetric warfare, but most of its forces are lightly equipped infantry trained and equipped for internal security missions. These forces are reported to have between 120,000 and 130,000 men, but such totals are uncertain. They also include conscripts recruited from the same pool as regular army conscripts, and training and retention levels are low. The IRGC land forces also control the Basij (Mobilization of the Oppressed) and other paramilitary forces if they are mobilized for war.

This makes the IRGC the center of much of Iran's effort to develop asymmetric warfare tactics to counter a U.S. invasion. Work by Michael Connell notes that the IRGC has been systematically equipping, organizing, and retraining its forces to fight decentralized partisan and guerrilla warfare.[13]

This assessment of the IRGC has been echoed in more recent studies including one by Frederick W. Kagan, Kimberly Kagan, and Danielle Pletka at the American Enterprise Institute;[14] another by Jahangir Arasli, at the George C. Marshall

European Center for Security Studies;[15] as well as one by Fariborz Haghshenass at the Washington Institute for Near East Policy.[16]

The IRGC has studied and continues to learn from the U.S. operations in Iraq and Afghanistan, as well as Hezbollah's continued role in Israel and Lebanon. From the reporting of exercises that the IRGC has conducted, it can be assessed that the IRGC is continuing to develop a strategy that takes advantage of its potential enemies' weaknesses posed by conventional warfighting doctrine and current counterinsurgency shortfalls.

It has strengthened the antitank and antihelicopter weaponry of IRGC battalions and stressed independent battalion-sized operations that can fight with considerable independence even if Iran loses much of the coherence in its command, control, communications, and intelligence capabilities.[17] Its exercises have included simulated attacks on U.S. AH-64 attack helicopters with Iran's more modern manportable surface-to-air missiles, using mines and using IED-like systems to attack advancing armored forces.

The IRGC has attempted to develop and practice deception, concealment, and camouflage methods to reduce the effectiveness of U.S. and other modern imagery coverage, including dispersing into small teams and avoiding the use of uniformed personnel and military vehicles. While the credibility and effectiveness of such tactics are uncertain, the IRGC claims to be adopting tactics to avoid enemy radars and satellites. Both the IRGC and the army have also attempted to deal with U.S. signals and communications intelligence collection capabilities by making extensive use of buried fiber optics and secure communications and developing more secure ways to use the Internet and commercial landlines. Iran claims to be creating a relatively advanced secure communications system, but its success is uncertain.[18]

According to the Jane's report, the IRGC is to focus on "less traditional defense duties," such as enforcing border security, commanding the country's ballistic missile and potential weapons of mass destruction forces, and preparing for a closing of the Strait of Hormuz with military means.[19]

IRGC Air Force

The IRGC air force is believed to operate Iran's Shahab-3 intermediate-range ballistic missiles units and may have had custody of its chemical weapons and any biological weapons. While the actual operational status of the Shahab-3 remains uncertain, Iran's Supreme Leader, Ayatollah Ali Khamenei, announced in 2003 that Shahab-3 missiles had been delivered to the IRGC.[20]

It is not clear what combat formations exist within the IRGC, but the IRGC may operate Iran's 10 EMB-312 Tucanos. It also seems to operate many of Iran's 45 PC-7 training aircraft, as well as some Pakistani-made trainers at a training school near Mushshak, but this school may be run by the regular air force. It has also claimed to manufacture gliders for use in unconventional warfare. These are unsuitable delivery platforms, but could at least carry a small number of weapons.[21]

The IRGC could follow the path of Iraq in 1990 and create R&D programs to adapt modified aircraft drop tanks for biological agent spray operations. The Iraqi program attempted to create a tank that could be attached either to a piloted fighter or UAV guided by another piloted aircraft. The tank was designed to spray up to 2,000 liters of anthrax on target. The IRGC is certainly capable of duplicating this type of program at its current R&D levels and capabilities.

IRGC Naval Forces

From an Iranian military perspective, asymmetric naval warfare employs available equipment, flexible tactics, superior morale, and the physical and geographical characteristics of the area of operation to defend vital economic resources, inflict losses unacceptable to the enemy, and ultimately destroy technologically superior enemy forces. More specifically, the asymmetric naval warfighter exploits enemy vulnerabilities through the use of "swarming" tactics by well-armed small boats and fast-attack craft to mount surprise attacks at unexpected times and places.[22] The terrain of the Persian Gulf, the Strait of Hormuz, and the Gulf of Oman gives Iran's use of asymmetric forces a tactical advantage in harassing ships in the region, as well as in its greater defense strategy.

The roots of the IRGC navy (IRGCN) can be traced back to 1984 as a support entity for amphibious operations in the southern marshlands of Iraq; it was officially established as an independent military entity in 1985. Despite initial setbacks in regards to equipment, manpower, and adequate training, the IRGCN quickly became a serious threat during the Tanker War of 1987–1988 and quickly built up its tally of attacks on carefully identified oil tankers carrying Kuwaiti and Saudi oil, from 37 during the first year of the Tanker War to more than 96 in 1987.[23]

By the end of the war, the political leadership was convinced of the IRGC's ability to defend Iranian shipping, control sea lines of communication, and even to cross the Persian Gulf and take the fight to the enemy, if necessary. As a result, Iran identified the following requirements for its naval forces:[24]

Large numbers of antiship missiles on various types of launch platforms

Small fast-attack craft, heavily armed with rockets or antiship missiles

More fast mine-laying platforms

An enhanced subsurface warfare capability with various types of submarines and sensors

More small, mobile, hard-to-detect platforms, such as semisubmersibles and unmanned
    aerial vehicles

More specialized training

More customized or purpose-built high-tech equipment

Better communications and coordination between fighting units

More timely intelligence and effective counterintelligence/deception

Enhanced ability to disrupt the enemy's command, control, communications, and
    intelligence capability.

The importance of initiative, and the avoidance of frontal engagements with large U.S. naval surface warfare elements

Means to mitigate the vulnerability of even small naval units to air and missile attack.

To operate effectively, unconventional naval warfighters and logistical support units need secure bases, staging areas, and routes to and from their areas of operation. There are more than 10 large and 60 small ports and harbors along Iran's southern coastline, in addition to the many scattered fishing and sailing villages and towns, all of which offer excellent hiding places for small surface combatants.[25] The IRGC has numerous staging areas in such places and has organized its Basij militia among the local inhabitants to undertake support operations.[26]

In recent years, the role of the IRGCN has grown. The IRGC was put in charge of defending Iran's Persian Gulf coast in September 2008, is operational in the Persian Gulf and the Gulf of Oman, and could potentially operate elsewhere if given suitable sealift or facilities.[27] The IRGC has a naval branch consisting of approximately 22,000 men, including marine units of around 5,000 men, and the potential during a conflict to increase its manpower threefold with Basij militias from littoral provinces, according to claims by Admiral Morteza Saffari.[28] Such a force could deliver conventional weapons, bombs, mines, and CBRN weapons into ports and oil and desalination facilities. No common fleet structure has been identified, but the basic pattern seems to be small "naval guerrilla" formations. "Boghammar"-type patrol craft and coastal missile battery sites were under IRGC control.

Iran's unconventional naval warfare force consists of six elements: surface vessels, midget and unconventional submarines, missiles and rockets, naval mines, aviation, and military industries.[29] Iran uses these elements in its national defense strategy, but they can also be used in an asymmetric strategy to harass and disrupt shipping lanes.

Marines and sailors of the IRGC's navy are stationed in almost every Iranian port, harbor, and islands in the Persian Gulf.[30] The naval branch has bases and contingency facilities in the Gulf, many near key shipping channels and some near the Strait of Hormuz. These include facilities at Al-Farsiyah, Halul (an oil platform), Sirri, Abu Musa, Bandar Abbas, Khorramshahr, and Larak. Iran has also started constructing new naval bases along the coasts of the Persian Gulf and the Sea of Oman.

On October 27, 2008, Iran opened a new naval base at Jask, located at the southern mouth of the Strait of Hormuz, a strategic choke point for Persian Gulf oil. Iran's Deputy Army Commander Brigadier General Abdolrahim Moussavi announced that the new naval base at Jask would serve as an "impenetrable naval barrier" against Iran's potential adversaries. Moussavi stressed Iran's commitment to expanding its strategic reach, arguing, "In the past, our military had to brace itself for countering regional enemies. This is while today we are faced with extra-regional threats."[31]

In January 2005, Rear Admiral Abbas Mohtaj—then navy chief—said that instead of seeking to defeat the enemy, Iran's naval operations aim to make its enemies "fail to achieve its goals" and therefore should adopt "asymmetric defense." The opening of naval bases such as Jask was viewed by Mohataj, and has been repeated by other military commanders, as a way to increase Iran's power projection and allow it to close the Strait of Hormuz.[32]

Iran also upgraded a naval base at Assalouyeh in Iran's southern Bushehr Province. This base is the fourth in a string of IRGC bases along the waterway that will extend from Bandar Abbas to Pasa Bandar near the Pakistan border, as part of what IRGC's Navy Commander Rear Admiral Morteza Saffari says is the "new mission of the navy to establish an impenetrable line of defense at the entrance to the Sea of Oman."[33]

The IRGC is now reported to operate all mobile land-based antiship missile batteries and has an array of missile boats, torpedo boats, catamaran patrol boats with rocket launchers, motor boats with heavy machine guns, mines as well as Yono (Qadir)-class midget submarines, and a number of swimmer delivery vehicles.[34]

The IRGC controls Iran's coastal defense forces, including naval guns and an HY-2 Seersucker land-based antiship missile unit deployed in five to seven sites along the Gulf coast. Iran has repeatedly warned that in case of any attack by either the United States or Israel, it would target 32 American bases in the Middle East and close the strategic Strait of Hormuz; a report by the Washington Institute for Near East Policy released in September 2008 says that in the two decades since the Iran-Iraq War, the Islamic Republic has excelled in naval capabilities and is able to wage unique asymmetric warfare against larger naval forces.[35]

In January 2008, Iranian speedboats belonging to the IRGC became involved in an incident with the U.S. Navy near the Straits of Hormuz. Again in late April 2008, a U.S.-flagged cargo ship contracted by the U.S. Navy was harassed by two small boats in the Persian Gulf and subsequently fired warning shots at the ships.

The IRGC naval forces have at least 40 light patrol boats, 10 Houdong-guided missile patrol boats armed with C-802 antiship missiles, and a battery of HY-2 Seersucker land-based antiship missiles. Some of these systems could be modified to carry a small CBRN weapon, but hardly are optimal delivery platforms because of their limited-range payload and sensor/guidance platforms unsuited for the mission.

An Iranian version of the C-802 was, in fact, used by Hezbollah against an Israeli Saar 5-class missile boat during the Israel-Lebanon War of 2006. This same weaponry could be used by the IRGC against the U.S. Navy in the Persian Gulf.

Iran has a history of harassing and even confronting US forces in the Persian Gulf going back to 1987 during the "Tanker War," when Iran mined sea-lanes in the area and a U.S. frigate, the USS *Samuel B. Roberts*, was almost blown in half. The United States delivered an overwhelming retaliatory strike against the Iranian Navy and the IRGC.

Iran could launch a coordinated attack involving explosives-laden remote-controlled boats, swarming speedboats, semisubmersible torpedo boats, fast attack crafts (FACs), kamikaze UAVs, midget and attack submarines, and shore-based antiship missile and artillery fire, all concentrated on a U.S.-escorted convoy or surface action group transiting the Strait of Hormuz, and barrages of rockets with cluster warheads could be used to suppress enemy defensive fire and carrier air operations.[36]

The deputy commander of the IRGC's navy, Rear Admiral Ali Fadavi, told the Fars News Agency on November 11, 2008, that both unmanned speedboats and UAVs are now mass-produced in the country.[37]

The IRGC could also construct or purchase self-propelled, semisubmersible (SPSS) vessels from South American narcotraffickers. In a paper by U.S. Navy Captain Wade F. Wilkenson, he reports that "in dozens of secret, makeshift shipyards scattered throughout the lowlands of South America, narcotraffickers have been building SPSS vessels in record numbers. Designed to ferry illicit drugs from Colombia to staging points in Central America and Mexico, the SPSS vessels may seem yet another in a long string of innovative methods drug traffickers use to sneak past law enforcement." Due to "the craft's ability to evade detection, capacity to carry tons of any type of cargo thousands of miles,"[38] it could be assessed that SPSS vessels could very well have greater national security implications and could be an effective asymmetrical naval warfare weapon.

In his report, Captain Wilkenson goes on to describe these SPSS vessels as follows:

SPSS vessels vary in design and construction but share common characteristics. Size and capacity range from 10 to 25 meters in length and 3 to 15 metric tons of cargo space. Generally made from wood framing and fiberglass, some designs include steel hull construction for better seaworthiness and durability. Although typically ballasted with tons of lead, concrete, or rock, newer versions provide means to change draft under way. By filling fuel tanks with seawater as they empty, they maintain a steady, ultra-low profile that make them nearly impossible to spot by eye at any distance over one nautical mile.

Range of an SPSS is about 1,500 miles, but some store enough fuel to travel twice that distance. A small conning tower allows a wave-top view for steering. Piping redirects diesel engine exhaust back toward the boat's wake to lower the infrared signature. Equipped with GPS [global positioning system], SPSS vessels navigate independently without need for external communication. They can cruise faster than eight knots but tend to operate at slower speeds to minimize wake detection. Such technological enhancements and tactics make the SPSS increasingly complex and better capable of defying surveillance and detection.[39]

The IRGC could easily adapt this technology for its needs, which would create a stealthy addition to its asymmetric arsenal, which it could use in its own trafficking operations or as an added capability in harassing and hindering shipping operations in the Strait of Hormuz and the Persian Gulf. These vessels could also pose a serious threat to U.S. naval operations in the Persian Gulf and the Sea of Oman, taking advantage of known vulnerabilities in the U.S. Navy's capabilities to react to these types of threats.

The IRGC is also reported to have a variety of antiship missiles at its disposal. During a military exercise in 2006, the IRGC's navy test-fired a Hoot torpedo it claimed was capable of moving at 195 knots, or four times faster than a normal torpedo. Most military and industry analysts have concluded that the Hoot is derived from the Russian VA-111 Shkval supercavitation torpedo, which travels at the same speed.[40] IRGC Commander Major General Mohammed Ali Jafari announced in

August 2008 that Iran had test-fired a "new naval weapon that could destroy any vessel in a range of 300 km [kilometers]."[41]

The IRGC has a wide variety of assets at its disposal to threaten shipping lanes in the Persian Gulf, the Gulf of Oman, and the Caspian Sea. It has the capability to conduct hit-and-run operations, lay a variety of mines, target ships with shore-based missiles from an approximate range of 90 km, raid offshore facilities, and direct many of its speedboats at civilian and naval targets primarily in the Hormuz choke point, using swarming tactics.

Its forces can carry out extensive raids against Gulf shipping, carry out regular amphibious exercises with the land branch of the IRGC against objectives such as the islands in the Gulf, and could conduct raids against Saudi Arabia or other countries on the southern Gulf coast. They give Iran a major capability for asymmetric warfare. The Guards also seem to work closely with Iranian intelligence and appear to be represented unofficially in some embassies, Iranian businesses and purchasing offices, and other foreign fronts.

The IRGC Intelligence Branch

The roughly 2,000 staff members of the Islamic Revolution Guard Corps intelligence force are a largely politicized force with a political mission. According to Jane's, their conformity and loyalty to the regime are unquestionable.[42]

The main task of the IRGC Intelligence Branch is to gather intelligence in the Muslim world. As far as domestic security is concerned, the organization targets the enemies of the Islamic Revolution and also participates in their prosecution and trials.[43] In addition, it works closely with the IRGC's Qods Corps, which also operates covertly outside Iran.

Proxy and Covert CBRN Operations

As has been touched upon earlier, the IRGC plays a major role in Iran's military industries. Its lead role in Iran's efforts to acquire surface-to-surface missiles (SSMs) and WMDs gives it growing experience with advanced military technology. As a result, the IRGC is believed to be the branch of Iran's forces that plays the largest role in Iran's military industries.[44] It also operates all of Iran's Scuds, controls most of its chemical and biological weapons, and provides the military leadership for missile production and the production of all weapons of mass destruction.

The IRGC is a powerful economic force, controlling key elements of Iraq's defense industry. It seems to operate part of Iran's covert trading network, a system established after the fall of the Shah to buy arms and military parts through various cover and false flag organizations. It is not clear, however, how much of this network is controlled by the IRGC vs. the Ministry of Defense. For example, the same UN resolution dealing with Iran's nuclear proliferation listed a wide range of entities where the role of the IRGC is often unclear.[45]

The IRGC has become a leading contracting organization, bidding for other contracts including at least some oil and gas projects. Like most Iranian entities associated with government projects, it is reported to get many contracts out of favoritism and/or without competitive bidding. It is believed to now be as corrupt as civil entities and religious foundations such as the Bunyods.[46]

The IRGC has a complex structure that includes both political and military units. It has separate organizational elements for its land, naval, and air units, which include both military and paramilitary units. The Basij and the tribal units of the Pasdaran are subordinated to its land unit command, although the commander of the Basij often seems to report directly to the commander in chief and minister of the Pasdaran and through him to the Leader of the Islamic Revolution.

The IRGC has close ties to the foreign operations branch of the Iranian Ministry of Intelligence and Security (MOIS), particularly through the IRGC's Qods Force. The MOIS was established in 1983 and has an extensive network of offices in Iranian embassies. It is often difficult to separate the activities of the IRGC, the Vezarat-e Ettela'at va Amniat-e Keshvar, and the Foreign Ministry, and many seem to be integrated operations managed by a ministerial committee called the "Special Operations Council" that includes the Leader of the Islamic Revolution, the president, the Minister of Intelligence and Security, and other members of the Supreme Council for National Defense.[47]

Other elements of the IRGC can support proxy or covert use of CBRN weapons. They run some training camps inside Iran for outside "volunteers." Some IRGC still seem to be deployed in Lebanon and actively involved in training and arming Hezbollah, other anti-Israeli groups, and other elements.[48] The IRGC has been responsible for major arms shipments to Hezbollah, including large numbers of AT-3 antitank guided missiles, long-range rockets, and some Iranian-made Mohajer UAVs.[49]

Iran exported thousands of 122-mm rockets and Fajr-4 and Fajr-5 long-range rockets to Hezbollah in Lebanon, including the Arash with a range of 21–29 km. These reports give the Fajr-5 a range of 75 km with a payload of 200 kg. Iran seems to have sent such arms to Hezbollah and some various Palestinian movements, including some shiploads of arms to the Palestinian Authority.[50]

It has provided arms, training, and military technology to Shi'ite militias in Iraq and may have provided such support to Sunni Islamist extremists as well, which led to attacks on U.S. and Coalition forces. These transfers have included relatively advanced shaped charge and triggering components, which have sharply increased the lethality of militia and insurgent attacks using IEDs on U.S. and Coalition armor. There were also growing indicators that similar training, weapons, and other aid were being provided to Shi'ite forces and Taliban elements in Afghanistan in 2007.

Military Exercises

Iran also sends signals about its use of asymmetric warfare through its military parades and exercises. Tehran also uses such exercises, in part, as a display of force in order to look as if it is taking a harder stand against Western influence and as a distraction from its controversial nuclear activities. The follow is a brief chronology of Iran's military exercises between January 2006 and December 2008:

- **January 27, 2006:** Iran completed a huge military exercise that tested Teheran's ability to attack Western shipping and Arab oil facilities. Sources said the exercise was designed to test capabilities to strike U.S. and Arab targets throughout the area of the Persian Gulf. According to a diplomatic source, the exercise was meant to show the West that Iran could stop all oil shipments in the Gulf and destroy numerous oil facilities in Gulf Arab countries and included a range of fighter-jets and helicopters from the Iranian Air Force, with the Iranian Navy contributing surface vessels and submarines.[51]

- **August 19, 2006:** Iran launched a series of large-scale military exercises aimed at introducing the country's new defensive doctrine, state-run television reported. The military exercise, involving 12 infantry regiments, is called "The Blow of Zolfaghar." The television report said the military exercise would occur in 14 of the country's 30 provinces and could last as long as five weeks. The first stage of the maneuvers began with air strikes in the southeastern province of Sistan va Baluchistan, the report said. Iran has routinely held war games over the past two decades to improve its combat readiness and test locally made equipment such as missiles, tanks, and armored personnel carriers.[52]

- **November 2, 2006:** Iran's Revolutionary Guards began another series of military exercises dubbed "Great Prophet II" on November 2. Iran began the 10 days of maneuvers in the Persian Gulf by test firing dozens of missiles, including the long-range Shahab-3 (estimated range: 2000 km or 1,240 miles), Iranian state-run television said. Among other weapons tested was the Shahab-2, which Iran says can carry a cluster warhead that can deliver 1,400 bomblets at once.[53]

  ○ Major General Yahya Rahim Safavi, leader of the Revolutionary Guards, said on television that Iran's military exercises were not meant to threaten neighboring countries. "We want to show our deterrent and defensive power to trans-regional enemies, and we hope they will understand the message of the maneuvers," he said. "The first and main goal is to demonstrate the power and national determination to defend the country against possible threat." General Safavi said the exercises would last 10 days and would take place in the Persian Gulf, the Gulf of Oman, and several Iranian provinces.

- **March 22–30, 2007:** Iran launched week-long war-games on March 22 on its southern shores, state television reported. The military exercises are being carried out in the Persian Gulf by Iran's regular navy, the report said, adding that they would continue until March 30. Domestically designed military equipment would be used throughout the maneuvers, it added.[54]

- **January 7, 2008:** In what U.S. officials called a serious provocation, Iranian boats harassed and provoked three U.S. Navy ships in the strategic Strait of Hormuz, threatening to explode the American vessels. Five small boats began charging the U.S. ships, dropping boxes in the water in front of the ships and forcing the U.S. ships to take evasive maneuvers, a Pentagon official said.[55]

- ○ U.S. forces were on the verge of firing on the Iranian boats in the early Sunday incident, when the boats—believed to be from the Iranian Revolutionary Guard's navy—turned and moved away, a Pentagon official said. "It is the most serious provocation of this sort that we've seen yet," said the official, who spoke on the condition of anonymity because he was not authorized to speak on the record. U.S. Department of Defense spokesman Bryan Whitman called it a "serious incident. This is something that deserves an explanation."

- **July 7, 2008:** Iran's elite Islamic Revolutionary Guards Corps launched large-scale war-games dubbed "Exercise Stake Net." The Iranian military maneuvers took place on the same day the United States announced it, too, would be holding naval exercises in the Persian Gulf. Iranian state media said that the military maneuvers by the IRGC's navy and air force missiles unit were aimed at improving the force's military abilities.[56]

  - ○ Separately, Brigadier General Mahmoud Chaharbaghi, commander of the IRGC Ground Forces artillery and missiles unit, announced that 50 of his unit's brigades were being armed with smart weapons and cluster bombs.

  - ○ During the exercise, Iran's IRGC successfully test-fired advanced shore-to-sea, surface-to-surface, and sea-to-air missiles. Iran also tested the upgraded Shahab-3 missile equipped with a one-ton conventional warhead capable of hitting targets within a 2,000-km (1,245-mile) range. Iran's naval forces also made a breakthrough in building various types of "radar-evading" submarines to guard its territorial waters.

- **September 8, 2008:** On September 8, the IRGC and the army took part in three days of routine drills involving antiaircraft defense systems, the Iranian Students News Agency reported. The main purpose of the maneuvers was to maintain and promote the combat readiness of relevant units and to test new weapons and defense plans.[57]

  - ○ Iran's Chief Navy Commander, Rear Admiral Habibollah Sayyari, said Iran is upgrading its naval fleet with a new generation of domestically built submarines.

- **September 15, 20008:** The Islamic Republic Air Force will test Iran's domestic-made warfare in a joint military exercise with the IRGC, the Defense Ministry says. The joint aerial maneuver is aimed at boosting Iran's defensive capabilities and operational tactics, Iran's Defense Minister Brigadier General Mostafa Mohammad-Najjar said. The military exercise involves The Islamic Republic of Iran Air Force (IRIAF) and the IRGC.[58]

- **October 10, 2008:** Radical Islamist militiamen affiliated to Iran's IRGC staged military exercises in the suburbs of Tehran to defend the Iranian capital against "natural disasters" and "enemy assaults."[59]

  - ○ Members of the paramilitary Basij took part in military drills under the command of the Tharallah Garrison in Tehran. Similar war games will be held in Karaj, Islamshahr, Shahre Rey, Rabat Karim, and Varamin, said the acting deputy commandant of the IRGC, Brigadier General Mohammad Hejazi, who also commands the Tharallah Garrison.

  - ○ Meanwhile another senior Basij leader announced that the paramilitary force was giving "specialized training" to its units across Iran. "These units are receiving specialized air, sea and ground training to be prepared for defending the country, the ruling establishment, and the revolution," said Brigadier General Ahmad Zolqadr on the sidelines of a military parade in Zanjan, northwest Iran. Zolqadr is the operational commander of the Basij.

- **October 18, 2008:** The Iranian Air Force tested several surface-to-air missiles during the first stage of the Fadayan-e Harim-e Velayat (Devotees of Guardianship) military exercise. Iranian F-14s, F-4s and F-5s hit land targets with smart missiles during the second stage of the exercises.[60]

- **November 8, 2008:** Iran successfully tested a new missile near the Iraqi border during war games. Iranian media claimed that the Samen missile was domestically designed and manufactured and further boosted Iran's combat readiness.[61]

- **December 2–7, 2008:** On December 2, Iranian officials reported that they had begun six days of naval war games dubbed "Unity 87" in the Gulf and the Strait of Hormuz, the strategic transport route for global oil supplies that the Islamic Republic has threatened to close if it is attacked.[62]

  ○ The high-profile exercise included destroyers, missile boats, submarines, helicopters, fighters, and UAVs, bringing the total number of participating combat vessels to 60. Iran sought to accomplish a number of designated military objectives that include dealing with a potential Israeli and U.S. threat, closing the Strait of Hormuz to local and international shipping. and the testing of new and improved military assets.

  ○ "The aim of this maneuver is to increase the level of readiness of Iran's naval forces and also to test and to use domestically-made naval weaponry," Admiral Qasem Rostamabadi told state radio.

  ○ The radio said the naval maneuvers would cover an area of 50,000 square miles, including the Sea of Oman off Iran's southern coast. An Iranian naval commander was quoted as saying the country's navy could strike an enemy well beyond its shores and as far away as Bab al-Mandab, the southern entrance to the Red Sea that leads to the Suez Canal.

  ○ During the exercises Iran's military test-fired a new surface-to-surface missile from a warship as part of exercises along a strategic shipping route, state media reported. "The Nasr-2 was fired from a warship and hit its target at a distance of 30 km (19 miles) and destroyed it," the official Islamic Republic News Agency said, adding it was the first test of the new, medium-range missile.

- **May 26, 2009:** Iran sent six warships into international waters including the Gulf of Aden, a local newspaper reported, just days after it test-fired its Sajjil-2 missile. "We have dispatched six warships to international waters and the Gulf of Aden," naval commander Habibollah Sayari was quoted as saying in the Jomhuri Eslami. "This mission shows our increased capability in dealing with any foreign threat," he said. Iranian officials said on May 14 that the Islamic republic had dispatched two warships to the Gulf of Aden but it was unclear whether they were among the six announced by Sayari.[63]

One example mentioned above, in July 2008 , was when Tehran took a seemingly cooperative stance urging the Western powers to continue their negotiating efforts within the IAEA, while at the same time embarking on a bold and confrontational major naval exercise in the Persian Gulf.

The five-day Iranian naval exercise, dubbed Exercise Stake Net, was carried out in the Strait of Hormuz and the Sea of Oman, where an assortment of new weapons was brought into play. Media coverage of the exercise was rather unprecedented, leaving the impression that the Islamic regime intended to send a strong message to the West, especially the United States and Israel, that they must think twice before deciding to pass a harsh resolution against Iran in the Security Council or threaten the survival of Tehran's Islamic regime.

One important aspect of the exercise was the almost total absence of the regular Iranian Navy, whose functions are more oriented toward the classical tasks of sea denial and power projection ashore in the Persian Gulf and the Strait of Hormuz. This may well reflect that Iran understands that the Iranian Navy would not be able to sustain combat capability in a purely classical naval engagement. That was the case in the late 1980s where the Iranian Navy lost some of its warships in an unequal interface with the American units during the Tanker War of 1987–1988.

According to some experts, this experience led Iranian defense planners to devise new tactics with limited but effective light and fast units for hit-and-run operations in the Strait of Hormuz and the Sea of Oman. The strategy follows the classical guerrilla warfare doctrine, which emphasizes the strategy that when two unequal opponents face each other, the best way for the weak side is to resort to a war of attrition and asymmetric tactics. In the enclosed narrow and rather shallow waters of the Persian Gulf, this tactic can be very decisive against larger units and can deny the enemy from effective deployment, sea lines of communication, and power projection.

The IRGC often claims to conduct very large exercises, sometimes with 100,000 men or more. The exact size of such exercises is unclear, but they are often a small fraction of IRGC claims. With the exception of a limited number of more elite elements, training is limited and largely suitable for internal security purposes. Most forces would require substantial refresher training to act in any mission other than static infantry defense and using asymmetric warfare tactics such as hit and-run operations or swarming elements of forces when an invader appears vulnerable.

Iran has other ways of sending signals. One example came after the 2008 U.S. presidential elections. On November 12, 2008, Iran launched yet another new type of long-range ballistic missile with the by-now-customary mixture of fanfare, hype, self-congratulations, and threats. The Iranians dubbed the missile launched on November 12 "Sajeel," but its general layout was indistinguishable from the description of the "Ashura," which was flight-tested about a year before, apparently without success.

The launch of the Sajeel/Ashura displayed Tehran's continued commitment to its missile programs in an effort to possess a missile program with a global reach. This display can also be viewed as another example of Tehran's intention to destabilize the Gulf region with its ever-advancing missile capabilities and ambiguous nuclear program.

All of these examples can be viewed as part of Iran's psychological warfare strategy, which is just one component of its overall strategy. By displaying both its real and virtual military (e.g., naval) fighting capabilities through electronic, printed, and network media, and through endless official statements, Iran tends to achieve the following politico-diplomatic and propaganda ends (the "4Ds"):[64]

Defiance (to maintain a course of resistance, targeting primarily the Western political will and system)

Deception (on the real state of Iranian warfighting capabilities, targeting the Western military establishments)

Deterrence (with the Islamic Republic of Iran (IRI) military "might," targeting Western public opinion, delivered through the media)

Demonstration (of the outreach of its own power, targeting the Iranian people and the Muslim world)

Another example of the use of Iran's naval exercises as part of its asymmetric warfare efforts came on December 2, 2008, when the Iranian Navy began a six-day naval exercise dubbed Unity 87 in the Gulf of Oman and the Strait of Hormuz. The four-stage exercise involved destroyers, missile boats, submarines, helicopters, fighters, and UAVs.[65]

Commander of the Iranian Navy Rear Admiral Habibollah Sayyari said, "Over 60 combat vessels will take part in the exercise, codenamed 'Unity 87,' in the Gulf of Oman." He went on to state that "the goal of the exercise is to improve the combat readiness of the Iranian navy to counter potential external threats and to test modern weaponry developed by the Iranian defense industry," adding that it was also designed to "enhance the country's deterrence capability."[66]

The week prior to the exercise, Sayyari said, "All the movements of the enemy in Oman Sea, Persian Gulf and Hormuz Strait are under control and the enemy will never dare to enter Iran's waters."[67] Sayyari also confirmed the delivery of two new domestically built missile boats, Kalat (Fortress) and Derafsh (Flag), as well as a Ghadir-class light submarine to the Iranian Navy. Iran has launched a domestic weapons procurement campaign aimed at improving its defense capabilities and has announced the development of 109 types of advanced military equipment over the past two years.[68]

On December 3, 2008, Tehran announced the successful completion of the first stage of the exercises, which included exercises focusing on psychological warfare and the deployment of combat units in operations.[69] Later that day, the second stage of the exercise was announced as being successfully completed as well. "During Stage 2 of the Unity-87 exercise, destroyers, submarines, fighter jets, and unmanned aerial vehicles rehearsed the detection and effective engagement of aggressive forces," Deputy Navy Commander Admiral Qasem Rostamabadi said.[70]

On December 6, 2008, the Iranian Navy test-fired a new surface-to-surface missile from a warship as part of exercises along a strategic shipping route. "The Nasr-2 was fired from a warship and hit its target at a distance of 30 km (19 miles) and destroyed it," Iranian state-run radio reported.[71]

More recently, on June 1, 2009, the Iranian Air Force launched a large military exercise dubbed "Thunder 88" over its regional waters. During the exercises Iran commissioned three new Ghadir-class submarines for its naval fleet, bringing the total number of the sonar-evading vessels to seven. Iranian Defense Minister Mostafa Mohammad Najjar turned the three submarines over to naval officials at the Bandar Abbas port city near the Strait of Hormuz. Reports of the submarine in the Iranian Student News Agency say the launch is an effort to "arm the military with new strong capabilities." The Ghadir class is a smaller vessel with a displacement of around 120 tons. The semiofficial Fars News Agency in 2007 said the Ghadir class was equipped with stealth technology.[72]

The news comes amid a flurry of Iranian defense activity. Iran in May inaugurated a production line for a military hovercraft, dubbed the Younes 6. Iran also announced the military production of some 20 other military devices, including laser systems and electronic warfare devices. Production also began on a 40-mm anticruise cannon dubbed Fath, which is capable of reaching targets as far as 7 miles away with a firing rate of 300 rounds per minute.

The size and breadth of the exercises, coupled with the remarks leading up to the exercises and the public status reports throughout, are in line with the asymmetric strategy Iran continues to pursue, and the threatening nature of Iran's military posturing and continued advancements in its indigenous weapons programs further add to regional tensions while Iran continues to pursue its controversial nuclear program and threatens to close the Strait of Hormuz.

The IRGC Commander's Asymmetric Strategy[73]

IRGC commander Mohammad Ali Aziz Jafari has extensive military experience and proven organizational skills. He is considered a proven tactician and is credited with the development of effective intelligence warfare strategies. He has emphasized asymmetrical warfare and developing Iran's ballistic missile capabilities throughout his military career. A *Rooz* article from September 4, 2007, explained that "asymmetrical warfare" refers to "attacks in enemy territory based on dispersed commando strikes rather than on traditional warfare [between two armies]."[74]

Jafari held several senior positions in the IRGC, including head of operations at the joint headquarters and deputy commander of the ground forces. In 1992, he was appointed commander of the ground forces, a position he held for 13 years. One of the tasks he carried out in this capacity was "to study and assess the strengths and weaknesses of America [as reflected] in its attacks on Afghanistan and Iraq."[75] In 2005, he was appointed by Khamenei to head the Strategic Research Center of the Revolutionary Guards intelligence service.[76]

A *Rooz* article published on September 3, 2007, stated that Jafari focuses on military, rather than political, affairs. However, he is closely associated with Expediency Council secretary general and former IRGC commander Mohsen Rezai.

In speeches he has given since his appointment, Jafari has outlined the strategy he means to promote as IRGC commander, reiterating his commitment to developing

Iran's ballistic missile capabilities and the asymmetrical warfare capacities of the IRGC.[77]

"The IRGC is closely monitoring the enemy's movements in the region . . . We discern even their most minor movements . . . The IRGC's excellent defensive and ballistic [missile] capabilities [constitute] one of our present advantages, and we aim to attain superiority [in this area] . . . Informed response to threats, developing independent capabilities and preserving Iran's strength—these are among the goals of the IRGC . . . .

Asymmetrical warfare . . . is [our] strategy for dealing with the considerable capabilities of the enemy. A prominent example of this kind of warfare was [the tactics employed by Hezbollah during] the Lebanon war in 2006 . . . Since the enemy has considerable technological abilities, and since we are still at a disadvantage in comparison, despite the progress we have made in the area of equipment, [our only] way to confront [the enemy] successfully is to adopt the strategy [of asymmetric warfare] and to employ various methods of this kind.[78]

Jafari added that "the Revolutionary Guards [Corps] will invest efforts in strengthening its asymmetrical warfare capabilities, with the aim of successfully confronting the enemies."[79] On another occasion, Jafari stated, "After September 11, [2001], all [IRGC] forces changed their [mode of] operation, placing emphasis on attaining combat readiness. The first step [toward achieving] this goal was to develop [a strategy] of asymmetrical warfare and to hold maneuvers [in order to practice it]."[80]

Jafari has said in the past that, in the case of a confrontation with the West, Iran will be willing to employ the organizations under its influence. In a January 2005 speech to intelligence commanders from the Basij and the IRGC, Jafari—then commander of the ground forces—stated, "In addition to its own capabilities, Iran also has excellent deterrence capabilities outside its [own borders], and if necessary it will utilize them."[81]

IRGC Quds Force

The IRGC has a large intelligence operation and unconventional warfare component. Roughly 5,000 of the men in the IRGC are assigned to the unconventional warfare mission. The IRGC has the equivalent of one Special Forces division, plus additional smaller formations, and these forces are given special priority in terms of training and equipment. In addition, the IRGC has a special Quds Force that plays a major role in giving Iran the ability to conduct unconventional warfare overseas using various foreign movements as proxies.[82]

Some reports indicate that the budget for the Quds Force is a classified budget directly controlled by Supreme Leader Khamenei and is not reflected in the Iranian general budget.[83] It operates primarily outside Iran's borders, although it has bases inside and outside of Iran. The Quds troops are divided into specific groups or "corps" for each country or area in which they operate. There are directorates for Iraq; Lebanon, Palestine, and Jordan; Afghanistan, Pakistan, and India; Turkey and the Arabian Peninsula; Asian countries of the former Soviet Union, Western nations

(Europe and North America) and North Africa (Egypt, Tunisia, Algeria, Sudan, and Morocco).[84]

The Quds has offices or "sections" in many Iranian embassies, which are closed to most embassy staff. It is not clear whether these are integrated with Iranian intelligence operations or whether the ambassador in such embassies has control of, or detailed knowledge of, operations by the Quds staff. However, there are indications that most operations are coordinated between the IRGC and offices within the Iranian Foreign Ministry and the MOIS. There are separate operational organizations in Lebanon, Turkey, Pakistan, and several North African countries. There are also indications that such elements may have participated in the bombings of the Israeli Embassy in Argentina in 1992 and the Jewish Community Center in Buenos Aires in 1994—although Iran has strongly denied any involvement.[85]

The Quds Force seems to control many of Iran's training camps for unconventional warfare, extremists, and terrorists in Iran and countries such as the Republic of Sudan and Lebanon. In Sudan, the Quds Force is believed to run a training camp of unspecified nature. It has at least four major training facilities in Iran. The Quds Force has a main training center at Imam Ali University that is based in the Sa'dabad Palace in Northern Tehran. Troops are trained to carry out military and terrorist operations and are indoctrinated in ideology.

There are other training camps in the Qom, Tabriz, and Mashhad governorates and in Lebanon and the Sudan. These include the Al Nasr camp for training Iraqi Shi'ites and Iraqi and Turkish Kurds in northwest Iran and a camp near Mashhad for training Afghan and Tajik revolutionaries.

The Quds Force seems to help operate the Manzariyah training center near Qom, which recruits foreign students from the religious seminary and which seems to have trained some Bahraini extremists. Some foreigners are reported to have received training in demolition and sabotage at an IRGC facility near Isfahan, in airport infiltration at a facility near Mashad and Shiraz, and in underwater warfare at an IRGC facility at Bandar Abbas.[86]

The Quds Force has supported nonstate actors in many foreign countries. These include Hezbollah in Lebanon, Hamas and the Palestinian Islamic Jihad in the Gaza Strip and the West Bank, the Shi'ite militias in Iraq, and Shi'ites in Afghanistan. Links to Sunni extremist groups such as Al Qa'ida have been reported, but never convincingly confirmed.

On January 11, 2007, the director of the Defense Intelligence Agency stated in a testimony before the U.S. Senate Select Committee on Intelligence that the Quds Force of Iran's Islamic Revolutionary Guard Corps had the lead for its transnational terrorist activities, in conjunction with Lebanese Hezbollah and Iran's MOIS.[87] Other sources believe that the primary mission of the Quds has been to support Shi'ite movements and militias, and such aid and weapons transfers seem to have increased significantly in the spring of 2007.

The Quds Force is also believed to play a continuing role in training, arming, and funding Hezbollah in Lebanon and to have begun to support Shi'ite militia and Taliban activities in Afghanistan. Experts disagree on the scale of such activity, how much it has provided support to Sunni Islamist extremist groups rather than Shi'ite groups, and over the level of cooperation in rebuilding Hezbollah forces in Lebanon since the cease-fire in the Israel-Hezbollah War of 2006. The debates focus, however, on the scale of such activity and the extent to which it has been formally controlled and authorized by Supreme Leader Khamenei and President Ahmadinejad, and not over whether some level of activity has been authorized.

The exact relationship among the Quds Force, Hamas, and the Palestinian Islamic Jihad is even more speculative. Some Iranian arms shipments have clearly been directed at aiding antipeace and anti-Israeli elements in the Gaza Strip. There is some evidence of aid in training, weapons, and funding to hostile Palestinian elements in both the Gaza Strip and the West Bank. Open sources do not, however, provide a clear picture of the scale of such activity.

Many U.S. experts believe that the Quds Force has provided significant transfers of weapons to Shi'ite (and perhaps some Sunni) elements in Iraq. These may include the shaped charge components used in some IEDs in Iraq and the more advanced components used in explosively formed projectiles, including the weapon assembly, copper slugs, radio links used to activate such devices, and the infrared triggering mechanisms. These devices are very similar to those used in Lebanon, and some seem to operate on the same radio frequencies. Shaped charge weapons first began to appear in Iraq in August 2003, but became a serious threat in 2005.[88]

In January 2007, Iran's Supreme National Security Council (SNSC) decided to place all Iranian operations in Iraq under the command of the Quds Force. At the same time, the SNSC decided to increase the personnel strength of the Quds Force to 15,000.[89]

On January 11, 2007, the U.S. military in Iraq detained five men accused of providing funds and equipment to Iraqi insurgents. According to U.S. military sources, these men had connections to the Quds Force.[90] On January 20, 2007, gunmen dressed as U.S. soldiers entered the Provincial Joint Coordination Center in Karbala and killed or wounded several U.S. servicemen. According to some sources, including U.S. military intelligence, the gunmen were members of the Quds Force. The sophisticated planning and execution of this attack made it unlikely that any Iraqi group was involved.[91]

General David H. Petraeus, commander of U.S. forces in Iraq, stressed the growing role of the Quds Force and the IRGC in testimony to Congress in April 2007. He noted that the United States had found Quds operatives in Iraq and seized computers with hard drives that included a 22-page document that had details on the planning, approval process, and conduct of an attack that killed five U.S. soldiers in Karbala. Petraeus noted,

> They were provided substantial funding, training on Iranian soil, advanced explosive munitions and technologies as well as run-of-the-mill arms and ammunition . . . in some cases advice and in some cases even a degree of direction . . . Our sense is that these records were kept so that they could be handed in to whoever it is that is financing

them . . . And again, there's no question . . . that Iranian financing is taking place through the Quds force of the Iranian Republican Guards Corps.[92]

Israeli defense experts continue to state that they believe the IRGC and the Quds Force not only played a major role in training and equipping Hezbollah, but may have assisted it during the Israeli-Hezbollah War in 2006. Israeli intelligence officers claim to have found command-and-control centers, and a missile and rocket fire-control center, in Lebanon that was of Iranian design. They feel the Quds Force played a major role in the Hezbollah antiship missile attack on an Israeli Navy Sa'ar-class missile patrol boat and that Iranians and Syrians supported Hezbollah with intelligence from facilities in Syria during the fighting.

Iranian Paramilitary, Security, and Intelligence Forces

Iran has not faced a meaningful threat from terrorism since the isolation of the Mujahedin-e Khalq Organization (MEK or MKO) forces based in Iraq following the fall of Saddam Hussein's regime in 2003, and the MEK had long been little more than an ineffective Rajavi cult before Saddam's fall.[93]

While Iran does show concern over any outside source of criticism or opposition, and conducts covert foreign political and intelligence operations against such groups and movements, its internal security forces focus on countering political opposition. Since 1990, Iran has maintained the same force structure, and its key agencies have not changed since the early years of the Iranian Revolution.

The U.S. Department of State described the role of Iran's internal security apparatus as follows:

> Several agencies share responsibility for law enforcement and maintaining order, includ-ing the ministry of intelligence and security, the law enforcement forces under the interior ministry, and the IRGC [Islamic Revolutionary Guards Corps]. A paramilitary volunteer force known as the Basij and various informal groups known as the Ansar-e Hezbollah (Helpers of the Party of God) aligned with extreme conservative members of the leadership and acted as vigilantes. The size of the Basij is disputed, with officials citing anywhere from 11 to 20 million, and a recent Western study claiming there were 90 thousand active members and up to 300 thousand reservists. Civilian authorities did not maintain fully effective control of the security forces. The regular and paramilitary security forces both committed numerous, serious human rights abuses. According to HRW [Human Rights Watch] since 2000 the government's use of plainclothes security agents to intimidate political critics became more institutionalized. They were increas-ingly armed, violent, and well equipped, and they engaged in assault, theft, and illegal seizures and detentions.[94]

Dennis Blair, U.S. President Barack Obama's new Director of National Intelli-gence, summarized Iran's goals as follows in his survey of international threats in February 2009:

Militarily, Iran continues to strengthen the three pillars of its strategic deterrence: surface-to-surface missiles, long-range rockets and aircraft for retaliation; naval forces to disrupt maritime traffic through key waterways; and unconventional forces and surrogates to conduct worldwide lethal operations. Although many of their statements are exaggerations, Iranian officials throughout the past year have repeatedly claimed both greater ballistic missile capabilities that could threaten US and allied interests and the ability to close the Strait of Hormuz using unconventional small boat operations, anti-ship cruise missiles, and other naval systems. Some officials, such as Islamic Revolutionary Guard Corps Commander Major General Mohammad Ali Jafari-Najafabadi, have hinted that Iran would have a hand in attacks on "America's interests even in far away places," suggesting Iran has contingency plans for unconventional warfare and terrorism against the United States and its allies.

Iran's goals in Iraq include preventing the emergence of a threat from Iraqi from the government of Iraq itself, or from the United States. To achieve this, Iran probably seeks a government in Baghdad in which Tehran's Shia allies hold the majority of political, economic, and security power. Iran also has sought to make the United States suffer political, economic, and human costs in order to limit US engagement in the region and to ensure that Washington does not maintain a permanent military presence in Iraq or use its military to pressure or attack Iran.

- Iranian efforts to secure influence in Iraq encompass a wide range of activities, including using propaganda, providing humanitarian assistance, building commercial and economic ties, and supporting Shia elements fighting the Coalition. Iran has provided a variety of Shia militants with lethal support including weapons, funding, training, logistical and operational support, and intelligence training.

- We judge Iran will continue to calibrate its lethal aid to Iraqi Shia militants based on the threat it perceives from US forces in Iraq, the state of US-Iran relations, Tehran's fear of a Ba'thist resurgence, Tehran's desire to help defend Iraqi Shia against sectarian violence, and to maintain the ability to play a spoiler role in Iraq if Iran perceives the government of Iraq has become a strategic threat.

- Despite Tehran's efforts, we judge Iraqi nationalism and the growing capabilities of the Iraqi government will limit Iranian influence in Iraq. Baghdad, for example, signed the US-Iraq security agreement despite Iranian opposition.

In Afghanistan, Iran has focused on promoting a friendly central government in Kabul and limiting Western power and influence. Iran's policy in Afghanistan follows multiple tracks, including providing political and economic support to the Karzai government and developing relationships with actors across the political spectrum.

- Iran has opposed Afghan reconciliation talks with the Taliban as risking an increase in the group's influence and legitimacy.

- We judge Iran distrusts the Taliban and opposes its return to power but uses the provision of lethal aid as a way to pressure Western forces, gather intelligence, and build ties that could protect Iran's interests if the Taliban regains control of the country.

In the Levant, Tehran is focused on building influence in Lebanon and expanding the capability of key allies. Tehran continues to support groups such as Hizballah, HAMAS, and Palestine Islamic Jihad (PIJ), which it views as integral to its efforts to challenge Israeli and Western influence in the Middle East.

- Hizballah is the largest recipient of Iranian financial aid, training, and weaponry, and Iran's senior leadership has cited Hizballah as a model for other militant groups. We assess Tehran has continued to provide Hizballah with significant amounts of funding, training, and weapons since the 2006 conflict with Israel, increasing the group's capabilities to pressure other Lebanese factions and to threaten Israel.

- Iran's provision of training, weapons, and money to HAMAS since the 2006 Palestinian elections has bolstered the group's ability to strike Israel and oppose the Palestinian Authority.[95]

Iran maintains an extensive network of internal security and intelligence services. The main parts of the domestic security apparatus are made up of the Ministry of Intelligence and Security, the Basij Resistance Force, the intelligence unit of the IRGC, and the law enforcement forces within the Ministry of Interior that largely are responsible for providing police and border control. The leadership of each of these organizations appears to be fragmented and dispersed among several, often competing, political factions. Public information on all Iranian security and intelligence forces is extremely limited and subject to political manipulation.

The IRGC has control over several other organizations or parts thereof. All security organizations without exception report to the SNSC, as the highest body in the political chain of command. The phenomenon of the fragmented leadership of the security organizations is reflected in their relationship to the SNSC as different security organizations maintain special ties to certain elements of the SNSC.

Other state organizations, most notably the police services, exert varying control over internal security. As with virtually all other organizations, the IRGC is believed to have considerable leverage over these services.[96] The effectiveness of the internal security organizations is unclear and the political will to use them is hard to predict. After local unrest in the Iranian province of Baluchistan in May 2006, police were unable to seize control of the situation against regional tribal forces.[97]

Iran's Basij Resistance Force

The Basij Resistance Force is a popular reserve and paramilitary force of about 90,000 men, with an active and reserve strength of up to 300,000 and a mobilization capacity of nearly 1,000,000 men, mostly manned by elderly men, youth, and volunteers who have completed their military service. The Basij Force is organized in a regional, decentralized command structure and has up to 740 regional "battalions" of approximately 300–350 soldiers, each of which is organized into three to four sub-units. It maintains a relatively small active-duty staff of 90,000 and relies on mobilization in the case of any contingency.[98] The Basij was put under command of the IRGC on January 1, 1981.

Iran's Basij Force performs broader functions than simply serving as a reserve for the IRGC, as discussed earlier. The IRGC oversaw the creation of a people's militia, a volunteer group it named the Basij Resistance Force—which means Mobilization of the Oppressed—in 1980. The Basij derives its legitimization from Article 151 of the Iranian Constitution, which calls upon the government to fulfill its duty according to the Quran to provide all citizens with the means to defend themselves.

The Basij's mission has increasingly been broadened to providing reserves and small combat elements for the IRGC in defending against a U.S. invasion. It would serve as a mobilization base for the IRGC, as well as provide cadres and small units for independent action against invading forces. It would also serve as a "stay behind" force and attack isolated U.S. units and rear areas. According to Connell, the IRGC has formed a wartime mobilization plan for the IRGC called the "Mo'in Plan," where Basij battalions would be integrated into the IRGC in wartime as part of the IRGC regional defense structure.[99]

According to one source, about 20,000 Basij troops were organized in four brigades during the Great Prophet II military exercise in November 2006. According to an IRGC general, during the Great Prophet II exercise 172 battalions of the Basij Resistance Force were employed with the primary mission of guarding "public alleyways and other urban areas."[100]

The IRGC maintains tight control over the leadership of the Basij and imposes strict Islamic rules on its members. Comments by Iranian leaders indicate that the mission of the Basij is shifting away from traditional territorial defense to "defending against Iranian security threats." Furthermore, there are reports of an increased interest in improving the Basij under the leadership of President Mahmoud Ahmadinejad.[101]

It is far from clear how effective the Basij would really be in such missions. Similar forces have been created in a number of countries, including Iraq. In many cases, they have not materialized as a meaningful resistance force. Iran does, however, have extensive experience in creating and using such forces dating back to the Iran-Iraq War, and the fighting in Iraq since 2003 has shown that small cadres of activists using IEDs, car bombs, and suicide bombs can have a major political and military impact.

Iran's Ministry of Intelligence and Security

The MOIS, or Vezarat-e Ettela' at va Aminat-e Keshvar (VEVAK), was installed following the Revolution to replace the now-disbanded National Organization for Intelligence and Security (SAVAK), which in turn was created under the leadership of U.S. and Israeli officers in 1957. SAVAK fell victim to political leadership struggles with the intelligence service of the IRGC during the Iran-Iraq War. A compromise solution resulted in the creation of the MOIS in 1984.

The MOIS's major tasks include intelligence about the Middle East and Central Asia and domestic intelligence and monitoring of clerical and government officials[102] as well as work on preventing conspiracies against the Islamic republic.[103]

There is an ongoing debate within Iran's political system over limiting parliamentary control over the MOIS, indicating that the control over the MOIS can be used as a powerful political instrument. There have also been efforts in Iran to extract the counterintelligence unit of the MOIS and make it a separate entity. This proposal seems to be favored by Supreme Leader Ayatollah Ali Khamenei and some hard-line legislators.[104]

Until recently, the organization has remained under very limited public disclosure. In the 1990s, ministry personnel were accused of killing political dissidents in Iran. Ensuing investigations have been covered up systematically. Apparently, the MOIS has a comparatively large budget at its disposal and operates under the broader guidance of Ali Khamenei.[105]

Iran's Ministry of Interior

Iran also has 45,000–60,000 men in the Ministry of Interior (MoI) serving as police and border guards, with light utility vehicles, light patrol aircraft (Cessna 185/310s and AB-205s and AB-206s), 90 coastal patrol craft, and 40 harbor patrol craft. The rest of Iran's paramilitary and internal security forces seem to have relatively little capability in any form of warfighting mission.[106]

The exact role of Iran's MoI and its forces in covert and asymmetric operations is unclear. Open-source information regarding its structure and forces is limited. The same is true of other organizations in Iran's internal security apparatus. Ansar-e Hezbollah is a paramilitary force that has gained questionable notoriety. It remains unclear to what extent this force is attached to government bodies. Reportedly, the political right in the government has repeatedly made use of it to fight and intimidate liberal forces in society. The Ansar-e Hezbollah's military level of training appears to be poor.[107]

Tehran's Proxy and Terrorist Assets

As stated earlier, the IRGC is suspected of training and arming several paramilitary, terrorist, and proxy forces including its Quds Force and other elements that operate covertly or openly overseas; such as working with Hezbollah of Lebanon, Shi'ite militias in Iraq, and Shi'ites in Afghanistan, to name a few.

The Islamic Revolutionary Guard Corps and Ministry of Intelligence and Security have been implicated in the planning of and support for terrorist acts and continued to exhort a variety of groups that use terrorism to pursue their goals.

Iran has maintained a high-profile role in encouraging anti-Israeli activity, both rhetorically and operationally, while denying any involvement in such activity. Supreme Leader Khamenei praised Palestinian resistance operations. Matching this rhetoric with action, Iran provided Hezbollah and Palestinian resistance and liberation organization's—such as Hamas, the Palestine Islamic Jihad, and the Popular Front for the Liberation of Palestine–General Command—with funding, safe haven, training, and weapons. Iran hosted a conference in August 2003 on the Palestinian

Intifada, at which an Iranian official suggested that the continued success of the Palestinian resistance depended on suicide operations.

Iran has pursued a variety of policies in Iraq aimed at securing Tehran's interests. Iran has indicated support for the Iraqi Governing Council and promised to help Iraqi reconstruction, while running covert insurgent operations throughout the country and supporting domestic Shi'ite paramilitary forces, such as Muqtada al-Sadr's Mahdi Army.

The *Times* (London) in September 2005 identified at least a dozen active Islamic groups with ties to Tehran. Eight were singled out as having considerable cross-border influence:[108]

- **Badr Brigade:** A Shi'ite militia force of 12,000 trained by Iran's Revolutionary Guards and blamed for a number of killings of Sunni Muslims. They are thought to control several cities in southern Iraq.

- **Islamic Dawaa Party:** A Shi'ite party that has strong links to Iran. Its leader, Ibrahim al-Jaafari, former Iraqi prime minister, has vowed to improve ties between the two neighbors.

- **Mahdi Army:** Received arms and volunteers from Iran during its battle against U.S. and British troops last year. The group's commander in Basra, Ahmed al-Fartusi, was arrested by British forces in mid-September 2005.

- **Mujahideen for Islamic Revolution in Iraq:** A Tehran-backed militia blamed for the murder of six British Royal Military Police soldiers in Majar el-Kabir in 2003

- **Thar Allah (Vengeance of God):** An Iranian-backed terror group blamed for killing former members of the ruling Ba'ath Party and enforcing strict Islamic law

- **Jamaat al-Fudalah (Group of the Virtuous):** A paramilitary group that imposes Islamic rules on Shia areas and has attacked shops selling alcohol and music

- **Al-Fadilah (Morality):** A secret political movement financed by Iran. It is thought to have many members among the provincial officials.

- **Al-Quawaid al-Islamiya (Islamic Bases):** An Iranian-backed Islamic movement that uses force to impose Islamic law

Hezbollah and Hamas

Hezbollah was originally formed in 1982 by Iranian seminarians; its links to Tehran have strengthened as it has grown into a semiautonomous power of its own. Hezbollah has become a sophisticated political military-social organization, a key player in the Lebanese government, a dominant force in southern Lebanon, a potent militia, a trainer for regional terror groups, and an exporter of terror; all owing a great deal to Hezbollah's ties with Tehran.

Hezbollah is an important Iranian instrument over which Tehran exerts significant influence. According to former Hezbollah Secretary-General Sheik Subhi Al-Tufeili (who broke with Iran and Hezbollah in 1992), "Hezbollah is a tool, and it is an integral part of the Iranian intelligence apparatus. . . . Iran is the main nerve in the activity today in Lebanon. All Hezbollah activity [is financed] by Iranian funds. Syria has an important role, but Iran is the main and primary support of [the Lebanese opposition]."[109]

Ali Akbar Mohtashemi, one of the founders of Hezbollah, former Iranian ambassador to Syria and Lebanon, and former Iranian interior minister, has said that "Hezbollah is part of the Iranian rulership; Hezbollah is a central component of the Iranian military and security establishment; the ties between Iran and Hezbollah are far greater than those between a revolutionary regime with a revolutionary party or organization outside its borders."[110]

More recently, Hezbollah's second-in-command, Sheik Naim al Qassem, explained in an interview on Iranian television that Hezbollah yields to Iranian authority for all military issues, including suicide bombings, rocket launches, and other terrorist operations. Qassem references "'al-wali al-faqih' (the ruling jurisprudent), a title formerly used by Ayatollah Ruhollah Khomeini and presently used by his successor, leader Ali Khamenei . . . to describe Hezbollah's source of authority."[111]

Hezbollah has recovered from its 2006 confrontation with Israel and has been able to rearm and regroup, and Iran has been an important part of that recovery. In a February 2007 interview, Hezbollah leader Hassan Nasrallah openly stated that Iran is supplying his group.[112]

Weapons shipments come by land, sea, and air from Iran, often via Damascus. Shipments are frequent and large. For example, Israel's Intelligence and Terrorism Information Center reported that at least nine times between December 2003 and January 2004, the IRGC Quds Force "used Iranian and Syrian cargo planes flying humanitarian aid in to the earthquake victims in Southeastern Iran to take large quantities of weapons for Hezbollah on their return flights" with monetary aid and weapons.[113]

Iran has gone from supplying small arms, short-range missiles, and training to providing more sophisticated long-range missiles and other higher-end weaponry destined to escalate tensions between Lebanon and Israel.[114] In mid-2004, IRGC officers reportedly unloaded 220 missiles with a 250–350-kilometer range for Hezbollah at an airfield near Damascus.

According to calculations by the Middle East Media Research Institute (MEMRI), between 1992 and 2005, Hezbollah received approximately 11,500 missiles and rockets; four hundred short- and medium-range pieces of artillery; and Aresh, Nuri, and Hadid rockets and transporters/launchers from Iran.[115] In 2005, Iran sent Hezbollah a shipment of large Uqab missiles with 333-mm warheads and an enormous supply of SA-7 and C-802 missiles, two of which were used in a July 14, 2006, attack on an Israeli ship.[116]

As part of a package of aid to Hezbollah said to exceed $100 million per year, reported Iranian shipments to Hezbollah over the past five years have included the "Fajr" (dawn) and Khaybar series of rockets that were fired at the Israeli city of Haifa (30 miles from the border), and over 10,000 Katyusha rockets that were fired at cities within 20 miles of the Lebanese border.[117]

Iran also supplied Hezbollah with an unknown number of UAVs, the *Mirsad*, that Hezbollah briefly flew over the Israel-Lebanon border on November 7, 2004, and April 11, 2005; at least three were shot down by Israel during the summer 2006 war.[118]

During Hezbollah's summer 2006 war with Israel, Iran resupplied the group's depleted weapons stocks. In July of that year, secret IRGC airlifts from bases in Bandar Abbas transported supplies for Hezbollah to the Dumeir Syrian military airfield near Homs;[119] and the following month, Iran sent more advanced surface-to-air missiles, including Strela-2/2M, Strela-3, Igla-1E, and the Mithaq-1. The same missiles were reported to have been used to target Israeli helicopters.[120]

Iran also supported Hezbollah's demands and provided it with leverage by resupplying it with rockets, reportedly increasing its stockpile to 27,000 rockets, more than double what Hezbollah had at the start of the 2006 war.[121] Among the deliveries were 500 Iranian-made "Zelzal" (earthquake) missiles with a range of 186 miles, enough to reach Tel Aviv from south Lebanon. Iran also made at least $150 million available for Hezbollah to distribute to Lebanese citizens (mostly Shi'ite supporters of Hezbollah) whose homes were damaged in the Israeli military campaign.[122]

Hezbollah's performance during the 2006 war showed how effective Iranian support could be. Hezbollah fighters had benefited from serious, in-depth training from the IRGC at rear training facilities in Syria and Iran, as well as on the ground in Lebanon. Hezbollah also reportedly had hundreds of Iranian engineers who, with North Korean experts brought into Lebanon by Iranian diplomats, built a 25-km underground tunnel to move fighters. The IRGC also aided in the construction of underground storerooms in the Bekaa Valley to hold missiles and ammunition.[123]

In short, the fighting in Lebanon in 2006 seems to have increased Hezbollah's dependence on Iran even further. Both Hezbollah's loss of weapons and fighters in the conflict with Israel and the resulting damage to its reputation and position within Lebanon made it more reliant upon Iran. Moreover, Iran has shown every sign of drawing on the Lebanon-Hezbollah model to expand its ties to other nonstate actors such as Hamas and various Shi'ite militias in Iraq.

Iran took a similar stand in supporting Hamas in its recent clash with the Israel military in Gaza. During the fighting in Gaza between Israeli forces and Hamas militants between December 27, 2008 and January 17, 2009, Iran supported Hamas and spoke out against the lack of support for Hamas by Arab regimes throughout the Middle East, most notably Egypt and Saudi Arabia. The Iranian government also seized this opportunity to rally Islamic fundamentalists against Israel and its supporters.

There were numerous reports of support for Hamas by Iran during this period. Chairman of the Joint Chiefs Admiral Mike Mullen said on January 27, 2009, that the United States boarded but did not seize a ship carrying light arms to Hamas from Iran; the ship later went to Cyprus. Hamas appeared to corroborate allegations of Iranian weapons supplies when its exiled leader, Khaled Meshal, on February 1, 2009, publicly praised Iran for helping Hamas achieve "victory" over Israel in the conflict.[124]

Iran has been implicated in supplying Hamas with arms in its fight against the Israeli Air Force (IAF), and after a cease-fire agreement was reached, Israeli intelligence sources continued to report Iranian efforts to rearm Hamas. On March 11, 2009, a UN committee monitoring Iran's compliance with Resolution 1747, which bans Iranian arms exports, said Iran might have violated that resolution with an alleged attempted weapons shipment to Hamas, which was intercepted by the U.S. Navy and ordered to port in Cyprus. Iranian weaponry might also have been the target of a January 2009 strike on a weapons delivery purportedly bound for Gaza in transit via Sudan (and presumably through Egypt).[125] The suspected rearmament of Hamas following the 2008–2009 Gaza conflict comes on the heels of its rearmament of Hezbollah after its clash with the IAF in Lebanon in 2006.

Since the 2008–2009 Gaza Conflict between Hamas and Israeli forces, Sunni Arab leaders in Egypt, Jordan, Saudi Arabia, and throughout the region apparently fear Iran's growing regional influence and reported Iranian support for efforts to discredit these leaders for what Iran considers insufficient support for Hamas during this conflict. Some Iranian efforts reportedly involve establishing Hezbollah cells in some of these countries to stir up opposition to these governments and build public support for Hezbollah and Hamas.[126]

The continued support—both overt and covert—for groups such as Hezbollah and Hamas can be viewed as a continued Iranian policy to support terrorist organizations against Israel and spread its influence in the region through a variety of proxy assets.

Tehran's Influence in Iraq

Iran continues to play a major role in the security and political situation in Iraq and continues to take an aggressive approach in trying to shape Iraq's political future and security position in the Gulf. Some experts believed that Tehran had abandoned its efforts to export its "Shi'ite revolution" to the Gulf, but this view has changed since the invasion of Iraq. Officials across the Arab world, especially in Saudi Arabia and Jordan, have expressed concern over a new "strategic" Shi'ite alliance between Iran and Iraq, with ties to Syria and Lebanon.

Iran has sought to expand its influence in Iraq ever since the beginning of the U.S.-led invasion in 2003. Less than a week after the war started, U.S. Secretary of Defense Donald Rumsfeld referred to the "unhelpful" presence of small numbers of Iranian-backed Iraqi forces; a few days later he said hundreds of combatants from the Badr Corps were operating in Iraq and that more were waiting in Iran[127] and added, "The Badr Corps is trained, equipped, and directed by Iran's Islamic Revolutionary Guard, and we will hold the Iranian government responsible for their actions and will view Badr Corps activity inside Iraq as unhelpful. Armed Badr Corps members found in Iraq will have to be treated as combatants." A month later Rumsfeld reiterated his previous statement saying, "There is no question but that the government of Iran has encouraged people to go into the country [Iraq] and that they have people in the country attempting to influence the country."[128]

Furthermore, analysis of declassified interrogation and other intelligence material published by the West Point Counterterrorism Center, the Institute for Studying War, and the *Long War Journal* has helped to document what military intelligence professionals have been piecing together for longer than five years: Iran has been developing a covert action program in Iraq that is open-ended, resilient, and well funded and that utilizes a broad range of Iraqi proxies.[129]

Shortly after the fall of Saddam Hussein, individuals with ties to the IRGC attempted to infiltrate southern Iraq, and elements of the Iranian government have helped members of Ansar al-Islam transit and find safe haven in Iran. In a Friday Prayers sermon in Tehran in May 2003, Guardian Council member Ayatollah Ahmad Jannati publicly encouraged Iraqis to follow the Palestinian model and participate in suicide operations against Coalition forces in Iraq.

By mid-2004 there was an ongoing program in Iran to recruit volunteers for martyrdom operations in Iraq. It is organized by the Headquarters for Tribute to the Martyrs of the Global Islamic Movement. The Headquarters for Tribute to the Martyrs of the Global Islamic Movement, which is affiliated with the IRGC, began enrollment of volunteer suicide bombers in May 2004. Registration forms for suicide bombers are available all over Tehran, and the government does not seem to be trying to halt this phenomenon. By mid-2005 the effort had reportedly culled 40,000 volunteers to undergo special training to become suicide bombers for serving the Palestinian cause against the Israeli occupation.

A number of high-ranking individuals defended the registration of suicide bombers. At a late summer 2004 ceremony in the southern Iranian city of Bushehr organized by the Headquarters for Tribute to the Martyrs of the Global Islamic Movement, parliamentarian Shokrollah Atarzadeh registered as a martyrdom volunteer. Hussein Shariatmadari, the Supreme Leader's representative at the Kayhan Institute, said Iranians must be ready to use "martyrdom-seeking operations." He said Israel is vulnerable and added, "You don't know that the wish of martyrdom-seekers is to send the Israelis to hell. You don't know what a fury and vengeance burns in the hearts of each and every Muslim when they see you destroy the houses of Muslims over their heads or when you commit genocide." Shariatmadari asked, "Why should they be in peace and security in European cities while the people of Iraq, Palestine, and other Muslim countries have no security?"[130]

Supreme Leader Ayatollah Ali Khamenei has also defended the practice. According to a state radio report, he said during a May 2002 speech, "It is the zenith of honor for a man, a young person, boy or girl, to be prepared to sacrifice his life in order to serve the interests of his nation and his religion. This is the zenith of courage and bravery. . . . martyrdom-seeking operations demonstrate the pinnacle of a nation's honor."[131] In a May 2003 sermon in Tehran, Ayatollah Ahmad Jannati said that the Iraqi people "have no option but to resort to Intifada and martyrdom-seeking operations. That is the only solution. They are learning from the Palestinian experience."[132]

By late 2004, Iranian influence had expanded to the where Jordan's King Abdullah warned in an interview with the *Washington Post* that a Shi'ite crescent was forming among Iran, Iraq, Syria, and Lebanon. He was quoted as saying,

> It is in Iran's vested interest to have an Islamic republic of Iraq. If Iraq goes Islamic republic, then, yes, we've opened ourselves to a whole set of new problems that will not be limited to the borders of Iraq. I'm looking at the glass half-full, and let's hope that's not the case. But strategic planners around the world have got to be aware that is a possibility. Even Saudi Arabia is not immune from this. It would be a major problem. And then that would propel the possibility of a Shi'ite-Sunni conflict even more, as you're taking it out of the borders of Iraq.[133]

Former interim Iraqi president, Ghazi Al-Yawar, a Sunni, warned at the same time, "Unfortunately, time is proving, and the situation is proving, beyond any doubt that Iran has very obvious interference in our business—a lot of money, a lot of intelligence activities and almost interfering daily in business and many [provincial] governates, especially in the southeast side of Iraq."[134]

A number of experts have stated since 2005 that Tehran-backed militias had infiltrated Iraqi security forces. In September 2005, Iraq's National Security Adviser, Mouwafak al-Rubaie, admitted that insurgents had penetrated Iraqi police forces in many parts of the country, but he refused to speculate about the extent of the infiltration.[135]

In addition, both the U.S. and British ministers of defense complained that Iran is actively supporting various militias in Iraq, has supplied advanced triggering and motion detector systems for IEDS, and is using elements of the Quds Force to train death squads and militias.[136] Work by Nawaf Obaid and the Saudi National Security Assessment Project (SNSAP) stated the following:

> Iran is insinuating itself into Iraq. The first is through the activities of the al-Quds Forces, the special command division of the Iranian Revolutionary Guard (IRGC). The second approach is by funding and arming Shi'ite militias, the most prominent of which is the SCIRI's 25,000-strong armed wing, the Badr Organization of Reconstruction and Development. Senior members of the Badr Organization and the al- Quds Forces have a closely coordinated relationship. Intelligence reports have indicated that Iranian officers are directing operations under cover in units of the Badr Organization. The Mahdi Army also receives important Iranian assistance, but on a much smaller scale.
>
> The IRGC Commander is General Yahya Rahim-Safavi and the Deputy Commander is General Mohammad Bager Zulgadr. The al-Quds Forces Commander is General Qassem Soleimani. Generals Zulgadr and Soleimani are two most senior officers responsible for Iran's large covert program in Iraq and have a direct link to the Office of the Leader. Additionally, intelligence estimates have identified four other IRGC generals and nine IRGC colonels that are directly responsible for covert operations in Iraq.

The al-Quds Forces mainly functions as a large intelligence operation skilled in the art of unconventional warfare. Current intelligence estimates puts the strength of the force at 5,000. Most of these are highly trained officers. Within the al-Quds Forces, there is a small unit usually referred to as the "Special Quds Force" which consists of the finest case officers and operatives.

The senior officers attached to this unit conduct foreign covert unconventional operations using various foreign national movements as proxies. The forces operate mainly outside Iranian territory, but maintain numerous training bases inside Iran as well. Al-Quds international operations are divided into geographic areas of influence and various corps. The most important and largest cover Iraq, Saudi Arabia (and the Arabian Peninsula), and Syria/Lebanon. The smaller corps cover Afghanistan, Pakistan/India, Turkey, the Muslim Republics of the former Soviet Union, Europe/North America, and North Africa (Egypt, Tunisia, Algeria, Sudan, and Morocco).

The goal of Iran is to infiltrate all Iraq-based militias by providing training and support to their members. For example, al-Sadr's estimated 10,000-strong Mahdi Army, which gets logistical and financial support from al-Quds, also receives training in IRCG camps in Iran. Moreover, nearly all of the troops in the Badr.

Organizations were trained in these camps as well. In addition, most senior officers acquired their skills in specialized camps under the control of the al-Quds Forces. Intelligence estimates that al-Quds currently operates six major training facilities in Iran, with the main facility located adjacent to Imam Ali University in Northern Tehran. The other most important training camps are located in the Qom, Tabriz, and Mashhad governorates. There are also two similar facilities operating on the Syrian-Lebanese border.

According to a senior general in the Iraqi Defense Ministry and a critic of Iran, the Iranians have set up the most sophisticated intelligence-gathering network in the country, to the extent that they have infiltrated "every major Iraqi ministry and security service." There is also an intelligence directorate that has been set up within the Revolutionary Guard that is under the command of the al-Quds Forces devoted exclusively to monitoring the movements of US and Allied forces in Iraq.

Many members of the newly created police and Iraqi forces are controlled by Shi'ite officers who, in some form or another, previously belonged to SCIRI or other groups affiliated with Iran. Recent intelligence indicates that IRGC officers are currently operating in Iraq in certain Shi'ite militias and actual army and police units. The degree of penetration of these organizations is difficult to assess, and it is virtually impossible to distinguish between Iraqi Shi'ite militias and police units, both of which are profoundly influenced by Iran, and in some cases are under Iranian control.

Iranian manipulation has filtered down to street level as well. Ordinary police and military officers now have a stronger allegiance to the Badr Organization or the Mahdi Army than to their own units. And of course, these organizations are deeply connected to Iran. According to the head of intelligence of an allied country that borders Iraq, "the Iranians have not just pulled off an infiltration, in certain regions in Baghdad and Basra, it's been a complete takeover."[137]

Iran's approach to Iraq has since varied with time and has been highly opportunistic. Iran has offered aid in development and sought to invest in Iraq. It has worked with and against the Iraqi government. It has supported a variety of Shi'ite militias, including the Sadr faction, but sometimes aided Sunni insurgent groups such as Al

Qa'ida in Iraq as well. Tehran has repeatedly stated that it supports stability in Iraq. At the same time, several organizations with ties to the Iranian security apparatus are suspected of actively driving a wedge between rivaling factions in Iraq. The IRGC and its subordinate organizations appear to be the most important entities involved in assisting terrorist groups in neighboring Iraq.

The U.S. Department of Defense's September 2008 report on "Measuring Stability" in Iraq said that "malign" Iranian influence in Iraq poses the most significant long-term threat to Iraqi stability. This and the Department of State terrorism report for 2007, released April 30, 2008, complement the statements of U.S. officials that the Qods Force is providing arms (including highly lethal "explosively forced projectiles," EFPs, that have killed over 200 U.S. soldiers in Iraq), training, guidance, and financing to "special groups" of Shi'ite militias involved in sectarian violence and anti-U.S. activities.[138]

Iran's best-known militant proxy in Iraq is called *Asaib Ahl al-Haq* (League of the Righteous), often referred to as Special Groups; these cells specialize in certain types of signature attacks, such as the employment of Iranian-produced weapons or components, including the roadside bombs referred to as EFPs. The latter munitions are particularly significant because of their lethality; although they have been used in just 5–10 percent of roadside bombings, they account for 40 percent of U.S. casualties.[139]

Iranian support has also been visible in rocket attacks across Iraq. Taking a page from Lebanese Hezballah's book, Iranian-backed groups in Iraq have specialized in the use of long-range rocket attacks on Coalition bases. Iran has supplied bulky Fajr-3 240-mm rockets, positively identified by Multinational Forces technical specialists as newly constructed missiles, to insurgents to conduct these types of attacks.[140]

Reporting indicates that Iranian-backed insurgent groups in Iraq have suffered major disruptions since 2007, losing many leaders, arms caches, and safe havens. Yet by the end of 2008, they began to return from Iranian safe havens to resume operations in Iraq. On February 4, 2009, Lieutenant General Lloyd Austin noted, "We know that some elements that were working with Shiite extremists left the country, went into Iran, and came back, and we've captured . . . some of those elements."[141]

The March 2009 Department of Defense report on Iraq stability does indicate that Iranian interference in Iraq has been reduced, and there have been fewer Iranian weapons shipments. The Shi'ite militias and political parties that benefit most from Iranian support fared poorly in the January 31, 2009, provincial elections in Iraq, and the results were viewed as a setback for Iran's influence in Iraq. Iran also was unable to derail the U.S.-Iraq defense pact (which took effect January 1, 2009).[142]

It is hard to predict with any certainty whether or not the decrease in Iranian involvement in Iraq will continue in the long term. This is not the first time Iranian involvement has been reported as being reduced. General Ray Odierno, commander of the Multinational Force–Iraq, noted in October 2008 that Iran "dials it up and down" in respect to supporting militias, meaning that temporary restraint should not be confused with permanent dismantlement of proxy networks, which Iran has cultivated for decades. In fact, Iran's relationship with such proxies is arguably closer than ever.[143] In fact, recent increases in attacks and their lethality could very well be an indication of Iran "dialing up" its support to militias in Iraq.

U.S. troops reported that they captured more than 30 suspects in the month of November 2008 that the U.S. military says are sponsored by Iran.[144] Moving forward into 2009, reports and assessments of Iranian involvement continue to indicate a wide range of Iranian involvement in arming and training militant groups in Iraq covertly, while the Iranian government very openly tries to increase ties and build a relationship with the Iraqi government.

On February 14, 2009, U.S. Central Command (CENTCOM) Commander General David Petraeus—who commanded the U.S. military in Iraq prior to his appointment as CENTCOM Commander—said that Iranian military ties to "special groups" in Iraq was "one of the elements fueling" violence between Sunnis and Shias that brought Iraq to the verge of civil war in 2006 and 2007. General Petraeus went on to say, "There is absolutely no question about this, and there is also no question that some of this does continue to this day."[145]

Tehran's Influence in Afghanistan

Tehran also plays a significant role in Afghanistan's security and political situation. Iranian involvement is less noticeable in Afghanistan, but open-source reporting on the political and security situation has been lacking on the whole. Iranian involvement has still been substantial, especially considering Tehran's history of animosity toward some of the groups it is now supporting: most notably the Taliban elements that continue to conduct insurgent operations in Afghanistan and Pakistan.

Reporting suggests that in 2007, Iran offered economic, social, and cultural assistance to Afghanistan; pressured Kabul over Afghan refugees and migrant workers in Iran; lent limited military support to the Taliban and possibly other insurgent groups; tried to develop a deep bilateral relationship between Tehran and Kabul; attempted to create a gap between Kabul and the West; and possibly tried to destabilize the government of Hamid Karzai.[146]

On April 17, 2007, then Chairman of the Joint Chiefs of Staff General Peter Pace announced that U.S. forces "have intercepted weapons in Afghanistan headed for the Taliban that were made in Iran," and he went on to say, "We know that there are munitions that were made in Iran that are in Iraq and Afghanistan. And we know that the Quds force works for the IRGC. We then surmise from that one or two things. Either the leadership in the country knows what their armed forces are doing, or they don't. And in either case that's a problem."[147]

The shipment seized near Kandahar included mortars and plastic explosives. The shipment was later reported as including "RPG-7 launchers, light guns, and explosive devises," and that "the arms bore the distinct hallmarks of Iran," by International Security Assistance Force (ISAF) spokeswoman Lieutenant Colonel Maria Carl.[148]

The following day, when asked about the weapons shipments seized by General Pace, Brigadier General Joseph Votel, deputy commanding general for operations of Combined Joint Task Force-82 (CJTF-82) said, "I don't know all the particulars of those finds. I'm not sure I really have the visibility to address that particular problem. . . . Being in Regional Command East, you know, our focus is more over on the Pakistan border, so we certainly don't see [any] direct influence from Iran. . . . Right now it's not having an impact here in Regional Command East.[149]

Views differ, however, over the seriousness of Iran's actions. On June 5, 2007, ISAF Commander General Daniel McNeill announced that Coalition forces had intercepted two more weapons shipments that bore Iranian hallmarks, saying,

> We have intercepted at least two convoys that have contained munitions or weapons. Some of those munitions and weapons clearly of—are Iranian origin. . . . We do have two events in which we have recovered explosively formed penetrators [EFP]. . . . In one case, it was not highly sophisticated in terms of giving it a technology-type measurement; in the other case, it was fairly sophisticated. In both cases, they had characteristics of EFPs that I had read about that have been found and indeed used in Iraq and are said to have originated from Iran. . . . We intercepted those convoys . . . inside of Afghanistan. We intercepted them out west. In the case of one of them, there were mortar rounds that were clearly of Iranian origin. There were also explosives, plastic explosives, packaged to make it look like U.S.-made C-4, which is an up-scale version of plastic explosives. It's my understanding that similar types of explosives have been found in Iraq, and once again, the information says they originate from Iran. . . . The convoys were intercepted inside of the Afghan border with Iran—in one case, well inside; in the other case, inside.[150]

On June 13, 2008, Under Secretary of State R. Nicholas Burns stated, "There's irrefutable evidence the Iranians are now" transferring arms to Taliban fighters in Afghanistan. He added, "It's certainly coming from the government of Iran. It's coming from the Iranian Revolutionary Guard Corps command, which is a basic unit of the Iranian government."[151]

Later that day Secretary of Defense Robert Gates downplayed the link of the Iranian government in insurgent activities in Afghanistan, but did not alleviate it of responsibility completely, saying,

> I have seen additional analysis in the interval that makes it pretty clear there's a fairly substantial flow of weapons. I would say, I haven't seen any intelligence specifically to the effect—to this effect, but I would say, given the quantities that we're seeing, it is difficult to believe that it's associated with smuggling or the drug business or that it's taking place without the knowledge of the Iranian government. . . . My impression is that the weapons are intended for the Taliban. I don't know that we have seen any evidence of Qods Force in Afghanistan.[152]

But weapons shipments are not the only types of support that Iranian entities have been implicated in supplying to insurgents in Afghanistan. *Pajhwok Afghan News* reported, "The government of Iran has converted the military camps of former muja-hedeen into training camps for the opponents of the current Afghan government," according to an anonymous member of parliament (MP) from Heart. The *Pajhwok* report went on to say,

> [The anonymous MP] [q]uoting residents of Herat and Farah provinces, who had freshly returned from the neighboring country, said the former mujahedeen training camps in Turbat Jam, Birjand, Taibat and Haji Abad areas had now been converted into training camps for Taliban.
>
> He said People who had returned from Iran claimed that high ranking Taliban were also freely visiting those "training facilities."
>
> He added Yahya Khurdturk, a former commander of Islamic Movement of Sheikh Asif Mohsini and currently a member of the Islamic United Front of Ustad Akbari, leader of the Shi'a community, had also got training along with his colleagues at . . . those camps.
>
> The MP said Yahya was directly linked to the Revolutionary Guards known as Sipah-i- Pasdaran [the IRGC]. . . .
>
> Ahmad Behzad, another MP from Heart province, said: "We have information that Sepahi Qudus (sacred force) [the Quds Force], a wing of the Pasdaran, is organizing and equipping opposition inside Afghanistan as well as train[ing] them at the centers in Iran." He termed the alleged training facilities for Taliban as an open intervention in the internal affairs of Afghanistan by the neighboring country.
>
> "We have information that such centers are existing not only in the border areas, but also in remote provinces."[153]

Claims like these continue to emerge from the reporting by news and intelligence agencies in Afghanistan, as well as from Afghani government officials and ranking Coalition commanders in the area of operations.[154]

On February 14, 2009, CENTCOM Commander General David Petraeus asserted that Iran was continuing to provide assistance to Taliban insurgents in Afghanistan; he stated, "There is a willingness to provide some degree of assistance to make the life of those who are trying to help the Afghan people difficult." General Petraeus gave no details of the Iranian assistance, which he described as taking place at "a small level," but he did go on to say that Iran continues to train and equip Shi'-ite Muslim militias in neighboring Iraq.[155]

Iran has gained considerable influence in the western provinces of Afghanistan with infrastructure programs and providing services to the people in these provinces; which the Afghan government has not been able to provide. On the surface this type of influence is sometimes harmless and in many cases supports the humanitarian mission in Afghanistan and the nation-building efforts of the Coalition forces in sup-port of the Afghan government.

If one looks at the bigger picture of Iranian involvement, however, there are some-times indications that Iran is supporting attacks on security forces and aid workers and then using Iranian aid efforts to fill the voids that are created by the insecurity created by insurgent groups in the western provinces. It is able to play both games at once in an effort to increase Iran's role in the region and influence over this portion of the population.

NUCLEAR WEAPONS AND LONG-RANGE MISSILES AS PART OF IRAN'S ASYMMETRIC STRATEGY

Since the early 1990s, Iran has been trying to align its military doctrine with its capabilities by adopting ways of withstanding the superior power of the United States in the region. In doing so, Iran has placed heavy emphasis on creating missile-based deterrence.

Iran uses missile test launches and progress in its nuclear program in much the same way it uses its military exercises as part of its asymmetric strategy. The Iranian military conducts frequent and very public test launches of its indigenous weapons programs, but many times the reported results cannot be confirmed by sources outside the Iranian government and many times the results have been found to be widely exaggerated by Iranian officials and the state-run media.

Vice Admiral Ali Shamkhani, defense minister and former chief of the Islamic Republic of Iran Military's (IRIM) navy, who now heads the Defence Strategic Research Centre, told the Fars News Agency on October 29, 2008, "Today, there is an imbalance of power between Iran and those who threaten it. . . . Iran's deterrence strategy is not based on a balance of power." He went on to add that, therefore, focusing on Iran's missile program and its air defense system is the surest and most affordable way to strengthen the country's power of deterrence.[156]

One thing is clear. The effectiveness of all of Iran's military assets depends heavily on Iran's ability to use them, or the threat of their use, without provoking conventional wars and attacks. There are no definitive ways to tie Iran's possible nuclear weapons programs and missile programs to Iran's defense and deterrence strategy for using asymmetric forces. It is clear, however, that the acquisition of longer-range missiles and the possibility of the acquisition of nuclear warheads help Iran to bolster defense for itself while adhering to an evolving and expanding offensive asymmetric warfare strategy.

If one looks for a rationale behind an Iranian effort to acquire nuclear weapons, it is clear that adopting a strategy of combining ambiguity regarding its nuclear and missile programs intentions and capabilities with forces for asymmetric and covert warfare already gives Iran more freedom of movement in regard to low-level conflict through its proxies as well as in its diplomatic dealings.

Iran cannot afford to appear or act too threatening and risk provoking new coalitions against it or preventive or preemptive strikes. As a result, Iran seems to have developed a strategy that relies on ambiguity, coupled with misperception, denial, deception, compliance, and concealment. Tehran allows inspectors to see just enough to keep the international community leaders scratching their heads as to what Tehran's true intentions and capabilities are. At the same time, Iranian officials have also used the faulty intelligence leading to Operation Iraqi Freedom to discredit any intelligence collected that may support claims of any operational Iranian WMD programs.

Iranian officials often make public statements addressing the accusations by the international community, from its ties to terrorist organization and insurgent groups, to its suspected WMD programs and intentions. It is clear that Iranian officials have paid close attention to the role of the media in influencing Western policy and manipulating public policy, and they have used the lessons they have learned to smokescreen Iran's developing nuclear program.

Iran may be much weaker than its adversaries in conventional military terms, but in asymmetric warfare, a weaker force does not need traditional military victory over the enemy; it needs only to outlast its enemy. Iran is able to generate and project real strategic threats and create operational and tactical challenges through its asymmetric strategy by taking advantage of its real, potential, and perceived capabilities. The asymmetric capabilities that Tehran has at its disposal pose a serious threat to the regional balance and create new regional and international security concerns.

Iran's Missile Arsenal and Other Delivery Systems

Iran is clearly giving the development and deployment of ballistic and cruise missiles high priority, and it is creating warfighting capabilities based on systems that are sufficiently limited in payload and accuracy that can be effective only if armed with weapons of mass destruction. While such missiles can always be used as "terror weapons" with conventional warheads, they cannot be reliable ways of hitting key point targets or doing serious damage to an area target until they have proven reliability and warheads with sophisticated terminal homing capabilities.

Iran may acquire these capabilities in the future, but at least the current generation of Iranian systems can achieve significant lethality—even against large-area targets—only if armed with weapons of mass destruction. It is also doubtful that Iran can achieve such lethality with its current and near-term chemical, biological, or radiological weapons capabilities—although this will become progressively more uncertain in the case of biological weapons. Nuclear weapons are the only way of arming such missiles that provides a convincing way to do massive damage to an area target, given the limits to the accuracy, reliability, and warhead capability of Iran's current deployments and more advanced development efforts.

The analysis of Iran's nuclear programs is, therefore, directly tied to the fact Iran is deploying new medium-range surface-to-surface missiles such as the Shahab-3, and it has much longer-range systems in development. It is equally important to note that the Iranian government has placed these systems under the command of hard-line elements in the Iranian military: the Islamic Revolutionary Guards Corps (IRGC). [1]

The IRGC is believed to play a critical role in Iran's efforts to acquire nuclear weapons technology and to control all of Iran's longer-range ballistic missiles. The key leaders of the IRGC also report directly to the Supreme Leader, Ali Hoseini-Khamenei, although Iran's president, Mahmoud Ahmadinejad, plays a role in the

Iranian National Security Council. Arms control experts may have the luxury of focusing on Iran's nuclear efforts, but this is only part of the story. There are reasons why key U.S. officials such as U.S. Secretary of Defense Robert M. Gates have seen Iran's missile programs as a key element in Iran's overall program.[2]

At the same time, there are many uncertainties as to how far Iran has gotten in developing effective ballistic and cruise missiles, and as to the nature of its current development programs. Much of the unclassified reporting is contradictory or makes assumptions that are not based on clear or reliable sources. In some cases, the motive the Iranian government gives for a given action or program may not be accurate or describe the whole truth. It is often unclear whether Iran is providing accurate technical data or even suitably advanced test and evaluation programs.

More broadly, it is necessary to speculate about the future path Iran is going to pursue in virtually every area of missile development, and as to how it will mix missile, aircraft, and covert delivery capabilities. As is the case with many other aspects of Iran's efforts, Iran is pursuing so many options that its future path may be more a matter of opportunism than some fixed master plan.

THE RANGE OF IRANIAN PROGRAMS

As Figure 4.1 shows, Iran has a variety of short-, medium-, and long-range missiles. While many are based on missiles developed in other countries, Iran has either developed them further or renamed them. Figure 4.2 shows the range of Iranian missiles that are deployed or under development, and Figure 4.3 shows an estimate of their nominal range. The reader should be aware that very different estimates exist of the nature and configuration of Iran's Shahab-3 and development missile programs and that the range data shown are highly nominal.

Missile Performance Issues

Missiles, like aircraft, make trade-offs between range and payload. The figures shown for range generally assume a nominal 1,000-kilogram payload and often make rough estimates of the capabilities of a given missile booster and stage. Iran can increase range significantly by using a smaller warhead, although this can create risks in terms of reliability and overall design, and it forces reductions in lethality that increase the need to use a nuclear weapon or highly lethal biological weapon. At the same time, it is possible to deliver much larger payloads by reducing range.

Moreover, Iran might make trade-offs in range for other reasons. Real-world reliability and accuracy can vary with range. Altering the apogee to increase reentry speed is one way to counter missile defenses. Increasing warhead weight could provide a limited decoy or countermeasure capability, or the inclusion of some form of terminal guidance. Alternatively, an improved booster, or change in the number and nature of other stages in a missile, is a way to rapidly increase the range-payload of a mature and well-proven system.

Figure 4.1 Estimated Iranian Missile Profiles, 2009

Designation	Stages	Progenitor Missiles	Propellant	Range (Kilometers)	Payload (Kilograms)	IOC (Year)	Inventory
Fateh A-110 (NP-110)	1	Zelzal-2 variant, DF-11, CSS-8	Solid	210	500	2003	?
Tondar 69	1	CSS-8	Solid	150	150–200	?	200
M-9 variant	1	CSS-6, DF-15	Solid	800	320	?	?
M-11 variant	1	CSS-7, DF-11	Solid	400	?	?	80
Mushak-120	1	CSS-8, SA-2	Solid	130	500	2001	200
Mushak-160 (Fateh 110)	1	CSS-8, SA-2	So id, liquid	160	500	2002	?
Mushak-200 (Zelzal-2)	1	SA-2	So id, liquid	200	500	N/A	?
Saegheh	1?	?	Solid	75–225	?	?	?
Shahab-1	1	Soviet SSN-4, N. Korean Scud-B	Liquid	285–330	987–1,000	1995	250–300

Shahab-2	1	Soviet SSN-4, N. Korean Scud-C	Liquid	500–700	750–989	?	50–450
Shahab-3	1	N. Korea No-Dong 1	Liquid	1,280–1,600	760–1,158	2002	25–100
Shahab-4	2	N. Korea Taep'o-dong-1	Liquid	2,000–3,000	1,040–1,500	N/A	0
Ghadr 101	Multi	Pakistan Shaheen-1	Solid	2,500	N/A	N/A	0
Ghadr 110	Multi	Pakistan Shaheen-2	Solid	3,000	N/A	N/A	0
IRIS	1	China M-18	Solid	3,000	760–1,158	2005	N/A
Kh-55	1	Soviet AS-15 Kent, Ukraine	Jet engine	2,900–3,000	200 kgt nuclear	2001	12
Shahab-5	3	N. Korea Taep'o-dong-2	Liquid	4,000–5,500	390–1,000	N/A	0
Shahab-6	3	N. Korea Taep'o-dong-2	Liquid	6,000–10,000	270–1,220	N/A	0
Sajjil-2	2	?	Solid	1,500–2,000	?	2008	?

N/A = not available.

Source: Adapted from GlobalSecurity.org, http://www.globalsecurity.org/wmd/world/iran/missile.htm; the Federation of American Scientists, http://www.fas.org/nuke/guide/iran/missile; The Claremont Institute: Ballistic Missiles of the World, http://www.missilethreat.com/missiles/index.html, The International Institute for Strategic Studies, http://www.iiss.org/publications/strategic-comments/past-issues/volume-15-2009/volume-15-issue-1/irans-missile-development/.

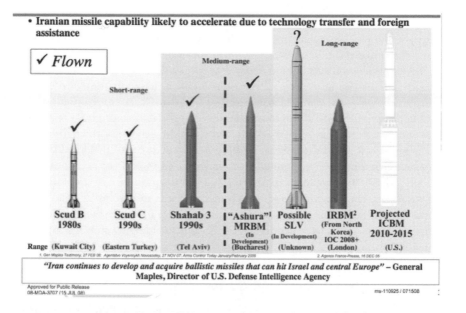

Figure 4.2   Iranian and North Korean Missiles

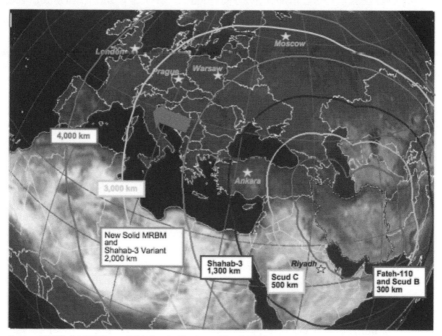

Source: NASIC, B&CM Threat 2006, Jacoby Testimony March 2005

Figure 4.3   Estimated Iranian Missile Ranges

Any given system can evolve over a decade or more, and it can be altered significantly in the process. Reliability can be improved, and so can inertial guidance systems and quick reaction launch capabilities. Iran may not have terminal homing guidance packages for its missiles today, but it may develop or import them in the future. Iran may acquire decoys or maneuvering warhead capabilities to try to defeat missile defenses—and some, such as "spiraling" warheads, are not that sophisticated.

The International Institute for Strategic Studies (IISS) suggests there are three such obstacles that Iran must overcome that would take at least three to five years and require a test and demonstration program involving multiple test flights that can be tracked by Western intelligence agencies and should provide considerable warning. First, Iran would need to establish a production line for solid-fuel motors to strict performance criteria; second, Iran still needs to develop and incorporate sophisticated navigation, guidance, and control systems for future missiles; and third, Iran has yet to show that it has developed thermal shielding to protect a long-range missile warhead during reentry into the atmosphere.[3]

The Rationale for Long-Range Systems

Iran has made no secret of the fact that it includes Israel and the United States as key reasons for these programs, and it looks beyond its neighbors in developing them. One senior IRGC officer has described the strategic and tactical rationale behind such a weapons program as follows:

> Our enemy's strategy is based on air and sea operations. That is, we believe that any future threat to us will come from the countries beyond our region. In our military analyses, we particularly consider the Americans and the Zionist regime as the two threats from beyond our region. Their strategy will be aerial operations, be it by long-range missiles or fighter planes. In the face of their air raids or missile attack, we have adopted the strategy of utilizing long-range or surface-to-surface missiles.[4]

The Iranian government stated as early as 1999 that it was developing a large missile body or launch vehicle for satellite launch purposes and repeatedly denied that it was upgrading the Shahab series (especially the Shahab-3) for military purposes. Iran also continued to claim that the "Shahab-4" program is aimed at developing a booster rocket for launching satellites into space. In January 2004, Iran's Defense Minister claimed that Iran would launch a domestically built satellite within 18 months. This had still not taken place as of September 2008.[5]

In December 2005, the U.S. government announced its belief that Iran had built underground missile factories that were capable of producing Shahab-1s, Shahab-2s, and Shahab-3s, as well as testing new missile designs. It was also believed that Karimi Industries was housed at one of the secret bases, which is where work is taking place on perfecting Iran's nuclear warheads.[6] Most of Iran's missile development industry reportedly is located in Karaj near Tehran. Apparently, there are two large, underground tunnels between Bandar Abbas and Bushehr.[7]

One source notes that with improvements in its Shahab missile program, Iran has attained the capability to strike any place in the Middle East from hardened, fixed sites. Apparently, launch silos for its long-range missiles exist near Isfahan.[8]

U.S. officials insisted that information on the underground facilities did not come from Iranian opposition sources such as the terrorist group Mujahadin-e Khalq (MEK) and that it was reliable. They feel Iran has made significant strides in recent years using North Korean, Chinese, and Russian technology. If Iran begins work on the Shahab-5 and the Shahab-6 series, it may acquire delivery systems with the range to make it a global nuclear power, instead of merely a regional one. One observer has concluded that Iran is becoming self-sufficient in the production of ballistic missiles.[9] Another source claims that Iran is covering almost all the technological bases necessary to administer an advanced missile program;[10] reports of a possible space launch program support such assertions.

Iran claimed to have test-launched a suborbital rocket in early 2007, and on February 2, 2009, Iran successfully launched its first indigenously produced satellite into space, further raising concerns throughout the international community. According to Iranian media outlets, Iran used a Safir-2 rocket to carry the Omid satellite. Iranian officials have also announced that it is planning to launch four more satellites by 2010.[11] According to experts, a satellite launch capability might improve Iran's ability to produce intercontinental ballistic missiles.[12] Also, it is possible that Iran may master cruise-missile technology in the near future. As one Israeli analyst concludes, "Iran's missile program is not a paper tiger."[13]

IRANIAN SHAHAB MISSILE PROGRAMS

Iran can use shorter-range rockets to deliver chemical, radiological, and biological weapons, but it is most likely to link the delivery of its weapons of mass destruction to longer-range missile systems. These begin with the Scud system—with a nominal range of some 300 kilometers, but they are growing to missile systems with ranges approaching 4,000 kilometers.

Shahab-1/Scud-B

The Soviet-designed Scud-B (17E) guided missile currently forms the core of Iran's ballistic missile forces. The missile was used heavily in the latter years of the Iran-Iraq War. In 2006, it was estimated that Iran had between 300 and 750 Shahab-1 and Shahab-2 variants of the Scud-B and Scud-C missiles in its inventory, although some earlier estimates for the Scud-B ranged as low as 50.[14] These seem to be deployed in three to four battalions in a Shahab brigade.

Iran acquired its first Scud missiles in response to Iraq's invasion. It obtained a limited number from Libya and subsequently a larger number from North Korea. Some 20 such missiles and two MAZ-543P transporter-erector-launchers (TELs) were delivered in early 1985.[15]

The Iranians deployed these units with a special Khatam ol-Anbya force attached to the air element of the Pasdaran. Iran fired its first Scud missiles in March 1985. While experts differ over the exact numbers involved, Iran seems to have fired as many as 14 Scuds in 1985, 8 in 1986, 18 in 1987, and 77 in 1988. Iran fired 77 Scud missiles during a 52-day period in 1988, during what came to be known as the "War of the Cities." Sixty-one were fired at Baghdad, 9 at Mosul, 5 at Kirkuk, 1 at Tikrit, and 1 at Kuwait. Iran fired as many as 5 missiles on a single day, and once fired 3 missiles within 30 minutes. This still, however, worked out to an average of only about 1 missile a day, and some experts believe that Iran was down to only 10–20 Scuds when the War of the Cities ended.

Iran's missile attacks were initially more effective than Iraq's attacks. This was largely a matter of geography. Many of Iraq's major cities were comparatively close to its border with Iran, but Tehran and most of Iran's major cities that had not already been targets in the war were outside the range of Iraqi Scud attacks. Iran's missiles, in contrast, could hit key Iraqi cities such as Baghdad. This advantage ended when Iraq deployed extended-range Scud missiles.

The Iranian Shahab-1 version of the Scud-B is a relatively old Soviet design that first became operational in 1967, designated as the R-17E or R-300E. Its thrust is 13,160 kgf (kilogram-force), its burn time is between 62 and 64 seconds, and it has an Isp (specific impulse) of 62-Sl due to vanes steering drag loss of 4–5 seconds. The Scud-B possesses one thrust chamber and is a one-stage rocket (it does not break into smaller pieces). Its fuel is TM-185, and its oxidizer is the AK-27I.[16]

The Shahab-1 is reported to have a nominal range of 285–330 kilometers with its normal conventional payload. The export version of the missile is about 11 meters long, 85–90 centimeters in diameter, and weighs 6,300 kilograms. It has a nominal circular error probable (CEP) of 1,000 meters. Various reports claim that the Russian versions can be equipped with conventional high explosives, fuel air explosives, runway penetrating submunitions, and chemical and nuclear warheads. Its basic design comes from the old German V-2 rocket design of World War II. It has moveable fins and is guided only during powered flight.

The original Scud-B was introduced on the JS-3 tracked chassis in 1961 and appeared on the MAZ-543 wheeled chassis in 1965. The Scud-B missile later appeared on the TEL based on the MAZ-543 (8×8) truck. The introduction of this new cross-country wheeled vehicle gave this missile system greater road mobility and reduced the number of support vehicles required.

The export version of the Scud-B comes with a conventional high-explosive warhead weighing about 1,000 kilograms (kg), of which 800 kg are the high-explosive payload and 200 are the warhead structure and fusing system. It has a single-stage storable liquid rocket engine and is usually deployed on the MAZ-543, an eight-wheel TEL. It has a strap-down inertial guidance system, using three gyros to correct its ballistic trajectory, and it uses internal graphite jet vane steering. The warhead hits at a velocity above Mach 1.5.

The following timeline tracks the history of the Shahab-1 (Scud-B) after it was first introduced in Iran in 1985:

- **1985:** Iran began acquiring Scud-B (Shahab-1) missiles from Libya for use in the Iran-Iraq War.[17] About 20 Scud-Bs were delivered along with two MAZ-543P TELs.[18]

- **1986:** Iran turned to Libya as a supplier of Scud-Bs.[19] Syria is believed to have supplied Iran with a small number of Scud-B missiles.[20]

- **1987:** A watershed year. Iran attempted to produce its own Scud-B missiles, but failed. Over the next five years, it purchased 200–300 Scud-B missiles plus 6–12 TELs from North Korea.[21]

- **1988:** Iran began producing its own Shahab-1s, though not in large quantities.[22]

- **1988:** The Iranian government is reported to have made its first test launch of a ballistic missile, which was believed to be a Scud-B variant with a range of 320 kilometers (km) (199 miles) and a payload of 985 kg, developed with the assistance of either North Korea or the People's Republic of China (PRC).[23]

- **1991:** It is estimated that at approximately the time of the Gulf War, Iran stopped producing its own Shahab-1s and began purchasing the more advanced Scud-Cs (Shahab-2). This is said to be a system with an 800-kg warhead and a 500-km range vs. comparable profiles of 1,000 kg with a 300-km range for the Shahab-1.[24]

- **1993:** Iran sent 21 missile specialists, led by Brigadier General Manteghi, to North Korea for training.[25]

- **1998:** The Iranian government publicly test-fired a Shahab-1 in the Caspian Sea. This test is very important to the study of Iran's ballistic missile program. The Shahab-1 that was tested in the Caspian was tested from its TEL, on board a commercial vessel. This constitutes a different kind of missile threat to the United States and coastal range countries.[26]

- **2001:** Reports indicate nearly 70 missiles of varying class and designation were fired into Iraq from Iran. Iran is reported to have purchased a number of Syrian and 120 North Korean Scud-B missiles. The U.S. Air Force reports from 1996 indicate that number could be in the 200s. The same report implicates North Korea in the sale of approximately 170 Scud-Cs to Iran. The precise number of these missiles, however, is quite uncertain.[27]

- **October 2007:** Jane's indicates development of the Shahab-3 program has obviated the need for Iran to acquire additional Shahab-1s and 2s.

Some sources estimate Iran bought 200–300 Scud-Bs (Shahab-1s) and Scud-Cs (Shahab-2s), or the suitable components for Iranian reverse-engineered systems, from North Korea between 1987 and 1992 and may have continued to buy such missiles after that time.[28]

Israeli sources have estimated that Iran had at least 250–300 Shahab-1 missiles and at least 8–15 launchers on hand in 1997. Some current estimates indicate that Iran now has 6–12 launchers and up to 200 Scud-B (R-17E)/Shahab-1 missiles with a 230–310-km range. Some estimates give higher figures. The IISS estimates in 2008 that Tehran had up to 18 launchers and 300 Shahab-1 and Shahab missiles.[29] It is, however, uncertain how many of those are Shahab-1s and how many are Shahab-2s.

The IISS estimates that Iran's IRGC has at least one brigade of Shahab-1 missiles with 12–18 missile launchers and that the Iranian Army has a matching capability with the same number of launchers. Other estimates put the total as high as three brigades with higher numbers of launchers and missiles.

U.S. experts also believe that Iran can now manufacture virtually all of the Shahab-1, with the possible exception of the most sophisticated components of its guidance system and rocket motors. Some estimates have put production rates as high as 10–12 missiles per month, although experts feel the actual numbers may be an order of magnitude lower, and considerable confusion exists in unclassified estimates as to whether the production estimates being reported apply to the Scud-B, Scud-C, or a mixture of both. This makes it difficult to estimate how many missiles Iran has in its inventory and how many it can acquire over time, as well as to estimate the precise performance characteristics of Iran's missiles, since it can alter the weight of the warhead and adjust the burn time and improve the efficiency of the rocket motors.

Several factors contribute to the uncertainty of Iran's arsenal. Iran tends to be extremely secretive and often redesignates systems without warning or notification. Also, Iran has several production facilities that build their own variants of the original systems purchased from North Korea or China. Therefore, the exact numbers of domestically produced and foreign-bought missile systems is unclear.

As mentioned in the timeline, there are reports that at least one experimental ship-based Shahab weapon system was publicly tested in 1998 in the Caspian Sea, from its TEL, on board a commercial vessel, which constitutes a different kind of missile threat to the United States and coastal range countries. It means the Scud might be covertly deployed near a coastline and launched without notice. Then, as quickly as the weapon is fired, it could return to covert status. This method of delivery brings the weapon in closer range, which improves its accuracy and decreases its chance of being spotted by radar. Due to the flight time of the missile, it could be delivered without a major radar signal.[30] This seems to have been done to examine the options for extending the attack range of the missile into Iraq, but it does at least raise the possibility of covert ship-based missile launches against Israel or even the United States.

Shahab-2/Scud-C

Iran served as a transshipment point for North Korean missile deliveries during 1992 and 1993. Part of this transshipment took place using the same Iranian B-747s that brought missile parts to Iran. Others moved by sea. For example, a North Korean vessel called the *Des Hung Ho,* bringing missile parts for Syria, docked at Bandar Abbas in May 1992. Iran then flew these parts to Syria. An Iranian ship coming from North Korea and a second North Korean ship followed, carrying missiles and machine tools for both Syria and Iran. At least 20 of the North Korean missiles have gone to Syria from Iran, and production equipment seems to have been transferred to Iran and to Syrian plants near Hama and Aleppo.

The Scud-C is the NATO (North Atlantic Treaty Organization) terminology for improved versions of the Scud-B, but is often used to describe system variants developed in North Korea and modified in countries such as Iraq and Iran. All are reported to have significantly better range and payload than the Scud-B.

North Korea seems to have completed development of the Iranian version of the missile in 1987, after obtaining technical support from China. While it is often called a "Scud-C," it seems to differ substantially in detail from the original Soviet Scud-B. It seems to be based more on the Chinese-made DF-61 than on a direct copy of the Soviet weapon.

Experts estimate that the North Korean version of the missile has a range of around 500 km (310 miles), a conventional warhead with a high-explosive payload of 700 kg, and relatively good accuracy and reliability. While some experts feel the payload of its conventional warhead may be limited for the effective delivery of chemical agents, Iran might modify the warhead to increase payload at the expense of range and restrict the using of chemical munitions to the most lethal agents such as persistent nerve gas. It is also possible that North Korea may have armed its Scud-C forces with biological agents and have done development work on a nuclear warhead.

Iran seems to have acquired its first versions of the missile by 1990. Iran formally denied the fact it had such systems long after the transfer of these missiles became a fact. Hassan Taherian, an Iranian foreign ministry official, stated in February 1995, "There is no missile cooperation between Iran and North Korea whatsoever. We deny this."[31]

There were, however, many reports during the 1990s about North Korean missile technology transfers to Tehran. For example, a senior North Korean delegation traveled to Tehran to close the deal on November 29, 1990, and met with Mohsen Rezaei, the former Commander of the IRGC. Iran either bought the missile then or placed its order shortly thereafter. North Korea then exported the missile through its Lyongaksan Import Corporation. Iran imported some of these North Korean missile assemblies using its B-747s and seems to have used ships to import others.

There are reports it fired them in the early 1990s from mobile launchers at a test site near Qom to a target area about 500 km (310 miles) away south of Shahroud. There are also reports that units equipped with such missiles deployed as part of Iranian exercises such as the Saeqer-3 (Thunderbolt 3) exercise in late October 1993.[32]

Iran probably had more than 60 of the longer-range North Korean missiles by 1998, although other sources report 100, and one source reports 170. Iran may have 5–10 Scud-C launchers, each with several missiles. This total seems likely to include 4 North Korean TELs received in 1994.[33]

A number of reports indicate that Iran may have modified some aspects of the system or provided contradictory specifications. As a result, many of the details of performance of what is now normally referred to as the Shahab-2 are unclear. Various reports indicate, however, that it has a diameter of 0.885 meters, a height of 11–12 meters, a launch weight of 6,370–6,500 kg, an unknown stage mass, an unknown dry mass, and an unknown propellant mass. In terms of propelling ability, its thrust is unknown, its burn time is unknown, and it has an effective Isp of 231. It is reported to have one thrust chamber and is a one-stage rocket (it does not break into smaller pieces). Its fuel is Tonka-250, and its oxidizer is the AK 20P.[34]

These reports indicate that it has an approximate range of between 804 and 1,127 km, or 500 and 700 miles, a CEP of 50 meters, and it carries a 750–989-kg warhead. Even the most conservative estimates of the missile's range indicate that it has enough range-payload to give Iran the ability to strike all targets on the southern coast of the Gulf and all of the populated areas in Iraq, although not the West. Iran could also reach targets in part of eastern Syria, the eastern third of Turkey, and cover targets in the border area of the former Soviet Union, western Afghanistan, and western Pakistan.

Accuracy and reliability still present important operational uncertainties, as does the missile's operational CEP. Much would depend on the precise level of technology Iran deployed in the warhead. Neither Russia nor the People's Republic of China seems to have transferred the warhead technology for biological and chemical weapons to Iran or Iraq when they sold them the Scud-B missile and the CSS-8. However, North Korea may have sold Iran such technology as part of the Scud-C sale. If it did so, such a technology transfer would save Iran years of development and testing in obtaining highly lethal biological and chemical warheads. In fact, Iran would probably be able to deploy far more effective biological and chemical warheads than Iraq had at the time of the Gulf War.

It is currently estimated that Iran has 50–150 Shahab-2s/Scud-Cs in its inventory.[35] While early development of the Scud-C tracks closely with that of the Scud-B, the following timeline tracks the development of Iranian Shahab-2s/Scud-C missiles since the Gulf War:

- **1991:** Iran apparently received its first shipment of about 100–170 North Korean Scud-C missiles.
- **1994:** By this year, Iran had purchased 150–200 Scud-Cs from North Korea.[36]
- **1997:** Iran began production of its own Scud-C missiles. This is generally considered a technological leap for Iran, and it is believed that a large portion of its production capability and technology came from North Korea.[37]
- **2004–2006:** According to Iranian sources, Iran fired Shahab-2 missiles in most of its major military exercises. In 2004, the Shahab-2 became an active participant in all military drills and exercises, being consistently tested and with successful results. An additional public test was in April 2006 beginning a regional war game.[38]
- **November 2006:** Iran was reported to have successfully fired Shahab-2 and Shahab-3 missiles in military exercises.[39]
- **Undated and unconfirmed:** According to one report, Iran set up a production line for Shahab-2 missiles in Syria.[40]
- **October 2007:** Jane's indicates development of the Shahab-3 program has obviated the need for Iran to acquire additional Shahab-1s and 2s.

Most experts agree that Iran can now assemble Shahab-2s missiles using foreign-made components. There is less agreement as to whether it can now make every component of the entire Shahab-2 missile system and warhead package in Iran, but this seems increasingly likely. Iran also is continuing to modify and improve some components of the missile. It may be working with Syria in such development efforts, as well as North Korea, although some experts note that Middle Eastern nations have problems in cooperating in such sensitive areas.[41]

Iran has now deployed enough Shahab-2 missiles and launchers to make its missile force highly dispersed and difficult to attack. According to some reports, Iran has also created shelters and tunnels in its coastal areas that it could use to store these and other missiles in hardened sites to reduce their vulnerability to air attack. These reports give Iran a potential mix of launch on warning and launch under attack capabilities and the ability to ride out preventive or preemptive attacks. There is no hard reporting, however, to confirm that Iran has put such plans into action.

Shahab-3

Iran began to shift from a reliance on missile imports to a technological partnership with North Korea in creating new missiles and missile production capabilities in the early 1990s. The visit to North Korea in 1993 by General Manteghi and his 21 specialists seems to be a possible date when Iran shifted from procurement to development.

One key reason for this shift was to ensure that Iran could not be sanctioned or interdicted by U.S. and other international action or military embargos. Iran may also, however, have seen acquiring longer-range and more capable missiles as a key to being able to use relatively heavy nuclear weapons, and to threatening targets outside the region in Israel and Europe that could help intimidate or deter U.S. military action. As Figure 4.2 shows, even the Scud-C did not guarantee that Iran could attack all of Israel or key regional allies of the United States such as Egypt and Turkey with large payloads.

As a result, Iran turned to designs for the North Korean No-Dong medium-range ballistic missile in an attempt to manufacture its own version of the missile, the Shahab-3. Between 1997 and 1998, Iran began testing the early versions of a missile now called the Shahab-3. While Iran claimed the Shahab-3's purpose was to carry payloads of conventional submunitions, it is more likely that Iran sought to use the Shahab-3's superior range to carry a chemical, nuclear, or biological weapon.

Missile Development

The Shahab-3 series seems to be based on the design of the North Korean No-Dong 1/A and No-Dong B missiles—which some analysts claim were developed with Iranian financial support. The initial versions of the Shahab-3 also had strong similarities to Pakistan's Ghauri I missile, which benefited from transfers of North Korean technology and possibly Chinese technology as well.

While the Shahab-3 may have been based on North Korean designs and technology, it was developed and produced in Iran and evolved steadily over time. This development effort is controlled and operated by the IRGC. Iranian officials also claimed that the development and production of the Shahab-3 missiles were entirely domestic. Former Iranian Defense Minister Ali Shamkhani stated in May 2005 that the production was comprised of locally made parts and that the production was continuing.[42]

The following timeline shows that the Shahab-3 has been tested in a number of variants:

- **October 1997:** Russia began training Iranian engineers on missile production for the Shahab-3.[43]

- **1998:** Iran began testing its own Shahab-3s. Problems with finding or making an advanced guidance system hindered many of Iran's tests, however. Meanwhile, Iran begins experimenting with the Shahab-4.[44]

- **July 23, 1998:** Iran launched its first test flight of the Shahab-3. The missile flew for approximately 100 seconds, after which time it was detonated. It is not known whether the missile malfunctioned or if this was an apogee test because the Iranians did not want to risk discovery.[45]

- **July 15, 2000:** Iran had its first successful test of a Shahab-3, using a new North Korean engine.[46]

- **Summer 2001:** Iran claimed to have begun production of the Shahab-3.[47]

- **July 7, 2003:** Iran completed the final test of the Shahab-3. Allegations emerged that Chinese companies such as Tai'an Foreign Trade General Corporation and China North Industries Corporation had been aiding the Iranians in overcoming the missile's final technical glitches.[48] The missile was seen in Iranian military parades and displayed openly. Iran announced at the same time an increase in the production rate of the Shahab-3 to several a month and introduction into service.[49]

- **September 22, 2003:** The Shahab-3 was displayed on mobile launchers at a military parade. Reportedly, the parade announcer said that the missile shown had a range of 1,000 miles.[50]

- **October 2003:** Iran claimed it was abandoning its Shahab-4 program, citing that the expected increase in range (2,200 to 3,000 km) would cause too much global tension.

- **Late 2003:** Some sources indicated that Iran had begun only limited production of the Shahab-3.

- **August 11, 2004:** Iran decreased the size of the Shahab-3 warhead with a significantly modified reentry vehicle and propulsion system, making a move toward being able to mount a nuclear warhead to a Shahab-3. At this point, the modified Shahab-3 is often referred to as the Shahab-3M.[51] The missile had a new, smaller, and "bottleneck" warhead. This kind of warhead has a slower reentry than a cone-shaped warhead and has advantages using warheads containing chemical and biological agents. Some estimated that it had a range of 2,000 km for a 700-kg warhead, but this may be confused with another solid-fueled system. A second variant may exist with a larger fin, a meter less length, and less than a 1,500-km range.[52]

- **September 19, 2004:** Another test took place, and the missile was paraded on September 21 covered in banners saying "we will crush America under our feet" and "wipe Israel off the map."[53]

- **May 31, 2005:** Iranian Defense Minister Ali Shamkhani claimed that Iran successfully tested a new missile motor using solid-fuel technology with a range of 1,500–2,000 km, and a 700-kg warhead. Shamkhani was quoted as saying, "Using solid fuel would be more durable and increase the range of the missile."[54] It remains uncertain if this referred to the Shahab-3 or the modified Shahab-3, the IRIS missile.

- **September 2005:** Two new missiles were tested, again with a triconic or baby-bottle warhead some 3 meters long. Some experts speculate that it can disperse chemical and biological weapons or is better suited to a nuclear warhead. Others feel it is an air-burst warhead, capable of better dispersing chemical and/or biological weapons. Two Shahab-3 missiles with triconic warheads were displayed at a parade. These missiles were believed to be new variants of the Shahab-3.

- **February 16, 2006:** Iran is reported to have successfully completed four successful missile test launches this year, including one of a Shahab-3 and a Shahab-4 missile with ranges of 1,300 km and 2,200 km, respectively.

- **April 7, 2006:** The *Telegraph* (London) reports that Iran has succeeded in adapting the nose cone of the Shahab-3 missile to deliver a nuclear weapon. Allegedly, a modified Shahab-3 could carry the Pakistani version of a nuclear warhead, and it is rumored that Iran possesses this design.

- **September 2006:** Iran is reported to have more than 30 Shahab-3s and 10 TELs, but this is not confirmed.[55]

- **November 23, 2006:** It is reported that Iran for the first time fired Shahab-3 missiles in an exercise in early November. Allegedly, a Shahab-3 version with a range of 1,900 km (with cluster bombs) was fired. According to Iranian sources, the missiles carried cluster warheads, had a strike range of about 1,900 km, and landed "a few meters away" from its intended target.[56] The military exercise was termed "Great Prophet II." During the 10-day war games, the IRGC claimed to have deployed 10 infantry divisions, including several mechanized and armored brigades, and to have launched 15 missiles including Shahab-2 and Shahab-3 ballistic missiles. Some reports alleged that some of the Shahab-3 missiles were equipped with cluster warheads.[57]

- **August 2007:** There are reports that Iran has developed a remote-controlled launch system that can be used to operate dozens of unmanned Shahab-3 ballistic missile launchers in underground bunkers.[58]

- **October 2007:** Jane's indicates development of the Shahab-3 program has obviated the need for Iran to acquire additional Shahab-1s and 2s.

- **July 8–10, 2008:** Iran reports a series of missile tests at the Holy Prophet III exercises, including a Shahab-3 with a conventional warhead weighing one ton and a 2,000-km range. Iranian media depicted what appeared to be two Shahabs lifting off within seconds of one another.[59] Iranian Revolutionary Guards Commander Hossein Salami tells an Iranian reporter that the Shahab-3 had undergone further improvements, including to its navigation and ignition systems, and featured enhanced maneuverability and reaction time. Iranian media claims that the Shahab-3 can now be launched "at night and in adverse weather conditions."[60]

- **July 9, 2008:** The IRGC conducted another military exercise, the "Great Prophet III," on July 9, 2008. During the exercise, nine medium- and short-range missiles were fired from the Iranian desert, including an upgraded Shahab-3, the 150-km range Fateh, and the 400-km Zelzal.[61] A still picture showing four missiles taking off in the desert was used by the international media. However, closer examination revealed that the image had been doctored. The original image from the Iranian news Web site Jamejam clearly showed that one missile had not taken off, but another image altered by the public relations arm of the IRGC and widely circulated, showed otherwise.[62] While these tests did not reveal any new capability beyond what has already been seen, they do signal Iran's continuing determination to advance and demonstrate its missile capability. Although no reliable estimates exist of the exact number of Shahabs produced to date, these tests lead some analysts to now assume that Iran is capable of producing Shahab-3s in large quantities.[63]

- **August 16, 2008:** Iran successfully launched the Safir (Messenger) rocket into space from its new space center 60 km southeast of Semnan City. According to Reza Taghizadeh, "The firing paved the way for placing the first Iranian satellite in orbit." The Safir is said to be based on the Shahab-3 ballistic missile, and TV footage of the launch indicated that Iran has mastered the transition from first- to second-stage rocket power. Prior to this test launch, Iran had not tested a two-stage rocket system.[64]

- **September 16, 2008:** Herman Nackaerts, head of Middle East Monitoring for the International Atomic Energy Agency (IAEA), showed pictures and diagrams to IAEA representatives of Iran's retrofits to the Shahab-3 missile. The retrofits would reportedly enable the missile to carry a nuclear warhead. Mohamed El-Baradei, Director General of the IAEA, calls the information "very credible" and asked Iran for a "political explanation." Iran's representative to the IAEA, Ali-Asghar Soltaniyeh, called the diagrams and pictures baseless and ridiculous.[65]

This Iranian test and development program seems to have been driven by changes in performance requirements and specifications as much as by problems in technology, systems integration, and manufacturing. As of early 2006, Iran had conducted some 10 launches at a rate of only 1–2 per year. Roughly 30 percent had fully malfunctioned, and 6 launches had some malfunction.

Uncertain Performance and Range-Payload[66]

Discussions of the Shahab-3's range-payload, accuracy, and reliability are uncertain and will remain speculative until the system is far more mature. A long-range ballistic missile requires at least 10–30 tests in its final configuration to establish its true payload and warhead type, actual range-payload, and accuracy—and some experts put the number much higher for a nation that does not have a long history of advanced missile production and development.

While there are many detailed unclassified estimates of the Shahab-3's performance, they at best are uncertain and sometimes are speculative to the point of being sheer guesswork using rounded numbers. Its real-world range will depend on both the final configuration of the missile and the weight of its warhead.

Various sources now guess that the Shahab-3 has a range of between 1,280 and 2,000 km, but the longer-range estimate seems to be based on Iranian claims and assumptions about an improved version, not full-scale operational tests.[67] U.S.

experts believe that the original Shahab-3 missile had a nominal range of 1,100 to 1,300 km, with a 1,200-kg payload. The basic system is said to have been 16.5 meters long, have a diameter of 1.58 meters, with a launch weight of 17,410 pounds. Iran has claimed that the Shahab-3 has a range of 2,000 km. This may reflect different estimates of different versions of the missile.

In June 2003, Iran conducted a test fight of the Shahab-3. Details concerning the test are lacking; however, Israeli sources suggest that this launch was the most successful to date. A foreign ministry spokesman stated that "it was a final test before delivering the missile to the armed forces. It was within the same range that we had declared before."[68] This report suggests that Iran's Shahab-3 missile program is improving to the point of being deployed to Iranian military units.

Nasser Maleki, the head of Iran's aerospace industry, stated on October 7, 2004, "Very certainly we are going to improve our Shahab-3 and all of our other missiles." Tehran claimed in September 2004 that the Shahab-3 could now reach targets up to 2,000 km away, presumably allowing the missiles to be deployed a greater distance away from Israel's Air Force and Jericho-2 ballistic missiles.[69]

IRGC Political-Bureau Chief Yadollah Javani stated in September 2004 that the modified Shahab-3—sometimes called the Shahab-3A or Shahab-3M—could be used to attack Israel's Dimona nuclear reactor.[70] Iran performed another test on October 20, 2004, and Iran's Defense Minister, Ali Shamkhani, claimed it was part of an operational exercise. On November 9, 2004, Iran's Defense Minister also claimed that Iran was now capable of mass producing the Shahab-3 and that Iran reserved the option of preemptive strikes in defense of its nuclear sites. Shamkhani claimed shortly afterward that the Shahab-3 now had a range of more than 2,000 km (1,250 miles).[71]

One leading German expert has stressed the uncertainty of any current estimates and notes that range-payload trade-offs would be critical. He puts the range for the regular Shahab-3 at 820 km with a 1.3-ton payload and 1,100 km with a 0.7-ton payload. (An analysis by John Pike of GlobalSecurity.org also points out that missiles—such as combat aircraft—can make trade-offs between range and payload. For example, the No-Dong B has a range of 1,560 km with a 760-kg warhead and 1,350 km with a 1,158-kg warhead.[72])

The German analyst notes that an improved Shahab could use a combination of a lighter aluminum airframe, lightweight guidance, reduced payload, increased propellant load, and increased burn time to increase range. He notes that little is really known about the improved Shahab-3, but estimates the maximum range of an improved Shahab-3 as still being 2,000 km, that a 0.7–0.8-ton warhead would limit its range to 1,500 km, and that a 0.8–1.0-ton warhead would reduce it to 1,200 km. A 1.2-ton warhead would limit it to around 850 km. He feels Iran may have drawn on Russian technology from the R-21 and the R-27. Photos of the system also show progressive changes in cable duct position, fins, and length in 2004 and 2005.[73]

Some aspects of the differences in range estimates may be a matter of Iranian propaganda, but a number of experts believe that Iranian claims refer to the modified Shahab-3D or the Shahab-3M and not the regular Shahab-3. There are reports that such modified versions use solid fuel and could have a range of up to 2,000 km. They also indicate that the standard Shahab-3 remains in production, but the improved Shahab is now called the Shahab-3M.[74]

Some sources report that the Shahab-3 has a height of 16 meters, a stage mass of 15,092 kg, a dry mass of 1,780–2,180 kg, and a propellant mass of 12,912 kg. In terms of propelling ability, its thrust is between 26,760–26,600 kgf, its burn time is 110 seconds, and it has an effective Isp of 226 and a drag loss of 45 seconds. According to this source, the Shahab-3 possesses one thrust chamber. Its fuel is TM-185, and its oxidizer is the AK 27I.[75]

Missile Accuracy

If the system uses older guidance technology and warhead separation methods, its CEP could be anywhere from 1,000 to 4,000 meters (approximately 0.0015 to 0.001 CEP). If it uses newer technology, such as some of the most advanced Chinese technology, it could have a CEP as low as 190–800 meters. Some analysts argue that Iran may have advanced to the point where relatively high levels of accuracy are possible for the Shahab and that Iran may be developing a version with terminal homing.

As for other aspects of performance, it is again easy to find many highly precise estimates, but impossible to know if any are correct even for the versions of the Shahab-3 that Iran has tested to date. A German expert feels, for example, that the operational CEP of the improved Shahab-3 is likely to be around 3 km, but the maximum deviation could be 11 km.[76] Iran makes very different claims. In 2007, Yahya Safavi, Commander of the IRGC, announced on Iranian state television that Iran test-fired its latest version of the Shahab-3. According to the general, the missile used had a CEP of "several meters."[77] Another source reports that the Shahab-3 has a CEP of 190 meters and carries a 750–989–1,158-kg warhead.

There are other problems in estimating operational accuracy. CEP is a theoretical engineering term that states that 50 percent of all the missiles launched will hit within a circle of the radius of the CEP. It also assumes that all missiles are perfectly targeted and function perfectly throughout their entire flight. It makes no attempt to predict where the 50 percent of the missiles that hit outside the circle will go, or missile reliability.[78]

Engineering estimates basing CEP on the theoretical accuracy of the guidance platform have often proved to be wrong in the past until they are based on the actual performance of large numbers of firings of mature deployed systems (the derived aim point method). This means real-world missile accuracy and reliability cannot be measured using technical terms such as CEP even if they apply to a fully mature and deployed missile. True performance can be derived only from observing reliability under operational conditions and by correlating actual point of impact to a known aim point.[79]

At present, unclassified estimates of the Shahab-3's accuracy and reliability available from public sources seem to be based on speculation rather than on such tests.

No unclassified source has credibility in describing its performance in real-world, warfighting terms.

Payload Configurations

There has been some official reporting on the missile warhead, and Iran is known to have tested several major payload configurations for the Shahab.[80] In 2004, then U.S. Secretary of State Colin Powell accused Iran of modifying its Shahab-3 to carry a nuclear warhead based on documents the U.S. government had received from a walk-in source. While experts argued that this information was yet to be confirmed, others claimed that Iran obtained "a new nosecone" for its Shahab-3 missile.[81]

Other U.S. officials claimed that the source of the information provided "tens of thousands of pages of Farsi-language computer files" on Iran's attempts to modify its Shahab-3 missile to deliver a "black box," which U.S. officials believed to "almost certainly" refer to a nuclear warhead. These documents were said to include diagrams and test results, weight, detonation height, and shape, but did not include warhead designs.[82]

Media reporting indicates that the United States was able to examine drawings on a stolen laptop from Iran and found that Iran had developed 18 different ways to adapt the size, weight, and diameter of the new nose cone on its Shahab-3 missile. It was also reported, however, that Iran's effort to expand the nose cone would not work and that Iran did not have the technological capabilities to adapt nuclear weapons into its Shahab-3 missile. U.S. nuclear experts claimed that one reason for this failure was that the project "wasn't done by the A-team of Iran's program."[83]

Some experts believe that the new bottleneck warhead tested in 2004 was for the Shahab-3M and made it more accurate and capable of air-burst detonations, which could be used to more effectively spread chemical weapons. Others believe a smaller warhead has increased its range. According to one source, the baby-bottle shaped missiles, which surfaced in 2004, would represent an entirely new missile development if they carry a triconic warhead. Reportedly, the latter warhead does not fit on a Shahab-3 missile. Other analysts believe that this warhead would be the prime vehicle for a nuclear weapon.[84] The same source states that the SHIG (a unit known as Department 2500 or Shahid Karimi) started a project (project 111) between 2001 and 2003 to fit a nuclear warhead on a Shahab-3.[85]

The uncertainties in such reporting are not a casual issue, since actual weaponization of a warhead requires extraordinarily sophisticated systems to detonate a warhead at the desired height of burst and to reliably disseminate the munitions or agent. Even the most sophisticated conventional submunitions are little more than area weapons if the missile accuracy to target location has errors in excess of 250–500 meters, and a unitary conventional explosive warhead without terminal guidance is little more than a psychological or terror weapon almost regardless of its accuracy.

The effective delivery of chemical agents by either spreading the agent or the use of submunitions generally requires accuracies less than 1,000 meters to achieve lethality against even large point targets. Systems with biological weapons are inherently area weapons, but a 1,000-kg nominal warhead can carry so little agent that accuracies less than 1,000 meters again become undesirable. Nuclear weapons require far less accuracy, particularly if a "dirty" ground burst can be targeted within a reliable fall-out area. There are, however, limits. For example, a regular fission weapon of some 20 kilotons requires accuracies under 2,500–3,000 meters for some kinds of targets such as sheltered airfields or large energy facilities.

It does seem clear that the Shahab could carry a well-designed nuclear weapon in a well-designed warhead to ranges well over 1,000 km, and Iran may have access to such warhead designs. As noted earlier, the Shahab-3 missile has been tested in ways that indicate it has a range of 2,000 km, which is enough to reach the Gulf and Israel. As later chapters indicate, A. Q. Khan seems to have sold a Chinese nuclear warhead design to Libya with a mass of as little as 500 kg and a one-meter diameter. IAEA and U.S. background briefings in 2008 indicate that such designs, or key elements of such designs, were sold to Iran as well.

Mobility and Deployment

The Shahab-3 is mobile, but requires numerous launching support vehicles for propellant transport and loading and power besides its TELs.[86] The original version was slow in setting up, taking five hours to prepare for launch.[87] Some five different TELs have been seen, however, and some experts believe the current reaction time is roughly an hour.[88] One report states that the latest TELs used for launching a Shahab-3 need one hour to arrive at the launch site, set up the TEL, and fire the missile.[89]

As is discussed later, speculation about changing the Shahab's reaction times by replacing the liquid propulsion fuel with solid fuel for the Shahab-3 do not seem realistic. Reengineering the current design with solid fuel propulsion would effectively create a completely different and more sophisticated missile than the Shahab-3.[90]

Operational Status and Force Size

The Shahab-3's deployment status is uncertain. Some reports have claimed that the Shahab-3 was operational as early as 1999. Reports surfaced that development of the Shahab-3 was completed in June 2003 and that it underwent "final" tests on July 7, 2003. Other sources claim that around 20 missiles were operational in May 2004. By February 2006 it is believed that 30–50 were operational.[91]

A Central Intelligence Agency (CIA) report to Congress, dated November 10, 2003, indicated that upgrading of the Shahab-3 was still under way, and some sources indicated that Iran was now seeking a range of 1,600 km. The CIA then reported in 2004 that Iran had "some" operational Shahab-3s with a range of 1,300 km. Some experts feel the missile has since become fully operational and Iran already possesses 25–100 Shahab-3s in its inventory.[92] Iranian opposition sources have claimed that Iran has 300 such missiles.

According to other sources, the IRGC operated six batteries in the spring of 2006 and was redeploying them within a 35-km radius of their main command-and-control center every 24 hours because of the risk of a U.S. or Israeli attack. The main operating forces were deployed in the west in the Kermanshah and Hamadan provinces with reserve batteries farther east in the Fars and Isfahan provinces.[93]

A substantial number of other experts believe the Shahab-3 may be in deployment, but only in the form of "showpiece" or "test-bed" units using conventional warheads and with performance Iran cannot accurately predict. The IISS reports that the IRGC has one battalion of Shahab-3 missiles with six launchers, each of which has 4 missiles (total operational force of 24).[94]

High Apogee Tests and the Shahab's Possible Use as an Electromagnetic Pulse Weapon

Some Shahab tests have been high apogee tests where the missile was destroyed in mid flight to keep the missile within Iranian territory. This has led some analysts to speculate that Iran might be developing a capability to use the Shahab-3 as a launch vehicle for a nuclear electromagnetic pulse (EMP) weapon and that it might develop a covert ship-based launch capability to attack the United States. These analysts have voiced the following concerns over the possibility of these types of attacks by Iran:[95]

> Testifying before the US Senate Committee on the Judiciary's Subcommittee on Terrorism, Technology and Homeland Security on 8 March 2005, Peter Pry, a senior staff member of the Congressional EMP Commission, said that these flights were reported to have been terminated by a self-destruct mechanism on the missile. "The Western press has described these flight tests as failures because the missiles did not complete their ballistic trajectories," he told the subcommittee. "Iran has officially described all of these same tests as successful. The flight tests would be successful if Iran were practicing the execution of an EMP attack."
>
> As evidence of Iranian interest in EMP weapons, he quoted an article from an unidentified Iranian political military journal as saying: "Once you confuse the enemy communication network you can also disrupt the work of the enemy command and decision-making centre . . . when you disable a country's military high command through disruption of communications, you will, in effect, disrupt all the affairs of that country. If the world's industrial countries fail to devise effective ways to defend themselves against dangerous electronic assaults then they will disintegrate within a few years."[96]
>
> In testimony before the House Armed Services Committee and in remarks to a private conference on missile defense, Dr. William Graham warned that the U.S. intelligence community "doesn't have a story" to explain the recent Iranian tests. One group of tests that troubled Graham, the former White House science adviser under President Ronald Reagan, were successful efforts to launch a SCUD missile from a platform in the Caspian Sea. "They've got [test] ranges in Iran which are more than long enough to handle SCUD launches and even Shahab-3 launches," Dr. Graham said. "Why would they be launching from the surface of the Caspian Sea? They obviously have not explained that to us."

Another troubling group of tests involved Shahab-3 launches where the Iranians "detonated the warhead near apogee, not over the target area where the thing would eventually land, but at altitude," Graham said. "Why would they do that?" Graham chairs the Commission to Assess the Threat to the United States from Electromagnetic Pulse (EMP) Attack, a blue-ribbon panel established by Congress in 2001.

"The only plausible explanation we can find is that the Iranians are figuring out how to launch a missile from a ship and get it up to altitude and then detonate it," he said. "And that's exactly what you would do if you had a nuclear weapon on a SCUD or a Shahab-3 or other missile, and you wanted to explode it over the United States."[97]

Since this report, some experts have stated that in at least two earlier ballistic missile launches, the Iranians launched in ways that "appear they were designed to optimize an EMP burst," according to a Pentagon source with detailed knowledge of the Iranian's efforts and of space technology.[98]

Other analysts are more cautious.[99] Although an asymmetric EMP attack is a technically feasible launch option, high apogee tests have many other explanations—including the limits of test ranges, technical problems in flight, and a desire to avoid disclosing the full range of the missile. Such a threat cannot be ignored, but it also should not be exaggerated.

Shahab-3A/3B/3M

There are many speculative reports on the state of follow-on missiles and variants of Iran's evolving Shahab-3 program. In October 2004, the MEK claimed that Iran was developing an improved version of the Shahab with a 2,400-km range (1,500 miles). The MEK has an uncertain record of accuracy in making such claims, and such claims could not be confirmed.

Such a "Shahab-3B" or "Shahab 3M" is sometimes reported to have a solid propellant serving as first- or second-stage propulsion. However, the supposed payload was only 800 kg, 500 kg less than the standard Shahab-3.[100]

Mortezar Ramandi, an official in the Iranian delegation to the United Nations, denied that Iran was developing a missile with a range of more than 2,000 km (1,250 miles).[101]

The Shahab 3D, the IRIS, and the Ghadr 101 and Ghadr 110

There are other reports of solid fuel missile programs that are compounded by reports of separate missile development programs. Some experts believe that a new solid fueled missile, using part of the Shahab-3, is under development, rather than a modification of the Shahab-3. This program is sometimes called the Shahab-3D, or the IRIS missile.

If there is an IRIS vehicle, reporting suggests that it consists of the No-Dong/ Shahab-3 first stage with a bulbous front section ultimately designed to carry the IRIS second-stage solid motor, as well as a communications satellite or scientific payload.[102] The IRIS solid fuel missile itself may be the third-stage portion of the North Korean Taep'o-dong-1.[103]

The Shahab-3D alone is not capable of launching a large satellite probe into space, and it is possible that it is a test for the second- and third-stage portions of the IRBM Ghadr designs and the limited-range intercontinental ballistic missile (LRICBM) Shahab-5 and Shahab-6.[104]

No test flights of the Shahab-3D have been recorded on video, but it is believed that they have taken place at a space launch facility.[105] The following timeline shows the reported tests of the Shahab-3 variants and IRIS:

- **July 22, 1998:** First test flight (exploded 100 seconds after takeoff)
- **July 15, 2000:** First successful test flight (range of 850 km).
- **September 21, 2000:** Unsuccessful test flight (exploded shortly after takeoff). After the test, an Iranian source claimed that the missile was a two-stage/solid fuel propulsion system.
- **May 23, 2002:** Successful test flight
- **July 2002:** Unsuccessful test flight (missile did not function properly)
- **June 2003:** Successful test flight. Iran declared this was the final test flight before deployment.
- **August 11, 2004:** Successful test flight of the Shahab-3M. The missile now had a "baby-bottle" warhead.
- **October 20, 2004:** Another successful test flight of the Shahab-3M. Iran now claimed the modified missile had a range of 2,000 km.[106]
- **February 25, 2007:** Shahab-3A, suborbital sounding flight test. The details of this launching are not clear, yet this firing appears to be in conjunction with Iranian efforts to launch commercial satellites into orbit.[107]
- **September 22, 2007:** In an Iranian military exercise, a missile with the range of 500 km more than the Shahab-3 is displayed. The missile known as "Qadr-1" and its launcher were displayed at the parade held to commemorate the 27th anniversary of the Iran-Iraq War. Qadr-1 is a ballistic missile with a warhead and an explosive-impact and surface fuse system that is launched vertically.[108]
- **February 4, 2008:** Iran conducts a successful test launch of the Kavoshgar-1 (Explorer-1) research rocket to inaugurate its first domestically built space center 60 km southeast of Semnan City. The Kavoshgar-1 is a variant of the single-stage Shahab-3 intermediate-range ballistic missile, specifically the Shahab-3B variant with the baby-bottle nose.[109]
- **August 16, 2008:** Iran successfully launched the Safir (Messenger) rocket into space from its new space center 60 km southeast of Semnan City. According to Reza Taghizadeh, "the firing paved the way for placing the first Iranian satellite in orbit." The Safir is said to be based on the Shahab-3 ballistic missile, and TV footage of the launch indicated that Iran has mastered the transition from first- to second-stage rocket power. Prior to this test launch, Iran had not tested a two-stage rocket system.[110]

• **February 2, 2009:** Iran successfully launched its first indigenously produced satellite into space. According to Iranian media outlets, Iran used a Safir-2 rocket to carry the Omid satellite. Iran's use of the indigenously developed Safir-2 rocket to place a satellite in orbit raises concerns that Iran could use similar technology to help build intercontinental ballistic missiles (ICBMs).[111]

There are also reports of a different type of solid-fueled system. The hard-line Iranian exile group National Council of Resistance of Iran (NCRI)—an organization that the U.S. Department of State reports has strong ties to the terrorist group MEK—claimed in December 2004 that Iran had developed the Ghadr-101 and the Ghadr-110. These were said to be new missile types that used solid fuel and were, in fact, intermediate-range ballistic missiles (IRBMs). Their existence has never been confirmed, and conflicting reports make an exact description difficult. One analyst claims that the Russian Kh-55 cruise missile (see below) is being reengineered by Iran under the name Ghadr.[112]

At the time, U.S. experts indicated that the Ghadr is actually the same as the Shahab-3A/Shahab-3M/Shahab-4, which seemed to track with some Israeli experts who felt that Iran was extending the range/payload of the Shahab-3 and that reports of both the Ghadr and the Shahab-4 were actually describing the Shahab-3A/3M.[113] Another source claims that Ghadr missiles can be compared to Scud-E missiles.[114] The Scud-E designation has been used to describe Taep'o-dong-1 and No-Dong 2 missiles.

In May 2005, Iran tested a solid fuel motor for what some experts then called the Shahab-3D, possibly increasing its range to 2,500 km, making space entry possible, and setting the stage for the Shahab-5 and the Shahab-6 to be three-stage rockets resembling ICBMs.[115] This test showed that Iran had developed some aspects of a successful long-range, sold fuel missile design, but did not show how Iran intended to use such capabilities.

In March 2006 the NCRI claimed that Iran was moving forward with the Ghadr solid fuel IRBM. It also claimed that Iran had scrapped the Shahab-4 because of test failures and performance limitations. It reported that Iran had substantial North Korean technical support for the Ghadr, that it was 70 percent complete, and had a range of 3,000 km. One Israeli expert felt that the NCRI was confusing a solid-state, second-stage rocket for the liquid-fueled Shahab-4 with a separate missile.[116]

Jane's has reported that unnamed intelligence sources have stated that a parallel, indigenously built IRBM is being built by the Shahid Bagheri Industrial Group with range of 2,000 km and a payload of about 900 kg. The Iranian government announced in November 2007 that it was developing this new missile, Ashura (or Ashoura). An Israeli report in April 2008 reported that Ashura is a two-stage solid propellant missile with a triconic nose shape similar to the Shahab-3A. A Russian report in November 2007 said that the Ashura had a failed flight test, and an Israeli report said that the solid propellant motors were tested but not launched.[117]

Work by Dr. Robert Schmucker indicates that Iran is working on solid-fueled systems, building on its experience with solid fuel artillery rockets such as its Fateh

A-110 and with Chinese support in developing solid fuel propulsion and guidance. The Fateh, however, is a relatively primitive system with strap-down gyro guidance that is not suited for long-range ballistic missiles, although it is reported to be highly accurate.[118]

On September 21, 2008, Iran quietly paraded a version of what might be the Ghaadr-110 tactical solid propellant ballistic missile. Two images of the ballistic missile were shown by the FARS News Agency, and the only noticeable difference between the Iranian Ghadr-110 and the Chinese M-9—which is the missile the Ghadr is reportedly based on—is a shortened conical nose cone. The appearance of the Ashura/Ghadr seems to be further evidence of two things: Chinese missile proliferation to Iran and the claims made by the MEK regarding this particular program were true.[119]

As is the case with longer-range variants of the Shahab, it is probably wise to assume that Iran is seeking to develop options for both solid- and liquid-fueled IRBMs and will seek high-range payloads to ensure it can deliver effective chemical, biological, radiological, and nuclear (CBRN) payloads even if it cannot produce efficient nuclear weapons. It is equally wise to wait for systems to reach maturity before reacting to vague possibilities, rather than real-world Iranian capabilities.

Shahab-4

Iran may also be developing larger designs with greater range-payload using a variety of local, North Korean, Chinese, and Russian technical inputs. These missiles have been called the Shahab-4, the Shahab-5, and the Shahab-6. As of September 2006, none of these missiles were being produced, and the exact nature of such programs remained speculative.[120]

Some experts believe the "Shahab-4" has an approximate range between 2,200 and 2,800 km. Various experts have claimed that the Shahab-4 is based on the North Korean No-Dong 2, the three-stage Taep'o-dong-1 missile, the Russian SS-N-6 SERB, or even some aspects of the Russian SS-4 and SS-5,[121] but has a modern digital guidance package rather than the 2,000–3,000-meter (m) CEP of early missiles such as the Soviet SS-4, whose technology is believed to have been transferred to both North Korea and Iran.

Russian firms are believed to have sold Iran special steel for missile development, test equipment, shielding for guidance packages, and other technology. Iran's Shahid Hemmat Industrial Group is reported to have contracts with the Russian Central Aerohydrodynamic Institute, Rosvoorouzhenie, the Bauman Institute, and Polyus. It is also possible that Iran has obtained some technology from Pakistan.

One source has provided a precise estimate of some performance characteristics. This estimate of Shahab-4 gives it an estimated height of 25 meters, a diameter of 1.3 meters, and a launch weight of 22,000 kg. In terms of propelling ability, its thrust is estimated to be around 26,000 kgf and its burn time is around 293 seconds. It is said to be a two- and/or three-stage rocket that possesses three thrust chambers, one for each stage. Its fuel for the first stage is heptyl, and its oxidizer is inhibited red fuming nitric acid.[122]

Iran has sent mixed signals about the missile development status. In October 2003, Iran claimed it was abandoning its Shahab-4 program, citing that the expected increase in range (2,200 to 3,000 km) would cause too much global tension.[123] Some then speculated that Iran may have scrapped its Shahab-4 program because it either was not innovative and large enough and/or to avoid controversy. The reason announced by some Iranians for creating a missile such as the Shahab-4 was for satellite launches. Other sources felt that the improved range and bottleneck warhead design offered by the Shahab-3M (which began testing in August 2004) may make the Shahab-4 simply not worth the effort or controversy.[124]

The NCRI—which the U.S. Department of State, as previously stated, reports has strong ties to MEK—has provided mixed reporting, but indicated that Iran persisted and launched a Shahab-4 missile for the first time on August 17, 2004.[125]

In May 2005, Ali Shamkhani, Iran's Minister of Defense announced the successful development of a "twin engine" booster, which subsequently was interpreted as a two-stage missile with a solid propellant. Initial assumptions over an improved version of the Shahab-3 were refuted, as observers claimed that introducing a solid propellant, two-stage motor into a Shahab-3 made little sense.[126]

Iranian sources did not clarify their statements about the alleged new motor, therefore leaving open speculations whether the new engine was in use at all, perhaps in use with the Shahab-4 and Shahab-5 missiles, or whether it existed at all. The Pakistani Shaheen, on the other hand, is solid fueled. The IISS *The Military Balance 2007* reports that Iran holds an unspecified number of Shaheen missiles. Perhaps Iran has modified the motor of that engine for its own program.

Iranian Defense Minister Mostafa Mohammad-Najjar indicated in a public press conference in 2006 that the nation was in the process of "researching and building" the Shahab-4.[127]

According to German press reports, Iran is moving ahead in its development of the Shahab-4. In February 2006, the German news agency cited "Western intelligence services" as saying that Iran successfully tested the Shahab-4 missile with a range of 2,200 km on January 17, 2006, and the test was announced on Iranian television several days later by the commander of the IRGC.[128] Additionally, reports indicate that the test was terminated after the separation of the nose reentry vehicle.[129]

In the first week of February 2008, reports indicate that Iran tested a missile. Russian reports claim that it was possibly a more advanced Shahab-3, indicating either the 4 series or 5 series. Russian officials expressed concern over the test, citing a missile test is an integral part of nuclear weapons program.[130] These reports remain unverifiable.

Shahab-5 and Shahab-6

Israeli intelligence has reported that Iran is attempting to create a Shahab-5 and a Shahab-6, with a 3,000–5,000-km range. Israeli sources indicate such missiles would be based on the North Korean Taep'o-dong-2 and would be three-stage rockets. Some report that the Shahab-5 and the Shahab-6 would have a liquid fuel first stage and a third stage, but such details are speculative. If these reports are correct and the missiles are deployed, the Shahab-5 and the Shahab-6 would give Iran ICBMs and enable Iran to target the U.S. eastern seaboard.

It is alleged that Russian aerospace engineers are aiding the Iranians in their efforts. It is believed that the engineers will employ a version of Russia's storable liquid propellant RD-216 in the missile's first stage. The RD-216 is an Energomash engine originally used on the Skean/SS-5/R-14, IRBM, Saddler/SS-7/R-16, ICBM, and Sasin/R-26 ICBM missiles used in the Cold War. The effort to develop an ICBM with the Russian RD-216 engine in some sources has been named Project Koussar.[131] These reports remain uncertain, and Israeli media and official sources have repeatedly exaggerated the nature and speed of Iranian efforts.[132]

Due to the deception and denial strategy of the Iranian government regarding its missile programs, it is unknown whether or not the Shahab-5 or the Shahab-6 has been tested or constructed. Because little is known about the Shahab-5 project and even less is known about Shahab-6, much of the data is speculative at best.

Extrapolations for the Shahab-5 have been made based on the North Korean Taep'o-dong-2. The Shahab-5 has an approximate range between 4,000 and 4,300 kilometers. The Shahab-5 has an unknown CEP, and its warhead capacity is between 700 and 1,000 kg. It has a height of 32 meters, a diameter of 2.2 meters, and a launch weight of 80,000–85,000 kg. In terms of propelling ability, some experts estimate its thrust to be 31,260 kgf and its burn time to be 330 seconds. The Shahab-5 is a three-stage rocket that possesses six thrust chambers, four for stage one, and one each for the two remaining stages. The Shahab-5 and the Shahab-6 would be considered long-range ICBMs.[133]

As stated previously, in the first week of February 2008, reports indicate that Iran tested a missile in the first week of February 2008. Russian reports claimed that it was a more advanced Shahab-3, indicating either the 4 series or 5 series. Russian officials expressed concern over the test, citing a missile test is an integral part of a nuclear weapons program.[134] Again, these reports remain unverifiable.

Analysts have suggested that the Shahab-6 is a two- or three-stage liquid/solid fuel rocket. The missile uses most of the same systems as the Shahab-5, but economies in weight and payload increase the range to approximately 6,000 km (3,728 miles). The missile is intended to carry one single warhead with a substantial yield, most likely in the area of 500–1,000 kg. As a result of its inaccuracy, the missile's utility it probably restricted to attacking population centers and spreading radiation rather than hitting military targets. Thus, the Shahab-6 is more likely a blackmail/terrorist weapon than a military asset. Significant reports indicate that the Shahab-5 and the Shahab-6 have the possibility of being developed into satellite launch vehicles (SLVs).[135] Little is known about the Shahab-5 project and even less is known about Shahab-6.

The integration of technology from the Taep'o-dong 2 missile into the Shahab-5 represents a substantial security risk for the United States. If its 6,000-km reported range is accurate, the Shahab-6 will be able to target most of Europe, Russia, and Asia. Reports indicate its engine's possible burn time would be up to 330 seconds, which would classify the system as an ICBM.[136] At this time there has been no credible reporting of a Shahab-6 launch. This information is dependent on the uncertain intelligence available on these systems.

SATELLITE LAUNCH VEHICLE PROGRAMS

As early as 1998 Iran announced its objective to establish a space program. One source reports that when Iranian Supreme Leader Ali Khamenei visited a defense fair the same year, images of a SLV surfaced that apparently showed a SLV resembling the Shahab-3 with the letters IRIS painted on it.[137] Iran has never openly declared its space program assets, but on February 25, 2007, proclaimed that it had fired a test rocket into a suborbital altitude. This apparently was based on a vehicle identified as Shahab-4.[138]

There are a number of speculations about this satellite launch, but claims of the Shahab-4 with a two-stage, solid propellant motor seem to be the most prevalent. This may, however, simply be attributed to the fact that Iranian official sources distributed such information and other sources lacked any convincing evidence. Parts of the missile that was fired on February 25, 2007, apparently fell back to the earth by parachute. This test caused considerable concern among Western observers. It may or may not be the case that Iran signaled its intentions to speed up its ballistic missile program; there is simply not enough reliable data available that can give credible evidence to whether the launch is a step toward the acquisition of an ICBM or not.

According to one source, Iran is working on the following satellite projects:

- **Zohreh:** Allegedly, Iran was the contractor for this communication satellite, but did not engineer any of the parts for it. The satellite was supposed to be launched by a Russian vehicle.
- **Safir 313:** This is a 20-kg heavy, Iranian-made satellite that was supposed to be launched in early 2005, but the first reported launches did not take place until 2008.
- **Mesbah:** Reportedly, this is a 70-kg satellite produced by an Italian-Iranian joint venture. It was supposed to be launched by a Russian vehicle.
- **Sina-1:** This is a Russian communication and observation satellite. Apparently, the Iranian role consisted of a tracking and data retrieval station and possibly to expand cooperation with a successor satellite named Sina 2.[139] Reportedly, the Sina-1 was Iran's first satellite that it launched into space. The launch occurred in October 2005.[140]
- **Safir-2:** On February 2, 2009, Iran successfully launched its first indigenously produced satellite into space. According to Iranian media outlets, Iran used a Safir-2 rocket to carry the Omid satellite.[141]

One analyst speculates about the difficulties in discerning Iranian space vehicle launch capabilities as follows:

Though an indigenously built Iranian satellite launch vehicle could exist, the launch of a North Korean-manufactured Taepodong-2 with an Iranian flag painted on it is far more likely (although any Iranian-built missile would likely be nearly identical to the Taepodong-2 and in grainy imagery of such a launch it could be impossible to tell one from the other). Either way, any Iranian satellite launch vehicle will look strikingly similar to the Taepodong family, and there would almost certainly be North Korean scientists on the ground at the launch site.[142]

In late January 2007, it was reported that Iran had converted a ballistic missile into a satellite launch vehicle. Reports assume that the missile is either a version of the Shahab-3 or the Ghadar-110, based on the reported weight of 30 tons.[143] According to the latest Defense Intelligence Agency estimates, Iran may develop a 3,000-mile ICBM by the year 2015. The advances in missile technologies have substantiated evidence that there is close cooperation between North Korean and Iranian space missile programs, but no reliable information about this is available.[144]

On February 4, 2008, Iran was reported to have inaugurated its first domestically built space center by launching the Kavoshgar-1 (Explorer-1) research rocket, according to Russian news sources. This platform was apparently capable of carrying a satellite into low orbit. Iran also unveiled its first domestically built satellite, Omid, or Hope, during this inauguration. The Iranian spokesman said, "The launch of the Explorer rocket into space was conducted strictly for scientific purposes. Our achievements in space research, as well as our progress in nuclear research, serve peace and justice."[145]

Iran reportedly test-fired a new rocket, named Safir-e Omid, capable of carrying a satellite into orbit on August 17, 2008, as part of its rapidly developing space program. The White House said Iran's rocket announcement was "troubling," calling it part of a pattern of Iranian activity to build a nuclear program and the means to potentially launch a weapon. "The Iranian development and testing of rockets is troubling and raises further questions about their intentions," said White House spokesman Gordon D. Johndroe. Rocket scientists agree that the same technology that puts satellites into orbit can deliver warheads.[146] The launch was assessed as a failure by U.S. and Israeli intelligence reporting, which claimed that the Safir failed to separate in its second-stage launch.[147]

On September 25, 2008, President Mahmoud Ahmadinejad announced that Iran planned to launch a satellite into space soon using its own satellite carrier rocket. Ahmadinejad said the Persian nation will soon "launch a rocket, which has 16 engines and will take a satellite some 430 miles" into space.[148]

On February 2, 2009, Iran successfully launched its first indigenously produced satellite into space. According to Iranian media outlets, Iran used a Safir-2 rocket to carry the Omid satellite. Iran's use of the indigenously developed Safir-2 rocket to place a satellite in orbit raises concerns that Iran could use similar technology to help build ICBMs.[149]

Although Iranian officials continued to stress that their nuclear program is solely for peaceful energy purposes and that its space program has no military aims, some analysts and international leaders expressed their concerns following Iran's joining of the space club. U.S. Missile Defense Agency spokesman Rick Lehner said, "In the case of Iran, one of the biggest concerns we've always had is that any country that can put a satellite into orbit has thereby demonstrated that they can send a nuclear weapon to intercontinental distances."[150]

White House spokesman Robert Gibbs stated that the rocket launch "does not convince us that Iran is acting responsibly to advance stability or security in the region," and added that "efforts to develop missile delivery capability, efforts to continue an illicit nuclear program, or threats that Iran makes towards Israel and its sponsorship of terror are of acute concern to this administration."[151]

One military official affiliated with NATO stated, "If this is confirmed, it would mean that their rockets are capable of [flying 1,250 to 1,850 miles], and would therefore have the range to hit part of Europe and Israel."[152] Perfecting solid fuel technology would also move Iran's missile systems a long way toward the successful creation of a LRICBM, which is what the Shahab-5 and Shahab-6 are intended to accomplish.[153]

IRAN'S OTHER SURFACE-TO-SURFACE MISSILE PROGRAMS

There are a number of reports that Iran has shorter-ranged missiles that might be used to deliver weapons of mass destruction at shorter ranges, or that it is obtaining medium-range ballistic missiles, IRBMS, and air-to-surface missiles from other sources. Some reports seem credible—at least in part. Others are little more than sporadically reported rumors.

Iranian Fateh A-110 (PRC CSS-8)

One indigenous Iranian Zelzal program that is of interest is the Fetah A-110, Zelzal-2 variant that is reportedly based on China's CSS-8. Jane's reports that Iran may have some 200 Chinese CSS-8, or M-7/Project 8610, short-range missiles. These are Chinese modifications of the SA-2 surface-to-air missile for use as a surface-to-surface system. It has a 190-kg warhead and a 150-km range. Up to 90 may have been delivered to Iran in 1992, and another 110 may have been delivered later. The system is reported to have poor accuracy.[154] Iran has since used this PRC system as a base model for its Fateh system developments.

The Fateh A-110 may be designed to replace many of its aging Scud systems. While the program is based in Iran, the missile is believed to incorporate components from Chinese contractors. In 2006 the U.S. Department of the Treasury accused Great Wall Industry, a Chinese corporation, and its partners for playing a lead role in the development of the Fateh missile system.[155]

The Fateh A-110 is part of Iran's indigenous Zelzal missile program. The Fateh missile program was started in 1997 by the Iranian government–owned Aerospace Industries. The Fateh A-110 is a single-staged, solid-propelled, guided variant of the Zelzal-2 short-range ballistic missile (SRBM).[156] Reporting indicates that the

Fateh A-110 has a range of anywhere between 160 and 210 km, but it is possible that Iran will add, if it has not already added, an extra booster to increase the range of the missile to 400 km (249 miles).[157]

The Fateh A-110 was released for distribution by the Iranian Aerospace Industries Organization in 2003 after three successful launches—May 2001, September 2002, and February 2003—with a reported range "in excess of 200 km" by Iranian media agencies.[158] The missile entered low-rate production in October 2002, and initial operational achievement is believed to have occurred in 2004.[159] The Fateh A-110 has since been tested three times—at the "Holy Prophet II" exercises of 2006, as well as tests in January and September 2007.

The Fetah A-110 is similar in shape to the Zelzal-2, but it has two delta-shaped control fins at the nose and four delta control fins just in front of the rear wings. This aerodynamic control arrangement is new for a ballistic missile and was developed by Iran to provide improved accuracy.[160] From the available information, analysts have assessed the missile as having an accuracy of 100-m CEP and using a combination of inertial guidance and a global positioning satellite (GPS) system to locate its target.[161]

Iranian sources claim that the weapon has a high degree of accuracy, which would require it to have a more sophisticated guidance system. It can carry a payload of some 500 kg and is most likely intended to deliver only high explosive, chemical, or submunitions warheads. The possibility remains, however, that Iran could deploy the Fateh A-110 with biological or nuclear warheads.[162]

It is also noteworthy that there are reports that claim that the Fateh A-110 missile may be based on the Chinese DF-11A missile, which has a range of 200 to 300 km and is capable of carrying nuclear warheads.[163] This is yet another example of the uncertainties that are still surrounding Iran's domestic missile programs, as well as its stockpile numbers and capabilities.

Iran's deceptive behavior, as well as the fact that the Fateh A-110 is domestically made, has made it impossible to know the number of Fateh A-110 and other PRC CSS-8 variants that are in Iran's missile stockpile. This is a problem in assessing the amount of missiles, of any type, Iran possesses.

Iranian Sajjil Missile Program

Another indigenous missile program that is reportedly under way in Iran is the Sajjil missile program. The Iranian reports of a November 2008 test launch of the Sajjil is an important milestone for Iran's missile development program, in that it is a shift from the liquid-fueled Shahab program to a new generation of multistage, solid propelled missile. Neither the range nor the payload capacity of the Sajjil is substantially greater than that of Iran's existing Shahab-3 missile. However, the transition from the liquid-propelled Shahab to production of the multistage, solid-fuel Sajjil would be important if shown by further tests to be sustainable.

An IISS assessment of the Sajjil missile provides some insight into Iran's developing long-range, solid-fuel, multistage missile programs.

While full details of the *Sajjil* missile and its test launch are unavailable, it is obviously much larger than any solid-propellant missile previously produced by Tehran. Judging from videos and pictures, the *Sajjil's* first-stage rocket motor alone contains up to ten tonnes of solid propellant and is capable of generating 55–65 tonnes of thrust (see above). The knowledge, equipment and experience needed to produce such a motor go far beyond that behind the two-tonne motor used by the *Zelzal* and *Fateh*-110. The technological leap represented by the *Sajjil* missile is further underlined when the difference between liquid-fuelled and solid-fuelled rocket engines is considered.

Photographs reveal that the first stage is approximately 1.25 metres in diameter, and 9m long. This suggests that the solid-propellant grain in the first stage is about 7m long, with an average web thickness of 31–32cm. This corresponds to a web fraction of 0.53, which is consistent with a motor of this size. Assuming a linear burn rate of 0.75cm per second would result in a total burn time of 42 seconds. (These calculations use a specific impulse of 245 seconds.) Reasonable variations in these assumptions provide a thrust of between 55–65 tonnes.

Less is known about the *Sajjil's* second stage, although it does appear to be steered by four small vernier rockets mounted externally at the aft end of the stage. The presence of these steering engines suggests the second stage may be powered by the same liquid-propellant engine used by the *Shahab*-3, which produces about 25 tonnes of thrust. In this case, some of the propellant intended for the main engine would be diverted to the vernier engines. Many Soviet missiles utilised such a configuration.

Alternatively, the second stage could employ a 4–5 tonne solid-propellant motor, which would also generate about 25 tonnes of thrust. The lift-off mass of the missile is likely to be 18–20 tonnes. The one-tonne estimated payload capacity is the minimum necessary to accommodate a first-generation nuclear warhead.

The *Sajjil* is estimated to be able to carry a maximum one-tonne payload 1,500–1,800 kilometres. While these capabilities are similar to those of the *Shahab*, the technical capacity required to build a medium-range, solid-fuel missile is of a different order to that needed for its liquid-fuel equivalent. If progress could be extended beyond the initial *Sajjil* launch, Iran might be able to begin the design and development of a new generation of long-range missiles. Solid-fuel missiles can be launched more quickly and are thus less vulnerable to pre-emptive strike.[164]

The November 2008 Sajjil launch illustrates the increasing range of Iran's missile programs. Some analysts—such as Uzi Rubin, former director of Israel's Ballistic Missile Defence Organization—have argued, "This is a whole new missile," adding, "Unlike other Iranian missiles, the Sajjil bears no resemblance to any North Korean, Russian, Chinese or Pakistani [missile technology]. It demonstrates a significant leap in Iran's missile capabilities. This missile places Iran in the realm of multiple-stage missiles, which means that they are on the way to having intercontinental ballistic missile capabilities."[165]

More recently, on May 20, 2009, Iran test-fired a solid-fuel missile capable of reaching Israel or U.S. bases in the Middle East. Iranian officials claim that the two-stage, solid-fuel Sajjil-2 surface-to-surface missile has a range of approximately 2,000 km (1,240 miles); which is slightly longer than the Sajjil missile tested in November 2008.

Iranian Defense Minister Mostafa Mohammad Najjar claimed that, in addition to the increase in range, the Sajjil-2 differs from the Sajjil missile launched in November 2008 because it "is equipped with a new navigation system as well as precise and sophisticated sensors," according to Iran's official news agency, and added that the missile landed "precisely on the target."[166]

Mark Fitzpatrick, an analyst at the International Institute for Strategic Studies, said the development of the Sajjil missile was significant because of the type of fuel it used, rather than its range. "To be able to build a solid-fuel missile of medium range represents a significant technological breakthrough," Fitzpatrick said. "It is technically more difficult than a liquid-fuel missile, and militarily more significant because it is not as vulnerable to attack while being fuelled."[167]

The IISS analysis indicates, however, that even if Iran is able to produce long-range, solid-propellant missiles capable eventually of hitting targets in Europe, and possibly a future ICBM, there are still a number of obstacles that Iran must overcome in order to attain this capability and deploy the Sajjil missile on any kind of scale. These obstacles would take at least three to five years and require a test and demonstration program involving multiple test flights, which can be tracked by Western intelligence agencies and should provide considerable warning. First, Iran would need to establish a production line for solid-fuel motors to strict performance criteria; second, Iran still needs to develop and incorporate sophisticated navigation, guidance, and control systems for future missiles; and third, Iran has yet to show that it has developed thermal shielding to protect a long-range missile warhead during re-entry into the atmosphere.[168]

Reports also indicate that the Sajjil-2's reaction times may be about 50–20 minutes faster than the Shahab series that came before it. Its solid fuel booster may also be reliable, particularly in a mobile basing, and have less need for maintenance. Its mobility launcher might also be harder to detect since the TEL requires fewer support vehicles—although the Shahab does use storable liquid fuels and the difference might not be as serious as some sources indicate.

In short, the November 2008 and May 2009 Sajjil and Sajjil-2 test launches can be viewed as further advancement in Iran's highly controversial indigenous missile programs. But although Iranian officials claim that the Sajjil is an indigenous program, further developments toward ICBM capabilities in such missile programs would likely require foreign assistance. At this time the Sajjil is not capable of deployment and does not pose an immediate threat, but programs such as this do not help to ease regional and international security concerns over any relationship between Iran's parallel nuclear and missile programs.

M-9 and M-11 Missiles

For over a decade there has been occasional speculation whether or not Iran acquired Chinese M-9 and M-11 missiles, which are based on the Russian Scud designs. It seems evident that Iran expressed interest in these missiles, but apparently China did not deliver any missiles because of U.S. pressure. One source notes that

China may have delivered one or two M-11 SRBMs with a 300-km range in the early 1990s.[169]

Yet other sources report that Iran could have received 80 M-11 systems along with TELs, but these reports are unconfirmed, and Iran has never publicly tested the weapon.[170] Reports confirm that the M-11 is the nuclear-capable Pakistani Shaheen-1.[171] Reports also confirm that transfers of M-11 technology and support have taken place between Pakistan and Iran, with Chinese aid.[172]

Some experts speculate whether deliveries have taken place illegally, despite China's pledge not to sell the missiles, although most reports do not confirm that any of the missiles are in stock with Iranian forces. Although on September 22, 2005, the BBC (British Broadcasting Corporation) translated Iranian media reports of an Iranian military parade that included numerous ballistic missiles including an M-11 Variant/Tondar-68, purchased from China, with a range 400 km and possibly an M-9 missile, with a range 600 km, also purchased from China.[173]

Since Iran has shown itself to be capable of reverse engineering and altering ballistic missiles for the purpose of domestic production, it is possible that if Iran received any of these missiles or their components, it may have been able to start domestic production of a variant of the PRC's M-11 and/or DF-11. Some reports have stated that Iran is doing just this, although the status of its M-11 variant project is uncertain. Also due to the lack of consistent public display of the M-9, reports from 1996 on suggest possible termination of the Iranian M-9 program,[174] although this could be due to continued Iranian secrecy and deception in regard to its missile programs.

It has also been reported that the Syrian missile program was developed in a joint project with Iran. These reports indicate that the Iranian M-11 variant would likely be similar, if not the same as, the Syrian single-stage, solid-propelled SRBM, with a range of 280–400 km—within the limits of the Missile Technology Control Regime; with a 500- or 800-kg warhead that can be equipped with high explosives, chemicals, submunitions, fuel air explosives, or a nuclear yield of 2, 10, or 20 kilotons; and an accuracy of 600 meters CEP. The accuracy of the weapon could be increased with a projected separating warhead. The separating warhead is a design feature that requires the warhead to detach itself from the missile body and continue on to its objective. The warhead is then able to adjust its trajectory based on fin design and its range due to weight redistribution. This attribute would be unique to the Iranian version.[175]

As with a majority of the Iranian and Syrian missile programs and their capabilities, this information remains unconfirmed, making the status of the projects as well as the stockpile numbers rough estimates, if not unknown.

BM-25/SS-N-6

Some sources have reported that Iran has concluded an agreement with North Korea to buy 18 IRBMs (initially called BM-25) that in return are reverse-engineered Russian SS-N-6 submarine-launched ballistic missiles (SLBM).

Apparently, Iran tested a BM-25 in January 2006; the missile is reported to have flown more than 3,000 km. Several sources claim that the BM-25 has a range of up to 4,000 km.[176]

Iran is believed to have received 18 missiles; an Israeli source reportedly confirmed the delivery, but claimed that the missile's range was 2,500 km.[177] This report seems to be confirmed by German intelligence that stated that Iran had taken delivery of 18 disassembled medium-to-intermediate range ballistic missiles from North Korea in 2005, which were described as BM-25 models with a range of 2,500 km.[178]

One source claims that the initial SS-N-6 used a complicated propulsion as well as guidance system, and it appears questionable that North Korea and/or Iran is capable of making the necessary adjustments to create a land-launched version and achieving a range of over 2,000 miles.[179]

Raduga KH-55 Granat/Kh-55/AS-15 Kent

Ballistic missiles are scarcely the only platforms Iran has to deliver weapons of mass destruction. In addition to covert means or using proxies, Iran can use cruise missiles, drones or unmanned combat aerial vehicles (UCAVs), or aircraft equipped with either air-to-surface missiles or free-fall bombs. Little is known about the extent to which Iran has explored many of these options, but some of its actions make it clear that it is examining them.

One confirmed example is Iran's covert acquisition of long-range cruise missiles. The Raduga Kh-55 Granat is a Ukrainian-/Soviet-made armed nuclear cruise missile first tested in 1978 and completed in 1984.[180] The Russian missile carries a 200-kiloton nuclear warhead, and it has a range of 2,500–3,000 km. It has a theoretical CEP of about 150 meters and a speed of Mach 0.48–0.77.

Its guidance system is reported to combine inertial-Doppler navigation and position correction based on in-flight comparison of terrain in the assigned regions with images stored in the memory of an on-board computer. It was designed to deliver a high-yield nuclear weapon against fixed-area targets and has little value delivering conventional warheads. While it was originally designed to be carried by a large bomber, and its weight makes it a marginal payload for either Iran's Su-24s or F-14As, it has land and ship launch capability. It can also be adapted to use a much larger nuclear or other CBRN warhead by cutting its range, and it may be a system that Iran can reverse engineer for production.[181]

Russian President Boris Yeltsin made further manufacture of the missile illegal in 1992.[182] Still, the Ukraine had 1,612 of these missiles in stock at the end of 1991, and it agreed to give 575 of them to Russia and scrap the rest.[183] The plans to give the missiles to Russia in the late 1990s proved troublesome, however, and an organization was able to forge the documents regarding 20 missiles and listed them as being sold to Russia, while in fact 12 seem to have been distributed to Iran and 6 to China (the other two are unaccounted for).[184] It was estimated that the missiles were smuggled to Iran in 2001.[185]

Ukrainian officials confirmed the illegal sale on March 18, 2005, but the Chinese and Iranian governments were silent regarding the matter. While some U.S. officials downplayed the transaction, the U.S. Department of State expressed concern that the missiles could give each state a technological boost.[186] The missiles did not contain warheads at the time of their sale, and they passed their service life in 1995 and were in need of maintenance.[187] It is, however, feared that Iran could learn from the cruise missiles technology to improve its own missile program and the missiles could be fitted to match Iran's Su-24 strike aircraft.[188] According to one source, Parchin Missile Industries and CSIG are to reverse engineer the missile, but as of March 2007 are likely still at an early stage of the process.[189]

The availability of the Kh-55 is impeded by the fact that this missile was designed to be launched only from long-range Tupolev bombers, which Iran does not possess. It is therefore not unlikely that the Kh-55 is primarily for research purposes and/or reverse engineering of its small fan jet engine, especially since the turbo fan engine for the Kh-55 was manufactured in Ukraine. The Kh-55 therefore may serve as an important stepping-stone in the development of cruise missile capabilities.[190]

If Iran could make the Kh-55 cruise missile fully operational, rather than simply use it for reverse-engineering purposes, Iran would acquire a capability to strike targets in Western Europe, an option that is widely believed to alter strategic and political considerations between the United States and its allies. Iran's capability in this regard, however, remains a theoretical one. It is highly doubtful that Iran possesses the means to employ a Kh-55 according to its widely stated technical capabilities. Even though the Kh-55 may have a maximum range of 3,000 km, there are numerous technical obstacles that Iran would have to overcome before launching a cruise missile.

Iran would need to adapt its aircraft or naval vessels to be operational to fire a Kh-55, or to convert it to a land-based system. There is currently no indication that Iran possesses aircraft or ships with such capability, but Iran has a number of ships with search-track radars that might be modified to launch cruise missiles The Kilo-class submarines in Iran's possession are not fitted to launch Kh-55 missiles, only short-range SS-N-27 cruise missiles, but it is possible that some kind of deck chamber could be rigged.

Guidance would be a potential problem. The full technical details of the KH-55 guidance system are not clear, but Iran would need to access the equivalent of the GPS, TERCOM (Terrain Contour Matching), or GLONASS (Global Navigation Satellite System) systems. In 2000, the Iranian defense minister announced that Iran was beginning to produce its own laser gyros, which are at the core of any modern navigation system, but the CEP of a modified KH-55 missile that flew ranges approaching 3,000 km could be well over 1,000 meters, and reliability could be a very serious issue.

Iran might be able to use unmanned aerial vehicles or aircraft to provide additional guidance data during the launch and course correction phase, or plant some kind of covert homing signal. One analyst also claims that Iran might develop the capability to launch a cruise missile based on the Kh-55 from its Su-24 and F-14A aircraft.[191]

AIRCRAFT DELIVERY

The uncertainty surrounding Iran's military intentions and capabilities makes it imperative to examine any and all credible means of delivery of CBRN munitions. The Iranian Air Force is headquartered in Tehran with its training, administration, and logistics branches, as well as a major central Air Defense Operations Center. The headquarters has a political directorate and a small naval coordination staff. It has three major regional headquarters: Northern Zone (Badl Sar), Central Zone (Hamaden), and Southern Zone (Bushehr). Iran has large combat air bases at Mehrabad, Tabriz, Hamadan, Dezful, Bushehr, Shiraz, Isfahan, and Bandar Abbas. It has smaller bases at least at 11 other locations.

Iran's Current Air Strength

The Iranian Air Force (IAF) is still numerically strong, but most of its equipment is aging, worn, and has limited mission capability. Reports indicate that Iran has approximately 319 combat aircraft in the inventory.[192]

As is the case with most aspects of Iranian military forces, estimates of Iran's air strength differ by source. The IISS estimates that the IAF has 14 main combat squadrons. These include nine fighter ground-attack squadrons, four with at least 65 U.S.-supplied F-4D/Es, four with at least 60 F-5E/F, and one with 30 Soviet-supplied Su-24MK, 13 Su-25K, and 24 French F-1E Mirage aircraft. Iran possesses some MiG-29, Su-25K, and 24MK, and Mirage F-1E Iraqi aircraft it seized during the Gulf War. Another source reports that Iran has five fighter squadrons; two with 25 U.S.-supplied F-14s each, two with 25–30 Russian/Iraqi-supplied MiG-29A/-UBs, and one with 24 Chinese-supplied F-7Ms.[193] How many of these are operational is not known.

Many of Iran's aircraft are either not operational or cannot be sustained in extended air combat operations. This applies to 50–60 percent of Iran's U.S.- and French-supplied aircraft and some 20–30 percent of its Russian- and Chinese-supplied aircraft. It has nine fighter-ground attack squadrons with approximately 192 aircraft; seven fighter squadrons with 74–79 aircraft; a reconnaissance unit with 4–8 aircraft; and a number of transport aircraft, helicopters, and special purpose aircraft.

This situation may change in the future. On July 28, 2008, Brigadier General Ahmad Miqani was quoted as saying that the IAF has achieved self-sufficiency in the repair, maintenance, and overhaul of its equipment. He added that Iranian military experts are capable of overhauling F-5 two-seaters, F-14 Tomcat fighter jets, 707 and 747 aircraft with only 40 days of work: "We have upgraded our air force fleet, state-of-the-art radar-systems, and rocket launchers over the past few years."[194]

Mission Capability and Possible Upgrades

Most Iranian squadrons can perform both air-defense and attack missions, regardless of their principal mission—although this does not apply to Iran's F-14 (air-defense) and Su-24 (strike/attack) units. Iranian sources claim that the IAF's F-14s have been modified to increase its AWG-9's radar range and capability and that Iran has integrated the R-73 air-to-air missile (AAM) and various air-to-ground weapons with the aircraft.[195]

Iran's F-14s were, however, designed as dual-capable aircraft, and it has not been able to use its Phoenix AAMs since the early 1980s. Iran has claimed that it is modernizing its F-14s by equipping them with Improved Hawk (I-Hawk) missiles adapted to the air-to-air role, but it is far from clear that this is the case or that such adaptations can have more than limited effectiveness. In practice, this means that Iran might well use the F-14s in nuclear strike missions. They are capable of long-range, high payload missions and would require minimal adaptation to carry and release a nuclear weapon.[196]

According to *Flight International* magazine, Iran has managed to keep large number of its F-14 fleet operational.[197] Iran has acquired spare parts for F-14 aircraft from U.S. stocks through various cutouts, intermediaries, and arms smugglers.[198] As a consequence, the U.S. Defense Logistics Agency tightened its supervision of surplus goods sales. One source states that Iran claims to be able to produce up to 70 percent of all F-14 parts indigenously. However, Iran continues to make constant efforts to acquire F-14 and other U.S. aircraft parts on the world market. It is questionable whether or not Iran can keep more than 30 F-14 aircraft serviceable.[199]

Flight International also reports that Iran is comprehensively upgrading its F-14 fleet involving new radar, engines, and a glass cockpit—with the help of Russian experts and technology. This could not only keep Iranian F-14s operational but also improve the Iranian F-14s and allow them to be armed with modern Russian missiles.[200]

According to one source, Iran has improved its Su-24s with in-flight refueling capability, a Upaz-A buddy refueling system to extend the range of other aircraft, installed active radar jammers and electronic countermeasures, and upgraded some aspects of the weapons launch and target software.[201] These reports cannot be fully confirmed.

Possible Purchases

Some reports indicate that Iran ordered an unknown number of TU-22M-3 "Backfire C" long-range strategic bombers from either Russia or the Ukraine.[202] While discussions to buy such aircraft seem to have taken place, no purchases or deliveries have ever been confirmed.

Iran is also reportedly seeking to acquire up to 250 Russian-built Su-30 MKs to update its land-based aircraft fleet. The Su-30, an advanced fighter-bomber, has a range of 1,620 nautical miles that can be extended with in-flight refueling. Its weapons payload of 17,000 pounds and advanced avionics make it a much more capable delivery system.[203]

An unknown number of "new" Su-25s were delivered to the Iranian Revolution Guards Corps Air Force in 2003. Where these Frogfoots originated from was unclear. Since the number was said to include advanced Su-25T and Su-25UBK aircraft, reports suggested that these aircraft could have come from Russia or Ukraine, two countries Iran had significant contact with during the 1990s, especially regarding aircraft manufacture.

In July 2003, Chengdu Aircraft Industrial Corporation unveiled the new "Super-7" or Chao Qi fighter plane to the public. The new Super-7 is an all-purpose light fighter, required to have all-weather operation capabilities, be capable of performing the dual tasks of dogfight and air-to-ground attack, and have the ability to launch medium-range missiles. Mass production of the fighter will not begin until two and a half years of research are completed. The plane is being produced to be sold abroad to developing nations. China said it had received orders from Iran and some African countries. Production of the Super-7 aircraft, now called the FC-1 (with an export designation of JF-17) was supposed to begin in 2006, but this was believed to have been delayed. Iran had not received any such aircraft by 2008.[204]

On July 30, 2007, the *Post* (Jerusalem) reported that Iran was negotiating with Russia to buy 250 Sukhoi Su-30 "Flanker" fighter-bombers. Israeli defense officials were investigating the potential Iran-Russia deal, in which Iran would pay $1 billion for a dozen squadrons' worth of the jets. Iran would also buy 20 Ilyushin Il-78 Midas tankers that could extend the fighters' range as part of the deal. The move was seen as a response to the new American plans to sell billions of dollars' worth of weapons to potential Iranian adversaries in the Middle East, including Saudi Arabia, Egypt, and Israel. The report came soon after other deals to sell advanced Su-27 and Su-30 combat fighters to Indonesia, Malaysia, and Venezuela.[205]

It should be noted that in addition to conventional warfighting capabilities, Iran has a large number of attack and air-defense aircraft that could carry a small- to medium-sized nuclear weapon long distances, particularly since such strikes are likely to be low-altitude one-way missions. (These were the mission profiles in both NATO and Warsaw Pact theater nuclear strike plans.) Several might conceivably be modified as drones or the equivalent of "cruise missiles" using autopilots, on-board computers, and an add-on GPS.

Unmanned Aerial Vehicles and Drones

Iran has the technology to convert some of its fighters to the equivalent of unmanned aerial vehicles (UAVs) that would be programmed to fly a fixed flight profile and crash at a given target area. It might be able to achieve GPS levels of accuracy, although the flight profile would probably have to be high enough to make detection and interception relatively easy, and reliability would be a major problem.

Iran began developing UAVs in the early 1990s. Since 2005, it has reportedly used them to shadow U.S. fleet movements in the Gulf and to monitor events in Iraq and

Afghanistan. In 2007, Iran claimed to have begun producing "suicide drones" invisible to radar and usable as guided missiles to attack U.S. ships.[206]

Iran is also developing regular UAVs, some of which are reported to be relatively large and capable of carrying combat payloads. On July 28, 2008, Brigadier General Ahmad Miqani stated that Iran was mass producing different types of drones used in reconnaissance missions, pinpointing enemy bases, and carrying explosives.[207]

In mid-February 2009, Iranian Deputy Defense Minister Brigadier General Ahmad Vahidi announced that Iran had developed a new generation of unmanned aerial vehicles with a range of 1,000 km (620 miles).[208] If Iran should arm its UAVs with chemical, biological, radiological, or nuclear warheads—which soon may be within Iranian capabilities—its UAVs will be strategic, offensive weapons systems. Iran has also shown that it is willing to place less lethal UAVs directly in the hands of terrorists and nonstate actors. Hezbollah has penetrated Israeli air defenses using Iranian-supplied drones and has claimed to have attacked an Israeli warship.[209] Figure 4.4 outlines Iran's known UAV programs and capabilities as of early 2009.[210]

IRAN'S UNCERTAIN PATH

The Iranian missile program has been shrouded in secrecy, deception, and the unknown. Iran obtains weapons of various design and origin and frequently retains a single name and reclassifies its physical missile assets, which adds to the confusion. At present, the future of the Iranian missile program is uncertain, but the existence of these missiles must continue to raise questions in the international community as to what Iran's military intentions are in conventional and unconventional terms, regionally and globally.

U.S. President Barack Obama's new Director of National Intelligence, Dennis C. Blair, summarized the situation as follows in his testimony to the Senate Intelligence Committee in February 2009,

> Beyond its WMD potential, Iranian conventional military power threatens Persian Gulf states and challenges US interests. Iran is enhancing its ability to project its military power, primarily with ballistic missiles and naval power, with the goal of dominating the Gulf region and deterring potential adversaries. It seeks a capacity to disrupt the operations and reinforcement of US forces based in the region, potentially intimidating regional allies into withholding support for US policy, and raising the political, financial, and human costs to the United States and our allies of our presence.
>
>   . . . Iran's growing inventory of ballistic missiles—it already has the largest inventory in the Middle East—and its acquisition of anti-ship cruise missiles provide capabilities to enhance its power projection. Tehran views its conventionally armed missiles as an integral part of its strategy to deter and if necessary retaliate against forces in the region, including US forces. Its ballistic missiles are inherently capable of delivering WMD and if so armed would fit into this same strategy.[211]

Iran is the only country not in possession of nuclear weapons to have produced or flight-tested missiles with ranges exceeding 1,000 km. The Iranian missile program is

Figure 4.4 Iranian UAV Projects/Assets 2009

Prime Manufacturer	Designation	Development/Production	Operation	Payload Wt.	Endurance (hr)	Range	Ceiling (ft)	Mission
Unknown	Stealth	Under way/Under way	Deployed			700 km		R/S*
HESA	Ababil (Swallow)	Complete/Under way	Deployed	45 kg	1.5+	150 km	14,000	Multiple variants for R/S*—attack—ISR†
Shahbal Group, Sharif Univ.	Shahbal	Under way		5.5 kg		12 km	4,500	R/S*
Asr-e Talai Factories	Mini-UAV	Under way						Surveillance
FARC	Sobakbal	Under way/Under way	Deployed	0.35 kg	2	2.7–13.5 mi	19,686	Surveillance
Qods Aeronautics Industries	Mohajer II/III (Dorna); Mohajer IV (Hodhod); Saeqeh I/II; Tallash I/Endeavor; Tallash II Hadaf 3000	Complete/Under way	Deployed					Multirole; aka Lightning Bolt Target drone—aka Target 3000

Notes:

* R/S: Reconnaissance/Surveillance.

† ISR: Intelligence/Surveillance/Reconnaissance.

largely based on North Korean and Russian designs and has benefited from Chinese technical assistance.[212] It is very important to remember this when analyzing and assessing Iran's motives, intentions, and capabilities in regard to its ballistic missile programs and how they relate to Iran's existing and possible WMD programs.

Iran is putting immense effort into programs that can deliver weapons of mass destruction, and many of which make sense only if they can eventually be equipped with a nuclear or highly lethal biological weapon. It must be stressed, however, that Iran's problems are evolutionary, opportunistic in character and execution, and reliable unclassified reports do not exist on many of their key details.

Accordingly, any analysis of Iran's efforts to acquire weapons of mass destruction has to both look beyond its nuclear programs, but recognize that much of the same degree of uncertainty that surrounds Iran's nuclear, chemical, and biological weapons efforts exists in analyzing its delivery systems. This does not, however, mean that the analysis of Iran's nuclear programs cannot be credible; it means that all of Iran's relevant efforts need more analysis in net assessment terms and that both official and unofficial analytic efforts that examine only part of Iran's programs have limited value and credibility.

Iran's Chemical Weapons (CWs) Program

Iran has declared that it has been a chemical weapons power in the past. It never, however, has declared the full nature of its past efforts or been subject to inspection of any of its suspected facilities. The end result is a level of ambiguity that has grown, rather than declined, over time. This ambiguity raises important questions about both Iran's claims to have destroyed all of its chemical weapons capability, as well as past weapons capabilities.

Officially, the Islamic Republic of Iran denies that it now has any biological, chemical, or nuclear weapons in its arsenal, or that it has plans to acquire such weapons. Some current intelligence assessments indicate, however, that Iran remains a chemical weapons state. They indicate that Iran may possess secret stockpiles of chemical weapons, and opinions that Iran is seeking to enhance the quality of its chemical weapons capabilities through the acquisition of technical knowledge, precursor chemicals, and process equipment from abroad have been regularly reinforced by new revelations of Iranian imports of dual-use chemicals and process equipment.

The facts are unclear, but Iran has shown itself to be deceptive in its military, as well as in unconventional research and development (R&D) programs, including its suspect chemical programs. Its lack of transparency leads to further international suspicion and scrutiny regarding these suspected chemical weapons programs, as well as Iran's intentions in possibly researching, developing, and stockpiling dual-use technology in possible production of chemical munitions.

OFFICIAL ESTIMATES OF IRANIAN CAPABILITY

Iran's involvement with chemical weapons began with the Iran-Iraq War of 1980–1988. Beginning in 1983, Iran suffered the effects of escalating Iraqi CW attacks, initially using blister agents (mustard gas) but later including nerve agents such as tabun

(GA) and sarin (GB). According to the U.S. Defense Intelligence Agency (DIA), Iran initiated a chemical weapon development program in 1983 "in response to Iraqi use of riot control and toxic chemical agents" during the war.[1]

The weak international response, particularly by the United Nations and the international community to the Iraqi use of chemical weapons against Iranian forces, left Iran increasingly bitter about what it perceived to be a double standard in the enforcement of international agreements. Many Iranian officials concluded that their country had to develop the ability to retaliate in kind in order to deter chemical weapons use against it.

Iranian Use or Nonuse of Chemical Weapons during the Iran-Iraq War

Open sources on Iran's efforts are limited and conflicting. Governments have provided a few useful summary assessments of Iranian chemical weapons program, but few details and none look beyond the potential use of chemical weapons for tactical purposes. Though there is no concrete evidence that Iran is currently developing CWs, there have been several instances where CW technology, equipment, and possible feedstocks were purchased from foreign sources.

For example, the U.S. intelligence community claimed during the Iraq-Iraq War that Iran had used chemical weapons against Iraqi forces, but Iran has disputed this. Other analysts do feel Iran employed CW agents on a small scale between 1984 and 1988; and some analysts feel that if such use did occur, it was because Iranian troops captured some Iraqi chemical munitions and used them against Iraqi forces. However, an intensive review of the open literature (including United Nations [UN] reports from that era) has failed to verify such claims.[2]

U.S. statements that Iran used chemical weapons at Halabja have never been substantiated. A UN Security Council report issued on May 14, 1987, did indicate that Iraqi military personnel had been injured by CW agents, but never claimed that Iran had used such weapons; some experts feel that any such injuries came from Iraqi uses of the weapons that went into areas with Iraqi troops.[3] Iran, in turn, has claimed that it had 100,000 casualties from chemical weapons during the war, 30,000 of which were serious, and of whom perhaps 5,000 died, while many others suffered debilitating long-term health effects. Tehran has never provided details for claims made in round numbers that may well be exaggerated.[4]

While several Iranian leaders felt that developing a CW program would offset the Iraqi threat and prove to be a strong deterrent, others within the clerical Islamic regime publicly condemned any use of chemicals on moral grounds, calling them un-Islamic. In 1988, however, Ayatollah Ali Akbar Rafsanjani was quoted as saying that "chemical and biological weapons are a poor man's atomic bombs and can easily be produced. We should at least consider them at least for our defense; although the use of such weapons is inhumane, the [Iran-Iraq] war taught us that international laws are only scraps of paper."[5]

Iran Chemical Weapons Developments since the Iran-Iraq War

The United States accused German firms of selling dual-use materials and technology to Iran during the 1980s. In 1989, U.S. authorities found Alcolac International Inc., a pharmaceutical firm based out of Baltimore, Maryland, guilty of illegally shipping almost 120 tons of thiodyglycol (a mustard gas precursor) to Iran. The same year, the U.S. Department of Commerce put export controls on 23 specific chemicals that could aid CW proliferation. Also in 1989, the State Trading Corporation of India admitted that it had sold Iran over 60 tons of thionyl chloride (a nerve agent precursor) and that its supplier was planning to ship an additional 257 tons of the chemical to Iran.

According to a report released by the Russian Federal Intelligence Service, in early 1993 Iran established the "industrial production . . . of sarin." During this period, other sources claim that Rafsanjani created a chemical weapons–related entity called the Special Industries Organization (SIO). This 250-man agency is reported as being independent of the Council of Ministers.[6]

Soon after Iran signed the Chemical Weapons Convention on January 13, 1993, Iran was placed under the Iraq Sanctions Act of 1990 (PL 101-513) with Title XVI of the U.S. Department of Defense Authorization Act. Under this act, the United States opposes, and seeks that other states oppose, transfers of goods or technology to Iran that would contribute to its acquisition of biological, chemical, or nuclear weapons, or destabilizing numbers of advanced conventional weapons.[7]

In July 1996, the Central Intelligence Agency (CIA) and the DIA released new details about the chemical and biological weapons programs in Iran, in response to questions from the Senate Select Committee on Intelligence. According to both agencies, Iran's chemical weapons program is continually expanding and improving. The current stockpile of agents held by Tehran includes 2,000 or more tons of sulfur mustard, phosgene, and cyanide agents. They also concluded that Iran was enhancing its chemical weapons infrastructure and munitions capabilities in order to develop nerve agents.[8]

In 1997, as part of a reported multimillion dollar deal, India agreed to construct a "sophisticated chemical plant at Qazvim, on the outskirts of Tehran."[9] India also agreed to sell Iran phosphorous pentasulfide, a dual-use chemical used in the production of pesticides as well as the nerve agent VX. The deal eventually fell apart, but a similar deal was eventually concluded with China in 1998. China reportedly agreed to sell Iran 500 tons of phosphorus pentasulfide.[10]

The CIA reported that Chinese entities were selling Iran chemical warfare–related chemicals between 1997 and 1998. The U.S. sanctions imposed in May 1997 on seven Chinese entities for knowingly and materially contributing to Iran's CW program remain in effect. In addition, the CIA estimated in January 1999 that Iran obtained material related to chemical warfare from various sources during the first half of 1998.

By 1998, the Iranian government had publicly acknowledged that it began a chemical weapons program during the war. According to the DIA, the program began under the Islamic Revolutionary Guard Corps (IRGC), with the role of the Ministry of Defense increasing over time.

An unclassified U.S. intelligence assessment of Iranian CW capabilities issued in 2001 provided the following broad summary:

> Iran has acceded to the Chemical Weapons Convention (CWC) and in a May 1998 session of the CWC Conference of the States Parties, Tehran, for the first time, acknowledged the existence of a past chemical weapons program. Iran admitted developing a chemical warfare program during the latter stages of the Iran-Iraq war as a "deterrent" against Iraq's use of chemical agents against Iran. Moreover, Tehran claimed that after the 1988 cease-fire, it "terminated" its program. However, Iran has yet to acknowledge that it, too, used chemical weapons during the Iran-Iraq War.
>
> Nevertheless, Iran has continued its efforts to seek production technology, expertise and precursor chemicals from entities in Russia and China that could be used to create a more advanced and self-sufficient chemical warfare infrastructure. As Iran's program moves closer to self-sufficiency, the potential will increase for Iran to export dual-use chemicals and related equipment and technologies to other countries of proliferation concern.
>
> In the past, Tehran has manufactured and stockpiled blister, blood and choking chemical agents, and weaponized some of these agents into artillery shells, mortars, rockets, and aerial bombs. It also is believed to be conducting research on nerve agents. Iran could employ these agents during a future conflict in the region. Lastly, Iran's training, especially for its naval and ground forces, indicates that it is planning to operate in a contaminated environment.[11]

In mid-May 2003, the Bush administration released a statement to the Organisation for Prohibition of Chemical Weapons in which the United States accused Iran of continuing to pursue production technology, training, and expertise from abroad. The statement asserted that Iran was continuing to stockpile blister, blood, choking, and some nerve agents.

This was followed by an unclassified report that the CIA released in November 2003, which stated that

> Iran is a party to the Chemical Weapons Convention (CWC). Nevertheless, during the reporting period it continued to seek production technology, training, and expertise from Chinese entities that could further Tehran's efforts to achieve an indigenous capability to produce nerve agents. Iran likely has already stockpiled blister, blood, choking, and probably nerve agents—and the bombs and artillery shells to deliver them—which it previously had manufactured.[12]

Statements and actions by ranking Iranian officials continued to make it difficult to assess Iran's intentions and capabilities. All too often Iranian decision makers made statements that condemned the use of chemical weapons, while at the same time advocating the strategic and tactical advantages of possessing such weapons, as well as Iran's right to possess this "defensive" capability. Ayatollah Rafsanjani made many statements to this effect:

With regard to chemical, bacteriological, and radiological weapons training, it was made very something missing here "clear" perhaps during the war that these weapons are very decisive. It was also made clear that the moral teachings of the world are not very effective when war reaches a serious stage and the world does not respect its own resolutions and closes its eyes to the violations and the aggressions which are committed on the battlefield. We should fully equip ourselves both in the offensive and defensive use of chemical, bacteriological, and radiological weapons. From now on you should make use of the opportunity and perform the task.[13]

Intelligence Estimates since 2005

In later unclassified Director of National Intelligence (DNI) reports released in 2005, 2006, and 2007, the findings were similar to the November 2003 CIA report, but the report released in 2007 states that "Russian entities also remained a source of dual-use biotechnology equipment and related expertise. Such entities have been a source of dual-use biotechnology, chemicals, production technology, and equipment for Iran."[14]

According to an unclassified report to Congress, Iran continued to seek production technology, training, and expertise from foreign entities in order to further its efforts to achieve an indigenous capability to produce nerve agents during the time period of January 1, 2004, and December 31, 2004. This report also concluded that Iran continued to receive dual-use chemical production and technology from China.

John R. Bolton, then Under Secretary for Arms Control and International Security at the U.S. Department of State, reported on Iran's chemical program in testimony to the House International Relations Committee Subcommittee on the Middle East and Central Asia in 2005. He again reported only in summary terms:

> We believe Iran has a covert program to develop and stockpile chemical weapons. The U.S. Intelligence Community reported in its recent unclassified Report to Congress on the Acquisition of Technology Relating to Weapons of Mass Destruction and Advanced Conventional Munitions, also known as the "721 Report," that Iran continues to seek production technology, training, and expertise that could further its efforts to achieve an indigenous capability to produce nerve agents. A forthcoming edition of the 721 report is expected to state that, "Iran may have already stockpiled blister, blood, choking, and nerve agents—and the bombs and artillery shells to deliver them—which it previously had manufactured."
>
> Iran is a party to the Chemical Weapons Convention (CWC). The CWC's central obligation is simple: no stockpiling, no development, no production, and no use of chemical weapons. The overwhelming majority of States Parties abide by this obligation. Iran is not, and we have made this abundantly clear to the Organization for the Prohibition of Chemical Weapons (OPCW). Although Iran has declared a portion of its CW program to the OPCW, it is time for Iran to declare the remainder and make arrangements for its dismantlement and for the destruction of its chemical weapons.[15]

Some European assessments have agreed with those of the U.S. Department of Defense and the CIA, but there have been only limited public reports. The German

Federal Customs Administration (ZKA) published a report in November 2004 that stated,

> Iran has an emerging chemical industry. Its CW program obtains support, according to accounts received, from China and India. It probably possesses chemical agents such as sulfur mustards, Tabun, and hydrogen cyanide, possibly also Sarin and VC. Iran is attempting to acquire chemical installations and parts thereof, as well as technology and chemical precursors.[16]

In January 2006, another ZKA report with the Federal Office of Criminal Investigations was published on illegal arms transfers by German companies to Iran. The report claims that Iran is working to increase its stockpiles of chemical weapons.[17]

Israeli reports continue to assert that Iran has chemical weapons capabilities and that these capabilities pose a grave threat to Israeli national security. In a January 14, 2008, interview before the Israeli Knesset, the Israeli Military Intelligence research chief Brigadier General Yossi Kuperwasser said that "the possibility certainly exists" for Iran to supply chemical weapons to Hezbollah. This suggested that Israeli intelligence held open the possibility either that Iran had covertly retained undeclared stocks of chemical weapons or that such agents could be quickly (and possibly covertly) manufactured.[18]

Work by GlobalSecurity.org does, however, raise important questions about the nature of some more recent U.S. intelligence estimates and whether the U.S. intelligence estimates cited earlier are still valid:

> According to the CIA's first of two Unclassified Report to Congress on the acquisition of Technology Relating to Weapons of Mass Destruction and Advanced Conventional Munitions (Sect. 721 reports) in 1997 "Iran already has manufactured and stockpiled CW, including blister, blood and choking agents and the bombs and artillery shells for delivering them." The DoD in the Proliferation: Threat and Response of the same year confirmed the CIA's findings and also concluded that Iran was researching various nerve agents as well.
>
> In the first half of 2000, according to both the Director and the Deputy Director of the Director of Central Intelligence's Nonproliferation Center, Iran was estimated to have an inventory of several thousand tons of various agents. These agents included sulfur mustard, phosgene, cyanide, and nerve agents, both weaponized and bulk. In the second of the Sect. 721 reports in 2000 said only that Iran "probably" had nerve agents.
>
> From 2003 to the latest reports in 2007 the U.S. intelligence community seems to have been softening its view on the extent of Iran's chemical weapons production and stockpiles. The first Sect 721 report of 2003 claimed Iran "likely has already stockpiled blister, blood choking, and probably nerve agents." The Sec. 721 report, publicly released in May 2006, but covering activities in 2004, made no reference to stockpiles and delivery systems. What remained was a statement that Iran "continued to seek production technology, training, and expertise from foreign entities that could further Tehran's efforts to achieve an indigenous capability to produce nerve agents." The 2007 report stated that "Iran has a large and growing commercial chemical industry that could be used to support a chemical agent mobilization capability."

The February 2008 testimony to the SSCI [Senate Select Committee on Intelligence] by DNI Mike McConnell stated that: "Tehran maintains dual-use facilities intended to produce CW agent in times of need and conducts research that may have offensive applications. We assess Iran maintains a capability to weaponize CW agents in a variety of delivery systems."

The reasoning behind the change in the intelligence community's stance is not known, but two theories have been suggested. It is possible that since 2003 there has been evidence which required that a change in the projected size and scope of Iran's CW program. It is also possible that the consequences of the problematic intelligence from the CIA concerning Iraq prompted a second look at the chemical weapon intelligence that has been collected.[19]

At the same time, U.S. intelligence officials continue to stress that Iran has a chemical weapons program, and it should be noted that Iran may have chosen not to produce and stockpile chemical weapons—as distinguished from maintaining a production base and development effort—because of the political risk involved and the instability of many chemical weapons designs once actually placed in a weapon and put into storage. A chronology the Nuclear Threat Initiative (NTI) has prepared of U.S. statements regarding Iran's chemical weapons during 2008 indicates that the United States feels Iran does maintain a stockpile of chemical weapons and that Iran continues to import material that can be used for chemical weapons:[20]

- **5 February 2008:** In testimony before the US Senate Select Committee on Intelligence the Director of National Intelligence addresses the question of Iran's pursuit of WMD [weapons of mass destruction] capabilities. On the issue of chemical weapons Mr. McConnell says: "We know that Tehran had a chemical warfare program prior to 1997, when it declared elements of its program. We assess that Tehran maintains dual-use facilities intended to produce CW agent in times of need and conducts research that may have offensive applications. We assess Iran maintains a capability to weaponize CW agents in a variety of delivery systems."[21]

- **27 February 2008:** Testifying before the US Senate Committee on Armed Services the Director of the Defense Intelligence Agency (DIA), Lt. General Michael D. Maples states: "We assess that Tehran maintains dual-use facilities intended to produce chemical warfare agents in times of need and conducts research that may have offensive applications.[22]

- **3 March 2008:** The US Office of the Director of National Intelligence (ODNI) releases its Unclassified Report to Congress on the Acquisition of Technology Relating to Weapons of Mass Destruction and Advanced Conventional Munitions for the period 1 January to 31 December 2005. In the section addressing Iranian chemical programs the report states: "Iran is a party to the Chemical Weapons Convention (CWC). Nevertheless, during the reporting period it continued to seek production technology, training, and expertise from foreign entities that could advance its assessed chemical warfare program." (This language differs slightly from that of the 2004 report. It does not refer to "efforts to achieve an indigenous capability to produce nerve agents.").[23]

- **3 March 2008:** ... US Office of the Director of National Intelligence (ODNI) releases its Unclassified Report to Congress on the Acquisition of Technology Relating to

Weapons of Mass Destruction and Advanced Conventional Munitions for the period 1 January to 31 December 2006. In the section addressing Iranian chemical programs the report states: "We judge that Iran maintains a Chemical Warfare (CW) research and development program which began in response to Iraqi use of CW during the Iran-Iraq War during the 1980s. . . . [Iran] continues to seek production technology, training, and expertise from foreign entities that could advance a CW program. We judge that Iran maintains a small, covert CW stockpile."[24]

- **8 July 2008:** U.S. designates a number of Iranian entities and individuals as being of proliferation concern under the terms of Executive Order 13382. . . . Although Parchin Chemical Industries is designated for its import of solid rocket motor fuel precursors the company has been previously accused of involvement in the production or development of chemical warfare agents.[25]

A Congressional Research Service (CRS) Report to Congress, dated September 24, 2008, continues to assert that Iran has continued to seek a self-sufficient CW infrastructure and casts doubts on Iran's compliance to the CWC.

Official U.S. reports and testimony continue to state that Iran is seeking a self sufficient chemical weapons (CW) infrastructure, and that it "may have already" stockpiled blister, blood, choking, and nerve agents—and the bombs and shells to deliver them. This raises questions about Iran's compliance with its obligations under the Chemical Weapons Convention (CWC), which Iran signed on January 13, 1993, and ratified on June 8, 1997. These officials and reports also say that Iran "probably maintain[s] an offensive [biological weapons] BW program . . . and probably has the capability to produce at least small quantities of BW agents."[26]

ARMS CONTROL ESTIMATES OF IRANIAN CAPABILITY

Iran's stated position is clear; its actions are not. Iran signed the CWC on January 13, 1993, and deposited the instruments of ratification with the UN on November 3, 1997. The treaty required Iran to formally declare the nature of chemical weapon stockpiles and relevant facilities within 60 days from the dates of ratification. It also required Iran to accept inspections by the Organization for the Prohibition of Chemical Weapons (OPCW)—the treaty's implementing body—at any site that any other state that is a party suspected it of housing chemical weapon activities.

Iran's actions seemed to reflect the impact of having been the target of Iraqi chemical weapons, and its statement on the treaty implied it would fully comply:

The Islamic Republic of Iran, on the basis of the Islamic principles and beliefs, considers chemical weapons inhuman, and has consistently been on the vanguard of the international efforts to abolish these weapons and prevent their use.

1. The Islamic Consultative Assembly (the Parliament) of the Islamic Republic of Iran approved the bill presented by the Government to join the [said Convention] on 27 July 1997, and the Guardian Council found the legislation compatible with the Constitution and the Islamic Tenets on 30 July 1997, in accordance with its required Constitutional process. The Islamic Consultative Assembly decided that:

The Government is hereby authorized, at an appropriate time, to accede to the [said Convention]—as annexed to this legislation and to deposit its relevant instrument.

The Ministry of Foreign Affairs must pursue in all negotiations and within the framework of the Organization of the Convention, the full and indiscriminate implementation of the Convention, particularly in the areas of inspection and transfer of technology and chemicals for peaceful purposes. In case the aforementioned requirements are not materialized, upon the recommendation of the Cabinet and approval of the Supreme National Security Council, steps aimed at withdrawing from the Convention will be put in motion.

2. The Islamic Republic of Iran attaches vital significance to the full, unconditional and indiscriminate implementation of all provisions of the Convention. It reserves the right to withdraw from the Convention under the following circumstances:

– Non-compliance with the principle of equal treatment of all States parties in implementation of all relevant provisions of the Convention;

– Disclosure of its confidential information contrary to the provisions of the Convention;

– Imposition of restrictions incompatible with the obligations under the Convention.

3. As stipulated in article XI, exclusive and non-transparent regimes impeding free international trade in chemicals and chemical technology for peaceful purposes should be disbanded. The Islamic Republic of Iran rejects any chemical export control mechanism not envisaged in the Convention.

4. The Organization for Prohibition of Chemical Weapons (OPCW) is the sole international authority to determine the compliance of States Parties regarding chemical weapons. Accusations by States Parties against other States Parties in the absence of a determination of non-compliance by OPCW will seriously undermine the Convention and its repetition may make the Convention meaningless.

5. One of the objectives of the Convention as stipulated in its preamble is to "promote free trade in chemicals as well as international cooperation and exchange of scientific and technical information in the field of chemical activities for purposes not prohibited under the Convention in order to enhance the economic and technological development of all States Parties." This fundamental objective of the Convention should be respected and embraced by all States Parties to the Convention. Any form of undermining, either in words or in action, of this overriding objective is considered by the Islamic Republic of Iran a grave breach of the provisions of the Convention.

6. In line with the provisions of the Convention regarding non-discriminatory treatment of States Parties:

– Inspection equipment should be commercially available to all States Parties without condition or limitation.

– The OPCW should maintain its international character by ensuring fair and balanced geographical distribution of the personnel of its Technical Secretariat, provision of assistance to and cooperation with States Parties, and equitable membership of States Parties in subsidiary organs of the Organization.

7. The implementation of the Convention should contribute to international peace and security and should not in any way diminish or harm national security or territorial integrity of the States Parties.[27]

The Iranian Majlis noted in approving the ratification, however, that "accusations by States Parties against other States Parties in the absence of a determination of non-compliance by OPCW will seriously undermine the Convention and its repetition may make the Convention meaningless."

Compliance with the CWC

In practice, Iran has treated the CWC in much the same way that it has treated the nuclear nonproliferation treaty. Iran did not meet its schedule for issuing a declaration, and Iran's initial declaration was considered incomplete by the OPCW Verification Division. Tehran did file an amended declaration, but it was only in 1999 that Iran told the OPCW that it was a country that could be listed as having had chemical weapons in the past. Iran also claimed that it had destroyed all of its chemical weapons before it became a party to the CWC and that there was nothing for the OPCW to verify.[28]

Iran's ambassador to the 3rd Conference of States Parties (CSP) to the CWC in The Hague—which was held in November 1998—stated that Iran had worked on chemical weapons during the Iran-Iraq War, but, "following the establishment of the cease fire (in July 1998), the decision to develop chemical weapons capabilities was reversed and the process was terminated." H.E. Dr. G. Ali Khoshro, Iran's Deputy Foreign Minister of Legal and International Affairs, made a similar statement to the CWC Review Conference, held April and May 2003. He said,

> I have to recall the fact that due to the lack of reaction by the international community against Iraqi chemical weapons attack during the 8 year imposed war, in the last phase we got the chemical capabilities, but we did not use it, and following the cease fire we did decide to dismantle. We did destroy the facilities under the supervision of the OPCW inspectors and we got the certificate of the destruction of CWPF [chemical weapons production facility].[29]

Iran did declare the existence of two "former" chemical weapons facilities to the OPCW, and it staged a model inspection of the Shahid Razakani multipurpose chemical plant in Tehran when it hosted a Regional Seminar on National Implementation of the Chemical Weapons Convention, in Tehran during April 22–25, 1996. It never, however, has had any challenge inspection of any facility. At the same time, U.S. and other intelligence agencies that report that Iran has chemical weapons have never made allegations that the OPCW could pursue through challenge inspections.[30]

At a press conference during the 10th International Chemical Weapons Demilitarisation Conference (CWD 2007) in Brussels, Belgium, OPCW Director-General Ambassador Rogelio Pfirter stated, "Iran is a full member of CWC. We have carried out several inspections in Iran and so far it has proven to comply with the CWC."[31]

In October 2007, the OPCW reported that Iran was 1 of 18 countries that met the deadline for submission of annual declarations regarding projected activities and anticipated production in 2008 at schedule 1 facilities. The report does not specify the nature of the Iranian facility that may be a single small-scale facility, a facility for protective purposes, or a facility for medical, pharmaceutical, or research purposes.[32]

As has been noted earlier, various intelligence agencies and open-source reporting have continued to allege that Iran has continued to seek production technology, training, and expertise from various national governments and firms that could further Tehran's efforts to achieve an indigenous capability to produce nerve agents and that Iran likely has a stockpile of chemical munitions, which it previously had manufactured.

There are also reports that Iran has imported CW technology from China and Russia.[33] Other reports claim that Iran has made deals to export chemical munitions and technology to Syria.[34] The latter claim was supported by another article in *Jane's Defence Weekly* alleging that an unspecified number of Iranian missile weaponization engineers were killed in an accidental explosion during an attempt "to weaponize a 500 km [range] 'SCUD C' with a mustard gas warhead" at a Syrian military facility in the vicinity of Aleppo.[35]

On April 8, 2008, in its national statement to the Second CWC Review conference in The Hague, Iran highlighted concerns over CW possessor states' slow progress, and the possible need for extensions beyond the final allowable treaty deadline, in fulfilling their obligations to totally destroy their CW stockpiles. The statement observes that "failure to meet this deadline (April 2012) is a clear and serious case of non-compliance. It would also raise the concern that domestic policies have resulted in preferences for retaining certain stockpiles as 'Security Reserves.'"

In addition, the statement calls on member states to take "concrete measures to bring to justice those who assisted Saddam in development and use of chemical weapons." Finally the Iranians expressed their dissatisfaction with Western efforts to refocus the OPCW's industry verification activities away from Schedule 1, 2, and 3 facilities and onto other chemical production facilities noting that "attempts at redefining the hierarchical risks envisaged in the Convention for three schedules of chemicals would endanger the focus of the verification regime of the Convention."[36]

A Strategy of Ambiguity?

Iran's signing of conventions such as the CWC, the Biological Weapons Convention (BWC), and the Nuclear Non-Proliferation Treaty (NPT) can be viewed as yet another part of Iran's attempts to deceive the international communities in regard to its WMD intentions and capabilities. As a senior U.S. administrative official stated, in regard to Iran's BW program, "If Iran has an offensive biological weapons program, Iran would not be signing a document that prevents it from cheating."[37] This comment is indicative of Tehran's diplomacy with regard to its WMD conventions.

Tehran seems to have adopted and implemented Rafsanjani's policy of deception and denial in regard to its WMD programs. Publicly, Iranian officials appear to follow and support most international conventions in which they are a signatory to, but in reality they may be using these conventions as a smoke screen for Iran's WMD programs and as a means to further its programs by keeping lines of trade open for precursor materials.

Ayatollah Rafsanjani's follower, President Mohammad Khatami, did his part in Rafsanjani's WMD strategy of ambiguity. Khatami maintained a stance of "plausible deniability" in regard to Iran's chemical and biological weapons.[38] During his presidency, Khatami continually indicated that he favored Iran's strategic weapons programs and that he believed Iran's security depended upon the success of these programs, while being careful not to admit knowledge of Iran's WMD programs.[39]

Other statements by Iranian officials have contradicted their previous statements or the statements of other officials. One such example of this is comments made by Iranian nuclear negotiator Saeed Jalil to the UN, which contradict statements made by Ambassador Mohammad R. Alborzi, director general of the Iranian Foreign Ministry, to the OPCW regarding Iran's chemical weapons history.

On January 23, 2008, speaking in Brussels Iranian nuclear negotiator Saeed Jalil states that: "I assure you that the (chemical) weapons have no place in our defense doctrine." The context is made in the context of a discussion about Iranian actions during the Iran-Iraq war of 1980–1988 and is intended to support the proposition that Iran made no use of chemical weapons during that conflict. [This assertion may contradict a statement made at the OPCW in 1998 that Iran possessed CW in the latter stages of the war.][40]

But previously, on November 18, 1998, Ambassador Mohammad R. Alborzi, director general of the Iranian Foreign Ministry, delivered Iran's CW declaration during a session of the Conference of the States Parties (CSP) to the CWC in The Hague, Netherlands. In his statement, he admitted for the first time that Iran had once possessed CW, in the waning years of the Iran-Iraq War. But he claims that, ". . . following the establishment of cease fire, the decision to develop chemical weapons capabilities was reversed and the process was terminated."[41]

NONGOVERNMENTAL ORGANIZATION ESTIMATES OF IRANIAN CAPABILITY

Nongovernmental organization (NGO) reporting emphasizes potential capability over current production, stockpiling, and deployment. The International Institute for Strategic Studies pointed out in its 2005 study of Iran's weapons that "despite a similar record with respect to nuclear weapons and the NPT, Iran conducted undeclared nuclear activities in violation of the treaty for over 20 years. Whether Iran has carried out similar activities in violation of its CWC and BWC obligations cannot be determined definitively from the available public information."[42]

The same basic judgments occur in the reporting of the Federation of American Scientists, GlobalSecurity.org, and the Nuclear Threat Initiative. These NGOs do, however, provide a level of detail that raises additional questions about Iran's past and present capabilities. For example, a study by the Monterey Institute of International Studies indicated there are a number of sites in Iran that might be related to Iran's chemical warfare effort:[43]

- **Abu Musa Island:** Iran holds a large number of chemical weapons, principally 155-millimeter artillery shells, in addition to some weaponized biological agents. According to a study by the National Defense University from April 1997, "The United States believes that Iran has some weaponized biological weapons and a large chemical weapons stockpile, some of which are deployed on Abu Musa Island in the Gulf near the Strait of Hormuz."[44]

- **Bandar Khomeini:** This is allegedly the location of a chemical weapons facility, run by the Razi Chemical Corporation, established during the Iran-Iraq War to manufacture chemical weapons.

- **Damghan:** According to several sources, Iran's primary suspected chemical weapons production facility is located in the city of Damghan. This is the location of either a chemical weapons plant or warhead assembly facility, primarily involved in 155-millimeter artillery shells and Scud warheads. According to the Federation of American Scientists, there are uncorroborated reports that Iran had a chemical weapons plant in operation at this location as early as March 1988.

- **Isfahan:** This is a suspected location of a chemical weapons facility, possibly operated by the Poly-acryl Iran Corporation, Linear Alkyl Benzene Complex, and/or Chemical Industries Group (CIG). Unconfirmed reports from the National Council of Resistance of Iran claim that nerve gas produced in a facility near Semnan was transported to a missile plant in Isfahan for weaponization on ballistic missiles, including the Scud-B. Located in Isfahan, the Chemical Industries Group is the backbone of the Iranian weapons industry. According to U.S. intelligence sources, CIG is making solid-fuel propellant powders for Iran's ballistic missile and artillery rocket programs. Within the CIG, a state-of-the-art chemical plant was built by the Swedish group Bofors in Isfahan starting in the late 1970s as a dual-use fertilizer and explosives factory; however, the plant did not open until 1987 due to Iraqi artillery and missile barrages.

- **Karaj:** Located about 14 kilometers from Tehran, this is the site of an alleged storage and manufacturing facility for chemical weapons. The National Council of Resistance of Iran reports that a considerable number of long-range missiles, including Scud-Bs, are held in the Balal Habashi garrison of the Guards Corps on Karaj Road. Reports suggest that this facility was built with Chinese assistance and may also be used as part of Iran's nuclear-related research programs.

- **Marvdasht:** The Chemical Fertilizers Company is suspected to have been a manufacturing facility for mustard agents during the Iran-Iraq War.

- **Parchin:** This is the location of at least one munitions factory and is suspected of being a major chemical weapons production facility. Reports of uncertain reliability indicate that the plant was in operation no later than March 1988. In April 1997, a German newspaper reported that, according to the German Federal Intelligence Service, the factories at Parchin were producing primary products for chemical warfare agents. In 2002, the National Council of Resistance of Iran asserted that the Hungarian company

Lampert had refurbished Parchin Chemical Industries, described as an aging CW plant. Headed by S. J. Seyyedi, this plant legitimately produces chemical intermediates as well as explosives, including sulfuric acid, ethyl alcohol, dynamite, gun powder, nitrocellulose, acetic acid, acetic anhydride, diethyl ether, ethyl acetate, nitric acid, and antifreeze. The plant has reportedly resumed production of chemical weapons agents.

- **Qazvin:** A large pesticide plant at this location that was built in 1987 by a German consortium including the German companies Lurgi Metallurgie GmbH, Bayer AG, and BASF (formerly of VEB Bitterfeld), Ciba-Geigy of Switzerland, and an unidentified Yugoslav company is widely believed to produce nerve gas. Signed by Iran's state-controlled Nargan Consulting Engineers, the contract stipulated that Iran would use the Qazvin facility to make Amiton, a powerful organophosphorus pesticide classified as a nerve agent by Western governments in the 1950s and withdrawn from the market because of its lethality. To handle the deal, Bayer set up a subsidiary in Iran called Bayer-Iran Chemie and began importing equipment from the United States in 1987.

- **Mashar:** Iranian opposition groups have made allegations, of uncertain reliability, that a warhead filling facility is operated at this location.

GlobalSecurity.org cites the existence of possible facilities at Damqhan, Esfahan, Karaj, Parchin, and Qazvin and also raises serious questions about Iran's potential use of chemical weapons to paramilitary proxies such as the terrorist organization Hezbollah:

> As Iran became more self-sufficient at producing chemical agents, there was a potential that it could become a supplier to others trying to develop CW capabilities. Iran supplied Libya with chemical agents in 1987. In a January 14, 2008, interview before the Israeli Knesset the Israeli Military Intelligence research chief Brigadier General Yossi Kuperwasser said that "the possibility certainly exists" for Iran to supply chemical weapons to Hezbollah. This suggests that Israeli intelligence holds open the possibility either that Iran has covertly retained undeclared stocks of chemical weapons, or that such agents could be quickly [and possibly covertly] manufactured.[45]

The NTI gives rise to similar uncertainties about what is and is not known about the status of Iran's chemical weapons:

> Despite its acquisition of precursors from abroad, Iran is allegedly working to develop an indigenous CW production capability. The CIA believes that "Teheran is rapidly approaching self-sufficiency and could become a supplier of CW-related materials to other nations." As of 1996, the Department of Defense claimed that Iran had stockpiled almost 2000 tons of toxic chemical agents and was continuously working on expanding its CW program. Iran has several advanced research institutions employing various chemicals for a variety of reasons, including pesticide production, pharmaceutical research, and other medical studies. Iran has also conducted several military exercises to date that have included defensive chemical and biological weapons maneuvers.
>
> Iran continues to deny any allegations that it is actively pursuing an offensive CW program. In 1996, it held the first regional seminar on the national implementation of the CWC in Tehran so that government authorities could familiarize themselves with

their duties and obligations under the treaty. It also held a mock "trial inspection" at the Shahid Razkani chemical factory to allow inspectors to see how such a procedure was conducted. Iran submitted a declaration on its chemical facilities and its past CW stockpile, it has destroyed chemical weapons production equipment in the presence of OPCW inspectors, and it has undergone a number of OPCW inspections of its chemical industrial facilities. Iran continues to play an active role at the Organization for the Prohibition of Chemical Weapons (OPCW), is recognized as a member in good standing, and currently serves on its executive council. Although U.S. and Israeli intelligence agencies continue to insist Iran maintains a stockpile of chemical weapons, no challenge inspections of Iranian facilities have been requested, and none of the allegations made regarding the stockpiling of CW can be verified in the unclassified domain. However, Iran continues to retain a strong incentive for developing a defensive CW program.[46]

STOCKPILES, PRODUCTION, BREAKOUT CAPABILITY, OR NOTHING?

Iran has a sophisticated base for the development of a chemical weapons program dating back to the Iran-Iraq War, a conflict that gave Iran strong incentives for developing a robust chemical defense capability. There are several unclassified allegations and reports that suggest Iran has developed an offensive CW program as well. Most of these claims cannot be verified in open sources, but some deserve special attention.

In 2005, *Jane's Defence Weekly* quoted an unidentified "diplomatic source" alleging that Iran and Syria had concluded an agreement whereby Iran would construct a number of facilities intended to give Syria an independent capability for the production of CW agent precursors, eliminating its current dependence on imports. The report notes that a contract had not yet been officially signed, but Iran would reportedly "supply Syria with reactors, pipes, condensers, heat exchangers, storage and feed tanks, as well as NDCAM equipment (to detect CW agents in the air)."[47]

Another article from *Jane's Defence Weekly* also reports that an agreement between Syrian and Iranian officials, which describes the signing of a "confidential strategic accord . . . which includes a sensitive chapter dealing with co-operation and mutual aid during times of international sanctions, or scenarios of military confrontation with the West," appears to have taken place. Among other provisions the accord allegedly requires the Iranian government to provide "co-operation and continuous transfer of technology and equipment in the areas of weapons of mass destruction [particularly the upgrade of Syrian missile and chemical warfare capabilities]." In return Syria will reportedly "allow Iran to safely store weapons, sensitive equipment or even hazardous materials on Syrian soil should Iran need such help in a time of crisis."[48]

Reports such as these point toward an advanced R&D program for the production of CW agents. Although this does not give a clear picture of Iran's capabilities, it does indicate that Iran has significant production capabilities if the reports are true. This also creates concern as to Iran's intentions and policy toward WMD proliferation. But these inquiries remain difficult to assess without further reporting.

The Impact of Using Chemical Weapons

It is equally difficult to determine how Iran would plan to use such weapons, or the somewhat similar threat of radiological weapons. Lethality is an issue. Most lists of weapons of mass destruction include chemical, biological, radiological, and nuclear weapons. In practice, however, currently deployed chemical weapons, and virtually all radiological weapons, have far less real-world lethality than nuclear weapons.

Radiological weapons can contaminate a facility or limited area, and be used for area denial, but it is far from clear that most radiological weapons are more effective than high explosive weapons in this role; they are also very difficult to weaponize in a form that produces significant casualties unless they can somehow be introduced covertly into the target area. Even then, their prompt kill effect may be very limited. There is no evidence that Iran has ever developed or deployed radiological weapons, although any such effort would be difficult to detect, and it is always possible that Iran has done so for use in terror operations or irregular war.

Chemical weapons are a better known threat, with a history of use dating back to World War I. While Iranian casualty claims may be exaggerated, it is clear that Iraq did use chemical weapons effectively during the Iran-Iraq War, which produced a significant number of Iranians killed and wounded. The main impact of Iraqi chemical weapons, however, was to disrupt Iranian operations and provide area denial. They were effective only when employed in large numbers, and in persistent form—such as the Iraqi use of mustard gas during the Iraqi counteroffensive in Faw in 1988.

There is no way to know what would have happened if Iraq or Iran had been able to weaponize and employ persistent nerve agents in large numbers during the Iran-Iraq War, and so-called "third-generation" weapons—which cannot be described in unclassified literature—may well present a far more lethal threat than any of the nerve agents that have been deployed to date.

The fact remains, however, that chemical weapons have rarely produced anything like the theoretical estimates of their effects. They have had to be delivered in very large amounts to have a significant tactical impact, usually by large numbers of rockets and artillery shells.

Chemical weapons are difficult to weaponize for delivery by aircraft or unmanned combat air vehicles (UCAVs) unless they are deployed slowly along a carefully calculated path—a method called "line source" distribution—that ensures the agent covers a wide area and moves along a path where the wind ensures suitable coverage of the target area. Delivering chemical weapons effectively by bomb or missile alternative requires the use of advanced cluster munitions that can scatter canisters of munitions over large areas, which then release their agent at precisely the right altitude. This is a difficult challenge for bomb design, and an extremely difficult challenge in a missile warhead.

At the same time, the psychological, terror, and political impacts of chemical (and radiological) weapons are likely to be much greater than their lethality or actual area denial effects. This might make Iranian possession of chemical weapons a significant factor if Iran was seeking to create a deterrent to preventive or preemptive strikes on its nuclear facilities, or a more convincing threat of escalation from conventional to nuclear war.

An Iranian missile force known to be armed with chemical warheads—even less effective unitary warheads—would give Iran a rapid way of deploying a form of weapon of mass destruction that would almost certainly have a major impact on how its neighbors view the risk of supporting U.S. military action and might have a deterrent impact on Israel. The threat of using such weapons against key facilities such as oil export terminals or desalination plants would have a global impact, given the world's dependence on Gulf oil exports.

None of these *possibilities* can be described in terms of *probabilities*. It is impossible to prove a negative, and the various unclassified claims and counterassertions about Iran's chemical weapons capabilities show that they are as hard to substantiate as they are to rebut. There currently are no inspection or detection efforts that can guarantee that Iran has not, or will not, covertly deploy such a capability. Iran has had all of the technology to develop and deploy at least unitary chemical bomb warheads since the late 1980s to early 1990s. It may well have acquired the capability to deploy more advanced cluster weapons from nations such as North Korea or modify cluster weapons design to delivered high-explosive bomblets.

Tests and Exercises Involving Chemical Weapons

Iran has not publicly declared any doctrine for the offensive use of chemical weapons or discussed in its open military literature how Iran might use such weapons. Reports of Iranian exercises involving the use of chemical weapons cannot be confirmed. Instead, Iran continued to state its objection to the use of CBW in war—often on religious grounds based on Khomeini's statements in the 1980s—and its legal obligation under international conventions.

Iran's technology base is advanced enough, however, so that Iran retains some capability to make chemical weapons, and it may have inactive or mothballed facilities. While there have been no public reports of active production, this is possible and such efforts can occur at low levels and be easy to conceal. Iraq produced small lots of mustard gas weapons at the laboratory level before its major production facilities came online and showed that it could produce at the batch level with relatively small and easy-to-conceal facilities. Iran's purchases also indicate that it could have a significant stock of precursors, and some less lethal weapons can be made out of refinery and petrochemical by-products.

It seems clear that Iran has the technology base to produce mustard gas and non-persistent nerve agents—including reasonable stable agents and binary weapons—and may have the technology to produce persistent nerve agents as well. It probably has technical knowledge of third-generation and "dusty" agents. It has had the opportunity to reverse engineer captured Iraqi weapons and may have received aid in weapons design from Russian, Chinese, and North Korean sources. It certainly has monitored UN reporting on the Iraqi chemical and biological programs and may have acquired considerable detail on these programs, their strengths and weaknesses, and Iraq's sources abroad.

Any assessment of potential Iranian capabilities must also take account of the fact that Iran has had at least a quarter of a century in which to weaponize chemical agents in ways it can effectively deliver. It also has had to react to a real-world threat and has spent six years fighting Iraq—a nation seeking to acquire chemical, biological, and nuclear weapons to destroy it. Discussions with Iranian officials confirm that Iranian military literature also has reprinted Western and other literature on chemical, biological, radiological, and nuclear weapons, and Iran actively collects such literature on a global basis.

Iran almost certainly has the ability to make effective chemical artillery shells and bombs and unitary rocket and missile warheads. It can probably design effective cluster bombs and warheads. It may have sprayers for use by aircraft, helicopters, and unmanned aerial vehicles. Iran's ability to develop lethal missile warheads is far more problematic. The timing and dissemination problems are far more difficult and may be beyond Iran's current technical skills.

The past history of Iranian efforts at complex program management and systems integration, however, has shown that Iran has serious problems in translating its technical expertise into practice. The knowledge of how to do things rarely leads to similar capability to actually do them, particularly when programs remain concealed and are largely "mothballed" or have low levels of activity.

Testing chemical weapons presents serious problems when the test goes beyond static tests or relatively crude measurements of how well given weapons disseminate the agent. It is particularly difficult in the case of missile warheads. It is possible to determine lethality in rough terms from residues, but this requires repeated testing using actual weapons in a variety of real-world conditions. There are no reports of such testing, but it is more than possible that they could be successfully concealed. Unlike most biological weapons, the operational lethality of chemical weapons can be safely tested against live animals. Again, there are no reports of such testing, but it is more than possible that they could be successfully concealed.

The history of actual chemical warfare, however, indicates that the results of such tests can be extremely unrealistic and that operational lethality has rarely approached anything like engineering and test predictions. The "scale-up" of individual weapons results in predictions of real-world results from using large numbers of weapons that have produced particularly misleading results. Moreover, as is the case with biological weapons, temperature, weather, sunlight, wind, surface conditions, and a number of external factors can have a major impact on lethality.

These factors, coupled with the difficulty in measuring incapacity or deaths in less than hours to days, also means Iran and other users would have to carry out any chemical campaign with little ability to predict its actual lethality or carry out effective battle damage assessment. Such considerations might not be important, however, when the goal was terror, panic, area denial, forcing an enemy to don protection gear and decontaminate, or accept these casualties in addition to other casualties from military operations.

This means that even if Iran does have plans and doctrine for using chemical weapons, and has made serious efforts to estimate their lethality and effectiveness, such plans are unlikely to survive engagement with reality. Iran's past reports on its military exercises may be propaganda driven, but some of Iran's conventional war-fighting exercises do have a strong element of ideology and wishful thinking and a lack of demanding realism. This could lead military officers and civilian decision makers to make serious miscalculations based on the war they want to fight rather than the war they can fight.

Such considerations would have less impact if Iran chose to use proxies or covert means of attack to strike at high-value targets or for the purposes of terrorism and intimidation. The IRGC has conducted the kind of conventional exercise that could be adapted to such ends, and Iran has long supplied conventional weapons to movements such as Hezbollah and Hamas.

Even so, an Iranian ship that was hijacked by pirates off the Horn of Africa on August 21, 2008, is of some concern when assessing Iran's CW intentions. Hijackings occur quite frequently in this area, but this hijacking is of particular interest in this assessment due to the cargo it was carrying. Its declared cargo consists of minerals and industrial products; however, Somali and regional officials directly involved in the negotiations over the ship stated that they were convinced that it was heading to Eritrea to deliver small arms and chemical weapons to Somalia's Islamist insurgents.

The ship is owned and operated by Islamic Republic of Iran Shipping Lines—a state-owned company run by the Iranian military. This firm was sanctioned by the U.S. Department of the Treasury on September 10, 2008, shortly after the ship's hijacking. According to the U.S. government, the company regularly falsifies shipping documents in order to hide the identity of end users, uses generic terms to describe shipments to avoid the attention of shipping authorities, and employs the use of cover entities to circumvent UN sanctions to facilitate weapons proliferation for the Iranian Ministry of Defense.[49]

Options for Tactical Use of Chemical Weapons

Iranian military use of chemical weapons offers some potential benefits, but it would also present a number of problems:

- Any use of chemical weapons may have a powerful psychological and political impact, but it also may not be lethal enough to deter or intimidate, and it may well provoke and lead any opponent that can to escalate. It may discredit the initial user and can justify a massive level of escalation, potentially even the use of biological or nuclear weapons in retaliation.

- Arming aircraft or missiles with unitary chemical weapons can potentially produce high rates of lethality against exposed troops or populations, but real-world lethality is extremely difficult to predict. Actual area coverage can be limited, particularly with a ballistic missile warhead where preserving the integrity of a fully loaded warhead and dissemination at precisely the right altitude presents major technical challenges.

- Cluster munitions and other advanced ways of disseminating chemical weapons from a bomb or warhead offer more potential lethality, but also present more technical challenges and even worst-case persistent nerve agents will have limited lethality compared to a nuclear weapon.

- Line source dissemination by an aircraft, cruise missile, drone, or UCAV offers a simpler and more lethal way of disseminating chemical agents than unitary or cluster weapons, but means flying a large air system to the target area and flying a vulnerable penetration profile.

- Effective air strikes require high confidence in the ability to penetrate enemy air defenses and good intelligence, surveillance, and reconnaissance (IS&R) assets. In many cases, a chemical weapon would have only marginally greater lethality than a conventional precision-guided weapon or cluster weapon. Again, such use might do more to provoke than terrify, intimidate, or damage.

- Chemical weapons have proven to be effective in disrupting tactical operations, denying areas to enemy forces, but such weapons have to be used in large numbers. They are not individually lethal enough to have a major impact on ground battles and take time to be effective. They are best suited to relatively static battles, dominated by ground forces that do not have armored and protected vehicles and which cannot mass airpower effectively. This describes Iran and Iraq in 1980–1988. It does not describe the United States or most of Iran's opponents today. Airpower and sea power are largely immune to the kind of chemical attack Iran could launch, with the possible exception of fixed, targetable area targets—many of which could be denied for any significant time only by large numbers of accurate attacks. Rapidly maneuvering ground forces would be a difficult target for Iran's much more static forces. Nations such as the United States would have extensive amounts of detection, protection, and decontamination gear. They also would not have large, static, rear area, and support operations near the forward edge of the battle area.

- Iranian artillery tends to be slow moving and lacks the ability to rapidly target and switch fires. It relies heavily on static massed fires. This requires relatively short-range engagement against an equally slow-moving or static opponent. In reality, Iran will probably face opponents that maneuver more quickly and have superior IS&R assets. A repetition of the battlefield conditions of the Iran-Iraq War seems unlikely.

- Chemical weapons could be more effective as area weapons that forced enemy forces to abandon positions, denied the ability to use rear areas, or acted as a barrier to movement. The tactical and maneuver effects were more important in the Iran-Iraq War than using CWs as a killing mechanism. They again, however, tend to be most useful against relatively static opponents that do not have air superiority or supremacy.

- Iran has a number of potential long-range artillery rockets and missiles. A single chemical warhead, however, is more a terror weapon than a killing mechanism. Such systems have limited accuracies, and Iran has limited long-range targeting capability against mobile targets. The use of a few chemical rounds would be highly provocative and justify massive escalation by an enemy. As such, it might do more to provoke than terrify, intimidate, or damage. Iran might, however, be able to use persistent nerve and mustard agents to deny the use of a key facility such as an air base, key supply facility, mobilization center, oil export facility, or desalination or power plant.

- The use of chemical weapons against targets at sea presents significant targeting and meteorological problems. These are certainly solvable, but do require exceptional planning and skill. Similarly, firing against coastal targets requires high volumes of CW fire or good meteorological data.

- Covert or proxy use presents serious problems in wartime. Plausible deniability is doubtful, and an opponent simply may not care if it can prove Iran is responsible for any given use of CWs.

- Operation lethality is dependent on an opponent's CW defense and decontamination facilities, level of depth, and speed of maneuver. Iran may be dealing with much more sophisticated opponents than the Iraq of the 1980s.

None of these problems or issues implies that Iran could not use chemical weapons effectively under some conditions. They might, however, deter Iran from stockpiling such weapons or using them except under the most drastic conditions. Iran has to understand that their use would tend to make Iran lose the political and information battle and act as a license to its opponent to escalate. While such concerns might well deter Iran under most circumstances, it is also important to understand that wars and drastic crises are not "most circumstances." One inherent problem in any such analysis is that even the most prudent decision maker in peacetime can panic, overreact, or drastically miscalculate in war.

6

Iran's Biological Weapons Programs

Any analysis of Iran's biological weapons effort must be more speculative than an analysis of its chemical and nuclear weapons efforts and the details of its missile programs. Many claims can be traced back to hard-line opponents of the regime that have uncertain to dubious credibility. Others provide important insights into Iran's potential capability, but do not prove Iran has an active program, or that it has ever produced such weapons.

As is the case with Iran's other potential efforts to develop weapons of mass destruction, Iran denies that it currently has such programs, although—as is the case with chemical weapons—some statements imply that it may have had such programs in the past. Similarly, the statements of the U.S. government have the same internal problems and contradictions as those relating to chemical weapons, while too little data are available from other governments to get a picture of their official position or the judgments of their intelligence communities.

Another problem in trying to gain insight into Iran's biological weapons programs is that these types of programs are easy to conceal due to the small-scale equipment and dual-use raw materials needed in the production process. Biological agents are easier and cheaper to produce than either nuclear materials or chemical warfare agents, and the necessary technology is widely available and relatively easy to acquire. The fact of the matter is that any nation with even modestly sophisticated biopharmaceutical industrial capabilities is capable of producing biological agents. But weaponizing and storing weaponized biological agents is a much more complex process.

A number of nongovernmental organizations (NGOs) have made considerable contribution to the analysis of Iran's programs, but they are forced to rely on uncertain reports and unreliable sources. Biological weapons also present the problem that there is no meaningful separation between defensive and offensive efforts. Effective defense requires access to effective biological agents. The facilities necessary to develop, and produce, such weapons can be very small compared to those for chemical and nuclear weapons.

Biological weapons activities can easily be concealed in organizations, facilities, and even universities; which serve medical, biological manufacturing, and research purposes—although sometimes at the cost of a significant risk in safety. Moreover, the steady expansion of civil biotechnology, food processing, and pharmaceutical activities makes dual-use equipment commercially available that can be used to produce even the most advanced biological agents, and a combination of Iran's use of covert purchasing networks and steadily weakening controls—particularly over used and surplus equipment—has further weakened already weak export control efforts.

A HISTORY OF UNCERTAIN JUDGMENTS AND INDICATORS

There have been reports that Iran has had biological weapons programs ever since the first years of the Iran-Iraq War. For example, U.S. officials began to provide background briefings in 1982 that Iran had imported suitable type cultures from Europe and was working on the production of mycotoxins—a relatively simple family of biological agents that require only limited laboratory facilities for small-scale production. One of the first research facilities was established in 1986 under the Pasteur Institute of Iran, and around the same time a similar research program on producing myotoxins began at Vira Laboratory.

Many experts believed that an Iranian biological weapons effort had been placed under the control of the Islamic Revolutionary Guards Corps (IRGC), whose elements and subsidiaries are known to have tried to purchase some equipment that could be used for the development and production of such weapons.

Actual Programs or Potential Capability

A long chronology of reports surfaced from 1982 onward, many in the form of official, unofficial, and opposition group background briefings. For example, U.S. and British intelligence sources reported in August 1989 that Iran was trying to buy two new strains of fungus from Canada and the Netherlands that can be used to produce mycotoxins. German sources indicated that Iran had successfully purchased such cultures several years earlier.

Some universities and research centers were linked to the biological weapons program. The Imam Reza Medical Center at Mashhad University of Medical Sciences and the Iranian Research Organization for Science and Technology were identified as the end users for this purchasing effort, but it is likely that the true end user was an Iranian government agency specializing in biological warfare.

These reports intensified in the early 1990s, after the post–Gulf War discovery of Iraq's massive biological weapons (BWs) program. It is not clear, however, whether these reports describe real or potential activities and whether the increase in reports since the early 1990s was the result of increases in Iranian activity or the assumption that Iran either had paralleled Iraq's efforts or was reacting to their disclosure.

Reports surfaced in the spring of 1993 that Iran had succeeded in obtaining advanced biological weapons technology in Switzerland and containment equipment and technology from Germany. According to these reports, this led to serious damage to computer facilities in a Swiss biological research facility by unidentified agents. Similar reports indicated that agents had destroyed German biocontainment equipment destined for Iran. More credible reports by U.S. experts indicate that Iran might have begun to stockpile anthrax and botulinum in a facility near Tabriz, can now mass manufacture such agents, and has them in an aerosol form. None of these reports, however, can be verified.

As is the case with chemical weapons, the fact some reports were relatively specific did not mean that they proved to be accurate. But Iran does have increasingly sophisticated industries, and its sophisticated research facilities and universities could easily serve as a front for illicit BW activities and offer legitimate excuses for dual-use imports, as was the case in Iraq prior to 1990. It can also be reasonably assessed that except for Pakistan, Iran is the most advanced nation in the Muslim world in the production and use of industrial chemicals and biotechnology. All of this information compounds the uncertainties and ambiguities associated with Tehran's biological warfare intentions and capabilities.

Uncertain and Ambiguous Intelligence Judgments

Once again, U.S. and other official intelligence reporting has been so summary in form, and so ambiguous or contradictory in character, that one must be as cautious about whether Iran has an effort as cautious about the dangers such an effort can pose. The U.S. intelligence community has always limited its unclassified judgments to summary statements. Some have been little more than repetitions of past statements. Others have had serious potential contradictions.

For example, the Central Intelligence Agency (CIA) reported in 1996, "We believe that Iran holds some stocks of biological agents and weapons. Tehran probably has investigated both toxins and live organisms as biological warfare agents. Iran has the technical infrastructure to support a significant biological weapons program with little foreign assistance." It also reported that Iran has "sought dual-use biotech equipment from Europe and Asia, ostensibly for civilian use," and that Iran might be ready to deploy biological weapons.[1] Beyond this point, little unclassified information exists regarding the details of Iran's effort to "weaponize" and produce biological weapons.

Iran continued to deny that it had such programs, but its imports continued to raise intelligence concerns. Iran again announced in June 1997 that it would not produce or employ chemical weapons including biological toxins. However, the CIA reported in June 1997 that Iran had obtained new dual-use technology from China and India during 1996.

At the same time, one element of the U.S. government did not always seem to be talking to another, and some statements by given intelligence agencies became self-contradictory over time. In 1997, the U.S. Department of Defense (DOD) asserted that the Iranian biological warfare program "is in the research and development stage, [but] the Iranians have considerable expertise with pharmaceuticals, as well as the commercial and military infrastructure needed to produce basic biological warfare agents."[2]

The CIA reported in January 1999 that Iran continued to pursue dual-use biotechnical equipment from Russia and other countries, ostensibly for civilian uses. Its BW program began during the Iran-Iraq War, and Iran may have some limited capability for BW deployment. Outside assistance is both important and difficult to prevent, given the dual-use nature of the materials and equipment being sought and the many legitimate end uses for these items.

The Department of State updated its findings in 2001 as follows:

> Iran has a growing biotechnology industry, significant pharmaceutical experience and the overall infrastructure to support its biological warfare program. Tehran has expanded its efforts to seek considerable dual-use biotechnical materials and expertise from entities in Russia and elsewhere, ostensibly for civilian reasons. Outside assistance is important for Iran, and it is also difficult to prevent because of the dual-use nature of the materials and equipment being sought by Iran and the many legitimate end uses for these items.
>
> Iran's biological warfare program began during the Iran-Iraq war. Iran is believed to be pursuing offensive biological warfare capabilities and its effort may have evolved beyond agent research and development to the capability to produce small quantities of agent. Iran has ratified the BWC [Biological Weapons Convention].[3]

A detailed chronology prepared by the Nuclear Threat Initiative (NTI) shows that the Department of State has announced sanctions on 13 foreign companies and individuals under the Iran Nonproliferation Act of 2000 for transferring items that could be used in chemical weapons, biological weapons, or long-range missile programs.[4] The CIA reported in 2004 that "even though Iran is part of the Biological Weapons Convention (BWC), Tehran probably maintained an offensive BW program. Iran continued to seek dual-use biotechnical materials, equipment, and expertise that could be used in Tehran's BW program. Iran probably has the capability to produce at least small quantities of BW agents."[5]

In 2006, Lieutenant General Michael D. Maples, Director of the Defense Intelligence Agency (DIA), stated, "We believe that Iran maintains offensive chemical and biological weapons capabilities in various stages of development."[6] That same year, a CIA report to Congress stated, "As of 2004, the status of Iran's biotechnology infrastructure indicated that at a minimum, Iran probably had the capability to produce at least small quantities of BW agents for offensive purposes. Iran continued to seek dual-use biotechnology materials, equipment, and expertise that is consistent with its growing legitimate biotechnology industry but could benefit Tehran's BW program."[7]

Lieutenant General Maples modified his judgment in 2007 in ways that stressed that Iran might have a biological program, but he did not state that it did: "Iran has a growing biotechnology industry, significant pharmaceutical experience and the overall infrastructure that could be used to support a biological warfare program. DIA believes Iran is pursuing development of biological weapons."[8] He repeated a statement with these qualifications again in 2008: "Tehran continues to seek dual-use biotechnical materials, equipment and expertise which have legitimate uses, but also could enable ongoing biological warfare efforts."[9]

J. Michael McConnell, then Director of National Intelligence, provided a somewhat different interpretation in his comments, which implied that Iran had had an active program but might no longer have one: "We assess that Iran has previously conducted offensive BW agent research and development. Iran continues to seek dual-use technologies that could be used for biological warfare."[10]

The U.S. Office of the Director of National Intelligence (ODNI) provided yet another view in its "Unclassified Report to Congress on the Acquisition of Technology Relating to Weapons of Mass Destruction and Advanced Conventional Munitions, 1 January–31 December 2005." This report was issued in March 2008, lagging years behind the normal reporting date. It stated, "As of 2005, the status of its [Iran's] biotechnology infrastructure indicated that at a minimum, Iran probably had the capability to produce at least small quantities of biological warfare (BW) agents for offensive purposes. Iran continued to seek dual-use biotechnology materials, equipment, and expertise that are consistent with its growing legitimate biotechnology industry but could benefit Tehran's assessed probable BW program."[11]

Oddly enough, ODNI released its update of the same report for the period January 1–December 31, 2006, at virtually the same time, and this report stated, "Our assessment of Iran's biotechnology infrastructure indicates that Iran probably has the capability to produce large-quantities of some Biological Warfare (BW) agents for offensive purposes, if it made the decision to do so. Iran continues to seek dual-use biotechnology materials, equipment, and expertise consistent with its growing legitimate biotechnology industry but these components could also advance Tehran's BW capability."[12]

As is the case for U.S. intelligence reporting on chemical weapons and nuclear weapons, the U.S. intelligence community seems to find it extraordinarily difficult to decide exactly what it is trying to communicate. It simply is not clear whether such statements reflect any knowledge that there was or is an actual program and whether the judgments involved reflect suspicion, potential capability, a strong probability, or a fact.

Continued Iranian Denials

As might be expected, Iran continued to deny that it had biological weapons programs. It also continued to be a party to the BWC, which Iran signed in 1972, ratified in 1973, and went into force on March 25, 1975. Iran has not, however, provided full disclosure of two statements under the BWC: A-2, the Declaration of national biological defense research and development programs, and F, the Declaration of Past activities in offensive/defense biological research and development programs.[13]

Work by the NTI shows that the Iranian position has not changed in recent years.[14] For example, the Iranian delegation issued a statement in July 2004 as part of the preparations for the Second Meeting of the States Parties to the BWC in Geneva in December 2004: "Although the BWC lacks a verification mechanism, we do believe that assigning security and politically oriented responsibilities, such as investigation of suspicious cases of use of biological weapons, to certain international organizations such as WHO [World Health Organization], puts the humanitarian and fundamental objectives and mandate of these organizations in jeopardy." In regard to the issue of alleged use of biological or toxin weapons; "even though according to the Geneva Protocol of 1925, the 'Use' is prohibited, but [. . .] regrettably some States Parties have still kept their reservations to that effect, that is keeping the right of retaliation for any case of use against them."[15]

Several weeks later, however, the chairman of the Iranian Supreme National Security Council Foreign Policy Committee, Seyyed Hoseyn Musavian, stated that Iran had taken defensive measures against chemical, biological, and nuclear attacks since the Iran-Iraq War. He also said that the Ministry of Defense and Armed Forces Logistics is responsible for enforcement of the policy.[16] Later that year, an officer in the IRGC was also quoted as saying that a military exercise, "Ashura-5," showed that Iranian armed forces could operate even against invaders equipped with "the most destructive bacteriological and chemical weapons."[17] These statements are important because the only way to develop defenses against biological agents is to do research using biological weapons, and the only way to create defenses against advanced militarized agents is to possess them.

Iranian officials responded by continuing to deny that Iran had biological weapons, and they have criticized other countries for their lack of transparency and compliance with the terms and spirit of the BWC. They also, however, continued to describe control regimes such as the Australia List and other export controls as ineffective.

For example, in August 2007, the Iranian representative to the Biological Weapons Convention Meeting of Experts in Geneva, Switzerland, warned about the lack of any legally binding compliance mechanism:

[T]he Fifth and Sixth Review Conferences decided by consensus on the follow-up mechanism aiming at promotion of common understanding among the States Parties with the hope that real multilateralism would be revived and the negotiations on the Protocol on strengthening the Convention would be resumed in a foreseeable future. We strongly believe that the present follow-up mechanism which is of limited scope and nature cannot be considered as a substitute to afore-mentioned negotiations.[18]

Other countries' governments and intelligence services also raised questions about Iran's efforts, although they have not been as explicit in making summary judgments. For example, in February 2005, the German Customs Office of Criminal Investigations (ZKA) reported that Iran is engaged in biological weapons programs being conducted "in small laboratories of universities, strictly guarded from the outside world." The ZKA also observed that "Iran has long-standing experience in the field of bio-technology so that is has the necessary know-how for operating biological combat agent programs."[19]

In September 2006, the United Kingdom's Department of Trade and Industry issued an updated list of Iranian entities that had raised concern that they might be developing weapons of mass destruction, and that had been denied licensed exports. These included the Amir Kabir University of Technology, M/S Iran Electromotor, and Oil Industries Engineering and Construction, aka LG/OIEC/IOEC. At least one was suspect for biological activities.[20]

A 2006 staff report by a subcommittee of the House Intelligence Committee just further adds to the complexity of assessing Iran's chemical and biological weapons (CBW) programs. In the report the subcommittee complained that the intelligence regarding potential Iranian chemical and biological weapons was "neither voluminous nor conclusive,"[21] while the U.S. intelligence reports concluded that "Iran likely is pursuing chemical and biological weapons."[22]

The available open-source information from the Iranian Science and Technology Group neither proves nor disproves the allegations that have been made regarding its biological research and suspected weaponization programs. The ambiguity and uncertainty of intelligence judgments have made it increasingly difficult to assess the true nature of Iran's biotechnology programs.

Opposition Claims

Most NGOs do not go beyond describing Iran's potential programs and capabilities. At least one Iranian opposition group, however, has made very detailed claims. The National Council of Resistance of Iran has long been a major source of information and misinformation on Iran's weapons of mass destruction (WMD) efforts. It provided the following description of Iran's programs in a press conference at the Willard Hotel in Washington, D.C., on May 15, 2003:

> The activities of the clerical regime with respect to acquiring biological weapons began in 1985, during the Iran-Iraq War. In 1985 and 1986, the regime established a secret research complex in Teheran's Pasteur Institute to work on toxic fungus and microbial substances.
>
> The center succeeded in producing toxic fungus, including aflatoxin. At the same time, similar research was being undertaken at Vira Laboratory under the supervision of Mr. Gholamhossein Riazi. In subsequent years, as the regime succeeded in mass production of microbial material, it moved the production centers to a military facility. Centers such as Pasteur Institute are now being used for research purposes.
>
> Under then-President Rafsanjani, these activities took on new dimensions in the 1990s. The regime originally imported fermenters from European countries, particularly France and Switzerland. Due to international restrictions and major needs on the part of the regime, domestic production of fermenters was put on the agenda.
>
> In June 2001, a plan called Comprehensive National Microbial Defense Plan was adopted by the Supreme National Security Council chaired by Khatami. A senior cleric,

Hassan Rowhani, the SNSC secretary, personally pursued the implementation of this plan and reported directly to Khamenei, the supreme leader.

In addition to the principal members, the relevant ministers and competent officials from the armed forces command headquarters also took part in that SNSC meeting. The Comprehensive National Plan for Microbial Defense is prepared in four pages and kept in the secretariat of the SNSC [Iran's Supreme National Security Council]. It contains an introduction and specific task of each ministry.

On the basis of this plan, the biological weapons capacity of the regime must be increased three-fold in the next two years. The biological weapons activities are centered around the following elements: Anthrax, produced at the Revolutionary Guard Imam Hussein University in Teheran; next, aflatoxin, also produced at the Imam Hussein University; production of microbial bombs using anthrax; production of microbial bombs using smallpox virus; production of microbial bombs using typhoid fever; production of microbial bombs using high dosage of aflotoxin; production of microbial bombs using plague microbes; production of microbial bombs using chloromicrobes.

Genetic cloning or alteration is being carried out at Malek Ashtar University, which is headed by Maqsudi, the head of Center for Scientific and Growth Technology.

Agencies involved in the plan: The Armed Forces Command headquarters, the Ministry of Defense, the Revolutionary Guard Joint Command headquarters, the Revolutionary Guard Imam Hussein University and Ministry of Intelligence and Security are involved in acquiring and stockpiling of microbial weaponry.

New warhead directorate. A senior Revolutionary Guards commander, Nasser Toqyani, is in charge of the directorate pursuing weapons of mass destruction in the Armed Forces Command headquarters. He is coordinating the biological activities of all relevant organs. Major General Hassan Firouzabadi, the chairman of the Joint Command headquarters, takes part in these meetings.

Special chemical, biological and nuclear industries in the Ministry of Defense. A special organization dubbed Special Chemical, Biological and Nuclear Industries has been set up in the Ministry of Defense. This entity is also involved in chemical and biological activity. Brigadier General Seyyedi is in charge of this organization. His predecessor was named Dr. Abbass-pour, who had been appointed by Rafsanjani.

This organization is in charge of arming the regime with microbial and chemical bombs and has been strengthened during Khatami's presidency. The organization is also responsible for procuring technological needs of microbial and chemical weapons as well as chemical and microbial bombs.

A number of foreign microbial weapons experts from China, North Korea, India, and Russia are cooperating with the Ministry of Defense of the Iranian regime. A number of them have been hired by this organization. The Biological Research Center of Special Industries Organization is located at Shahid Meisami, Martyr Meisami complex on Special Karaj Highway, 27 kilometers near the steel factory.

During the Khatami's presidency, the Ministry of Defense formed a new biological weapons center to expand biological bomb. That was called Malek Ashtar University and is based in Lavizan Shian Technological Research Center.

Dr. Maqsudi heads this center, which is the most important research center for biological WMD. Imam Hussein University has been a bio-technology section which works on microbial bombs with aflatoxin. Major investments have been made in this university to acquire weapons of mass destruction, including chemical, biological and missile warheads.

Students are given foreign scholarships to study abroad and use western technology. The Revolutionary Guards' Baqiyatollah Research Center, affiliated with the Guards' Baqitollah Hospital, is another Revolutionary Guard Baqiyatollah center which works on microbial bombs.

Dr. Karami is the head of this center. He's a member of the Guard Corps Imam Hussein University scientific staff and has been working on biological weapons for 18 years. He is also a member of the national body of Biological Weapons Disarmament Convention and travels to Geneva regularly.

The Revolutionary Guards Joint Command headquarters has started new activities dealing with microbial weaponry. Brigadier General Abroumand is heading the activities and organized them in different committees.

At the Ministry of Intelligence, the directorate to access weapons of mass destruction is run by Asgari. Its task is to steal foreign technology on WMD, especially biological weapons. The directorate has planted its spies on foreign countries.

Next, the Research Center for Direct Biotechnology is headed by San'ati. This center does not directly work on microbial bombs, but it's used as the research supplement for biological weapons and actively works with Malek Ashtar and Imam Hussein University, as well as the Guards' Baqiyatollah Biological Research Center.

Experts. On the basis of the decisions reached by the Supreme National Security Council, the regime intends to increase the number of experts in biological field from current 3,000 to 11,000 in the coming years. Dr. Maqsudi, head of Centers for Science and Technological Growth of the Biological Research Center of Malek Ashtar, affiliated with the defense industries, are in charge of mass production of biological weapons.

Dr. Mirza'i. He supervises all Defense Ministry plans on biological weapons. He has been active in this field since the 1980s.

Dr. Hossein San'ati. He is the head of the National Center for Genetic Technology and Growth Technology. He has been working on biological weapons since the war and, along with Mirza'i and Karami, are known as the architect of the regime microbial bombs. San'ati has allocated the capabilities of the National Center for Genetic Technology and Growth Technology to the development of microbial bomb and is using this center as cover.

Gholamhossein Rizai. He is among the founders of the regime's weapons-of-mass-destruction program. Due to his age, he has become the dean of the university, but actively advises the regime.

Dr. Mirza Khalil Bahmani. He has been working on defensive and offensive plans at Imam Hussein University.

Dr. Toula'i. He is an expert on biotechnology and works at the Ministry of Defense and Biological Research Center at Imam Hussein University.

. . . in addition . . . the Sina Industry, SINA, Sina Industry, that are concentrated on production of the biological materials . . . The head of this Sina Industry is Dr. Yousefi. This is a center that was previously named Vira Laboratories—Vira Laboratories. This is one of the most important biological and chemical laboratories of the Iranian regime. This basically was used as a front, as a cover for doing their research and their activities on biological weapons under the cover and the name of medical research.

In this center, the Sina Industry Center, the microbial tests are done on animals. This is a center that has been active since the early '90s. The previous head of this laboratory was Dr. Riazi, Gholamhossein Riazi. You mentioned the name earlier. And his deputy was Dr. Yousefi, who is now heading the Sina Industry.

During the time of presidency of Khatami, obviously the regime has escalated their efforts in the field of weapons of mass destruction, particularly in the field of biological weapons. And as a result, the organizational structure of the Defense Ministry went through significant changes to be able to comply with the rising demands of Iranian regime in this field. And they formed—they call it Special Industry Group headed by a brigadier general whose name is—the Revolutionary Guards' brigadier general, Farmanesh, F-A-R-M-A- N-E-S-H. So that's the purpose.

Now, what they do in the Special Industry Group, which deals with different aspects of what they need for their biological weapons program, and depending on the issue and the subject, they have distributed the work in different centers and industrial places in the country. I give you—I name a few for you.

One is the Milad Industry, M-I-L-A-D, Milad Industry that is located in Mard-Abad. The second one is called Be'ethat Industry, Be'ethat Industry, which is located in the city of Qom. And the next one is Sard-Shimi Industry or Sard Chemical Industry, which is located in Shiraz, which is located in the central part of the country.

The next one is Raja-Shimi Industry, which is located in Malard, near Karaj, which is west of Teheran.

The next one is Shahid Salehi Industry, which is also located in the city of Qom.

Next is the Shahid Meysami Industry that Ms. Samsami referred to earlier, which is located close to Karaj; and then the Sina Industry itself, which is located in Karaj, and then the Valasr Industry, Valasr Industry, that is located in Teheran.

. . . Dr. Yousefi, given the extensive many years of working first under Dr. Riazi and then in other parts, he has really concentrated and moved all the experience he had had to this Sina Industry now. In other words, the Sina Industry is now a consolidation or concentration of all the experiences that the regime had built over the years, both in biological and chemical weapons program.[23]

The practical problem with such statements is that the Middle East is filled with extremely detailed conspiracy claims that cannot be validated. The National Council also is affiliated with the Mujahadin-e Khalq (MEK), a group with a history of attacking and killing Americans during the time of the Shah (Mohammad Reza Shah Pahlavi), conducting terrorist operations during the power struggles after his fall, and of acting as an Iraqi proxy to oppose the regime for Saddam Hussein. The MEK has also been designated as a terrorist organization by the U.S. Department of State.[24] At the same time, past reporting has sometimes proved to be accurate in regard to Iran's missile programs, as well as Iran's nuclear program. The National Council's claims cannot be trusted, but they also cannot be dismissed.

SUSPECT ORGANIZATIONS AND FACILITIES

As is the case with Iran's chemical, nuclear, and missile facilities, various sources cite so many different organizations and facilities as being linked to Iran's biological weapons efforts that it is impossible to determine the credibility of any given source —if any are credible. The sheer volume of information and the detail do not mean that reports are accurate. Iranian opposition groups, and some U.S. and Israeli groups, have virtually made an industry out of making such claims.

The Federation of American Scientists, GlobalSecurity.org, the Monterrey Institute, and the Nuclear Threat Initiative have all done more balanced and objective work in compiling such lists. The NTI list of Iranian institutions that may be involved in Iran's biological weapons program makes a good case study, and one that could just as easily have been used to explain the list of possible chemical weapons facilities in the previous chapter. The NTI list includes the following:[25]

- Amir Kabir University of Technology
- Biotechnology Institute of the Iranian Research Organization for Science and Technology
- Damghan
- Institute for Pestilence and Plant Disease Research
- Institute for Plant and Seed Modification Research
- Iranian Research Organization for Science and Technology (IROST)
- National Research Center of Genetic Engineering and Biotechnology (NRCGEB)
- Pasteur Institute
- Persian Type Culture Collection (PTCC)
- Razi Institute for Serums and Vaccines
- Research Center of the Construction Crusade (Jihad-e Sazandegi)
- Science and Technology Group
- Sharif University of Technology Biochemical and Bioenvironmental Engineering Research Center
- Special Industries Organization (SIO)
- Tehran University Institute for Biochemistry and Biosphysics Research (IBB)
- Vira Laboratory

It is important to note, however, that the NTI and other NGOs make it clear that most of the institutions listed have the capability to contribute to a biological weapons program, rather than a proven track record of action. Moreover, the reason that many are listed is that hard-line opposition groups have made charges that have never been confirmed by other reporting. For example, the Persian Type Culture Center is listed largely because it maintains a stockpile of type cultures of various diseases. In practice, a weapons development center might well obtain more lethal cultures in the field or from a patient.

Iranian opposition groups have been far more categorical in identifying such facilities. The National Council of Resistance of Iran has identified Amir Kabir University of Technology in Tehran as a potential center for Iran's programs. The

University could play such a role. It has the first major biomedical engineering department in Iran, which was established in October 1993. It has graduate programs in bioelectrics, biomaterials, and biomechanics, and its biomaterials laboratory has all of the specialties needed to go from biological research to designing and testing the production of weaponized agents. The National Council of Resistance of Iran also claims that it has been used as a cover for purchasing dual-use equipment. It also has a mutual scientific cooperation agreement with Damascus University.[26]

Once again, however, these reports cannot be verified, and the long lists of institutions that various NGOs indicate *might* be linked to biological weapons efforts becomes far shorter if one considers only those institutions that are specifically tied to the Iranian military and to actual biological weapon activities. The NTI, for example, includes four such institutions that appear in the previous list:

- *Damghan:* A facility in or near the city of Damghan located some 375 miles to the southwest of Mashad, or 300 kilometers east of Teheran. It is claimed to be a biological weapons research center under the control of the Islamic Revolutionary Guard Corps, to have been set up with Russian assistance, and to be near a similar facility for chemical weapons research. U.S. intelligence sources have mentioned this facility in the past, but no recent mention has occurred.[27]

- *Engineering Research Center of the Construction Crusade, Jihad e-Sazandegi, Jahaad-e Saazandegi, Construction Jihad, Jahad-e Sazandegi, and Jahad; also Jahad Engineering Research Center, Jahad Sazandegi Research Center. Tehran:* According to NTI and the National Council of Resistance of Iran, the Ministry of Jihad-e Sazandegi (Ministry of Construction Crusade and Ministry of Construction Jihad) has 12 divisions and research centers in 20 provinces. It has four affiliated research institutes in the cities of Isfahan, Shiraz, Tabriz, and Mashad that are involved in biological weapons research and production. It should be noted that the Construction Crusade is more a construction group than a research or production group. The National Council of Resistance of Iran claims, however, that the Construction Crusade was affiliated with the Islamic Revolutionary Guards Corps (IRGC) during the Iran-Iraq War, was originally supposed to be part of the Defense Ministry, but was established separately by IRGC Minister Muhsin Rafiqdust to avoid detection.[28]

- *Vira Laboratory, Teheran:* The National Council of Resistance of Iran claims that Vira is the chemical laboratory of the Defense Ministry's Special Industries Organization and worked on research, testing, and production of chemical and biological warfare–related materials. Some sources claim it has worked on bioagents designed to contaminate soil and affect agriculture.[29]

- *Science and Technology Group (STG), Mahsa Building, Teheran:* The National Council of Resistance (NCR) of Iran claims that STG provides broad oversight for all of Iran's weapons of mass destruction programs. It stays that it "oversees the regime's plans and projects in the area of biological, nuclear, and chemical weapons." It also claims that it

  ○ Formed the Revolutionary Guards' 24th Bessat Brigade for Chemical Attacks
  ○ Stockpiled huge quantities of nerve agents

- ○ Expanded biotechnology research centers and the NBC (Nuclear, Biological, Chemical) Special Industries Organization
- ○ Hired Chinese, Korean, and Russian experts under cover of research projects, and
- ○ Procured the required materials and technology from European countries through the use of dual-use technology
- The NCR has also claimed that the STG oversees four major efforts: the Defense Ministry's Special Industries Organization, the Jihad Construction Research Center, the Revolutionary Guards' study center at the Imam Hoseyn University, and the Biotechnology Research Center. The National Council of Resistance on Iran reports that in only one branch of the STG, the regime has already developed three biological agents—VX (though in fact a chemical agent), aflatoxin, and *Bacillus anthracis*—with the help of at least 18 Russian, Chinese, and Korean experts.[30]

What is clear is that Iran has become a country with a relatively advanced base in biotechnology, which has extensive laboratory and research capability, and steadily improving industrial facilities with dual-use production capabilities with all of the equipment necessary to produce wet and dry storable biological weapons. Iran's biological weapons research and production programs are scattered among a number of sites, many of which are at university laboratories. This creates an ambiguity that cannot be resolved by either U.S. claims or Iranian denials, and this is a problem with most current known and potential proliferators.

Many nations now have the biotechnology, the industrial base, and the technical expertise to acquire biological weapons. Not only does most civil technology have "dual use" in building weapons, but the global dissemination of biological equipment has made control by supplier nations extremely difficult. Even when such controls do still apply to original sellers, they have little or no impact on the sellers of used equipment, and a wide range of sensitive equipment is now available for sale to any buyer on the Internet or to any purchasing effort that closely examines the used and surplus equipment sold or disposed of by university and commercial laboratories.

This makes it almost impossible to disprove a nation's interest in biological weapons. Moreover, there is little meaningful distinction between a "defensive" and an "offensive" capability. Nations can claim to be conducting defensive research, acquiring key gear for defensive purposes, and practicing defensive training and maneuvers.

REQUIRED TECHNOLOGY AND MANUFACTURING CAPABILITY AND THE UNCERTAIN ROLE OF OUTSIDE SUPPLIERS

The world market in biotechnology, food processing, pharmaceutical, and other related equipment has grown so large, has so many dual-use items, and has such weak controls that it is impossible to know what Iran has purchased and is purchasing, and from whom Iran is purchasing such items from. What is clear is that Iran has been able to develop a relatively advanced base in biotechnology and is advancing in its ability to use its dual use biotechnology infrastructure to produce and store biological weapons.

Iran was able to enlist plenty of help in acquiring biotechnology and know-how in the early 1990s. The fall of the Soviet Union—which had been involved in extensive WMD research, development, and production throughout the Cold War—left many unemployed Russian scientists looking for new clients. Tehran was able to lure many of these unemployed scientists with knowledge and experience in weaponizing deadly toxins to its program with its abundant reserve of petrodollars.

According to former Soviet scientists, several military biologists were recruited by Iran throughout the 1990s. A *Sunday Times* (London) article in August 1995 reported that "by hiring Russian biological weapons experts, Iran had made a quantum leap forward in its biological weapons program."[31]

In testimony to the U.S. Senate Committee on Foreign Relations, John A. Lauder, the Director of the Nonproliferation Center at the CIA, asserted the following in 2000:

> Iran is seeking expertise and technology from Russia that could advance Tehran's biological warfare effort. Russia has several government-to-government agreements with Iran in a variety of scientific and technical fields.
>
> —Because of the dual-use nature of much of this technology, Tehran can exploit these agreements to procure equipment and expertise that could be diverted to its BW effort.
>
> —Iran's BW program could make rapid and significant advances if it has unfettered access to BW expertise resident in Russia.[32]

The CIA has continued to provide virtually the same assessments of sales and technology transfer over time. For example, it reported in November 2003, "Even though Iran is part of the BWC, Tehran probably maintained an offensive BW program. Iran continued to seek dual-use biotechnical materials, equipment, and expertise. While such materials had legitimate uses, Iran's biological warfare (BW) program also could have benefited from them. It is likely that Iran has capabilities to produce small quantities of BW agents, but has a limited ability to weaponize them."[33]

John R. Bolton, then Under Secretary for Arms Control and International Security at the U.S. Department of State, provided a more detailed version of such views in testifying the following to the House International Relations Committee in 2004:

> The U.S. Intelligence Community stated in its recent 721 Report that, "Tehran probably maintains an offensive BW program. Iran continued to seek dual-use biotechnical materials, equipment, and expertise. While such materials had legitimate uses, Iran's biological warfare (BW) program also could have benefited from them. It is likely that Iran has capabilities to produce small quantities of BW agents, but has a limited ability to weaponize them."
>
> Because BW programs are easily concealed, I cannot say that the United States can prove beyond a shadow of a doubt that Iran has an offensive BW program. The

intelligence I have seen suggests that this is the case, and, as a policy matter therefore, I believe we have to act on that assumption. The risks to international peace and security from such programs are too great to wait for irrefutable proof of illicit activity: responsible members of the international community should act to head off such threats and demand transparency and accountability from suspected violators while these threats are still emerging. It would be folly indeed to wait for the threat fully to mature before trying to stop it.

Iran is a party to the Biological Weapons Convention (BWC) and the 1925 Protocol for the Prohibition of the Use in War of Asphyxiating, Poisonous or Other Gases, and of Bacteriological Methods of Warfare. Like the CWC [Chemical Weapons Convention], the central obligation of the BWC is simple: no possession, no development no production and, together with the 1925 Protocol, no use of biological weapons. The overwhelming majority of States Parties abide by these obligations. We believe Iran is not abiding by its BWC obligations, however, and we have made this abundantly clear to the parties of this treaty. It is time for Iran to declare its biological weapons program and make arrangements for its dismantlement.[34]

This creates a level of ambiguity that cannot be resolved by either U.S. claims or Iranian denials, and this is a problem with characterizing the efforts of most current known and potential proliferators. Many nations now have the biotechnology, the industrial base, and the technical expertise to acquire biological weapons.

Development and proliferation is made much easier because of the dual-use nature of many of the components necessary for a biological weapons program. According to multiple reports, Chinese, Russian, North Korean, Swiss, Indian, Dutch, German, Italian, Cuba, and Spanish companies—among others—have all provided Iran with biotechnological components and dual-use biological agents that may well have since been incorporated into its biological weapons program.

It is clear, however, that Russia has been a key source of biotechnology for Iran. No U.S. official has ever indicated that Russia has deliberately supplied Iran with technology or equipment for a biological weapons effort. However, Russia's world-leading expertise in biological weapons makes it a particularly attractive target for Iranians seeking technical information and training on BW agent production processes. This has led to speculation that Iran may have the production technology to make dry storable and aerosol weapons. This would allow it to develop suitable missile warheads, bombs, and covert devices.

POSSIBLE BIOLOGICAL AGENTS AND CBW WARFIGHTING CAPABILITY

These factors make it almost impossible to know how Iran may use any capabilities it is developing or does possess. They also create a situation where if Iran has developed agents for defensive purposes, it also has a relatively rapid "breakout" capability to produce offensive agents. Iraq, for example, showed it could rapidly convert a pharmaceutical plant to anthrax production several decades ago, although there is no clear way to determine how lethal its agents would have been.

Potential Threats

It is impossible to know what biological agents Iran might actually have weaponized, if only for defensive purposes. Over the years, various sources have cited a range of different possible agents. These included anthrax, a botulin toxin, other biotoxins, hoof and mouth disease, Marburg, plague, smallpox, and tularemia. All of these are biological weapons that Iran has long had the technological and manufacturing capability to weaponize, but none has yet been described as having had known tests, as having actually been weaponized, or having been deployed with Iranian forces. Iran also has a sufficiently developed technology base so that it could develop advanced biological agents and weapons and could take advantage of a variety of ways of producing far more lethal weapons than were available during the Cold War.

Figure 6.1 provides a summary overview of some of the agents Iran might use. It draws upon a study by the Chemical and Biological Arms Control Institute that estimates the impact of a line source attack using 50 kilograms of agent along a two-kilometer line upwind of a population center of 500,000.[35]

There are no empirical data to base such estimates upon, and they are little more than "guesstimates."[36] It also is not clear that Iran would use a single agent. Most U.S. and former Soviet Union (FSU) planning for biological warfare during the Cold War called for a mix of biological agents to be used—so-called "biological cocktails." At least some study was given to mixes that would create a focus on the first source of lethality and lead to the wrong response. Other attacks modeled the use of one biological agent to greatly increase the lethality of another. The modeling of simultaneous and sequential attacks with one agent is uncertain enough, but there are no rules that say a sophisticated terrorist group, or one aided by a state actor, could not use similar "cocktails."

Iran might also attack livestock and agriculture. Annual accidental "attacks" on American agriculture in the form of inadvertent transfers of new pests, diseases, etc., are the rule rather than the exception and have often had a major impact. Such

Figure 6.1   Area Coverage and Casualty Impact of Different Types of Biological Attack

Agent	Downwind Area Kilometers	Number of Casualties Dead	Incapacitated
Rift Valley Fever	1	400	35,000
Tick-Borne Encephalitis	1	9,500	35,000
Typhus	5	19,000	85,000
Brucellosis	10	500	125,000
Q Fever	20+	150	125,000
Tularemia	20+	30,000	125,000
Anthrax	20+	95,000	125,000

Note: Assumes 50 kilograms of agent along a two-kilometer line upwind of a population center of 500,000.

Source: George Christopher et al., "Biological Warfare: A Historical Perspective," *Journal of the American Medical Association* 278, no. 5 (August 6, 1997).

attacks have consisted of importing the wrong pet, diseases brought in the form of a few infected animals or plants, and insects and parasites that have arrived on birds, aircraft, cars, and ships. These have all had a major impact on given crops and have affected the ecology of whole states, particularly in the southern and western United States and Hawaii.

What is clear is that Iran should be able to deploy weapons with at least the lethality that militarized anthrax had reached during the Cold War. Figure 6.2 illustrates typical estimates of how the lethality of such weapons compares to the chemical weapons discussed in the previous chapter. It is clear that such biological weapons *could* be as or more lethal than the fission nuclear weapons Iran is likely to be able to acquire within the next half decade. Unlike radiological and chemical weapons, biological weapons can be true weapons of mass destruction.

Anthrax as a Case Study

The attacks analyzed by the OTA in Figure 6.2 assumed the use of highly advanced, weaponized, dry storable, and coated anthrax powder of precisely the right particle size, and like many studies of the day, ignored many of the major uncertainties affecting the real-world lethality of biological weapons. There is little doubt that Iran has the technology base to achieve at least this level of sophistication, but the data do assume a worst-case scenario in terms of the lethality of such attacks. Even though anthrax qualifies as the most studied biological weapon, the effectiveness of any given weaponization of the agent is impossible to simulate or test even by limited use of human subjects. It can be determined only when it is actually used, and its real-world lethality could range from negligible to catastrophic.[37]

While Iraq produced over 8,000 liters of concentrated anthrax solution before the Gulf War, there is little practical experience with anthrax as a human disease. Only 18 cases of inhalation have been recorded in the United States from 1900 to 1978, two of which were the result of laboratory experiments. In contrast, some 2,000 cases of cutaneous anthrax are reported each year, a total of 224 cases were reported in the United States during 1944–1994, and some 10,000 people died during an epidemic in Zimbabwe between 1979 and 1985. This helps explain why estimates of the lethality of weaponized inhalational anthrax have to be based on primate data, and why the range of uncertainty for a lethal dose of a 1–5 microns of dry agent ranges from 2,500 to 55,500 spores.[38] The Department of Defense *Medical NBC Battlebook* does not give lethality data per se, but shows a range of 8,000–50,000 spores for an infective dose.[39]

Unlike nuclear weapons, a weapon such as anthrax also is not a prompt killing mechanism and creates large uncertainties over detection and treatment. The Soviet experience with a biological weapons accident in Sverdlovsk showed that cases occurred over a period of 2 to 43 days after exposure. Primate data indicate that weaponized spores retained lethal effects for at least 58 to 98 days after exposure, and spores can last for years or decades in a natural environment.

Figure 6.2   Comparative Effects of Biological, Chemical, and Nuclear Weapons Delivered against a Typical Urban Target

Using missile warheads: Assumes one Scud-sized warhead with a maximum payload of 1,000 kilograms. The study assumes that the biological agent would not make maximum use of this payload capability because this is inefficient. It is unclear whether this is realistic.

	Area Covered in Square Kilometers	Deaths Assuming 3,000–10,000 People per Square Kilometer
Chemical: 300 kilograms of sarin nerve gas with a density of 70 milligrams per cubic meter	0.22	60–200
Biological: 30 kilograms of anthrax spores with a density of 0.1 milligram per cubic meter	10	30,000–100,000
Nuclear: One 12.5 kiloton nuclear device achieving 5 pounds per cubic inch of overpressure	7.8	23,000–80,000
One 1 megaton hydrogen bomb	190	570,000–1,900,000

Using one aircraft delivering 1,000 kilograms of sarin nerve gas or 100 kilograms of anthrax spores: Assumes the aircraft flies in a straight line over the target at optimal altitude, dispensing the agent as an aerosol. The study assumes that the biological agent would not make maximum use of this payload capability because this is inefficient.

	Area Covered in Square Kilometers	Deaths Assuming 3,000–10,000 People per Square Kilometer
Bright Sunny Day		
Sarin Nerve Gas	0.74	300–700
Anthrax Spores	46	130,000–460,000
Overcast Day or Night, Moderate Wind		
Sarin Nerve Gas	0.8	400–800
Anthrax Spores	140	420,000–1,400,000
Clear Calm Night		
Sarin Nerve Gas	7.8	3,000–8,000
Anthrax Spores	300	1,000,000–3,000,000

Source: Adapted by the Anthony H. Cordesman from Office of Technology Assessment (OTA), *Proliferation of Weapons of Mass Destruction: Assessing the Risks*, U.S. Congress OTA-ISC-559, Washington, D.C., August, 1993, pp. 53–54.

Soviet diagnostics and postmortems at Sverdlovsk found a wide range of symptoms and effects that made diagnosis difficult. If an attack was covert, it is also unlikely that the disease would be recognized quickly. The limited experience with weaponized forms of disease indicated that the first stage symptoms were similar to those of the flu—a problem that could make initial diagnosis difficult. Even if a deliberate early effort is made to use diagnostic testing for anthrax, it would take 6–24 hours to confirm the disease, and the course of the disease normally lasts only three days before death, presenting serious problems in organizing the proper response. A delay of even hours in administering antibiotics can be fatal.[40]

Treatment presents further problems because there are no clinical studies of inhalational anthrax in human beings. Moreover, a weaponized agent can be tailored to increase both its lethality and its resistance to treatment, and rapid vaccination would not be practical even if the vaccine was known to be effective against the strain used in the weapon. The U.S. vaccine, which may or may not be effective, normally is given in a six-dose series, and the United States does not regard the human-live attenuated vaccine developed by the FSU as safe. The communicability of a weaponized version of the disease is unclear, and containment and quarantine might be necessary. Serious problems could also arise in dealing with dead bodies since cremation seems to be the only safe form of corpse disposal.[41]

Smallpox as a Case Study

Iran might be willing to use infectious agents at long ranges against targets such as Israel. Smallpox is often used as an example, although there is no practical evidence as yet that Iran has access to smallpox. In theory, smallpox was eradicated in 1977, and only two tightly controlled samples are supposed to exist in the United States and Russia. However, the FSU was still involved in the large-scale weaponization of the agent in 1980, and little data exist on whether any current stockpiles exist or what controls exist.[42] A number of developing states began their biological warfare programs in the 1960s, and they may have retained cultures. Unclassified U.S. statements have indicated that Iran, Libya, North Korea, and Syria may have retained cultures for military purposes, but it is unclear whether this is speculation or based on substantive data.[43]

Other highly infectious diseases present far more practical problems from the viewpoint of handling, "weaponization," and dissemination. An epidemic with a smallpox agent could be far more lethal than anthrax, although far harder to limit in effect and control.

Many games and models have tended to assume that a disease such as small pox could be easily used to create highly lethal epidemics and pandemics. This is questionable, but once infection actually takes hold, it is extremely lethal. The WHO notes that in natural outbreaks, "Variola major and variola minor are characterized by similar lesions but variola minor is accompanied by milder symptoms and a case-fatality rate of less than 1%, while the fatality rate of variola major is 20–40%."[44]

There is no real-world experience with deliberate efforts to infect, thus there is no way to translate the normal behavior of the disease into the effectiveness of a military agent, or to predict its transmissibility between human beings, and the natural aerosolized version of variola major is vulnerable to heat and humidity. This could present problems in any agent used by terrorists. However, each generation of infection can also expand the number of cases by 10–20 times. Only a few virons seem to be needed to infect a human being, and they are only 200 nanometers in diameter, but there are still serious questions as to what dose would be lethal and how much agent would be required. The Department of Defense *Medical NBC Battlebook* does not give lethality data per se, but shows an *assumed* range of 10–100 organisms for an infective dose.[45]

Like most known biological weapons, smallpox is not a prompt killing mechanism. It could, however, be difficult to detect in time to respond, and a covert attack might remain unknown until a major outbreak. Smallpox has an incubation period of 7–17 days, with the normal period beginning around 12 days. It then takes 1–3 days for clear symptoms to appear in the form of typical skin eruptions, followed by a 7–10-day progression of the disease requiring constant isolation and intensive medical treatment.[46] As a result, warning and detection would be difficult, and death usually occurs 5 or 6 days after the appearance of the characteristic rash, leaving limited time for treatment.

Vaccination is effective only through a maximum of 2–4 days after exposure, although the first symptoms do not appear for roughly two weeks, supportive therapy has only moderate effectiveness, and cases require isolation to prevent further transmission of the disease. In one case, a single patient infected people on three floors of a hospital because of transmission through the air vents. Decontamination is difficult and must be very thorough.[47] The problem of deciding whom to contain and/or quarantine would again force largely speculative decisions, and in several simulations where smallpox is assumed to get out of control, armed force has had to be used to contain fleeing populations because of the inability to characterize infection.

Biotoxins as a Case Study

At the other extreme, Iran might employ biotoxins—which are sometimes included in the list of chemical weapons—but these are much less lethal. Ricin, for example, can theoretically be some 30 times more lethal than VX nerve gas by weight. However, it is anything but easy to disseminate in lethal form. Planned and actual ricin attacks to date have involved targeted killings and have had little potential for producing serious casualties. As a CIA report notes, "Terrorists have looked at delivering ricin in foods and as a contact poison, although we have no scientific data to indicate that ricin can penetrate intact skin."[48] Some planned or actual attacks have reflected an almost morbid fascination with new killing mechanisms, and most of the efforts involved have probably made the terrorists involved much less lethal than if they had devoted the same effort to conventional explosives.

Similarly, botulinum toxin has received extensive attention by a number of terrorist groups, and a CIA study showed that "crude but viable methods to produce small quantities of this lethal toxin have been found in terrorist training manuals." Botulinum, however, is even more difficult to use in large-scale attacks than ricin, and the CIA notes that "botulinum toxin would be effective in small-scale poisonings or aerosol attacks in enclosed spaces, such as movie theaters. The toxin molecule is likely too large to penetrate intact skin."[49]

This does not mean that even a low-level bioterrorism incident, with minimal casualties, cannot have massive impact in terms of panic and political and economic effects, and a series of well-distributed low-level attacks might well substitute for one massive attack, or at least produce far more serious effects than a single incident. The anthrax attacks in the United States in the fall of 2001 killed only 4 and infected a total of 18, but still led to widespread panic, closing U.S. government and postal facilities, massive public expenditures, and preventive actions such as treating some 20,000 people for possible exposure to anthrax.

The Use of Covert, Proxy, and Low-Level Attacks

Iran can also deliver biological attacks by covert or proxy means. A study of possible attack scenarios, developed for defense and response planning by the Department of Homeland Security, was inadvertently put on the Internet. Among many other cases, it cited the following examples of real-world, near-term possibilities, ones based on current options that states or nonstate actors could actually use:[50]

- Spreading pneumonic plague in the bathrooms of an airport, sports arena, and train station, killing 2,500 and sickening 8,000 worldwide.
- Infecting cattle with foot-and-mouth disease in several places, resulting in hundreds of millions of dollars in losses.
- Exposing an estimated 350,000 people to an anthrax attack by terrorists spraying the biological weapon from a truck driving through five cities over two weeks, according to the report. An estimated 13,200 people could die.

There is a wide range of other agents that Iran might weaponize that differ very sharply in terms of lethality, ease of weaponization, infectiousness, persistence, warning, and treatability. It should also be stressed that lethality is only one measure of the impact of biological weapons, and in most real-world attacks, it may be far less important than the other impacts of such attacks. The immediate and long-term effects of the anthrax scare following 9/11, as well as the Japanese subway attacks, are a prime example that lethality is not the only measure of success in terms of biological attacks. At the same time, great care should be exercised in assuming that biological attacks necessarily become "weapons of mass media," "weapons of mass panic," or "weapons of mass expenditure." Initial attacks may produce such effects, but governments, media, and populations may well have a more rapid learning curve than some analysts expect.

Weaponization Issues

Like chemical weapons, it might well be harder for Iran to effectively weaponize biological weapons than for it to develop and produce the biological agent. A number of studies indicate that the manufacture, weaponization, and dissemination process were technically difficult and required major resources. A report by the WHO summarizes such as follows:

Extensive research, development and testing by military establishments have shown that large-scale production of certain infective agents and their incorporation into weapons for atmospheric dispersal of pathogens is feasible in suitably designed facilities with specialized equipment and appropriate precautions to protect the workers and prevent accidental release to the environment.

The selection of the agent and strain, its large-scale growth and its further processing present numerous technical problems and require specialized technologies and associated effort in research, development and testing. Several modes of delivery have received attention in military offensive programs but by far the greatest emphasis has been placed on methods of disseminating biological agents as inhalable aerosols.

Numerous additional technical difficulties must be overcome in order to develop munitions or other devices that produce stable aerosols, and specific delivery and atmospheric conditions must be met if the aerosol is to reach the target population. Throughout all these steps, including that of aerosol cloud travel, special techniques and conditions are required to maintain the inhalability, infectivity and virulence of the agent.[51]

This same WHO report notes, however,

Nevertheless, despite the fact that the development of strategic biological weapons within military establishments historically required large-scale efforts over several years, some infective agents could be produced and used as weapons of terror on a smaller scale using relatively simple techniques.

A DOD study, conducted in the early 2000s, makes the following points:

A state might elect to build large-scale facilities unique to this function, as was done in the United States prior to 1969. Such facilities would be, in principle, more susceptible to detection. However, there is no requirement to do this. The lower cost (by a considerable margin) and less readily observable approach would be to employ an in-place civilian facility as the site for agent production.

Production equipment will vary, depending on the quantity of material desired, the methods selected for production, and the agent selected. Unlike CW [chemical weapons] agents, where production is measured in the tons, BW agent production is measured in the kilograms to tens of kilograms. Assessments of BW verification sometimes assume that the problem is to detect production of as little as 10 kilograms of BW agent.

There is nothing unique about the types of equipment (or technology) that might be employed in a BW program. For example, biological safety cabinets have been adopted universally for biomedical research as well as commercial production of infectious disease products, reagents, and so forth. Fermenters, centrifuges, purification, and other laboratory equipment are used not only by the biomedical community, but have other academic and commercial applications as well, such as wineries, milk plants, pharmaceutical houses, and agricultural products. Production of beer, antibodies, enzymes, and other therapeutic products, such as insulin and growth hormone, involves the use of fermenters ranging in size from 10,000 to 1 million liters; such fermenters could produce significant quantities of BW agent. Key technologies have an intrinsic dual-use character.[52]

Iran almost certainly has the ability to produce dry, storable, biological agents and agents that can be disseminated through aerosols, either as droplets from liquid suspensions or by small particles from dry powders, which is by far the most efficient method.[53] Tests conducted during the 1950s and 1960s showed that an aerosol cloud of fine (2–5 microns) particles behaves more like a gas than a suspension and penetrates interior spaces as well as exterior spaces. The United States found that release from ships, aircraft, and tall buildings could achieve some lethality over distances of 50–100 miles, although without anything approaching uniform density.[54]

Iran also has an advanced-enough technology and industrial base to potentially develop "next-generation" biological weapons. The U.S. National Intelligence Council noted in its study, Mapping the Global Future: 2020,

> Major advances in the biological sciences and information technology probably will accelerate the pace of BW agent development, increasing the potential for agents that arte more difficult to detect or defend against. Through 2020, some countries will continue to try to develop chemical agents designed to circumvent the chemical weapons regime.[55]

Genetic engineering and other new technologies can now be employed to overcome product deficiencies in the classic agents and toxins normally addressed in such discussions. Moreover, toxins that exist in nature in small amounts were once considered not to be potential threat agents because of their limited availability.[56] Studies such as those of the Jason project show that genetically engineered pathogens can be designed to have any or all of the following attributes:[57]

- *Safer handling and deployment,* including the elimination of risks from accidents or misuse—the "boomerang effect"
- *Easier propagation and/or distribution,* eliminating the need for a normally hydrated bioagent or any use of aerosols; microorganisms with enhanced aerosol and environmental stability
- *Improved ability to target the host,* including the possible targeting of specific races or ethnic groups with given genetic characteristics
- *Greater transmissivity and infectivity,* engineering a disease such as Ebola to be as communicable as measles; microorganisms resistant to antibiotics, standard vaccines, and therapeutics

- *New weapons:* benign microorganisms genetically altered to produce a toxin, venom, or bioregulator

- *Increased problems in detection:* immunologically altered microorganisms able to defeat standard identification, detection, and diagnostic methods, causing problems in diagnosis, false diagnosis, lack of detection by existing detectors, long latency, and binary initiation

- *Greater toxicity, more difficult to treat:* very high morbidity or mortality, resistant to known antibacterial or antiviral agents, defeats existing vaccines, and produces symptoms designed to saturate available specialized medical treatment facilities

- *Combinations of some or all of the above*

While any such analysis is speculative, scientists postulate that the following new types of biological weapons are now deployable or can be manufactured during the coming decade:[58]

- *Binary biological weapons* that use two safe-to-handle elements that can be assembled before use. This could be a virus and a helper virus such as Hepatitis D or a bacterial virulence plasmid such as *E. coli*, plague, anthrax, and dysentery.

- *Designer genes and life forms,* which could include synthetic genes and gene networks, synthetic viruses, and synthetic organisms. These weapons include DNA shuffling, synthetic forms of the flu—which killed more people in 1918 than died in all of World War I and which still kills about 30,000 Americans a year—and synthetic microorganisms.

- *"Gene therapy" weapons* that use transforming viruses or similar DNA vectors carrying Trojan horse genes (retrovirus, adenovirus, poxvirus, or HSV-1). Such weapons can produce single individual (somatic cell) or inheritable (germline) changes. They can also remove immunities and wound healing capabilities.

- *Stealth viruses* can be transforming or conditionally inducible. They exploit the fact that humans normally carry a substantial viral load, and examples are the herpes virus, cytomegalovirus, Epstein-Barr, and SV40 contamination, which are normally dormant or limited in infection but can be transformed into far more lethal diseases. They can be introduced over years and then used to blackmail a population.

- *Host-swapping diseases:* Viral parasites normally have narrow host ranges and develop an evolutionary equilibrium with their hosts. Disruption of this equilibrium normally produces no results, but it can be extremely lethal. Natural examples include AIDS, hantavirus, Marburg, and Ebola. Tailoring the disruption for attack purposes can produce weapons that are extremely lethal and for which there is no treatment. A tailored disease such as AIDS could combine serious initial lethality with crippling long-term effects lasting decades.

- *Designer diseases* involve using molecular biology to create the disease first and then constructing a pathogen to produce it. It could eliminate immunity, target normally dormant genes, or instruct cells to commit suicide. Apoptosis is programmed cell death, and specific apoptosis can be used to kill any mix of cells.

Storage and delivery of weaponized biological agents are serious technical challenges that Iran would have to overcome in order to create a serious biological missile arsenal and carry out effective biological attacks. Some of the problems, and possible alternative delivery methods, posed by the weaponization process of biological agents follow:[59]

- Biological agents are far less controllable and predictable in effects than chemical weapons.
- Biological agents are dependent on temperature, weather, and topographical conditions, both for storage and delivery purposes.
- Most biological agents must be inhaled or ingested to be effective, and skin contact is unlikely to cause infection, making it easier to defend against a biological attack than a chemical attack with sufficient warning.
- Most biological agents degrade rapidly, although dry agents such as anthrax spores and some toxins are persistent—making prolonged storage (stockpiling) more difficult, and in some cases making use of the agents less effective.
- Biological agents are best dispersed as low-altitude aerosol clouds; explosive methods may destroy the organisms.
- High stress, gravitational force (G-force) and heat generated by acceleration and reentry of ballistic missiles make them a less-than-ideal method of delivering live biological agents.
- Considerable technical efforts are required to package live biological weapon agents in missile warheads and ensure that agents are dispersed at correct height and angle of delivery to create an airborne aerosol.
- Mounting biological dispersal systems onto cruise missiles may overcome disadvantages associated with aircraft and ballistic missile delivery systems.
- Aerosol dispersal systems mounted on unmanned aerial vehicles (UAVs) or cruise missiles, creating remote-piloted crop dusters, are other possibilities.

When other state and nonstate actors perusing biological and chemical weaponization were posed with similar issues, they found ways to improvise their existing technology to double as delivery systems. Delivery systems have included—but have not been limited to—spray tanks, bombs, cluster bombs, and bomblet dispensers. Iraq worked to adapt modified aircraft drop tanks for biological agent spray operations in 1990. The tank could be attached to either a piloted fighter aircraft or a UAV guided by another piloted aircraft and was designed to spray up to 2,000 liters of anthrax on a target. Similarly, the Japanese Aum Shinrikyo cult planned to use Russian helicopters or radio-controlled drone aircrafts with modifications to deliver chemical and biological agents.

The past history of Iranian efforts at complex program management and systems integration, however, has shown that Iran has serious problems in translating its technical expertise into practice. The knowledge of how to do things rarely leads to similar capability to actually do them, particularly when programs remain concealed and are largely "mothballed" or have low levels of activity.

Testing biological weapons also presents even more serious problems in determining their actual effects than chemical weapons. Testing requires human subjects, and it is far from clear that limited testing under controlled conditions can be scaled to indicate real-world effects. It is possible to determine lethality in rough terms by sampling residues of the agent after dissemination, but this requires repeated testing using actual weapons in a variety of real-world conditions. This is particularly true of missile warheads.

WARFIGHTING: BIOLOGICAL WEAPONS

Doubts about the military effectiveness of biological weapons in tactical combat have resulted in very limited use in recent history, with the exception of the Japanese biological attacks on China during World War II. Biological weapons do present a wide range of drawbacks in addition to the uncertainties regarding their real-world lethality. But despite the uncertainties about performance of biological weapons, some states, such as Iran, continue to research and develop biological agents for the purpose of possible weaponization.

While biological agents in relatively small quantities are theoretically capable of causing massive casualties, their military utility as an instrument of war has long been questioned. Most biological agents that would be weaponized are too slow acting and unpredictable for surprise attacks or repelling the immediate attacks of others. Biological attacks may be more suitable for use against fixed defensive positions in long wars of attrition or against reserve combat units, formations massing in preparation for an offensive, air force squadrons, or rear-area support units—where immediate results are not required and the danger to friendly forces is minimal.

Nevertheless, biological weapons were stockpiled during both world wars, and research and development continued throughout the Cold War by the United States and the Soviet Union.

The world showed during the Iran-Iraq War that it would tolerate the use of chemical weapons. Any use of biological weapons, however, raises far deeper concerns and fears, particularly any use of biological agents. The level of international reaction—or reaction by Iran's neighbors and the United States—could include preventive war, invasion, or crippling sanctions. Iranian use of biological weapons could be used to justify virtually any level of escalation or retaliation, including all-out nuclear war against Iran's population centers.

While biological weapons offer a wide range of potential covert or proxy delivery means, this may be as much a threat as an advantage. Iran also would face a serious risk of massive retaliation if any use was made of biological weapons against any potential enemy of Iran unless that use could be clearly and decisively attributed to some other state. Proxy uses by any nonstate actor known—or suspected—to have any association with Iran might also trigger such retaliation. Existential warfare will not be an exercise in international law, or the subject of debates in the Security Council. The suspect can be unilaterally attacked just as easily as the guilty.

At the same time, biological weapons do offer Iran potential advantages. There is no practical way that any power, or combination of powers, can deny Iran the ability to covertly develop and produce such weapons. All of the uncertainties Iran faces in deploying and using such weapons create major problems for its neighbors, the United States, and Israel. There is no way, short of an inspection regime that does not now exist and for which there are no plans or precedents, that any outside power can know how far Iran has gone, or the lethality of its weapons.

No potential target can ignore even worst-case scenarios and effects. Short of invasion and occupation, no state or combination of states can prevent Iran from responding to any preventive attack on its nuclear facilities and other military capabilities and then going on to a biological option. It is doubtful that intelligence could provide reliable warning that Iran was preparing for or conducting a biological attack or deploying biological warheads that could give it a sudden launch on warning or launch under attack capability. Dry storable agents could potentially be prepositioned in a target country. The threat of retaliating to a major attack by using infectious agents could not be casually dismissed.

A world whose attention is fixed on nuclear weapons has not yet developed any clear countermeasures to this form of proliferation or to the fact that Iran could mix biological and nuclear capabilities. At the same time, biological weapons do present many of the same problems in using chemical weapons and are less suited for tactical use except in rear areas that are a substantial distance from the front and friendly territory.

Any broader Iran military use of chemical weapons would present a number of problems:

- While biological weapons have a powerful psychological and political impact, and are be lethal enough to deter or intimidate, they too may well provoke and lead any opponent that can to escalate. Any use also justifies a massive level of escalation, including the use of biological or nuclear weapons in retaliation.

- Arming aircraft or missiles with unitary, cluster, or forms of biological weapons can potentially produce high rates of lethality against exposed troops or populations, but real-world lethality is extremely difficult to predict. Actual area coverage can be limited, particularly with a ballistic missile warhead where preserving the integrity of a fully loaded warhead and dissemination at precisely the right altitude presents major technical challenges.

- Cluster munitions and other advanced ways of disseminating chemical weapons from a bomb or warhead offer more potential lethality, but also present more technical challenges.

- Line source dissemination by an aircraft, cruise missile, drone, or unmanned combat air vehicle offers a simpler and more lethal way of disseminating biological agents than unitary or cluster weapons, but means flying a large air system to the target area and flying a vulnerable penetration profile.

- Effective air strikes require high confidence in the ability to penetrate enemy air defenses and good intelligence, surveillance, and reconnaissance assets. In many cases, a chemical weapon would have only marginally greater lethality than a conventional precision-guided weapon or cluster weapon. Again, such use might do more to provoke than terrify, intimidate, or damage.

- Biological weapons have never been used in combat. They are an abstract and uncertain threat until employed and they achieve proven lethality, or until some form of test or "accident" gives them tangible credibility.

- The time required to achieve incapacitating, lethal, or agricultural effects presents major problems. It may be unimportant in "broken back" or existential exchanges, in avoiding defensive action, and/or limiting attribution, but it limits the ability to promptly disrupt tactical operations and deny areas to enemy forces. Rapidly maneuvering ground forces would be a difficult to impossible target. Nations such as the United States would have extensive amounts of detection, protection, and decontamination gear. They also would not have large, static, rear-area and support operations near the forward edge of the battle area.

- The use of biological weapons against targets at sea presents significant targeting and meteorological problems. These are certainly solvable, but do involve substantial problems, delayed effects, and require exceptional planning and skill. Similarly, firing against coastal targets requires high volumes of CW fire or good meteorological data.

- Covert or proxy use presents serious problems in wartime. Plausible deniability is doubtful, and an opponent simply may not care if it can prove Iran is responsible for any given use of BW. The risk to Iran of having dry storable weapons that could get out of control or be used against it would also be significant.

None of these problems and issues implies that Iran cannot benefit from deploying biological weapons or creating a level of ambiguity that forces any potential enemy to take these threats far more seriously than they are taken today. It is also clear that Iran has the incentive to use biological weapons under some conditions and that such use might be effective.

Biological weapons also present special problems in terms of deterrence in peacetime and controlling escalation in a conflict. This does not mean that Iran will act on the basis of ideology or ignore risk. As extreme as some Iranian statements are, Iran tends to be pragmatic in practice. Once again, however, crises create new conditions, perceptions, misunderstandings, and levels of risk taking. Rational bargainers with perfect insight and all the necessary transparency in terms of full knowledge of the situation and risks are theoretical constructs. It is dangerous to assume that even the most prudent decision maker will not take exceptional risks, overreact, or drastically miscalculate in war.

Possible Nuclear Weapons Programs

There is more information available on Iran's nuclear programs than on its chemical and biological programs, but this scarcely eliminates major areas of uncertainty. The flood of information regarding Iran's nuclear programs includes many gaps and conflicting reports and assessments, and there are major problems in assessing the credibility of information that often has to be collected from questionable sources.

Estimating Iranian nuclear capabilities is further complicated by three key factors:

- First, the United States, the European Union (EU), and the United Nations (UN) all agree that Iran has the right to acquire a full nuclear fuel cycle for peaceful purposes under the Nuclear Non-Proliferation Treaty (NPT), but there is no clear way to distinguish many of the efforts needed to acquire a nuclear weapon from such "legitimate" activities or pure research.

- Second, Iran has never denied that it carries out a very diverse range of nuclear research efforts. In fact, it has openly claimed that it is pursuing nuclear technology and has a "national" right to get access to nuclear energy. This has given it a rationale for rejecting Russia's offer to provide Iran nuclear fuel without giving Tehran the technology and the expertise needed to use it for weaponization purposes. The United States agrees with this position.

- Third, it has never been clear whether Iran does have a "military" nuclear program that is separate from its "civilian" nuclear research. American and French officials have argued that they believe that Iran's nuclear program would make sense only if it had military purposes. Both governments have yet to provide evidence to prove these claims.

If Iran is actively developing nuclear weapons, as seems steadily more likely, it has shown that it can conduct a skilled program capable of hiding many aspects of its activities, that it can mask its activities by sending confusing and contradictory signals, and that it can simultaneously exploit both deception and the international inspection process. It has also shown that it can rapidly change the character of given facilities, pausing and retreating when this is expedient.

A CASE STUDY IN DECEPTION, OBFUSCATION, AND MISDIRECTION?

Iran learned from the U.S. invasion of Iraq in 2003 and used these lessons to its advantage. The 2003 invasion of Iraq took place under the pretense of finding and destroying Iraq's weapons of mass destruction (WMDs) programs, which turned out to be greatly exaggerated, and possibly nonexistent; which in turn showed the shortcomings of the intelligence community and created credibility issues for future operations, especially in regard to the Middle East and WMD programs.

Iran is taking full advantage of this situation by developing a strategy that focuses on creating just enough uncertainty in the international community that any use of force could very well be taken as further signs of U.S. imperialism. Tehran's posture would seem to indicate that it is betting on a strategy that by maintaining a high level of ambiguity while showing some level of compliance, it can create enough uncertainty to avoid a unilateral preventive strike by the United States or Israel.

Tehran has shown how well it can use the media, public speaking engagements, international forums, and contradicting officials' statements as invaluable weapons in its continuing war of deception. Misdirection has become a cornerstone of Iran's strategy in concealing its true intentions and capabilities in its WMD programs, missile programs, asymmetric forces, and use of proxies and nonstate actors.

As Figure 7.1 indicates, Iran repeatedly demonstrated in recent years that denial can be a weapon; by consistently finding an alternative explanation for all its actions, including concealment and actions that are limited violations of the NPT, it can maintain some degree of "plausible deniability" for a long chain of ambiguous actions and events.

As is the case in assessing every aspect of Iran's missile programs and efforts to acquire nuclear weapons, the devil really does lie in the details. Figure 7.1 shows that Tehran has learned from the failures of other nation's nuclear programs in terms of denial and deception. Iran learned from Saddam Hussein that the perception of compliance, limited transparency, and plausible deniability are more effective than constant denial and the concealment strategy that were the cornerstone to the Iraqi nuclear program. Iran also learned that too much transparency and overtly threatening actions and strategy, such as in the case of North Korea, can be counterproductive and lead to greater isolation coupled with the constant fear of preventive or preemptive action against the regime.

Jose Goldemberg, Brazil's former Secretary of State for Science and Technology, made this point in commenting on the denuclearization of Brazil and Argentina. He observed that a country developing the capability to produce nuclear fuel "does not have to make an explicit early [political] decision to acquire nuclear weapons. In some countries, such a path is supported equally by those who genuinely want

Figure 7.1   Major Developments in Iran's Nuclear Program 2006–2009[1]

- **Early January 2006:** Iran removes 52 International Atomic Energy Agency (IAEA) seals on Natanz, Pars Trash, and Farayand centrifuge projects.
- **February 4, 2006:** The IAEA Board of Governors votes to refer Iran to the United Nations Security Council (UNSC).
- **February 27, 2006:** IAEA Director General Mohamed ElBaradei reports that the IAEA is still tracking enriched uranium activity, the status of the P-1 centrifuge program is still uncertain, P-2 centrifuge acquisition remains uncertain, there are still uranium tetrafluoride (UF4) to uranium metal conversion issues and outstanding issues related to both uranium enrichment and the plutonium experiments; still assessing mining, polonium, beryllium, site inspection "transparency" issues (e.g., Lavisan-Shian) dating back to 2004.
- **Early March 2006:** Twenty cascade machines are reported running at Natanz and Farayand.
- **April 2006:** The Iranian parliament passes a resolution for Iran to withdraw from the NPT.
- **April 28, 2006:** IAEA Director General Mohamed ElBaradei reports that there is no clarification on enrichment, highly enriched uranium (HEU) contamination issues remain, and P-1 and P-2 centrifuge issues have not been addressed; there are new issues over P-2 designs, new issues over uranium hexafluoride (UF6) to metal and casting of uranium hemispheres (Iran refused to hand over a 15-page document about the casting of enriched and depleted uranium metal into hemispheres), still no clarification on plutonium experiments, the heavy-water reactor at Arak is still under construction, and new transparency issues. Iran is building a second and third cascade at the Pilot Fuel Enrichment Plant.
- **May 30, 2006:** IAEA Director General Mohamed ElBaradei states that Iran's nuclear activity "does not present an immediate threat."[2]
- **May 31, 2006:** U.S. Secretary of State Condoleezza Rice acknowledges Iran's right to civil nuclear energy, supports the EU-3 (British, French, and German) offer to Iran, offers "new and positive relationship . . . looks forward to a new relationship," "as soon as Iran fully and verifiably suspends its enrichment and reprocessing activities, the U.S. would come to the table with our EU-3 colleagues and meet with Iran's representatives"[3]; Rice repeats this willingness to hold talks on August 29.
- **June 8, 2006:** Director General Mohamed ElBaradei reports that there is no further resolution on contamination, P-1, P-2, or uranium metal and casting, warns that Iran has started centrifuge cascade activity for 164-machine cascade and has started work on a second 164-machine unit (second cascade launched on October 23, 2006, but without UF6 insertion), no improvement in transparency, especially plutonium and heavy-water reactor, new UF6 conversion campaign had begun in the Isfahan Uranium Conversion Facility (UCF) on June 6, 2006, following up on "Green Salt" project, investigating high explosives testing and design of missile reentry vehicle.
- **July 31, 2006:** United Nations Security Council Resolution (UNSCR) 1696 (July 31, 2006) finds that there is "serious concern" over IAEA DG reports of February 27, April 28, and June 8, "Demands . . . that Iran shall suspend all enrichment-related and reprocessing activities, including research and development", expressed intention (if Iran did not comply by August 31) to adopt appropriate measures under Article 41 of Chapter VII of Charter of UN to "persuade Iran to comply . . . and underlines that further decisions will be required should such additional measures prove necessary."[4]

- **August 13–November 2, 2006:** According to the IAEA, during this time period Iran reported that approximately 34 kilograms of UF_6 was fed into the centrifuges and enriched to levels below 5 percent U-235. Iran had reported by August 31 that a total of 6 kilograms of UF_6 was fed into the then single cascade between June 23 and July 8. This would represent an almost 500-percent increase in the inserted quantity of UF_6, which in return may be an indication of additional and/or more efficient cascades.
- **August 20, 2006:** Ayatollah Ali Khamenei says in a speech, "The Islamic Republic of Iran has made up its mind based on the experience of the past 27 years to forcefully pursue its nuclear program and other issues it is faced with."[5]
- **August 26, 2006:** Mahmoud Ahmadinejad inaugurates the Arak heavy-water production plant.
- **August 27, 2006:** Chief nuclear negotiator Ali Larijani rejects the UN deadline. Ahmadinejad says Iran will never abandon its purely peaceful program. He repeats the rejection of the deadline on August 29, and he verbally attacks the United Kingdom and the United States.
- **August 31, 2006:** IAEA Director General Mohamed ElBaradei reports that Iran tested a 164-machine cascade to 5-percent enrichment, a second 164-centrifuge cascade is to start in September (reportedly it started on October 23), limiting access to Natanz, possibly in the future to Arak and Isfahan, no indications of ongoing reprocessing, no resolution of HEU contamination (still partly unaccounted for), P-1 and P-2 issues, machining of uranium remains unresolved, uranium conversion stepping up but is inspected, and transparency issues on environmental sampling and missile reentry vehicles (Green Salt) are unresolved.
- **September 11, 2006:** Secretary of State Condoleezza Rice says that a temporary suspension of the uranium enrichment program might be sufficient for holding direct negotiations with Iran.[6]
- **October 1, 2006:** Ahmadinejad announces that Iran is planning to construct 100,000 centrifuges.
- **November 14, 2006:** The IAEA Board of Governors reports that the testing of the second 164-machine cascade with UF6 was begun; as of November 7, Iran had produced 55 tons of uranium (in the form of UF_6) out of the 160 tons of uranium ore it started processing at its Isfahan UCF in June 2006.
- **December 23, 2006:** The UNSC passes resolution 1737, which calls on Iran to stop all uranium enrichment activities and heavy-water experiments within 60 days, allows monitoring and verification of its enrichment activities, and imposes sanctions on several Iranian persons and organizations that are believed to be linked to the nuclear program.
- **January 2007:** Iran blocks the entry of 38 IAEA inspectors in retaliation for sanctions.[7] The Islamic Republic News Agency (IRNA) reports that inspectors from countries that voted in favor of the UNSCR placing sanctions on Iran would be banned. The IRNA did not name the diplomat, saying he spoke on the condition of anonymity.[8]
- **February 19, 2007:** Mohamed ElBaradei says that Iran may be six months away from enriching uranium on an industrial scale. He adds that according to U.S. and British intelligence, Iran was 5–10 years away from developing a nuclear bomb.[9]
- **February 22, 2007:** The IAEA Board of Governors issues a report (Gov/2007/8) that addresses Iran's compliance with the provisions set forth in UNSCR 1737. The February 22 report concludes that not only has Iran not complied with any of the calls set forth in UNSCR 1737, but it has informed the IAEA that it is installing two additional 164-

machine cascades for uranium enrichment. Further, Iran informed the IAEA that it is planning to build a module of 18 164-machine cascades underground by mid-2007. However, by the time IAEA report Gov/2007/8 was issued, apparently no UF_6 had been fed into the centrifuges.

- **March 15, 2007:** The five permanent members (China, France, Russian Federation, the United Kingdom, and the United States) of the UN Security Council plus Germany (P5 +1) agree on a draft resolution on further sanctions on Iran. Apparently, the draft contained an arms embargo and broader economic sanctions such as a halt on international loans and freezing assets on individuals connected to the nuclear as well as the ballistic missile development programs. However, by the end of March 2007, the UNSC had not taken up a vote on the matter of further UN sanctions, and it was not clear what the smallest common political denominator at the UNSC would be on the matter.
- **April 5, 2007:** Iran's head of its Atomic Energy Agency, Ali Larijani, tells a European Union group, "The Islamic Republic of Iran is ready to negotiate only on non-diversion of its nuclear program for military purposes, and not on its nuclear rights . . . . Iran will not accept any preconditions or suspension for a time. Nor can suspending enrichment be a precondition or the result of negotiations (with the Permanent Members of the U.N. Security Council)."[10]
- **April 9, 2007:** Iranian President Ahmadinejad announces that Iran is now capable of nuclear fuel production on an "industrial scale."[11]
- **May 14, 2007:** Inspectors for the IAEA concluded that Iran had solved most of its technical problems in enriching uranium and is doing so on a much larger scale than before. A short-notice inspection of Natanz found up to 1,300 active centrifuges, with 300 more being tested and another 300 under construction. Iran seems to be capable of installing up to 3,000 centrifuges as early as June 2007 in "cascades" of 164 centrifuges each. Some diplomats speculate that Iran could have as many as 5,000 centrifuges installed by the end of the year, and some estimates go as high as 8,000. There is, however, no data on the efficiency of this effort or its real-world capability to produce given amounts of weapons-grade uranium.[12]
- **October 20, 2007:** Ali Larijani, the top Iranian negotiatior over nuclear program issues, resigns from his post because of differences with President Ahmadinejad. He is replaced by the deputy foreign minister Saeed Jalili.[13]
- **November 22, 2007:** The head of the IAEA, Mohamed ElBaredei, tells the Board that although Iran has been positively cooperating about many important aspects of its nuclear activities, it needs to be more forthcoming on the remaining outstanding issues.[14]
- **December 3, 2007:** A declassified U.S. National Intelligence Estimate on Iran states that work on a nuclear weapons program was abandoned in 2003 and that the halt lasted at least several years.[15]
- **January 22, 2008:** The permanent U.N. Security Council members plus Germany (P5+1) reach an agreement on a new sanctions resolution targeting Iran's nuclear program. The IAEA and Iran agree to a four-week deadline for Iran to clear up the remaining outstanding questions on its nuclear activities.[16]
- **February 22, 2008:** Director General ElBaradei presents the latest nuclear safeguards report to the IAEA Board. The report states that good progress has been made but that a final verdict cannot be offered.[17]

- **March 3, 2008:** The U.N. Security Council authorizes Resolution 1803. This is the third round of sanctions targeting Iran over its nuclear activities. The resolution also demands the Director General of the IAEA to report within 90 days on whether Iran has ceased its uranium enrichment process, as previously demanded by the Security Council.[18]
- **April 11, 2008:** The IRNA reports that three sets of 164-machine cascades from a second series of 3,000 are in motion at Natanz. Previous reports stated that 18 sets of 164-machine cascades were already active in uranium enrichment. During the National Nuclear Technology Festival, President Ahmadinejad declares that activities have started for the installment of 6,000 P-1 centrifuges.[19]
- **May 27, 2008:** The IAEA report on Implementation of the NPT Safeguards Agreement states that the alleged studies in the development of nuclear weapons remain "a matter of serious concern" and that Iran still owes "substantial explanations" on its nuclear activities. Using unprecedented blunt language, the report accuses Iran of "willful lack of cooperation."[20]
- **June 7, 2008:** A senior member of the Israeli cabinet, Shaul Mofaz, says that an attack on Iran would be "inevitable" if Iran is to be stopped from developing nuclear weapons.[21] The comments by the Israeli minister were credited for a record one-day jump in oil prices by $11, setting a new price record of $139 per barrel.[22]
- **June 14, 2008:** EU foreign affairs representative Javier Solana delivers the "carrots and stick" package to Tehran.[23] The package was meant as an incentive to the halt of uranium enrichment and the beginning of negotiations to resolve the nuclear crisis. In case of rejection, sanctions could be in place within a month.[24]
- **June 16, 2008:** Ongoing investigations revealed that the Tinners, a Swiss family with a middle-man role in the A. Q. Khan network, were in possession of electronic blueprints for a sophisticated and compact nuclear weapon. The new weapon design was reported to be more sophisticated than the old designs that emerged in 2003 when Libya gave up its nuclear weapons program. Prior evidence indicated that the network led by the Pakistani scientist had sold uranium-enrichment technology to Libya, Iran, and North Korea.[25] According to David Albright of the Institute for Science and International Security (ISIS), the design in Switzerland "would have been ideal for two of Khan's other major customers, Iran and North Korea. They both faced struggles in building a nuclear warhead small enough to fit atop of their ballistic missiles, and these designs were for a warhead that would fit."[26]
- **June 18, 2008:** Iran responds to the Solana package with a counteroffer of comprehensive negotiation, of which the nuclear issue is only one part.[27] The IAEA circulates a communication from Iran (issued as INFCIRC/729) that forwards the text of the "Islamic Republic of Iran's proposed package for constructive negotiation."
- **June 20, 2008:** IAEA Director General Mohamed ElBaradei says in an interview that if Iran wants a nuclear weapon, it will have to leave the NPT, expel IAEA inspectors, and then it "would need at least six months to one year" to produce a nuclear weapon. ElBaradei adds that at the moment there is no justification for a strike on Iran because this is not a scenario "where we would wake up one morning to an Iran with a nuclear weapon."[28]
- **June 20, 2008:** Reports emerge in the media that the Israeli Air Force (IAF) conducted a major military exercise earlier in the month of June. The exercise involved more than 100 Israeli F-15 and F-16 fighters alongside rescue helicopters and refueling tankers. The

maneuvers took place across 900 miles over the eastern Mediterranean and Greece and were largely seen as rehearsal for an eventual attack on Iranian nuclear facilities.[29]

• **June 23, 2008:** The EU agrees on new sanctions aimed at companies and individuals seen as links to the Iranian ballistic missile and nuclear programs. The punitive measures include the freeze of Bank Melli assets and a ban on select Iranian officials. Iran condemns the measures by calling them illegal and damaging to the diplomatic process.[30]

• **June 25, 2008:** Media report alleged claims by an adviser to the Israeli National Security Council that Syria plans to supply Iran with spent nuclear fuel for reprocessing into weapons-grade plutonium. If confirmed, these reports would indicate greater nuclear co-operation between Syria and Iran than previously known.[31]

• **June 28, 2008:** Iran is reported as having repositioned its Shahab-3B missiles targeting Israeli sites, including the Dimona nuclear plant. The move is perceived as a deterrence response against possible Israeli air strikes, given the "dress rehearsal" IAF long-range exercises earlier in June.[32]

• **June 29, 2008:** Saber rattling occurs between Israel and Iran. The former head of the Mossad and current adviser to the Israeli parliament's foreign and defense committees, Shabtai Shavit, says that Israel "should do whatever necessary" to prevent Iran from obtaining nuclear weapons. His assessment is that Israel has a 12-month window of opportunity to destroy Iran's nuclear program. The worst-case scenario analysis is that Iran will use nuclear weapons against Israel once it has the capability and that in case sanctions fail, military action is the only option.[33] Major General Mohammad Ali Jafari of the Revolutionary Guard declares to Iranian media that "Iran will definitely act to impose control on the Persian Gulf and Strait of Hormuz," stemming the flow of oil and putting pressure on Western economies. Additionally, Jafari noted that Israel is well within the reach of Iranian missiles and that Iran would retaliate against regional countries that partake in attacks on Iran.[34]

• **June 30, 2008:** Anonymous U.S. Department of Defense officials report to ABC News that Israel is likely to strike Iran by the year's end. The Israeli decision is contingent upon two "redlines": (a) whether Iran produces enough enriched uranium at Natanz to make a nuclear weapon and (b) whether Iran deploys the SA-20 air defense system it is reportedly purchasing from Russia. The Israeli government declined to comment on the allegations, but former head of the Mossad, Ephraim HaLevy, said that a potential Israeli strike has been "in the air" for a long time. However, for Hirsch Goodman of the Jaffee Center for Strategic Studies in Tel Aviv, these comments are "the latest in the hype." According to Goodman, "It's all total rubbish by anonymous officials who want to create an atmosphere of pressure on those who need to make decisions and implement sanctions." Goodman does not believe these attacks to be militarily and politically feasible.[35] Furthermore, according to a recent report by Jane's, the Russian-Iranian deal over the SA-20 (S-300) air defense system "has since been shelved because of disagreements over the price."[36] U.S. Secretary of Defense Robert Gates later says that it is "unlikely that those air-defense missiles would be in Iranian hands any time soon."[37]

• **July 2, 2008:** Admiral Mike Mullen, Chairman of the Joint Chiefs of Staff, expresses his concern about a conflict with Iran upon his return from Israel, where he consulted with the Israeli defense minister and the chief of defense staff. Mullen says, "Opening up a third front right now would be extremely stressful on us" and that "[t]his is a very unstable part of the world, and I don't need it to be more unstable."[38] Manouchehr Mottaki, the Iranian foreign minister, dismissed the possibility of an attack upon Iran as psychological warfare, adding that Iran did not believe that the United States was in a position to wage another war. Nevertheless, Iranian officials appeared to be giving greater consideration to the package of political and economic incentives offered by Western diplomats. There were also talks of a "freeze-for-freeze" deal, where Iran would stop adding new uranium-enrichment capabilities and the West would stop pushing for sanctions, resulting in a period of preliminary talks.[39]

- **July 4, 2008:** Iran responds to the P5+1 package of incentives saying that it is willing to begin comprehensive negotiations with EU foreign policy representative Javier Solana. The letter from Iran's foreign minister, Manouchehr Mottaki, does not address the issue of stopping uranium-enrichment activities.[40] The following day a spokesperson for the Iranian government comments that Iran's nuclear policy has not changed and that Iran would not comply with any UN Security Council resolution requiring a halt of uranium enrichment.[41]

- **July 7, 2008:** The *Daily Telegraph* (London) reports that according to the latest intelligence circulated among Western diplomats, Iran's Revolutionary Guard has set up a network of civilian companies to manufacture components for the advanced P-2 centrifuges. The operation is allegedly based on the 2004 plot involving Kalaye Electric Company and was exposed by UN nuclear inspectors.[42]

- **July 9, 2008:** The U.S. Navy's Fifth Fleet and allied navies conduct "Exercise Stake Net," a five-day drill in the Persian Gulf aimed at protecting the oil-rich region. The drill is seen as a response to Iranian threats against regional U.S. interests and oil flows through the Strait of Hormuz.[43] At the same time, the State and Treasury departments proceed to place greater financial sanctions on key Iranian public and private officials, as well as companies, accused of being involved in the alleged nuclear weapons program.[44]

- **July 9, 2008:** The Iranian media broadcast the Iranian Revolutionary Guard Corps (IRGC) test-firing nine missiles 100 miles south of Tehran; all the while Iran is also conducting "The Great Prophet III" naval games at the mouth of the Strait of Hormuz.[45] One of the fired missiles was presumed to be a Shahab-3 with a one-ton warhead and a range of 1,200 miles, capable of reaching Israel and U.S. targets within the region.[46] According to Charles Vick of GlobalSecurity.org, the launched Shahab-3s appear to have a conic warhead indicating that they may have been older models with a 900-mile range. Vick suggests that these may have been the Shahab-3A, rather than the more advanced tri-conic nose cone Shahab-3B, which is suspected to be Iran's delivery system for a potential nuclear weapon. The other missiles were identified as Zelzal and Fateh.[47] Thomas Fingar, head of the National Intelligence Council, described Iran as pursuing a "hedgehog strategy," coupling bellicose rhetoric and display of military capabilities with offers of comprehensive negotiations.[48] The test firing did not seem to show any new capabilities, mostly involving middle-range to close-range battlefield rockets.[49]

- **July 19, 2008:** The P5+1 group holds a meeting with Iran in Geneva, Switzerland, to hear the Iranian response to its diplomatic offer. The Under Secretary for Political Affairs of the U.S. Department of State, Ambassador William J. Burns, is present as an observer in what is considered to be the highest-level contact between the United States and Iran since the 1979 revolution.[50] While Iranian foreign minister Saeed Jalili described the talks as "constructive and progressing," the European officials expressed disappointment in the Iranian response.[51] The two-page document that Iran circulated at the meeting did not substantially address the major demands, and it ignored the freeze-for-freeze offer. The paper called for three more meetings with Javier Solana and gave the impression that Iran intended to prolong the talks. U.S. Secretary of State Rice said that Iran could not continue to stall the process and warned of more sanctions in case Iran failed to respond positively within a two-week period.[52]

- **July 21, 2008:** British Prime Minister Gordon Brown tells the Knesset, the Israeli parliament in Jerusalem, that he is ready to back another round of sanctions if Iran does not take concrete steps to meeting Security Council demands.[53]

- **July 23, 2008:** Iranian President Mahmoud Ahmadinejad says the Persian Gulf nation will resist pressure from world powers to halt its nuclear program, following the July 19 Geneva talks that failed to produce a breakthrough in the dispute over the project.[54]

- **July 24, 2008:** Just five days after Tehran stonewalled demands from the P5+1 that it halt activities capable of producing the fissile core of warheads, Iranian Vice President Gholam Reza Aghazadeh signals that Iran will no longer cooperate with UN experts probing for signs of clandestine nuclear weapons work, confirming the investigation is at a dead end a year after it began.[55]

- **July 26, 2008:** Iran's President Mahmoud Ahmadinejad claims that Iran now possesses 6,000 centrifuges, which is double the 3,000 uranium-enriching machines Iran had previously said it was operating. Iran says it plans to move toward large-scale uranium enrichment that will ultimately involve 54,000 centrifuges. President Ahmadinejad also calls the U.S. participation in the latest round of nuclear talks "a victory for Iran." In the past, the United States said it would join talks only if Iran suspended uranium enrichment first. Ahmadinejad was quoted as saying, "The presence of a U.S. representative . . . was a victory for Iran, irrespective of the outcome. . . . The U.S. condition was for Iran to suspend enrichment but they attended (the talks) without such a condition being met."[56]

- **July 28, 2008:** "Today, we see new behavior shown by the United States and the officials of the United States. My question is, is such behavior rooted in a new approach?" President Ahmadinejad tells NBC in a rare interview with a U.S. broadcaster. "In other words, mutual respect, cooperation and justice? Or is this approach a continuation in the confrontation with the Iranian people, but in a new guise?" he says from Tehran, speaking through an interpreter. If U.S. behavior represents a genuine change, "we will be facing a new situation and the response by the Iranian people will be a positive one."[57] Although Iran's tone has softened, "they haven't agreed to a slowdown in progress, not withstanding all the hints they would be doing so," Mark Fitzpatrick, a senior fellow for nonproliferation at the London-based International Institute for Strategic Studies policy group, says in a telephone interview. "Of course he says they aren't producing a bomb, but they are producing the wherewithal to make a bomb once they have the enrichment capability."[58]

- **August 1, 2008:** Iran fails to win support from the nonaligned nations to remove UN Security Council sanctions. A U.S. official says that the conference was deadlocked on portions of the draft statement presented by Iran, which demands the removal of sanctions, dismissed UN authority, and affirmed Iran's right to possess the entire nuclear fuel cycle. Iran did receive broad endorsement to pursue a peaceful nuclear program.[59]

- **August 4, 2008:** The P5+1 nations agree to seek new sanctions against Iran after the country failed to respond to an incentives package aiming to resolve the nuclear dispute. "We are disappointed that we have not yet received a response from Iran," U.S. Department of State spokesman Gonzalo Gallegos tells reporters. "We agreed in the absence of a clear, positive response from Iran [that] we have no choice but to pursue further measures against Iran."[60]

- **August 16, 2008:** Iran test-fires a new rocket, named Safir-e Omid, capable of carrying a satellite into orbit. The White House says Iran's rocket announcement is "troubling," calling it part of a pattern of Iranian activity to build a nuclear program and the means to potentially launch a weapon. "The Iranian development and testing of rockets is troubling and raises further questions about their intentions," said White House spokesman Gordon D. Johndroe. Rocket scientists agree that the same technology that puts satellites into orbit can deliver warheads.[61]
- **August 28, 2008:** In the wake of the Russian invasion of Georgia, the Russian ambassador to Iran, Alexander Sadovnikov, tells the official IRNA news agency that Moscow will not support a new round of UN Security Council sanctions against Iran. "The Russian move into Georgia has begun a tectonic shift in the (Mideast) region," said Joshua Landis, a Syria expert in the United States. "It has emboldened Syria, Hezbollah and Iran to push harder against Israel and the U.S."[62] Also on this date it is reported that Iran offered to share its nuclear technology with Nigeria to boost electricity production. The deal was signed at the end of three days of talks between the oil-producing nations. Both countries stress that the nuclear program is for peaceful purposes only.[63]
- **August 29, 2008:** Iranian Deputy Foreign Minister Ali Reza Sheikh announces that Iran has increased the number of centrifuges at its uranium enrichment plant to 4,000 and is preparing to install 3,000 more in the Natanz plan. By reaching 4,000 centrifuges, the program is moving into an industrial-scale program that could churn out enough enriched material for dozens of nuclear weapons.[64]
- **September 5, 2008:** According to Iranian President Mahmoud Ahmadinejad, Iran was considering imposing unilateral sanctions against Western powers in response to measures to punish Tehran over its nuclear program.[65]
- **September 6, 2008:** President Hu Jintao of China urges other nations to negotiate a resolution to Iran's nuclear issue during a meeting with Iranian President Mahmoud Ahmadinejad, making it clear again that China disapproves of any move by Western countries to attack Iran with military force.[66]
- **September 7, 2008:** The Kremlin is reported to be discussing sending teams of Russian nuclear experts to Tehran and inviting Iranian nuclear scientists to Moscow for training, according to sources close to the Russian military.[67]
- **September 8, 2008:** A senior Russian nuclear official is quoted by the Russian ITAR TASS news agency as saying that the start-up of the first reactor at Iran's Bushehr nuclear plant will be "irreversible" by February next year. "Between December 2008 and February 2009 various technical measures will be carried out . . . that will make the physical start-up process of the first Bushehr reactor irreversible," the report quoted the head of the Russian company working on the facility, Atomstroiexport, as saying. He says further high-level meetings between Russian and Iranian officials will be held September 29. Russia, using Bushehr as a lever in relations with Tehran, has repeatedly put back the start-up date. Moscow has said it expects the plant to be started up sometime this year.[68]
- **September 10, 2008:** The U.S. imposes sanctions on the Islamic Republic of Iran Shipping Lines (IRISL) and 18 of its affiliates over its alleged support for Tehran's nuclear program. The U.S. Department of the Treasury says that the IRISL's U.S.-based assets will be frozen and its transactions banned. "Not only does IRISL facilitate the transport of cargo for UN-designated proliferators, it also falsifies documents and uses deceptive schemes to shroud its involvement in illicit commerce," Stuart Levey, Under Secretary for Terrorism and Financial Intelligence, says in a statement, and adds that the "IRISL's actions

are part of a broader pattern of deception and fabrication that Iran uses to advance its nuclear and missile programs."[69]

• **September 12, 2008:** IAEA nuclear experts say they believe Iran has renewed work on developing nuclear weapons. "The inspectors only have limited access at Isfahan and it looks as though Iranian officials have removed significant quantities ... at a stage in the process that is not being monitored," an IAEA nuclear official tells the *Daily Telegraph* (London). "If Iran's nuclear intentions are peaceful, then why are they doing this?" Nuclear experts responsible for monitoring Iran's program said they discovered that enough uranium, which if enriched could make up to six bombs, was no longer at the Isfahan nuclear production facility and that spy satellites identified suspicious sites that Iran has not declared to nuclear inspectors.[70]

• **September 15, 2008:** In its latest report on the Iranian nuclear program, the IAEA says it has failed to make meaningful progress in assessing Iran's past nuclear activities. In its report, the IAEA says that Iran is failing to cooperate with its investigators. In May, the UN watchdog said Tehran was withholding information about projects to develop a nuclear warhead, convert uranium, and test high explosives. It called for access to key sites, documents, and officials so that investigators could assess Iran's position that its nuclear work was for peaceful purposes. But, says the IAEA, no such access has been granted. "Regrettably the agency has not been able to make any substantial progress on the alleged studies and other associated key remaining issues which remain of serious concern," and that without greater transparency from Iran, the IAEA would "not be able to provide credible assurances about the absence of undeclared nuclear material and activities in Iran." The IAEA also says that Iran is continuing to install new cascades of centrifuges to enrich uranium in defiance of a UN Security Council order. Around 3,800 centrifuges are now in operation at Iran's enrichment plant in Natanz, an increase of 300 since May, the report says. Responding to the report, the United States says Iran could face more punitive measures.[71]

• **September 15, 2008:** The ISIS writes that the IAEA reported that it had recently obtained information about the possibility of Iran drawing on "foreign expertise" in conducting experiments connected with the symmetrical initiation of a hemispherical high-explosive charge suitable for an implosion-type nuclear weapon. The official notes that the IAEA has not linked this expertise to the A. Q. Khan proliferation network.[72]

• **September 16, 2008:** The IAEA shows the UN documents and photographs suggesting Iran secretly tried to modify a missile cone to fit a nuclear bomb. Tehran said the alleged weapon-related studies were based on fabricated documents or pertained only to conventional arms, and it provided the IAEA a 117-page response in May addressing some of the agency's questions. This evidence heightened Western concerns that Iran may have had foreign expertise helping in experiments on a detonator applicable to an implosion-type nuclear blast occurring at high altitude.[73]

• **September 17, 2008:** "We are against offering the [IAEA] an open door once more and that they expect Iran to respond to any claim," says Alaeddin Borujerdi, the head of parliament's national security and foreign affairs commission, adding, "We do not think there should be an open forum so America can bring up a new claim every day and pass it on to the [IAEA], expecting Iran to address any claim," and, "We continue cooperating with the IAEA but they should not expect us to apply the additional protocol." Iran stopped applying the additional protocol, which gives inspectors broader access to its nuclear sites, after the nuclear case was referred to the UN Security Council in 2006.[74]

- **September 20, 2008:** The Russian Foreign Minister states that Russia's position in regard to the Iran situation is that Russia is against the UN taking any extra measures on Iran over its nuclear program for now and thinks efforts toward dialogue should continue. The comments came after talks between majors powers over a fourth round of UN sanctions against Iran ended with no firm commitment on September 19. The United States, Britain, France, and Germany are pushing for harsher measures over Tehran's defiance of UN demands for full disclosure and a halt to uranium enrichment, which can have both civilian and military purposes. These are moves that Russia and China have resisted.[75]

- **September 23, 2008:** Iranian President Mahmoud Ahmadinejad addresses the UN General Assembly 63rd Session in New York. The following are remarks made by President Ahmadinejad regarding Iran's nuclear program and the Iranian perception of the international system:[76]

  - *Iraq was attacked under the false pretext of uncovering weapons of mass destruction and overthrowing a dictator. The dictator is toppled and WMDs are not uncovered. A democratic government is established by the votes of the people but, after six years, the occupiers are still there. They insist on imposing colonial agreements on the people of Iraq by keeping them under Chapter 7 of the UN Charter. The occupiers, without sense of shame, are still seeking to solidify their position in the political geography of the region and to dominate oil resources.*

  - *The UN is not capable enough to solve the problems and to remove aggression, occupation and imposition.*

  - *The Security Council cannot do anything and sometimes, under pressure from a few bullying powers, even paves the way for supporting these Zionist murderers. It is natural that some UN resolutions that have addressed the plight of the Palestinian people have been relegated to the archives unnoticed.*

  - *The people of Afghanistan are the victims of the willingness of NATO [North Atlantic Treaty Organization] member states to dominate the regions surrounding India, China, and South Asia The Security Council cannot do anything about it because some of these NATO members also happen to be the major decision makers in the Security Council.*

  - *The never-ending arms race and the proliferation stockpile of nuclear and other weapons of mass destruction and the threats to use them, and the establishment of missile defense systems, have made the system unstable.*

  - *With regards to Iran's peaceful nuclear program, despite the inalienable right of all nations including the Iranian nation, in producing nuclear fuel for peaceful purposes, and despite such facts as the transparency of all Iranian activities and our country's full cooperation with the inspectors of the IAEA and the Agency's repeated confirmation of the fact that Iran's activities are peaceful, a few bullying powers have sought to put hurdles in the way of the peaceful nuclear activities of the Iranian nation by exerting political and economic pressures against Iran, and also through threatening and pressuring the IAEA. These are the same powers that produce new generations of lethal nuclear arms and possess stockpiles of nuclear weapons that no international organization is monitoring; and, the tragedies of Hiroshima and Nagasaki were perpetuated by one of them.*

  - *Indeed, they are not against weapons, but they oppose other nations' progress, and tend to monopolize technologies and to use those monopolies in order to impose their will on other nations. But it is very natural that the great Iranian people, with their trust in God, and with determination and steadfastness and will continue to defend its rights. The Iranian nation is for dialogue. But it has not accepted and will not accept illegal demands. The time has come for the IAEA to present a clear report to the international community on its monitoring of the disarmament of these nuclear powers and their nuclear activities, and for a disarmament committee to be established by independent states to monitor the disarmament of these nuclear powers.*

- *The theories of development that are in line with the hegemonic system and not in accordance with the true needs of humankind and human societies.*
- *A universal resistance against the acquisitiveness, aggression and selfishness of the bullying powers is being formed. Today, the bullying powers' thoughts, practices and strategies are rejected by nations and governments, and all are seeking to establish new human relations based on justice with a view to attain prosperity, perfection, security, and sustainable welfare.*
- *Today, the Zionist regime is on a definite slope to collapse, and there is no way for it to get out of the cesspool created by itself and its supporters.*
- *The American empire in the world is reaching the end of its road, and its rulers must limit their interference to their own borders.*

- **September 23, 2008:** The Russian Foreign Ministry reports that it will not participate in a meeting with the United States to discuss Iran's nuclear program, the most significant indication yet of how Russia's war with Georgia has spoiled relations regarding other security issues. Russia and the United States, with China, Britain, France, and Germany, had been scheduled to meet in New York to discuss additional punitive actions against Iran in the wake of a report by the IAEA criticizing Iran's failure to fully answer questions about its nuclear activities. But Russia's refusal to attend meetings and support further sanctions led to a cancellation of the UN Security Council meeting regarding Iran's nuclear program.[77]

- **September 25, 2008:** The *Guardian* (Manchester) reports that on May 14, 2008, then Israeli Prime Minister Ehud Olmert raised the issue of a military strike on Iranian nuclear sites, but was told by President George W. Bush that he would not support it and did not expect to revise that view for the rest of his presidency, says senior European diplomatic sources. The decision to refuse to offer any support for a strike on Iran appeared to be based on two factors, the sources said. One was U.S. concern over Iran's likely retaliation, which would probably include a wave of attacks on U.S. military and other personnel in Iraq and Afghanistan, as well as on shipping in the Persian Gulf. The other was U.S. anxiety that Israel would not succeed in disabling Iran's nuclear facilities in a single assault even with the use of dozens of aircraft. It could not mount a series of attacks over several days without risking full-scale war. So the benefits would not outweigh the costs. If Israel were to launch an attack on Iran without U.S. approval, its planes could not reach their targets without the United States becoming aware of their flight path and having time to ask them to abandon their mission. In this context Iran would be bound to assume Bush had approved it, even if the White House denied foreknowledge, raising the prospect of an attack against the United States.[78]

- **September 26, 2008:** The UN Security Council reaffirms three earlier rounds of sanctions against Iran. No new sanctions were imposed, but the resolution declares that it is "our determination to ensure that the international rules are upheld in this very important area," U.K. Foreign Secretary David Miliband says. Russia's UN ambassador Vitaly Churkin states that "there were some concerns" that the P5+1 were not working together. In order to dispel those concerns "the ministers have decided to introduce this very brief draft resolution which would reaffirm the previous decisions of the Security Council."[79]

- **October 5, 2008:** Iranian Foreign Minister Manouchehr Mottaki states, "Iran's uranium enrichment policy remains unchanged. Enrichment will continue until Iran becomes self-sufficient in fuel production for nuclear plants." Mottaki indicates that Iran is willing to supply other countries with nuclear fuel after it is self-sufficient.[80]

- **October 9, 2008:** The IAEA reports that it is investigating whether a Russian scientist helped Iran conduct nuclear weapons–related experiments. The agency obtained a five-page document written in Farsi from undisclosed sources, detailing precision detonator experiments allegedly conducted by Iran with the Russian scientist's help. The Russian scientist appears to have been working for Iran without the sanction of the Russian government. Iranian officials are calling the charges "groundless" and claiming that the experiments were for conventional arms. In response, IAEA Chief Weapons Inspector Olli Heinonen asserts the experiments were "not consistent with any application other than the development of a nuclear weapon."[81]

- **October 11, 2008:** The United States and a number of Western allies begin discussions regarding imposing new financial sanctions on Iran outside of the UN Security Council. The sanctions would target oil-refining products and refined petroleum. According to one Western diplomat, "The idea would be to get together a coalition of the willing . . . given the difficulties we would have getting this past Russia and China."[82]

- **October 14, 2008:** Approximately 700 Iranian nuclear engineers who received their training in Russia are reported to be ready to begin work on the Bushehr reactor. Iranian nuclear official Ahmad Fayyazbakhsh reports that Bushehr will become operational in March 2009.[83]

- **October 17, 2008:** Russia will reportedly ship nearly 1,000 tons of equipment to Iran for construction of the nuclear power plant at Bushehr. Iranian officials expect Bushehr to be commissioned early next year.[84]

- **October 19, 2008:** According to Mohammad Qods, managing director of Iran's Power Plant Construction Company, some Western countries are interested in cooperating with Iran on the Darkhovin reactor's design and construction. Qods indicated that the design of the 360-megawatt (MW) light-water reactor would be completed in six years and construction would begin in 2013.[85]

- **October 20, 2008:** Mohamed ElBaradei assesses that Iran still lacks the key components to produce nuclear weapons. According to ElBaradei, "They do not have even the nuclear material, the raw un-enriched uranium to develop one nuclear weapon if they decide to do so. Even if you decide to walk out tomorrow from the NPT (Nuclear Nonproliferation Treaty) and you go into a lot of scenarios, we're still not going to see Iran tomorrow having nuclear weapons."[86]

- **October 31, 2008:** A three-page intelligence assessment by an unidentified IAEA member state alleges that Iran has recently tested ways of recovering highly enriched uranium from waste reactor fuel. The report asserts, "Procedures were evaluated for recycling fuel by dissolving fuel rods," which would be taken from the Iranian nuclear reactor and reprocessed into uranium with weapon-usable concentrations. The document also alleges that Iran's Atomic Energy Organization is in the final stages of producing a report for the Iranian leadership to consider whether or not to approve the project. The fuel would be taken from the Tehran Nuclear Research Center (TNRC) research reactor, which is unlikely to yield enough fissile material for a nuclear warhead.[87]

- **November 14, 2008:** According to Deputy Foreign Minister Sergei Riabkov, Russia will oppose any new sanctions aimed at pressuring Iran to halt its atomic work during talks among the P5+1 members meeting, stating, "The Western countries are for the sanctions. China like Russia did not back it."[88]

- **November 18, 2008:** Mohsen Delaviz, spokesman for the Atomic Energy Organization of Iran (AEOI), announces that preparations for the Bushehr nuclear power plant inauguration have started, stating, "The preliminary stages of the inauguration of Bushehr nuclear plant are being carried out and we hope that the power plant will be inaugurated in 2009, in accordance with the agreements reached with the Russian side."[89]
- **November 19, 2008:** According to the IAEA report dated November 19, 2008, Iran has manufactured 630 kilograms (kg) of low-enriched uranium (LEU) and is assembling significantly more centrifuge cascades. In addition, Iran is testing a small number of more advanced IR-2 and IR-3 centrifuges at the Pilot Fuel Enrichment Plant (PFEP) and feeding them with UF_6. IAEA environmental sampling indicates that the Fuel Enrichment Plant (FEP) and the PFEP are operating as declared and only enriching U-235 to 5 percent. At the time of the report Iran was still refusing to address the IAEA's concerns over alleged weaponization experiments. According to the IAEA report, "regrettably, as a result of the lack of cooperation by Iran in connection with the alleged studies and other associated key remaining issues of serious concern, the agency has not been able to make substantial progress on these issues."[90]
- **November 20–21, 2008:** The *New York Times* reports that Iran has produced roughly enough LEU that, if further enriched, could be used to make a single nuclear device. This estimate is based on the latest IAEA report indicating that Iran has manufactured 630 kg of LEU. Experts caution that the milestone is mostly symbolic, because Iran would have to further enrich the LEU for use in a nuclear bomb. According to Richard L. Garwin, a top nuclear physicist who helped invent the hydrogen bomb, "[T]hey [Iran] know how to do the enrichment. Whether they know how to design a bomb, well that is another matter." "They have a weapon's worth," Thomas Cochran, a senior scientist in the nuclear program of the Natural Resources Defense Council, said in an interview with the *New York Times*. He added that if Iran were to further enrich its stockpiled LEU, the amount would be suitable for an implosion-type device. Iranian officials rejected the *New York Times*' claims, asserting that this would require taking additional steps such as ejecting IAEA inspectors and withdrawing from the NPT. Ambassador Ali Asghar Soltanieh says, "This information has no technical basis and gives wrong and misleading information to the public." Iran's envoy to the IAEA indicates that in order for Iran to militarize its enrichment capabilities, it would require substantial centrifuge modification that inspectors would undoubtedly notice.[91]
- **November 26, 2008:** Iran announced that it is now operating 5,000 centrifuges at Natanz, a significant increase from the 4,000 it claimed it was operating in August 2008. According to Gholam Reza Aghazadeh, head of the AEOI, "Iran will continue to install centrifuges and enrich uranium in order to produce nuclear fuel for the country's future nuclear power plants."[92]
- **December 1, 2008:** Ahmad Fayyazbakhsh, deputy head of the AEOI, announces, "Our organization has decided to build two new plants with a capability of 1,000 MW each instead of completing the second unit of the Bushehr nuclear power plant." The two new plants will be built near Bushehr.[93]
- **February 19, 2009:** The IAEA releases its report on the implementation of NPT safeguards in Iran and the status of Iran's compliance with Security Council Resolutions 1737, 1747, and 1803. The report includes three important findings. The first is that while Iran has dramatically increased its installation of centrifuges (now numbering more than 5,400), it has not increased the number of centrifuges enriching uranium, which is

holding steady at just under 4,000. The second is that Iran has accumulated a total of 1,010 kg of low-enriched uranium in the form of UF_6. The third concerns Iran's manufacture of uranium fuel rods for the Arak heavy-water reactor and its continued refusal to allow IAEA inspection of the reactor under construction.[94]

- **February 25, 2009:** Multiple news outlets report that Iranian and Russian officials began a test run of Iran's first nuclear plant after repeated delays in making the plant operational. An Iranian official says the test run was done with computers and uranium was not used. Reports also say that Iranian nuclear scientists will schedule a date to insert uranium fuel rods, if the test is deemed a success.[95] Iran's nuclear chief also claimed that the country has increased the number of centrifuges enriching uranium to 6,000.[96]

- **June 5, 2009:** The IAEA releases its latest report on the implementation of NPT safeguards in Iran and the status of Iran's compliance with Security Council Resolutions 1737, 1747, and 1803. The report includes several important findings:[97]

  - The first is that the number of centrifuges enriching uranium at the Natanz Fuel Enrichment Plant (FEP) has increased to 4,920 (up from 3,936) with an additional 2,132 installed and operating under vacuum. **This brings the total number of centrifuges either enriching uranium or installed and ready to begin enrichment, to 7,052.** Since the last IAEA report, Iran has produced an additional 329 kg of low-enriched uranium (LEU) hexafluoride, or a total of 1,339 kg of LEU hexafluoride reflecting a 20-percent improvement in Iran's daily rate of LEU production. Of note, the IAEA states that given increases in the number of centrifuges operating and the rate of production of LEU, improvements to "containment and surveillance measures" at the FEP are necessary.

  - The second issue highlighted in the report is Iran's continued refusal to allow the IAEA access to the IR-40 reactor under construction at Arak and to provide the Agency with design information for a planned reactor to be built at Darkhovin. The report notes that the IAEA has not visited the Arak reactor since August 2008 and that with the completion of the containment structure over the reactor, it is impossible to continue following progress remotely. Regarding Darkhovin, the IAEA adds that Iran is the only country with "significant nuclear activities" not implementing safeguard provisions that provide the IAEA with access to design information prior to construction.

  - Finally, the IAEA notes that in addition to a small, 10-machine cascade of next-generation IR-2 centrifuges, Iran has recently installed a 10-machine IR-3 cascade and is now operating as single machines, the IR-4 centrifuge.

---

to explore an energy alternative and by government officials who either want nuclear weapons or just want to keep the option open."[98] This statement seems to sum up the dangers of allowing Iran to further its nuclear programs.

PROBLEMS IN ANALYZING IRAN'S WEAPONS OF MASS DESTRUCTION PROGRAM: NUCLEAR WEAPONS AS A CASE STUDY

Given this background, it is scarcely surprising that Iran's nuclear programs present major problems in intelligence collection and analysis. The details of U.S.,

British, and other intelligence efforts to cover Iran remain classified. At the same time, studies of U.S. and British intelligence failures in covering Iraq have provided considerable insights into the difficulties in covering a nation such as Iran, and background discussions with intelligence analysts and users reveal the following general problems in analyzing the WMD threat:

- The uncertainties surrounding collection on virtually all proliferation and weapons of mass destruction programs are so great that it is impossible to produce meaningful point estimates. As the Central Intelligence Agency (CIA) has shown in some of its past public estimates of missile proliferation, the intelligence community must first develop a matrix of what is and is not known about a given aspect of proliferation in a given country, with careful footnoting or qualification of the problems in each key source. It must then deal with uncertainty by creating estimates that show a range of possible current and projected capabilities—carefully qualifying each case. In general, at least three scenarios or cases need to be analyzed for each major aspect of proliferation in each country—something approaching a "best," "most likely," and "worst case."[99]

- Even under these conditions, the resulting analytic effort faces serious problems. Security compartmentation within each major aspect of collection and analysis severely limits the flow of data to working analysts. The expansion of analytic staffs has sharply increased the barriers to the flow of data and has brought a large number of junior analysts into the process that can do little more than update past analyses and judgments. Far too little analysis is subjected to technical review by those who have actually worked on weapons development, and the analysis of delivery programs, warheads and weapons, and chemical, biological, and nuclear proliferation tends to be compartmented. Instead of the free flow of data and exchange of analytic conclusions, or "fusion" of intelligence, analysis is "stovepiped" into separate areas of activity. Moreover, the larger staffs get, the more stovepiping tends to occur.

- Analysis tends to focus on technical capability and not on the problems in management and systems integration that often are the real-world limiting factors in proliferation. This tends to push analysis toward exaggerating the probable level of proliferation, particularly because technical capability is often assumed if collection cannot provide all the necessary information.

- Where data are available on past holdings of weapons and the capability to produce such weapons—such as data on chemical weapons feedstocks and biological growth material—the intelligence effort tends to produce estimates of the maximum size of the possible current holding of weapons and WMD materials. While ranges are often shown, and estimates are usually qualified with uncertainty, this tends to focus users on the worst case in terms of actual current capability. In the case of Iraq, this was compounded by some 12 years of constant lies and a disbelief that a dictatorship obsessed with record keeping could not have records if it had destroyed weapons and materials. The end result, however, was to assume that little or no destruction had occurred whenever the United Nations Special Commission, the United Nations Monitoring, Verification and Inspection Commission, and the IAEA reported that major issues still affected Iraqi claims.

- Intelligence analysis has long been oriented more toward arms control and counterproliferation rather than warfighting, although the Defense Intelligence Agency and the military services have attempted to shift the focus of analysis. Dealing with broad national trends and assuming capability is not generally a major problem in seeking to push nations toward obeying arms control agreements or in pressuring possible suppliers. It also is not a major problem in analyzing broad military counterproliferation risks and programs. The situation is very different in dealing with warfighting choices, particularly issues such as preemption and targeting. Assumptions of capability can lead to preemption that is not necessary, overtargeting, inability to prioritize, and a failure to create the detailed collection and analysis necessary to support warfighters down to the battalion level. This, in turn, often forces field commanders to rely on field teams with limited capability and expertise and to overreact to any potential threat or warning indicator.

- The intelligence community does bring outside experts into the process, but often simply to provide advice in general terms rather than a cleared review of the intelligence product. The result is often less than helpful. The use of other cleared personnel in U.S. laboratories and other areas of expertise are inadequate and often present major problems because those consulted are not brought fully into the intelligence analysis process and given all of the necessary data.

- The intelligence community does tend to try to avoid explicit statements of the shortcomings in collection and methods in much of its analysis and to repeat past agreed judgments on a lowest common denominator level—particularly in the form of the intelligence products that get broad circulation to consumers. Attempts at independent outside analysis or "B teams," however, are not subject to the review and controls enforced on intelligence analysis teams, and the collection data and methods used are generally selected to prove given points rather than to provide an objective counterpoint to finished analysis.[100]

- There often is no reliable methodology for estimating capability at the technical level. Models for estimating missile range-payload, accuracy, and reliability are extremely uncertain unless based on observation of actual missile testing and access to classified national data or telemetry. There is no way to reliably estimate the amount of weapons-grade material a given country needs for a functioning warhead or bomb, or its level of progress in design for fission, boosted, and fusion weapons. Estimates of reactor and centrifuge production of weapons-grade material are extremely uncertain, and estimates of the timelines to use such devices to produce given numbers of nuclear weapons are often worst-case speculations. On the other hand, many analyses of such capabilities can be overconservative because they assume an unrealistic emphasis on reliability or conventional production techniques and/or that a nation cannot "leapfrog" into weapons designs using minimal amounts of weapons-grade material.

Few of these problems have been explicitly addressed in open-source reporting on Iran, and it is uncertain from the reporting on past intelligence failures in the intelligence analysis of Iraq before the 2003 invasion that the intelligence community has covered them at the classified level.

Part of the problem lies with the user. Policy-level and other senior users of intelligence tend to be intolerant of analysis that consists of a wide range of qualifications and uncertainties even at the best of times, and the best of times does not exist when urgent policy and warfighting decisions need to be made. Users inevitably either force the intelligence process to reach something approaching a definitive set of conclusions or else they make such estimates themselves.

Intelligence analysts and managers are all too aware of this fact. Experience has taught them that complex intelligence analysis—filled with alternative cases, probability estimates, and qualifications about uncertainty—generally go unused or make policy makers and commanders impatient with the entire intelligence process. In the real world, hard choices have to be made to provide an estimate that can actually be used and acted upon, and these choices must be made either by the intelligence community or by the user.[101]

These problems are compounded by the fact that so many sources report on parts of the picture—some conflicting and some almost endlessly repeating information and speculation provided in previous reports. These sources also have very different motives.

Opposition Groups

One key source has been an opposition group largely associated with the Mujahadin-e Khalq (MEK). Its information has proven to be useful at times, yet some of the data it provided have been "too good to be true." Revelations by the National Council of Resistance of Iran (NCRI) about Iran's secret nuclear program did prove to be the trigger point in inviting the IAEA into Tehran for inspections, but its claims about "5,000 centrifuges" were premature and came to be seen by many as an exaggeration or at least an unconfirmed allegation.[102]

Later IAEA inspections have shown these numbers to be greatly exaggerated, although the inspectors have been denied access to a number of suspected sites, and Iran may have numerous undisclosed facilities, some of which may be concealed in underground facilities.

The source of such claims must be taken into account. Alireza Jafarzadeh is the former President of NCRI, which is associated with MEK—an organization that is considered by the U.S. Department of State as a terrorist organization and until recently was on the EU list of terrorist groups. Its motives are well known, and its information must be considered with skepticism. As a former CIA counterintelligence official said, "I would take anything from them with a grain of salt."[103]

The NCRI claimed that it relied on human sources, including scientists and civilians working in the facilities or locals who live near the sites. In addition, the NCRI claimed at times that its sources are inside the Iranian regime and added, "Our sources were 100 percent sure about their intelligence."[104] The NCRI did not provide any confirmation about its sources, and its information is considered by some in the U.S. and European governments as less than credible. Another example was the NCRI's claim in September 2004 that Tehran allocated $16 billion to build a nuclear bomb by mid-2005. This again was proven to be inaccurate.[105]

U.S. "Walk-In" Sources

In contrast, U.S. officials have cited walk-in sources to prove the existence of an Iranian nuclear program. It is unclear who those sources are, but the United States insisted that they were not associated with the MEK or NCRI. In November 2004, for example, U.S. officials claimed that a source provided U.S. intelligence with more than 1,000 pages worth of technical documents on Iranian "nuclear warhead design" and missile modifications to deliver an atomic warhead. In addition, it was reported that the documents also included "specific" warhead design based on implosion and adjustments, which was thought to be an attempt at fitting a warhead to Iranian ballistic missiles.[106]

According to the *Washington Post*, the walk-in source that provided the documents was not previously known to U.S. intelligence. In addition, it was not clear if this source was connected to an exile group. The same source was, apparently, the basis for the comments by then Secretary of State Colin Powell on November 17, 2004, when he said, "I have seen some information that would suggest that they have been actively working on delivery systems . . . You don't have a weapon until you put it in something that can deliver a weapon . . . I'm not talking about uranium or fissile material or the warhead; I'm talking about what one does with a warhead."[107]

Press reports indicate that walk-in documents came from one source and were without independent verification. The uncertainty about this source, reportedly, stopped many in the U.S. government from using the information, and some expressed their surprise when Secretary Powell expressed confidence in the information provided. Some saw it as a reminder of the problems in his presentation to the UN regarding Iraqi WMDs and hoped that he had not made those remarks before they were confirmed. Some U.S. officials even went as far as saying that Powell "misspoke" when he was talking about the information.[108]

Other U.S. officials described the intelligence as "weak."[109] Other press reports claimed that the source, who was "solicited with German help," provided valuable intelligence that referred to a "black box," which U.S. officials claim was a metaphor to refer to a nuclear warhead design. One U.S. official was quoted by the *Wall Street Journal* as saying the documents represented "nearly a smoking gun," yet the same official claimed that this was not definitive proof.[110]

Iranian Sources

There are sources within Iran that have cooperated with the IAEA. According to IAEA reports, Iranian nuclear scientists were interviewed on specific questions. For example, in November 2003, the Agency requested clarification on the bismuth irradiation. The IAEA reported that in January 2004, it "was able to interview two Iranian scientists involved in the bismuth irradiation. According to the scientists, two bismuth targets had been irradiated, and an attempt had been made, unsuccessfully, to extract polonium from one of them."[111]

The credibility of these scientists depends on how much freedom they have to talk about specific issues, their level of involvement, and the nature of the questions posed to them. The nature of access and the type of information provided to the IAEA by Iranian scientists remain uncertain.

The IAEA and the UN have been major sources of data, much of which are verified by on-the-scene visits or more detailed inspections. IAEA reports have often provided the most concrete data on what Iran is, and is not, known to be doing, as well as on the major uncertainties affecting Iran's actions and possible nuclear programs. The IAEA, however, is limited in what it can say by the fact it is an international organization focused on one aspect of arms control—nuclear proliferation. It also often has to be moderate or tactful in its summary reporting even if the detailed portions of its reports raise more serious questions and challenges.

Finally, there are sources such as background briefings based on intelligence gathered by the United States, the European Union, and regional powers. These are based on sources such as satellite images, electronic intercepts, human intelligence, and various forms of information gathering and intelligence analysis. The IAEA and the UN do not have their own intelligence and have to rely on member states to provide them with the necessary information. The history of the U.S. and the U.K. intelligence provided to UN inspectors in Iraq, however, has shown the limits to the ability of intelligence agencies to get a full picture of a country's nuclear, biological, chemical, and missile programs.

IRAN'S NUCLEAR PROGRAMS: KEY MILESTONES

It is clear that Iran has sought to acquire nuclear reactors and technology since the 1960s and that the Shah (Mohammad Reza Shah Pahlavi) imported suspect technology that could be used to produce fissile material long before the 1979 Revolution. It is also clear from IAEA discoveries that Iran has pursued two key tracks toward acquiring nuclear fuel or fissile material since the revolution: uranium enrichment and production of plutonium.[112] Both of these tracks can produce the materials that can be used for nuclear reactors and for nuclear weapons.

While some of the details of Iran's history of nuclear activities are controversial, work by the IAEA, the Nuclear Threat Initiative, and other sources provides the following chronology of the key milestones in Iran's nuclear programs from 1959 to 2008:[113]

- **1959:** The Shah ordered the establishment of a nuclear research center at Tehran University.
- **1960:** Iran arranged to establish a 5-MW research center at Tehran University. The United States was supplying a research reactor; it also sold Iran many hot cells.
- **1964:** During his visit to the United States, the Shah decided to start an ambitious plan for nuclear power.

- **1967:** The start-up of the U.S.-supplied 5-MW research reactor occurred at Tehran University.
- **July 1, 1968:** Iran signed the Nuclear Non-Proliferation Treaty (NPT) on the day it was opened for signature.
- **February 2, 1970:** Iran ratified the NPT.
- **1974:** The AEOI was established. The Shah announced that Iran intended to generate 23,000 MW at nuclear power plants "as soon as possible." The U.S. Department of State said that the United States considered cooperation with Iran in the field of nuclear energy as an alternative means for energy production to be a suitable area for joint collaboration and cooperation. The majority of reactors were to be built by the United States. The Shah stated that Iran would have nuclear weapons "without a doubt and sooner than one would think."[114] France and Iran ratified a preliminary agreement for France to supply five 1,000-MW reactors, uranium, and a nuclear research center to Iran. The United States and Iran reached a provisional agreement for the United States to supply two nuclear power reactors and enriched uranium fuel. A Department of State document says the United States and Iran were preparing to negotiate an agreement that would permit the sale of nuclear reactors as well as enriched fuel "at levels desired by the Shah." The United States also notified the Shah of its support for Iran's proposal to buy up to 25-percent interest in a commercial uranium enrichment plant. Iran signed agreements to purchase two 1,200-MW pressurized water reactors from the German firm Kraftwerk Union (KWU) to be installed at Bushehr and two 900-MW reactors from Framatome of France to be installed at Bandar Abbas. Under the contracts, France and Germany would provide enriched uranium for the initial loading and 10 years' worth of reloads. The French reactors were to be built under license from Westinghouse of the United States.
- **1975:** U.S. Secretary of State Henry Kissinger and Iranian Finance Minister Hushang Ansari signed a broad trade agreement that called for the purchase of eight reactors valued at $6.4 billion. The U.S. Atomic Energy Commission agreed to supply Iran with fuel for two 1,200-MW light-water reactors and signed a provisional agreement to supply fuel for as many as six additional reactors with a total power capacity of 8,000 MW.
- **1979:** German construction at the Bushehr reactors was suspended because of the Islamic Revolution in Iran, which in turn put an end to Iran's nuclear program.
- **1980:** Iraq invaded Iran and triggered a war that lasted eight years.
- **1987–1988:** The Bushehr reactors were heavily damaged by Iraqi bombing raids.
- **1990:** Iran signed a 10-year nuclear cooperation agreement with China.
- **July 1989:** Iranian President Akbar Hashemi-Rafsanjani signed the 10-point Iran-Russia cooperation pact on peaceful utilization of "nuclear materials and related equipment."[115]
- **1992:** After a week-long inspection in Iran, an IAEA team found no evidence that Iran had a nuclear weapons program.
- **1993:** The Iranian Majlis (Parliament) ratified bills on cooperation pacts with Russia and China. China provided Iran with an HT-6B Tokamak fusion reactor that was installed at the Plasma Physics Research Centre of Azad University. Iran asked Russia

for heavy-water reactors. U.S. President Bill Clinton convinced Russian President Boris Yeltsin to kill negotiations with Iran on the sale of a natural-uranium-burning (heavy-water) reactor. Germany refused to resume construction of the 80-percent-complete Siemens-built nuclear power plant at Bushehr. Russian Ambassador to Iran Sergei Tretyakov confirmed that Russia would help Iran complete the nuclear reactor in Bushehr, indicating that a preliminary agreement had been reached but that financing was still being negotiated. The CIA assessed Iran is 8–10 years away from acquiring nuclear weapons and asserted that foreign assistance would be critical to the effort.

- **1994:** Russian experts started work on the first unit of Iran's 1,000-MW plant, according to a source at the plant. The Bushehr nuclear power plant was scheduled to be finished in four years. Iran signed a contract with China's National Nuclear Corporation for the supply of two 300-megawatt power reactors and continued to shop for a heavy-water research reactor.

- **1995:** Iran signed a contract with Russia to complete one of the Bushehr reactors and tried to buy a uranium enrichment plant.

- **1997:** China canceled plans to build a nuclear power plant in Iran.

- **1998:** American pressure forced Turboatom, a Ukrainian manufacturer of steam turbines, to abandon its $45-million deal to supply turbines to Bushehr. Russia proposed to build a research reactor in Iran using 20-percent enriched uranium.

- **1999:** Iran threatened to withhold further nuclear contracts from Russia for failing to complete the Bushehr plant in time.

- **2000:** The CIA speculated that Iran might be able to make a nuclear weapon. The finding apparently was not based on reliable evidence, but on the fact that it was unable to track Iran's covert efforts to acquire nuclear materials and technology on the international black market. The U.S. Senate approved legislation that would impose sanctions on entities assisting Iran's chemical, biological, and nuclear weapons programs. Iran announced that it was no longer working with China on nuclear projects. Russia's Ministry of Atomic Energy acknowledged that the Bushehr project was running 18 months behind schedule. The Czech government, under pressure from the United States, banned companies from supplying parts to Bushehr. The ZVVZ Milevsko Company had planned to provide Bushehr with air conditioning equipment. Russia's deputy minister for atomic energy said the Bushehr plant would be completed in 2002. In its report on worldwide proliferation, the CIA stated that Iran sought nuclear-related equipment, material, and technical expertise from a variety of sources, especially in Russia, during the second half of 1999, and that Russian entities continued to interact with Iranian research centers on various activities.

- **2002:** An opposition group that the U.S. government lists as a terrorist organization, the National Council of Resistance of Iran, reported the existence of a uranium enrichment facility at Natanz and a heavy-water plant at Arak. Satellite photographs of Natanz and Arak were publicized in the media, suggesting that Natanz is probably a centrifuge uranium enrichment site and Arak is a heavy-water production plant. Russian technicians restarted work on the abandoned Bushehr reactor despite strong U.S. objection. White House spokesman Ari Fleischer and CIA Chief George Tenet reported that revelations regarding Natanz and Arak reinforce U.S. fears about Iran's "across-the-board pursuit of weapons of mass destruction and missile capabilities."[116]

- **2003:** The IAEA report, after February inspections of Natanz and Arak, stated that Iran had failed to comply with the nuclear Non-Proliferation Treaty. Iran told France, Britain, and Germany—the "EU3" negotiating for the European Union—that it would suspend all enrichment-related activities. Iran signed a protocol allowing snap inspections of nuclear facilities.

- **2004:** The IAEA board complained of inadequate cooperation from Iran. In retaliation, Iran said it would resume production and testing of centrifuges. Iran agreed to suspend voluntarily all of its uranium-enrichment activity as part of a deal with the EU3 (Paris Agreement). Iranian scientists broke the seals on centrifuges that can be used to create weapons-grade material. Iran claimed that they had started to prepare 37 metric tons of raw uranium for processing in centrifuges.

- **2005:** President Mohammad Khatami asserted that no Iranian government would give up nuclear technology programs. The Iranian parliament voted to continue the enrichment program. Iran said it had resumed uranium conversion at its Esfahan plant. A report by IAEA chief Mohamed ElBaradei confirmed Iran had resumed uranium conversion at Isfahan. New Iranian President Mahmoud Ahmadinejad stated that Iran was ready to transfer nuclear know-how to other Muslim nations.

- **2006:** The IAEA Board of Governors voted to refer Iran to the UNSC. Iran stated that it had developed machinery to separate uranium from its ore. Iranian President Mahmoud Ahmadinejad said that Iran will have "completed its fuel cycle" by February–March 2007 and bragged about bringing thousands of centrifuges online. Twenty cascade machines were reported running at Natanz and Farayand. Mahmoud Ahmadinejad inaugurated the Arak heavy-water production plant. IAEA Director General Mohamed ElBaradei reported that Iran tested a 164-machine cascade to 5-percent enrichment, and a second 164-centrifuge cascade started October 23. The IAEA Board of Governors reported the testing of the second 164-machine cascade with UF_6 was begun; as of November 7, Iran had produced 55 tons of uranium (in the form of UF_6) out of the 160 tons of uranium ore it started processing at its Isfahan UCF in June 2006. Iran reported that approximately 34 kilograms of UF_6 were fed into the centrifuges and enriched to levels below 5 percent U-235. Iran had reported by August 31 that a total of 6 kilograms of UF_6 were fed into the then-single cascade between June 23 and July 8. This would represent an almost 500-percent increase in the inserted quantity of UF_6, which in return may be an indication of additional and/or more efficient cascades.

- **2007:** Mohamed ElBaradei said that Iran may be six months away from enriching uranium on an industrial scale. He added that according to U.S. and British intelligence, Iran was 5 to 10 years away from developing a nuclear bomb.[117] The IAEA reported that the Iranian Centrifuge Facility at Natanz had completed the 164-unit cascade, adding to the 10- and 24-unit cascades in the Pilot Fuel Enrichment Plant that already existed. The 164-unit cascade is at the production EFP and in which the first 18 will be tested shortly. The current enrichment quality is at 4.2 percent U-235, proving the design efficiency of the facility. Iran continues to deny remote monitoring of the 3,000-machine hall but pledges to allow frequent inspector visits. Iran also stated that once the hall reaches 500 machines, all monitoring will cease. The IAEA reports that Iran's publicly visible (as inspected by the IAEA) uranium enrichment capacity has doubled since its last look in March, now operating some 164 separation centrifuges in the gallery; Iran hopes to have 3,000 such devices in operation. Iranian President Ahmadinejad announced that Iran is now capable of nuclear fuel production on an "industrial scale."[118] Inspectors for the IAEA concluded that Iran had solved most of its technical problems in enriching uranium and is doing so on a much larger scale than before. A short-notice inspection of Natanz found up to 1,300 active centrifuges, with 300 more being tested and another 300 under construction. Iran seems to be capable of installing up to 3,000 centrifuges as early as June 2007 in "cascades" of 164 centrifuges each. Some diplomats speculate that Iran could have as many as 5,000 centrifuges installed by the end of the year, and some estimates go as high as 8,000. There is, however, no data on the efficiency of this effort or its real-world capability to produce given amounts of weapons-grade uranium.[119]

- **2008:** Iranian officials confirmed they had begun installing IR-2 centrifuges that churn out enriched material at a rate more than double that of Iran's earlier centrifuges. The IRNA reports that three sets of 164-machine cascades from a second series of 3,000 are in motion at Natanz. Previous reports stated that 18 sets of 164-machine cascades were already active in uranium enrichment. During the National Nuclear Technology Festival, President Ahmadinejad declared that activities have started for the installment of 6,000 P-1 centrifuges.[120] Iran has stated its intent to move to full-rate production using some 54,000 centrifuges. A *Washington Post* article citeed a report that indicates that Pakistani nuclear proliferator A. Q. Kahn may have sold Iran the design for a so-called "compact" nuclear weapon—a higher-technology nuke that weighs less and is smaller—ideal for mounting in a ballistic missile nose cone. The information comes from drawings discovered in the investigation in 2006 of Swiss businessmen Maroc, Urs, and Friedrich Tinner who were identified by the U.S., U.K., and IAEA investigators as black market smugglers of nuclear secrets. The *Daily Telegraph* (London) reported that according to latest intelligence circulated among Western diplomats, Iran's Revolutionary Guard had set up a network of civilian companies to manufacture components for the advanced P-2 centrifuges. The operation was allegedly based on the 2004 plot involving Kalaye Electric Company and was exposed by UN nuclear inspectors.[121]

- **September 2008:** In its latest report on the Iranian nuclear program, the UN nuclear watchdog, the IAEA, said it had failed to make meaningful progress in assessing Iran's past nuclear activities. The IAEA also said that Iran was continuing to install new cascades of centrifuges to enrich uranium in defiance of a UN Security Council order. Around 3,800 centrifuges were now in operation at Iran's enrichment plant in Natanz, an increase of 300 since May, the report said. Iran had 3,800 centrifuges operating, with increasing stability, at Natanz. Under optimal—if unlikely—conditions, a fully functional capacity of 3,000 P-1 class centrifuges could give Iran enough material for one fission device in 18–27 months, and some private experts give the worst-case estimate in as little as 12 months—some point to 2008.[122] According to estimates made by the ISIS and based on data obtained in IAEA inspections, Iran had fed 7,600 kg of UF_6 into its centrifuges as of August 30, 2008, and had produced approximately 480 kg of LEU.[123] The ISIS writes that the IAEA reported that it has recently obtained information about the possibility of Iran drawing on foreign expertise in conducting experiments connected with the symmetrical initiation of a hemispherical high-explosive charge suitable for an implosion-type nuclear weapon. The official noted that the IAEA has not linked this expertise to the A. Q. Khan proliferation network.[124] The

IAEA showed the UN documents and photographs suggesting Iran secretly tried to modify a missile cone to fit a nuclear bomb.[125]

- **October 2008:** Approximately 700 Iranian nuclear engineers who received their training in Russia were reported to be ready to begin work on the Bushehr reactor. Iranian nuclear official Ahmad Fayyazbakhsh reported that Bushehr will become operational in March 2009.[126] Russia will reportedly ship nearly 1,000 tons of equipment to Iran for construction of the nuclear power plant at Bushehr. Iranian officials expect Bushehr to be commissioned early next year.[127] According to Mohammad Qods, managing director of Iran's Power Plant Construction Company, some Western countries are interested in cooperating with Iran on the Darkhovin reactor's design and construction. Qods indicated that the design of the 360-MW light-water reactor would be completed in six years and construction would begin in 2013.[128]

- **November 2008:** According to the IAEA report dated November 19, 2008, Iran had manufactured 630 kg of LEU and is assembling significantly more centrifuge cascades. In addition, Iran is testing a small number of more advanced IR-2 and IR-3 centrifuges at the PFEP and feeding them with UF_6. IAEA environmental sampling indicated that the FEP and the PFEP were operating as declared and only enriching U-235 to 5 percent. At the time of the report, Iran was still refusing to address the IAEA's concerns over alleged weaponization experiments. According to the IAEA report, "regrettably, as a result of the lack of cooperation by Iran in connection with the alleged studies and other associated key remaining issues of serious concern, the agency has not been able to make substantial progress on these issues."[129] The *New York Times* reported that Iran had produced roughly enough LEU that, if further enriched, could be used to make a single nuclear device. This estimate was based on the latest IAEA report indicating that Iran has manufactured 630 kg of LEU. Experts caution that the milestone is mostly symbolic, because Iran would have to further enrich the LEU for use in a nuclear bomb.[130] Iran announced that it was operating 5,000 centrifuges at Natanz, a significant increase from the 4,000 it claimed it was operating in August 2008. According to Gholam Reza Aghazadeh, head of the AEOI, "Iran will continue to install centrifuges and enrich uranium in order to produce nuclear fuel for the country's future nuclear power plants."[131]

- **February 2009:** On February 19, 2009, the IAEA released its latest report on the implementation of NPT safeguards in Iran and the status of Iran's compliance with Security Council Resolutions 1737, 1747, and 1803. The report includes three important findings. The first is that while Iran has dramatically increased its installation of centrifuges (now numbering more than 5,400), it has not increased the number of centrifuges enriching uranium, which is holding steady at just under 4,000. The second is that Iran has accumulated a total of 1,010 kg of low-enriched uranium in the form of UF_6. The third concerns Iran's manufacture of uranium fuel rods for the Arak heavy-water reactor and its continued refusal to allow IAEA inspection of the reactor under construction.[132] On February 25, 2009, multiple news outlets reported that Iranian and Russian officials began a test run of Iran's first nuclear plant after repeated delays in making the plant operational. An Iranian official says the test run was done with computers and uranium was not used. Reports also say that Iranian nuclear scientists will schedule a date to insert uranium fuel rods, if this test run is deemed a success.[133] Iran's nuclear chief also claimed that the country has increased the number of centrifuges enriching uranium to 6,000.[134]

• **June 2009:** The IAEA released its latest report on the implementation of NPT safeguards in Iran and the status of Iran's compliance with Security Council Resolutions 1737, 1747, and 1803. The report includes several important findings. The first is that the number of centrifuges enriching uranium at the Natanz Fuel Enrichment Plant (FEP) has increased to 4,920 (up from 3,936) with an additional 2,132 installed and operating under vacuum. **This brings the total number of centrifuges either enriching uranium or installed and ready to begin enrichment, to 7,052.** Since the last IAEA report, Iran has produced an additional 329 kg of low-enriched uranium (LEU) hexafluoride, or a total of 1,339 kg of LEU hexafluoride reflecting a 20-percent improvement in Iran's daily rate of LEU production. The report also notes that the IAEA has not visited the Arak reactor since August 2008 and that with the completion of the containment structure over the reactor, it is impossible to continue following progress remotely. Regarding Darkhovin, the IAEA adds that Iran is the only country with "significant nuclear activities" not implementing safeguard provisions that provide the IAEA with access to design information prior to construction. Finally, the IAEA notes that in addition to a small, 10-machine cascade of next-generation IR-2 centrifuges, Iran has recently installed a 10-machine IR-3 cascade and is now operating as single machines, the IR-4 centrifuge.[135]

IRAN'S KEY NUCLEAR FACILITIES

Iran has numerous facilities associated with its various nuclear programs and activities. Some of these sites are still suspected sites, and the details of the true activities taking place at these sites are still speculative and cannot be confirmed due to Iran's lack of transparency and full cooperation with IAEA inspectors. Based on numerous open sources—including (but not limited to) reporting by the IAEA, the Federation of American Scientists, GlobalSecurity.org, NTI, the University of Wisconsin's Iran Watch program, and multiple media outlets—it is possible to put together the following list of declared and suspected nuclear facilities:[136]

• **Jabr Ibn Hayan Multipurpose Laboratory (JHL):**

  ○ Radioisotope Research and Development (R&D) and Uranium Conversion. At least a laboratory-scale capability to convert uranium. In a letter to the IAEA, Iranian authorities confirmed that in 1991, the facility had received natural uranium that was not previously reported. Iran stated that in 1991, they received 1,000 kg of UF_6, 400 kg of UF_4, and 400 kg of uranium dioxide (UO_2). This material was being held, and likely remains, at the JHL. Iran further stated that some of the imported UO_2 was used to test uranium purification and conversion processes. In 2000, Iran converted almost all of the UF_4 that it had obtained in 1991 to uranium metal. Subsequently, Iran stored the conversion equipment at that facility and began refurbishing it to create a dedicated metal reprocessing laboratory. JHL is a primary training facility for nuclear science and technology. It was established in 1990. The staff at JHL is involved in all aspects of Iran's research and development program. It comprises a nuclear spectrometry laboratory, nuclear production fuel facility, conversion laboratory, an instrumental analysis laboratory, and a health physics section.

- **Suspected Rudan Conversion Facility at Fasa:**

  ○ This facility is thought to be the site of a uranium hexafluoride gas conversion plant, or some other form of nuclear research center. Indications of the existence of this facility (wherever it might be located) included Russian press reports of a shipment of uranium hexafluoride gas from China to Iran in late 1994, as well as purchases of hydrogen fluoride from Germany and attempts to buy fluorification equipment from the United Kingdom. U.S. officials asserted that in the mid-1990s, China built a uranium hexafluoride conversion plant in Rudan as part of a secret nuclear co-operation agreement signed in 1991. The agreement came as the result of a two-day Chinese visit of Iran's nuclear facilities in July 1991. According to media reports, in late 1994, China delivered equipment for the plant to Iran. The last list of declared Iranian nuclear facilities, published in 2004, did not include any additional uranium conversion facilities. IAEA reports as of July 2008 had not mentioned a facility near Fasa or referred to as Rudan.

  ○ In mid-2001 Israel's Eros A1 imaging spacecraft photographed what its operators believed to be the construction site for a facility that could be used to store large missiles. Fasa had not previously been associated with missile-related activities. The image taken by the spacecraft showed excavation works for large underground bunkers. The roads on the site formed two hexagons and below these the start of what might have been intended as an octagon. Between the hexagons and the main road were around 20 buildings, some of which were contained in a small pentagonal-shaped area.

- **Isfahan (Esfahan) Nuclear Technology Center (INTC); Isfahan Uranium Conversion Facility; Isfahan Fuel Manufacturing Plant (FMP); Isfahan Fuel Element Cladding Plant; Isfahan Nuclear Fuel Research and Production Center (NFRPC); Isfahan Nuclear Waste Storage Facility:**

  ○ Large-scale multipurpose facility: R&D, uranium conversion, nuclear waste storage, etc. Some sources assess Isfahan to be the primary location of the Iranian nuclear weapons program.

  ○ The NFRPC was founded in 1974 for scientific and technical support of the country's comprehensive nuclear power plant program. It is involved in various aspects of fuel analysis and research. The Metallurgical Engineering and Fuel Department at the center operates the Fuel Fabrication Laboratory and is involved in "experimental production of fuel for WWER reactors."[137] The NFRPC may be the future location of the FMP. Construction at the site of the INTC may have included a hexafluoride plant that was built with Chinese assistance, as part of the nuclear cooperation deal, which was later canceled under U.S. pressure.

  ○ Located at the University of Isfahan, the INTC is one of Iran's largest nuclear research complexes. In 1975, France signed an agreement to build the facility and train personnel to operate the Bushehr reactor. Isfahan is a multipurpose research center. It operates two research reactors, a critical assembly, and a subcritical assembly. It also operates a hexafluride conversion facility, a fuel production plant, a zirconium cladding plant, and other facilities and laboratories. The INTC may also operate a laboratory-scale heavy-water production facility on its premises. In a letter to the IAEA dated August 19, 2003, the AEOI reported that the decision to conduct research in heavy research production was made in the early 1980s. By the mid-1980s, laboratory-scale experiments were undertaken at the INTC. The results of those experiments prompted subsequent decisions in the mid-1990s to construct a heavy-water reactor.

○ The Isfahan UCF was constructed to facilitate the conversion of yellowcake into uranium oxide, uranium hexafluoride, and uranium metal at the INTC. In July 2003, Iran revealed to the IAEA that it had obtained the designs for the UCF from abroad and that this information was sufficient to complete a more detailed design of the facility and manufacture conversion equipment indigenously. The facility was planned with the intention of supplying UO_2 as fuel to the 40-MW heavy-water reactor under construction at Arak and to meet the needs of UF_6 for the Natanz enrichment facility. IAEA chief Mohamed ElBaradei confirmed Iranian statements that it had resumed uranium conversion at Isfahan in 2005. In 2006, IAEA Director General Mohamed ElBaradei reported that Iran tested a 164-machine cascade to 5-percent enrichment, and a second 164-centrifuge cascade started October 23. The IAEA Board of Governors reported the testing of the second 164-machine cascade with UF6 was begun; as of November 7, Iran had produced 55 tons of uranium (in the form of UF_6) out of the 160 tons of uranium ore it started processing at its Isfahan UCF in June 2006. Iran reported that approximately 34 kg of UF_6 was fed into the centrifuges and enriched to levels below 5 percent U-235. Iran had reported by August 31 that a total of 6 kg of UF_6 was fed into the then-single cascade between June 23 and July 8. This would represent an almost 500-percent increase in the inserted quantity of UF_6, which in return may be an indication of additional and/or more efficient cascades.

○ Waste from the "testing of processes envisioned for UCF, isotope production experiments at TRR [Tehran Research Reactor], and the use of pellets for testing chemical processes for the MIX facility" is said to have been transferred to storage facilities at Isfahan.

• **Natanz Enrichment Facility (FEP and PFEP):**

○ The Natanz facility is believed to be the third stage in the three stages of Iran's centrifuge enrichment program. The program is believed to have begun in 1985 on the AEOI's premises in Tehran, before moving to the second stage at the Kalaye Electric Company, also in Tehran, in 1997. In 2002, assembly activities were moved to Natanz.

○ The Natanz Enrichment Plant comprises at least three main areas: an above-ground area, three large underground structures, and one large building standing alone. The above-ground area consists of six large buildings. Two of these are twin 2,500 meter halls. The function of the above-ground buildings is to assemble gas centrifuges. The underground structures are primarily centrifuge halls. The first two buildings each measure 190 meters by 170 meters, with a surface area of approximately 32,000 square meters. The third structure is smaller, with a gross ground area of approximately 7,700 square meters. It is intended to provide support and administrative services to the two larger structures.

- The Natanz Enrichment Plant is a large facility holding a PFEP and a commercial FEP. The PFEP is a test facility located at Natanz before industrial-scale enrichment takes place at the FEP, Iran's main uranium enrichment facility. The PFEP, when completed, will hold 1,000 centrifuges. The Director General of the IAEA visited the facility in February 2003 and observed over 100 (as many as 160) centrifuges already installed. The PFEP was originally scheduled to be completed and begin operation in June 2003. On June 25, 2003, Iran introduced UF_6 into a centrifuge for single-machine testing and subsequently on August 19, 2003, began testing a small 10-machine cascade with UF_6. At the time, both tests were conducted with safeguard measures in place. Questions remain as to how the Iranians tested their centrifuges.

- Since the removal of the seals at the Natanz facility, Iran has conducted substantial renovation of the gas-handling system at the PFEP. Following the release of updated design information for the PFEP to the IAEA on February 8, 2006, on February 11, 2006, Iran started enrichment tests by feeding a single P-1 centrifuge machine with UF_6 gas. Subsequently, by February 15 and February 22, the feeding of a 10-machine cascade and a 20-machine cascade were carried out at the PFEP, respectively. In 2007, the IAEA reported that the Iranian Centrifuge Facility at Natanz had completed the 164-unit cascade, adding to the 10- and 24-unit cascades in the Pilot Fuel Enrichment Plant that already existed.

- In April 2006, Iran successfully completed a UF_6 feeding campaign using a 164-machine cascade at the PFEP. The level of the enriched product from the aforementioned process was estimated to be between 3.5 and 4.8 percent uranium-235. In May 2006, the IAEA took samples to confirm the enrichment levels of the product. Since the April campaign, Iran has fed UF_6 into a single machine, and one machine of the 10-machine cascade. Beginning June 6, Iran started feeding UF_6 into the 164-machine cascade and is working on the installation of another 164-machine cascade at the PFEP. While the enrichment process and products at the PFEP, including the feed and withdrawal station, are under IAEA containment and surveillance measures, Iran has thus far declined to discuss implementation of remote monitoring for verification of its enrichment facilities.

- During his February 2003 visit, the International Atomic Energy Agency's Director General learned that the FEP at Natanz, when completed, would house 50,000 centrifuges at full operational capacity. The IAEA received updated design information from Iran for the FEP on February 8, 2006. Also, as per IAEA reports, equipment such as process tanks and an autoclave are being moved into the FEP. At the present time, the number of complete centrifuges in Iran's possession is yet uncertain. It is estimated that once completed, the FEP operating at full capacity of 50,000 centrifuges will have the potential to produce, at a minimum, 500 kg of weapons-grade uranium per year. Twenty cascade machines were reported running at Natanz in 2005. A short-notice IAEA inspection of Natanz in 2007 found up to 1,300 active centrifuges, with 300 more being tested and another 300 under construction. In its September 2008 report the IAEA stated that Iran was continuing to install new cascades of centrifuges to enrich uranium in defiance of a UN Security Council order. The number of centrifuges enriching uranium at the Natanz Fuel Enrichment Plant (FEP) has increased to 4,920 with an additional 2,132 installed and operating under vacuum. This brings the total number of centrifuges either enriching uranium or installed and ready to begin enrichment, to 7,052. Israeli experts believe that Natanz will come online in 2013.

- **Suspected Additional Enrichment Sites at Lashkar-Abad and Ramandeh:**

  ○ On May 27, 2003, the People's Mojedin Organization (MKO) revealed that two additional secret uranium enrichment facilities were being constructed by the Iranian government. The first is at Lashkar-Abad, which is close to Hashtgerd, and the second is at Ramandeh. The MKO asserted that construction at both facilities is complete and there may already be "a number" of centrifuges installed there. The MKO also stated that the additional facilities are "complimentary" to the larger Natanz site and may support the larger facility or even take over for Natanz if it were destroyed. The MKO claims that these additional sites may be under the management of the front company, "Noor-Afza-Gostar." In July 2003, the IAEA sought permission to take environmental samples at these two sites, but the Iranian authorities refused access.

  ○ IAEA inspectors were permitted visits to these locations on August 13, 2003. During that visit, they determined that the Lashkar-Abad facility was operating a laser laboratory. Iranian officials claim that the facility was originally devoted to laser fusion research and laser spectroscopy, but that its focus has since changed. The IAEA inspectors noted that the facility was engaging in the production of copper vapor lasers of up to 100 watts, but that no experiments involving laser spectroscopy or enrichment appeared to be under way. The officials claimed that in the past, the laser division of the AEOI had cooperated with a university student to write a thesis in laser spectroscopy of SF_6. The IAEA noted in its August 2003 to its board of governors, "While the study could be seen as relevant to laser enrichment, the underlying experiments appear not to have involved nuclear material."[138] IAEA inspectors were not able to take environmental samples at Lashkar-Abad.

- **Khondab Water Production Plant; Arak Heavy-Water Reactor (IR-40):**

  ○ The heavy-water production plant is under construction in Khondab, near Arak. According to the May 2003 Nuclear Suppliers Group Plenary notes, the production capacity for this plant is approximately 100 tons per year.

  ○ On August 14, 2002, members of an Iranian resistance group, the National Council of Resistance of Iran, alleged that the Iranian government was involved in the construction of "at least two secret sites that support its nuclear weapons program." One of these was a heavy-water production plant in Arak. These allegations prompted the IAEA to question the Iranian authorities about the existence of a heavy-water program. On May 5, 2003, the Iranian authorities informed the IAEA of their intention to construct a heavy-water research reactor at Arak. However, the decision to supplement Iran's nuclear program with a heavy-water reactor was made in the mid-1990s. Construction of the Arak reactor, a 40-MW thermal heavy-water reactor began in 2004. The Arak reactor will use natural UO_2 fuel and heavy water as both cooler and moderator. At present, construction continues at the reactor site and is scheduled for completion in 2009. It is believed that the IR-40 will be used for research and development activities, radioisotope production, and training. To meet the isotope production requirements, Iranian officials believe that the reactor must have a neutron flux of 1,013 to 1,014 n/cm^2/s. This would require a reactor capable of producing 30–40 MW thermal when using UO_2 as fuel. Once fully operational, it is believed that the Arak reactor will be able to produce about 9 kg of weapons-grade plutonium each year, or enough for about two nuclear weapons each year. IAEA inspectors confirmed that a heavy-water production plant was under construction in Arak. In 2006 Iranian President Mahmoud Ahmadinejad inaugurated the Arak heavy-water production plant.

○ The Iranian state-owned heavy manufacturing firm Machine Sazi Arak bought eight vertical turning and boring machines (three Model SKJ-12As, three Model SKJ-20As, and two SKD-32As), and the Czech firm TST Kovosvit Semimovo Usti provided Machine Sazi Arak with at least five computer numerical-controlled drilling machines. These machines are used in the construction of uranium centrifuges.

• **Bushehr Nuclear Power Generators:**

○ Bushehr is nearing completion and expected to come online sometime in early 2009. Israeli experts claim that Russia has transferred fuel to Iran for Bushehr and expect the plant to be active in no more than year. On February 25, 2009, a test run of the Bushehr plant was conducted and Iranian officials stated that if this test run proves to be successful, the plant could be scheduled to have uranium fuel rods installed and be up and running in a matter of months.[139] It is similar to the technical configuration of Unit Four at Russia's Balakovskaya plant in Balakovo.

○ The Bushehr project began in 1975, before the 1979 revolution. The West German company KWU started building what would have been a pair of 1,300-MW pressurized water reactors at that time. Bushehr-1 was 90 percent built and Bushehr-2 was partly built when a series of problems began to plague the project. The first came in 1979 after the new government under Ayatollah Ruhollah Khomeini decided to freeze construction of the reactors. The project was restarted shortly after the new government came to power. However, from 1980 to 1988, Iraqi warplanes conducted a series of bombing raids on the reactors and damaged them severely. Subsequently, the government requested assistance from foreign commercial contractors to rebuild and complete the power plants. Iran contacted various countries including Argentina, China, Russia, and West Germany. Finally, in 1995, Tehran and Moscow signed an $800 million agreement for the completion of Bushehr-1. Minatom assumed overall management of the work, utilizing organizations such as Zarubezhatomenergostroy (Nuclear Energy Construction Abroad) and Novosibirsk Chemical Concentrate Plant, which is contributing nuclear fuel. In addition, Russia has been training at least 10–20 graduate students and Ph.D. students annually in Russian facilities such as the Kurchatov Institute. Other Iranian technicians have been trained in Russia at various reactors and institutes over the years. The experience that these students and technicians gain may be used to operate Bushehr, but may also be used to develop new indigenous reactors, or other more discreet military applications.

○ With Bushehr nearing completion and scheduled to come online in early 2009, as per a deal signed between Iran and Russia in February 2005, fuel for the reactor will be supplied by Russia. Under the terms of the deal, Iran is also required to return spent fuel rods from the Bushehr reactor to Russia.

○ Approximately 700 Iranian nuclear engineers who received their training in Russia were reported to be ready to begin work on the Bushehr reactor in October 2008. Iranian nuclear official Ahmad Fayyazbakhsh reported that Bushehr will become operational in March 2009.[140] Russia will reportedly ship nearly 1,000 tons of equipment to Iran for construction of the nuclear power plant at Bushehr. Iranian officials expect Bushehr to be commissioned early next year.[141] Although the reactor is not yet fully operational, on February 25, 2009, a test run of the Bushehr plant was conducted and Iranian officials stated that if this test run proves to be successful, the plant could be scheduled to have uranium fuel rods installed and be up and running in a matter of months.[142] In its June 5, 2009, report, the IAEA Director General stated that "Iran has informed the Agency that the loading of fuel into the Bushehr Nuclear Power Plant is now scheduled to take place in September/October 2009."[143]

○ On August 14, 2003, Iran's First Vice President Mohammad-Reza Aref authorized the AEOI to sign contracts for the construction of a second reactor at the Bushehr nuclear power plant, with a capacity of 1,000 MW.

• **Tehran Nuclear Research Center (TNRC); TRR (IR-0001); Laboratory Scale Milling Facility; Kalaye Electric, Sharif University of Technology (SUT); Atomic Energy of Iran; Molybdenum, Iodine, and Xenon Radioisotope Production Facility (MIX Facility):**

○ The TNRC is located at the University of Tehran. The center was constructed in the early 1960s and became operational in 1965. The University of Tehran originally oversaw the center, but in 1974 it was transferred to its present management, the AEOI. The TNRC is composed of the following: Reactor Research and Operation Department, Radioisotopes Research and Production Department, Nuclear Physics Department, Theoretical Physics and Mathematics Departments, Analytical Chemistry Department, Engineering Department, Solid State Physics Section, Health Physics Department, Electronics Department, and the Chemistry & Physics Department. Iran may have separated gram quantities of plutonium from spent fuel at a laboratory at the TNRC. In 1988, an Iranian nuclear engineer stated that he took part in experiments at the TNRC in which he and his colleagues cold-tested a plutonium extraction laboratory, but did not reprocess any plutonium. Akbar Etemad, former head of the AEOI, also confirmed that experiments were performed on a laboratory scale related to the reprocessing of spent fuel. The TNRC operates several hot cells that were supplied by the United States in 1967. These provide a basic capability for separating plutonium from spent fuel, but do not constitute a dedicated program by themselves. However, there are other facilities at the TNRC such as a radiation measurements laboratory, chemistry laboratory, and radioisotope production unit that may contribute to a reprocessing capability. In the 1990s, the TNRC radiochemistry section conducted some "laboratory-scale experiments," presumably at this laboratory, to produce UF_4 from depleted UO_2 that was imported by Iran in 1997.

○ The TNRC is also on the site of the TRR. In 1967, this U.S.-made 5-MWt pool-type light-water research reactor went critical. Intelligence analysts believe that the TNRC is the location of Iran's secret nuclear program, including plutonium reprocessing, laser enrichment, and weapons-design efforts. It is capable of producing up to 600 grams of plutonium annually. In 1987, the AEOI paid Argentina's Applied Research Institute $5.5 million to convert the reactor's fuel from 93-percent enriched uranium to 20-percent enriched uranium. The Argentine Nuclear Energy Commission has subsequently supplied the reactor with 115.8 kg of safeguarded 20-percent enriched uranium fuel. In the 1990s, TRR was used to irradiate UO_2 targets for subsequent separation of I-131 at the MIX facility. The facility remains in operation.

○ The Kalaye Electronic Company comprises several facilities, one of which is a workshop where open sources have reported on the possible conduct of enrichment activities. When questioned about the reports, the Iranian authorities acknowledged that the workshop was used for the production of centrifuge components, but stated that no nuclear material had been used in the operation of this workshop or the assembly of centrifuges, either at the Kalaye Electric Company or at any other location in Iran. During later visits, IAEA officials noted that much construction had taken place since the previous visit in March 2003.

○ In its February 2005 declaration to the IAEA, Iran informed the Agency that it had prepared a small amount of UO_2 for use in pellets to test the chemical processes of the MIX facility. The material was used to fabricate targets, irradiate it at the TRR, and separate it in a lead-shielded cell at a laboratory in the MIX facility to obtain the resulting I-131 isotope. Analysts are concerned that other activities may have occurred during these experiments. According to David Albright and Corey Hinderstein, "The question is whether plutonium was also separated from these targets, or whether other undeclared targets were produced, irradiated, and processed to obtain separated plutonium."[144]

○ SUT is one of the largest engineering schools in Iran. There are approximately 8,000 students supported by 300 full-time faculty and 430 adjunct staff. SUT was established in 1966 under the name of Aryamehr University of Technology. Western intelligence once believed that Sharif University was at the center of research in uranium enrichment and spent fuel reprocessing. To prove this, some analysts cite a 1991 attempt by SUT staff to purchase ring magnets from the German firm Thyssen. This attempt ultimately failed. The Iranian government may have supported SUT's efforts by clandestinely procuring nuclear-related and dual-use technologies, and buying small companies, particularly in Germany, to serve as export fronts for sensitive equipment. The status of these activities is unknown.

- **Gorgan al-Kabir Center:**

  ○ Possible nuclear weapon production: In the early 1990s, the media reported that there was a secret nuclear research facility at Gorgan. According to one report, scientists from Iran, Ukraine, Russia, and Kazakstan were working at the Gorgan al-Kabir Center to develop nuclear weapons. These reports have never been substantiated.

- **Weapons development facility at Chalus:**

  ○ Chalus had been reported as the location of an underground nuclear weapons development facility located inside a mountain south of this coastal town. The facility had been variously reported as being staffed by experts from Russia, China, and North Korea. The reports came in 1995 from Iranian exiles living in Europe. In March 2002 the claims resurfaced in a report by the *Middle East Intelligence Bulletin*. It was described as an alleged underground nuclear weapons development facility built in the Alborz Mountains. Iranian authorities reportedly told their citizens that the facility was an electricity generation plant operated by Canadians.

- **Moallem Kaleyah:**

  ○ The IRGC reportedly operates a gas centrifuge uranium enrichment plant and suspected nuclear weaponization research site. In 1987, Iran acquired equipment from French, German, and Italian companies to construct and outfit the facility. Some sources report that the facility was for weaponization. Other sources state that Moallem Kaleyah may be used for laser enrichment. In 1992, IAEA inspectors visited the site and found only a small training center under construction. Some believe that the inspectors were taken to the wrong location, away from the real site.

- **Saghand Uranium Mine:**

  ○ The Saghand uranium mine is divided into two distinct deposits: Saghand 1, which is approximately 16 meters below the surface and encompasses an area 200 meters by 300 meters, and Saghand 2, which is approximately 70 meters below the surface. Identified reserves for Saghand 1 are estimated at 1,927 metric tons of uranium and for Saghand 2 at 1,367 metric tons of uranium. Undiscovered reserves for the Saghand mine are estimated at 7,500 metric tons of uranium.

  ○ Iran has received assistance in exploiting its uranium deposits at various times and from various countries. Specialists have come from Argentina, Germany, Czechoslovakia, Hungary, and Russia. Most notably, the Chinese have provided the greatest assistance. In the early 1990s, over 600 Chinese and Iranian specialists formed a working group to investigate the deposits. Experts from the Beijing Research Institute of Uranium Geology have assisted Iran in prospecting for uranium in the past. Additionally, the NCRI has previously alleged the presence of approximately 50 Chinese experts at Saghand and is reportedly host to approximately 230 workers comprising of Iranian specialists and engineers.

- **Talmesi and Meskani Uranium Mines:**

  ○ These mines contain approximately 200 tons of EAR-II uranium. They are among the oldest known ore deposits in Iran. However, they have been systematically exploited only since 1935. The mines have experienced intermittent operations since then and were closed in 1968 after copper mining operations were shut down. Upon discovering uranium at the sites in the 1990s, the AEOI began operating the mines to exploit the deposits.

- **Bonab Atomic Energy Research Center:**

  ○ In 1989, Iran began the first phase of Bonab's development, but it did not become operational until 1995. The center conducts research on nuclear technology for agricultural applications. In July 1997, IAEA Director General Hans Blix visited Bonab and found that all was in order. However, there have been allegations that not all activities at Bonab have been declared to the IAEA.

- **Ardakan Pilot Yellowcake Production Facility and Uranium Ore Processing Plant:**

  ○ This large-scale facility will be able to process between 100 and 200 tons of ore annually. Iran may have received assistance in developing the plant from various countries. In 1989, Argentina signed an agreement to build a series of structures, but that deal fell through due to U.S. input. In the mid-1990s, Russia drew designs for the plant. Later, Chinese specialists helped Iran begin constructing the plant.

- **Yazd Radiation Processing Center (YRPC); Beneficiation and Hydrometallurgical Center (BHRC):**

  ○ The YRPC is one of the newest industrial complexes of Iran. It is engaged in geophysical research to analyze the mineral deposits surrounding the city. The AEOI expects this center to play an important role in supporting the medical and polymer industries. The YRPC is equipped with a Rhodotron TT200 accelerator, made by IBA, Belgium, with outputs of 5- and 10-MeV (megaelectron volt) beam lines and a maximum power of 100 KW (kilowatts). The YRPC was organized to apply radiation research in the field of applied radiation chemistry. The facility provides buildings for accelerator equipment, administration offices, and laboratory equipment. Professor M. Haji Saeid, Director of YRPC, leads the group to engage technology implementation and to collaborate with the Agriculture and Medical Center in Karaj and other scientific institutions in Iran.

  ○ AEOI personnel working at the BHRC examine the mineralogy, mineral processing, beneficiation, preparation, and leaching of uranium ores to determine the best method for mining and recovery of uranium in Yazd. The BHRC operates research labs and engineering facilities that undertake the following: sampling, crushing, grinding, preparation, and mineral processing of uranium, thorium, and phosphates; research to determine the process flow for the hydrometallurgy of resources in the bench scale and pilot plant; studies to compare lab and pilot-plant conditions; expansion of heap-leaching methods, in-place, in-situ, and bacteria leaching; preparation of technical specifications and the layout of the pilot plant for production of yellowcake; and all areas of purification and milling operation at a laboratory scale.

- **Karaj Agricultural and Medical Research Center (30 MeV Cyclotron) (1-Millamp Calutron):**

  ○ On May 11, 1991, the AEOI began operating this research center. It comprises the Departments of Nuclear Agriculture, Ion Beam Applications, Materials Engineering, Nuclear Electronics, Nuclear Medicine, and Health Physics. It also operates a 30-MeV cyclotron accelerator, a 1-milliamp calutron, and a secondary standard dosimetry laboratory. The C30 is a fixed-field, fixed-frequency, variable-energy dual-proton beam cyclotron. In 1991, Belgium's Ion Beam Applications supplied C30 to Iran. C30 produces "Single Photon-Emission Tomography" and "Positron Emission Tomography" isotopes. The cyclotron has 10 ports that are capable of holding a wide range of target and chemistry systems to produce a variety of isotopes. This calutron was provided by the Chinese. The existence of these devices has led to allegations that China was installing a uranium-enrichment facility using calutrons at Karaj. A large hydroelectric dam located nearby could provide the facility with the great amounts of electricity it would require. However, the Chinese-supplied calutron is housed in a gymnasium-sized building that uses an unprotected ventilation system that would normally exclude it from working with radioactive substances.

- **Azad University Plasma Physics Research Center at Damarand:**

  ○ The research center conducts research to examine plasma activities. It houses a HT-6B Tokamak nuclear fusion research reactor. In 1993, China's Institute of Plasma Physics agreed to transfer the Tokamak to Azad University. Under the agreement, two teams of Chinese scientists and engineers assisted Iran to install the reactor.

- **Engineering Research Center for the Constructions Crusade (Jihad-e Sazandegi) at Tabriz:**

  ○ Engineering defense research, possible chemical, biological, radiological, and nuclear (CBRN) weaponization research facility.

- **Gchine:**

  ○ Uranium mine in the south of Iran, near Bandar Abbas, with co-located mill. Low but variable grade uranium ore found in near-surface deposits will be open-pit mined and processed. GlobalSecurity.org indicates that the estimated production design capacity is 21 tons of uranium per year. Iran has stated that, as of July 2004, mining operations had started and the mill had been hot tested, during which testing a quantity of about 40–50 kg of yellowcake was produced.

- **Karazj:**

  ○ Radioactive Waste Storage (under construction, but partially operating).

- **Koloduz:**

  ○ Possible nuclear-related facility located about 14 km west of Tehran; the plant is reportedly concealed within a large military complex. The U.S. Geological Survey's National Imagery and Mapping Agency's only rendering of this name is Kolah Duz, but the name of this facility is also transliterated as Kolahdouz, Kolahdooz, or Kolahdoz.

- **Darkhovin, also variously referred to as Ahvaz, Darkhouin, Esteghlal, and Karun:**

  ○ Located on the Karun River south of the city of Ahvaz. A facility at this location is reportedly under the control of the Islamic Revolution Guard Corps and is said to be suspected of being an underground nuclear weapons facility of unspecified nature.

- **Tabas:**

  ○ Reported as a possible site of a nuclear reactor of North Korean origin. This is probably an unfounded speculation.

- **Anarak:**

  ○ Waste storage site (waste to be transferred to JHL).

IRAN'S CURRENT NUCLEAR DEVELOPMENTS

No consensus exists regarding the degree to which Iran's current nuclear activities are or are not designed to help give it nuclear weapons, and especially over the critical question of how close Iran is to having a nuclear device. Few now believe that Iran has nuclear weapons, or is so close to acquiring them that it presents a time-urgent threat. Many believe, however, that Iran is no more than several years away from having a viable nuclear weapons program and that it is a matter of when—rather than if —Tehran acquires nuclear weapons. That is, once Iran gets the capability to produce the materials necessary to closing the nuclear cycle, Iran would acquire the capabilities to produce nuclear weapons.

As of summer 2006, U.S. intelligence estimates still projected that Iran was five to eight years away from a bomb.[145] Some Israeli estimates in early 2007, however, indicated that Iran might acquire a nuclear device as early as 2009. This Israeli time-line gathered more credibility in the spring of 2007, when Iran claimed that it had succeeded in deploying some 1,312 centrifuges and would have 3,000 by the summer of 2007.

The U.S. National Intelligence Estimate (NIE) released December 3, 2007, judged that late 2009 is the earliest Iran would be technically capable of producing enough HEU for a weapon, but that this is very unlikely and that the more likely time frame remains 2010–2015 or later.

The IAEA does not believe that Iran is yet capable of making fissile material, or that it can do so in the near future, but its assessments have also reacted to Iran's progress. In 2006, Mohamed ElBaradei, the Director General of the IAEA, stated, "To develop a nuclear weapon, you need a significant quantity of highly enriched uranium or plutonium, and no one has seen that in Iran."[146] The IAEA has not changed that position since, but the IAEA has made it clear that Iran is coming steadily closer to the point where it could produce fissile material, and it has identi-fied Iranian activities and possible attempts at acquiring a wide range of technology and manufacturing capabilities necessary to produce a bomb.

In April 2007, Mohamed ElBaradi discounted such Iranian claims, however, and felt Iran had far less than 3,000 centrifuges, and other experts put the maximum number of functional units at around 650 actually operating in series. They felt many of these were still running empty, although IAEA experts felt some were now running UF_6 at low pressure.[147] It should also be noted that some experts speculate Iran may face a special problem because its uranium ore is contaminated with heavy metals such as molybdenum; this would limit enrichment to 20 percent without out-side technical aid from an advanced power such as Russia.[148]

The IAEA issued a report on September 15, 2008, that assessed that Iran had 3,800 centrifuges operating, with increasing stability, at Natanz. Under optimal—if unlikely—conditions, a fully functional capacity of 3,000 P-1 class centrifuges could give Iran enough material for one fission device in 18–27 months; some private experts predict this capability in as little as 12 months—some point to 2008.

The key variable in gauging the timeline is how soon Iran can get the cascades functioning smoothly to produce enriched uranium around the clock. In the most plausible breakout scenario, Iran would produce a stockpile of low-enriched uranium under IAEA verification, and only when it had a sufficient quantity, in one or two years, expel the inspectors and enrich this stockpile to weapons grade in five to eight weeks.

According to the ISIS analysis of the September 15, 2008, IAEA findings, Iran has largely overcome previous centrifuge problems, which is reflected in the increased feed rates and LEU production. One official close to the IAEA stated that Iran may have reached a point where its cascades are operating in a stable manner, noting that fewer centrifuges are breaking.[149]

No one knows the actual current or final design output of Iran's P-1 centrifuges or the efficiency of its cascades and overall production systems. Some speculate, however, that the annual output of each P-1 could be 2.5 separative work units (SWUs) or some 0.013 kg of HEU a year (European P-2 centrifuges are about twice as efficient and produce 5 SWUs a year). Under some conditions, a total system of 3,000 Iranian P-1s could produce as much as 7,500 SWUs per year or enough to provide 40 kg of HEU per year. This would be enough for one weapon a year and possibly two.[150]

On October 20, 2008, Mohamed ElBaradei assessed that Iran still lacked the key components to produce nuclear weapons. According to ElBaradei, "They do not have even the nuclear material, the raw un-enriched uranium to develop one nuclear weapon if they decide to do so. Even if you decide to walk out tomorrow from the NPT (Nuclear Nonproliferation Treaty) and you go into a lot of scenarios, we're still not going to see Iran tomorrow having nuclear weapons."[151]

But on October 27, 2008, ElBaradei also reiterated that Iran is continuing to block the IAEA inspectors from verifying whether the nation has any ambitions for nuclear weaponry. "I regret that we are still not in a position to achieve full clarity regarding the absence of undeclared nuclear material and activities in Iran," ElBaradei asserted. He urged Tehran to do more to ensure transparency, but emphasized that the Vienna-based IAEA "does not in any way seek to pry into Iran's conventional or missile-related military activities";[152] which Iran has continued to assert that the IAEA, under the corrupt thumb of the West, is trying to do.

On February 19, 2009, the IAEA released a report on the implementation of NPT safeguards in Iran and the status of Iran's compliance with Security Council Resolutions 1737, 1747, and 1803. The report includes three important findings. The first is that while Iran has dramatically increased its installation of centrifuges (now numbering more than 5,400) it has not increased the number of centrifuges enriching uranium, which is holding steady at just under 4,000. The second is that Iran has accumulated a total of 1,010 kg of low-enriched uranium in the form of uranium hexafluoride (UF_6). The third concerns Iran's manufacture of uranium fuel rods for the Arak heavy-water reactor and its continued refusal to allow IAEA inspection of the reactor under construction.[153]

Although much of the analysis following the February 19, 2009, IAEA report argues that Iran has achieved a "breakout capability," other analysts and intelligence officials from a number of agencies have argued that Iran would not achieve a true breakout capability until it has enough weapons-grade uranium for 10–12 weapons, and at the present time Iran has only enough LEU for a single nuclear weapon.[154]

Another important development came on February 25, 2009, when a test run of the Bushehr plant was conducted and Iranian officials stated that if this test run proves to be successful, the plant could be scheduled to have uranium fuel rods installed and be up in running in a matter of months.[155] Iran's nuclear chief also claimed that the country has increased the number of centrifuges enriching uranium to 6,000.[156]

On June 5, 2009, the IAEA released its latest report on the implementation of NPT safeguards in Iran and the status of Iran's compliance with Security Council Resolutions 1737, 1747, and 1803. The report includes several important findings that have raised further concern over Iran's nuclear progress, especially in regard to Iran's Fuel Enrichment Plant (FEP) at Natanz:

> The first is that the number of centrifuges enriching uranium at the Natanz FEP has increased to 4,920 (up from 3,936) with an additional 2132 installed and operating under vacuum, bring the total number of operational centrifuges to 7,052. Since the last IAEA report, Iran has produced an additional 329 kg of low enriched uranium (LEU) hexafluoride, or a total of 1,339 kg of LEU hexafluoride reflecting a 20 percent improvement in Iran's daily rate of LEU production. Of note, the IAEA states that given increases in the number of centrifuges operating and the rate of production of LEU, improvements to "containment and surveillance measures" at the FEP are necessary.
>
> The second issue highlighted in the report is Iran's continued refusal to allow the IAEA access to the IR-40 reactor under construction at Arak and to provide the Agency with design information for a planned reactor to be built at Darkhovin. The report notes that the IAEA has not visited the Arak reactor since August 2008 and that with the completion of the containment structure over the reactor, it is impossible to continue following progress remotely. Regarding Darkhovin, the IAEA adds that Iran is the only country with "significant nuclear activities" not implementing safeguards provisions that provide the IAEA with access to design information prior to construction.
>
> Finally, the IAEA notes that in addition to a small, 10 machine cascade of next-generation IR-2 centrifuges, Iran has recently installed a 10 machine IR-3 cascade and is now operating as single machines, the IR-4 centrifuge.[157]

The IAEA report also points out developing issues in the oversite of Iran's nuclear program. In addition to Iran denying U.N. inspectors access to facilities involved in its nuclear program, the UN is running into new oversite issues as Iran continues to expand it nuclear program. With Iran significantly and rapidly expanding its uranium enrichment capabilities, this has made it harder for UN inspectors to keep track of the disputed nuclear activity.

According to a *Los Angeles Times* article, "so rapidly is Iran's nuclear program growing that the agency said it has begun talks to upgrade its 'containment and surveillance' systems. The agency often uses mounted cameras to keep track of nuclear material stockpiles around the world. It has long wanted to install remotely monitored cameras in Iran's uranium-enrichment facility in the central city of Natanz, so that it doesn't incur the cost and hassle of sending inspectors to Iran to change the film."[158]

U.S. President Barack Obama has said that he will continue with the provisions currently in place regarding Iran's nuclear program and reassess the situation at the end of 2009, but Iran's nuclear progress and lack of cooperation with the IAEA coupled with the recent developments in its rapidly advancing missile programs have increased tension over Iran's nuclear program and have sparked more concern over prospects and the options available to the international community for dealing with a defiant Iran.

FISSILE MATERIAL AND WEAPONS PRODUCTION

Many experts believe that the key factor limiting Iran is obtaining fissile material. Here it should be noted that there is also a major debate over how much fissile material Iran would need and much depends on the sophistication of its weapons-design efforts. Figure 7.2 shows the range of material required for older weapons designs. Advanced weapons designs require only a fraction of this material, but Iran is unlikely to have access to such designs. As a result, it seems doubtful than Iran could make nuclear weapons using less than 50–70 percent of the fissile material shown in Figure 7.2 during the next decade.

The U.S. NIE on Iran's nuclear programs issued in November 2007 made the importance of fissile material clear:

> We continue to assess with low confidence that Iran probably has imported at least some weapons-usable fissile material, but still judge with moderate-to-high confidence it has not obtained enough for a nuclear weapon. We cannot rule out that Iran has acquired from abroad—or will acquire in the future—a nuclear weapon or enough fissile material for a weapon. Barring such acquisitions, if Iran wants to have nuclear weapons it would need to produce sufficient amounts of fissile material indigenously—which we judge with high confidence it has not yet done.
>
> We assess centrifuge enrichment is how Iran probably could first produce enough fissile material for a weapon, if it decides to do so. Iran resumed its declared centrifuge enrichment activities in January 2006, despite the continued halt in the nuclear weapons program. Iran made significant progress in 2007 installing centrifuges at Natanz, but we judge with moderate confidence it still faces significant technical problems operating them.
>
> Iranian entities are continuing to develop a range of technical capabilities that could be applied to producing nuclear weapons, if a decision is made to do so. For example, Iran's civilian uranium enrichment program is continuing. We also assess with high confidence that since fall 2003, Iran has been conducting research and development projects with commercial and conventional military applications—some of which would also be of limited use for nuclear weapons.[159]

Figure 7.2   Amount of Fissile Material Needed to Build a Basic Fission (Nonboosted) Weapon

Highly Enriched Uranium HEU (90% U-235)	Simple gun-type weapon	90–110 lb/40–50 kg
	Simple implosion weapon	33 lb/15 kg
	Sophisticated implosion weapon	20–26 lb/9–12 kg
Weapons-Grade Plutonium	Simple implosion weapon	14 lb/6 kg
	Sophisticated implosion weapon	4.5–9 lb/2–4 kg

Source: Extract from the unclassified estimates in Union of Concerned Scientists, "Preventing Nuclear Terrorism Fact Sheet," April 2004, and work by Abdullah Toukan.

PLUTONIUM PRODUCTION

Plutonium is one of the two key sources of fissile material, and Iran has followed a number of different paths it could use to develop the capacity to produce plutonium:

First, Iran is building heavy-water production plants, which U.S. officials claim that their only purpose is to supply heavy water that is optimal for producing weapons-grade plutonium. The Iranian government, on the other hand, has claimed that their purpose is for isotope production for its civilian nuclear energy program.[160]

Second, Iran is building light-water power reactors. The main reactor is at Bushehr, which is designed to produce civilian nuclear technology. Bushehr is also the reactor that Russia agreed to supply its fuel and recover the spent fuel from the reactor. According to an agreement between Russia and Iran dating from September 2006, Russia agreed to provide low-enriched uranium for the reactor by March 2007, regardless of UN sanctions.[161] The U.S. Under Secretary for Arms Control and International Security, John R. Bolton, claimed that Bushehr would produce enough plutonium per year to manufacture nearly 30 nuclear weapons.[162]

Third, Iran is developing new heavy-water reactors. Iran is seeking to replace or supplant its small, 35-year-old research reactor in Tehran with a more modern, 40-megawatt, thermal-cooled, heavy-water reactor at Arak. Some outside experts feel that Iran's IR-40 heavy reactor could be operational by 2011 and allow Iran to begin producing significant amounts of weapons-grade material by 2014.

Such a reactor could be used to produce up to 8 kg of weapons-grade plutonium a year—enough for one to two weapons a year. Iran might also need far less weapons-grade plutonium per weapons than uranium. One outside expert quotes a figure of 5 kg for plutonium vs. 25 kg of uranium—although such calculations are based on nominal figures used for arms control purposes that have little relevance to actual weapons designs employed since the 1960s.[163]

Fourth, Iran has experimented extensively with plutonium separation, which extracts plutonium that can be used for weapons from irradiated nuclear reactor fuels such as those used in Iran's new nuclear power reactor at Bushehr. The following chronology shows the history of Iran's plutonium separation experiments reported in IAEA documents:[164]

- **1987–1988:** The separation process was simulated using imported unirradiated uranium dioxide (UO2); dissolution and purification took place in the Shariaty Building at TNRC [Tehran Nuclear Research Center]; pressed and sintered pellets were manufactured using imported UO2 (DU) at Fuel Fabrication Laboratory (FFL); the UO2 pellets were further manipulated into aluminum and stainless steel capsules at FFL.

- **1988–1993:** The capsules (containing a total of 7 kilograms of UO2 in the form of powder, pressed pellets, and sintered pellets) were irradiated in Tehran Research Reactor (TRR).

- **1991–1993:** Plutonium was separated from some of the irradiated UO2 targets in the capsules (about 3 kilograms of the 7 kilograms of UO2) and plutonium solutions produced; these activities were carried out at the Shariaty Building and, after the activities were transferred in October/November 1992, at the Chamaran Building at TNRC; the research and development related irradiation and separation of plutonium were terminated in 1993.

- **1993–1994:** The unprocessed irradiated UO2 was initially stored in capsules in the spent fuel pond of TRR and later transferred into four containers and buried behind the Chamaran Building.

- **1995:** In July, purification of the plutonium solution from the 1988–1993 period was carried out in the Chamaran Building; a planchet (disk) was prepared from the solution for analysis.

- **1998:** In August, additional purification of plutonium from the 1988–1993 period was carried out in the Chamaran Building; another planchet (disk) was prepared from the solution for analysis.

- **2000:** The glove boxes from the Chamaran Building were dismantled and sent to ENTC [Esfahan Nuclear Technology Center] for storage; one glove box was moved to the Molybdenum Iodine Xenon Facility.

- **2003:** Due to construction work being carried out behind the Chamaran Building, two containers holding the unprocessed irradiated UO2 were dug up, moved, and reburied.

- **2003:** Iran in February confirmed that it was building a heavy-water production plant at Arak.

- **2003:** The IAEA DG report of November 10 (GOV/2003/71) asserts that "between 1992 and 1998 it [Iran] had irradiated 7 kg of UO2 targets and extracted small quantities of plutonium."

- **2003:** John Bolton, U.S. Under Secretary of State for Arms Control and International Security, stated at a conference on December 2: "In what can only be an attempt to build a capacity to develop nuclear materials for nuclear weapons, Iran has enriched uranium with both centrifuges and lasers, and produced and reprocessed plutonium [. . .] Iran is trying to legitimize as "peaceful and transparent" its pursuit of nuclear fuel cycle capabilities that would give it the ability to produce fissile material for nuclear weapons. This includes uranium mining and extraction, uranium conversion and enrichment, reactor fuel fabrication, heavy-water production, a heavy-water reactor well-suited for plutonium production, and the "management" of spent fuel—a euphemism for reprocessing spent fuel to recover plutonium."

- **2004:** The IAEA in its March 17 Board of Governors Resolution (GOV/2004/21) stated that the nature and the scope of Iranian research into laser isotopic enrichment and the question of experiments in the production of polonium-210 remained not satisfactory disclosed.

- **2004:** IAEA DG report (GOV/2004/82) from November 15: "Between 1988 and 1993, Iran carried out plutonium separation experiments at TNRC. The shielded glove boxes in which these experiments were carried out were dismantled in 1993, relocated to JHLand used for other purposes [. . .] In its letter of 21 October 2003, Iran acknowledged the irradiation of depleted UO_2 targets at TRR and subsequent plutonium separation experiments in shielded glove boxes in the Nuclear Safety Building of TNRC. Neither the activities nor the separated plutonium had been reported previously to the Agency [. . .] Iran stated that the Am-241 had been imported from abroad prior to the Iranian revolution in 1979, and explained that, in 1990, the glove box that had been used in connection with the Am-241 had been transferred to the building where the plutonium separation took place, but that it had been used for training purposes and not for plutonium experiments [. . .] In addition, while Iran has provided preliminary design information on the IR-40 heavy-water research reactor, the construction of which should commence in 2004, the Agency has raised some questions regarding Iran's attempts to acquire manipulators and lead glass windows for the hot cells. With respect to the latter issue, in October and November 2004, Iran provided some clarifications, which are now being assessed."

- **2005:** In June, Iran admitted that it conducted small-scale experiments to produce plutonium. Iran had declared to the IAEA that it ended certain plutonium experiments in 1993, but disclosed to the IAEA that those experiments were still being undertaken in 1998.

- **2008:** In June, media reports alleged claims by an adviser to the Israeli National Security Council that Syria was planning to supply Iran with spent nuclear fuel for reprocessing into weapons-grade plutonium. If confirmed, these reports would indicate greater nuclear cooperation between Syria and Iran than previously known.[165]

The IAEA reported in September 2005, "A final assessment of Iran's plutonium research activities must await the results of the destructive analysis of the disks and targets."[166] The IAEA analysis of Iran's plutonium separation experiments concluded, however, that the solutions that were tested were 12–16 years old, which seemed to corroborate Iran's claims. In addition, the IAEA carried out verification tests for unprocessed irradiated UO_2 targets stored in four containers. These results also supported Iranian claims, although the IAEA argued that the number of targets provided by Iran was much lower than the actual ones it has.

URANIUM ENRICHMENT

Many weapons experts believe that the Iranian uranium enrichment program is more advanced than its plutonium programs and does not rely on Iran's nuclear reactors. The former chief UN weapons inspector in Iraq, Hans Blix, has said that Tehran's plans to build a 1,000-MW power reactor at Bushehr, which is considered Iran's main plutonium production facility, should not be the main concern. He argued that the light-water reactor used only low-enrichment (3.5 percent) uranium and is scarcely ideal for plutonium production.

He added,

"What is uncomfortable and dangerous is that they have acquired the capacity to enrich uranium of their own uranium that they dig out of the ground . . . If you can enrich to five percent you can enrich it to 85 percent."[167] Others note, however, that the reactor will use some 103 tons of uranium contained in 193 fuel assemblies and still generate some 250 kilograms of plutonium a year. They speculate that there would be enough plutonium in every four irradiated fuel assemblies to produce a single nuclear weapon, and if Iran broke its fuel agreement with Russia and dedicated the reactor to weapons production, it could provide enough plutonium for 40–50 weapons a year. Given Iran's stated plans to acquire a total of six 1,000-megawatt reactors, it is hard to dismiss these concerns.[168]

Iran has a long history of research into uranium enrichment. According to one report, Iran had made earlier attempts just after the oil crisis of 1974.[169] It is likely that work on uranium enrichment was conducted between 1974 and 2003; however, it is not known to what extent.

In October 2003, during negotiations with the EU-3, Iran agreed to suspend its uranium enrichment program, most likely because it feared an escalation of the issue with interference by the UN Security Council. Two months later, Iran also signed the IAEA Model Additional Protocol. Reportedly, Iran resumed enrichment activities in 2004, but then agreed to suspension again in 2005, after facing referral to the UN Security Council again. In August 2005, the EU-3 proposal failed and Iran began enrichment activities anew.

Iran showed it was determined to continue the enrichment program even though it faced IAEA referral to the UN Security Council—a referral that eventually took place in February 2006. Mohammad Saeedi, Iran's Deputy Nuclear Chief, reiterated that Iran aimed to expand uranium enrichment to industrial scale at Natanz. In addition to installing 3,000 centrifuges at Natanz by 2006, Saeedi claimed that Iran aims at expanding the total number of centrifuges to 54,000, which would be used to fuel a 1,000-MW nuclear power plant.[170] Iran's Deputy Foreign Minister Mohammad Reza Bagheri pointed out Iran's stance on the uranium enrichment program: "It is our red line. We will never do it."[171]

While some believe that these Iranian claims were credible, others speculated that Iran made the announcement to send a message that military strikes or sanctions would not deter Iran from achieving a full nuclear cycle. Much depends on what the announcement really meant. Iran had previously obtained at least 2-percent enrichment from the experimental use of centrifuges and possibly significantly higher levels. The IAEA had previously made it clear that it lacked the data to determine how far Iran had actually progressed. Iran also had reached enrichment levels as high as 8 percent making experimental use of laser isotope separation, although it seemed far from being able to scale such efforts up beyond laboratory tests.

President Mahmoud Ahmadinejad announced on April 11, 2006, that Iran was successful at enriching uranium. "At this historic moment, with the blessings of God almighty and the efforts made by our scientists, I declare here that the laboratory-scale nuclear fuel cycle has been completed and young scientists produced enriched uranium needed to the degree for nuclear power plants [on April 9]." The head of the AEOI and Iran's Vice President, Gholamreza Aghazadeh, and Iranian nuclear scientists stated Iran's accomplishments and/or goals as follows:[172]

- Started enriching uranium to a level—3.5 percent—needed for fuel on a research scale using 164 centrifuges, but not enriched enough to build a nuclear bomb;

- Produced 110 tons of uranium hexafluoride (UF6)—this amount is nearly double the amount that Iran claimed to have enriched in 2005;

- Aim[s] to produce a gas high with an increased percentage of U-235, the isotope needed for nuclear fission, which is much rarer than the more prevalent isotope U-238; and

- Plan[s] to expand its enrichment program to be able to use 3,000 centrifuges at the nuclear center at Natanz by the end of 2006.

According to estimates made by the ISIS and the University of Wisconsin Project on Nuclear Arms Control, and based on data obtained in IAEA inspections, Iran had fed 9956 kg of UF_6 into its centrifuges as of February 2009 and had produced approximately 357 kg of LEU.[173]

Furthermore, in the June 2009 IAEA report, the Director General reported an increase in the rate of LEU being produced in Iranian facilities. During the prior reporting period, from November 18 through January 31, Iran produced approximately 171 kg of LEU hexafluoride, corresponding to an average of approximately 2.3 kg per day. In the period covered in the latest report, from February 1 through May 31, Iran produced 329 kg of LEU hexafluoride, corresponding to approximately 2.75 kg per day, or an increase of approximately 20 percent from the previous period.[174]

Figures 7.3 and 7.4 illustrate Iran's progress in the area of enrichment areas as of June 1, 2009.

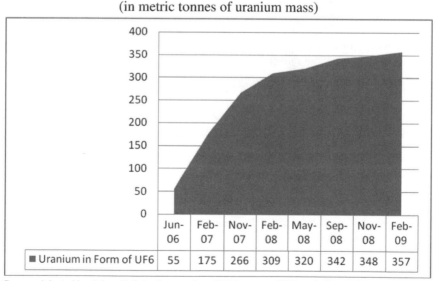

(in metric tonnes of uranium mass)

	Jun-06	Feb-07	Nov-07	Feb-08	May-08	Sep-08	Nov-08	Feb-09
■ Uranium in Form of UF6	55	175	266	309	320	342	348	357

Source: Adapted by Adam C. Seitz from various IAEA reports, ISIS analysis, and University of Wisconsin Project on Nuclear Arms Control.

Figure 7.3   Cumulative UF$_6$ Production at Esfahan

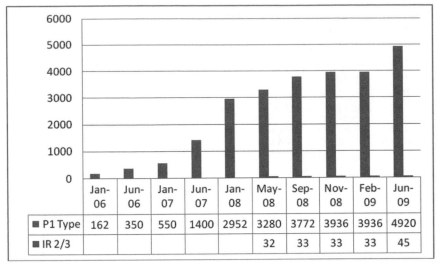

	Jan-06	Jun-06	Jan-07	Jun-07	Jan-08	May-08	Sep-08	Nov-08	Feb-09	Jun-09
■ P1 Type	162	350	550	1400	2952	3280	3772	3936	3936	4920
■ IR 2/3						32	33	33	33	45

Source: Adapted by Adam C. Seitz from various IAEA reports, ISIS analysis, and University of Wisconsin Project on Nuclear Arms Control.

Figure 7.4   Number of Centrifuges Enriching Uranium at Natanz FEP

THE CENTRIFUGE CHALLENGE

Iran has experimented with two different methods of uranium enrichment ever since the time of the Shah. First, Iran has manufacturing and testing centrifuges. Second, Iran also pursued enriching uranium through laser enrichment. According to Mohamed ElBaradei, the Director General of the IAEA, Iran was able to enrich uranium up to 1.2 percent using centrifuges and up to a peak enrichment grade of 13 percent using lasers.[175]

The Origin's of Iran's Centrifuge Program

Many of Iran's experiments took place between 1981 and 1993 at the TNRC and at the INTC. One source reports that uranium enrichment in centrifuges began in 1985.[176] In this case, however, it is clear that some of these activities continued throughout 2002. According to the IAEA, Iran's uranium enrichment activities also received some foreign help in 1991. The IAEA outlined its findings regarding Tehran's uranium enrichment as follows:

In 1991, Iran entered into discussions with a foreign supplier for the construction at Esfahan of an industrial scale conversion facility. Construction on the facility, UCF, was begun in the late 1990s. UCF consists of several conversion lines, principal among which is the line for the conversion of UOC to UF6 with an annual design production capacity of 200 t uranium as UF6. The UF6 is to be sent to the uranium enrichment facilities at Natanz, where it will be enriched up to 5% U-235 and the product and tails returned to UCF for conversion into low enriched UO2 and depleted uranium metal. The design information for UCF provided by Iran indicates that conversion lines are also foreseen for the production of natural and enriched (19.7%) uranium metal, and natural UO2. The natural and enriched (5% U-235) UO2 are to be sent to the Fuel Manufacturing Plant (FMP) at Esfahan, where Iran has said it will be processed into fuel for a research reactor and power reactors. [. . .]

In March 2004, Iran began testing the process lines involving the conversion of UOC into UO2 and UF4, and UF4 into UF6. As of June 2004, 40 to 45 kg of UF6 had been produced. A larger test, involving the conversion of 37 t of yellowcake into UF4, was initiated in August 2004. According to Iran's declaration of 14 October 2004, 22.5 t of the 37 t of yellowcake had been fed into the process and that approximately 2 t of UF4, and 17.5 t of uranium as intermediate products and waste, had been produced. There was no indication as of that date of UF6 having been produced during this later campaign.[177]

IAEA inspections found traces of contamination from advanced enrichment effects at Natanz. Iran claimed that these contaminations were from equipment it purchased in the 1980s from abroad (presumably from Pakistan). Reports by the IAEA, however, showed that Iran may well have started its enrichment program in the 1970s and that the Iranians were already partially successful at uranium conversion.

Some of Iran's gas centrifuge program initially depended on help it received from Pakistan. Although reports by the Director General of the IAEA do not mention Pakistan by name, Iran's gas centrifuges could be traced back to the mid-1990s when A. Q. Khan approached an Iranian company and offered it P-1 documentation and components for 500 centrifuges. Iran claimed that it received only the P-1 and not the P-2 design (the P-1 and the P-2 refer to two designs for centrifuges by Pakistan). Both Iran and Pakistan would later admit to this transaction and provide the documents to support these allegations.[178]

According to the IAEA, Tehran received P-1 components and documentation in January 1994. Tehran, however, claimed that it did not receive the first of these components until October 1994. Regardless of the month of delivery, there is one more important element that remains unresolved. The IAEA refers to this as the "1987 offer," which reportedly provided Iran with a sample machine, drawings, descriptions, and specifications for production and material for 2,000 centrifuge machines.[179]

In addition, Iran received the P-2 design in 1994/1995 from Pakistan, but all of its components were designed and manufactured in Iran. According to Iran's official statements, the AEOI awarded a contract to a company in Tehran to build P-2 centrifuges.[180] Furthermore, Iran claimed that it did not pursue any work on the P-2 design between 1995 and 2002 due to shortages in staff and resources at the AEOI and that Tehran focused on resolving outstanding issues regarding the P-1 design. The IAEA, however, was not convinced that Iran did not pursue further development of the P-2 design and called on Iran in September 2005 to provide more information on the history of its P-2 development.[181]

Iran No Longer Is Dependent on Imports

The IAEA's discoveries have made it clear that Iran no longer needs imports of technology and equipment to move forward. It has functioning centrifuge design and manufacturing capability. Revati Prasad and Jill Marie Parillo state that the AEOI purchased designs and components for the P-1 centrifuges through the A. Q. Khan network in 1987.[182] It also seemed highly likely that it had acquired P-2 centrifuge designs and the same basic Chinese design data for a fissile weapon suitable for mounting on a ballistic missile that North Korea had sold to Libya.

Iran also has reactor development capability and plutonium separation capability. As has been touched upon earlier, it has experimented with polonium in ways that show it can make a neutron initiator, it has the technology to produce high-explosive lenses and beryllium reflectors, it can machine fissile material, and it has long had a technology base capable of designing nuclear weapons and performing nonfissile simulation tests of its weapons designs of the kind used by Pakistan in its nuclear weapons-design efforts.

In early February 2008, reports by European and American diplomats began to surface that Iran had tested a new domestically engineered centrifuge design to enrich uranium. The IR-2 is an Iranian improvement on a Pakistani design that President Mahmoud Ahmadinejad boasted in an April 2006 speech would quadruple Iran's enrichment powers. A report released February 7, 2008, by the Institute for Science and International Security states that 1,200 centrifuges of the new design could produce enough weapons-grade uranium for a bomb in one year. Iran would need 3,000 of the current generation of machines for the equivalent output.[183]

As a result, both the claims Mahmoud Ahmadinejad made on April 11, 2006, that Iran had made a major breakthrough by successfully enriching uranium and the response by U.S. President George W. Bush that Iran would not be allowed to acquire the technology to build a nuclear weapon were little more than vacuous political posturing. Ahmadinejad's statement seems to have been an effort to show the UN that it could not take meaningful action and to exploit Iranian nationalism.

The Bush statement seems to have been the result of a combination of basic technical ignorance on the part of his speechwriters and of an effort to push the UN toward action and to convince Iran that it could face the threat of both serious sanctions and military action if diplomacy and sanctions failed. It effectively ignored the fact that Iran not only already had the technology, but could disperse it to the point where it was extremely unlikely that any UN inspection effort could find it, even if Iran allowed this, or any military option could seriously affect Iran's technology base—as distinguished from its ability to create survivable large-scale production facilities and openly deploy nuclear-armed delivery systems.

In reality, Iran's progress in developing its centrifuge program has been steady, dependent on past imports of technology, and evolutionary. In fact, diplomats and officials from the IAEA were quick to point out that the announcement by Iran should not be a sign of concern and that Iran may face many technical hurdles before it can enrich enough quantities of uranium at high levels to produce a nuclear weapon.

The Uncertain Status of Iran's Current Centrifuge Programs

One European official said that while the 164-machine centrifuges were more industrial, "it's not like they haven't come close to achieving this in the past." This assessment has been reflected in reports by the IAEA, which argues that Iran has used centrifuges and laser to enrich uranium throughout the 1990s and even before.[184]

This helps explain why experts have argued that Iran's goal of producing 50,000 centrifuges in Natanz should be considered a sign of serious concern for the international community. As far as the future developments of Natanz are concerned, Iran established its additional cascades underground, and the IAEA GOV/2007/8 confirms that Iran moved about 10 tons of unenriched uranium into the cavernous halls in Natanz.

David Albright and Corey Hinderstein of the ISIS have argued that Iran planned in January 2006 to install centrifuges in modules of 3,000 machines that were designed to produce low-enriched uranium for civilian power reactors. If half of these machines were to be used to create HEU instead, they could produce enough HEU for one nuclear weapon a year. Furthermore, if the Iranians do achieve their ultimate goal of 50,000 centrifuges, Albright and Hinderstein argue, "At 15–20 kilograms per weapon that would be enough for 25–30 nuclear weapons per year."[185]

Key Centrifuge Facilities

Natanz is the primary uranium enrichment site in Iran. It contains installations both above and below ground and covers an area of about 100,000 square meters.[186] The commercial enrichment plant reportedly is buried underground and is located in three structures that are to be capable of housing 50,000 cascades.

Until early 2007, Iran was believed to have two 164-cascade machines running in its Natanz facility. In February 2007, however, the IAEA reported that Iran installed four additional cascades underground, which would equal a total of 1,018 centrifuges in Natanz, most of them underground. IAEA report GOV/2007/8 described the situation as follows:

> During the design information verification (DIV) carried out at FEP on 17 February 2007, Agency inspectors were informed that two 164-machine cascades had been installed and were operating under vacuum and that another two 164-machine cascades were in the final stages of installation. In light of this, in a letter dated 19 February 2007, the Agency requested that arrangements be made for the relocation of cameras into the cascade hall during the Agency's next visit to FEP, which is scheduled to take place between 3 and 5 March 2007. The issue of remote monitoring remains to be resolved.[187]

This meant that in addition to the two cascade machines with 164 centrifuges each that were confirmed to be running in the Natanz pilot plant, Iran had installed another two machines with 164 cascades each. As of the time of the report, 656 cascades were reported by the IAEA to be running, half of them under vacuum. It also meant that if Iran installed yet another two "chains," "cascades," or "links" of 164 centrifuges, the total number of running cascades would amount to 984.

The IAEA gave no indication in this report when any additional chains of centrifuges would be operational. A report by David Albright and Jacqueline Shire from November 14, 2006, had expressed doubt about how quickly this could happen.[188] It then became clear, however, that Iran fed an unexpectedly large amount of UF_6 into its cascades in late 2006 and 2007. An ISIS report by Jacqueline Shire and David Albright dated March 15, 2007, concluded that Iran fed about 100 kilograms of UF_6 into its cascades at the Natanz plant between mid-August 2006 and mid-February of 2007.[189] It should be noted that by March 2007, Iran had reached its highest rate of UF_6 insertions, a trend that had continually grown since Iran agreed to resume uranium enrichment in early 2006.

The authors of the ISIS report also computed that at that rate of enrichment activity, Iran could feed about 613 kilograms of UF_6 into its existing centrifuges. The uranium, according to Iranian estimates, was enriched to a 5-percent enrichment level. Shire and Albright conclude that Iran operated its centrifuges for an average of about five hours a day.[190]

Problems in Estimating the Efficiency of Iran's Centrifuge Programs

David Albright noted Iran's potential difficulties in mastering, i.e., linking, all its centrifuge cascades. According to Albright, there are four likely reasons Iran has problems:

- The centrifuges have experienced an unknown technical problem that prevents continuous operation;
- Iran is slowing its program down so as not to alarm the international community;
- Iran is already competent in operating cascades to enrich uranium, but that competency is being hidden. For example, Iran may have received undeclared assistance from the Khan network in this area; or
- Iran is simply implementing its own plan for cascade installation that includes its own method to become proficient, according to its own timetable, and has chosen not to share it with the IAEA or the outside world.[191]

Shire and Albright acknowledged in March 2007, however, that Iran's centrifuges were running better than commonly expected by most observers.[192] Moreover, in April 2007, Iran claimed that it had succeeded in deploying some 1,312 centrifuges and would have 3,000 by the summer of 2007. As has been noted earlier, a fully functional capacity of 3,000 P-1 class centrifuges could give Iran enough material for one fission device in 18–27 months under optimal—if unlikely—conditions.

The problem in making such estimates is there are no data on the operational status and efficiency of Iran's units. Mohamed ElBaradei, the Director of the IAEA, discounted Iranian claims in April 2007, for example, and felt Iran had far less than 3,000 centrifuges, and other experts put the maximum number of functional units at around 650 actually operating in series. They felt many of these were still running empty, although IAEA experts felt some were now running UF_6 at low pressure.[193]

At the same time, a smaller facility might be adequate. A study by Frank Barnaby for the Oxford Research Group estimates Iran's current centrifuges could produce about 2.5 SWUs a year, with a range of 1.9–2.7 SWUs. If Iran had the P-2, each centrifuge would produce roughly 5 SWUs a year. A fully operational 3,000-centrifuge facility could then produce some 7,500 SWUs or about 40 kg of HEU a year, and it would probably take a total capacity of 5,000 machines to keep 3,000 online at all times.[194] As is discussed later, the 1,500-centrifuge pilot facility that Iran is now seeking to operate could conceivably produce a single weapon in two to three years.

Continuing Iranian Efforts

The IAEA reported on September 15, 2008, that Iran is continuing to install new cascades of centrifuges to enrich uranium in defiance of a UN Security Council order. Around 3,800 centrifuges were now in operation at Iran's enrichment plant in Natanz, an increase of 300 since May.[195]

The IAEA reported that on August 30, 2008, five 164-machine cascades were being fed with UF_6, another cascade was in a vacuum without UF_6, and installation continued on the remaining 12 cascades at the unit. Approximately 7,600 kg of UF_6 has been fed into the cascades at Natanz, and based on Iran's daily operating records, as of August 30, 2008, Iran had produced approximately 480 kg of LEU. This indicates that Iran's centrifuges are running at approximately 85 percent of their stated previous target capacity, which is a significant increase over previous rates.[196]

According to an ISIS analysis of the IAEA findings, this report shows that Iran has largely overcome previous centrifuge problems, which is reflected in the increased feed rates and LEU production. One official close to the IAEA stated that Iran may have reached a point where its cascades are operating in a stable manner, noting that fewer centrifuges are breaking.[197]

The findings by the ISIS in their analysis of the September 2008 IAEA report were echoed in their analysis of the June 5, 2009 IAEA report. David Albright and Jacqueline Shire found that the number of centrifuges enriching uranium at the Natanz Fuel Enrichment Plant (FEP) had increased to 4,920 (up from 3,936) with an additional 2,132 installed and operating under vacuum, bringing the total number of centrifuges either enriching uranium or installed and ready to begin enrichment, to 7,052. Since the previous IAEA report, Iran had produced an additional 329 kg of LEU hexafluoride, or a total of 1,339 kg of LEU hexafluoride. Albright and Shire found that this reflected a 20-percent improvement in Iran's daily rate of LEU production. The IAEA also stated that improvements to "containment and surveillance measures" at the FEP are necessary because of increases in the number of centrifuges operating and the rate of production of LEU.[198]

Based on data from the September 15, 2008, IAEA report, the ISIS estimates that under optimal conditions, Iran could use between 700 and 800 kg of LEU to produce in its P-1 centrifuges 20–25 kg of weapons-grade uranium, enough for a crude fission weapon. Other estimates are more pessimistic about Iran's ability to enrich the LEU up to weapons grade, estimating that 1,000–1,700 kg of LEU would be necessary to produce 25–30 kg of weapons-grade uranium, generally considered more than enough for one nuclear weapon. Whatever the actual amount of LEU, Iran is progressing toward this capability and can be expected to reach it in six months to two years.[199]

Figure 7.5 gives estimates of Iran's centrifuge and LEU status from the University of Wisconsin's Iran Watch Web page and estimates of Iran's progress in moving from weapons reactor-grade to weapons-grade uranium. Figure 7.6 gives the estimated number of centrifuges deployed over time according to IAEA inventories. These estimates are based on open-source information collected and analyzed by the University of Wisconsin's Iran Watch program, which was primarily initially attained via IAEA reporting.

Reports by Israeli experts assess that Iran will get enough low-enriched uranium— 1.0 to 1.5 tons—for one device in the next year but not go ahead with one weapon, but instead will build up enough stocks for multiple weapons before it violates the NPT. These same experts claim that enrichment to weapons grade will take place at a separate site.

LASER ISOTOPE SEPARATION

As for Iran's other route to uranium enrichment, Iran has acknowledged it had started a laser enrichment program in the 1970s. Iran has claimed that it used two different tracks in using laser enrichment: (1) atomic vapor laser isotope separation (AVLIS) and (2) molecular isotope separation (MLIS). Iran, however, depended on key contracts with four (unnamed) different countries to build its laser enrichment program. The following chronology was presented by the IAEA:[229]

- **1975:** Iran contracted for the establishment of a laboratory to study the spectroscopic behavior of uranium metal; this project was abandoned in the 1980s as the laboratory did not function properly.

- **Late 1970s:** Iran contracted with a second supplier to study MLIS, under which four carbon monoxide lasers and vacuum chambers were delivered, but the project was ultimately terminated due to the political situation before major development work was begun.

- **1991:** Iran contracted with a third supplier for the establishment of a "Laser Spectroscopy Laboratory" (LSL) and a "Comprehensive Separation Laboratory" (CSL), where uranium enrichment would be carried out on a milligram scale based on the AVLIS process. The contract also provided for the supply of 50 kg natural uranium metal.

- **1998:** Iran contracted with a fourth supplier to obtain information related to laser enrichment and the supply of relevant equipment. However, due to the inability of the supplier to secure export licenses, only some of the equipment was delivered (to Lashkar Ab'ad).

Figure 7.5   Iran's Centrifuge and LEU Status June 1, 2009, and Estimates in Moving toward Weapons-Grade Uranium[200]

The following estimates are based on information in quarterly reports by the International Atomic Energy Agency—which is responsible for nuclear inspections in Iran—analysis of these reports by the Institute for Science and International Security, and data compiled from these sources by the "Iran Nuclear Timetable," IranWatch.org, University of Wisconsin Project on Nuclear Arms Control:

Iran's progress toward this status as of June 1, 2009, is *estimated* below:
- Amount of U-235 contained in Iran's stockpile of low-enriched uranium: 31.7 kg[201]
- Amount of this U-235 produced each month: 2 kg[202]
- Amount of this U-235 required to fuel a first-generation implosion bomb:[203] 21.6 kg[204]
- Date by which Iran is likely to have stockpiled the above: December 2008[205]
- Number of additional months needed to convert this low-enriched uranium to weapons grade: 2–3[206]
- Date by which Iran may have enough U-235 to fuel a second bomb: October 2009[207]
- Date by which Iran may have enough U-235 to fuel a third bomb: November 2009[208]

Additional estimates: *Moving from reactor-grade to weapons-grade uranium*
- Amount of uranium hexafluoride (UF$_6$) enriched to 3.5 percent U-235 now on hand: 1,339 kg[209]
- Average daily production rate of this low-enriched UF$_6$: 2.75 kg[210]
- Average monthly production rate of this low-enriched UF$_6$: 71.4 kg[211]
- Amount of this LEU needed to produce a bomb's worth of weapons-grade UF$_6$: 914 kg[212]
- Number of separative work units (SWUs)[213] needed to accomplish the above: 840[214]
- Number of first-generation IR-1 centrifuges being fed with UF$_6$ at the Natanz Fuel Enrichment Plant as of January 1,2009: 4,920[215]
- Average number of SWUs each centrifuge now appears to be producing per year: 0.3[216]
- Average number of SWUs each centrifuge produced per year between December 2007 and November 2008: 0.5[217]
- Total number of centrifuges installed at Natanz: 7,052[218]
- Number of SWUs these 7,052 centrifuges are assumed to be capable of producing per year: 7,000[219]
- Number of months needed for these 7,052 centrifuges operating at such a capacity to produce 840 SWUs: 1.5[220]

Additional estimates: *Low-enriched uranium production*
- Amount of UF$_6$ produced through November 7, 2008: 357 metric tons[221]
- Approximate number of first-generation implosion bombs that this amount of UF$_6$ could fuel if enriched to weapons grade: 45–50[222]
- Amount of UF$_6$ fed into centrifuges through November 7, 2008: 9,956 kg[223]
- Average monthly feed rate of UF$_6$ as of November 7, 2008: 1,024 kg[224]
- Monthly feed rate of UF$_6$ from December 12, 2007 to August 30, 2008: 698 kg[225]
- Average monthly percentage of natural uranium feed converted to low-enriched UF$_6$ product from February 2007 to December 12, 2007: 0.43[226]
- Average monthly percentage of natural uranium feed converted to low-enriched UF$_6$ product from December 12, 2007 to August 30, 2008: 0.80[227]
- Percentage increase in feed rate: 47%

Figure 7.6   Number of Centrifuges Deployed over Time[228]

Date of IAEA Inventory	Centrifuges Being Fed with UF$_6$	Centrifuges Being Tested without UF$_6$	Centrifuges Being Installed
2/17/2007	0	328	328
5/13/2007	1312	328	492
8/19/2007	1968	328	328
11/3/2007	2952	0	0
12/12/2007	2952	0	?
5/7/2008	3280	164	2460
8/30/2008	3772	164	2132
11/7/2008	3772	?	2132
2/1/2009	3936	125	1968
6/1/2009	4920	169	2296

Source: Adapted by Adam C. Seitz from various IAEA reports, ISIS analysis, and University of Wisconsin Project on Nuclear Arms Control.

The IAEA seems to be more confident about its findings regarding Iran's laser enrichment developments than gas centrifuges. This is largely due to Iranian co-operation, but it also stems from the fact that Iran had nothing to hide since its foreign contractors failed to deliver on the four contracts Tehran signed between the 1970s and the 1990s.

According to the IAEA, Iran claimed that the laser spectroscopy laboratory and the MLIS laboratory (the first two contracts) were never fully operational.

As for the third contract, the IAEA estimated the contract was finished in 1994, but that CSL and LSL had technical problems and were unsuccessful between 1994 and 2000. Iran responded by claiming that the two labs were dismantled in 2000. In addition, the IAEA concluded, "As confirmed in an analysis, provided to the Agency, that had been carried out by the foreign laboratory involved in the project, the highest average enrichment achieved was 8%, but with a peak enrichment of 13%."[230]

Finally, the fourth contract was signed in 1998, but failed due to the supplier's inability to obtain export licenses. Tehran claimed that it attempted to procure these equipment and parts, but it was unsuccessful.[231]

These failures almost certainly did strain Tehran's ability to effectively use the laser enrichment track to advance its uranium enrichment activities. This may explain why Iran did less to try to conceal its laser enrichment program than conceal the details of its centrifuge program. According to the IAEA, Tehran's declarations largely tracked with the IAEA inspectors' findings. For example, Iran claimed that its enrichment level was 0.8 percent U235, and the IAEA concluded that Iran reached an enrichment level of 0.99 percent 0.24 percent U235.[232]

The IAEA findings regarding this aspect of Tehran's enrichment program are summarized in the following two paragraphs:

> The Agency has completed its review of Iran's atomic vapor laser isotope separation (AVLIS) program and has concluded that Iran's descriptions of the levels of enrichment achieved using AVLIS at the Comprehensive Separation Laboratory (CSL) and Lashkar Ab'ad and the amounts of material used in its past activities are consistent with information available to the Agency to date. Iran has presented all known key equipment, which has been verified by the Agency. For the reasons described in the Annex to this report, however, detailed nuclear material accountancy is not possible.
>
> It is the view of the Agency's AVLIS experts that, while the contract for the AVLIS facility at Lashkar Ab'ad was specifically written for the delivery of a system that could achieve 5 kg of product within the first year with enrichment levels of 3.5% to 7%, the facility as designed and reflected in the contract would, given some specific features of the equipment, have been capable of limited HEU production had the entire package of equipment been delivered. The Iranian AVLIS experts have stated that they were not aware of the significance of these features when they negotiated and contracted for the supply and delivery of the Lashkar Ab'ad AVLIS facility. They have also provided information demonstrating the very limited capabilities of the equipment delivered to Iran under this contract to produce HEU (i.e. only in gram quantities).[233]

The accuracy of such findings is critical because isotope separation is far more efficient than centrifuge separation, much less costly once mature, uses far less power, and is much harder to detect.[234]

OTHER ASPECTS OF IRANIAN ACTIVITY

Other aspects of Iranian activity have been less than reassuring. Following Iran's announcement that it converted 37 tons of yellowcake into UF_4 in May 2005, experts believed that this amount of uranium could "theoretically" produce more than 200 pounds of weapons-grade uranium, which would be enough to produce five to six crude nuclear weapons. The head of Iran's Supreme National Security Council, Hasan Rowhani, was quoted in 1995 saying, "Last year, we could not produce UF_4 and UF_6. We didn't have materials to inject into centrifuges to carry out enrichment, meaning we didn't have UF_6 [...] But within the past year, we completed the Isfahan facility and reached UF_4 and UF_6 stage. So we made great progress."[235]

In February 2006, ahead of the IAEA board meeting, it was reported in the press that a report was circulated to IAEA member states regarding what press reports called "the Green Salt Project." The report largely used information provided by U.S. intelligence. The project name was derived from "green salt," or uranium tetrafluoride. The materials are considered intermediate materials in uranium conversion ore into uranium hexafluoride, UF_4, which is central to producing nuclear fuel.[236]

This project was reportedly started in the spring of 2001 by an Iranian firm, Kimeya Madon, under the auspices of the IRGC. U.S. officials believe that

Kimyea Madon completed drawings and technical specifications for a small UCF, and they argue that the drawings provide "pretty compelling evidence" for Iran's clandestine uranium conversion program. In addition, there was evidence that the Iranians envisioned a second UCF. It remains uncertain why the operation of Kimeya Mado stopped in 2003. Some speculated that this was a plan to replace Isfahan in case of a military strike against it. Another view is that Iran scratched the plan after it was revealed that the new UCF was not "as good as what they had" at Isfahan.[237]

Another important development was the IAEA's discovery of "a document related to the procedural requirements for the reduction of UF6 to metal in small quantities, and on the casting and machining of enriched, natural and depleted uranium metal into hemispherical forms," as the IAEA February 4, 2006, resolution emphasized.[238]

The description of this document first appeared in an IAEA report on November 15, 2005. This "one-page document" apparently was related to the Pakistani offer in 1987, and the IAEA made the following assessment:

> As previously reported to the Board, in January 2005 Iran showed to the Agency a copy of a hand-written one-page document reflecting an offer said to have been made to Iran in 1987 by a foreign intermediary for certain components and equipment. Iran stated that only some components of one or two disassembled centrifuges, and supporting drawings and specifications were delivered by the procurement network, and that a number of other items of equipment referred to in the document were purchased directly from other suppliers. Most of these components and items were included in the October 2003 declaration by Iran to the Agency.
>
> The documents recently made available to the Agency related mainly to the 1987 offer; many of them dated from the late 1970s and early to mid-1980s. The documents included: detailed drawings of the P-1 centrifuge components and assemblies; technical specifications supporting component manufacture and centrifuge assembly; and technical documents relating to centrifuge operational performance. In addition, they included cascade schematic drawings for various sizes of research and development (R&D) cascades, together with the equipment needed for cascade operation (e.g. cooling water circuit needs and special valve consoles). The documents also included a drawing showing a cascade layout for 6 cascades of 168 machines each and a small plant of 2000 centrifuges arranged in the same hall. Also among the documents was one related to the procedural requirements for the reduction of UF6 to metal in small quantities, and on the casting and machining of enriched, natural and depleted uranium metal into hemispherical forms, with respect to which Iran stated that it had been provided on the initiative of the procurement network, and not at the request of the Atomic Energy Organization of Iran (AEOI).[239]

As noted earlier, the foreign intermediary is believed to have been A. Q. Khan, the Pakistani nuclear scientist. The United Kingdom argued that the document, on casting uranium into hemispheric form, had no other application other than nuclear weapons. Experts agreed with this assessment.[240] IAEA officials, however, were more cautious. One senior IAEA official was quoted as saying that the document "is damaging," but he argued that the handwritten document was not a blueprint for making nuclear weapons because it dealt with only one aspect of the process.[241]

Many experts believe that in order to understand Iran's nuclear program, one must understand its gas centrifuge program—particularly whether Tehran's ability to establish a test run of 1,500 centrifuges at Natanz would give Iran enough capacity to produce HEU. David Albright and Corey Hinderstein of the ISIS argued that Iran may well be on its way to achieving this capacity:

> Each P1 centrifuge has an output of about 3 separative work units (swu) per year according to senior IAEA officials. From the A. Q. Khan network, Iran acquired drawings of a modified variant of an early-generation Urenco centrifuge. Experts who saw these drawings assessed that, based on the design's materials, dimensions, and tolerances; the P1 in Iran is based on an early version of the Dutch 4M centrifuge that was subsequently modified by Pakistan. The 4M was developed in the Netherlands in the mid-1970s and was more advanced than the earlier Dutch SNOR/CNOR machines. Its rotor assembly has four aluminum rotor tubes connected by three maraging steel bellows.
>
> With 1,500 centrifuges and a capacity of 4,500 swu per year, this facility could produce as much as 28 kilograms of weapon-grade uranium per year, assuming a tails assay of 0.5 percent, where tails assay is the fraction of uranium 235 in the waste stream. This is a relatively high tails assay, but such a tails assay is common in initial nuclear weapons programs. As a program matures and grows, it typically reduces the tails assay to about 0.4 percent and perhaps later to 0.3 percent to conserve uranium supplies.
>
> By spring 2004, Iran had already put together about 1,140 centrifuge rotor assemblies, a reasonable indicator of the number of complete centrifuges. However, only about 500 of these rotors were good enough to operate in cascades, according to knowledgeable senior IAEA officials. The November 2004 IAEA report stated that from the spring to October 10, 2004, Iran had assembled an additional 135 rotors, bringing the total number of rotors assembled to 1,275. As mentioned above, a large number of these rotors are not usable in an operating cascade.
>
> Iran is believed to have assembled more centrifuges prior to the suspension being reimposed on November 22, 2004. Without more specific information, it is assumed that Iran continued to assemble centrifuges at a constant rate, adding another 70 centrifuges, for a total of 1,345 centrifuges. However, the total number of good centrifuges is estimated at about 700.[242]

These developments led some observers to question whether Iran received more help from Pakistan than it admitted. Some experts argued that the A. Q. Khan network tended to hand over the "whole package" as was the case with Libya, and they question whether Iran received only the few pages that it shared with the IAEA.[243] These revelations point out how little is known about how advanced Iran's uranium enrichment program is.

Most experts, however, believe that Iran's uranium enrichment program is far more dangerous and far more advanced than its plutonium production activities. They argue that the danger of the enrichment program is that regardless of how high Iran's enrichment level of uranium is, if Iran were able to enrich it at a low level, Iran will have the know-how to enrich it at higher levels and produce the weapons-grade uranium to produce nuclear weapons.[244]

In addition, experts are concerned that Iran may acquire uranium from other nations. For example, during a visit by Iranian Parliament Speaker Gholam Ali Haddad-Adel in early 2006, Iran and Venezuela signed a deal that allowed Iran to explore Venezuela's strategic minerals. Venezuelan opposition figures to President Hugo Chávez claimed that the deal could involve the production and transfer of uranium from Venezuela to Iran. The United States, however, downplayed such reports. A U.S. Department of State official was quoted as saying, "We are aware of reports of possible Iranian exploitation of Venezuelan uranium, but we see no commercial activities in Venezuela."[245]

DOES IRAN HAVE A NUCLEAR WEAPONS PROGRAM? THE NIE ON IRAN'S NUCLEAR FORCES

The most authoritative document the U.S. intelligence community has ever released on how these developments can be linked to Iran's military programs is the unclassified summary of a U.S. National Intelligence Estimate on Iranian nuclear weapons, "Iran: Nuclear Intentions and Capabilities," which was issued in November 2007. This unclassified summary is a striking document in many ways:

- On the one hand, it indicates that Iran suspended a nuclear weapons effort in 2003 and is susceptible to international pressure and negotiation. The U.S. intelligence community analysis indicates that it is highly probable that the United States and the international community have some four to seven years to negotiate before Iran could become a nuclear power. It provides a major argument against any early military action against Iran, and it refutes much of the hard-line rhetoric emerging from various neoconservatives. In broad terms, it reinforced the moderate, pronegotiation positions of key officials and officers such as Secretary of State Condoleezza Rice, Secretary of Defense Robert Gates, Admiral Michael Mullen, and Admiral William J. Fallon.

- On the other hand, it provides the first solid indication that the U.S. intelligence community had the equivalent of a "smoking gun" to confirm that Iran had an active nuclear weapons program. It shows far less confidence that this program has continued to be halted than that it was halted for a time in 2003. It states Iran's enrichment programs allow it to move forward toward a nuclear weapons effort in spite of any continuing suspension of a formal nuclear weapons program, and it raises serious doubts as to whether Iran's longer-term efforts to acquire nuclear weapons are negotiable. It does not in any way indicate that the UN effort to prevent further Iranian weapons development is unnecessary or that further sanctions are not needed to limit or halt Iran's efforts.

- The document is the summary of a 150-page NIE that the *Washington Post* reports was based on some 1,500 intelligence indicators, including intercepts of communications from Iranian military officers. It is not an intelligence report. It does not portray the range of opinion or most dissenting views. It does not describe the nature of the indicators and analytic methods used. This is a critical point because past outside commentary on NIEs, and attempts to parse out the words in summary judgments, have proven to be highly unreliable. Moreover, a "war of leaks" almost inevitably follows advocates of one policy position or another.

- The summary does not address what the U.S. intelligence community does and does not know about Iran's efforts in each of the following five areas the NIE addressed:

    ○ What are Iran's intentions toward developing nuclear weapons?

    ○ What domestic factors affect Iran's decision making on whether to develop nuclear weapons?

    ○ What external factors affect Iran's decision making on whether to develop nuclear weapons?

    ○ What is the range of potential Iranian actions concerning the development of nuclear weapons, and the decisive factors that would lead Iran to choose one course of action over another?

    ○ What is Iran's current and projected capability to develop nuclear weapons? What are our key assumptions, and Iran's key choke points/vulnerabilities?

- The NIE only indirectly addresses the limits in U.S. ability to detect and track Iranian covert efforts. It does not address related military developments such as Iran's missile programs, many of which only seem to make sense if they are being armed with a nuclear warhead.

- No mention is made of the progress Iran has made in nuclear weapons design before 2003 or to date. It does not address any of key issues indicating that Iran was developing nuclear missile warheads. It does not address the transfer of nuclear weapons designs from North Korea and the A. Q. Khan network, the Green Salt and "laptop" issues being addressed by the IAEA, or what kind of nuclear weapons Iran was found to be working on in 2003. No hint is made of Iranian progress in completing fission, boosted, or thermonuclear weapons designs.

The Need for Careful Review

It is very important for anyone using or making judgments about the document to actually read the full text of the judgments the NIE makes about Iran's nuclear program. Press summaries and outside commentary are not a substitute for responsible literacy and attention to details.[246]

This level of careful attention is particularly important because the first few pages carefully define the meaning of the words used in assessing Iran's efforts. The definition of levels of confidence is particularly important in understanding what the document actually says:[247]

- *High confidence* generally indicates that our judgments are based on high-quality information, and/or that the nature of the issue makes it possible to render a solid judgment. A "high confidence" judgment is not a fact, nor is it a certainty, however, and such judgments still carry a risk of being wrong.

- *Moderate confidence* generally means that the information is credibly sourced and plausible but not of sufficient quality or corroborated sufficiently to warrant a higher level of confidence.

- *Low confidence* generally means that the information's credibility and/or plausibility is questionable, or that the information is too fragmented or poorly corroborated to make solid analytic inferences, or that we have significant concerns or problems with the sources.

It is also important to point out that the U.S. intelligence community has made major changes and improvements in its intelligence methods in recent years. Accordingly, while the document does provide the summary comparison of the judgments in the new document with past judgments made in a May 2005 NIE shown at the end of this report, it should be noted that the intelligence collection and analytic efforts that created the two documents are not directly comparable and that outside attempts to make word-for-word comparisons, and judge credibility, can be highly misleading.

Examining the NIE's Key Judgments

A careful reading shows that the U.S. intelligence community made careful caveats about its knowledge of whether Iran has continued to halt its program and the level of confidence the intelligence community has regarding Iran's actions.

The full text of the key portions of the NIE's judgments are shown below, and key points are in bold text:

> We judge with high confidence that in fall 2003, Tehran halted its nuclear weapons Program (For the purposes of this Estimate, by "nuclear weapons program" we mean Iran's nuclear weapon design and weaponization work and covert uranium conversion-related and uranium enrichment-related work; **we do not mean Iran's declared civil work related to uranium conversion and enrichment.**);
> ... **we also assess with moderate-to-high confidence that Tehran at a minimum is keeping open the option to develop nuclear weapons.**
> We judge with high confidence that the halt, and Tehran's announcement of its decision to suspend its declared uranium enrichment program and sign an Additional Protocol to its Nuclear Non-Proliferation Treaty Safeguards Agreement, **was directed primarily in response to increasing international scrutiny and pressure resulting from exposure of Iran's previously undeclared nuclear work.**
> • **We assess with high confidence that until fall 2003, Iranian military entities were working under government direction to develop nuclear weapons.**
> • We judge with high confidence that the halt lasted at least several years. (**Because of intelligence gaps discussed elsewhere in this Estimate, however, DOE and the NIC [U.S. National Intelligence Committee] assess with only moderate confidence that the halt to those activities represents a halt to Iran's entire nuclear weapons program.**)

• We assess with moderate confidence Tehran had not restarted its nuclear weapons program as of mid-2007, but we do not know whether it currently intends to develop nuclear weapons.

• We continue to assess with moderate-to-high confidence that Iran does not currently have a nuclear weapon.

• **Tehran's decision to halt its nuclear weapons program suggests it is less determined to develop nuclear weapons than we have been judging since 2005. Our assessment that the program probably was halted primarily in response to international pressure suggests Iran may be more vulnerable to influence on the issue than we judged previously.**

B. We continue to assess with **low confidence that Iran probably has imported at least some weapons-usable fissile material**, but still judge with moderate-to-high confidence it has not obtained enough for a nuclear weapon. We cannot rule out that Iran has acquired from abroad—or will acquire in the future—a nuclear weapon or enough fissile material for a weapon. **Barring such acquisitions, if Iran wants to have nuclear weapons it would need to produce sufficient amounts of fissile material indigenously—which we judge with high confidence it has not yet done.**

C. We assess centrifuge enrichment is how Iran probably could first produce enough fissile material for a weapon, if it decides to do so. Iran resumed its declared centrifuge enrichment activities in January 2006, despite the continued halt in the nuclear weapons program. **Iran made significant progress in 2007 installing centrifuges at Natanz, but we judge with moderate confidence it still faces significant technical problems operating them.**

• We judge with moderate confidence that the earliest possible date Iran would be technically capable of producing enough HEU for a weapon is late 2009, but that this is very unlikely.

• **We judge with moderate confidence Iran probably would be technically capable of producing enough HEU for a weapon sometime during the 2010–2015 time frame. (INR [U.S. Department of State's Bureau of Intelligence and Research] judges Iran is unlikely to achieve this capability before 2013 because of foreseeable technical and programmatic problems.)** All agencies recognize the possibility that this capability may not be attained **until after 2015.**

D. **Iranian entities are continuing to develop a range of technical capabilities that could be applied to producing nuclear weapons**, if a decision is made to do so. For example, Iran's civilian uranium enrichment program is continuing. We also assess with high confidence that since fall 2003, **Iran has been conducting research and development projects with commercial and conventional military applications— some of which would also be of limited use for nuclear weapons.**

E. **We do not have sufficient intelligence to judge confidently whether Tehran is willing to maintain the halt of its nuclear weapons program indefinitely** while it weighs its options on whether it will or already has set specific deadlines or criteria that will prompt it to restart the program.

• Our assessment that Iran halted the program in 2003 primarily in response to international pressure indicates **Tehran's decisions are guided by a cost-benefit approach rather than a rush to a weapon irrespective of the political, economic, and military costs.** This, in turn, suggests that some combination of threats of intensified international scrutiny and pressures, along with opportunities for Iran to achieve its security, prestige, and goals for regional influence in other ways, might—if perceived by Iran's leaders as credible—prompt Tehran to extend the current halt to its nuclear weapons program. It is difficult to specify what such a combination might be.

• We assess with moderate confidence that convincing the Iranian leadership to forgo the eventual development of nuclear weapons will be difficult given the linkage many within the leadership probably see between nuclear weapons development and Iran's key national security and foreign policy objectives, and given Iran's considerable effort from at least the late 1980s to 2003 to develop such weapons. **In our judgment, only an Iranian political decision to abandon a nuclear weapons objective would plausibly keep Iran from eventually producing nuclear weapons—and such a decision is inherently reversible.**

F. We assess with moderate confidence that Iran probably would use covert facilities —rather than its declared nuclear sites—for the production of highly enriched uranium for a weapon. A growing amount of intelligence indicates Iran was engaged in covert uranium conversion and uranium enrichment activity, but we judge that these efforts probably were halted in response to the fall 2003 halt, and that these efforts probably had not been restarted through at least mid-2007.

G. We judge with high confidence that Iran will not be technically capable of producing and reprocessing enough plutonium for a weapon before about 2015.

H. We assess with high confidence that Iran has the scientific, technical and industrial capacity eventually to produce nuclear weapons if it decides to do so.

The Key Issues That Were Not Addressed

It is important to note several things about these judgments:

• No mention is made of exactly what nuclear weapons efforts Iran halted and whether this included all covert and dual-use programs.

• The NIE unambiguously says that U.S. intelligence did have high confidence Iran was actively working on nuclear weapons until 2003, and the intelligence community expresses important levels of uncertainty over whether Iran has resumed its nuclear weapons effort.

• Iran's current enrichment efforts have and will continue to move it closer to being able to deploy nuclear weapons even if key elements of its weapons design and production activity have been halted or suspended.

• The NIE does not address any of the major issues and uncertainties still being examined by the IAEA. The omission of any discussion of the Green Salt, laptop, and warhead issues is particularly important.

• The commentary on the uncertainty relating to research and dual-use activity is particularly important. Iran is known to have worked on technology that could be used to produce the high-explosive lens, uranium machining, neutron initiator, neutron reflector, and other components needed for a fission weapon. Ongoing covert research in each area would be very easy to disperse and conceal. Passive and conventional high-explosive testing of actual warhead and weapons designs using nonfissile material would not provide any indicators other than—at most—those associated with conventional high explosives. Missile testing using warheads with such assemblies and similar bomb testing would probably be detectable only through a major leak of human intelligence.

- Moreover, no mention is made of Iran's long-range missile programs, but Iran is clearly continuing to improve its ability to develop advanced nuclear delivery systems and has announced two new missile programs within the last month [October 2007].

In short, the NIE is good news in that it indicates that past efforts to pressure Iran have had some impact, and there is time for negotiation and to find alternatives to attacking Iran—such as the containment approach suggested by General John Abizaid. It does not, however, make any promises for the future or resolve the major credibility problems the United States incurred in providing incorrect intelligence on Iraq.

The bad news is that many will focus only on taking the more positive news out of context and judge credibility of the basis of comparisons between the 2005 and 2007 estimates, while ignoring the full text of the key judgments and the many areas where the unclassified summary leaves more questions than answers. Figure 7.7 outlines the key differences between the key judgments of the May 2005 Intelligence Community Assessment Estimate on Iran's nuclear program and the 2007 NIE.

THE DNI'S FOLLOW-UP TO THE NIE

It is also important to note that the NIE is scarcely the last word of the U.S. intelligence community. J. Michael McConnel, then Director of National Intelligence (DNI) stated on February 27, 2008,

Over the past year we have gained important new insights into Tehran's activities related to nuclear weapons and the Community recently published a National Intelligence Estimate on Iranian intent and capabilities in this area. I want to be very clear in addressing the Iranian nuclear capability. First, there are three parts to an effective nuclear weapons capability:

1. Production of fissile material
2. Effective means for weapons delivery
3. Design and weaponization of the warhead itself

We assess in our recent NIE on this subject that warhead design and weaponization were halted, along with covert military uranium conversion- and enrichment-related activities. Declared uranium enrichment efforts, which will enable the production of fissile material, continue. This is the most difficult challenge in nuclear production. Iran's efforts to perfect ballistic missiles that can reach North Africa and Europe also continue.

We remain concerned about Iran's intentions and assess with moderate-to-high confidence that Tehran at a minimum is keeping open the option to develop nuclear weapons. We have high confidence that Iranian military entities were working under government direction to develop nuclear weapons until fall 2003. Also, Iranian entities are continuing to develop a range of technical capabilities that could be applied to producing nuclear weapons. Iran continues its efforts to develop uranium enrichment technology, which can be used both for power reactor fuel and to produce nuclear weapons. And, as noted, Iran continues to deploy ballistic missiles inherently capable of delivering nuclear weapons, and to develop longer-range

Figure 7.7   Key Differences between the Key Judgments of This Estimate on Iran's Nuclear Program in the May 2005 Intelligence Community (IC) Assessment Estimate and the 2007 National Intelligence Estimate

2005 IC Estimate	2007 NIE
Assess with high confidence that Iran currently is determined to develop nuclear weapons despite its international obligations and international pressure, but we do not assess that Iran is immovable.	Judge with high confidence that in fall 2003, Tehran halted its nuclear weapons program. Judge with high confidence that the halt lasted at least several years. (DOE [Department of Energy] and the NIC have moderate confidence that the halt to those activities represents a halt to Iran's entire nuclear weapons program.) Assess with moderate confidence Tehran had not restarted its nuclear weapons program as of mid-2007, but we do not know whether it currently intends to develop nuclear weapons. Judge with high confidence that the halt was directed primarily in response to increasing international scrutiny and pressure resulting from exposure of Iran's previously undeclared nuclear work. Assess with moderate-to-high confidence that Tehran at a minimum is keeping open the option to develop nuclear weapons.
We have moderate confidence in projecting when Iran is likely to make a nuclear weapon; we assess that it is unlikely before early-to-mid next decade.	We judge with moderate confidence that the earliest possible date Iran would be technically capable of producing enough highly enriched uranium (HEU) for a weapon is late 2009, but that this is very unlikely.
Iran could produce enough fissile material for a weapon by the end of this decade if it were to make more rapid and successful progress than we have seen to date.	We judge with moderate confidence that the earliest possible date Iran would be technically capable of producing enough highly enriched uranium (HEU) for a weapon is late 2009, but that this is very unlikely. We judge with moderate confidence Iran probably would be technically capable of producing enough HEU for a weapon sometime during the 2010–2015 time frame. (INR judges that Iran is unlikely to achieve this capability before 2013 because of foreseeable technical and programmatic problems.)

missiles. We also assess with high confidence that even after fall 2003 Iran has conducted research and development projects with commercial and conventional military applications—some of which would also be of limited use for nuclear weapons.

We judge with high confidence that in fall 2003, Tehran halted its nuclear weapons design and weaponization activities, as well as its covert military uranium conversion and enrichment-related activities, for at least several years. Because of intelligence gaps, DOE and the NIC assess with only moderate confidence that all such activities were halted. We assess with moderate confidence that Tehran had not restarted these activities as of mid-2007, but since they comprised an unannounced secret effort that Iran attempted to hide, we do not know if these activities have been restarted.

We judge with high confidence that the halt was directed primarily in response to increasing international scrutiny and pressure resulting from exposure of Iran's previously undeclared nuclear work. This indicates that Iran may be more susceptible to influence on the issue than we judged previously.

We do not have sufficient intelligence information to judge confidently whether Tehran is willing to maintain the halt of its nuclear weapons design and weaponization activities indefinitely while it weighs its options, or whether it will or already has set specific deadlines or criteria that will prompt it to restart those activities. We assess with high confidence that Iran has the scientific, technical and industrial capacity eventually to produce nuclear weapons. In our judgment, only an Iranian political decision to abandon a nuclear weapons objective would plausibly keep Iran from eventually producing nuclear weapons—and such a decision is inherently reversible. I note again that two activities relevant to a nuclear weapons capability continue: uranium enrichment that will enable the production of fissile material and development of long-range ballistic missile systems.

We assess with moderate confidence that convincing the Iranian leadership to forgo the eventual development of nuclear weapons will be difficult given the linkage many within the leadership see between nuclear weapons development and Iran's key national security and foreign policy objectives, and given Iran's considerable effort from at least the late 1980s to 2003 to develop such weapons.

We continue to assess with moderate-to-high confidence that Iran does not currently have a nuclear weapon. We continue to assess with low confidence that Iran probably has imported at least some weapons-usable fissile material, but still judge with moderate-to-high confidence it has not obtained enough for a nuclear weapon. We cannot rule out that Iran has acquired from abroad—or will acquire in the future—a nuclear weapon or enough fissile material for a weapon. Barring such acquisitions, if Iran wants to have nuclear weapons it would need to produce sufficient amounts of fissile material indigenously—which we judge with high confidence it has not yet done.

Iran resumed its declared centrifuge enrichment activities in January 2006, despite the 2003 halt in its nuclear weapons design and weaponization activities. Iran made significant progress in 2007 installing centrifuges at Natanz, but we judge with moderate confidence it still faces significant technical problems operating them.

We judge with moderate confidence that the earliest possible date Iran would be technically capable of producing enough highly enriched uranium (HEU) for a weapon is late 2009, but that is very unlikely.

We judge with moderate confidence Iran probably would be technically capable of producing enough HEU for a weapon sometime during the 2010–2015 time frame. INR judges Iran is unlikely to achieve this capability before 2013 because of foreseeable technical and programmatic problems. All agencies recognize the possibility that this capability may not be attained until *after* 2015.

> We know that Tehran had a chemical warfare program prior to 1997, when it declared elements of its program. We assess that Tehran maintains dual-use facilities intended to produce CW agent in times of need and conducts research that may have offensive applications. We assess Iran maintains a capability to weaponize CW agents in a variety of delivery systems.
>
> We assess that Iran has previously conducted offensive BW agent research and development. Iran continues to seek dual- use technologies that could be used for biological warfare.[248]

President Barack Obama's new Director of National Intelligence, Dennis C. Blair, provided a significantly clearer estimate in his testimony to the Senate Intelligence Committee in February 2009,

> The Iranian regime continues to flout UN Security Council restrictions on its nuclear programs. There is a real risk that its nuclear program will prompt other countries in the Middle East region to pursue nuclear options conducive to the development of nuclear weapons, and the advent of additional nuclear weapons programs might lead countries in other regions to reassess their nuclear options.
>
> I want to be very clear in characterizing the Iranian nuclear program. First, there are three key parts to an effective nuclear weapons capability:
>
> (1) Production of fissile material,
>
> (2) Effective means for weapon delivery, and
>
> (3) Design, weaponization, and testing of the warhead itself.
>
> We assessed in our 2007 NIE on this subject that Iran's nuclear weapon design and weaponization work was halted in fall 2003, along with its covert uranium conversion and enrichment-related activities. Declared uranium enrichment efforts were suspended in 2003 but resumed in January 2006 and will enable Iran to produce weapons-usable fissile material if it chooses to do so. Development of medium-range ballistic missiles, inherently capable of delivering nuclear weapons, has continued unabated.
>
> We assess Iranian military entities were working under government direction to develop nuclear weapons until fall 2003. Iranian entities are continuing to develop a range of technical capabilities that could be applied to producing nuclear weapons, if a decision were made to do so.
>
> • Iran continues its efforts to develop uranium enrichment technology, which can be used both to produce low-enriched uranium for power reactor fuel and to produce highly enriched uranium for nuclear weapons.
>
> • As noted, Iran continues to deploy and improve ballistic missiles inherently capable of delivering nuclear weapons.
>
> • We assess Iran since fall 2003 has conducted research and development projects with commercial and conventional military applications, some of which would be of limited use for nuclear weapons.
>
> We judge in fall 2003 Tehran halted its nuclear weapons design and weaponization activities and that the halt lasted at least several years. We assess Tehran had not restarted these activities as of at least mid-2007. Although we do not know whether Iran currently intends to develop nuclear weapons, we assess Tehran at a minimum is keeping open the option to develop them.
>
> We judge the halt was directed primarily in response to increasing international scrutiny and pressure resulting from exposure of Iran's previously undeclared nuclear work.

This indicates Iran may be more susceptible to influence on the issue than we had judged in the 2005 National Intelligence Estimate.

We do not have sufficient intelligence reporting to judge confidently whether Tehran is willing to maintain indefinitely the halt of its previously enumerated nuclear weapons-related activities while it weighs its options, or whether it will or already has set specific deadlines or criteria that will prompt it to restart those activities. We assess Iran has the scientific, technical, and industrial capacity eventually to produce nuclear weapons. In our judgment, only an Iranian political decision to abandon a nuclear weapons objective would plausibly keep Iran from eventually producing nuclear weapons—and such a decision is inherently reversible. I reiterate that two activities of the three relevant to a nuclear weapons capability continue: development of uranium enrichment technology that will enable production of fissile material, if Iran chooses to do so, and development of nuclear-capable ballistic missile systems.

We assess convincing the Iranian leadership to forgo the eventual development of nuclear weapons will be difficult given the linkage many within the leadership see between nuclear weapons and Iran's key national security and foreign policy objectives, and given Iran's considerable effort from at least the late 1980s to 2003 to develop such weapons. Our analysis suggests that some combination of threats of intensified international scrutiny and pressures, along with opportunities for Iran to achieve its security and goals might—if perceived by Iran's leaders as credible—prompt Tehran to extend the halt to the above nuclear weapons-related activities. It is difficult to specify what such a combination might be.

We continue to assess Iran does not currently have a nuclear weapon. We continue to assess Iran probably has imported at least some weapons-usable fissile material but still judge it has not obtained enough for a nuclear weapon. We cannot rule out that Iran has acquired from abroad or will acquire in the future a nuclear weapon or enough fissile material for a weapon.

Barring such acquisitions, if Iran wants to have nuclear weapons it would need to produce sufficient amounts of fissile material indigenously. We judge it has not yet done so. Iran made significant progress in 2007 and 2008 installing and operating centrifuges at its main centrifuge enrichment plant, Natanz. We judge Iran probably would be technically capable of producing enough highly enriched uranium (HEU) for a weapon sometime during the 2010- 2015 time frame. INR judges Iran is unlikely to achieve this capability before 2013 because of foreseeable technical and programmatic problems.[249]

THE IRANIAN COMMITMENT TO NUCLEAR PROGRAMS

It is not clear how future Iranian leaders will treat either Iran's nuclear weapons programs or the issue of nuclear power. Iran did, however, express an interest in acquiring two more nuclear power reactors in April 2007, and its statements in reaction to both the new Security Council sanctions passed in early 2007 and the announcement in April 2007 that it was scaling up its centrifuge program provide at least some indication of how deep Iran's commitment may be.

The following quotes all come from Iranian statements made on Iran's "Nuclear Day" on April 10, 2007, and show little sign of giving way to international pressure:[250]

- **President Mahmoud Ahmadinejad, speaking on Iran's Nuclear Day, April 10, 2007:** "I declare today, in all pride, that from this day, Iran is among the countries producing nuclear fuel on an [industrial] scale . . . Today, Iran's enemies are embarrassed by Iran's progress in various areas . . . According to a pre-set program, the Iranian government is determined to produce at least 20,000 megawatts of nuclear electricity according to a specific timetable . . . We warmly shake the hands of all governments interested in holding talks with us and in cooperating with us in this area.

  "I [address] the governments that have so far refused to come to terms with today's reality and with the Iranian people's right [to develop nuclear technology], and demand that they stop acting aggressively, illogically, hostilely, and in violation [of the law] towards Iran. [They had better know] that every member of the Iranian people stands fast behind its leaders, out of knowledge, faith, and absolute unity, and [that the Iranian people] will defend its right to the end . . . The [Western countries] should know that the path of the progress of the Iranian people is irreversible They must pay attention, and do nothing to cause this brave and brave people to reconsider the way it deals with them. [Western countries] have tried this [hostile] approach several times, and have seen that the [Iranian] people are capable of [reconsidering its approach toward them]."[251]

- **Ali Larijani, Iran's Chief Nuclear Negotiator, April 10, 2007:** "[The Western countries] must in any event accept a nuclear Iran . . . We are moving vigorously along the path of obtaining . . . 54,000 centrifuges . . . The sanctions against us [UN Resolution 1747] have had no effect, and will have no effect, on our government towards this goal [in the future] . . . The number of centrifuges doesn't matter. But we have a work output of 3,000 centrifuges. This level and above is considered industrial."[252]

- **Gholam Reza Aghazadeh, Vice President for Atomic Energy of the Islamic Republic of Iran and President of the Atomic Energy Organization of Iran, April 10, 2007:** "Iran's program is not to install and operate only 3,000 centrifuges at the Natanz uranium enrichment facilities, but 50,000 . . . We planned and invested for [the installation of] 50,000 centrifuges. The infrastructure that has been established— including equipment for air filtering, electricity, a new air supply, and everything required for this industry—was for 50,000 centrifuges . . . I intentionally did not indicate any number [in my speech at the Natanz celebrations] . . . because I wanted no misunderstandings in the foreign media, [and I did not want] them to think that Iran's [nuclear program] included [only] 3,000 centrifuges.

  "[The situation is] quite the opposite. As we enter the industrial stage, the installation of the centrifuges will be carried out on an ongoing basis, until all 50,000 [centrifuges] are installed . . . Our declaration that we have entered the stage [of producing nuclear fuel] on an industrial [scale means] that there is no turning back."

  At the Natanz celebrations, Aghazadeh stressed that "despite the commitments we have received from [various] countries, no expert of [external] company has stood by us . . . but despite these challenges, obstacles, and problems, Iran was determined to realize, by means of its creative young people, its nuclear program—which includes peaceful purposes, with the first priority being to produce a nuclear fuel cycle as supreme science in nuclear technology . . . and in the past year, our young scientists have managed to produce 270 tons of UF6."

  "Not long ago, [producing] this important substance was far from the imagination of our country's nuclear researchers and scientists. But finally, we managed to attain [enrichment of] uranium, at [a level of] 3.5% to 5% . . . Now, as we enter mass production of centrifuges and begin to produce [nuclear fuel] on an industrial [scale], we are taking one more step towards the flowering of Iran . . ."

"Now that Iran has entered into production of nuclear fuel on an industrial [scale], there will be no limit on the production of nuclear fuel in Iran . . . This is the accomplishment of some 3,000 expert scientists and the best of the forces that worked in the best year night and day at the Natanz facility."[253]

- **Keyhan editorial, "The West Must Expect a Shock from Iran at Any Moment, April 10, 2007:** "Under the current threatening and unjust conditions, Iran has decided to employ a strategy of ambiguity. Since Iran's nuclear dossier was illegally returned to the UN Security Council, the eyes of the IAEA—the intelligence agency of the West—are finding it more difficult every day [to monitor Iran's activities]. When [the IAEA] reported on [Iran's nuclear dossier] to the Security Council last winter, Iran announced that it would no longer be implementing the Additional Protocol. A few months later, when sanctions resolution 1737 was issued, Iran began to install 3,000 centrifuges in Natanz . . . When sanctions resolution 1747 was passed, Iran further reduced IAEA access [to its nuclear facilities] by stopping the implementation of the agreements connected to the 'Safeguards Agreement.' "[254]

- **Keyhan editorial, "Duel with an Unloaded Gun," April 11, 2007:** "Now America has expended all the bullets in its clip. Now, it is Iran that will decide, in the face of the shocked world, on the 'news' and the 'event' with which it will strike the superpowers at their weak points and their Achilles heel. Iran still has great wisdom in its clip—each bullet of wisdom prepares the ground for new opportunities, and makes Iran's hands more skilled . . . America is now dealing with the deadly hail of Iran's wisdom."[255]

Since these statements were made, Iranian officials have continued to assert that Tehran will not be deterred from its current policy regarding its "civilian" nuclear program. On October 5, 2008, Iranian Foreign Minister Manouchehr Mottaki stated, "Iran's uranium enrichment policy remains unchanged. Enrichment will continue until Iran becomes self-sufficient in fuel production for nuclear plants." Mottaki indicates that Iran is willing to supply other countries with nuclear fuel after it is self-sufficient.[256]

Recent reports, statements, and activities reaffirm Tehran's commitment to its nuclear program. Reports from October 2008 out of Iran and Russia assess that Iran's Bushehr reactor could be operational in March 2009, with the assistance of Russian engineers and equipment in the final stages of its completion.[257]

On February 25, 2009, Iranian and Russian scientists carried out successful tests at the Bushehr nuclear reactor. The tests at the nuclear plant in the southern city of Bushehr brought the power station closer to full operation. Iran and Russia's top nuclear officials have not stated when exactly electricity production would begin. But Iranian officials have stated that the reactor will be operational by the end of the year.[258]

As of the IAEA report by the Director General dated June 5, 2009, the Bushehr nuclear reactor was not yet fully operational.[259]

A CONTINUING PROCESS OF DISCOVERY

It is clear that there is still much more to learn, and it is equally clear that Iran may well have a program that is opportunistic, which constantly evolves, and where it is impossible to predict the rate of Iranian progress or the end result. As noted earlier, in early 2006, the *New York Times* reported on new U.S. intelligence estimates that suggested Iran's "peaceful" program included a "military-nuclear dimension." This assessment was reportedly based on information provided by the United States to the IAEA and referred to a secret program called the Green Salt Project. This project was started to work on uranium enrichment, high explosives, and on adapting nuclear warheads to Iranian missiles. The report suggested that there was evidence of "administrative interconnections" between weaponization and nuclear experts in Iran's nuclear program. Tehran argued that these claims were "baseless" and promised to provide further clarifications on the matter.[260]

The IAEA report on Iran's nuclear activities in August 2006 made it clear, however, that Iran was not clarifying any major issues that have arisen relating to its nuclear activities, and this raised new questions about Iran's activities in highly enriching uranium that could not be linked to any contamination of centrifuges imported from Pakistan.

Claims that there was a link between Iran's civilian and military nuclear tracks seem to support the comments made by then Secretary of State Colin Powell in November 2004, yet it remains uncertain if the sources of intelligence were the same. Mr. Powell argued that the U.S. intelligence had information that showed Iranian efforts to adapt their nuclear research to fit their Shahab-3 missile. He argued that it made no sense that Iran would work on advancing its delivery systems unless it was also working on the warheads. Other U.S. officials, however, argued that the information Colin Powell used came from unconfirmed sources with uncertain information and should not be seen as a definitive proof.[261]

The source for this information seems to be a stolen laptop computer, which contained designs of a small-scale uranium gas production facility by Kimeya Madon, an Iranian company. In addition, the documents contained modification to the Shahab-3 missile in a way, U.S. officials believe, to fit a nuclear warhead. U.S. intelligence experts, reportedly, believe that the files on the computer were authentic, but they argue that there was no way to prove it. They argue that while there was the possibility that the document was forged by Iranian opposition groups or fabricated by a third country such as Israel, it was unlikely. In addition, the authenticity of the document also seemed to have been confirmed by British intelligence.[262]

What concerns U.S. officials is that while there was no mention of the word "nuclear" on the laptop, the documents mentioned the names of military officers that were linked to Mohsen Fakhrizadeh, who is believed to direct "Project 111." U.S. intelligence believes that this project has been responsible for weaponizing Iran's nuclear research efforts and missile developments. In addition, the United States believes that this project is the successor to Project 110, which used to be the military arm of Iran's nuclear research program. These revelations, however, are "cloaked" with uncertainty, and the United States believes that the only way to know is if Fak-rizadeh cooperates with IAEA inspectors.[263]

These concerns about Iranian weaponization efforts were exacerbated by the IAEA's discovery of a document relating to the requirement of reducing UF_6 to small quantities of metal as well as casting enriched and natural depleted uranium into hemispherical forms.[264] This is believed to be the first link the IAEA has shown between Iran's military and civilian nuclear program. Many argue that this discovery was the turning point in the IAEA negotiation efforts with Tehran and that the failure to disclose this document early in the inspections was a cause for concern for the Agency.

Press reports have also claimed that there was further evidence of Iran's effort to weaponize its nuclear research. A U.S. intelligence assessment was leaked to the *Washington Post*. According to U.S. officials, Iran's nuclear researchers have completed the drawing of "a deep subterranean shaft." The drawings outlined the plans for a 400-meter underground tunnel with remote-controlled sensors to measure pressures and temperatures. U.S. experts believed that the tunnel was being prepared for an underground nuclear test. One U.S. official was quoted saying, "The diagram is consistent with a nuclear test-site schematic." This assessment was based on the fact that the drawings envisioned a test control team to be so far away—10 kilometers—from the test site, but the United States believes that the tunnel was still in the drawing stage and no developments have taken place. The evidence for this tunnel and Iranian weaponization efforts were the closest thing to a smoking gun in proving an Iranian nuclear weapons program.[265]

This illustrates the point that Iran can gain as much from concealing and obfuscating its weaponization activities as from hiding or obfuscating the nature of its nuclear program. As long as Iran does not actually test a full nuclear explosion, it can develop and test potential weapons and warhead designs in a wide range of ways. It can also prepare for underground testing and test simulated weapons underground to validate many aspects of the test system—including venting—without exploding a bomb until it is ready for the international community to know it has actually tested a weapon.

Iran can develop and deploy its missile program with conventional warheads and create considerable confusion over the nature of its warhead and bomb tests, concealing whether it has carried out extensive research on CBRN weaponization as part of what it claims is the testing of conventional weapons. Telemetry can be encrypted, avoided, and made deliberately misleading. The same is true of static explosive testing or the use of air-delivered warheads and bombs. So far, for example, the international community and outside experts have generally failed to explore the rationale for Iran's missile efforts and other weaponization activities. The IAEA and the Chemical Weapons Convention lack any clear mandate for inspection and analysis of such activities, and the Biological Weapons Convention does not address the issue.

Following the September 15, 2008, report by the IAEA, the ISIS wrote that the IAEA reported that it had obtained information about the possibility of Iran drawing on foreign expertise in conducting experiments connected with the symmetrical initiation of a hemispherical high-explosive charge suitable for an implosion-type nuclear weapon. The official noted that the IAEA has not linked this expertise to the A. Q. Khan proliferation network.[266]

In addition to the report by the ISIS, IAEA Director General Dr. Mohamed ElBaradei showed the UN documents and photographs suggesting Iran secretly tried to modify a missile cone to fit a nuclear bomb. Tehran said the alleged weapon-related studies were based on fabricated documents or pertained only to conventional arms, and it provided the IAEA with a 117-page response in May addressing some of the agency's questions. This evidence heightened Western concerns that Iran may have had foreign expertise helping in experiments on a detonator applicable to an implosion-type nuclear blast occurring at high altitude.[267]

While addressing the UN General Assembly on October 28, 2008, IAEA Director General Dr. Mohamed ElBaradei made the following statements regarding Implementation of the NPT Safeguards Agreement in the Islamic Republic of Iran:

> Six years have elapsed since the Agency began working to clarify Iran's nuclear programme. Substantial progress has been made under a work plan agreed with Iran to clarify outstanding issues, including the nature of Iran's enrichment activities. The Agency has been able to continue to verify the non-diversion of *declared* nuclear material in Iran.
>
> However, I regret that we are still not in a position to achieve full clarity regarding the absence of *undeclared* nuclear material and activities in Iran. This is because the Agency has not been able to make substantive progress on the so-called alleged studies and associated questions relevant to possible military dimensions to Iran's nuclear programme.
>
> I reiterate that the Agency does not in any way seek to "pry" into Iran's conventional or missile-related military activities. Our focus is clearly on nuclear material and activities. I am confident that arrangements can be developed which enable the Agency to clarify the remaining issues while ensuring that Iran's legitimate right to protect the confidentiality of sensitive information and activities is respected. I therefore urge Iran to implement all the transparency measures required to build confidence in the exclusively peaceful nature of its nuclear programme at an early date. This will be good for Iran, good for the Middle East region and good for the world.[268]

New information is constantly being uncovered regarding Iran's controversial nuclear program; but due to the factors discussed previously, uncertainty remains, and without greater transparency the truth will remain elusive. The IAEA and the UNSC P5+1 continue to stress that their patience is running thin with Iran, but they have not taken a united, decisive stance against Iran's noncompliant actions.

It is important to note that much of what Iran has done or is suspected of doing, in regards to its nuclear program, to date has been covert. Many of Iran's nuclear-related sites and activities have been discovered not by Iranian declaration, but through collection of intelligence. Given past Iranian behavior, it is entirely possible that Iran will continue working on, or restart, a covert nuclear weapons program.

The IAEA continues to press Iran for greater cooperation and transparency, but the IAEA cannot force Tehran to comply to requests for transparency. Without greater international cooperation on the nuclear issue, threats become "paper tigers" and Iran gets closer to its goal. Whether that goal is creating a civilian nuclear reactor or a nuclear weapons arsenal, the international community cannot stand by and let Iran continue along its current path unchecked.

IF IRAN BECOMES A SERIOUS NUCLEAR WEAPONS POWER

The situation will change strikingly if Iran does go from developing nuclear weapons and long-range missiles to deploying an effective nuclear strike capability. At this point in time, there is no way to be certain what such a force would look like or how capable it would be. There is no way to know the yield, reliability, or any other aspect of Iran's first nuclear devices or weapons, or how soon it could move on to boosted or thermonuclear weapons.

One thing, however, is clear. Even the political-psychological impact of a limited fissile surface or underground test would be enormous, and the strategic debate would immediately shift from trying to deny Iran nuclear capability to preemption, containment, defense, and nuclear or conventional deterrence. Even the prospect of an Iranian weapon has created a de facto nuclear arms race with Israel, which is quietly improving its own capabilities and is making Arab states reconsider acquiring such weapons and delivery systems.

There are many different ways in which Iran can proliferate, deploy nuclear-armed or other CBRN weapons, and use them to deter, intimidate, and strike against other nations. All have only one thing in common: they are all provocative and dangerous to any nation Iran may choose to try to intimidate and target, *and* they are all provocative and dangerous to Iran.

Even Iranian ambiguity will probably lead Israel and the United States—and possibly India, Pakistan, and Russia—to develop nuclear options to deter or retaliate against Iran. Israeli and/or U.S. restraint in striking Iran does not have to stop at the first convincing Iranian threat to use nuclear or highly lethal biological weapons, but it could do so.

As of regional options, Iranian nuclear ambiguity might be enough to trigger Saudi, Egyptian, and Turkish efforts to become nuclear powers and some form of Israeli sea basing to enhance the survivability of its nuclear forces while increasing range and/or yield to strike Iran. Saudi Arabia has already said that it has examined nuclear options and rejected them, but this is no certainty and inevitably depends on Iranian action. The successful deployment of a highly capable Iranian force, and Israel's existential vulnerability, would almost certainly lead Israel to develop a retaliatory capability to destroy Iran's cities and kill most of its population.

Regional powers might show restraint if the United States could provide convincing ballistic and cruise missile defenses and the same form of extended deterrence it once provided to Germany during the Cold War. But these options are speculative and do not yet exist. Successfully deploying a nuclear warhead is one achievement;

second-strike capability is another that must be considered by Iranian decision makers. It borders on certainty that Iran's reaching a second-strike nuclear capability will take at least a decade if it will ever be achieved.

Any form of major nuclear confrontation could be a nightmare for all concerned. Iran's effort to limit or control the game will probably end at the first ground zero. Any actual Iranian use of such weapons is likely to provoke a nuclear response and may well provoke one targeted on Iranian cities and its population. Moreover, while Israel may technically be a more vulnerable "one bomb" country, it is highly questionable whether any form of Persian state could emerge from nuclear strikes on Iran's 5–10 largest cities.

The end result is the prospect of a far more threatening mix of CBRN capabilities in the Gulf region and the area that most models project as the main source of continued world oil and gas exports beyond 2015. It is also the near certainty of an Israeli-Iranian nuclear arms race that means crossing Arab territory, U.S. nuclear targeting of Iran in some form of extended deterrence, the threat of more polarization between Sunni and Shi'ites, and broader regional tensions and actions that spill over out of the confrontation over Iran's nuclear activities. As the next chapter shows, none of these prospects are pleasant.

8

Strategic and Warfighting Implications

It is still possible that Iran may not develop a nuclear weapons capability or deploy other weapons of mass destruction (WMDs). Diplomacy may change Iranian actions, the regime may change, sanctions and economic problems might halt or delay Iran's efforts, and/or Iran may develop other security priorities. These options do, however, seem less probable with time.

Nearly two decades of sanctions, diplomacy, and dialog have had some impact in delaying Iran's programs, in making it keep its programs more covert, and in highlighting the risks Iran runs in moving forward. It has not, however, prevented Iran from acquiring steadily more capable long-range missiles and the technology and production facilities needed to make nuclear weapons. Iran also has retained the technology and production base to make chemical weapons, and even if it does not have covert active programs, its civil sector is steadily improving its dual capabilities and ability to develop and deploy advanced biological weapons.

It is also far from clear that any power can carry out preventive attacks at this point that would do more than delay a determined Iranian effort to acquire nuclear weapons for several years. Israel and Iran's neighbors do not have the capability to launch more than limited strikes. It might be militarily possible for the United States to carry out effective initial strikes, follow them up with immediate restrikes, and then maintain a restrike capability that it used to systematically deny Iran the ability to create new, dispersed facilities. This kind of U.S. posture, however, would pose major political challenges in terms of both the willingness of friendly powers such as the Gulf States and Turkey to support any phase of such operations, and it is clear that the United States would have major problems in obtaining broad international support.

These are not reasons to give up on diplomacy or dialog, or to abandon sanctions and efforts to develop military options to prevent or limit Iranian capabilities. They are, however, realities that indicate that the Gulf States, the region, and the world may have to learn how to live with Iranian proliferation, coupled with growing Iranian capabilities for asymmetric warfare.

If that happens, there are two major strategic alternatives: (1) accept a major increase in Iran's ability to influence and intimidate key oil exporters and other states throughout the region; (2) create the capability to contain Iran through defense and deterrence. In both cases, the result may still be a regional nuclear arms race and at least the possibility of a devastating nuclear exchange.

IRAN'S UNCERTAIN PATH TO PROLIFERATION

Any examination of the options to change Iran's behavior must begin by looking at Iran's future options and how these evolve over time. The impact and risks of proliferation cannot be measured simply in terms of whether Iran does or does not have a nuclear weapon. Any realistic examination of Iran's options, and those of its neighbors and the United States, must consider what Iran may do over at least the next decade and the different ways in which it may deploy forces armed with weapons of mass destruction and other nations may respond.

Such an analysis is necessarily speculative. As the previous chapters have made clear, there is no definitive evidence that Iran is planning to make or deploy nuclear and biological weapons. Iran does not have a public strategy for proliferating, much less any public force plan or goals for creating a nuclear posture.

It is also likely that even if Iran has secret plans, its actual behavior will be opportunistic and dictated at least as much by its future circumstances as by its current intentions. Reality intervenes in even the best-made plans of the most powerful states, and Iran is neither a regional superpower nor a state that has demonstrated any capability to formulate the "best-made plans." It has obvious major limitations in both areas.

It is equally dangerous to assume that Iran will follow some linear path in proliferating based on some form of game theory or rational events. Wild cards and unanticipated events dominate history over time. Behavior is often less than rational, at least in the sense of taking optimal actions or avoiding crises and sometimes catastrophes. This is particularly true once conditions reach the crisis or warfighting level, where perceptions can be drastically wrong and driven by time pressures that push decision makers down poorly chosen paths where they cannot reverse course. There is no reason to assume worst cases dominate, but there is every reason to assume that they are possible.

Iran's Paths to Nuclear Proliferation

Iran has already advanced beyond the point where its choices consist of whether or not it should actually create some form of nuclear weapons capability. Its missile capabilities are giving it steadily better delivery options. Its technology and manufacturing base is approaching a "breakout" capability where it could choose to build a nuclear weapon within a year or so. Iran already has chemical weapons and has the technology base for a breakout capability in biological weapons.

There are many different ways, however, in which Iran could move forward, and it could halt its efforts to proliferate at many different levels of capability and risk. Iran has a wide range of nuclear options to create new military capabilities over the next decade, many of which could also be implemented in a similar form using advanced biological weapons:

- *Technology Creep:* Iran has reached the point where even if it fully complied with the terms of the Nuclear Non-Proliferation Treaty (NNPT), United Nations (UN) resolutions, and International Atomic Energy Agency (IAEA) inspections, its technology and manufacturing base will steadily improve its future capabilities to design and manufacture nuclear weapons. There currently are no proposals to limit its development of ballistic or cruise missiles, or procurement of advanced strike aircraft—although UN resolutions do call for restraint in such arms transfers. Unless totally new inspection regimes are developed, and a firm halt can be made to Iran's research programs, centrifuge programs, and heavy-water reactor programs, Iran's capabilities will improve under the best possible circumstances.

- *Modular Progress:* Iran can speed progress beyond technology creep. There are many aspects of weapons and warhead design that can be broken out into modules of peaceful research and manufacturing capability—avoiding any formal nuclear weapons program. Improved centrifuge technology and the ability to link centrifuges into efficient production chains will overcome Iran's most serious problem: the rapid and efficient production of fissile material in ways that can be highly disperse, concealed, and made redundant.

- *Breakout Capability:* At some point between 2009 and 2011, Iran's uranium enrichment capabilities will reach the point where Iran could build at least one fissile device within a 12–15-month period. This could quickly increase to several nuclear weapons a year. Iran can leverage this level of capability in many different ways. The threat to test and deploy will give it added negotiating leverage that can be increased by providing proof of capability or leaking a mix of real and exaggerated claims.

  Iran can also avoid going beyond its present policy of denial and leave its capabilities ambiguous. At the same time, it can covertly or overtly increase its ability to rapidly make a number of weapons: test bomb and missile warheads that simulate arming its delivery systems with nuclear weapons. Iran can improve the yield of its fissile weapons designs without actual testing and move toward a breakout capability in "boosted," higher-yield fissile weapons, or even move toward thermonuclear weapons designs.

  No outside power will be certain how soon Iran could acquire given nuclear capabilities under such circumstances. Iran could also continue to negotiate, and partially cooperate with the IAEA. It might negotiate agreements that effectively limit overt testing and proliferation while tacitly signaling to other states that they must treat Iran as a "quasinuclear" power, giving it added influence and the ability to intimidate, and be cautious about challenging its use of asymmetric warfare.

  In many ways, Iran has already advanced to this position. Moreover, barring a far more comprehensive set of limits and inspection options that has yet been imposed on any state to date, it is unclear that even the most successful negotiation by the "Six" [the United States, EU3 (France, Germany, and Great Britain), Russia, and China], the UN, and the IAEA can really change this. If Iran moves ahead in improving its enrichment capabilities, technology base, and in acquiring nuclear power, every year will increase Iran's potential capability to build better nuclear weapons more quickly and in greater numbers. There is no credible path to a truly secure negotiation or arms control agreement that would not require Iran to be totally open and forthcoming and to have a very different type of regime.

- *Undeclared Possession: "Bomb in the Basement":* There is no clear dividing line between a breakout capability and high confidence that a nation actually has nuclear weapons. The difference is largely one in terms of timelines and indicators. Much depends on whether possession is clearly credible, the country clearly had the technology and production capabilities, and delivery systems and exercises show potential nuclear capability.

    In the past, some evidence of testing was generally required, although this did not apply to Israel—which was credited with nuclear capabilities more than a decade before a suspect "event" occurred. Today, however, the mathematics and engineering have been available to Iran at least since 1992, and it seems to have acquired many of the details of a Chinese weapons design.

    Iran has the technology and equipment to do many critical tests using actual weapons designs that have nonfissile uranium or some other form of heavy metal. Pakistan and India made successful use of cruder approaches to such simulation tests before they tested. Some experts also feel that subcritical or marginally critical—ultralow yield—tests would be enough and that simulation would work with large boosted weapons designs. These, however, are controversial areas that only an actual weapons designer could really comment upon.

    There are questions as to whether Iran could create a reliable actual bomb or missile warhead with sufficient safety and reliability to build up a stockpile of weapons without testing. Once again, however, Iran could build actual weapons and warheads and test many aspects of their performance using nonfissile material. In fact, such simulations would be a key part of any realistic program, since testing of live weapons in flight would present major political problems and is inherently "destructive" and does not reveal the details of engineering performance or many of the causes of potential failure.

    This is also the threshold at which the "Nth weapon" becomes a critical problem. Once any weapons have actually been made, it becomes very difficult to create any kind of arms control or inspection regime that can be certain that all weapons have been turned over or destroyed. The possible existence of one or more dispersed weapons hidden somewhere in country becomes a possibility that no outside power can dismiss unless Iran turns over all its records and provides a level of unprecedented transparency and access to any suspect facility.

- *Test/Suspect Event:* Any surface test of a nuclear weapon provides clear evidence of possession of a nuclear device, although not of a functioning bomb or missile warhead unless a country deliberately provides considerable supporting evidence. Underground tests can be more ambiguous, both in a positive or negative sense.

    Some experts feel a nuclear underground test could be faked using massive amounts of conventional explosives. This has been an issue in terms of test ban verification, although other experts believe that this would not be possible even with an unvented underground test. Other experts feel that a subfractional or very low-yield nuclear test could be concealed in an area with earth tremors or a seismic event or be so small that it would not be detected and characterized. Another approach would be remote testing in a sensitive seismic area in the Indian Ocean.

Iran could test and deny, knowing that many low-yield tests would create some degree of uncertainty or that outside powers would not contest the issue. It could also create enough plausible or implausible deniability to both send a signal that it had weapons and still publicly deny this.

There are also potential trade-offs in testing vs. not testing that affect weapons design. Some experts feel testing is needed to use a small or minimal amount of fissile material, reduce weapons size and weight, and to verify weapons safety. Others feel it could be critical if Iran is to move beyond basic fission weapons to highly sophisticated fission weapons, or to boosted or fusion weapons.

This could be a major consideration if Iran becomes involved in a nuclear arms race with Israel or another state. Pure fission guns or implosion weapons (Iran might need an implosion design for effective missile warheads) can produce high yields, but Iran might initially be limited to maximum yields of around 20–30 kilotons and weapons using relatively large amounts of fissile material—with much depending on the sophistication of the design and factors such as the number of explosive lenses, tamper, reflector, and pit. Such yields are highly destructive against any target, but are not large enough to achieve a decisive level of lethality over large-area targets such as a major city, or to compensate for real-world problems in missile accuracy—which can be considerably greater than the nominal circular error probable (CEP) may indicate.

Boosted weapons allow yields in the 100-kiloton range, but are more complex. They essentially use a pure fission device to generate enough heat and pressure to trigger a thermonuclear explosion from an integrated mix of tritium and deuterium gas (heavy isotopes of hydrogen), "The hydrogen fuses to form helium and free neutrons. The energy release from fusion reactions is relatively negligible, but each neutron starts a new fission chain reaction, greatly reducing the amount of fissile material that would otherwise be wasted."[1] Boosting can double or even triple a fission weapon's yield.

Thermonuclear weapons are even more complex, and there are indications that both India and Pakistan had failures to achieve their design goals even when they carried out actual tests. A rough idea of the complexity involved is apparent in the following explanation of how thermonuclear weapons work: "Two-stage thermonuclear weapons are essentially a daisy chain of fusion-boosted fission weapons, with only two daisies, or stages, in the chain. The second stage, called the 'secondary,' is imploded by x-ray energy from the first stage, called the 'primary.' This radiation implosion is much more effective than the high-explosive implosion of the primary. As a result, the secondary can be many times more powerful than the primary, without being bigger."[2]

The secondary can be designed to maximize fusion energy release, but in most designs fusion is employed only to drive or enhance fission, as it is in the primary. More stages can be added, but the result would be a heavy multimegaton weapon with yields much higher than the United States and the Soviet Union found useful during most of the Cold War. (Yields of 500 kilotons to 5 megatons have been deployed. The United States briefly deployed 25-megaton weapons. The Soviet Union did build a 50-megaton weapon but did not deploy it.)

These considerations may seem arcane or pointless to an observer who does not have to design a functional force or ensure that a limited number of weapons can produce

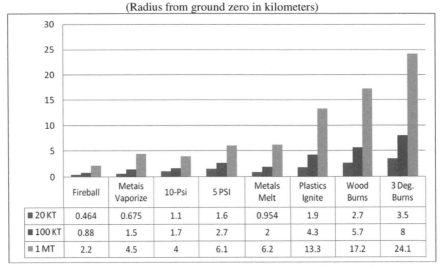

(Radius from ground zero in kilometers)

	Fireball	Metais Vaporize	10-Psi	5 PSI	Metals Melt	Plastics Ignite	Wood Burns	3 Deg. Burns
■ 20 KT	0.464	0.675	1.1	1.6	0.954	1.9	2.7	3.5
■ 100 KT	0.88	1.5	1.7	2.7	2	4.3	5.7	8
■ 1 MT	2.2	4.5	4	6.1	6.2	13.3	17.2	24.1

Source: Data compiled from multiple including; http://www.fas.org/nuke/intro/nuke/effects.htm, http://www.unitedstatesaction.com/nuclear_terrorism.htm, http://www.globalsecurity.org/wmd/intro/nuke-blast.htm, http://www.princeton.edu/~aglaser/lecture2007_weaponeffects.pdf.

Figure 8.1   The Impact of Yield on Nuclear Weapons Effects

decisive killing effects, but as Figure 8.1 shows, they have a major impact on area coverage—and this shapes their impact in terms of intimidation and deterrence as well as lethality.

- *Initial Deployment:* Like the early steps in becoming a nuclear power, deployment can take a wide range of forms. Its impact will also be shaped by the nature of the steps a country has taken previously and the credibility and nature of its weapons programs. It is easy, for example, for a nation such as Iran to go from denial to claims of possession and having nuclear armed forces, but such claims are far more credible if Iran has tested a weapon, has overtly or covertly shown it has the technology base to build functional weapons, and intelligence sources can confirm that the operators of nuclear armed forces train for nuclear warfare and have high confidence they have real weapons.

   Much then depends on the number and type of weapons Iran possesses. Iran might, for example, begin its deployments with a few fission bombs. This would eliminate many of the technical and reliability risks in arming its missiles, and creating freefall bombs is a simpler design task and would present fewer weight and reliability problems. Iran would, however, have problems with the performance of its current fighter attack aircraft that are all aging U.S. and Russian designs, and any fighter attack would be much more vulnerable to defensive operations than a ballistic missile.

   Small inventories of nuclear weapons also require trade-offs between safety (heavily guarded central facilities and devices that either require complex arming codes or assembly of the core from a separate location) and the kind of quick reaction capability that can ensure the survival of weapons and the ability to retaliate. The North Atlantic

Treaty Organization (NATO), for example, stored its weapons in dispersed secure sites and maintained an air component of quick reaction alert aircraft that could be kept armed with nuclear weapons in a crisis and that could take off for strike missions before their bases could be struck by aircraft or medium- and intermediate-range ballistic missiles. Over time, the strike aircraft went from pilot-armed weapons to requiring arming codes.

Iran would have to contend with both the potential use of U.S. stealth aircraft and extremely precise conventional weapons, as well as the risk of nuclear preemption and preventive strikes by Israel or its neighbors. This, and the problem of arming aircraft and maintaining them on nuclear-armed alert, could either require the aircraft to be put into flight with very ambiguous levels of warning or risk losing them. Reliance on a small number of weapons storage sites could lead to preventive/preemptive strikes. High levels of dispersed nuclear weapons storage sites risk unauthorized use.

Missile deployments offer a higher probability of penetrating today's defenses. They also offer the option of pretargeting key cities and high-value area targets such as key energy facilities and then authorizing or ordering a nuclear armed missile force to either launch on warning or at the first verified evidence that Iran and/or its nuclear forces are under attack. This is called launch under attack. Highly mobile missiles, or deeply sheltered missiles, can also offer the ability to ride out an attack on Iran and then decide what or if to strike, but designing a small force on the basis of guaranteed survival and riding out attacks increases the risk Iran might lose much of its capability in a preventive/preemptive strike.

Small, early deployments of nuclear weapons on missiles have other potential draw-backs. Reliability can be very hard to predict both in terms of accuracy and how well a warhead will function. Small missile forces face steadily improving Israeli and U.S. missile defenses, and the probable acquisition of such defenses by other Gulf States, Turkey, and Europe. Older liquid-fueled missiles have slow reaction times and limited time spans in which they can be kept fueled and on alert. Security and control require the use of reliable coded systems to arm the warhead—ideally in flight and outside Iranian territory but in practice probably before launch.

Small forces present another problem. Regardless of the delivery system, how release is authorized, and choices about reaction times and ride out or launch, a small force has to be used to produce decisive results rather than carefully structured levels of escalation over time. This does not rule out one or two demonstrative strikes, but it probably does mean Iran would target enemy population centers and seek to do as much damage as possible to that population and an enemy's economy. It is also important to note that once a war begins, weapons numbers are not the number in inventory, but the number Iran can count on to actually penetrate to a target. In general, this means devoting at least two weapons to any given city or area target to ensure that it is hit.

Moreover, Iran would probably want to communicate its broad targeting plans in some way to maximize deterrence and minimize the risk or preventive or preemptive attack. Any such communication of a counterpopulation targeting plan does, however, lead to countertargeting by any potential nuclear power. It also compounds the level of confusion that is almost certain as to the intentions and actions of all the sides involved. It would be hard for Iran to predict the end result of aircraft and missile launches in terms of penetration, accuracy, and damage inflicted. An enemy such as Israel or the United States—with much larger nuclear forces—might seek to use its nuclear weapons to both retaliate in kind and limit damage by striking at any suspect Iranian installation or facility. Under these conditions, "battle management" could easily become a matter of unconstrained nuclear war.

• *Large-Scale Deployment:* Iran is probably a decade or more away from deploying a force of 60 or more weapons—a force large enough to offer tactical, air, and missile options; a range of strike options that did not stress counterpopulation targets; and deploy enough delivery systems to make preventive or preemptive strikes against Iran an unacceptable risk. It is impossible, however, to determine either Iran's capabilities or the interaction among Iran and Israel, the United States, and Iran's neighbors.

Large forces offer a kind of increased safety and stability, particularly as they mature into forces with mobile or hardened basing modes, as warning and command-and-control systems become better, as weapons reliability and accuracy become more predictable, and it becomes possible to use security codes and built-in safety devices such as permissive actuation systems both to keep delivery systems armed and to prevent unauthorized use.

Every act Iran takes, however, will produce a hostile or defensive response. Israel is probably already developing sea-basing options for its nuclear forces and may be increasing the range-payload of its weapons. It must have examined options for deterring any Iranian strike on Israel, and Iran is highly vulnerable. Its economy and structure of government is highly centralized in Tehran, and it is uncertain that a Persian society could recover from strikes on even 10 of its major cities. The fact that Israel is potentially vulnerable to "existential" strikes on its population means that it virtually has to develop existential strike options to destroy Iran's ability to recover from an Israeli strike and secure basing modes to demonstrate that it can exercise such options regardless of the scale of an Iranian attack on Israel.

It is unclear whether Egypt, Turkey, or Saudi Arabia could or would seek to match Iran's evolving nuclear capability, but a regional nuclear arms race is a real possibility. The U.S. response is harder to predict, but it could consist of some form of guarantees of extended deterrence, and the United States might well conclude that the Gulf is so critical to the U.S. and global economy that it could not allow Iran to create nuclear forces without targeting Iran in return.

In short, Iran cannot act in a vacuum. The more forces it deploys, the more it will be targeted in return. The kinds of safety it will gain from larger or less vulnerable forces may create a kind of mutual assured destruction, but this may not create a stale pattern of deterrence as Iran's neighbors and the United States steadily increase their nuclear targeting of Iran. It is also important to note that it is extremely unlikely that the United States will not comprehensively target Iran with nuclear weapons if Iran deploys long-range, nuclear-armed missiles that can strike NATO and European targets, and the United States is virtually certain to do so if Iran develops any kind of nuclear strike option against it. It is equally likely that if Iran makes any overt—or serious covert—nuclear threats, it will be met with threats in kind.

The complex mix of players involved, and their very different levels of situational awareness, will also create a risk that if any one nation escalates to the use of nuclear weapons, or moves a crisis toward potential nuclear release, it will become progressively harder to control the situation and limit the ultimate pattern of escalation that results.

It is important to note in this regard that the nuclear arms race during the Cold War, and the level of deterrence created by mutual assured destruction, did not produce stability. The United States and the Union of Soviet Socialist Republics (USSR), and the NATO-Warsaw Pact, steadily increased the number of warheads and weapons on each side for several decades. They kept competing in deploying new delivery systems and creating new nuclear strike options. Their relative willingness to rely on conventional options was never clear, and they targeted both military forces and population centers—to the point where the USSR seems to have deployed biological weapons as a follow-up option to nuclear strikes on U.S. cities. Missile defenses added a further destabilizing element to this process as did arms control agreements that sometimes did as much to stimulate new forms of nuclear competition as to limit the forces on each side. If Iran moves to deployment, it will almost certainly trigger a similar kind of regional arms race; it may not end as well.

- *Proxy Nuclear Posture:* Most experts question whether any nation with only limited nuclear assets would ever transfer a nuclear weapon to a terrorist group or another state. This is not simply a matter of limited resources; it is a matter of trust. Nonstate actors presented very serious risks in terms of loyalty and restraint. Even state actors that are close allies still have different leaders and strategic priorities and may act independently —particularly in a crisis. Nevertheless, the risk exists. A nonstate actor might be a way of attacking while reducing the risk of attribution and retaliation. Arming nonstate actors is a way of dispersing weapons that makes them far harder to attack. The same is true of state actors, and Iran might find Syria or a Shi'ite-dominated Iraq to be a way of creating a nuclear bloc that reduces the risks an isolated nuclear Iran would face in the future.

- *Covert Nuclear Posture:* Iran might conclude that it could create a secure capability to deliver a nuclear weapon and create some degree of plausible deniability by smuggling a nuclear weapon into an enemy state, detonating it in a port or coastal area, or launching a short-range missile from a ship or forward-deployed covert location in a neighbor state.

    Experts differ over the extent to which an Iranian nuclear weapon would have a unique radiological and material "fingerprint," intelligence could warn or confirm that it was Iran that was responsible for a given attack, and any state could launch retaliatory strikes on Iran without 100-percent confirmation of Iranian responsibility.

    These are valid concerns, although it is one thing to debate legal, political, and moral-ethical considerations before an attack and another to assume that they will lead to restraint after the devastation caused by being the victim of a nuclear explosion. This is particularly true in the case of an existential attack on a small state such as Israel or a nuclear-armed Gulf or neighboring state. Israel, for example, might well feel it necessary to launch an all-out nuclear retaliatory strike on Iran's population unless there was decisive evidence that Iran was not responsible.

    Other scenarios have considered Iranian covert attacks on the United States using ship-based missiles in cargo ships off the U.S. coast. There are reports that Iran did test a Scud launch from a ship, and this is certainly technically feasible. Other scenarios assume Iran would use a high-altitude nuclear explosion to create an electromagnetic pulse to destroy an enemy's electronic infrastructure, satellite, and communications capabilities over a wide area. The lethality of such an explosion is sometimes exaggerated, but it offers both a way of attacking without provoking the same kind of counterstrike on Iranian cities and a potential covert means of attack that would also reduce the risk of retaliation.

These scenarios involve a wide range of risks for Iran and present the problem that they could provoke truly massive retaliation for limited damage on an enemy. They are, however, technically feasible, and it is actually dangerous to assume that there are no future conditions under which Iran might take such action.

It should be stressed that all but the first of these postures represent *possibilities and not probabilities or predictions*. Iran could stop at virtually any point in this escalation ladder of rising nuclear capabilities and could potentially roll back any production and deployment of nuclear devices and weapons. At the same time, there is a grim natural progression in the creation of nuclear forces, driven in part by the fact that proliferation never occurs on a unilateral level. One way or another, it drives other states to respond.

The end result could be a nuclear arms race, heavily oriented toward destroying the population of potential enemies. It could also be to create a nuclear Gulf or Middle East. This is not a minor consideration when the U.S. Department of Energy estimates the Gulf will produce 23.7 million barrels a day of crude oil in 2010 (27 percent of the world supply of 89.2 million barrels a day, and 31.8 million barrels a day of crude oil in 2030 (28 percent of the world supply of 112.5 million barrels a day; plus a major part of its exports is natural gas.[3]

Biological Weapons as an Alternative or Supplement

One of the problems in analyzing Iran's options and that of any other real or potential proliferators is the tendency to divide the analysis of proliferation into separate studies of chemical, radiological, biological, and nuclear activities and options. This compartmentation is made worse by dividing the analysis of weapons and delivery systems and the analysis of arms control issues from warfighting impacts. One key aspect of Iran's potential future behavior, however, is that it does not have to develop and deploy nuclear weapons to be a major proliferator.

Chapter 5 showed that Iran has considerable potential as a chemical weapons power and may have a stockpile of nerve and other chemical weapons. These weapons can be effective as deterrents in greatly complicating enemy operations because of the need for protection and decontamination, as actual killing mechanisms, and as ways of disrupting military operations and area denial. They are, however, far less lethal than nuclear weapons and biological weapons. Iran also has to know that the deterrent or shock effect of threatening to use—or actually using—chemical weapons can also be provocative and be used to justify massive conventional escalation. As a result, their value may be greatest as a defensive weapon, and they do not have the lethality to greatly intimidate or deter a potential opponent.

Radiological weapons have not been separately analyzed because most forms are essentially terror weapons that can contaminate a given building or small area, but which have more limited lethality than any similar investment of effort in conventional explosives and chemical weapons. There are designs for advanced forms of such weapons that may have wide area coverage, but their effectiveness is controversial and there are no indications that Iran is pursuing this path.[4]

Chapter 6, however, showed that biological weapons can be a very different story. They can have equal or greater lethality than nuclear weapons, programs require fewer resources and are far easier to conceal, they can be tailored to have a wide range of different effects, and they lend themselves to covert delivery as well as use in missile warheads and bombs.

The report of the Commission on the Prevention of WMD Proliferation and Terrorism has warned,

> Iran has been rapidly developing capabilities that will enable it to build nuclear weapons; Dr. A. Q. Khan, of Pakistan, led a nuclear proliferation network that was a one-stop shop for aspiring nuclear weapons countries; and nuclear arms rivalries have intensified in the Middle East and Asia. If not constrained, this proliferation could prompt nuclear crises and even nuclear use at the very time that the United States and Russia are trying to reduce their nuclear weapons deployments and stockpiles.
>
> ... Meanwhile, biotechnology has spread globally. At the same time that it has benefited humanity by enabling advances in medicine and in agriculture, it has also increased the availability of pathogens and technologies that can be used for sinister purposes. Many biological pathogens and nuclear materials around the globe are poorly secured—and thus vulnerable to theft by those who would put these materials to harmful use, or would sell them on the black market to potential terrorists.
>
> ... In addition to the current threat of bioweapons proliferation and terrorism, a set of over-the-horizon risks is emerging, associated with recent advances in the life sciences and biotechnology and the world-wide diffusion of these capabilities. Over the past few decades, scientists have gained a deep understanding of the structure of genetic material (DNA) and its role in directing the operation of living cells. This knowledge has led to remarkable gains in the treatment of disease and holds the promise of future medical breakthroughs. The industrial applications of this knowledge are also breathtaking: it is now possible to engineer microorganisms to give them new and beneficial characteristics.
>
> Activity has been particularly intense in the area of biotechnology known as synthetic genomics. Since the early 1980s, scientists have developed automated machines that can synthesize long strands of DNA coding for genes and even entire microbial genomes. By piecing together large fragments of genetic material synthesized in the laboratory, scientists have been able to assemble infectious viruses, including the polio virus and the formerly extinct 1918 strain of the influenza virus, which was responsible for the global pandemic that killed between 20 million and 40 million people. As DNA synthesis technology continues to advance at a rapid pace, it will soon become feasible to synthesize nearly any virus whose DNA sequence has been decoded—such as the smallpox virus, which was eradicated from nature in 1977—as well as artificial microbes that do not exist in nature. This growing ability to engineer life at the molecular level carries with it the risk of facilitating the development of new and more deadly biological weapons. The only way to rule out the harmful use of advances in biotechnology would be to stifle their beneficial applications as well—and that is not a realistic option. Instead, the dual-use dilemma associated with the revolution in biology must be managed on an ongoing basis. As long as rapid innovations in biological science and the malevolent intentions of

terrorists and proliferators continue on trajectories that are likely to intersect sooner or later, the risk that biological weapons pose to humanity must not be minimized or ignored.

... The Commission further believes that terrorists are more likely to be able to obtain and use a biological weapon than a nuclear weapon. The Commission believes that the U.S. government needs to move more aggressively to limit the proliferation of biological weapons and reduce the prospect of a bioterror attack.[5]

Iran could develop biological weapons as a substitute for nuclear weapons or to supplement them. It would be possible to do so under the guise of developing biological defenses, medical research, or in small, dispersed cells that would be far harder to detect than nuclear or chemical weapons facilities. The fact that there is a Biological Weapons Convention places virtually no limits on a determined proliferator. There are no enforcement or inspection provisions.

Moreover, the costs of such an effort to a country already moving toward modern biological research and production capabilities in its civil sector is likely to be no higher than a single battalion of modern main battle tanks and is virtually certain to be lower than the cost of a single squadron of fighter aircraft. It is doubtful that Iran faces a massive financial burden in producing nuclear weapons—given the investments it has already made in nuclear power, delivery systems, and dual-use technology. The financial burden of a biological weapons effort in military terms is negligible.

Some experts do argue that biological weapons have far less deterrent impact because it is impossible to show their lethality until they are used, and there is no serious precedent that has demonstrated that they can produce massive casualties. There are also questions about Iran's ability to build advanced bombs and warheads, or a survivable penetrator that could distribute such weapons as a line source delivery system.

At the same time, unknowns produce fear as well as uncertainty. It is also possible to demonstrate some of the effectiveness of such weapons by leaking data about human testing against prisoners and conducting more open tests against livestock or crops. Much would depend on whether Iran chose to use a mix of different agents to ensure the effectiveness of an attack as well as complicate detection and treatment. Iran could also effectively experiment in covert attacks to see which agents actually worked—carrying out tests on an enemy country.

Alternatively covert tests and proof of effectiveness allow the potential use of covert delivery with less risk of being identified as an attacker. Covert delivery can take advantage of attacks that mix a variety of different agents, appear to be natural outbreaks of human disease, or have an impact on agriculture similar to the constant spread of diseases and pests across national boundaries.

There also is the possibility that Iran would escalate to highly lethal infectious agents in response to any nuclear exchange or replace or supplement one. The restraints that exist before this kind of war could cease to have much practical meaning in a "broken back" conflict.

Once again, these are possibilities, not predictions. A nation committed to asymmetric warfare must, however, at least have studied all of these options and the decades of unclassified literature that describe them in far more detail. It is also a grim reality that no purely nuclear arms control regime can ever limit Iran's—or any other nation's—ability to deploy truly lethal weapons of mass destruction.

THE OPTIONS FOR DEALING WITH IRANIAN PROLIFERATION

This does not mean that other regional states and outside powers cannot contain and deter Iran, or that diplomatic and arms control options do not have value. There are a wide range of ways that outside states can react to Iran's options, many of which are already in play:

- *Diplomacy and Dialog:* Efforts to persuade Iran not to proliferate by convincing Iran that it does not face a sufficient threat to proliferate and cannot make major gains in power or security by doing so
- *Sanctions:* Controls and measures designed to put economic pressure on Iran, limit its access to technology, and/or limit its access to arms
- *Incentives:* Options that give Iran security guarantees and/or economic and trade advantages.
- *Regime Change:* Efforts to change the regime and create one that will not proliferate
- *Preventive or Preemptive Strikes before Iran Has a Significant Force:* Military options that would destroy Iran's ability to proliferate and/or deploy significant nuclear forces
- *Containment:* Creation of a mix of defensive and offensive measures that would both deny Iran the ability to exploit its WMD capabilities and show that any effort to use such weapons to intimidate or gain military advantage would be offset by the response
- *Deterrence:* Creation of military threats to Iran so great that no rational Iranian leader could see an advantage from using weapons of mass destruction.
- *Defense:* A mix of measures such as missile defense, air defense, counterterrorism, countersmuggling/covert operations capability, civil defense, and passive defense that would both deter Iran and protect against any use it made of its WMD capabilities

DIPLOMACY AND DIALOG

Diplomacy and dialog have not succeeded so far, but this does not mean they will fail in the future. They can also provide important options even if they do not prove to be able to keep Iran from moving to the breakout stage and beyond. Diplomacy and dialog may still persuade Iran to limit the threat or provocation posed by the way in which it proliferates or help create a climate where the risk of miscalculation and conflict are sharply reduced even if Iran moves ahead in developing and building nuclear weapons.

The way in which outside powers approach the diplomacy and dialog will, however, be critical. Purely negative efforts have already failed. Basing engagement and negotiation on offers that include incentives or "carrots" as well as sanctions or "sticks" is likely to be critical. The record to date shows that threatening, sanctioning, or even attacking Iran is not going to produce any of the desired changes in Iranian behavior. It is more likely to lead to broader direct or proxy conflicts, Iranian overreaction and extremism, and help hard-liners in Iran discredit more moderate elements on the ground of disloyalty.

The United States has been a key factor in pushing for sticks by trying to isolate Iran and by creating unilateral and UN sanctions. It has differed with its allies over both the need for negotiations and the way they should be approached. The United States did move away from charges that Iran was part of the "axis of evil" during the latter years of the Bush administration, however, and gave low real-world priority to efforts at regime change.

Senior U.S. officials did repeatedly make it clear that the United States would not take military options off the table. At the same time, they stressed that the United States has no immediate interest in military intervention inside Iran and is actively pursuing diplomatic options with its European allies and within the context of the UN Security Council (UNSC). The United States also showed that was willing to engage in dialogue with Iran and did so—albeit at arms length—and at least considered setting up a U.S. interests section in Iran.

In contrast, the collective actions of the Six—the United States, the United Kingdom, France, Germany, Russia, China—and the work of the UN and the IAEA—have offered at least some chance of success. Evolving a mix of diplomatic pressures, sanctions, incentives, and UN inspections and reports in a step-by-step response to Iranian nuclear noncompliance has sometimes seemed to produce a positive impact. The question is whether key members of the Security Council will have the courage to take more decisive action if Iran does not eventually respond. The previous chapters strongly indicate that the going may also get tougher for some years to come. Iran is simply too close to being able to build a nuclear device and may well conclude that Europe, Russia, China, and other key elements of the UN are now prepared to live with its possession of nuclear weapons.

Diplomacy and dialog will serve little purpose if all they do is produce more meetings, reports, and ineffective sanctions. The problem is whether it is possible to find the right international balance of pressure and incentives that could gradually change Iran's behavior. This means simultaneously offering Iran more security as an incentive not to proliferate while not offering it new "windows of opportunism." This requires all of the nations involved, not just the United States, to move toward a new degree of realism. Europe needs to understand that dialogue and negotiation are only a means to an end, not ends in themselves. All carrots and no sticks can be just as dangerous and ineffective as all sticks and no carrots.

It is also important to note that diplomacy and dialog will still have great value if they restrain Iran, rather than totally prevent it from having a nuclear and/or biological capability. Breakout capabilities, bombs in the basement, and tests that prove limited capability present serious problems, but—as the following analysis shows—they are likely to have a very different impact on any arms race from actual deployment of a nuclear or biologically armed force.

The same is true of arms control measures. No one can ignore the fact that 100-percent verification is better than 100-percent trust. In the real world, however, no agreement is perfect. There are always ways to cheat or bypass an agreement, or to use arms control as a method of "war" by other means. At the same time, an agreement that did nothing more than show Iran has not armed its aircraft and missiles with active online nuclear or biological weapons would still have some value, and there is a wide range of alternative agreements and inspection regimes in between. Dialog and diplomacy should not sell options such as the NNPT and the IAEA short simply because they cannot be perfect.

SANCTIONS AND ECONOMIC VULNERABILITY

Sanctions can have value, but there already is convincing historical evidence that they have severe limits. The United States and the UN already have tried a wide range of sanctions. The impact of international sanctions on trade financing in Iran is difficult to gauge.

Because the United States does not trade significantly with Iran now, it must depend on other countries to reduce trade with Iran in an effort to change Iran's policies. In December 2005, President George W. Bush remarked, "We are relying on others because we have sanctioned ourselves out of influence with Iran."[6]

There is considerable debate on the extent to which Iran's trading partners are susceptible to U.S. pressure to limit economic engagement with Iran. According to one Asian diplomat in Iran, "The situation over sanctions is a huge opportunity for China, former Soviet republics and regional countries."[7]

Since 2006, European Union countries, including France, Germany, and the United Kingdom, have curtailed export credits to companies doing business in Iran.[8] Germany does not actively dissuade companies from doing business in Iran, but it is conducting extra scrutiny of export authorization requests and evaluating the financial risks of doing business with Iran more closely.[9]

The problem is that it is far from clear that such sanctions can change the attitudes or actions of the Iranian government and Iranian public attitudes toward acquiring nuclear technology. The Iranian nuclear research program does not depend on the ability of the Iranian president to visit Paris, and Iran has already reached the point where it can probably sustain a nuclear weapons effort with its own capabilities and those it can smuggle in ways UN sanctions cannot prevent.

Food imports and agricultural sanctions, for example, do not seem practical. It would be difficult for the United States, its allies, and members of the UN to justify the use of sanctions or attacks against any aspect of Iran's agricultural products or imports—except possibly certain carefully selected dual-use technologies and fertilizers that can be used in the production of WMDs.

Political sanctions seem unlikely to do more than send vague signals of disapproval. The UN has already acted to restrict Iranian officials, including President

Mahmoud Ahmadinejad, as well as other top officials and clerics, from traveling outside Iran. It has also acted to target Iran's nuclear industry, in particular, components and processes. These sanctions have the advantage that they do little harm to the general population, and they send a message to the Iranian government and the world that the world does not approve of Iran's nuclear weapons. Beyond that, however, they have little impact or coercive effect.

More drastic sanctions targeting specific parts of the industrial sector might be a different story, particularly in the middle of a global financial crisis. Iran has a relatively weak and badly managed, statist economy that is vulnerable to sanctions. It has spent much of its budget on poorly run state industries and investments, and some 20 percent of Iran's total annual gross domestic product (GDP) is spent on a complex mix of subsidies. Its stock market suffered a serious crash in late 2008.[10] It admitted that it suffered from 30-percent inflation and more than 10-percent unemployment in 2008, and the real figures could be substantially higher. (The Central Intelligence Agency describes unemployment as "double digit."[11])

The Energy Information Agency (EIA) of the Department of Energy described Iran's preglobal economic crisis economy as follows:

> Despite higher oil revenues, Iranian budget deficits remain a chronic problem, in part due to large-scale state subsidies on foodstuffs and gasoline. Thus, the country's parliament (the Majlis) decided in January 2005 to freeze domestic prices for gasoline and other fuels at 2003 levels. In March 2006, parliament reduced the government's gasoline subsidy allocation for FY [fiscal year] 2006/07 to $2.5 billion, compared with a request of $4 billion and costs of over $4 billion for imports last year. As of July 2006, the Iranian government is still debating how to handle gasoline subsidies. NIOC [National Iranian Oil Company] has said it has used nearly its entire $2.5 billion budget for gasoline imports, but legislators have stated their opposition to providing the additional $3.5 billion necessary to pay for imports through the end of the fiscal year, in March 2007 . . .
>
> Another problem for Iran is the lack of job opportunities for the country's young and rapidly growing population. Unemployment in Iran is around 11 percent, but is significantly higher among young people. Iran is attempting to diversify its economy by investing some of its oil revenues in other areas, including petrochemicals production. In 2004, non-oil exports rose by a reported 9 percent. Iran also is hoping to attract billions of dollars worth of foreign investment to the country through creating a more favorable investment climate by reducing restrictions and duties on imports and creating free-trade zones. However, there has not been a great deal of progress in this area. Foreign investors appear to be cautious about Iran, due to uncertainties regarding its future direction under new leadership, as well as the ongoing international controversy over the country's nuclear program . . .
>
> During 2005, Iran produced about 4.24 million bbl/d [barrels per day] of total liquids. Of this, 3.94 million bbl/d is crude oil, roughly 5 percent of world crude production. Iran's current sustainable crude oil production capacity is estimated at 3.8 million bbl/d, which is around 310,000 bbl/d below Iran's latest (July 1, 2005) OPEC [Organization of the Petroleum Exporting Countries] production quota of 4.110 million bbl/d. . . . Through the first half of 2006, the EIA places Iran's crude oil production

at 3.75 million bbl/d. Iran's domestic oil consumption, 1.5 million bbl/d in 2005, is increasing rapidly as the economy and population grow. Iran subsidizes the price of oil products heavily, which contributes to rising domestic consumption.

Iran's existing oilfields have a natural decline rate estimated at 8 percent onshore and 10 percent per year offshore. The fields are in need of upgrading, modernization, and enhanced oil recovery (EOR) efforts such as gas reinjection. Current recovery rates are just 24–27 percent, compared to a world average of 35 percent. Iran also needs to increase its search for new oil, with only a few exploration wells being drilled in 2005.

With sufficient investment, Iran could increase its crude oil production capacity significantly. The country produced 6 million bbl/d of crude oil in 1974 but has not come close to recovering to that level since the 1978/79 Iranian revolution. Still, Iran has ambitious plans to increase oil production to more than 5 million bbl/d by 2010, and 5.8 million bbl/d by 2015. The country will require billions of dollars in foreign investment to accomplish this.[12]

The problem with several economic sanctions, however, is that many could do more to hurt Iran's people, and/or damage the global economy, than force Iran's leaders to change their behavior.

Petroleum Export Sanctions

Iran is heavily dependent on oil export revenues. Iran's oil export revenues increased from $32 billion in 2004 to $45.6 billion in 2005, to $54 billion in 2006, to $57 billion in 2007, and to $79 billion in 2008 (between January and November).[13] While the global economic crisis means these will be lower in 2008, and could be much lower in 2009, this will not reduce Iran's dependence on exports, but rather shrink a key source of national income that accounts for some 80–85 percent of government revenues. In December 2008, it was selling oil at prices below $40 a barrel when it needed $90 a barrel to avoid pushing its budget into deficit.[14] Figures 8.2 and 8.3 illustrate the trend in oil export revenues for the OPEC, more importantly Iran's oil export revenues.

Although Iran is still a major oil exporter, it badly needs outside investment and technology to modernize its petroleum sector and maintain and expand its oil and gas production. Even sanctions that slow down outside investment and technology transfer have already proven capable of putting continuous pressure on the Iranian economy and leadership, and Iran now faces a global economic crisis that makes any outside economic pressure more effective.

According to the Iran Transactions Regulations, administered by the U.S. Department of the Treasury's Office of Foreign Assets Control (OFAC), U.S. persons may not directly or indirectly trade, finance, or facilitate any goods, services, or technology going to or from Iran, including goods, services, or technology that would benefit the Iranian oil industry. U.S. persons are also prohibited from entering into or approving any contract that includes the supervision, management, or financing of the development of petroleum resources located in Iran.[15]

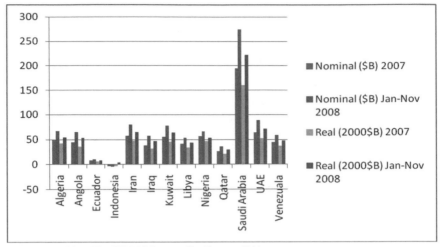

Source: Adapted from EIA OPEC Oil Revenues Fact Sheet, available at:
http://www.eia.doe.gov/cabs/OPEC_Revenues/Factsheet.html.

Figure 8.2   OPEC Net Oil Export Revenues

Iran's economy, particularly its transportation sectors and heavier industries, also relies on imports of refined products. Since 1982, Iran's dependence on imports of gasoline have surged due to the fact that its refineries were damaged by the Iran-Iraq War, the mismanagement of these refineries, and the lack of foreign investment in its refinery sector. According to the International Energy Agency, Iran's refining

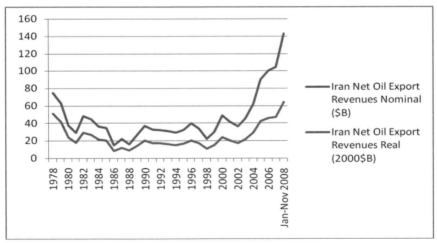

Source: Adapted from EIA OPEC Oil Revenues Fact Sheet, available at:
http://www.eia.doe.gov/cabs/OPEC_Revenues/Factsheet.html.

Figure 8.3   Iran Net Oil Export Revenues, 1978–2008

sector is inefficient. For example, only 13 percent of the refinery output is gasoline—which is estimated to be half of what European refineries produce.[16] Iran plans to ease its dependence on product imports by expanding its refinery capabilities, but this will remain an important vulnerability in the near to mid future.[17] Figure 8.4 gives a list of Iranian refinery projects and how much they are projected to produce in an effort toward easing Iran's reliance on gasoline imports.

The U.S. EIA estimates that Iran has 136 billion barrels of proven oil reserves, approximately 10 percent of the world's total known reserves. The oil is extracted from 27 onshore and 13 onshore oil fields. The majority of crude oil production is concentrated in the southwestern Khuzestan region in the proximity of the Iraqi border.[18] Iran produces approximately 4 million barrels of oil a day—5 percent of global output—and exports about 2.5 million barrels. Iran's oil export revenues represent around 80–90 percent of total export earnings and 40–50 percent of the government budget. It estimates that strong oil prices the past few years have boosted Iran's oil export revenues and helped Iran's economic situation. It estimates that Iran's real GDP increased by around 6.1 percent in 2005, but that inflation officially has reached 16 percent per year and unofficial estimates put inflation as high as 40–50 percent.

Virtually all outside sources agree that Iran's average oil output is decreasing. According to one source, the average Iranian oil production fell by 200,000 barrels

Figure 8.4   Iran Refinery Projects through 2012

Refinery	Project Type	Online	Additional Production Capability (Thousands bbl/d)	Notes
Bandar Abbas	Upgrades & Expansion	2012	300	Heavy crude processing
Bushehr	New Refinery	TBD	170	
Abadan	Upgrades	2009	140	
Abadan	New Refinery	2012	80	Gasoline production
Arak	Expansion	2009	80	
Bandar Assaluyeh	New Refinery	TBD	80	
Bandar Abbas	Expansion	2012	60	
Tehran	Expansion	2012	50	Gasoline production
Tabriz	Expansion	2012	25	Gasoline production
Total New Refinery Capacity: 985				

Note: TBD = to be determined.

Source: Adapted by Adam C. Seitz from the EIA's "Iran, Country Analysis Brief."

per day between 2002 and 2006.[19] Reportedly, Iran's oil output capacity has stagnated for the past 10 years; natural declines in oil field reserves have broadly been offset by investments of Western companies that resulted in higher productivity.[20]

Much depends on how the international economic crisis that began in late 2008 plays out over time. Iran may face far more serious economic problems, and importing countries may be less willing to invest and be less concerned with future energy supplies. In a worst case, Iran will face much more serious internal economic problems over time and have less leverage in world energy markets. These events cannot be predicted, nor can their impact on Iran's military forces, search for nuclear weapons, or actions. The most that can be said is that in the near term, Iran will be far less wealthy as it repeatedly lobbied OPEC members to decrease output dramatically, while at the same time continuing to assert that Iran could survive and would continue on a nuclear path even on oil prices that drop to $5 per barrel.[21]

At the same time, most mid- and long-term projections still indicate that growing global demand will put increasing pressure on supply, and sustained sanctions on Iranian production and exports will have a major impact on the world's importers and global economy as well as on Iran's. One analyst claimed that broad sanctions against Iran were "no longer feasible" before the international financial crisis reduced at least short-term demand because of fear that rising oil prices and supply constraints would have a negative impact on global economic growth.[22] These fears have scarcely ended. Sanctions on energy resources remain politically difficult, and key potential partners in sanctions such as the European Union (EU) still support such projects as constructing a multibillion-dollar gas pipeline partly fed by Iranian gas.[23]

Product Sanctions

Sanctions on Iran's imports of product and ability to increase its refinery capability might be a different story (as would precision attacks that temporarily halted all refinery output). Declining production and increasing demand raise growing doubts as to whether Iran can reduce its reliance on imports of refined petroleum products at anything like the schedule it desires. In 2006, Iran imported an estimated 0.192 MMBD (million barrels per day) of oil equivalent of gasoline (40 percent of its domestic consumption).

Iran's dependence on gasoline imports increased steadily in 2005 and 2006. Iran does not have sufficient refining capacity to meets its domestic gasoline and other light fuel needs. Therefore Iran imports gasoline from India, Turkmenistan, Azerbaijan, the Netherlands, France, Singapore, and the United Arab Emirates. Iran also imports from large, multinational wholesalers such as BP, Shell, Total, Vitol, LUKoil, and several Chinese companies. Iran is the second biggest gasoline importer in the world after the United States. Iran imported an estimated 0.170 MMBD of gasoline (41 percent of its domestic consumption) in 2005 and 0.192 MMBD (43 percent of its domestic consumption) in 2006.[24]

These trends are likely to continue. The Iranian parliament did vote to ration gasoline in March 2007, starting in May 2007. Iran's gasoline consumption dropped 30 percent immediately after the rationing scheme was adopted. Iranian gasoline imports for August 2007 dropped 14 percent, although an additional $1.5 billion was requested by the Iranian Oil Ministry to increase gasoline imports through March 2008.

The International Energy Agency reported that as of December 2008, Iranian domestic gasoline consumption would continue to rapidly increase over the next 20 years due to the fact that Iran allows advance purchase of gasoline at a subsidized rate.[25] The combination of rationing, price hikes, increased refining capacity, as well as compressed natural gas production will reduce Iranian gasoline import demand by an estimated 30,000 bbl/d in the next three years according to FACTS Global Energy.[26] For example, Iran paid an estimated $2.8 billion for its gas imports in 2004, about $5 billion in 2006, rising to about $8 billion in 2007.[27] Iran had to import 60 percent of the refined gasoline that it used in 2006. Iran's electricity demand is projected to grow 6 percent annually through 2015.[28]

The Iranian government set aside $2.5 billion for oil imports in its 2006–2007 budgets, but it is not clear if this sum was to cover all refined products.[29] Other experts estimate that the cost of importing refined products was as high as $6 billion or even $10 billion in 2005.[30] This total seems to have included jet fuels, diesel, residual oil, kerosene, and other products. While Iran is heavily subsidizing gasoline with funds from the reserve fund for oil revenues, it must import an increasing share of refined gasoline that it has to buy at world market prices. It is difficult to estimate foregone revenues, but guesses range from $10 billion to $50 billion per year. Further, it is believed that gasoline worth a total of $1 billion is getting smuggled out of Iran every year.[31] Indicators show that in 2006 gasoline subsidies are believed to have increased by 30 percent as compared to the year before.

Before the global financial crisis and major reduction in its export income, Iran planned to spend $16 billion between 2003 and 2030 to expand its refinery capacity from 1.5 MMBD in 2004 to 1.7 MMBD in 2010, 2.2 MMBD in 2020, and 2.6 MMBD in 2030. The director of the state-run Iranian refinery company allegedly revised these goals in early 2007, saying that refinery capacity was to increase from 1.6 to 2.6 MMBD in 2006. According to the director, this capacity expansion requires investment of $16 billion, $4 billion of which is already secured. Given that only a quarter of the necessary funds now seems to be available, and reaching the stated objective will depend on the application of modern technology, it appears doubtful that Iran can meet its goal.

Freezing of foreign investment and technology transfer for Iran's oil refineries could, therefore, be a productive target for internationally imposed sanctions.[32] Iran might get around some of the impact of such sanctions through unofficial deals and smuggling, but the price for gasoline and refined products is a sensitive issue because price hikes regularly upset the Iranian population, and, on the other hand, they are likely to lead to higher inflation rates, a long-standing and pervading problem for the Iranian economy. The Iranian parliament's decision to ration gasoline as of May 2007 is already acting to increase gas prices. Subsidized Iranian gasoline sells for 9 cents per liter at the pump, while a liter of imported gasoline costs about 40 cents a liter.[33]

Financial Sanctions

The U.S. Department of the Treasury has repeatedly employed targeted financial measures against Iran in an attempt to isolate Iran from the international financial and commercial system in an effort to promote policy change in Iran regarding its nuclear program and purported terror. The United States also hopes that financial isolation will limit Iran's resources for its nuclear program and its alleged support for terrorist organizations.

In his April 17, 2008, congressional testimony, the Deputy Assistant Secretary for Terrorist Financing and Financial Crimes, Daniel Glaser, stated, "Iran utilizes the international financial system as a vehicle to fund these terrorist organizations . . . the Iranian regime operates as the central banker of terrorism, spending hundreds of millions of dollars each year to fund terrorism."[34]

Several major Iranian banks are under U.S. and UN sanctions. A few examples of recent sanctions against Iranian banks follow:[35]

- Under E.O.13224, the Treasury has designated several Iranian entities for supporting terrorism. On October 25, 2007, the Treasury designated Bank Saderat, a major Iranian state-owned financial institution, for terrorism support.[36]
- On January 9, 2007, the Treasury sanctioned Bank Sepah, another major Iranian financial enterprise, under E.O. 13382 for assisting with Iran's missile program.[37]
- U.N. Security Council Resolution 1747 named Bank Sepah and Bank Sepah International as financial institutions involved in financing nuclear or ballistic missile activities.[38]
- On October 25, 2007, under E.O. 13382, the Department of the Treasury sanctioned Bank Melli and Bank Mellat, other major Iranian financial institutes, as WMD proliferators or supporters. In June 2008, the European Union also decided to sanction Bank Melli.[39]
- In a signal to Arab countries, the United States sanctioned the Bahraini Future Bank B.S.C. in March 2008 under E.O. 13382 for reportedly assisting in Iran's nuclear and missile programs, contending that Future Bank B.S.C. is controlled by the embargoed Bank Melli.[40]

The United States and some European countries also continue to assert that certain Iranian banks and their branches continue in their attempts to circumvent international financial sanctions in order to engage in proliferation-related activity and terrorist financing. Iranian government officials have denied these claims.[41]

Most of the financial assets Iran has in the West belong to the government or the ruling elite of Iran. The combination of freezing assets held in Western banks and travel restrictions might have a limited impact on the general population but a serious impact on Iran's ruling elites.

While U.S. capital markets have been closed to the Iranian government since the Revolution, Iran has maintained alternative sources. Some large European banks have reduced business with sanctioned Iranian bodies, and many European banks that have curtailed business with Iran are leaving offices open on a minimal basis in case there is a change in the international climate toward Iran.[42]

Iran relies on loans particularly from European and Asian banks to finance domestic projects in its energy sector.[43] For example, Iran's shipbuilding and car-making sectors are growing faster than Iranian domestic financial institutions.

These industries have relied on European banks for investment loans. Some European banks stopped doing business with Tehran, but many other banks continue to finance projects in Iran including major European banks such as HSBC, BNP Paribas, Deutsche Bank, Commerzbank, Standard Chartered, and Royal Bank of Scotland. Observers have argued that targeting loans from European banks could have a major impact on the Iranian economy, particularly since the Iranian capital market is still small and key industries in Iran cannot survive without investment loans from the outside.[44]

As Iranian businesses experience setbacks in obtaining trade financing from international banking partners, they may turn to lesser known banks or to other banking partners not susceptible to international pressure, but potentially raising the cost of business. In particular, the Islamic Republic has turned toward banks in Gulf Cooperation Council countries. Bahrain, Qatar, and Dubai in the United Arab Emirates are viewed as especially critical in propping up Iran's economy.[45]

Another option would be to freeze Iranian assets in European and Asian banks. There are no reliable estimates of how much Iran's hard currency deposits are. It is, however, safe to assume that it is a large amount given the surge in oil prices during the mid-2000s. Some estimates put it at $36 billion in 2005, $60 billion in 2006, and $64.46 billion in foreign exchange reserves in 2007.[46]

The Iranian government also began to react following the IAEA referral of Iran's case to the UNSC. In January 2006, the governor of Iran's Central Bank announced that Iran had started transferring its assets out of European banks. It is unclear where the funds have been moved, but there are indications and an initial admission that they may have been transferred to Southeast Asia.[47] Other reports indicate that Iranian government figures moved money from European financial institutions to Dubai, Hong Kong, Malaysia, Beirut, and Singapore. Iranian officials were quoted as saying that an amount as high as $8 billion was moved out of Europe.[48]

A still further option would be to restrict Western investment in Iran. It already is comparatively low, but it provides some key technology transfers to Iran. According to one source, the Management and Planning Organization of Iran permitted foreign investments worth $27.4 billion between 2000 and 2005, or $4.6 billion on average per year, but only $8.2 billion were carried out.[49] Given that several international organizations estimate the actual amount of foreign investments as between $300 million to $700 million, this would equal a $50 million to $117 million average inflow of foreign investment per year.

Sanctions can reach beyond European financial institutions to include Asian banks and international nongovernmental organizations such as the World Bank and the International Monetary Fund. This would drain another key source of financial support to the Iranian government. For example, in May 2005, the World Bank approved a $344-million loan to Iran to support the Caspian provinces in managing scarce water resources, $200 million for rebuilding following the Bam earthquake in October 2004, and $359 million in loans to the Government of Iran in order to improve housing, sanitation, and access to clean water in Ahwaz and Shiraz.[50] These loans, however, are focused toward humanitarian projects, but that does not mean that they could not be delayed to force Iran back to the bargaining table.

As sanctions take their toll on many Iranian businesses and individuals, they have also come to rely more on *hawala* money transfers. These use an informal trust-based money transfer system that exists in the Middle East and other Muslim countries. *Hawala* transactions are based on an honor system, with no promissory instruments exchanged between the parties and no records of the transactions. Some analysts consider the *hawala* system as particularly susceptible to terrorist financial transactions.

The use of *hawala* transfers by Iranians has reportedly increased since the imposition of U.S. and UN financial sanctions on Iran. It is considered by many Iranians as a more cost-effective way to transfer money in light of the added expenses incurred through working through the formal financial system in light of the sanctions. According to an Iranian merchant, "If we wanted to send money through the banking system it would cost a small fortune, so we move money to dealers and they send the money through Dubai to China." While some assert that the use of *hawala* shows that Iran is able to successfully circumvent international sanctions, others suggest that the increased use of *hawala* is a sign of the sanctions' effectiveness in making it more difficult for Iran to finance transactions.[51]

The United States and some European nations continue to place a variety of the sanction packages targeted at the areas listed above and continue to freeze assets of suspect entities that are reported to have connections to some aspect of Iran's nuclear and missile development programs. Amid the pressure posed by these sanctions, Iran's nuclear and missile programs continue to progress. This is in part due to the fact that many Iranian entities involved in these programs have been able to go around these barriers and thus continue to receive considerable outside aid.[52]

INCENTIVES

The P5+1 (the permanent five members of the UNSC plus one—China, France, Russian Federation, the United Kingdom, and the United States plus Germany) have provided incentives as well as sanctions. On May 31, 2006, the administration offered a multilateral incentive package through the UN to join the nuclear talks with Iran if Iran first suspended its uranium enrichment. Such talks would center on a package of incentives and possible sanctions—formally agreed to on June 1, 2006—by a newly formed group of negotiating nations, the so-called "Permanent

Five Plus 1." EU representative Javier Solana formally presented the P5+1 offer to Iran on June 6, 2006.[53]

The incentives in the package included the following:[54]

- Negotiations on an EU-Iran trade agreement and acceptance of Iran into the World Trade Organization

- Easing of U.S. sanctions to permit sales to Iran of commercial aircraft or aircraft parts

- Sale to Iran of a light-water nuclear reactor and guarantees of nuclear fuel (including a five-year buffer stock of fuel), and possible sales of light-water research reactors for medicine and agriculture applications

- An "energy partnership" between Iran and the EU, including help for Iran to modernize its oil and gas sector and to build export pipelines

- Support for a regional security forum for the Persian Gulf, and support for the objective of a WMD-free zone for the Middle East

- The possibility of eventually allowing Iran to resume uranium enrichment if it complies with all outstanding IAEA requirements and can prove that its nuclear program is purely peaceful

The practical question is whether incentives will work any better than sanctions. The answer may well be no—at least in persuading Iran not to move to the bomb in the basement or breakout stage. There may have been a time window following the U.S.-led invasion of Iraq, and the fall of Saddam Hussein, where Iran felt weak enough to respond to a mix of sanctions and incentives. The course of the fighting in Afghanistan and Iraq, however, has empowered Iran and made the United States seem weaker.

As was illustrated by statements made by ranking Iranian decision makers in Chapters 2 and 7, it simply is not clear whether Iran will feel it faces enough risks to accept any feasible incentives, and some Iranian leaders may feel that their bargaining position will actually improve over time if Iran does proliferate.

REGIME CHANGE

The Bush administration made a largely cosmetic effort to encourage regime change in Iran as a result of pressure from the U.S. Congress. The administration's focus on this option became apparent after the September 11, 2001, attacks, when President George W. Bush described Iran as part of an axis of evil in his January 2002 State of the Union message. President Bush's second inaugural address on January 20, 2005, and his State of the Union messages of February 2, 2005, and January 31, 2006, suggested a clear preference for a change of regime by stating, in the latter speech, that "our nation hopes one day to be the closest of friends with a free and democratic Iran." Indications of affinity for this option include increased public criticism of the regime's human rights record as well as the funding of Iranian prodemocracy activists.[55]

However, the administration never put serious resources into this effort and publicly shifted away from the option in 2006, as a strategy employing multilateral sanctions and diplomacy took priority, in part because European countries and other partners in the effort to pursue diplomatic options believed that efforts at regime change harmed diplomacy without offering any significant hope of success.[56]

Legislation in the 109th Congress did reflect the continuing support of some members for regime change in Iran. The Congress authorized funding for democracy promotion, among other provisions. In the 109th Congress, H.R. 282 passed the House on April 26, 2006, by a vote of 397–21. A companion, S. 333, was introduced in the Senate.[57] The Bush administration supported the democracy-promotion sections of these bills. Major provisions were included in H.R. 6198, which was introduced on September 27, 2006, passed by both chambers, and signed September 30, 2006 (P.L. 109-293). Entitled the Iran Freedom Support Act, it authorizes funds (no specific dollar amount) for Iran democracy promotion and modifies the Iran Sanctions Act.[58]

Many experts feel, however, that Iranian opposition groups are so weak, and U.S. efforts have such a limited impact, that U.S.-led efforts at regime change through democracy promotion and other means will never succeed without some form of U.S. military action. Providing overt or covert support to antiregime organizations, in the view of such experts, would not make them more viable or attractive to Iranians. The regime purportedly also conducts extensive regime surveillance of democracy activists or other internal dissidents.[59]

It is unclear whether any Gulf power, any European state, Russia, or China feels direct outside efforts at regime change will succeed or is willing to support such efforts. The outside movements that do exist are also weak and sometimes are as much of a problem as the current Iranian regime. While there is a long list of such groups outside Iran, most are largely ineffective political and propaganda voices with little impact inside Iran.[60] The remnants of the movement led by the son of the Shah of Iran, for example, seem totally ineffective.

The one possible exception is a terrorist group—the Mujahadin-e Khalq (MEK), aka People's Mujahedin of Iran—which has been discussed in previous chapters.[61] Many of its claims regarding action in Iran, however, either exaggerate its actions or cannot be verified. The MEK forces that Saddam Hussein set up have been disarmed and have been under guard by U.S. forces since 2003, and Iraq has made it clear that it will not tolerate the continued existence of these forces once it takes over from U.S. forces in 2009.[62]

Iran is deeply divided, but that does not mean the United States or any other outside power will be any more successful in exploiting Iran's fracture lines by encouraging regime change from the outside than it was in Iraq. What the outside states can do is find subtler ways to encourage Iran's moderates and reformers.

Only Iranians in Iran can accomplish real regime change, but outside powers can do far more with positive rather than negative influence. Exchanges, second track meetings and dialog, visits and scholarships, and all of the other ways of improving contacts that can show Iranians that other nations want Iran to succeed in its political and economic development and will deal with it on peaceful terms are key steps. Backing human rights movements, providing transparency to Iranians to the nature of the Iranian regime's actions, and repeatedly and constantly making it clear that other states want good relations are additional steps.

PREVENTIVE AND PREEMPTIVE STRIKES, AND STRIKES BEFORE IRAN HAS A SIGNIFICANT FORCE

It is clear that the United States and Israel have examined preventive and/or preventive attack options. Israel and the United States do differ over the timing and level of risk posed by Iran's nuclear efforts. The United States sees a mature or serious Iranian nuclear threat as coming well after 2010. Israel claims to see it as coming as early as 2009—although much of this may be Israeli hype designed to push the United States into diplomatic action, and military action if that fails.

Reports began to surface in late 2008 and early 2009 that in the summer of 2008 Israeli officials had approached President Bush for support for operations against Iran's nuclear facilities, including specialized bunker busters for an attack on Iran's main nuclear complex and covert actions intended to sabotage other suspected facilities. A report by the *New York Times* suggests that President Bush was convinced by top administration officials—led by Secretary of Defense Robert M. Gates—that any overt attack on Iran would probably prove to be ineffective, lead to the expulsion of international inspectors, and drive Iran's nuclear effort further out of view. Mr. Bush and his aides also discussed the possibility that an air strike could ignite a broad Middle East war in which America's 140,000 troops in Iraq would inevitably become involved.[63]

Official U.S. policy is to leave all options on the table and to emphasize diplomatic activity through the EU3 (France, Germany, and Great Britain) and the UN. The U.S. estimates of timelines for Iran's nuclear and missile efforts also leave at least several years in which to build an international consensus behind sanctions and diplomatic pressure, and a consensus behind military options if diplomacy fails. The United States would also have the potential advantage of finding any Iranian "smoking gun," improving its targeting and strike options, and being able to strike targets in which Iran had invested much larger assets. The fact that Iran can exploit time as a weapon in which to proliferate does not mean that the United States cannot exploit time as a weapon with which to strike Iran.

Israel, on the other hand, sees Iran as an existential threat. A single strike on Tel Aviv and/or Haifa would raise major questions about Israel's future existence.

The Problem of Targeting

There are no risk-free military options for Israel, the United States, or neighboring states. Tehran's known nuclear research facilities are dispersed around the country, generally large, and have constant new construction. There are at least six major complexes in Iran's public program, at least 18 major suspect facilities, and more facilities are under construction.

As discussed in Chapter 7, Iran has numerous facilities associated with its various nuclear programs and activities. Some of these sites are still suspected sites, and the details of the true activities taking place at these sites are still speculative and cannot be confirmed due to Iran's lack of transparency and full cooperation with IAEA inspectors.

The lack of knowledge about site locations is further exacerbated by the lack of knowledge about the types of activities that take place at known facilities. In creating target decks, it is important to know how destruction of a particular target would affect or cripple Tehran's nuclear programs and future efforts. Without this information the overall effectiveness of targeting Iran's known and suspect facilities is largely unknown.

Unclassified satellite photos show over 100 buildings in the major complexes, and many more in lesser areas.[64] Key facilities, including facilities for centrifuge manufacture, are at relatively distant points from the Gulf and particularly from Israel in locations such as Mashad. There is no way to know the level of knowledge the Israeli or U.S. intelligence community has, or the quality of their targeting data. Work by Frank Barnaby, reporting by the IAEA, ISIS, FAS, GlobalSecurity.org, NTI, the University of Wisconsin's Iran Watch program, and multiple media outlets have identified the following declared, confirmed, suspected, and potential nuclear centers, many of which are also potential major target complexes:[65]

- Jabr Ibn Hayan Multipurpose Laboratory (JHL)
- Suspected Rudan Conversion Facility at Fasa
- Isfahan (Esfahan) Nuclear Technology Center (INTC); Isfahan Uranium Conversion Facility (UCF); Isfahan Fuel Manufacturing Plant (FMP); Isfahan Fuel Element Cladding Plant; Isfahan Nuclear Fuel Research and Production Center (NFRPC); Isfahan Nuclear Waste Storage Facility
- Natanz Enrichment Facility (FEP and PFEP)
- Suspected Additional Enrichment Sites at Lashkar-Abad and Ramandeh
- Khondab Water Production Plant; Arak Heavy-Water Reactor (IR-40)
- Bushehr Nuclear Power Generators
- Tehran Nuclear Research Center (TNRC); TRR (IR-0001); Laboratory Scale Milling Facility; Kalaye Electric, Sharif University of Technology (SUT); Atomic Energy of Iran; Molybdenum, Iodine, and Xenon Radioisotope Production Facility (MIX Facility)
- Gorgan al-Kabir Center
- Weapons Development Facility at Chalus
- Moallem Kaleyah
- Saghand Uranium Mine
- Talmesi and Meskani Uranium Mines

- **Bonab Atomic Research Center**
- **Ardakan Pilot Yellowcake Production Facility and Uranium Ore Processing Plant**
- **Yazd Radiation Processing Center (YRPC); Beneficiation and Hydrometallurgical Center (BHRC)**
- **Karaj Agricultural and Medical Research Center (30-MeV Cyclotron) (1-Millamp Calutron)**
- **Azad University Plasma Physics Research Center at Damarand**
- **Engineering Research Center for the Constructions Crusade (Jihad-e Sazandegi) at Tabriz**
- **Gchine**
- **Karazj**
- **Koloduz**
- **Darkhovin, also variously referred to as Ahvaz, Darkhouin, Esteghlal, and Karun**
- **Tabas**
- **Anarak**

As was discussed in Chapter 7, this list is partial and uncertain. There are no reliable unclassified data on the number and function of sites related to Iran's nuclear program, and estimates vary from organization to organization in their assessments. Some key sites are underground or spread out in complexes with many buildings and in areas with peaceful or non-nuclear functions. Others are unknown or cannot be characterized reliably and in detail. IAEA inspections have identified at least 18 sites, but others argue that there might be more than 70. A great deal of the equipment other than major centrifuge facilities is also easy to move or relocate. Iran may already be playing a shell game with key research facilities and equipment, constantly changing the targeting pattern.

Tehran has had a quarter of a century to learn from the experience of Israel's attack on Iraq in 1981. Iran may have built redundant sites, underground facilities, and constructed a high level of protection around its known nuclear research centers. Others have argued that Iranian nuclear sites may have been deliberately built near populated areas or in facilities with many other "legitimate" purposes so Israel and the United States would be confronted with the problem of collateral damage or being charged with having hit an "innocent target." The previous chapters have also strongly suggested that many of Iran's research, development, and production activities are almost certainly modular and can be rapidly moved to new sites, including tunnels, caves, and other hardened facilities.

U.S. and Israeli officials have publicly identified key nuclear research sites that may have been placed underground to shield them against airborne assaults. For example, the United States identified the Parchin military complex, located south of Tehran, as a "probable" location for nuclear weaponization research. This site alone has many sections, hundreds of bunkers, and several tunnels. It is also a site that is being used to manufacture conventional armaments and Iranian missiles. This is one possible site that could be attacked, but even the evidence linking this to military nuclear weapons manufacturing was ambiguous. The site has civilian and conventional military use. The IAEA's initial assessment was that the site was not linked to nuclear weapons manufacturing, but most agree that there was not definitive proof.

Figures 8.5–8.8 illustrate the geographic complexities of targeting facilities suspected of being associated with various aspects of Iran's nuclear and missile programs.[66]

It is equally important to note that Iran has increased its protection of sites against possible U.S. or Israel air strikes. It has been reported that the IRGC launched a program to protect major nuclear facilities. The program was recommended by the Nuclear Control Center of Iran and endorsed by Iran's Supreme Leader, Ali

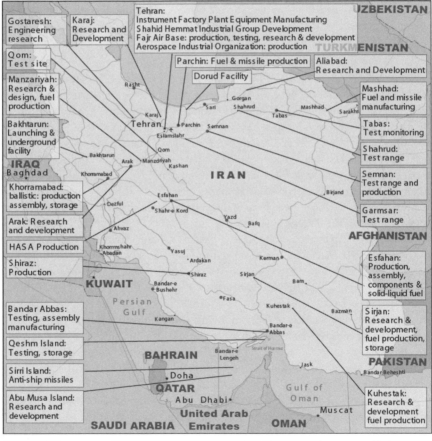

Iran Missile Sites   Copyright 2006 Nuclear Threat Initiative (NTI). All rights reserved.   http://www.nti.org

Made available for this publication Courtesy of the Nuclear Threat Initiative

Figure 8.5   Iran's Missile Facilities

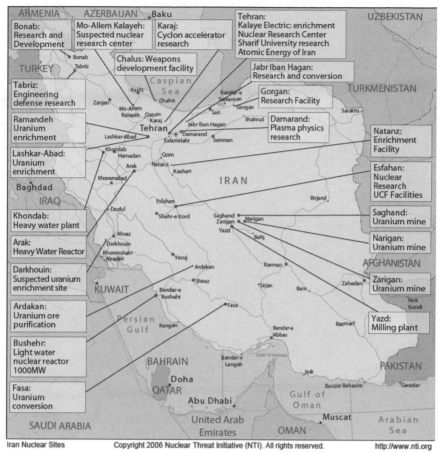

Iran Nuclear Sites   Copyright 2006 Nuclear Threat Initiative (NTI). All rights reserved.   http://www.nti.org

Made available for this publication Courtesy of the Nuclear Threat Initiative

Figure 8.6   Iran's Nuclear Sites

Khamenei. The program's mission was to build a defense infrastructure for Iran's nuclear research facilities.

This program, which some sources indicate has been coordinated with North Korea, is to build underground halls and tunnels at the cost of "hundreds of millions of dollars."[67] Some key sites such as Isfahan and Natanz are high on the list of the program to protect. The Isfahan facility, which reached fully operational status in February 2006, is most likely the primary source for converting yellowcake into UF_6. The logistic defense infrastructure would include natural barriers (tunnels into mountains and cliffs), manufactured barricades (concrete ceilings and multiple floors), and camouflage activities around key sites. The construction, a joint venture between Iranian and North Korean companies, was estimated to finish by June 1, 2006.

Made available for this publication Courtesy of the Nuclear Threat Initiative

Figure 8.7   Iran's Nuclear Enrichment Sites

In January 2006 *Jane's Defence Weekly* reported,

[T]he "Shahid Rajaei" company, which belongs to the IRGC, is involved in the project. It specialises in the excavation of underground tunnels and ducts and has accumulated extensive experience in such construction work, for instance at the underground nuclear site at Natanz. Company experts have divided the shielding project into two major stages, relating to topographic conditions in the area of the nuclear facility and branching tunnels.[68]

The report went on to say, "JDW has learned that the Islamic Revolutionary Guards Corps (IRGC) is accelerating a programme to protect Iran's major nuclear facilities," and added that "the office of Iran's Supreme Leader Ayatollah Ali Khomeini endorsed a decision by the Nuclear Control Centre to complete construction

Figure 8.8   Iran's Nuclear Reactors

of a logistic defence infrastructure for the Iranian military nuclear programme by no later than 1 July."[69]

The lack of reporting following this Jane's article, along with the information provided in the January 2006 JDW, suggests that phases of the initial contract with North Korea have been completed, but the overall status of the program is largely unknown, and shrouded in secrecy, much like the rest of Iran's nuclear program.

Israeli Options

A number of Israeli officers, officials, and experts have said that Israel must not permit the Iranians to acquire nuclear capabilities, regardless of Tehran's motivations. Some have called for preemptive strikes by Israel. Ephraim Inbar, President of the

Jaffee Center for Strategic Studies, said, "For self-defense, we must act in a pre-emptive mode."[70]

Senior U.S. officials have warned about this capability. Then Vice President Dick Cheney suggested on January 20, 2005, "Given the fact that Iran has a stated policy that their objective is the destruction of Israel, the Israelis might well decide to act first, and let the rest of the world worry about cleaning up the diplomatic mess afterwards."[71]

General Moshe Ya'alon, the Israeli Chief of Staff, was quoted as saying in August 2004 that Iran must not be permitted to acquire nuclear weapons. He added that Israel must not rely on the rest of the world to stop Iran from going nuclear because he said a nuclear Iran would change the Middle East where "Moderate States would become more extreme."[72]

Israeli military officials were quoted in press reports in January 2006 as saying that the Israel Defense Forces (IDF) received the order to get ready for a military strike against Iranian nuclear sites by March 2006.[73] Reports also surfaced in late 2008 stating that the IDF was readying to carry out unilateral strikes against Iranian nuclear facilities.[74]

Israeli officials reportedly asked U.S. President George W. Bush about support in acquiring bunker busters for use against Iran's main facility, as well as support for covert operations against Iran's other suspect facilities in the summer of 2008.[75]

In February 2009, following the elections to the 18th Knesset, Benjamin Netanyahu was charged with forming the next government and was sworn in as prime minister on March 31, 2009. Throughout his political career, Netanyahu has been very hawkish in his statements about Iran's WMD program and Iranian intentions for a global conflict. Since his appointment to prime minister, not much has changed. Netanyahu continues to make it clear that he is strongly against Iran's pursuit of unranium enrichment and other potention WMD progrms. On numerous occasions, Netanyahu has publicly stated that Israel will not stand by while Iran continues to progress its nuclear and missile programs.

Prime Minister Netanyahu has made numerous threats of military strikes against Iran if it does not halt its uranium enrichment, among other activities that Netanyahu perceives as threats to Israeli security. Since his appointment, the talk of unilateral strikes by Israel against Iran's suspected WMDs, and other military facilities, has been more prominent in official Israeli statements.

It is unclear what type of military strikes Israel may choose, if it decides to respond preemptively. Some have argued that Israel may declare its nuclear weapons and establish deterrence through "mutually assured destruction." While the impact of an Israeli declaration remains uncertain, it might have limited impact on Israel's strategic posture in the region, since most states factor Israel's nuclear weapons into their strategic thinking.

Possible Methods of Israeli Attack

Some experts argue that Israel does not have viable military options to deal with Iran's capabilities to make nuclear weapons, much less deal with a deployed force once Iran is able to disperse its warheads and missiles. They argue it does not have U.S. targeting capability and simply cannot generate and sustain the necessary number of attack sorties. Some argue that Israel might do little more than drive Iranian activity further underground, provoke even more Iranian activity, make it impossible for diplomatic and UN pressure to work, and make Israel into a real, rather than a proxy or secondary, target.

In April 2005, it was reported that a senior Israeli Air Force (IAF) officer dismissed plans to strike Iran's nuclear facilities because it was too risky and too complex both in terms of executing the mission as well as in long-term consequences, although he did not rule out the feasibility of military action against Iran. The officer further said that the most critical targets were concentrated near Tehran and 150 kilometers to the south of the city. He also noted that Iran possesses only 20 ballistic missile launchers, which should not present insurmountable difficulties when planning attacks.[76]

There is no doubt that such a strike would face problems. Israel does not have conventional ballistic missiles or land-/sea-based cruise missiles suited for such a mission. The shortest flight routes would be around 1,500–1,700 kilometers through Jordan and Iraq, 1,900–2,100 kilometers through Saudi Arabia, and 2,600–2,800 kilometers in a loop through Turkey.

There have been reports that Israel approached the United States in order to obtain permission for overflying Iraq in case of a contingency.[77] Another report has stated that Israeli forces have obtained U.S. permission to establish a military base in Iraq near the Iranian border. None of these reports seem accurate or founded on more than speculation.

There are many other problems in launching such a strike. Even if Israel had the attack capabilities needed for the destruction of the all elements of the Iranian nuclear program, it is uncertain whether Israel has the kind of intelligence needed to be certain that all the necessary elements of the program were traced and destroyed fully. Israel has good photographic coverage of Iran with the Ofeq series of reconnaissance satellites, but being so distant from Iran, one can assume that other kinds of intelligence coverage are rather partial and weak.

Retired Brigadier General Shlomo Brom has argued that Israel's capabilities may not be enough to inflict enough damage on Iran's nuclear program:

> [A]ny Israeli attack on an Iranian nuclear target would be a very complex operation in which a relatively large number of attack aircraft and support aircraft (interceptors, ECM [electronic countermeasure] aircraft, refuelers, and rescue aircraft) would participate. The conclusion is that Israel could attack only a few Iranian targets and not as part of a sustainable operation over time, but as a onetime surprise operation.[78]

All that said, this does not mean that Israel and the United States cannot target and strike much or most of Iran's capabilities. One great danger in open-sourced analysis is that it is not targeting intelligence and cannot provide a meaningful picture of what the United States or other potential attackers know at the classified level.

It is also dangerous, if not irresponsible, for analysts with no empirical training and experience in targeting and modern weapons effects to make sweeping judgments about strike options. They simply lack basic professional competence and even minimal credibility.

Israel could launch and refuel two to three full squadrons of 36–54 combat aircraft for a single set of strikes with refueling. It could use either its best F-15s (28 F-15C/Ds and 25 F-15I Ra'ams) or part of its 126 F-16CDs and 23 F-16I Sufas. It has at least three specially configured squadrons with conformal fuel tanks specially designed for extended-range use. It could add fighter escorts, but refueling and increased warning and detection would be major problems.

For the purposes of guessing how Israel might attack, its primary aircraft would probably be the F-15I, although again this is guesswork. GlobalSecurity.org has excellent reporting on the F-15I:

> The key aspects are that Boeing's (formerly McDonnell Douglas) F-15E Strike Eagle entered service with the IDF/Heyl Ha'Avir (Israeli Air Force) in January of 1998 and was designated the F-15I Ra'am (Thunder). The F-15E Strike Eagle is the ground attack variant of the F-15 air superiority fighter, capable of attacking targets day or night, and in all weather conditions.
>
> The two seat F-15I, known as the Thunder in Israel, incorporates new and unique weapons, avionics, electronic warfare, and communications capabilities that make it one of the most advanced F-15s. Israel finalized its decision to purchase 25 F-15Is in November 1995. The F-15I, like the U.S. Air Force's F-15E Strike Eagle, is a dual-role fighter that combines long-range interdiction with the Eagle's air superiority capabilities. All aircraft are to be configured with either the F100-PW-229 or F110-GE-129 engines by direct commercial sale; Night Vision Goggle compatible cockpits; an Elbit display and sight helmet (DASH) system; conformal fuel tanks; and the capability to employ the AIM-120, AIM-7, AIM-9, and a wide variety of air-to-surface munitions.
>
> Though externally the Ra'am looks similar to its USAF [United States Air Force] counterpart, there are some differences, mainly in the electronic countermeasures gear and the exhaust nozzles. The Ra'am has a counterbalance on the port vertical stabilizer instead of the AN/ALQ-128 EWWS (Electronic Warfare Warning System) antenna found on USAF Strike Eagles. The Ra'am uses two AN/ALQ-135B band 3 antennas, one mounted vertically (starboard side) and one horizontally (port side). These are located on the end of the tail booms. They are distinguished by their chiseled ends, unlike the original AN/ALQ-135 antenna, which is round and located on the port tail boom of USAF Eagles.
>
> The Ra'am utilizes extra chaff/flare dispensers mounted in the bottom side of the tail booms. Unlike USAF Eagles, the Ra'am still use engine actuator covers (turkey feathers) on their afterburner cans. The U.S. Air Force removed them because of cost and nozzle maintenance, though curiously, USAF F-16s still have their actuator covers installed. Israeli Strike Eagles and some USAF Eagles based in Europe use CFT air scoops. These scoops provide extra cooling to the engines.
>
> The 25 F-15Is operational since 1999 [and the 100 F-16Is] were procured first and foremost to deal with the Iranian threat. In August 2003 the Israeli Air Force demonstrated the strategic capability to strike far-off targets such as Iran [which is 1,300

kilometers away], by flying three F-15 jets to Poland 1,600 nautical miles away. After they celebrated that country's air force's 85th birthday, on their return trip, the IAF warplanes staged a fly-past over the Auschwitz death camp.[79]

Israeli aircraft would probably need to carry close to their maximum payloads to achieve the necessary level of damage against most targets suspected of WMD activity, although any given structure could be destroyed with one to three weapons. (This would include the main Bushehr reactor enclosure, but its real-world potential value to an Iranian nuclear program is limited compared to more dispersed and/or hardened targets.) At least limited refueling would be required, and backup refueling and recovery would be an issue.

They key weapon to be used against hard targets and underground sites such as Natanz might be the GBU-28, although the United States may have quietly given Israel much more sophisticated systems or Israel may have developed its own, including a nuclear armed variant.

The GBU-28 is carried by the F-15I. It is a "5,000-pound" laser-guided bomb with a 4,400-pound (lb) earth-penetrating warhead that can be upgraded by the IAF to use electro-optical or global positioning system (GPS) targeting. It is a vintage weapon dating back to the early 1990s, and the IAF is reported to have bought at least 100. It has been steadily upgraded since 1991, and the USAF ordered an improved version in 1996. It looks like a long steel tube with rear fins and a forward guidance module. It can glide some three to seven miles depending on the height of delivery. It is 153 inches long × 14.5 inches in diameter.[80]

Multiple strikes on the dispersed buildings and entries in a number of facilities would be necessary to ensure adequate damage without restrikes—which may not be feasible for Israel given the limits to its sortie generation capability over even Iranian soft targets. As for hardened and underground targets, the IAF's mix of standoff precision-guided missiles—such as Harpoon or Popeye—would not have the required lethality with conventional warheads, and Israel's use of even small nuclear warheads would cause obvious problems.

Israel may have specially designed or adapted weapons for such strikes. Some reports state that it bought 500 GBU-28, 5,000-lb laser-guided bombs from the United States in February 2005. These weapons are armed with BLU-113 penetrators and are sometimes called "bunker busters." They were first rushed into service during the Gulf War in 1991 and use a penetrating warhead. The bombs are modified U.S. Army artillery tubes, weigh 4,637 pounds, and contain 630 pounds of high explosives. The Federation of American Scientists reports that they are fitted with GBU-27 laser-guided bomb guidance kits, are 14.5 inches in diameter, and are almost 19 feet long. The operator illuminates a target with a laser designator and then the munitions are guided to a spot of laser energy reflected from the target.[81]

Experts speculated whether the purchase was a power projection move or whether Israel was, in fact, planning to use these conventional bombs against Iranian nuclear sites. These speculations were further exacerbated when Israeli Chief of Staff Lieutenant General Dan Halutz was asked how far Israel would go to stop Iran's nuclear program; he said, "2,000 kilometers."[82] According to some reports, The IAF took early delivery on some of these weapons during its war with the Hezbollah in 2006.[83]

The hard-target bombs it has acquired from the United States are, however, not systems designed to kill underground facilities. They could damage entrances, but not the facilities. What is not known is whether Israel has its own ordnance or has secretly acquired the more sophisticated systems described later.

Israel also has considerable precision-strike capability and is reported to have bought 1,000 GBU-39 small diameter, precision-guided bombs from the United States in September 2008.[84] These weapons have pop-out wings and a maximum range of up to 110 kilometers from very high altitudes and an accuracy of less than two meters. They can be launched from outside the range of most Iranian surface-to-air missiles, have considerable hard-target kill capability, can be used against surface targets in densely populated areas with minimal risk of collateral damage, and can be used to extend range by reducing payload or to increase the load a given aircraft can carry—allowing multiple strikes to ensure target damage or strikes at larger numbers of aim points per aircraft.[85]

The IAF would have problems in penetrating through Arab airspace, unless it could stage through Turkey, and would also have problems in refueling—its 5 KC-130H and 5 B-707 tankers are slow and vulnerable and would need escorts —and its ordinary B-707 airborne early warning (AEW), electronic intelligence (ELINT), and electronic warfare aircraft are also slow fliers, although the new G-550 Shaved ELINT aircraft is a fast flier and the IAF has some long-range unmanned aerial vehicles (UAVs) that could support its aircraft before, during, and after such missions.

These big-manned "slow fliers" would have serious problems penetrating and surviving in Arab and Iranian airspace. Israel has, however, specially configured some of its F-15s and F-16s with targeting, EW, surface-to-air missile (SAM)-suppression aids, and ELINT for this kind of mission. The full details of such capabilities are unknown.

Repeated strikes would be a problem because Israel could probably get away with going through Jordan and then through Saudi Arabia/Gulf or Iraq once, but any repeated effort would be too politically dangerous for Arab governments to easily tolerate. Israel has also had problems with its intelligence satellites, and its battle damage assessment and time-urgent retargeting capabilities for precision strikes with a target mix as complex as Iran's could be a major problem.

Much would depend on just how advanced Israel's long-range UAV capabilities really are and whether Israel could get access to U.S. intelligence and intelligence, surveillance, and reconnaissance (IS&R) capabilities for both its initial targeting and restrikes, but confirming the actual nature of damage, carrying out restrikes, and sending a clear signal that Israel can repeat its strikes if Iran rebuilds or creates new facilities would be a problem. Israel has kept the details of such programs classified, along with those of its long-range cruise missile and ballistic missile booster developments. Enough has leaked into the press, however, to indicate that the Israel Defense

Forces (IDF) have made very substantial progress in developing the long-range UAVs it would need for such missions.

The radars in the countries involved would probably detect IAF and U.S. missions relatively quickly, and very low-altitude penetration profiles would lead to serious range-payload problems. The countries overflown would be confronted with the need either to react or to have limited credibility in claiming surprise. There are gaps in Syrian air defenses in the north and along the Syrian-Jordanian border. An over-flight would still present political problems, however, and an overflight of Iraq would be a major violation of Iraqi sovereignty and seen in the region as having to have had a U.S. "green light." Iran would almost certainly see Jordanian, Turkish, and/or Saudi tolerance of such an IAF strike as a hostile act. It might well claim a U.S. green light in any case in an effort to mobilize hostile Arab and Muslim (and possibly world) reactions.

Many have compared current Israeli military options with Iran to that of the 1981 attack against Iraq's Osiraq reactor and have noted the conditions are very different. For example, Peter Brookes, a military expert and senior fellow at the Heritage Foundation, has argued that Israel has several options including satellite-guided Joint Direct Attack Munition (JDAM) bombs, cruise missiles on submarines, and Special Operation Forces. He, however, argued that attacking Iranian nuclear facilities are "much tougher" to target given the nature of the Iranian nuclear facilities and the strategic balance in the region.[86]

As for covert action, this demands significant operational capabilities and intelligence. It seems doubtful that Israel has the capability to conduct large-scale covert operations in Iran. The Iranian program is also hard to assess and covertly attack because it has reached the point where it is independent of external assistance. Moreover, much of the foreign assistance Iran has obtained came from nations such as Pakistan, which are not traditional areas of operations for the Israeli Secret Services, such as Europe or South America.

Reports have surfaced, however, about more drastic Israeli strike options. One report, dating from early 2007, states that Israel has created plans to strike Iran with nuclear bunker-buster bombs. This would apparently be used if the United States fails to neutralize Iran's nuclear facilities. The three prime targets in this plan include the enrichment facility in Natanz, the uranium conversion in Isfahan, and the heavy-water reactor in Arak.[87] Other, possibly longer-term options include deploying Israeli submarines in the Gulf or Gulf of Oman, which could respond to lower-level Iranian attacks on Israel by attacking Iran's oil exports and eventually being armed with nuclear cruise missiles to preempt or retaliate to an Iranian nuclear strike on Israel.

Iranian Defense against Israeli (and U.S.) Strikes

Iran would find it difficult to defend against U.S. forces using cruise missiles, stealth aircraft, standoff precision weapons, and equipped with a mix of vastly superior air combat assets and the IS&R assets necessary to strike and restrike Iranian targets in near real time. Iran might be able to intercept Israeli fighters; Iran has "quantity," but the previous chapters have shown that its air defenses have little "quality." It has assigned some 12,000–15,000 men in its air force to land-based air-defense functions, including at least 8,000 regulars and 4,000 IRGC personnel. It is not possible to distinguish clearly between the major air-defense weapons holdings of the regular air force and of the IRGC, but the air force appeared to operate most major SAM systems.

Although Iran has made some progress in improving and updating its land-based air-defense missiles, sensors, and electronic warfare capability—and has learned much from Iraq's efforts to defeat U.S. enforcement of the "no-fly zones" from 1992–2003—its defenses are outdated and poorly integrated. All of its major systems are based on technology that is now more than 35 years old, and all are vulnerable to U.S. use of active and passive countermeasures.

Iran's land-based air-defense forces are too widely spaced to provide more than limited air defense for key bases and facilities, and many lack the missile launcher strength to be fully effective. This is particularly true of Iran's SA-5 sites, which provide long-range, medium-to-high altitude coverage of key coastal installations. Too few launchers are scattered over too wide an area to prevent relatively rapid suppression. Iran also lacks the low-altitude radar coverage, overall radar net, command-and-control assets, sensors, resistance to sophisticated jamming and electronic countermeasures, and systems integration capability necessary to create an effective air-defense net.

Iran has, however, bought the advanced TOR-M short-range missile from Russia and can use this for point defense of key facilities—although Israel and the United States have standoff weapons that can launch from outside its range. Iran also claimed on December 22, 2008, that it had bought the far more advanced long-range Russian S-300 surface-to-air missile system from Russia.[88]

Statements and reporting by Iranian and Israeli officials suggest that such a sale has taken place and that Iran has received the S-300 system from Russia. Deputy Head of the National Security and Foreign Policy Commission in Iran's parliament, Esma'il Kowsari, on December 21, 2008, announced that Tehran had reached an agreement with Moscow on the delivery of the advanced S-300 surface-to-air missile system after years of negotiations. RIA (Russian Information Agency) Novosti quoted an unnamed Russian source as saying, "Moscow has earlier met its obligations on supplying Tor-M1 systems to Iran and is currently implementing a contract to deliver S-300 systems."[89]

Russia has repeatedly denied such a sale, but if Russia did sell the S-300—which some reporting indicates is likely—it would offer a fully modern surface-to-air missile, limited ballistic and cruise missile defense capability, much better electronic warfare capability, and a much better sensor and battle management (BM) system. Much would depend on delivery numbers and schedules, the exact variant of the S-300, and whether Russia also sold a modern command, control, communications, computers, and intelligence (C^4I)/BM radar system to go with it. It would also take some time for proper training of personnel to operate these systems, as well as to fully integrate them into the overall Iranian defense network. At a minimum, however, the

S-300 would make a major difference. Long-time Pentagon advisor Dan Goure stated, "If Tehran obtained the S-300, it would be a game-changer in military thinking for tackling Iran."[90]

Most Iranian squadrons can perform both air-defense and attack missions, regardless of their principal mission—although this does not apply to Iran's F-14 (air defense) and Su-24 (strike/attack) units. Iran's F-14s were, however, designed as dual-capable aircraft, and the Iranian Air Force has not been able to use its Phoenix air-to-air missiles since the early 1980s. Iran has claimed that it is modernizing its F-14s by equipping them with Improved Hawk missiles adapted to the air-to-air role, but it is far from clear that this is the case or that such adaptations can have more than limited effectiveness. In practice, this means that Iran might well use the F-14s in nuclear strike missions. They are capable of long-range, high-payload missions and would require minimal adaptation to carry and release a nuclear weapon.[91]

Iran's air forces are only marginally better able to survive in air-to-air combat than Iraq's were before 2003. Its land-based air defenses must operate largely in the point defense mode, and Iran lacks the battle management systems, and data links are not fast and effective enough to allow it to take maximum advantage of the overlapping coverage of some of its missile systems—a problem further complicated by the problems in trying to net different systems supplied by Britain, China, Russia, and the United States. Iran's missiles and sensors are most effective at high-to-medium altitudes against aircraft with limited penetrating and jamming capability.

Iranian Retaliation against Israel

For all the reasons outlined earlier in this chapter, however, Iran has other capabilities to strike back against Israel. In fact, it has threatened retaliation if attacked by Israel. Iranian Foreign Minister Manouchehr Mottaki was quoted as saying that an attack by Israel or the United States would have "severe consequence," and threatened that Iran would retaliate "by all means" at its disposal. Mottaki added, "Iran does not think that the Zionist regime is in a condition to engage in such a dangerous venture and they know how severe the possible Iranian response will be to its possible audacity . . . Suffice to say that the Zionist regime, if they attack, will regret it."[92]

On May 17, 2009, the head of the UN's nuclear watchdog, Mohamed ElBaradei, called any possible Israeli strike on Iran's nuclear facilities an "insane" move. "Attacking Iran would be insane," ElBaradei, the director general of the International Atomic Energy Agency, told Der Spiegel, and added that "this would trigger an explosion across the whole region and the Iranians would immediately start to construct a (nuclear) bomb and would be assured the support of the entire Muslim world."[93]

Iran has several options in responding to an Israeli attack:

- Multiple launches of Shahab-3 including the possibility of CBR warheads against Tel Aviv, Israeli military and civilian centers, and Israeli suspected nuclear weapons sites

- Using proxy groups such Hezbollah or Hamas to attack Israel proper with suicide bombings, covert CBR attacks, and missile attacks from southern Lebanon and Syria
- Covert attacks against Israeli interests by its intelligence and IRGC assets. This could include low-level bombings against Israeli embassies, Jewish centers, and other Israeli assets outside and inside Israel.
- Use of "suicide drone" UAVs possibly armed with CBR munitions against Israel overtly or through proxy groups such as Hezbollah

In addition, most Israeli military options would have to include an air strike that involved overflights of Arab territory that might seriously complicate Israel's fragile relations with Jordan and may provoke Saudi Arabia to respond. An Israeli strike against Iranian nuclear facilities may also strengthen the Iranian regime's stance to move toward nuclear capabilities and drive many neighboring states to support Iran's bid for nuclear weapons. In addition, it could lead to further escalation of the Iraqi insurgency and increase the threat of asymmetric attacks against American interests and allies in the region.

On the other hand, Israeli officials have expressed the concern that if Iran acquires nuclear weapons and the means to deliver them, this could spark further proliferation in the region. This would spread WMD capabilities around the Middle East and greatly increase the threat of CBRN attacks against Israel and the entire region. Waiting also has its penalties.

U.S. Options against Iran

A power as large as the United States would have far greater capabilities than Israel. It could strike on a scale that could destroy all highly suspect possible targets as well as confirmed targets. For Iran, this would present the problem that playing a shell game is dangerous when the opponent can strike at all the shells.

The United States also could strike at a wide range of critical Iranian military facilities, including its missile production facilities. Most are soft targets and would be extremely costly to Iran. Even if many of Iran's nuclear facilities did survive U.S. strikes, Iran would be faced with either complying with the EU3 (France, Germany, and United Kingdom) and UN terms or taking much broader military losses—losses its aging and limited forces can ill afford.

Possible U.S. Strike Methods

The United States has a wide range of attack assets it could use, including cruise missiles, standoff precision-guided weapons, and stealth aircraft. Military operations against Iran's nuclear, missile, and other WMD facilities and forces would still be challenging, however, even for the United States. Iran would find it difficult to defend against U.S. forces using cruise missiles, stealth aircraft, standoff precision weapons, and equipped with a mix of vastly superior air combat assets and the IS&R assets necessary to strike and restrike Iranian targets in near real time.

For example, each U.S. B-2A Spirit stealth bomber could carry eight 4,500-pound enhanced BLU-28 satellite-guided bunker busting bombs—potentially enough to take out one hardened Iranian site per sortie. Such bombers could operate flying from Al Udeid air base in Qatar, Diego Garcia in the Indian Ocean, RAF Fairford in Gloucestershire, United Kingdom, and Whiteman USAF Base in Missouri.

The United States also has a number of other new systems that are known to be in the developmental stage and can probably deploy systems capable of roughly twice the depth of penetration with twice the effectiveness of the systems known from its attacks on Iraq in 1991. There seems to be a follow-on version of the 2,000-pound BLU-109, with an advanced unitary penetrator that can go twice as deep as the original BLU-109.[94] The nature and characteristics of such systems are classified, but the newest development in the BLU series that has been openly reported is the 5,000-pound BLU-122, which was fielded in late 2007. Further, there is the Massive Ordnance Penetrator (MOP), weighing almost 30,000 pounds, carrying 5,300 pounds of explosives. According to some estimates, optimum penetrating distance is up to 200 feet. Possible future alternatives to these weapons include directed-energy and high-power microwave weapons, none of which are currently beyond the testing phase.

The JDAM GBU-31 version has a nominal range of 15 kilometers with a CEP of 13 meters in the GPS-aided Inertial Navigation System (INS) modes of operation and 30 meters in the INS-only modes of operation.[95]

More advanced systems that have been publicly discussed in the unclassified literature include the BLU-116 Advanced Unitary Penetrator, the GBU-24 C/B (USAF), or the GBU-24 D/B (U.S. Navy), which has about three times the penetration capability of the BLU-109.[96] The United States is investing in weapons that are supposed to destroy targets that are buried under more than 20 meters of dirt and concrete.

It is not clear whether the United States has deployed the AGM-130C with an advanced earth-penetrating/hard-target kill system. The AGM-130 Surface Attack Guided Munitions were developed to be integrated into the F-15E, so that the F-15E could carry two such missiles, one on each inboard store station. The AGM-130 is a retargetable, precision-guided standoff weapon using inertial navigation aided by GPS satellites and has a 15–40-nautical mile range.[97]

Northrop-Grumman announced in July 2007 that it had begun integrating a new 30,000-pound-class "penetrator bomb" for use by the B-2. In 2008, it was reported that USAF ordnance handlers at Whiteman Air Force Base, Missouri, had loaded a dummy version of the 20.5-foot long MOP into a mocked-up duplicate of the stealth bombers weapons bay on December 18, 2007. The USAF was reported to be checking in the test whether the B-2's existing mounting hardware was adequate, and if the bomb would fit in the bomb bay. The combined weight of the two MOPs was said to be 20,000 pounds—more than the published 40,000-pound maximum payload the B-2 is listed as carrying. However, the B-2 was believed to be able to carry the 60,000-pound payload of two conventional MOP weapons. Reports indicate that the USAF had asked Congress for nearly $88 million in development funds for the MOP in FY2008.[98]

It is not clear whether any combination of such weapons could destroy all of Iran's most hardened underground sites, although it seems likely that the BLU-28 could do serious damage at a minimum and might well collapse enough of them to make them unusable. Much depends on the accuracy of reports that Iran has undertaken a massive tunneling project with some 10,000 square meters of underground halls and tunnels branching off for hundreds of meters from each hall.

Iran is reported to be drawing on North Korean expertise and to have created a separate corporation (Shahid Rajaei Company) for such tunneling and hardening efforts under the IRGC, with extensive activity already under way in Natanz and Isfahan. The facilities are said to make extensive use of blast-proof doors, extensive divider walls, hardened ceilings, 20-centimeter-thick concrete walls, and double concrete ceilings with earth filled between layers to defeat earth penetrates.[99] Such passive defenses could have a major impact, but reports of such activity are often premature, exaggerated, or report far higher construction standards than are actually executed.

At the same time, the B-2A, other bombers, and U.S. land- and carrier-based attack aircraft—some with stealth-like features—could be used to deliver large numbers of precision-guided 250- and 500-pound bombs against dispersed surface targets or a mix of light and heavy precision-guided weapons. Submarines and surface ships could deliver cruise missiles for such strikes, and conventional strike aircraft and bombers could deliver standoff weapons against most suspect Iranian facilities without suffering a high risk of serious attrition. The challenge would be to properly determine what targets and aim points were actually valuable, not to inflict high levels of damage.

One analyst projects that strikes against some 400 targets would be necessary to dismantle the program. According to other reports, the U.S. Department of Defense is considering both conventional and nuclear weapons to use against reinforced underground targets and would strike at Iran's other WMD facilities, missiles, and missile production facilities and create an entry corridor by destroying part of Iran's air-defense system. This could easily require 800–1,200 sorties and cruise missile strikes.

One expert (Lieutenant General Thomas McInerny, the former retired Assistant Vice Chief of the USAF) speculates that this could require an initial strike force of 75 stealth aircraft, including B-2s, F-117s, and F-22s; and 250 nonstealth aircraft, including F-15s, F-16s, B-52s, and B-1s, It might include three carrier task forces with 120 F-18s, and large numbers of cruise missiles, supported by a large array of intelligence platforms, support aircraft, and UAVs.[100]

More generally, the United States could cripple Iran's economy by striking at major domestic gas production and distribution facilities, refineries, and electric power generations. There are no rules that would preclude the United States from immediate restrikes or restrikes over time. If the United States chose to strike at the necessary level of intensity, it could use conventional weapons to cripple Iran's ability to function as a nation in a matter of days with attacks limited to several hundred aim points.

Possible U.S. War Plans: Attacking, Delaying, and Waiting Out

If the United States does choose to respond militarily, it has several major types of military and strategic options. These options are summarized in Figure 8.9. Each of these options might have many of the following broad characteristics, although it should be stressed that these are only rough outlines of U.S. options and are purely speculative and illustrative points.

They are more warnings than recommendations, and they are not based on any inside knowledge of actual U.S. war plans and calculations. Those who argue strongly for and against such options should note, however, that there are many different ways in which the United States could act. There are no rules or certainties that say such attacks either could not succeed or that they would.

It is also important to point out that the United States cannot clearly separate its actions from those of Israel. Alliance never means identity of interest, and this is particularly true given the currently weak nature of Israel's political situation, its tendency to exaggerate and overreact, and the danger the United States could suddenly be pressured to finish what Israeli forces start. Either a U.S. attack is necessary in the U.S. national interest, or the United States should clearly oppose Israeli action. Israel is simply too weak a power, and too divisive in terms of regional politics, to be either a useful alternative or a proxy.

Iran's ride-out option is one that many commentators need to consider in more depth, particularly as long as Iran's capital investment is limited, its programs are not fully mature, the United States cannot be sure of destroying a target mix Iran cannot replace, and the United States does not have broad international support for its attacks. Unless the United States does find evidence of an imminent Iranian threat —which at this point might well require Iran to find some outside source of nuclear weapons or weapons-grade material—the United States may well simply choose to wait. Patience is not always a virtue, but it has never been labeled a mortal sin.

Furthermore, these options do deteriorate with time. The more Iran disperses its facilities and forces, and makes them redundant, the larger the attack the United States must launch and the greater the risk of at least partial failure. Iran's air defenses will improve if it gets modern fighters and a system such as the S-300. The risk that Iran has some form of covert weapons storage or an early form of launch of warning or launch under attack also grows with time, as does the fact that once it has fissile material, the key component in a nuclear weapon might well survive any U.S. strike.

Iranian Retaliation against U.S. Strikes

The United States would have political problems in exercising its military options, particularly if they require extended restrikes and coverage of Iran over time. Turkey and the southern Gulf States would be reluctant to provide bases and facilities. The United Kingdom, France, Germany, Russia, and China are not prepared to support

Figure 8.9   U.S. Strike Options against Iran

Demonstrative, Coercive, or Deterrent Strikes

1. Conduct a few cruise missile or stealth strikes simply as a demonstration or warning of the seriousness of U.S. intentions if Iran does not comply with the terms of the EU3 or UN.
2. Hit at least one high-value target recognized by the IAEA and the EU3 to show credibility to Iran, minimize international criticism.
3. Might strike at new sites and activities to show Iran cannot secretly proceed with, or expand, its efforts by ignoring the UN or EU3.
4. Could carrier base; would not need territory of Gulf ally.
5. International reaction would be a problem regardless of the level of U.S. action.
6. Might trigger Iranian counteraction in Iraq, Afghanistan, and dealing with Hezbollah.

Limited U.S. Attacks

1. A limited strike would probably take 16–20 cruise missile and strike sorties. (Total sorties in the Gulf and the area would probably have to total 100 or more including escorts, enablers, and refuelers.)
2. Might be able to combine B-2s and carrier-based aircraft and sea-launched cruise missiles. Might well need land base(s) in the Gulf for staging, refueling, and recovery.
3. Goal would be at least two to three of the most costly and major facilities critically damaged or destroyed.
4. Hit at high-value targets recognized by the IAEA and the EU3 to show credibility to Iran, minimize international criticism.
5. Might strike at new sites and activities to show Iran cannot secretly proceed with, or expand, its efforts by ignoring the UN or EU3.
6. Might slow down Iran if used stealth aircraft to strike at hard and underground targets, but impact over time would probably still be more demonstrative than crippling.
7. Hitting hard and underground targets could easily require multiple strikes during mission and follow-on restrikes to be effective.
8. Battle damage would be a significant problem, particularly for large buildings and underground facilities.
9. Size and effectiveness would depend very heavily on the quality of U.S. intelligence, and suitability of given ordnance, as well as the time the United States sought to inflict a given effect.
10. Iran's technology base would survive; the same would be true of much of the equipment even in facilities hit with strikes. Little impact, if any, on pool of scientists and experts.
11. Iranian response in terms of proliferation could vary sharply and unpredictably: deter and delay vs. mobilize and provoke.
12. Likely to produce cosmetic Iranian change in behavior at best. Would probably make Iran disperse program even more and drive it to deep underground facilities. Might provoke to implement (more) active biological warfare program.
13. Any oil embargo likely to be demonstrative.
14. Would probably trigger Iranian counteraction in Iraq, Afghanistan, and dealing with Hezbollah.
15. International reaction could be a serious problem; United States might well face same level of political problems as if it had launched a comprehensive strike on Iranian facilities.

Major U.S. Attacks on Iranian CBRN and Major Missile Targets

1. Period of attacks could extend from 3–10 days with 200–600 cruise missiles and strike sorties; would have to be at least a matching number of escorts, enablers, and refuelers.
2. Hit all suspect facilities for nuclear, missile, biological warfare (BW), and related C^4I/BM.
3. Knock out key surface-to-air missile sites and radars for future freedom of action.
4. Would need to combine B-2s, carrier-based aircraft, and sea-launched cruise missiles and use land base(s) in Gulf for staging, refueling, and recovery.
5. Threaten to strike extensively at Iranian capabilities for asymmetric warfare and to threaten tanker traffic, facilities in the Gulf, and neighboring states.
6. Would take at least 7–10 days to fully execute and validate.
7. Goal would be at least 70–80 percent of the most costly and major facilities critically damaged or destroyed.
8. Hit at all high-value targets recognized by the IAEA and the EU3 to show credibility to Iran, minimize international criticism, but also possible sites as well.
9. Strike at all known new sites and activities to show Iran cannot secretly proceed with, or expand, its efforts unless hold back some targets as hostages to the future.
10. Impact over time would probably be crippling, but Iran might still covertly assemble some nuclear devices and could not halt Iranian biological weapons effort.
11. Hitting hard and underground targets could easily require multiple strikes during mission and follow-on restrikes to be effective.
12. Battle damage would be a significant problem, particularly for large buildings and underground facilities.
13. Size and effectiveness would depend very heavily on the quality of U.S. intelligence and suitability of given ordnance, as well as the time the United States sought to inflict a given effect.
14. Much of Iran's technology base would still survive; the same would be true of many equipment items, even in facilities hit with strikes. Some impact, if any, on pool of scientists and experts.
15. Iranian response in terms of proliferation could vary sharply and unpredictably: deter and delay vs. mobilize and provoke.
16. A truly serious strike may be enough of a deterrent to change Iranian behavior, particularly if coupled to the threat of follow-on strikes in the future. It still, however, could as easily produce only a cosmetic Iranian change in behavior at best. Iran might still disperse its program even more and shift to multiple, small, deep underground facilities.
17. Might well provoke Iran to implement (more) active BW program.
18. An oil embargo might be serious.
19. Iranian government could probably not prevent some elements in Iranian forces and intelligence from seeking to use Iraq, Afghanistan, support of terrorism, and Hezbollah to hit back at the United States and its allies if it tried; it probably would not try.
20. International reaction would be a serious problem, but the United States might well face the same level of political problems as if it had launched a small strike on Iranian facilities.

Major U.S. Attacks on Military and Related Civilian Targets

1. Would take 1,000–2,500 cruise missiles and strike sorties.
2. Hit all suspect facilities for nuclear, missile, BW, and C^4I/BM, and potentially "technology base" targets including universities and dual-use facilities.

3. Either strike extensively at Iranian capabilities for asymmetric warfare and to threaten tanker traffic, facilities in the Gulf, and neighboring states or threaten to do so if Iran should deploy for such action.
4. Would require a major portion of total U.S. global assets. Need to combine B-2s, other bombers, and carrier-based aircraft and sea-launched cruise missiles. Would need land base(s) in the Gulf for staging, refueling, and recovery. Staging out of Diego Garcia would be highly desirable.
5. Would probably take several weeks to two months to fully execute and validate.
6. Goal would be 70–80-percent-plus of the most costly and major CBRN, missile, and other delivery systems, key conventional air and naval strike assets, and major military production facilities critically damaged or destroyed.
7. Hit at all high-value targets recognized by the IAEA and the EU3 to show credibility to Iran, minimize international criticism, but also possible sites as well.
8. Strike at all known new sites and activities to show Iran cannot secretly proceed with, or expand, its efforts unless hold back some targets as hostages to the future.
9. Hitting hard and underground targets could easily require multiple strikes during mission and follow-on restrikes to be effective.
10. Impact over time would probably be crippling, but Iran might still covertly assemble some nuclear device and could not halt Iranian biological weapons effort.
11. Battle damage would be a significant problem, particularly for large buildings and underground facilities.
12. Size and effectiveness would depend very heavily on the quality of U.S. intelligence and suitability of given ordnance, as well as the time the United States sought to inflict a given effect.
13. Much of Iran's technology base would still survive; the same would be true of many equipment items, even in facilities hit with strikes. Some impact, if any, on pool of scientists and experts.
14. Iranian response in terms of proliferation could vary sharply and unpredictably: deter and delay vs. mobilize and provoke.
15. Such a series of strikes might be enough of a deterrent to change Iranian behavior, particularly if coupled to the threat of follow-on strikes in the future. It still, however, could as easily produce only a cosmetic Iranian change in behavior at best. Iran might still disperse its program even more and shift to multiple, small, deep underground facilities.
16. Might well provoke Iran to implement (more) active biological warfare program.
17. An oil embargo might be serious.
18. Iranian government could probably not prevent some elements in Iranian forces and intelligence from seeking to use Iraq, Afghanistan, support of terrorism, and Hezbollah to hit back at the United States and its allies if it tried; it probably would not try.
19. International reaction would be a serious problem, and far greater than strikes that could be clearly associated with Iran's efforts to proliferate.

Delay and Then Strike
1. The United States could execute any of the above options and wait until after Iran provided proof it was proliferating. Such a smoking gun would create a much higher chance of allied support and international tolerance or consensus.
2. Iran will have committed major resources and created much higher-value targets.

3. The counter-risk is an unanticipated Iranian breakout: some form of Iranian launch on warning, launch under attack, or survivable "ride out" capability.
4. Iranian dispersal and sheltering may be much better.
5. Iran might have biological weapons as a counter.
6. Allied and regional reactions would be uncertain. Time tends to breed tolerance of proliferation.

Ride Out Iranian Proliferation
1. Announce or quietly demonstrate U.S. nuclear targeting of Iran's military and CBRN facilities and cities.
2. Tacitly signal U.S. green light for Israeli nuclear retaliation or preemption.
3. Deploy antiballistic and cruise missile defenses, and sell to Gulf and neighboring states.
4. Signal U.S. conventional option to cripple Iran by destroying its power generation, gas, and refinery facilities.
5. Provide U.S. guarantees of extended deterrence to Gulf States.
6. Tacitly accept Saudi acquisition of nuclear weapons.
7. Maintain preventive/preemptive option at constant combat readiness. Act without warning.
8. Encourage Israel to openly declare its strike options as a deterrent.
9. Announce doctrine that any Iranian use of biological weapons will lead to nuclear retaliation against Iran.

---

such strikes at this point, although they might if Iran tests or provides more evidence that it is moving forward. The UN would probably oppose such actions, as would most U.S. allies.

U.S. military options also are not risk-free. As is the case with Israeli attacks on Iran, Tehran has several retaliatory options:

- Retaliate against U.S. forces in Iraq and Afghanistan overtly using Shahab-3 missiles armed with CBR warheads
- Use suicide drone UAVs possibly armed with CBR munitions against U.S. military installations or naval units, diplomatic missions, or countries of interest in the Middle East
- Use proxy groups including Abu Musab al-Zarqawi and Muqtada al-Sadr in Iraq to intensify the insurgency and escalate the attacks against U.S. forces and Iraqi Security Forces
- Turn the Shi'ite majority in Iraq against the U.S. presence
- Attack the U.S. homeland with suicide bombs by proxy groups or deliver CBR weapons to Al Qa'ida to use against the United States
- Use its asymmetric capabilities to attack U.S. interests in the region, including soft targets, e.g., embassies, commercial centers, and American citizens.
- Use of suicide drone UAVs possibly armed with CBR munitions against Israel overtly or through proxy groups such as Hezbollah
- Attack U.S. naval forces stationed in the Gulf with antiship missiles, asymmetric warfare, and mines

- Attack Israel with missile attacks possibly with CBR warheads
- Retaliate against energy targets in the Gulf and temporarily shut off the flow of oil from the Strait of Hormuz
- Stop all of its oil and gas shipments to increase the price of oil and inflict damage on the global and U.S. economies

Iran has close relations with many Iraqi Shi'ites, particularly Shi'ite political parties and militias. While the consequences of U.S. military attacks against Iran remain unclear, the Shi'ite majority in Iraq can (1) ask the United States forces to leave Iraq, (2) instigate Shi'ite militia groups to directly attack U.S. forces, and/or (3) turn the new Iraqi security and military forces against U.S. forces in Iraq.

As has been described in earlier chapters, Iran has extensive forces suited to asymmetric warfare. It could not close the Strait of Hormuz, or halt tanker traffic, but it could threaten and disrupt it and create a high-risk premium and potential panic in oil markets. Iran could potentially destabilize part of Afghanistan and use Hezbollah and Syria to threaten Israel.

Iran can also use its IRGC asymmetric warfare assets to attack U.S. interests in the region. Iranian officials do not hide the fact that they would use asymmetric attacks against U.S. interests. For example, a brigadier general in the IRGC and the commander of the "Lovers of Martyrdom Garrison," Mohammad-Reza Jaafari, threatened U.S. interests with suicide operations if the United States were to attack Iran:

> Now that America is after gaining allies against the righteous Islamic Republic and wants to attack our sanctities, members of the martyrdom-seeking garrisons across the world have been put on alert so that if the Islamic Republic of Iran receives the smallest threat, the American and Israeli strategic interests will be burnt down everywhere.
>
> The only tool against the enemy that we have with which we can become victorious are martyrdom-seeking operations and, God willing, our possession of faithful, brave, trained and zealous persons will give U.S. the upper hand in the battlefield . . .
>
> Upon receiving their orders, our martyrdom-seeking forces will be uncontrollable and a guerrilla war may go on in various places for years to come . . .
>
> America and any other power cannot win in the unbalanced war against us.[101]

Iran could seek to create an alliance with extremist movements such as Al Qa'ida in spite of their hostility to Shi'ites. It can seek to exploit Arab and Muslim anger against U.S. ties to Israel and the invasion of Iraq on a global level, and European and other concerns that the United States might be repeating its miscalculation of the threat posed by Iraq and striking without adequate cause. Unless Iran is far more egregious in its noncompliance, or the United States can find a definitive smoking gun to prove Iran is proliferating, Iran would be certain to have some success in such efforts.

Iran's energy resources are another potential weapon. Shutting off exports would deeply hurt Iran but would also have an impact on global markets[102] As Iraq found, energy deals can also sharply weaken support for even diplomatic options, and Russia and China might well oppose any kind of U.S. military strike, regardless of the level of justification the United States could advance at the time.

CONTAINMENT: REACTING TO THE FACT IRAN BECOMES A SERIOUS NUCLEAR POWER

Iran already faces a kind of containment. The United States and Israel have a nuclear monopoly. A combination of U.S., British, French, and Gulf forces can decisively defeat Iran's forces in either conventional or asymmetric warfare, although scarcely without cost. The Gulf States, Israel, and the United States have limited missile defenses, and Iran does not even have effective fighter and surface-to-air missile capability. War with Iran is scarcely desirable, but Iran cannot escalate to the point where it wins any conflict unless its opponents fail to organize and fail to fight back. It also would lose any attempt to outescalate its opponents decisively and at a vastly greater cost.

The situation will change strikingly if Iran goes from developing nuclear weapons and long-range missiles to deploying an effective nuclear strike capability. At this point in time, there is no way to be certain what such a force would look like or how capable it would be, but certainly the political-psychological impact would be enormous.

As has been discussed earlier, there are many different ways in which Iran can proliferate, deploy nuclear-armed or other CBRN weapons, and use them to deter, intimidate, and strike against other nations. All have only one thing in common: they are all provocative and dangerous to any nation Iran may choose to try to intimidate and target.

At the same time, Iranian nuclear weapons and missiles are provocative and will almost certainly be dangerous to Iran. Iran has no monopoly on escalation. It almost certainly will provoke nuclear deterrence in kind, and this means creating a nuclear warfighting capability to strike at Iran at least as devastating as the damage Iran could do to any neighboring state, including Israel. Deterrence will be accompanied by defense, and this means a broader arms race in the region.

Iran's actions already are leading Iran's southern Gulf neighbors to consider buying missile defenses and modern combat aircraft and pushing them into clear relations with the United States. They are probably leading Israel to develop nuclear forces that can ride out any Iranian attack and destroy Iran's cities and population. They may lead other neighboring states to seek their own nuclear missile forces, and they may well lead the United States to deploy nuclear-armed submarines or other nuclear forces targeted on Iran.

DETERRENCE AND NUCLEAR WARFIGHTING

Deterrence almost certainly means nuclear targeting of Iran by Israel, the United States, and possibly neighboring countries. Even Iranian ambiguity will probably lead Israel and the United States—and possibly India, Pakistan, and Russia—to develop nuclear options to deter or retaliate against Iran. Israeli and/or U.S. restraint in striking Iran does not have to stop at the first convincing Iranian threat to use nuclear or highly lethal biological weapons, but it could do so.

Such targeting is almost certain to begin with countervalue options directed at Iran's cities and population, rather than countervalue targets directed against Iran's military forces. Iran already has mobile missile forces, and these will become steadily easier to disperse once their numbers and range increase, Iran acquires quick reaction liquid fuel or solid fuel missiles, Iran acquires more nuclear warheads, and/or Iran's warning and command-and-control systems improve. Iran also has the options of launch on warning, launch under attack, and covert sea basing on surface ships. Some form of counterforce strike may still be possible, but it seems likely that Iran will face retaliatory threats and deterrents that are largely "city busting" in character.

Israeli Deterrence

There already are reports that Israel is developing a sea-based launch capability and that its submarines will be able to launch nuclear-armed cruise missiles. It already has intelligence satellites with the capability to support nuclear targeting of Iran, and it may have much longer-range missiles than much of the literature indicates. Israel seems to have developed large boosters in the late 1980s, it has experience with satellite launches, and it may have developed or deployed missiles that can reach any target in Iran.[103]

If Israel has not already done so, it certainly has the capability to develop and deploy such weapons in a few years, and the nuclear stockpile to target every major city in Iran with multiple ground bursts. Iran faces a future where any existential attack on Israel would almost certainly lead to an existential attack on Iran, and Israel might well have the advantage, at least for the first decade of any nuclear-armed missile arms race. Israel probably has thermonuclear weapons while Iran may be limited to much lower-yield fission or early boosted weapons.

Ground bursts on Israeli cities would almost certainly affect the Palestinians and Jerusalem. Ground bursts on Iranian cities would have fallout that would be largely dissipated in Iran or affect weak border states such as Afghanistan. In practice, Israel will virtually have to find some way to demonstrate to Iran that it can target Iran's cities. It will not have to demonstrate intent. An Iranian nuclear strike on Israel might not destroy Israel, but Israel could not ride out such attacks and would have every reason to launch a pattern of retaliation that would destroy most of Iran's population and its ability to recover within any foreseeable amount of time.

U.S. Deterrence

The United States cannot leave a power vacuum in the Gulf. It is easy to talk about "withdrawing," but the Gulf is not Vietnam. Its location and the global dependence on Gulf energy exports will make it a critical U.S. strategic interest indefinitely into the future. This means the United States cannot ignore the unique security role that only it can perform in the region. Russia can still influence some of Iran's neighbors, but the United States still can play a unique role in working with Turkey, Afghanistan, Pakistan, and Iraq. Seeking regional action to both give Iran incentives for good behavior and clear collective deterrents to opportunism is going to be just as critical as broader international action.

The United States is also the only power other than Israel that can deter and defend against a serious Iranian military threat in the near to midterm. This deterrence can take a largely conventional form until Iran requires significant nuclear forces. The United States can maintain a high degree of deterrence-related warfighting capability by keeping its preventive and preemptive military options to strike at Iran's nuclear and missile facilities constantly up-to-date, work with its allies to prepare, and maintain the necessary capabilities and strength to secure the Gulf.

Turkey and Pakistan are strong enough to deter Iranian conventional and asymmetric attacks, but Iraq, Afghanistan, and the southern Gulf States are not. The United States needs to maintain the kind of military presence in the Gulf that makes it clear to Iran that it cannot take military action without the fear or reality of an American response. The United States must play a critical role in deterrence and containment.

The United States needs to work with the southern Gulf States to maintain the conventional military options that can ensure that Iran cannot block the flow of Gulf oil for more than a few days or weeks, be ready for limited action against any low-level Iranian adventures, be able to act quickly enough to prevent clashes from becoming war, and build up its regional allies. In the right political and strategic context, military containment and deterrence are both carrots *and* sticks. They deter without threatening, and they make diplomatic and economic incentives more attractive.

Once Iran has significant nuclear capabilities, however, the United States may have to deploy nuclear armed forces targeted on Iran. The United States should not leave the southern Gulf States, Turkey, and Israel vulnerable to Iranian attack without Iran's knowledge that any actual Iranian strike would be suicidal.

In fact, the United States should strongly consider making extended deterrence an option that covers the entire Middle East, including Israel, and do so in ways that leave Iran in no doubt as to the prospect of U.S. retaliation. Hopefully, Iran will never choose to really play the nuclear card. If it does, it must be certain that if it does play the game, the consequences will be suicidal. It must know long in advance that it will lose in ways from which it can never recover.

Regional Deterrence

As for regional options, Pakistan and India already have nuclear weapons. Other powers may follow. Even Iranian nuclear ambiguity may prove to be enough to trigger Saudi, Egyptian, and Turkish efforts to become nuclear powers, and actual deployment of nuclear-armed Iranian forces would provide a much stronger incentive for such action. Saudi Arabia has already said that it has examined nuclear options and rejected them, but this is no certainty and much depends on Iranian action.

Regional powers might show restraint if the United States provides the same form of extended deterrence it once provided to Germany during the Cold War. But, any form of a broad regional nuclear arms race would be a nightmare for all concerned. The end result would be a far more threatening mix of CBRN capabilities in the Gulf region. It would extend the near certainty of an Israeli-Iranian nuclear arms race to one where Israel and its Arab neighbors would consider targeting and deterring each other and raise the potential the threat of nuclear alliances and polarization between Sunni and Shi'ite states.

DEFENSE

Iran's neighbors, Europe, the United States, and Israel have important options for defense. Israel has already developed and deployed missile defenses and has long possessed advanced air defense capabilities. Most southern Gulf States have or are acquiring advanced surface-to-air missile systems such as the Patriot, and many seem likely to buy the U.S.-made Patriot PAC-3 or Theater High-Altitude Area Defense (THAAD) missile defense systems over time. The United States is acquiring the ability to project naval forces with Standard SM-2 or SM-3 missile defense, and the PAC-3 and THAAD. Russia already offers the S-300 surface-to-air missile system in configurations with significant missile defense capabilities and is developing the S-400 with substantially more advanced air and ballistic missile defense capabilities.

This would allow any power in the region to create a significant mix of antiair, antiballistic missile, and anticruise missile capabilities over the next decade. These capabilities could be reinforced by U.S. power projection capabilities and by the provision of U.S. intelligence and warning data. The United States can detect Iranian ballistic missile launches and has already agreed to provide real-time warning to some regional powers.

It should be stressed, however, that defenses are always relative and are as subject to arms races as offensive systems. Iran will probably be able to deploy decoys and warheads with limited maneuver or "spiral" capabilities by the time it can deploy a nuclear-armed missile force. Iran could launch saturation attacks using both short- and longer-range missiles against Gulf and other neighboring states. Larger and more powerful missiles can be used to launch mixes of multiple warheads and decoys and to increase closing velocities in ways that reduce the area coverage and probability of intercept of missile defenses. Iran can develop mixes of ballistic and cruise missiles to create more complicated patterns of attack.

Iran will have enough aircraft, UAVs, unmanned combat air vehicles, drones, and decoys to potentially saturate local air defenses—particularly if the southern Gulf States and Iraq do not develop truly integrated air-defense systems. It can attack coastal targets by having a ship or even small vessel move into the area or a port. This is a critical potential threat and deterrent if it involves a critical oil loading facility, water desalination plant, or port city. There are also reports that Iran has already experimented with Scud launchers from commercial ships. Effective air and missile defenses could also increase Iran's willingness to conduct covert or proxy nuclear and biological attacks.

It should be stressed that whatever defenses are deployed, much will depend on the overall architecture of the entire air-missile-naval-counterinfiltration systems that defending nations deploy, and the level of integration or interoperability involved. Simply buying ballistic missile defense fire units, for example, will at best involve uncertain point defense capabilities and might well simply mean acquiring expensive and ineffective "toys."

Creating wide area air and missile defenses that include the right mix of overall fire unit deployment and locations, wide area interceptors, warning, and battle management systems is a very different story. This will be particularly true if missile defenses are integrated with air-defense systems and are integrated or truly interoperable with neighboring and U.S. missile and air-defense systems. Iran's options for saturation, bypass, and "end runs" will be much more limited.

It is also important to note that civil and passive defenses and a mix of sensors and reporting systems that can quickly detect and characterize the nature of a nuclear and biological attack also offer important defensive options. Even a limited fallout shelter program could sharply reduce the casualties from an Iranian attack on most of the regions large, spread-out cities. Redundant and/or netted water facilities, energy export facilities, port facilities, and power grids could also reduce the impact of an Iranian attack—as could stockpiling components to replace or partially substitute for critical infrastructure nodes and facilities.

The problem with all of these options, however, is that they are likely only to reduce—not eliminate—the horrifying consequences of any nuclear or biological attack or exchange. They also can provoke a dual in which Iran seeks to increase its attack options in size and capability to match each increase in defense capability.

THE ONLY WAY TO WIN IS NOT PLAY

The danger in any analysis of this kind is that it may be viewed as alarmist or as crying wolf at a time when Iran's actions are uncertain, and many of the risks described are years in the future—if they materialize at all. *Once again, it must be stressed that this analysis deals with possibilities—not probabilities—and is not a prediction.* The paths described here, however, are ones that other nations have already taken. Their logic is scarcely inevitable, but it is a historical reality.

These paths also are easiest to avoid when they have not yet been taken, or when the risk they pose can be avoided or mitigated by dialog, diplomacy, and even limited forms of arms control such as transparency, inspection, and confidence-building measures. It is also important to look beyond the next stage in proliferation and consider the mid- and long-term courses it may take. The wolf may not be at the door or near the flock, but wolves do exist.

It is also important for Iran, Israel, and any other nuclear power to fully understand that actions produce reactions. Nuclear and biological weapons virtually force some form of response in kind. They also are not status symbols or tools that somehow guarantee security simply because their use can be so devastating. History does have long periods of peace and mutual deterrence; it also has periods of sudden and untended escalation to nearly total war.

Iranian officials need to seriously consider where their actions will take Iran if it does succeed in proliferating. It acquires only significant leverage over its neighbors or the United States if they do not respond. If they do respond, they can outspend, outdeploy, and outkill any capabilities Iran can create. They also can respond in kind to Iran's build of asymmetric warfare capabilities, and Iran gains only a tenuous advantage—if any—in using asymmetric attacks in conjunction with nuclear capabilities if it does not face a nuclear threat in response. Proliferation may offer Iran a more convincing deterrent to outright invasion, but this risk has always been more a matter of war scares and rhetoric than a reality, and it also involves a nuclear threat that is so risky that it may be seen as a bluff that can be called.

During the Cold War, a U.S. movie called *WarGames* (1983) raised a point that Iran and other potential proliferators need to carefully consider, as do all who consider military options centered around such risks.[104] The movie highlighted the fact that any U.S.-Soviet nuclear exchange had to be so costly to both sides that there was no way either side could gain an advantage. Iran might well wish to consider a line of dialog from the movie: "strange games . . . the only way to win is not to play."

Acronyms

AA	antiaircraft
AAM	air-to-air missile
AEI	American Enterprise Institute
AEOI	Atomic Energy Organization of Iran
AEW	airborne/aircraft early warning
APC	armored personnel carrier
AQ	Al Qa'ida
ATGM	antitank guided missile
AVLIS	atomic vapor laser isotope separation
BBC	British Broadcasting Corporation
BHRC	Benefication and Hydrometallurgical Center
BM	battlespace management
BW	biological weapons/warfare
CENTCOM	U.S. Armed Forces Central Command (Middle East and Central Asia)
CBRN	chemical, biological, radiological, and nuclear warheads
CBW	chemical and biological weapons
CEP	circular error probable
C^4I	command, control, communications, computers, and intelligence
CIA	U.S. Central Intelligence Agency
COIN	counterinsurgency
CRS	Congressional Research Service
CSL	Comprehensive Separation Laboratory
CSP	Conference of States Parties
CW	chemical weapons/warfare
CWC	Chemical Weapons Convention
CWD	Chemical Weapons Demilitarisation Conference

DG	director general
DIA	U.S. Defense Intelligence Agency
DIV	design information verification
DNI	Director of National Intelligence
DOD	U.S. Department of Defense
ECM	electronic countermeasure
EFP	explosively formed projectile
EIA	U.S. Energy Information Agency
ELINT	electronic intelligence
EMP	electromagnetic pulse
EOR	enhanced oil recovery
EU	European Union
EU3	Germany, France, and the United Kingdom
EW	early warning
FAC	fast attack craft
FEP	Fuel Enrichment Plant
FGA	fighter ground attack
FMP	Fuel Manufacturing Plant
FSU	former Soviet Union
GA	tabun (chemical nerve agent)
GB	sarin (chemical nerve agent)
GCC	Gulf Cooperation Council
GDP	gross domestic product
GLONAS	Global Navigation Satellite System
GNP	gross national product
GPS	global positioning system
HEU	highly enriched uranium
IAEA	International Atomic Energy Agency
IAF	Israeli Air Force
IC	Intelligence Community
IDF	Israeli Defense Force
IED	improvised explosive device
IISS	International Institute for Strategic Studies
INS	Inertial Navigation System
IRBM	intermediate-range ballistic missile
IR-40	Iran Nuclear Research
IRGC	Islamic Revolutionary Guards Corps
IRGCN	Islamic Revolutionary Guards Corps Navy
IRI	Islamic Republic of Iran
IRIAF	Islamic Republic of Iran Air Force
IRIM	Islamic Republic of Iran Military
ISAF	International Security Assistance Force
IS&R	intelligence, surveillance, and reconnaissance
Isp	specific impulse
JDAM	Joint Direct Attack Munitions
JHL	Jabr Ibn Hayan Multipurpose Laboratory
kg	kilogram

kgf	kilogram-force
km	kilometer
LEU	low-enriched uranium
LRICBM	limited-range intercontinental ballistic missile
LSL	Laser Spectroscopy Laboratory
MANPAD	man-portable air defense system
MEK	Mujahadin-e Khalq Organization
MEMRI	Middle East Media Research Institute
MIX	Molybdenum, Iodine, Xenon Radioisotope Production Facility Reactor
MLIS	molecular isotope separation
MLR	multiple rocket launcher
MMBD	million barrels per day
MNSTC-I	Multi-National Security Transition Command–Iraq
MoI	Ministry of Interior
MOIS	Iran's Ministry of Intelligence and Security
MOP	Massive Ordnance Penetrator
MP	member of parliament
MPA	maritime patrol aircraft
MR	maritime reconnaissance
MW	megawatt
NATO	North Atlantic Treaty Organization
NBC	nuclear, biological, and chemical
NCRI	National Council of Resistance of Iran
NGO	nongovernmental organization
NIE	U.S. National Intelligence Estimate
NIOC	National Iranian Oil Company
NPT	Non-Proliferation Treaty
NTI	Nuclear Threat Initiative
OCU	operational control unit
ODNI	U.S. Office of the Director of National Intelligence
OFAC	U.S. Department of Treasury's Office of Foreign Assets Control
OPCW	Organisation for the Prohibition of Chemical Weapons
P5	UNSC permanent members (China, France, Russia, the United Kingdom, and the United States)
P5+1	UNSC permanent members plus Germany
PFEP	Pilot Fuel Enrichment Plant
PIJ	Palestine Islamic Jihad
PRC	People's Republic of China
R&D	research and development
RECCE	reconnaissance
SAM	surface-to-air missile
SAR	search and rescue
SAVAK	National Organization for Intelligence and Security
SHIG	Shahid Hemat Industrial Group
SIO	Special Industries Organization
SLBM	submarine-launched ballistic missile
SLV	satellite launch vehicle

SNSAP	Saudi National Security Assessment Project
SNSC	Iran's Supreme National Security Council
SPSS	self-propelled, semisubmersible
SRBM	short-range ballistic missile
SSM	surface-to-surface missile
STG	Science and Technology Group
SUT	Sharif University of Technology
SWU	separative work units
TEL	transporter-erector-launcher
TERCOM	Terrain Contour Matching
THAAD	Theater High-Altitude Area Defense
TNRC	Tehran Nuclear Research Center
TRR	Tehran Research Reactor
UAE	United Arab Emirates
UAV	unmanned aerial vehicles
UCAV	unmanned combat aerial vehicles
UCF	Uranium Conversion Facility
UO_2/UO2	uranium dioxide
UF_4/UF4	uranium tetrafluoride
UF_6/UF6	uranium hexafluoride
USAF	United States Air Force
VEVAK	MOIS or Vezarat-e Ettela' at va Aminat-e Keshvar
WHO	World Health Organization
WMD	weapon of mass destruction
YRPC	Yazd Radiation Processing Center
ZKA	German Customs Office of Criminal Investigations

Notes

CHAPTER 1

1. Alex Bollfrass, "Arms Control and Proliferation Profile: Iran," Arms Control Association, January 2008, http://armscontrol.org/factsheets/iranprofile.

CHAPTER 2

1. "Iran's Statement at IAEA Emergency Meeting," *Mehr News Agency*, August 10, 2008, http://www.fas.org/nuke/guide/iran/nuke/mehr080905.html.

2. "Iran's Missing Anti-Nuclear Fatwa," *SECRECY NEWS* from the FAS Project on Government Secrecy, 2005, no. 79 (August 2005), http://www.fas.org/sgp/news/secrecy/2005/08/081105.html.

3. "Ayatollah Vows Iran's Nuclear Program Will Go On," *Associated Press*, June 3, 2008; "Iranian Supreme Leader Vows to Pursue Nuclear Program," *Voice of America News,* June 3, 2008.

4. Islamic Republic News Agency (IRNA), October 19, 1988.

5. Quoted in Kori N. Schake and Judith S. Yaphe, "The Strategic Implications of a Nuclear-Armed Iran," McNair Paper 64, Institute for National Strategic Studies, National Defense University, Washington, D.C., 2001, p. 3.

6. See the analysis in Global Security, "Weapons of Mass Destruction, Chemical Weapons, Iran," http://www.globalsecurity.org/wmd/world/iran/cw.htm.

7. Jalili: Chemical Weapons Have no Place in Iran's Defense Doctrine," IRNA, January 23, 2008, http://www2.irna.ir/en/news/view/line-17/0801239430180425.htm.

8. Itamar Eichner, "Iran Admits to Possessing Chemical Weapons," *Yedi'ot Aharonot*, November 20, 1998; FBIS Document FTS19981120000618, November 20, 1998; "Iran Pledges No Chemical Weapons Production," *Agence France-Presse*, November 17, 1998;

Mohammad R. Alborzi, "Statement to the Third Session of the Conference of the States Parties of the Chemical Weapons Convention," November 16–20, 2000.

9. "Iran Calls for the Destruction of Israel." See also "Iran Leader Urges Destruction of 'Cancerous' Israel," CNN, December 15, 2000, http://archives.cnn.com/2000/WORLD/ meast/12/15/mideast.iran.reut/. A similar quotation in Persian is at http://www.kheimeh.org/ kheimeh/index.php?po=fulltext&op=1&pg=1&id=455.

10. "Iran Calls for the Destruction of Israel."

11. Kasra Naji, Ahmadinejad: The Secret History of Iran's Radical Leader (Los Angeles: University of California Press, 2008), p. 144.

12. To link directly to a report on the speech, see Iranian Students News Agency, October 26, 2005, http://www.isna.ir/Main/NewsView.aspx?ID=News-603209. To view a similar report on Ahmadinejad's Web site (http://www.president.ir/fa), it is necessary to enter the archive of presidential speeches according to the Persian date, 4 Aban (8th month), 1384. Of the five items listed for that day, the "World without Zionism" speech is first.

13. http://sepahnews.com/nEWS/uNew.aspx?id=8482&pid=0, February 18, 2008.

14. According to the Fars News Agency; see http://www.aftab.ir/news/2008/feb/12/ c1c1202811597_politics_iran_jannati.php, February 12, 2008.

15. http://www1.irna.com/fa/news/view/line-5/8612021449121206.htm.

16. http://sepahnews.com/nEWS/uNew.aspx?id=8584&pid=0.

17. Iran Appears to Warm to Diplomacy," Washington Post, July 2, 2008; "Iranian FM Says 'New Process' Under Way in Nuclear Talks," Voice of America News, July 2, 2008.

18. "Wiping Israel Off the Map Is Iran's Official Policy," Iran Focus, October 30, 2005, http://www.iranfocus.com/en/ special-wire/wiping-israel-off-world-map-is-iran-s-official-policy-key-official.html.

19. http://www.aftab.ir/news/2007/oct/04/c1c1191492912_politics_iran_hossein _shariyat_madari.php, October 4, 2007.

20. Karim Sadjadpour, Reading Khanenei: The World View of Iran's Most Powerful Leader, Carnegie Endowment for International Peace, Washington, D.C., 2008. Khamenei's address to students in Yazd, January 3, 2008.

21. Emrooz (Tehran), May 3, 2008.

22. Asr-e Iran (Tehran), May 6, 2008.

23. Former member of the IRGC (Iranian Revolutionary Guards Corps).

24. Replaced Hojjatoleslam Hasan Rohani as both the Secretary of the Supreme National Security Council (SNSC) and Chief Nuclear Negotiator in 2005 before being replaced by Saeed Jalili in 2007.

25. Former president of Iran and front runner for Chief of State behind Khamenei.

26. Former member of the IRGC and former Deputy Foreign Affairs Minister for American and European Affairs.

27. Formerly deputy to IRGC Commander in Chief Yahaya Rahim Safavi.

28. Formerly Commander in Chief of the IRGC (1997–2007).

29. Akbar Ganji, "The Latter-Day Sultan: Power and Politics in Iran," Foreign Affairs, November/December 2008, http://www.foreignaffairs.org/20081001essay87604/akbar-ganji/ the-latter-day-sultan.html.

30. Hamid Algar, translation, The Constitution of the Islamic Republic of Iran (Berkeley: Mizan Press, 1980).

31. Ganji, "The Latter-Day Sultan: Power and Politics in Iran."

32. Sadjadpour, Reading Khanenei.

33. Algar, translation, *The Constitution of the Islamic Republic of Iran.*

34. Keith Crane, Rollie Lal, and Jeffrey Martini, "Iran's Political, Demographic and Economic Vulnerabilities," RAND Corporation, 2008, http://www.rand.org/pubs/monographs/2008/RAND_MG693.sum.pdf.

35. Ganji, "The Latter-Day Sultan: Power and Politics in Iran."

36. Ibid.

37. Daniel Byman, Shahram Chubin, Anoushiravan Ehteshami, and Jerrold D. Green, *Iran's Security Policy in the Post-Revolutionary Era* (Santa Monica, CA: RAND, 2001), http://www.rand.org/pubs/monograph_reports/MR1320/.

38. *Salam*, Aug. 17, 1994, as cited in Wilfried Buchta, *Who Rules Iran?* (Washington, DC: Washington Institute/Konrad Adenauer Stiftung, 2000), p. 73.

39. James Quinlivan, "Coup Proofing: Its Practice and Consequences in the Middle East," *International Security* 24, no. 2 (Fall 1999), pp. 131–165.

40. Byman et al., *Iran's Security Policy in the Post-Revolutionary Era.*

41. Ali Alfoneh, "Iran's Parliamentary Elections and the Revolutionary Guards' Creeping Coup d'Etat," *AEI Middle Eastern Outlook*, February 2008.

42. Frequent use is made of opposition reporting throughout this analysis. The reader should have no illusions about the character of one such source. The U.S. Department of State Country Reports on Terrorism, issued in April 2008, describes the MEK—and its front groups—as follows:

Mujahadin-e Khalq Organization (MEK) a.k.a. MKO; Mujahadin-e Khalq (Iranian government name for group); Muslim Iranian Students' Society; National Council of Resistance (NCR); Organization of the People's Holy Warriors of Iran; The National Liberation Army of Iran (NLA); The People's Mujahadin Organization of Iran (PMOI); National Council of Resistance of Iran (NCRI); Sazeman-e Mujahadin-e Khalq-e Iran.

Description: The Mujahadin-e Khalq Organization (MEK) advocates the violent overthrow of the Iranian regime and was responsible for the assassination of several U.S. military personnel and civilians in the 1970s. The MEK's armed wing is known as the National Liberation Army of Iran (NLA). In December 2006, the European Court of Justice ruled to overturn the designation of the MEK as a terrorist organization but was not supported by the Council of the European Union (EU).

The MEK emerged in the 1960s as one of the more violent political movements opposed to the Pahlavi dynasty and its close relationship with the United States. MEK ideology has gone through several iterations and blends elements of Marxism, Islam, and feminism. The group has planned and executed terrorist operations against the Iranian regime for nearly three decades from its European and Iraqi bases of operations. Additionally, it has expanded its fundraising base, further developed its paramilitary skills, and aggressively worked to expand its European ranks. In addition to its terrorist credentials, the MEK has also displayed cult-like characteristics.

Upon entry into the group, new members are indoctrinated in MEK ideology and revisionist Iranian history. Members are also required to undertake a vow of "eternal divorce" and participate in weekly "ideological cleansings." Additionally, children are reportedly separated from parents at a young age. MEK leader Maryam Rajavi has established a "cult of personality." She claims to emulate the Prophet Muhammad and is viewed by members as the "Iranian President in exile."

Activities: The group's worldwide campaign against the Iranian government uses propaganda and terrorism to achieve its objectives and has been supported by reprehensible regimes, including that of Saddam Hussein. During the 1970s, the MEK assassinated several U.S. military personnel and U.S. civilians working on defense projects in Tehran and supported the violent takeover in 1979 of the U.S. Embassy in Tehran.

In 1981, MEK leadership attempted to overthrow the newly installed Islamic regime; Iranian security forces subsequently initiated a crackdown on the group. The MEK instigated a bombing campaign, including an attack against the head office of the Islamic Republic Party and the Prime Minister's office, which killed some 70 high-ranking Iranian officials, including Chief Justice Ayatollah Mohammad Beheshti, President Mohammad-Ali Rajaei, and Prime Minister Mohammad-Javad Bahonar. These attacks resulted in a popular uprising against the MEK and an expanded Iranian government crackdown which forced MEK leaders to flee to France. For five years, the MEK continued to wage its terrorist campaign from its Paris headquarters. Expelled by France in 1986, MEK leaders turned to Saddam Hussein's regime for basing, financial support, and training. Near the end of the 1980–1988 Iran-Iraq War, Baghdad armed the MEK with heavy military equipment and deployed thousands of MEK fighters in suicidal, mass wave attacks against Iranian forces.

The MEK's relationship with the former Iraqi regime continued through the 1990s. In 1991, the group reportedly assisted the Iraqi Republican Guard's bloody crackdown on Iraqi Shia and Kurds who rose up against Saddam Hussein's regime. In April 1992, the MEK conducted near-simultaneous attacks on Iranian embassies and installations in 13 countries, demonstrating the group's ability to mount large-scale operations overseas. In April 1999, the MEK targeted key Iranian military officers and assassinated the deputy chief of the Iranian Armed Forces General Staff, Brigadier General Ali Sayyaad Shirazi.

In April 2000, the MEK attempted to assassinate the commander of the Nasr Headquarters, Tehran's interagency board responsible for coordinating policies on Iraq. The pace of anti-Iranian operations increased during "Operation Great Bahman" in February 2000, when the group launched a dozen attacks against Iran. One attack included a mortar attack against a major Iranian leadership complex in Tehran that housed the offices of the Supreme Leader and the President. In 2000 and 2001, the MEK was involved in regular mortar attacks and hit-and-run raids against Iranian military and law enforcement personnel, as well as government buildings near the Iran-Iraq border. Also in 2001, the FBI arrested seven Iranians in the United States who funneled $400,000 to an MEK-affiliated organization in the UAE, which used the funds to purchase weapons. Following an initial Coalition bombardment of the MEK's facilities in Iraq at the outset of Operation Iraqi Freedom, MEK leadership negotiated a cease-fire with Coalition Forces and voluntarily surrendered their heavy-arms to Coalition control. Since 2003, roughly 3,400 MEK members have been encamped at Ashraf in Iraq, under the protection of Coalition Forces.

In 2003, French authorities arrested 160 MEK members at operational bases they believed the MEK was using to coordinate financing and planning for terrorist attacks. Upon the arrest of MEK leader Maryam Rajavi, MEK members took to Paris' streets and engaged in self-immolation. French authorities eventually released Rajavi. Although currently in hiding, Rajavi has made "motivational" appearances via video-satellite to MEK-sponsored conferences across the globe.

According to evidence which became available after the fall of Saddam Hussein, the MEK received millions of dollars in Oil-for-Food program subsidies from Saddam Hussein from 1999 through 2003. In addition to discovering 13 lists of recipients of such vouchers on which the MEK appeared, evidence linking the MEK to the former Iraqi regime includes lists, as well as video footage of Saddam Hussein handing over suitcases of money to known MEK leaders, and video of MEK operatives receiving training from the Iraqi military.

Strength: Estimates place MEK's worldwide membership at between 5,000 and 10,000 members, with large pockets in Paris and other major European capitals. In Iraq, roughly 3,400 MEK members are gathered under Coalition protection at Camp Ashraf, the MEK's main compound north of Baghdad, where they have been treated as "protected persons" consistent with provisions of the Fourth Geneva Convention. This status does not affect the group's members outside of Camp Ashraf or the MEK's designation as a Foreign Terrorist Organization.

As a condition of the 2003 cease-fire agreement, the MEK relinquished more than 2,000 tanks, armored personnel carriers, and heavy artillery. A significant number of MEK personnel have voluntarily left Ashraf, and an additional several hundred individuals have renounced ties to the MEK and been voluntarily repatriated to Iran.

Location/Area of Operation: The MEK maintains its main headquarters in Paris and has concentrations of members across Europe, in addition to the large concentration of MEK located at Camp Ashraf in Iraq. The MEK's global support structure remains in place, with associates and supporters scattered throughout Europe and North America. Operations target Iranian regime elements across the globe, including in Europe and Iran. MEK's political arm, the National Council of Resistance of Iran (NCRI), has a global support network with active lobbying and propaganda efforts in major Western capitals. NCRI also has a well-developed media communications strategy.

External Aid: Before Operation Iraqi Freedom began in 2003, the MEK received all of its military assistance and most of its financial support from Saddam Hussein. The fall of Saddam's regime has led MEK increasingly to rely on front organizations to solicit contributions from expatriate Iranian communities.

Taken from Office of the Coordinator for Counterterrorism, "Chapter 6—Terrorist Organizations," *Country Reports on Terrorism*, U.S. Department of State, April 2008, http://www.state.gov/s/ct/rls/crt/2007/103714.htm.

43. Reza Shafa, "Who Are Political Guides in the IRGC," National Council of Resistance of Iran, August 31, 2008, http://ncr-iran.org/content/view/5562/153/.

44. "More Political Activities by the Passdaran: On the Eve of Elections, *Rooz*, October 31, 2008, http://www.roozonline.com/english/archives/2008/10/more_political_activities_by_t.html.

45. *Rooz* (Iran), September 3, 2007.

46. Reza Shafa, "Iran: The Strategic Organizational Shift within IRGC," NCRI—Foreign Affairs Committee, August 9, 2008, http://ncr-iran.org/index2.php?option=com_content&do_pdf=1&id=5483.

47. Ibid.

48. Ibid.

49. "IRGC Reshuffling Aimed at Boosting Political Role," National Iranian American Council (NAIC) US-Iran Policy Memo, July 2008.

50. Shafa, "Iran: The Strategic and Organizational Structure within IRGC."

51. UNSC Resolution 1737 (2006), December 23, 2008, http://www.iaea.org/News Center/Focus/IaeaIran/unsc_res1737-2006.pdf. Persons involved in the ballistic missile program: General Hosein Salimi, Commander of the Air Force, IRGC (Pasdaran). Persons involved in both the nuclear and ballistic missile programs: Major General Yahya Rahim Safavi, Commander, IRGC (Pasdaran).

52. Alireza Jafarzadeh is the president of Strategic Policy Consulting, Inc. and is the longtime Washington spokesman for the National Council of the Resistance of Iran (NCRI), the political wing of the Mujaheddin-e Khalq (MEK).

53. Alireza Jafarzadeh, "The Islamic Revolutionary Guards Corps Use Universities for Research to Build the Bomb: IRGC Imam Hossein University Involved in Clandestine Nuclear Weapons Program," statement by President of Strategic Policy Consulting, Inc. at the National Press Club in Washington, D.C., March 20, 2006, http://www.nci.org/06nci/03/Jafarzadeh_PC_Statement.htm.

54. Ibid.

55. Ibid.

56. Mathew Levitt, "Target Iranian Forces," *Washington Times*, February 16, 2007, http://www.washingtoninstitute.org/templateC06.php?CID=1026.

57. "Iran Offers Nuclear Technology to Nigeria," *Voice of America News*, August 29, 2008; "Iran, Nigeria Announce Peaceful Nuclear Deal," *Mobile Register*, August 29 2008.

58. "Iran: We Won't Halt Enrichment Even if Nuclear Fuel Supply Guaranteed," *Associated Press*, October 5, 2008; "Iran Refuses to Halt Enrichment for Fuel Guarantees," *Global Security Newswire*, October 6, 2008.

59. "Iran Vows not to Halt Its Nuclear Program Despite Western Pressure," *Associated Press Online*, May 5, 2008; "Iran Seems to Reject West's Offer," *New York Times*, May 5, 2008.

60. "Ayatollah Vows Iran's Nuclear Program Will Go On"; "Iranian Supreme Leader Vows to Pursue Nuclear Program."

61. "Iran Appears to Warm to Diplomacy"; "Iranian FM Says 'New Process' Under Way in Nuclear Talks."

62. "Iran Responds Obliquely to Nuclear Plan," *New York Times*, July 5, 2008; "Iran Indicates It Has No Plans to Halt Enrichment," *Associated Press*, July 5, 2008.

63. "Report: Iran Now Has 6,000 Centrifuges for Uranium," *Associated Press*, July 27, 2008; "Iran Claims It Has Added Enrichment Capability," *Virginian-Pilot*, July 27, 2008.

64. "Iran FM Rejects Deadline for Nuclear Incentives Package," *Voice of America News*, July 31, 2008; "Despite Call to Halt Iran Says It Will Continue Its Nuclear Program," *New York Times*, July 31, 2008.

65. "Iran: We Won't Halt Enrichment even if Nuclear Fuel Supply Guaranteed"; "Iran Refuses to Halt Enrichment for Fuel Guarantees."

66. "Emerging Threats: Iran Reacts to IAEA Reports," *UPI*, June 8, 2009, http://www.upi.com/Emerging_Threats/2009/06/08/Iran-reacts-to-IAEA-reports/UPI-41661244494331/.

67. David Albright, Jacqueline Shire, and Paul Brannan, "Has Iran Achieved a Nuclear Weapons Breakout Capability? Not Yet, But Soon." ISIS Report, December 2, 2008, http://www.isisnucleariran.org/assets/pdf/LEU_Iran.pdf; William J. Broad and David E. Sanger, "Iran Said to Have Nuclear Fuel for One Weapon," *New York Times*, November 20, 2008; "Iran Has Enough for A-Bomb: Agency," *The West Australian*, November 21, 2008. The *New York Times* reports that Iran has produced roughly enough LEU that, if further enriched,

could be used to make a single nuclear device. This estimate is based on the latest IAEA report indicating that Iran has manufactured 630 kg of LEU.

68. Michael Rubin, "Can a Nuclear Iran Be Contained or Deterred?" American Enterprise Institute for Public Policy Research, November 5, 2008, http://www.aei.org/publications/pubID.28896/pub_detail.asp.

CHAPTER 3

1. For two excellent and complementary looks at such options, see Fariborz Haghshenass, "Iran's Asymmetric Naval Warfare," Washington Institute for Near East Policy (WINEP), Policy Focus #87, September 2008, http://www.washingtoninstitute.org/templateC04.php?CID=298; and Jahangir Arasli, "Obsolete Weapons, Unconventional Tactics, and Martyrdom Zeal: How Iran Would Apply Its Asymmetric Warfare Doctrine in a Future Conflict," George C. Marshall European Center for Security Studies, Occasional Paper Series, No. 10, April 2007.

2. For a detailed analysis of the capabilities of Iranian naval forces, see Haghshenass, "Iran's Asymmetric Naval Warfare," pp. 12–25.

3. "Iran-Iraq War, 1980–1988," Global Security, http://www.globalsecurity.org/military/world/war/iran-iraq.htm/01/03/2005.

4. "Iran," *Jane's World Armies* (London: Jane's Information Group, October 26, 2006).

5. U.S. Department of State, "State Sponsors of Terrorism, Iran," *Country Reports on Terrorism, 2007*, Washington, April 2008, http://www.state.gov/s/ct/rls/crt/2007/103711.htm.

6. For another perspective on this issue, see Arasli, "Obsolete Weapons, Unconventional Tactics, and Martyrdom Zeal," especially Parts I and II.

7. Jacques Baud, *La Guerre asymétrique ou la défaite du vainqueur* (Monaco: Editions du Rocher, 2003).

8. Robert R. Tomes, "Relearning Counterinsurgency Warfare," *Parameters*, Spring 2004.

9. Michael Connell, "The Influence of the Iraq Crisis on Iranian Warfighting Doctrine and Strategy," CNA Corporation, Alexandria, April 2007; *Keyhan*, February 20, 2007, p. 14.

10. U.S. Department of State, *Country Reports on Terrorism 2008*, released April 30, 2009, http://www.state.gov/documents/organization/122599.pdf.

11. UNSC Resolution 1737 (2006), December 23, 2008, http://www.iaea.org/NewsCenter/Focus/IaeaIran/unsc_res1737-2006.pdf. Persons involved in the ballistic missile program: General Hosein Salimi, Commander of the Air Force, IRGC (Pasdaran). Persons involved in both the nuclear and ballistic missile programmes: Major General Yahya Rahim Safavi, Commander, IRGC (Pasdaran).

12. Michael Slackman, "Seizure of Britons Underlines Iran's Political Split," *New York Times*, April 4, 2007, p. 5; Sarah Lyall, "Iran Sets Free 15 Britons Seized at Sea in March," *New York Times*, April 5, 2007.

13. Connell, "The Influence of the Iraq Crisis on Iranian Warfighting Doctrine and Strategy"; Vision of the Islamic Republic of Iran Network, Network 1. 18:34 GMT, March 9, 2005.

14. Frederick W. Kagan, Kimberly Kagan, and Danielle Pletka, "Iranian Influence in the Levant, Iran, and Afghanistan," The American Enterprise Institute, February 2008.

15. Arasli, "Obsolete Weapons, Unconventional Tactics, and Martyrdom Zeal."

16. Haghshenass, "Iran's Asymmetrical Naval Warfare."

17. Connell, "The Influence of the Iraq Crisis on Iranian Warfighting Doctrine and Strategy"; Vision of the Islamic Republic of Iran Network.

18. Iran has said that experts at its Hossein and Sharif universities are working on an "impenetrable intranet communications network." Connell indicates that Iran claims such a system was fielded during the Eqtedar exercises in February 2007. *Baztab*, Web edition, February 20, 2007.

19. "Iran," *Jane's World Armies*.

20. "Iran Enhances Existing Weaponry by Optimizing Shahab-3 Ballistic Missile," *Jane's Missiles and Rockets*, January 20, 2004.

21. Reuters, June 12, 1996, 17:33.

22. Eshkboos Danekar, "Janghaye Gheyre Classic dar Khalij-e Fars" [Unconventional Wars in the Persian Gulf], in the proceedings of an event held at the Political and International Studies Bureau's Persian Gulf Studies Center, April 1988, Tehran (Tehran: Iranian Foreign Ministry, 1989), p. 272. Danekar was an Islamic Republic of Iran Navy captain and naval district commander during the Iran-Iraq War.

23. "A Brief Look at the Unconventional Warfare at Sea" [in Persian], *Faslnameye Tarikhe Jang* [*History of War Quarterly*] 2, no. 6 (Winter 1992) (IRGC War Studies Center).

24. Haghshenass, "Iran's Asymmetrical Naval Warfare."

25. Hossein Alaee, "How the IRGC Navy Was Formed" (Persian interview), in *Iran-Iraq War Strategic Issues* , ed. Madjid Mokhtari (Tehran: IRGC War Studies Center, 2002), p. 136.

26. Haghshenass, "Iran's Asymmetrical Naval Warfare."

27. "Iran Opens Fourth Naval Base in Persian Gulf," *Fars News Agency*, November 18, 2008, http://www.payvand.com/news/08/nov/1182.html.

28. "A New Line of Defence: Iran's Naval Capabilities," *Jane's Defence Weekly*, posted January 26, 2009.

29. Haghshenass, "Iran's Asymmetrical Naval Warfare."

30. "A New Line of Defence: Iran's Naval Capabilities."

31. "Iran Building Naval Bases along Sea of Oman Coast," www.news.cn, October 30, 2008, http://news.xinhuanet.com/english/2008-10/30/content_10281436.htm.

32. "A New Line of Defence: Iran's Naval Capabilities."

33. "Iran Opens Fourth Naval Base in Persian Gulf."

34. "A New Line of Defence: Iran's Naval Capabilities."

35. Haghshenass, "Iran's Asymmetrical Naval Warfare."

36. Ibid.

37. "A New Line of Defence: Iran's Naval Capabilities."

38. Captain Wade F. Wilkenson, U.S. Navy, "A New Underwater Threat," Proceedings, Military.com, October 14, 2008, http://www.military.com/forums/0,15240,177265,00.html.

39. Ibid.

40. Doug Richardson, "Leaked Documents Show Origin of Iran's Hoot Missile," *Jane's Missiles and Rockets*, posted February 3, 2009.

41. "A New Line of Defence: Iran's Naval Capabilities."

42. Jane's Sentinel Security Assessment, *The Gulf States: Armed Forces, Iran*, October 21, 2005.

43. Globalsecurity.org, *Qods (Jerusalem) Force: Iranian Revolutionary Guard Corps (IRGC - Pasdaran-e Inqilab)*, http://www.globalsecurity.org/intell/world/iran/qods.htm.

44. For typical reporting by officers of the IRGC on this issue, see the comments of its acting commander in chief, Brigadier General Seyyed Rahim Safavi, speaking to reporters during

IRGC week (December 20–26, 1995). FBIS-NES-95-250, December 25, 1995, IRNA 1406 GMT.

45. UNSC Resolution 1747, United Nations S/RES/1747 (2007), adopted by the Security Council at its 5647th meeting on March 24, 2007.

* Ammunition and Metallurgy Industries Group (AMIG) (aka Ammunition Industries Group) (AMIG controls 7th of Tir, which is designated under resolution 1737 (2006) for its role in Iran's centrifuge programme. AMIG is in turn owned and controlled by the Defence Industries Organisation (DIO), which is designated under resolution 1737 (2006))

* Esfahan Nuclear Fuel Research and Production Centre (NFRPC) and Esfahan Nuclear Technology Centre (ENTC) (Parts of the Atomic Energy Organisation of Iran's (AEOI) Nuclear Fuel Production and Procurement Company, which is involved in enrichment-related activities. AEOI is designated under resolution 1737 (2006))

* Kavoshyar Company (Subsidiary company of AEOI, which has sought glass fibres, vacuum chamber furnaces and laboratory equipment for Iran's nuclear programme)

* Parchin Chemical Industries (Branch of DIO, which produces ammunition, explosives, as well as solid propellants for rockets and missiles)

* Karaj Nuclear Research Centre (Part of AEOI's research division)

* Novin Energy Company (aka Pars Novin) (Operates within AEOI and has transferred funds on behalf of AEOI to entities associated with Iran's nuclear programme)

* Cruise Missile Industry Group (aka Naval Defence Missile Industry Group)

* (Production and development of cruise missiles. Responsible for naval missiles including cruise missiles)

* Bank Sepah and Bank Sepah International (Bank Sepah provides support for the Aerospace Industries Organisation (AIO) and subordinates, including Shahid Hemmat Industrial Group (SHIG) and Shahid Bagheri Industrial Group (SBIG), both of which were designated under resolution 1737 (2006)

* Sanam Industrial Group (subordinate to AIO, which has purchased equipment on AIO's behalf for the missile programme)

* Ya Mahdi Industries Group (subordinate to AIO, which is involved in international purchases of missile equipment) Iranian Revolutionary Guard Corps entities

46. Chris Hedges, "Islamic-Hard Liners Said to Gain Ground in Iran," *New York Times*, August 3, 1994, http://query.nytimes.com/gst/fullpage.html?res=9C0DE7DE1231 F930A3575BC0A962958260&sec=&spon=&pagewanted=all.

47. See *Time*, March 21, 1994, pp. 50–54, November 11, 1996, pp. 78–82; also see *Washington Post*, November 21, 1993, p. A-1, August 22, 1994, p. A-17; October 28, 1994, p. A-17, November 27, 1994, p. A-30, April 11, 1997, p. A-1, April 14, 1997, p. A-1; *Los Angeles Times*, November 3, 1994, pp. A-1, A-12; *Deutsche Presse-Agentur*, April 17, 1997, 11:02; Reuters, April 16, 1997, BC cycle, April 17, 1997, BC cycle; *The European*, April 17, 1997, p. 13; *Guardian* (Manchester), October 30, 1993, p. 13, August 24, 1996, p. 16 April 16, 1997, p. 10; *New York Times*, April 11, 1997, p. A1; *Associated Press*, April 14, 1997, 18:37. *Jane's Defence Weekly*, June 5, 1996, p. 15; *Agence France-Presse*, April 15, 1997, 15:13; BBC, April 14, 1997, ME/D2892/MED; Deustcher Depeschen via ADN, April 12, 1997, 0743; *Washington Times*, April 11, 1997, p. A22.

48. Riad Kahwaji and Barbara Opall-Rome, "Hizbollah: Iran's Battle Lab," *Defense News*, December 13, 2004, pp. 1, 6.

49. Amir Taheir, "The Mullah's Playground," *Wall Street Journal*, December 7, 2004, p. A10.

50. The estimates of such holdings of rockets are now in the thousands, but the numbers are very uncertain. Dollar estimates of what are significant arms shipments are little more than analytic rubbish, based on cost methods that border on the absurd, but significant shipments are known to have taken place.

51. "On Iran's 'Huge' Military Exercise," *Hyscience*, January 27, 2009, http://www.hyscience.com/archives/2006/01/on_irans_huge_m.php.

52. "Iran Exhibits Locally Made Warplane in War Games," Associated Press article in the *Jerusalem Post*, August 19, 2006.

53. "Iran: Making a Point with Military Exercises," STRATFOR, November 3, 2006, http://www.stratfor.com/iran_making_point_military_exercises.

54. "Iran Navy Begins Military Maneuvers in Gulf," *Iran Focus*, March 23, 2007, http://www.iranfocus.com/en/special-wire/iran-navy-begins-military-manoeuvres-in-gulf.html.

55. "Pentagon Says Ships Harassed by Iran," *Associated Press*, January 7, 2009.

56. "Iran Revolutionary Guards Launch Military Maneuvers in Gulf," *PressTV*, July 7, 2008.

57. "Iran to Launch Military Maneuvers," *PressTV*, September 7, 2008.

58. "Asemane Velayat Military Exercise," *PressTV*, September 15, 2008.

59. "Iran Readies to Fend Off 'Enemy Assaults' on Capital," *Iran Focus*, October 10, 2008, http://www.iranfocus.com/en/index2.php?option=com_content&do_pdf=1&id=16491.

60. "Iranian Air Force Hold Second Stage of Exercise in Tabriz," BBC Monitoring Trans Caucasus Unit, October 18, 2008.

61. "Iran Test-Fires Newly Designed Missile," *Fars News Agency*, November 8, 2008; "Iran Test Fires New Missile near Iraq: State Media," *Reuters*, November 11, 2008.

62. "Iran Tests New Missile from Warship: Reports," *Reuters*, Iran Focus, December 7, 2008, http://www.iranfocus.com/en/iran-general-/iran-tests-new-missile-from-warship-reports-16812.html; "Iran Starts Large-Scale Naval Drills," *Fars News Agency*, December 7, 2008, http://www.imra.org.il/story.php3?id=41642; Iran Early Bird Newsletter, December 3, 2008, http://www.kayhannews.ir/Detail.aspx?cid=1148; multiple Iran Focus Articles.

63. "Iran Sends 'Six Warships' to International Waters," *Agence France-Presse*, March 26, 2009.

64. Arasli, "Obsolete Weapons, Unconventional Tactics, and Martyrdom Zeal."

65. "Iran Starts Large-Scale Naval Drills."

66. "Iran Holds Naval War Games in Strategic Waterway," *International Herald Tribune*, December 2, 2008, http://www.iht.com/articles/reuters/2008/12/02/africa/OUKWD-UK-IRAN-WARGAMES.php.

67. "Iran Starts Large-Scale Naval Drills."

68. Ibid.

69. Iran Early Bird Newsletter, December 3, 2008.

70. "Iran Holds Second Stage of Naval Drills in Gulf of Oman," *Russian News and Information Agency*, December 3, 2008, http://en.rian.ru/world/20081203/118671711.html.

71. "Iran Tests New Missile from Warship: Reports."

72. "Iran Holds Air Exercises, Launches Ships," *UPI*, June 1, 2009; "Iran Commissions Stealth Submarine," *UPI*, June 1, 2009.

73. No one officer or Iranian official can provide a clear perspective on the range of Iranian views. For a good summary of quotes from a variety of Iranian sources, see Arasli, "Obsolete Weapons, Unconventional Tactics, and Martyrdom Zeal," pp. 39–45.

74. All primary sources translated by MEMRI in Special Dispatch Series, No. 1716 article, "New IRGC Commander: Asymmetrical Warfare Is Our Strategy for Dealing with Enemy's Considerable Capabilities; We Aspire to Ballistic Missile Superiority," September 19, 2007, translated statements available at http://www.memri.org/bin/articles.cgi?Page=archives& Area=sd&ID=SP171607; *Rooz* (Iran), September 3, 2007.

75. *Rooz* (Iran), September 3, 2007.

76. *Sharq* (Iran), August 21, 2005; *Baztab* (Iran), September 1, 2007; *Sobh-e Sadeq* (Iran), September 10, 2007.

77. All primary sources translated by MEMRI in Special Dispatch Series, No. 1716 article, "New IRGC Commander: Asymmetrical Warfare Is Our Strategy for Dealing with Enemy's Considerable Capabilities."

78. *Mehr* (Iran), September 3, 2007.

79. *Tehran Times* (Iran), September 5, 2007.

80. *Rooz* (Iran), September 3, 2007.

81. *Aftab* (Iran), January 21, 2005.

82. Much of the information relating to the Quds Force is highly uncertain. See the article from the Jordanian publication Al-Hadath in FBIS-NES-96-108, May 27, 1996, p. 9, and in Al-Sharq Al-Awsat, FBISNES- 96-110, June 5, 1996, pp. 1, 4; A. J. Venter, "Iran Still Exporting Terrorism," *Jane's Intelligence Review*, November 1997, pp. 511–516.

83. David Ignatius, "At the Tip of Iran's Spear," *Washington Post*, June 8, 2008, B07, http://www.washingtonpost.com/wp-dyn/content/article/2008/06/06/AR2008060603152_pf.html; Yaniv Berman, "Iran's al-Quds Octopus Spreads Its Arms," October 28, 2008, http://www.jpost.com/servlet/Satellite?cid=1225036820918&pagename=JPost%2FJPArticle%2FShowFull.

84. Anthony H. Cordesman and Khalid Al-Rodhan, "The Gulf Military Forces in an Era of Asymmetric Wars: Iran," CSIS Burke Chair in Strategy, June 28, 2006.

85. *New York Times*, May 17, 1998, p. A-15; *Washington Times*, May 17, 1998, p. A-13; *Washington Post*, May 21, 1998, p. A-29.

86. Venter, "Iran Still Exporting Terrorism," pp. 511–516.

87. Michael D. Maples, "Threat Assessment," Statement of Michael D. Maples, Director, Defense Intelligence Agency, U.S. Army, before the Committee on Senate Select Intelligence, January 11, 2007.

88. Michael Gordon and Scott Shane, "Iran Supplied Weapons in Iraq," *New York Times*, March 26, 2007.

89. "Tehran Targets Mediterranean," *IntelligenceOnline.com*, March 10, 2006.

90. "Coalition Targets Iranian Influence in Northern Iraq," Defense Department Documents and Publications, January 14, 2007.

91. Stephen Kaufman, "Bush Says Iranian Group "Certainly" Providing Weapons in Iraq," February 14, 2007, http://www.america.gov/st/washfile-english/2007/February/20070214171942esnamfuak0.7028467.html.

92. Bill Gertz, "US General Calls Al Qaeda 'Public Enemy No. 1' in Iraq," *Washington Times*, April 27, 2007, p. 4.

93. The Mujahedin-e Khalq Organization (MEK or MKO) has a wide range of names and cover groups. They include the National Liberation Army of Iran (NLA), People's Mojahedin

of Iran (PMOI), National Council of Resistance (NCR), National Council of Resistance of Iran (NCRI), and Muslim Iranian Student's Society. The United States, which lists the National Council of Resistance of Iran as a terrorist organization, closed the NCRI's Washington office in 2003.

The 2007 edition of the U.S. Department of State "Country Reports on Terrorism," which were released on April 30, 2008, list the MEK as a terrorist organization and describes it as follows (http://www.state.gov/s/ct/rls/crt/2007/103714.htm):

> Mujahadin-e Khalq Organization (MEK) a.k.a. MKO; Mujahadin-e Khalq (Iranian government name for group); Muslim Iranian Students' Society; National Council of Resistance (NCR); Organization of the People's Holy Warriors of Iran; The National Liberation Army of Iran (NLA); The People's Mujahadin Organization of Iran (PMOI); National Council of Resistance of Iran (NCRI); Sazeman-e Mujahadin-e Khalq-e Iran.
>
> Description: The Mujahadin-e Khalq Organization (MEK) advocates the violent overthrow of the Iranian regime and was responsible for the assassination of several U.S. military personnel and civilians in the 1970s. The MEK's armed wing is known as the National Liberation Army of Iran (NLA). In December 2006, the European Court of Justice ruled to overturn the designation of the MEK as a terrorist organization but was not supported by the Council of the European Union (EU).
>
> The MEK emerged in the 1960s as one of the more violent political movements opposed to the Pahlavi dynasty and its close relationship with the United States. MEK ideology has gone through several iterations and blends elements of Marxism, Islam, and feminism. The group has planned and executed terrorist operations against the Iranian regime for nearly three decades from its European and Iraqi bases of operations. Additionally, it has expanded its fundraising base, further developed its paramilitary skills, and aggressively worked to expand its European ranks. In addition to its terrorist credentials, the MEK has also displayed cult-like characteristics.
>
> Upon entry into the group, new members are indoctrinated in MEK ideology and revisionist Iranian history. Members are also required to undertake a vow of "eternal divorce" and participate in weekly "ideological cleansings." Additionally, children are reportedly separated from parents at a young age. MEK leader Maryam Rajavi has established a "cult of personality." She claims to emulate the Prophet Muhammad and is viewed by members as the "Iranian President in exile."
>
> Activities: The group's worldwide campaign against the Iranian government uses propaganda and terrorism to achieve its objectives and has been supported by reprehensible regimes, including that of Saddam Hussein. During the 1970s, the MEK assassinated several U.S. military personnel and U.S. civilians working on defense projects in Tehran and supported the violent takeover in 1979 of the U.S. Embassy in Tehran.
>
> In 1981, MEK leadership attempted to overthrow the newly installed Islamic regime; Iranian security forces subsequently initiated a crackdown on the group. The MEK instigated a bombing campaign, including an attack against the head office of the Islamic Republic Party and the Prime Minister's office, which killed some 70 high-ranking Iranian officials, including Chief Justice Ayatollah Mohammad Beheshti, President Mohammad-Ali Rajaei, and Prime Minister Mohammad-Javad Bahonar. These attacks resulted in a popular uprising against the MEK and an expanded Iranian government crackdown which forced MEK leaders to flee to France. For five years, the MEK continued to wage its terrorist campaign from its Paris headquarters. Expelled by France in

1986, MEK leaders turned to Saddam Hussein's regime for basing, financial support, and training. Near the end of the 1980–1988 Iran-Iraq War, Baghdad armed the MEK with heavy military equipment and deployed thousands of MEK fighters in suicidal, mass wave attacks against Iranian forces.

The MEK's relationship with the former Iraqi regime continued through the 1990s. In 1991, the group reportedly assisted the Iraqi Republican Guard's bloody crackdown on Iraqi Shia and Kurds who rose up against Saddam Hussein's regime. In April 1992, the MEK conducted near-simultaneous attacks on Iranian embassies and installations in 13 countries, demonstrating the group's ability to mount large-scale operations overseas. In April 1999, the MEK targeted key Iranian military officers and assassinated the deputy chief of the Iranian Armed Forces General Staff, Brigadier General Ali Sayyaad Shirazi.

In April 2000, the MEK attempted to assassinate the commander of the Nasr Headquarters, Tehran's interagency board responsible for coordinating policies on Iraq. The pace of anti-Iranian operations increased during "Operation Great Bahman" in February 2000, when the group launched a dozen attacks against Iran. One attack included a mortar attack against a major Iranian leadership complex in Tehran that housed the offices of the Supreme Leader and the President. In 2000 and 2001, the MEK was involved in regular mortar attacks and hit-and-run raids against Iranian military and law enforcement personnel, as well as government buildings near the Iran-Iraq border. Also in 2001, the FBI arrested seven Iranians in the United States who funneled $400,000 to an MEK-affiliated organization in the UAE, which used the funds to purchase weapons. Following an initial Coalition bombardment of the MEK's facilities in Iraq at the outset of Operation Iraqi Freedom, MEK leadership negotiated a cease-fire with Coalition Forces and voluntarily surrendered their heavy-arms to Coalition control. Since 2003, roughly 3,400 MEK members have been encamped at Ashraf in Iraq, under the protection of Coalition Forces.

In 2003, French authorities arrested 160 MEK members at operational bases they believed the MEK was using to coordinate financing and planning for terrorist attacks. Upon the arrest of MEK leader Maryam Rajavi, MEK members took to Paris' streets and engaged in self-immolation. French authorities eventually released Rajavi. Although currently in hiding, Rajavi has made "motivational" appearances via video-satellite to MEK-sponsored conferences across the globe.

According to evidence which became available after the fall of Saddam Hussein, the MEK received millions of dollars in Oil-for-Food program subsidies from Saddam Hussein from 1999 through 2003. In addition to discovering 13 lists of recipients of such vouchers on which the MEK appeared, evidence linking the MEK to the former Iraqi regime includes lists, as well as video footage of Saddam Hussein handing over suitcases of money to known MEK leaders, and video of MEK operatives receiving training from the Iraqi military.

Strength: Estimates place MEK's worldwide membership at between 5,000 and 10,000 members, with large pockets in Paris and other major European capitals. In Iraq, roughly 3,400 MEK members are gathered under Coalition protection at Camp Ashraf, the MEK's main compound north of Baghdad, where they have been treated as "protected persons" consistent with provisions of the Fourth Geneva Convention. This status does not affect the group's members outside of Camp Ashraf or the MEK's designation as a Foreign Terrorist Organization.

As a condition of the 2003 cease-fire agreement, the MEK relinquished more than 2,000 tanks, armored personnel carriers, and heavy artillery. A significant number of MEK personnel have voluntarily left Ashraf, and an additional several hundred individuals have renounced ties to the MEK and been voluntarily repatriated to Iran.

Location/Area of Operation: The MEK maintains its main headquarters in Paris and has concentrations of members across Europe, in addition to the large concentration of MEK located at Camp Ashraf in Iraq. The MEK's global support structure remains in place, with associates and supporters scattered throughout Europe and North America. Operations target Iranian regime elements across the globe, including in Europe and Iran. MEK's political arm, the National Council of Resistance of Iran (NCRI), has a global support network with active lobbying and propaganda efforts in major Western capitals. NCRI also has a well-developed media communications strategy.

External Aid: Before Operation Iraqi Freedom began in 2003, the MEK received all of its military assistance and most of its financial support from Saddam Hussein. The fall of Saddam's regime has led MEK increasingly to rely on front organizations to solicit contributions from expatriate Iranian communities.

According to work by Global Security (http://www.globalsecurity.org/military/world/para/mek.htm), they had a range of bases in Iraq, which were supported by Saddam Hussein's regime. These bases were located at

- Camp Ashraf, the MEK military headquarters, is about 100 kilometers [km] west of the Iranian border and 100 kilometers north of Baghdad near Khalis
- Camp Anzali near the town of Jalawla [Jalula] (120–130 km (70–80 miles) northeast of Baghdad and about 40–60 km (20–35 miles) from the border with Iran)
- Camp Faezeh in Kut
- Camp Habib in Basra
- Camp Homayoun in Al-Amarah
- Camp Bonyad Alavi near the city of Miqdadiyah in Mansourieh [about 65 miles northeast of Baghdad]

These bases were surrendered to V Corps of the U.S. Army on May 10, 2003. Coalition forces took control over some 2,139 tanks, armored personnel carriers, artillery pieces, air-defense artillery pieces, and miscellaneous vehicles formerly in the possession of the MEK forces. The 4th Infantry Division also reported it has destroyed most of the MEK munitions and caches. The voluntary, peaceful resolution of this process by the MEK and the Coalition significantly contributed to the Coalition's mission to establish a safe and secure environment for the people of Iraq. Some 3,400–4,000 MEK forces were disarmed and detained. Those now held at Camp Ashraf are "protected persons" under Article 27 of the Fourth Geneva Convention. This prevented extradition or forced repatriation to Iran as long as the United States maintained control. Their status following the implementation of the U.S.-Iraq Strategic Framework Agreement and the U.S.-Iraq Status of Forces Agreement is unclear.

Also see Holly Fletcher, "Mujahadeen-e-Khalq (MEK) (aka People's Mujahedin of Iran or PMOI)," Backgrounder, Council on Foreign Relations, updated April 18, 2008, http://www.cfr.org/publication/9158/. Her analysis provides a summary list of MEK attacks:

MEK terrorism has declined since late 2001. Incidents linked to the group include:

- the series of mortar attacks and hit-and-run raids during 2000 and 2001 against Iranian government buildings; one of these killed Iran's chief of staff;
- the 2000 mortar attack on President Mohammed Khatami's palace in Tehran;
- the February 2000 "Operation Great Bahman," during which MEK launched twelve attacks against Iran;
- the 1999 assassination of the deputy chief of Iran's armed forces general staff, Ali Sayyad Shirazi;
- the 1998 assassination of the director of Iran's prison system, Asadollah Lajevardi;
- the 1992 near-simultaneous attacks on Iranian embassies and institutions in thirteen countries;
- Saddam Hussein's suppression of the 1991 Iraqi Shiite and Kurdish uprisings;
- the 1981 bombing of the offices of the Islamic Republic Party and of Premier Mohammad-Javad Bahonar, which killed some seventy high-ranking Iranian officials, including President Mohammad-Ali Rajaei and Bahonar;
- the 1979 takeover of the U.S. embassy in Tehran by Iranian revolutionaries;
- the killings of U.S. military personnel and civilians working on defense projects in Tehran in the 1970s.

94. U.S. Department of State, "Iran," *Country Reports on Human Rights Practices*, 2005, http://www.state.gov/g/drl/rls/hrrpt/2005/61688.htm.

95. Dennis C. Blair, Director of National Intelligence, Annual Threat Assessment of the Intelligence Community for the Senate Select Committee on Intelligence, Office of the Director of National Intelligence, February 12, 2009, pp. 9–11.

96. Jane's Sentinel Security Assessment, *The Gulf States: Armed Forces, Iran*, October 21, 2005.

97. Alex Vatanka and Fatemeh Aman, "The Making of an Insurgency in Iran's Baluchistan Province," *Jane's Intelligence Review*, June 1, 2006.

98. Jane's Sentinel Security Assessment, *The Gulf States: Armed Forces, Iran*, October 21, 2005.

99. Connell, "The Influence of the Iraq Crisis on Iranian Warfighting Doctrine and Strategy," p. 4; Vision of the Islamic Republic of Iran Network.

100. BBC Monitoring Middle East, Iran's Guard Commander Comments on Tehran's Missile Power, November 13, 2006.

101. Globalsecurity.org, *Niruyeh Moghavemat Basij Mobilisation Resistance Force*, http://www.globalsecurity.org/intell/world/iran/basij.htm.

102. Jane's Sentinel Security Assessment, *The Gulf States: Armed Forces, Iran*, October 21, 2005.

103. Daniel Byman, Shahram Chubin, Anoushiravan Ehteshami, and Jerrold D. Green, *Iran's Security Policy in the Post-Revolutionary Era* (Washington, DC: RAND, 2006), 32.

104. Globalsecurity.org, *Ministry of Intelligence and Security*, http://www.globalsecurity.org/intell/world/iran/vevak.htm.

105. Jane's Sentinel Security Assessment, *The Gulf States: Armed Forces, Iran*, October 21, 2005.

106. Congressional Research Service, *Country Profile: Iran*, March 2006.

107. Globalsecurity.org, *Ansar-i Hizbullah Followers of the Party of God*, http://www .globalsecurity.org/intell/world/iran/ansar.htm.

108. Richard Beeston, "Two Years On, Iran Is the Only Clear Winner of War on Saddam," *London Times*, September 23, 2005.

109. Al-Siyassa (Kuwait), December 14, 2006, from Kagan, Kagan, and Pletka, "Iranian Influence in the Levant, Iraq, and Afghanistan."

110. Eitan Azani, "Hezbollah's Global Reach" (testimony, House Committee on International Relations Subcommittee on International Terrorism and Nonproliferation, September 28, 2006), 'www.ictconference.org/var/119/15436-Hezbollah's%20Global%20 Reach.pdf.

111. Intelligence and Terrorism Information Center (ITIC), "In an Interview Granted to an Iranian TV Channel, Sheikh Naim Qassem, Hassan Nasrallah's Deputy, Stresses That Hezbollah's Policy of Terrorist Operations against Israel (Including Suicide Bombings and Rocket Fire) Requires Jurisprudent Permission of the Iranian Leadership," April 29, 2007, www.terrorisminfo.org.il/malam_multimedia/English/eng_n/pdf/hezbollah_e0407.pdf.

112. The Israel Project, "Hezbollah, Hamas Rearm as Israel Works to Resume Peace Process," press release, February 22, 2007, https://www.kintera.org/site/apps/nlnet/content2. aspx?c=hsJPK0PIJpH&b=689705&t=3601455.

113. ITIC, "Using the Quds Force of the Revolutionary Guards as the Main Tool to Export the Revolution beyond the Borders of Iran," April 2, 2007, http://www.terrorism-info. org.il/malam_multimedia/English/eng_n/html/iran_e0307.htm.

114. *Al-Siyassa* (Kuwait), August 17, 2004.

115. MEMRI, "Iran and the Recent Escalation on Israel's Borders: Reaction in Iran, Lebanon, and Syria," Special Dispatch Series no. 1207, July 17, 2006, www.memri.org/bin/ articles.cgi?Page=archives&Area=sd&ID=SP120706.

116. Ali Nouri Zadeh, "130 Officers from the Iranian Revolutionary Guard Corps and Quds Force Aid Hezbollah: 11,500 Missiles and Rocket-Propelled Grenades Sent from Tehran to Hezbollah," *Asharq Al-Awsat*, July 16, 2006, www.aawsat.com/details.asp?section=4& issue=10092&article=373305&search=C802 &state=true; "New Iranian Capability Is Troublesome," *Washington Times*, February 19, 2009; Katzman, "Iran: U.S. Concerns and Policy Responses."

117. "Israel's Peres Says Iran Arming Hizbollah." *Reuters*, February 4, 2002.

118. Kenneth Katzman, "Iran: U.S. Concerns and Policy Responses," Congressional Research Service Report for Congress RL32048, April 14, 2009, http://www.fas.org/sgp/crs/ mideast/RL32048.pdf.

119. "Iran Takes 'Direct Command' of Hizballah War against Israel July 20," *DEBKAfile*, July 21, 2006.

120. Robin Hughes, "Iran Answers Hizbullah Call for SAM Systems," *Jane's Defence Weekly*, August 7, 2006, www.janes.com/defence/news/jdw/jdw060807_1_n.shtml.

121. Sebastian Rotella, "In Lebanon, Hezbollah Arms Stockpile Bigger, Deadlier." *Los Angeles Times*, May 4, 2008.

122. Anthony Shadid, "Armed with Iran's Millions, Fighters Turn to Rebuilding." *Washington Post*, August 16, 2006.

123. Ali Nouri Zadeh, "Iranian Officer: Hezbollah Has Commando Naval Unit," *Asharq Al-Awsat*, July 29, 2006, http://www.aawsat.com/english/news.asp?section=1&id=5801.

124. Katzman, "Iran: U.S. Concerns and Policy Responses"; Hamas Leader Praises Iran's Help in Gaza "Victory," *CNN.com*, February 1, 2009.

125. Katzman, "Iran: U.S. Concerns and Policy Responses"; Alon Ben-David, "Iranian Influence Looms as Fragile Gaza Ceasefire Holds," *Jane's Defence Weekly*, January 22, 2009; Mike Shuster, "Iranian Support for Hamas Running High Post-Gaza," *NPR*, February 4, 2009, http://www.npr.org/templates/rundowns/rundown.php?prgId=3.

126. Michael Slackman, "Egypt Accuses Hezbollah of Plotting Attacks in Sinai and Arms Smuggling to Gaza," *New York Times*, April 14, 2009; Katzman, "Iran: U.S. Concerns and Policy Responses."

127. Transcript from DoD News Briefing—Secretary Rumsfeld and General Myers, March 28, 2003, http://www.defenselink.mil/transcripts/transcript.aspx?transcriptid=2180.

128. Abbas William Samii, "The Nearest and Dearest Enemy: Iran after the Iraq War," *The Middle East Review of International Affairs* (MERIA), vol. 9, no. 3, article 3, September 2005, http://meria.idc.ac.il/journal/2005/issue3/jv9no3a3.html#_ednref70.

129. Michael Knights, "Iran's Ongoing Proxy War in Iraq," The Washington Institute for Near East Policy PolicyWatch #1492, March 16, 2009.

130. Ali Alfoneh, "Iran's Suicide Brigades: Terrorism Resurgent," *Middle East Quarterly* (Winter 2007), pp. 37–44.

131. Intelligence Iran Proxy Groups, Headquarters for Tribute to the Martyrs of the Global Islamic Movement, *Globalsecurity.org*, http://www.globalsecurity.org/intell/world/iran/proxy-groups.htm (accessed November 4, 2008).

132. Ibid.

133. Robin Wright and Peter Baker, "Iraq, Jordan See Threat to Election from Iran," *Washington Post*, December 8, 2004, http://www.washingtonpost.com/wp-dyn/articles/A43980-2004Dec7.html.

134. Ibid.

135. ABCTV News, Baghdad E-mail, September 20, 2005.

136. Robin Hughes, "Rumsfeld Alleges IRGC Al Qods Infiltrating Iraq," *Jane's Defence Weekly*, March 15, 2006.

137. Nawaf Obaid, "Meeting the Challenge of a Fragmented Iraq: A Saudi Perspective," CSIS, April 6, 2006, http://www.csis.org/media/csis/pubs/060406_iraqsaudi.pdf.

138. Katzman, "Iran: U.S. Concerns and Policy Responses."

139. Knights, "Iran's Ongoing Proxy War in Iraq."

140. Ibid.

141. Ibid.

142. Katzman, "Iran: U.S. Concerns and Policy Responses."

143. Knights, "Iran's Ongoing Proxy War in Iraq."

144. "U.S. Forces in Iraq Detain, Kill Iran-Backed Suspects," *Iran Focus*, Reuters, December 4, 2008, http://www.chinadaily.com.cn/world/2008-12/03/content_7267715.htm.

145. Henry Meyer, "Iran Is Helping Taliban in Afghanistan, Petraeus Says," *Bloomberg*, February 15, 2009.

146. Kagan, Kagan, and Pletka, "Iranian Influence in the Levant, Iran, and Afghanistan"; Kenneth Katzman, "Afghanistan: Post-War Governance, Security, and U.S. Policy," Congressional Research Service, updated January 14, 2008, www.fas. org/sgp/crs/row/RL30588.pdf; Alastair Leithead, "Iranian Influence in Afghanistan," *BBC News*, June 11, 2007; "Iran Steps Up Drive to Expel Afghan Refugees," *Agence France-Presse*, April 30, 2007; Peter Baker, "Bush Urges Karzai to Be More Wary of Iran," *Washington Post*, August 7, 2007.

147. Michael R. Gordon, "U.S. Says Iranian Arms Seized in Afghanistan," *New York Times*, April 17, 2007.

148. "Iran-Made Weapons Recovered in Operations: ISAF," *Pajhwok Afghan News*, May 9, 2007.

149. Brigadier General Joseph Votel, Department of Defense news briefing, Bagram, Afghanistan, April 18, 2007, www.defenselink.mil/transcripts/transcript.aspx?transcriptid=3934.

150. General Daniel McNeill, Department of Defense news briefing, Afghanistan, June 5, 2007, www.defenselink.mil/transcripts/transcript.aspx?transcriptid=3980.

151. "Iran Arming Taliban, U.S. Claims," *CNN.com*, June 13, 2007.

152. Robert Gates, media availability, Ramstein Air Force Base, Germany, June 13, 2007, www.defenselink.mil/transcripts/transcript.aspx?transcriptid=3987.

153. "Taliban Being Trained on Iranian Soil: MPs," *Pajhwok Afghan News*, July 21, 2007.

154. Kagan, Kagan, and Pletka, "Iranian Influence in the Levant, Iran, and Afghanistan"; Katzman, "Afghanistan: Post-War Governance, Security, and U.S. Policy"; Leithead, "Iranian Influence in Afghanistan"; "Iran Steps Up Drive to Expel Afghan Refugees"; Baker, "Bush Urges Karzai to Be More Wary of Iran"; Brigadier General Joseph Votel, Department of Defense news briefing, Bagram, Afghanistan; "Taliban Being Trained on Iranian Soil: MPs"; Robert Gates, media availability, Ramstein Air Force Base; General Daniel McNeill, Department of Defense news briefing, Afghanistan; "Iran Arming Taliban, U.S. Claims"; "Armed Men Crossed into Afghanistan from Iran: Police," *Indo-Asian News Service*, June 19, 2007; "Iran Accused of Training Taliban to Fight America," *Gulf Times*, July 21, 2007; "100 Iran-Made Bombs Seized, Claim Afghan Officials," *Pajhwok Afghan News*, August 14, 2007; "227 Civilians Killed in IED Blasts in 9 Months: Bashari," *Pajhwok Afghan News*, September 5, 2007; "Dumps of Iranian, Russian and Chinese Arms Found in Herat," *Pajhwok Afghan News*, September 6, 2007; Katzman, "Iran: U.S. Concerns and Policy Responses"; Bill Varner, "Iran Building Influence in Afghanistan," *Seattle Times*, July 19, 2008, http://seattletimes.nwsource.com/html/nationworld/2008060747_iranafghan19.html; Artie McConnell, "Iranian Conservatives Seek to Influence Developments in Afghanistan," February 14, 2002, http://www.eurasianet.org/departments/insight/articles/eav021402.shtml; David Rohde, "Iran Is Seeking More Influence in Afghanistan," *New York Times*, December 27, 2006, http://www.nytimes.com/2006/12/27/world/asia/27afghan.ready.html; Anne Mulrine, "Sphere of Influence," *U.S. News & World Report*, June 17, 2007, http://www.usnews.com/usnews/news/articles/070617/25afghan.htm; Brian Bennett, "Iran Raises the Heat in Afghanistan," *Time*, February 22, 2008, http://www.time.com/time/world/article/0,8599,1716579,00.html; NPR, "Afghan President Karzai Declares Iran Helper," August 7, 2007, http://www.npr.org/templates/story/story.php?storyId=12555916.

155. Meyer, "Iran Is helping Taliban in Afghanistan, Petraeus Says."

156. "A New Line of Defence: Iran's Naval Capabilities."

CHAPTER 4

1. Iran's military services include a wide range of different elements. The CIA reports that they include the Islamic Republic of Iran Regular Forces (Artesh): Ground Forces, Navy, Air Force of the Military of the Islamic Republic of Iran (Niru-ye Hava'i-ye Artesh-e Jomhuri-ye Eslami-ye Iran; includes air defense); Islamic Revolutionary Guard Corps (Sepah-e Pasdaran-e Enqelab-e Eslami, IRGC): Ground Forces, Navy, Air Force, Qods Force (special operations), and Basij Force (Popular Mobilization Army); Law Enforcement Forces (2008). Source: CIA, "Iran," *World Factbook, 2008.*

2. Stephen Kaufman, "Bush Says Iranian group Certainly Providing Weapons in Iraq, February 14, 2007, http://usinfo.state.gov/xarchives/display.html?p=washfile-english& y=2007&m=February&x=20070214171942esnamfuak0.7028467.

3. "Iran's Missile Development: Further Tests Needed to Cement Recent Advances," "Sizing up the *Sajjil*," The International Institute for Strategic Studies (IISS), Strategic Comments 15, no. 1 (February 2009), http://www.iiss.org/publications/strategic-comments/past-issues/ volume-15-2009/volume-15-issue-1/irans-missile-development/.

4. BBC Monitoring Middle East, Iran's Guard commander comments on Tehran's missile power, November 13, 2006.

5. "Iran Enhances Existing Weaponry by Optimizing Shahab-3 Ballistic Missile," *Jane's Missiles and Rockets*, January 20, 2004.

6. Iran has Built Underground Missile Factories," *Jane's Missiles and Rockets*, December 8, 2005.

7. Federation of American Scientists, *Iran*, http://www.fas.org/nuke/guide/iran/missile/ overview.html (accessed March 5, 2007).

8. Uzi Rubin, *The Global Reach of Iran's Ballistic Missiles*, Institute for National Security Studies, Tel Aviv, November 2006, pp. 21–22.

9. Kenneth Katzman, Congressional Research Service.

10. Rubin, *The Global Reach of Iran's Ballistic Missiles*, p. 7.

11. Alon Ben-David, "Iran Pushes Space Launch Limits with Research Rocket Test." *Jane's Defence Weekly*, March 7, 2007.

12. Ibid. "Iran appears to be well on the way to developing orbital launch capabilities, although they have not yet achieved them," Uzi Rubin, former director of Israel's Missile Defence Organisation, told *Jane's*. "Once they achieve satellite launch capabilities, it would signal their ability to produce an intercontinental ballistic missile, which could reach Europe and beyond."

13. Rubin, *The Global Reach of Iran's Ballistic Missiles*.

14. GlobalSecurity.org, "Iran: Missiles," http://www.globalsecurity.org/wmd/world/iran/ missile.htm; Federation of American Scientists, *Iran*.

15. Hughes, "Iran's Ballistic Missile Developments—Long-Range Ambitions," pp. 22–27.

16. Federation of American Scientists, "SCUD-B/Shahab-1," December 1, 2005, http:// www.fas.org/nuke/guide/iran/missile/shahab-1.htm.

17. Kenneth Katzman, *Commission to Assess the Ballistic Missile Threat to the United States*, 1998, http://www.globalsecurity.org/wmd/library/report/1998/rumsfeld/pt2_katz.htm.

18. Hughes, "Iran's Ballistic Missile Developments—Long-Range Ambitions."

19. Katzman, *Commission to Assess the Ballistic Missile Threat to the United States*.

20. Hughes, "Iran's Ballistic Missile Developments—Long-Range Ambitions."

21. Katzman, *Commission to Assess the Ballistic Missile Threat to the United States*; Hughes, "Iran's Ballistic Missile Developments—Long-Range Ambitions."

22. Katzman, *Commission to Assess the Ballistic Missile Threat to the United States*.

23. Missilethreat.com, The Claremont Institute, October 1, 2008, http://www .missilethreat.com/missilesoftheworld/id.180/missile_detail.asp.

24. Katzman, *Commission to Assess the Ballistic Missile Threat to the United States*.

25. Paul Beaver, "Iran's Shahab-3 IRBM 'Ready for Production,'" *Jane's Missiles and Rockets*, June 1, 1998.

26. Kenneth R. Timmerman, *Countdown to Crisis* (New York: Crown Publishing Group, 2005), 315–318.

27. Bill Gertz, "Iran's Regional Powerhouse," *Air Force Magazine Online,* June 1996, http://www.afa.org/magazine/June1996/0696iran.asp.

28. Hughes, "Iran's Ballistic Missile Developments—Long-Range Ambitions," pp. 22–27.

29. "Country Comparisons—Commitments, Force Levels and Economics," *The Military Balance,* 108:1 (2008), 419–450.

30. Timmerman, *Countdown to Crisis,* 315–318.

31. "Flashpoints: Iran," *Jane's Defence Weekly,* March 4, 1995, p. 18.

32. Anthony H. Cordesman, *Iran and Nuclear Weapons* (Washington, DC: Center for Strategic and International Studies, 2000), p. 36.

33. The CIA reports that North Korea has transferred at least four Scud TELs to Iran. The TELs were transferred in late 1994 and can launch Scud-B and Scud-C missiles. Tony Capaccio, *Defense Week,* May 1, 1995, pp. 1, 14.

34. "Shahab-2," Federation of American Scientists, December 1, 2005, http://www.fas.org/nuke/guide/iran/missile/shahab-2.htm.

35. GlobalSecurity.org, "Iran: Missiles," http://www.globalsecurity.org/wmd/world/iran/missile.htm.

36. Katzman, *Commission to Assess the Ballistic Missile Threat to the United States.*

37. Ibid.

38. Missilethreat.com, The Claremont Institute.

39. BBC Monitoring Middle East, Iran's Guard commander comments on Tehran's missile power; Ed Blanche, "Iran Stages Display of Missile Firepower," *Jane's Missiles and Rockets,* January 1, 2007.

40. Uzi Rubin: *The Global Reach of Iran's Ballistic Missiles,* Institute for National Security Studies, Tel Aviv, November 2006, p. 37.

41. Allegations of such cooperation echo in recent reports emerging out of Israel claiming that Syria was planning to supply Iran with spent nuclear fuel for reprocessing into weapons-grade plutonium. Ian Black, "Syria Planned to Supply Iran with Nuclear Fuel, Israel Says," *Guardian* (Manchester), June 25, 2008, http://www.guardian.co.uk/world/2008/jun/25/syria.iran.

42. "Iran Says Shahab-3 Missile Entirely Iranian, Production Ongoing," *Agence France-Presse,* May 5, 2005.

43. Katzman, *Commission to Assess the Ballistic Missile Threat to the United States.*

44. Ibid.

45. "Iran Tests Shahab-3 Ballistic Missile," *Jane's Missiles and Rockets,* August 1, 1998.

46. Global Security.org, "Shabab-3/Zelzal 3," www.globalsecurity.org/wmd/world/iran/shahab-3.htm.

47. David Isby, "Shahab-3 Enters Production," *Jane's Missiles and Rockets,* November 26, 2001.

48. Ed Blanche, "Shahab-3 Ready for Service, Says Iran," *Jane's Missiles and Rockets,* July 23, 2003.

49. Rubin, *The Global Reach of Iran's Ballistic Missiles,* p. 24.

50. Federation of American Scientists, *Iran.*

51. GlobalSecurity.org, "Shahab-3/Zelzal 3," www.globalsecurity.org/wmd/world/iran/shahab-3.htm.

52. Hughes, "Iran's Ballistic Missile Developments—Long-Range Ambitions," pp. 22–27.

53. Farhad Pouladi, "Iran Vows to Continue Nuclear Drive at All Costs," *Agence France-Presse,* September 22, 2004.

54. "Iran 'Tests New Missile Engine,'" *BBC News*, May 31, 2005, http://news.bbc.co.uk/2/hi/middle_east/4596295.stm.

55. Hughes, "Iran's Ballistic Missile Developments—Long-Range Ambitions," pp. 22–27.

56. BBC Monitoring Middle East, Iran's Guard commander comments on Tehran's missile power; Ed Blanche, "Iran Stages Display of Missile Firepower."

57. "Iran's 'Great Prophet' Military Drill," *Jane's Intelligence Digest*, November 17, 2006.

58. "Iran Develops Remote-Controlled Launch System for Shahab-3 Missiles," *Jerusalem Post*, August 22, 2007, http://www.nti.org/e_research/profiles/Iran/Missile/1788_6350.html.

59. Alan Cowell, "Iran Reports Missile Test, Drawing Rebuke," *International Herald Tribune*, July 9, 2008.

60. "Report: Iran Sends Missile Test Warning," *BBC News*, July 10, 2008; Alex Vatanka, "Iran Launches Dual-Purpose Missiles," *Jane's Intelligence Review*, July 18, 2008; Lauren Gelfand, "Tensions Rise in the Wake of Iranian Missile Tests," *Jane's Defence Weekly*, July 11, 2008.

61. Joshua Mitnick and Bill Gertz, "Tehran's Missile Tests Fail to Impress U.S., Israel; Revolutionary Guard Corps Flexes Muscles," *Washington Times*, July 10, 2008.

62. Cris Smyth, "Times—Picture: Iran 'Fakes' Missile Launch after Misfire," International Institute for Strategic Studies, July 10, 2008.

63. Ed Blanche and Doug Richardson, "Iran Gives Details of Latest Shabab-3 Missile," *Jane's Missiles and Rockets*, February 1, 2007.

64. "Iran Ministry Confirms Satellite Carrier Rocket," *BBC News*, August 17, 2008; Lauren Gelfand and Alon Ben-David, "Iranian Two-Stage SLV Passes Test Launch," *Jane's Defence Weekly*, August 20, 2008; Doug Richardson, "Safir Launch Paved Way for Placing Iranian Satellite in Space," *Jane's Missiles and Rockets*, September 1, 2008.

65. "Envoy Says Linking Iran Nuclear Activities and Missile Program Baseless," *BBC Monitoring Middle East*, September 17, 2008; "Iran Says IAEA Photos Are Forgeries," *BBC Monitoring Middle East*, September 17, 2008; "Iran not to Take Single Step beyond Commitments —Soltaniyeh," *Islamic Republic News Agency*, September 18, 2008.

66. For further details on the history and nature of the Shahab and Iran's programs, see Andrew Feickert, Missile Survey: Ballistic and Cruise Missiles of Selected Foreign Countries, Congressional Research Service, RL30427, (regularly updated); the work of Kenneth Katzman, also of the Congressional Research Service; the "Missile Overview" section of the Iran Profile of the NTI (http://www.nti.org/e_research/profiles/Iran/Missiles/); and the work of GlobalSecurity.org, including http://www.globalsecurity.org/wmd/world/iran/shahab-3.htm.

67. Ed Blanche, "Iran Claims Shahab-3 Range Now 2,000km," *Jane's Missiles and Rockets*, November 1, 2004.

68. "Iran Confirms Test of Missile That Is Able to Hit Israel," *New York Times*, July 8, 2003.

69. "Iran Boasts Shahab-3 is in Mass Production," *Jane's Missiles and Rockets*, November 19, 2004.

70. "Iran Threatens to Abandon the NPT," *Jane's Islamic Affairs Analyst*, September 29, 2004.

71. Douglas Jehl, "Iran Reportedly Hides Work on a Long-Range Missile," *New York Times*, December 2, 2004.

72. GlobalSecurity.org, "Iran: Missiles Development," http://www.globalsecurity.org/wmd/world/iran/missile-development.htm.

73. See the work of Dr. Robert H. Schmucker, "The Shahab Missile and Iran's Delivery System Capabilities," briefing to the James Shasha Institute conference on a nuclear Iran,

May 30–June 2, 2005; and "Iran and Its Regional Environment," Schmucker Technologies, Pease Research Institute Frankfurt, March 27, 2006, www.hsfk.de and http://www.hsfk.de/static.php?id=3929&language=de.

74. IISS, Iran's Strategic Weapons Programs: A Net Assessment, IISS Strategic Dossier, 2005, p. 102.

75. Federation of American Scientists, "Shahab-3," December 1, 2005, http://www.fas.org/nuke/guide/iran/missile/shahab-3.htm.

76. See the work of Schmucker, "The Shahab Missile and Iran's Delivery System Capabilities"; and "Iran and Its Regional Environment."

77. Blanche and Richardson, "Iran Gives Details of Latest Shabab-3 Missile."

78. There is a radical difference in the performance of proven systems, where actual field performance can be measured, and estimates based on engineering theory. With a proven system, the distribution of the impact of warheads relative to the target tends to be "bivariate normally distributed" relative to the aim point. Most are most reasonably close, and progressively fewer and fewer hit farther away, with only a few missing by long distances.

As an entry in Wikipedia notes, "One component of the bivariate normal will represent range errors and the other azimuth errors. Unless the munition is arriving exactly vertically downwards the standard deviation of range errors is usually larger than the standard deviation of azimuth errors, and the resulting confidence region is elliptical. Generally, the munition will not be exactly on target, i.e. the mean vector will not be (0,0). This is referred to as bias. The mean error squared (MSE) will be the sum of the variance of the range error plus the variance of the azimuth error plus the covariance of the range error with the azimuth error plus the square of the bias. Thus the MSE results from pooling all these sources of error. The square root of the MSE is the circular error probable, commonly abbreviated to CEP. Geometrically, it corresponds to radius of a circle within which 50% of rounds will land."

None of this has proven true, however, of estimates made in the design stage or with very limited tests. The actual hit distribution can be much farther away from the aim point and most or all missiles can fall outside the theoretical CEP.

It should also be noted that the concept of CEP is only strictly meaningful if misses are roughly normally distributed. This is generally not true for precision-guided munitions. As the Wikipedia entry also states, "Generally, if CEP is n meters, 50% of rounds land within n meters of the target, 43% between n and 2n, and 7% between 2n and 3n meters. If misses were exactly normally distributed as in this theory, then the proportion of rounds that land farther than three times the CEP from the target is less than 0.2%. With precision-guided munitions, the number of 'close misses' is higher."

79. See note 88, Chapter 4.

80. Schmucker, "Iran and Its Regional Environment."

81. Sonni Efron, Tyler Marshall, and Bob Drogin, "Powell's Talk of Arms Has Fallout," Los Angeles Times, November 19, 2004.

82. Carla Anne Robbins, "Briefing Iranian Missile to Nuclear Agency," Wall Street Journal, July 27, 2005, p. 3.

83. Dafna Linzer, "Strong Leads and Dead Ends in Nuclear Case against Iran," Washington Post, February 8, 2006, p. A01.

84. Hughes, "Iran's Ballistic Missile Developments—Long-Range Ambitions."

85. Ibid.

86. Federation of American Scientists, "Shahab-3D," December 1, 2005, http://www.fas.org/nuke/guide/iran/missile/shahab-3d.htm.

87. Doug Richardson, "Iran Is Developing an IRBM, Claims Resistance Group," *Jane's Rockets and Missiles*, December 14, 2004.

88. Hughes, "Iran's Ballistic Missile Developments—Long-Range Ambitions," pp. 22–27.

89. Ibid.

90. Rubin. *The Global Reach of Iran's Ballistic Missiles*, p. 25.

91. Duncan Lennox, ed., *Jane's Strategic Weapons Systems 42* (Surrey: Jane's Information Group, January 2005), 102–103.

92. GlobalSecurity.org, "Iran: Missiles."

93. "Iran Moves Its Shabab-3 Units," *Jane's Missiles and Rockets*, April 1, 2006.

94. IISS, "Iran," *The Military Balance, 2008*.

95. Dr. William R. Graham, Chairman, Commission to Assess the Threat to the United States from Electromagnetic Pulse (EMP) Attack, statement before the House Armed Services Committee, July 10, 2008, www.empcommission.org/docs/GRAHAMtestimony 10JULY2008.pdf.

96. "Shahab Break-Ups Suggest Possible EMP Trial," *Jane's Missiles and Rockets*, May 1, 2005.

97. Dr. William R. Graham, statement before the House Armed Services Committee.

98. Colin Clark, "Iran Joins Space Club; Why US Expresses 'Great Concern,'" posted on DoD Buzz, February 3, 2009, http://www.dodbuzz.com/category/homeland-security/.

99. Officials in Iran have also reported that in March 2006, they successfully tested their "Fajr-3" long-range missile, which they claim has a range of 2,000 miles, and which is invisible to radar. However, other intelligence sources reportedly argue that the Fajr-3 is merely an upgraded artillery shell with a very short range. "Iran Claims Test of Fajr-3 Missile 'Invisible' to Radar, Interceptors," April 3, 2006, *MissileThreat.com*, http://www.missilethreat.com/news/200604030826.html.

100. "Shabab-3/4," *Jane's Strategic Weapon Systems*, July 18, 2007.

101. Douglas Jehl, "Iran Is Said to Work on New Missile," *International Herald Tribune*, December 2, 2004, p. 7.

102. Federation of American Scientists, "Shahab-3D," December 1, 2005, http://www.fas.org/nuke/guide/iran/missile/shahab-3d.htm.

103. GlobalSecurity.org, "Iran: Missiles Development."

104. Federation of American Scientists, "Shahab-3D."

105. Ibid.

106. IISS, "Iran's Strategic Weapons Programs: A Net Assessment," IISS Strategic Dossier, 2005, p. 102.

107. "Iran Announces Rocket Launch," *International Herald Tribune*, February 25, 2007.

108. "Iran Displays Qadr-1 Missile at Military Exercise," *Fars News Agency*, September 22, 2007; "Iran Presents Ghadr—A 'New' Ballistic Missile," *Jane's Defence Weekly*, October 3, 2007.

109. "Iran Launches Rocket to Commemorate New Space Center," *New York Times*, February 5, 2008; Joseph Bermudez, "Iran Inaugurates Space Terminal and Launches Research Rocket," *Jane's Defence Weekly*, February 13, 2008; "Smoke and Mirrors—Analyzing the Iranian Missile Test," *Jane's Intelligence Review*, March 14, 2008.

110. "Iran Ministry Confirms Satellite Carrier Rocket," *BBC News*, August 17, 2008; Lauren Gelfand and Alon Ben-David, "Iranian Two-Stage SLV Passes Test Launch," *Jane's Defence Weekly*, August 20 2008; Doug Richardson, "Safir Launch Paved Way for Placing Iranian Satellite in Space," *Jane's Missiles and Rockets*, September 1, 2008.

111. "Iran Launches First Indigenous Satellite," *Agence France-Presse*, February 3, 2009, http://www.google.com/hostednews/afp/article/ALeqM5j2zKTDe8t9Hd8per7 Mc3yUYkAKAQ.

112. Richard Fisher Jr., "China's Alliance with Iran Grows Contrary to U.S. Hopes," http://www.strategycenter.net/research/pubID.109/pub_detail.asp, March 5, 2007.

113. Andrew Koch, "Tehran Altering Ballistic Missile,"*Jane's Defence Weekly*, December 8, 2004.

114. Doug Richardson, "Iran Is Developing an IRBM, Claims Resistance Group," *Jane's Missiles and Rockets*, January 1, 2005.

115. "Iran Tests Shahab-3 Motor," *Jane's Missiles and Rockets*, June 9, 2005.

116. Robin Hughes, "Iranian Resistance Group Alleges Tehran Is Developing New Medium Range Missile," *Jane's Defence Weekly*, March 22, 2006.

117. "Ashura," *Jane's Strategic Weapon Systems*, July 21, 2008.

118. Schmucker, "Iran and Its Regional Environment"; Hughes, Iran's Ballistic Missile Developments—Long-Range Ambitions."

119. Iranian military parade photographs of the FARS News Agency of September 21, 2008, reported by Charles P. Vick, "The Latest in North Korean & Iran Ballistic Missile & Space Booster Developments," *GlobalSecurity.org*, October 10, 2008, http://www.globalsecurity.org/space/world/iran/missile-developments.htm.

120. Hughes, Iran's Ballistic Missile Developments—Long-Range Ambitions," pp. 22–27.

121. Federation of American Scientists, *Iran*.

122. Federation of American Scientists, "Shahab-4," December 1, 2005, http://www.fas.org/nuke/guide/iran/missile/shahab-4.htm.

123. Doug Richardson, "Iran Is Developing an IRBM, Claims Resistance Group," *Jane's Rockets and Missiles*, December 14, 2004.

124. Federation of American Scientists, "Shahab-4."

125. Doug Richardson, "Iran Is Developing an IRBM, Claims Resistance Group," *Jane's Missiles and Rockets*, January 1, 2005.

126. Rubin, *The Global Reach of Iran's Ballistic Missiles*, p. 7.

127. Associated Press, "Iran: Russia Says New Rocket Raises Nuclear 'Suspicions,'" *New York Times*, http://www.nytimes.com/2008/02/07/world/worldspecial/07briefs-ROCKET.html?ref=world (accessed February 7, 2008).

128. "Western Intelligence Confirms Iranian Missile Developments—German Report," *BCC Monitoring International Report*, February 6, 2006, available through Lexus Nexus.

129. Lennox, ed., *Jane's Strategic Weapons Systems 46* , pp. 71–73.

130. GlobalSecurity.org, "Shahab-4," http://www.globalsecurity.org/wmd/world/iran/shahab-4.htm.

131. Hughes, "Iran's Ballistic Missile Developments—Long-Range Ambitions."

132. Federation of American Scientists, "Shahab-5," December 1, 2005, http://www.fas.org/nuke/guide/iran/missile/shahab-5.htm.

133. Federation of American Scientists, "Shahab-4."

134. Associated Press, "Iran: Russia Says New Rocket Raises Nuclear 'Suspicions.'"

135. Missilethreat.com, The Claremont Institute, October 1, 2008, http://www.missilethreat.com/missilesoftheworld/id.180/missile_detail.asp.

136. Anthony Cordesman and Martin Keliber, *Iran's Military Forces and Warfighting Capabilities: The Threat in the Northern Gulf* (Westport, CT: Praeger Security International, 2007), http://0-psi.praeger.com/.

137. Rubin, *The Global Reach of Iran's Ballistic Missiles*, p. 39.

138. Federation of American Scientists, *Iran*.

139. Rubin, *The Global Reach of Iran's Ballistic Missiles*, p. 7.

140. Nazila Fathi, "Iran Says It Launched Suborbital Rocket into Space, with Eye toward Lifting Satellites," *New York Times*, February 26, 2007.

141. Agence France-Presse, "Iran Launches First Indigenous Satellite," February 3, 2009, http://www.google.com/hostednews/afp/article/ALeqM5j2zKTDe8t9Hd8per7 Mc3yUYkAKAQ.

142. STRATFOR, "Iran: The Potential for a Satellite Launch," January 26, 2007.

143. "Iran Converts Missile into Sat Launch Vehicle," *Aerospace Daily & Defense Report*, January 29, 2007.

144. Ibid.

145. "Iran Says Space Program Poses No Threat to Peace," *Ria Novosti*, February 2, 2008.

146. William J. Broad, "Iran Reports Test of Craft Able to Carry a Satellite," *New York Times*, August 17, 2008, http://www.nytimes.com/2008/08/18/world/middleeast/18 iran.html.

147. Charles P. Vick, "Booster Orbital Launch Attempt," *GlobalSecurity.org*, August 19–28, 2008, http://www.globalsecurity.org/space/world/iran/orbital-attempt02_finally.htm.

148. Associated Press, "Iran to Launch Satellite Carrier Rocket to Space," September 25, 2008, http://washingtontimes.com/news/2008/sep/25/iran-to-launch-satellite-carrier-rocket-to-spac-1/.

149. Agence France-Presse, "Iran Launches First Indigenous Satellite."

150. "Space Launch Shows Iranian Missile Threat, Analysts Say," *Global Security Newswire (GSN)*, February 4, 2009, http://gsn.nti.org/gsn/nw_20090204_6997.php.

151. Agence France-Presse, "Iran's Satellite Spells Potential ICBM Threat: Experts," February 3, 2009, http://www.spacewar.com/2006/090204023334.6ec9ovm0.html.

152. Agence France-Presse, "Western Powers Worried about Iran Satellite Technology," February 3, 2009, http://www.spacewar.com/2006/090203213340.ewrvo3a8.html.

153. GlobalSecurity.org, "Iran: Missiles Development."

154. Hughes, "Iran's Ballistic Missile Developments—Long-Range Ambitions," pp. 22–27.

155. Michael Herald, "US Shows Muscle by Punitive Action," *New Zealand Herald*, August 30, 2006, http://www.nzherald.co.nz/.

156. Andrew Koch, Robin Hughes, and Alon Ben-David, "Tehran Altering Ballistic Missile," *Jane's Defence Weekly*, December 8, 2004.

157. MissileThreat.com, Fateh A-110, a project of the Claremont Institute, October 10, 2008, http://www.missilethreat.com/missilesoftheworld/id.39/missile_detail.asp; and GlobalSecurity.org, Fateh-110 / NP-110 / Mushak, April 28, 2004, http://www.global security.org/wmd/world/iran/mushak.htm.

158. Jane's Sentinel Security Assessment—The Gulf States, Armed Forces Iran Ballistic Missiles, Jane's, July 28, 2008, http://search.janes.com.

159. Lennox, ed., *Jane's Strategic Weapons Systems 46*, 67–68.

160. Jane's Sentinel Security Assessment—The Gulf States, Armed Forces Iran Ballistic Missiles.

161. MissileThreat.com, Fateh A-110.

162. Ibid.

163. GlobalSecurity.org, Fateh-110 / NP-110 / Mushak, April 28, 2004, http://www.globalsecurity.org/wmd/world/iran/mushak.htm.

164. "Iran's Missile Development: Further Tests Needed to Cement Recent Advances," "Sizing up the *Sajjil.*"

165. Lauren Gelfand and Alon Ben-David, "New Missile Marks 'Significant Leap' for Iran Capabilities," *Jane's*, November 14, 2008, http://www.janes.com/news/defence/systems/jdw/jdw081114_1_n.shtml.

166. Ali Akbar Dareini, "Iran Says It Tests Missile, Israel within Range," *Associated Press*, May 20, 2009.

167. Julian Borger, "Iran Test Fires Missile Capable of Reaching US Bases or Israel," *Guardian* (Manchester), May 20, 2009, http://www.iiss.org/whats-new/iiss-in-the-press/may-2009/iran-test-fires-missile-capable-of-reaching-us-bases-or-israel/.

168. "Iran's Missile Development: Further Tests Needed to Cement Recent Advances," "Sizing up the *Sajjil.*"

169. NTI, "Iran's Missile Capabilities—Long-Range Artillery Rocket Programs," http://www.nti.org/e_research/profiles/Iran/Missile/3367_3397.html.

170. Lennox, ed., *Jane's Strategic Weapons Systems 46*, 69.

171. Bill Gertz, "China's Broken Promises Outlined; Helms Makes List of Arms Offenses," *Washington Times*, July 23, 2001, www.washtimes.com/.

172. "Nukes for Sale," *The Statesman, India,* March 2, 2004, www.thestatesman.net.

173. BBC, "Iran Parades Missiles: Iranian Account of Parade"; and Agence France-Presse, "Iran Flaunts Ballistic Missiles with anti-US, Israeli Slogans," September 22, 2005, http://www.missilethreat.com/archives/id.1892/detail.asp.

174. Cordesman and Martin Keliber, *Iran's Military Forces and Warfighting capabilities: The Threat in the Northern Gulf.*

175. Lennox, ed., *Jane's Strategic Weapons Systems 46*, 169; and MissileThreat.com, M-11 variant, a project of the Claremont Institute, October 10, 2008, http://www.missilethreat.com/missilesoftheworld/id.66/missile_detail.asp.

176. Hughes, "Iran's Ballistic Missile Developments—Long-Range Ambitions."

177. Rubin, *The Global Reach of Iran's Ballistic Missiles*, p. 29.

178. Jane's Sentinel Security Assessment—The Gulf States, Armed Forces Iran Ballistic Missiles.

179. Reportedly, Iran concluded an agreement with North Korea to buy 18 IRBMs (BM-25), which in turn are reverse-engineered Russian SS-N-6 SLBMs. Apparently, Iran tested a BM-25 in January 2006; the missile is reported to have flown more than 3,000 km.

180. Federation of American Scientists, "KH-55 Granat," www.fas.org/nuke/guide/russia/bomber/as-15.htm.

181. Hughes, "Iran's Ballistic Missile Developments—Long-Range Ambitions," pp. 22–27; http://www.globalsecurity.org/wmd/world/russia/as-15specs.htm; http://www.globalsecurity.org/wmd/world/russia/kh-55.htm; http://www.globalsecurity.org/wmd/world/iran/x-55.htm.

182. Federation of American Scientists, "KH-55 Granat."

183. "Cruise Missile Row Rocks Ukraine," *BBC News*, March 18, 2005, http://news.bbc.co.uk/2/hi/europe/4361505.stm.

184. Bill Gertz, "Missiles Sold to China and Iran," *Washington Times,* April 6, 2005, http://washingtontimes.com/national/20050405-115803-7960r.htm.

185. Ibid.

186. Paul Kerr, "Ukraine Admits Missile Transfers," Arms Control Association, May 2005, http://www.armscontrol.org/act/2005_05/Ukraine.asp.

187. "Ukraine Investigates Supply of Missiles to China and Iran," *Jane's Missiles and Rockets,* May 1, 2005.

188. "18 Cruise Missiles Were Smuggled to Iran, China" *Associated Press,* March 18, 2005.

189. Hughes, "Iran's Ballistic Missile Developments—Long-Range Ambitions."

190. Rubin, *The Global Reach of Iran's Ballistic Missiles,* p. 28.

191. Fisher Jr., China's Alliance with Iran Grows Contrary to U.S. Hopes."

192. The IISS estimates 319 combat aircraft in 2009, "Chapter Five: Middle East and North Africa," *The Military Balance,* 109:1, 229–276, online publication date: February 1, 2009.

193. The range of aircraft numbers shown reflects the broad uncertainties affecting the number of Iran's aircraft that are operational in any realistic sense. Many aircraft counted, however, cannot engage in sustained combat sorties in an extended air campaign. The numbers are drawn largely from interviews; *Jane's Intelligence Review,* Special Report No. 6, May 1995; "Iran," *Jane's Sentinel: The Gulf Staffs,* various editions; the IISS, *The Military Balance,* various editions, Andrew Rathmell, "Iran;" *The Changing Balance in the Gulf,* Whitehall Papers 38 (London: Royal United Services Institute, 1996); Dr. Andrew Rathmell, "Iran's Rearmament: How Great a Threat?," *Jane's Intelligence Review,* July 1994, pp. 317–322; *Jane's World Air Forces* (CD-ROM).

194. "Iran Overhauls F-14 Fighter Jets," *Fars News Agency,* July 29, 2008.

195. Iran Defense Reports, http://www.irandefence.net/archive/index.php/t-744.html.

196. *Wall Street Journal,* February 10, 1995, p. 19; *Washington Times,* February 10, 1995, p. A-19.

197. *Flight International Magazine,* September 1999, http://info.flightinternational.com/?bbcam=adwds_z1&bbkid=flight+international&x=&jtid=83112&client_code=.

198. Cnn.com, "Iran, China exploit U.S. military surplus supermarket," January 16, 2007.

199. Guy Anderson, "Isonmainer Suspends Sale of F-14 Parts," *Jane's Defence Weekly,* February 7, 2007.

200. *Flight International Magazine.*

201. Iran Defense Reports.

202. Jane's Sentinel Security Assessment: The Gulf States, Armed Forces, Iran, October 7, 2004.

203. Philip Ewing, "Iran May Buy 250 Jets from Russia," *Navy Times,* August 1, 2007.

204. Globalsecurity.org, July 10, 2008, http://www.globalsecurity.org/military/world/iran/airforce.htm.

205. Yaakov Katz and Herb Keinon, "Reports: Russia to Sell Long-Range Fighter Jets to Teheran," July 30, 2007, http://pqasb.pqarchiver.com/jpost/access/1315547451.html?dids=1315547451:1315547451&FMT=ABS&FMTS=ABS:FT&type=current&date=Jul+30%2C+2007&author=YAAKOV+KATZ%3BHERB+KEINON&pub=Jerusalem+Post&edition=&startpage=01&desc=Reports%3A+Russia+to+sell+long-range+fighter+jets+to+%3B+Teheran.

206. "New Iranian Capability Is Troublesome," *Washington Times,* February 19, 2009.

207. "Iran Overhauls F-14 Fighter Jets," *Fars News Agency,* July 29, 2008, http://english.farsnews.net/newstext.php?nn=8705081124.

208. Associated Press, "Iran Claims It Has Unmanned Aircraft," February 18, 2009.

209. "New Iranian Capability Is Troublesome."

210. AIAA Aerospace, 2009 Worldwide UAV Roundup, http://www.aiaa.org/Aerospace/images/articleimages/pdf/UAVs_APR2009.pdf.

211. Dennis C. Blair, Director of National Intelligence. Annual Threat Assessment of the Intelligence Community for the Senate Select Committee on Intelligence, Office of the Director of National Intelligence, February 12, 2009, pp. 20–21.

212. Alex Bollfrass, "Arms Control and Proliferation: Iran," Arms Control Association, January 2008, http://armscontrol.org/factsheets/iranprofile.

CHAPTER 5

1. "Iran's Chemical Weapon Program," *Wisconsin Project on Nuclear Arms Control: Iran Watch*, July 2005, http://www.iranwatch.org/wmd/wmd-chemicalessay.htm.

2. U.S. Department of Defense, *Proliferation: Threat and Response*, November 25, 1997, http://www.defenselink.mil/pubs/prolif97/meafrica.html#middle.

3. GlobalSecurity.org, "Weapons of Mass Destruction, Chemical Weapons, Iran," http://www.globalsecurity.org/wmd/world/iran/cw.htm.

4. Gregory F. Giles, *Iranian Approaches to Chemical Warfare*, December 15, 1997, p. 5; Anthony Cordesman, "Creating Weapons of Mass Destruction, *Armed Forces Journal International* 126 (February 1989), p. 54. According to the Mostazafan and Janbazan (Veterans) Foundation of Iran, over 100,000 were exposed to chemical agents. See also Voice of the Islamic Republic of Iran, July 2, 2000.

5. Islamic Republic News Agency (IRNA), October 19, 1988.

6. Giles, *Iranian Approaches to Chemical Warfare*, pp. 13–14.

7. "Iran-Iraq Arms Non-Proliferation Act of 1992," *Arms Sales Monitor*, January 15, 1993, p. 3.

8. Laurie H. Boulden, "CIA, DIA Provide New Details on CW, BW Programs in Iran and Russia," *Arms Control Today*, August 1, 1996.

9. Con Coughlin Chief, "Iran in Secret Chemical Weapons Deal With India," *Sunday Telegraph*, June 24, 1996.

10. Con Coughlin, "China Helps Iran to Make Nerve Gas," *London Daily Telegraph*, May 24, 1998, p. 1.

11. *Proliferation: Threat and Response,* Office of Secretary of Defense, 2001, p. 36, http://www.defenselink.mil/pubs/ptr20010110.pdf.

12. CIA, Unclassified Report to Congress on the Acquisition of Technology Relating to Weapons of Mass Destruction and Advanced Conventional Munitions, November 2003, http://www.cia.gov/cia/reports/721_reports/pdfs/721report_july_dec2003.pdf.

13. Quoted in Kori N. Schake and Judith S. Yaphe, "The Strategic Implications of a Nuclear-Armed Iran," McNair Paper 64, Institute for National Strategic Studies, National Defense University, Washington, D.C., 2001, p. 3.

14. DNI, Unclassified Report to Congress on the Acquisition of Technology Relating to Weapons of Mass Destruction and Advanced Conventional Munitions, March 2008, http://www.dni.gov/reports2.htm.

15. John R. Bolton, "Iran's Continuing Pursuit of Weapons of Mass Destruction," testimony before the House International Relations Committee Subcommittee on the Middle East and Central Asia, June 24, 2004, http://www.state.gov/t/us/rm/33909.htm.

16. Quoted in the IISS, *Iran's Strategic Weapons Programs: A Net Assessment,* IISS Strategic Dossier, 2005, p. 67.

17. "German Investigators See Signs of 'Secret Military Nuclear Programme' In Iran," *BBC Monitoring International Reports*, January 31, 2006, http://web.lexis-nexis.com.

18. GlobalSecurity.org, "Weapons of Mass Destruction, Chemical Weapons, Iran," http://www.globalsecurity.org/wmd/world/iran/cw.htm.

19. The quotation is taken from Global Security, "Weapons of Mass Destruction, Chemical Weapons, Iran," http://www.globalsecurity.org/wmd/world/iran/cw.htm. Reprinted with permission. For a more detailed analysis of the uncertainties involved in recent U.S. intelligence reporting, see Marcus Binder, "Iran's First-Generation Chemical Weapons Evaporate, as Certainty Declines in U.S. Intelligence Reports," *WMD Insights*, February 2008 issue, http://www.wmdinsights.com/I22/I22_ME2_Iran1stGenCW.htm.

20. NTI, "Iran Profile: Chemical Chronology: 2004–2008," http://www.nti.org/e_research/profiles/Iran/Chemical/2340_4966.html.

21. J. Michael McConnell, Annual Threat Assessment of the Director of National Intelligence, statement for the record before the U.S. Senate Select Committee on Intelligence, February 5, 2008, http://www.dni.gov/testimonies/.

22. Lieutenant General Michael Maples, Current and Projected National Security Threats to the United States, statement for the record before the U.S. Senate Committee on Armed Services, February 27, 2008, http://www.dia.mil/publicaffairs/Testimonies/statement_30.pdf.

23. Unclassified Report to Congress on the Acquisition of Technology Relating to Weapons of Mass Destruction and Advanced Conventional Munitions for the period 1 January to 31 December 2005 (Washington, DC: Office of the Director of National Intelligence, 2008), p. 3, http://www.dni.gov/reports/CDA%2011-14-2006.pdf.

24. Unclassified Report to Congress on the Acquisition of Technology Relating to Weapons of Mass Destruction and Advanced Conventional Munitions for the period 1 January to 31 December 2006 (Washington, DC: Office of the Director of National Intelligence, 2008), p. 3, http://www.dni.gov/reports/.

25. Designation of Iranian Entities and Individuals for Proliferation Activities, July 8, 2008, www.state.gov.

26. CRS Report to Congress (RL32048), Iran: U.S. Concerns and Policy Response, updated September 24, 2008, http://www.fas.org/sgp/crs/mideast/RL32048.pdf.

27. Iran, "(ii) Instruments of ratification, acceptance (A), approval (AA), accession (a) and succession (s) deposited with the Secretary-General of the United Nations," http://disarmament.un.org/treatystatus.nsf/268c30bb29ee7d388525688f0060a3d0/3d08db771903b6818525688f006d2401?OpenDocument.

28. See the analysis in GlobalSecurity.org, "Weapons of Mass Destruction, Chemical Weapons, Iran," http://www.globalsecurity.org/wmd/world/iran/cw.htm.

29. Ibid.

30. Ibid.

31. "Chemical Weapons Watchdog Says Iran Complying with CWC," IRNA, May 16, 2007, http://www2.irna.ir/en/news/view/line-20/0705164594140044.htm.

32. *Status of Annual Declarations Regarding Projected Activities and Anticipated Production in 2008 at Schedule 1 Facilities, S-657-2007*, Organisation for the Prohibition of Chemical Weapons, October 10 2007, http://www.opcw.org/docs/snotes/2007/s-657-2007(e).pdf.

33. DNI, Unclassified Report to Congress on the Acquisition of Technology Relating to Weapons of Mass Destruction and Advanced Conventional Munitions.

34. *The CBW Conventions Bulletin*, nos. 76+77 (October 2007), p. 48.

35. Robin Hughes, "Explosion Aborts CW Project Run by Iran and Syria," *Jane's Defence Weekly*, September 26, 2007 (first posted on Jane's Web site on September 17, 2007).

36. Statement by H. E. Bozorgmehr Ziaran, Ambassador and Permanent Representative of the Islamic Republic of Iran to the OPCW before The Second Special Session of the Conference of the States Parties to Review the Operation of the Chemical Weapons Convention, April 8, 2008, www.opcw.org.

37. Judith Miller, "U.S. Explores Other Options on Preventing Germ Warfare," *New York Times*, July 25, 2001.

38. Michael Rubin, "Iran's Burgeoning WMD Programs," *Middle East Intelligence Bulletin (MEIB)*, 4, no. 3 (March 2002), www.meib.org/; and Michael Rubin, "What Are Iran's Domestic Priorities?" *Middle East Review of International Affairs (MERIA) Journal*, 6, no. 2 (June 2002), meria.idc.ac.il.

39. Statements by President Khatami regarding Iranian security and strategic weapons programs: statement by Khatami from *Associated Press* article, "Iran Provides Details of Missiles," August 12, 1998, quote: "Iran will not seek permission from anyone for strengthening its defense capability." And statement from Khatami from the *Washington Post* article "Rushdie Case Termed Finished," p. A21, September 23, 1998. Khatami addressing United Nations General Assembly quote: "We [Iranians] have over and over again expressed our concern that Israel has become a center for nuclear weapons and for WMD. We, too, have the right to defend ourselves."

40. Jalili: Chemical Weapons Have No Place in Iran's Defense Doctrine," IRNA, January 23, 2008, http://www2.irna.ir/en/news/view/line-17/0801239430180425.htm.

41. Itamar Eichner, "Iran Admits to Possessing Chemical Weapons," *Yedi'ot Aharonot*, November 20, 1998; FBIS Document FTS19981120000618, November 20, 1998; Agence France-Presse, "Iran Pledges No Chemical Weapons Production," November 17, 1998; Mohammad R. Alborzi, "Statement to the Third Session of the Conference of the States Parties of the Chemical Weapons Convention," November 16–20, 2000.

42. IISS, Iran's Strategic Weapons Programs: A Net Assessment, IISS Strategic Dossier, 2005, pp. 82–83.

43. Merav Zafary, "Iranian Biological and Chemical Weapons Profile Study," Center for Nonproliferation Studies, Monterey Institute of International Studies, February 2001.

44. Paula DeSutter, "Deterring Iranian NBC Use," *Strategic Forum* 110, National Defense University, April 1997, p. 3.

45. GlobalSecurity.org, "Weapons of Mass Destruction, Chemical Weapons, Iran," http://www.globalsecurity.org/wmd/world/iran/cw.htm.

46. "Iran: Chemical Overview," Nuclear Threat Initiative, revised in January 2006, http://www.nti.org/e_research/profiles/Iran/Chemical/#fnB15.

47. Robin Hughes, "Iran Aids Syria's CW Programme," *Jane's Defence Weekly*, October 21, 2005, http://www.janes.com.

48. Robin Hughes, "Iran and Syria Sign Mutual Assistance Accord," *Jane's Defence Weekly*, December 21, 2005.

49. Nick Grace and Abdiweli Ali, "Mystery Surrounds Hijacked Iranian Ship," *The Long War Journal*, September 22, 2008, http://www.longwarjournal.org/archives/2008/09/mystery_surrounds_hi.php.

CHAPTER 6

1. "The Acquisition of Technology Relating to Weapons of Mass Destruction and Advanced Conventions/ Munitions July–December 1996," Director of Central Intelligence, June 1997, http://www.fas.org/irp/cia/product/wmd.htm.

2. *Proliferation: Threat and Response,* Department of Defense, The Office of Secretary of Defense, 1997, http://www.fas.org/irp/threat/prolif97/index.html.

3. *Proliferation: Threat and Response,* Department of Defense, The Office of Secretary of Defense, 2001, p. 36, http://ftp.fas.org/irp/threat/prolif00.pdf.

4. As is noted in the text, this summary of U.S. positions draws heavily on the work of the Nuclear Threat Initiative (NTI) in its chronology of Iranian biological weapons, http://www.nti.org/e_research/profiles/Iran/Biological/2308_4698.html; Transcript: Department of State Noon Briefing by Deputy State Department Spokesman J. Adam Ereli, April 2, 2004, http://www.america.gov/st/washfile-english/2004/April/20040402171125xjsnommis0.6981012.html.

5. Report to Congress on the Acquisition of Technology Relating to Weapons of Mass Destruction and Advanced Conventional Munitions 1 July through 31 December 2003 (Washington, DC: Office of the Director of Central Intelligence, 2004), p. 3, www.cia.gov.

6. Lieutenant General Michael Maples, Current and Projected National Security Threats to the United States, statement for the record before the U.S. Senate Select Committee on Intelligence, February 28, 2006, p. 10, www.dia.mil.

7. Unclassified Report to Congress on the Acquisition of Technology Relating to Weapons of Mass Destruction and Advanced Conventional Munitions for the Period 1 January to 31 December 2004 (Washington, DC: Office of the Director of National Intelligence, 2006), p. 3, www.dni.gov. That November, John C. Rood, Assistant Secretary for International Security and Nonproliferation, stated, "We [the United States] believe that the regime in Iran probably has an offensive biological weapons program in violation of the BWC"; Richard Waddington, "Iran Probably Has Germ Weapons, Possibly N.Korea-US," *Reuters,* November 20, 2006, www.alertnet.org; John C. Rood, Assistant Secretary for International Security and Nonproliferation, remarks to the Sixth Biological Weapons Convention Review Conference, November 20, 2006, www.state.gov.

8. Lieutenant General Michael Maples, Current and Projected National Security Threats to the United States, statement for the record before the U.S. Senate Select Committee on Intelligence, January 11, 2007, intelligence.senate.gov.

9. Lieutenant General Michael Maples, Current and Projected National Security Threats to the United States, statement for the record before the U.S. Senate Committee on Armed Services, February 27, 2008, p. 12. www.dia.mil.

10. J. Michael McConnell, Annual Threat Assessment of the Director of National Intelligence, statement for the record before the U.S. Senate Select Committee on Intelligence, February 5, 2008, www.dni.gov.

11. Ibid.

12. Ibid.

13. Federation of American Scientists, The BWC Review Conferences and the Verification Protocol, http://www.fas.org/bwc/papers/review/bwcrc.htm.

14. Nuclear Threat Initiative (NTI), "Country Overviews: Iran: Biological Chronology," http://www.nti.org/e_research/profiles/Iran/Biological/2308_4698.html.

15. *The CBW Conventions Bulletin,* No. 65 (September 2004), p. 14.

16. The statement was made on August 2, 2004. See *The CBW Conventions Bulletin*, No. 66 (December 2004), p. 35.

17. As quoted in the NTI chronology. Also see Tehran Vision of the Islamic Republic of Iran Network, September 22, 2004, translated transcript provided by FBIS as "Guards Commander Says Iran Ready for Bacteriological, Chemical Warfare," FBIS document IAP20040922000086, www.opensource.gov.

18. NTI chronology and *The CBW Conventions Bulletin*, os. 76+77 (October 2007), p. 7.

19. "German Intelligence Services See Iran Possessing Biological, Chemical Weapons," February 20, 2005, FBIS document EUP2005022000035, www.opensource.gov.

20. Interview; NTI chronology; and WMD End-Use Control: License Applications for Iran, Amended May 2006, www.dti.gov.uk.

21. Director of National Intelligence John D. Negroponte, "Annual Threat Assessment of the Director of National Intelligence," testimony to the Senate Select Committee on Intelligence, February 2, 2006.

22. "Recognizing Iran as a Strategic Threat: An Intelligence Challenge for the United States," Staff Report of the House Permanent Select Committee on Intelligence Subcommittee on Intelligence Policy, August 23, 2006.

23. The group maintains an active Web site at http://ncr-iran.org/content/blogsection/18/154/.

24. Designation of National Council of Resistance and National Council of Resistance of Iran under Executive Order 13224, released on August 15, 2003, http://www.state.gov/r/pa/prs/ps/2003/23311.htm. The Secretary of State has amended the designation, under Executive Order 13224 on terrorist financing, of the Mujahedin-e Khalq, known as the MEK, to add its aliases National Council of Resistance (NCR) and National Council of Resistance of Iran (NCRI). That Executive Order blocks the assets of organizations and individuals linked to terrorism. The decision also clarifies that the designation includes the U.S. representative office of NCRI and all its other offices worldwide and that the designation of the People's Mujahedin of Iran ("PMOI") as an alias of the MEK includes the PMOI's U.S. representative office and all other offices worldwide.

The Secretary of State designated the MEK as a foreign terrorist organization in 1997 under the Immigration and Nationality Act, and again in 2001 pursuant to section 1(b) of Executive Order 13224. That order (as amended) authorizes the Secretary to designate foreign entities and individuals that he determines—in consultation with the Secretary of the Treasury, the Attorney General, and the Secretary of Homeland Security—to have committed, or to pose a significant risk of committing, acts of terrorism that threaten the security of U.S. nationals or the national security, foreign policy, or economy of the United States.

The action to amend the Executive Order 13224 designation of the MEK to include NCR and NCRI is based on information from a variety of sources that those entities functioned as part of the MEK and have supported the MEK's acts of terrorism.

25. NTI, Iran Profile, Biological Facilities, http://www.nti.org/e_research/profiles/Iran/Biological/2305_2380.html.

26. NTI, "Biological Facilities," http://www.nti.org/e_research/profiles/Iran/Biological/2305.html; and Clerical Remarks to the Press by Soona Samsami, U.S. Representative of the National Council of Resistance of Iran, January 26, 1999, p. 2; Amir Kabir University Web site, http://www.aku.ac.ir/; "Iranian, Syrian Universities Sign Mutual Scientific Cooperation Agreement," Tehran IRNA in English, March 20, 2002; in FBIS Document IAP20020320000059; "Iranian Procurement Fronts," *Middle East Defense News* (*Mednews*), 5, no. 17–18 (June 8, 1992).

27. See the NTI Web site and Federation of American Scientists, http://www.fas.org/nuke/ guide/iran/facility/damghan.htm; "Special Report: Chemical and Biological Warfare Programs," Jane's Intelligence Review-Special Report, June 1, 1995; Anthony H. Cordesman, *Iran's Military Forces in Transition: Conventional Threats and Weapons of Mass Destruction* (Westport, CT: Praeger Publishers, 1999), p. 236; "U.S. Suspects Iranian CW Facility Damaged in Quake," *Middle East Newsline*, 4, no. 243 (June 24, 2002); Exploring U.S. Missile Defense Requirements in 2010: What Are the Policy and Technology Challenges?, Institute for Foreign Policy Analysis, April 1997, chap. 4; James Adams, "Russia Helps Iran's Bio-Warfare" *Sunday Times*, Washington, D.C., August 27, 1995.

28. The NTI cites a wide range of sources. Key sources: Arnold Beichman, "Arsenal of Poison," *Hoover Digest*, no. 3 (1999); Remarks to the Press by Soona Samsami, U.S. Representative of the National Council of Resistance of Iran, January 26, 1999; Arnold Beichman, "Arsenal of Germs in Iran?" *Washington Times*, January 26, 1999, p. A17; Cordesman, *Iran's Military Forces in Transition: Conventional Threats and Weapons of Mass Destruction*, p. 237; Uzi Mahnaimi and James Adams, "Iran Builds Biological Arsenal: Israelis Warn of Teheran Plan to Poison Europe's Water Supplies," *Sunday Times*, August 11, 1996; "Israelis Warn of Teheran's Biological Arsenal," FBIS Document FTS19960811000139, August 11, 1996; Iran Trade Zone, http://www.irantradezone.com/ministriesdesc.asp?page=3&order=srno; Chemexcil; "The Internet in Iran: A Survey," Neda Rayaneh Institute, http://www.iranian.com/WebGuide/InternetIran/InternetIran.html; InternetIran-Government.html, 1997; "Jihad Striving for Development and Construction," Public Relations of Jihad-e-Sazandegi, Summer 1993, pp. 8–45, http://www.netiran.com/Htdocs/Clippings/DEconomy/930711XXDE01.html; Paula A. DeSutter, *Denial and Jeopardy: Deterring Iranian Use of NBC Weapons* (Washington, DC: National Defense University Press, 1997); FBIS, Tehran Domestic Service, April 27, 1986; The National Council of Resistance of Iran, Paris, August 13, 1997, http://www.iran-e-azad.org/english/ncr/970813.html.

29. NTI cites Remarks to the Press by Soona Samsami, p. 2; Arnold Beichman, "Arsenal of Germs in Iran?" *Washington Times*, January 26, 1999, p. A17; "Iran's Chemical Build-Up," Intelligence Newsletter, Indigo Publications, November 9, 1995; "Hungary Reportedly Helped Iran Report Parchin Chemical Weapons Facility," *Jerusalem Middle East Newsline*, e-mail text in English, August 22, 2002; FBIS document GMP20020822000212.

30. NTI cites Remarks to the Press by Soona Samsami, p. 2; Gudio Olimpio, "Khatami to Visit Rome on European Mission," Corriere della Sera (Internet version), February 4, 1999; "Italian Daily Cites MKO Report on Iran's CBW Program," FBIS Document FTS19990204000672, February 4, 1999; Beichman, "Arsenal of Germs in Iran?" p. A17; Rob Swanson, "Iranian Resistance Group Charges Iran Expediting Manufacture of Biological Weapons," *Washington Report on Middle East Affairs*, March 1999, pp. 111–115; "Iranian Opposition Highlights Regime's Biological, Chemical Projects," Iran Mojahedin WWW—text in English, August 14, 2002; FBIS document IAP20020816000037.

31. James Adams. "Russia Helps Iran's Bio-Warfare," *Sunday Times*, August 27, 1995.

32. Statement by John A. Lauder, to the Senate Committee on Foreign Relations on Russian Proliferation to Iran's Weapons of Mass Destruction and Missile Programs, October 5, 2000, http://www.cia.gov/cia/public_affairs/speeches/2000/lauder_WMD_100500.html.

33. CIA, Unclassified Report to Congress on the Acquisition of Technology Relating to Weapons of Mass Destruction and Advanced Conventional Munitions, July–December 2003, http://www.cia.gov/cia/reports/721_reports/pdfs/721report_july_dec2003.pdf.

34. John R. Bolton, "Iran's Continuing Pursuit of Weapons of Mass Destruction," testimony before the House International Relations Committee Subcommittee on the Middle East and Central Asia, June 24, 2004, http://www.state.gov/t/us/rm/33909.htm.

35. Adapted from Chemical and Biological Arms Control Institute (CBACI), Fighting Bioterrorism: Tracking and Assessing U.S. Government Programs, Washington, D.C., 2004, p. 9.

36. For interesting papers on the issue, although now seriously dated, see briefing on the JASON 1997 Summer Study, Lear Steven Block, "Biological Warfare Threats Enabled by Molecular Biology"; and Malcolm R. Dando, "The Impact of Biotechnology," in *Hype or Reality? The New Terrorism and Mass Casualty Attacks*, ed. Brad Roberts (Alexandria, VA: Chemical and Biological Arms Control Institute, 2000), pp. 193–206. Also see GAO/NSIAD-99-163, "Combating Terrorism: Need for Comprehensive Threat and Risk Assessments of Chemical and Biological Attacks," p. 12.

37. The range of uncertainty for a key agent such as anthrax, however, is illustrated in WHO reporting on the risk of the use of such an agent in a "deliberate epidemic": WHO, Deliberate Epidemics Annex 3: Biological Agents, http://www.who.int/csr/delibepidemics/biochemguide/en/index.html (accessed March 18, 2005).

Reported estimates of the dose required to infect 50 percent of a population of nonhuman primates in experimental studies of inhalational anthrax vary enormously, from 2,500 to 760,000 spores, apparently reflecting differences in the many variables involved in such experiments. While doses lower than the LD50 produce correspondingly lower rates of infection, the very large number of experimental animals that would be required makes it impractical to determine doses that would infect only a small percentage of those exposed.

The largest reported outbreak of human inhalational anthrax took place in 1979 in Sverdlovsk (Ekaterinburg), former Soviet Union. Of the 66 documented fatal cases, all were more than 23 years in age, suggesting that adults may be more susceptible to inhalational anthrax than younger individuals. The concomitant infection of sheep and cattle as far as 50 kilometers down wind of the apparent source points to the hazard of long-distance aerosol travel of infective spores.

An outbreak of inhalational anthrax and cutaneous anthrax in the United States during October and November 2001 was caused by *B. anthracis* spores intentionally placed in envelopes sent through the post office. Of the total of 11 reported inhalational cases, the probable date of exposure could be determined in six, and for these the median incubation period was four days (range four to six days). Prolonged antimicrobial prophylaxis administered to persons thought to be at the greatest risk may have prevented cases from occurring later. All 11 inhalational cases received antimicrobial and supportive therapy and 6 survived. As in the Sverdlovsk outbreak, there was a lack of young persons among the inhalational cases, whose ages ranged from 43 to 94.

38. Thomas V. Inglesby et al., "Anthrax as a Biological Weapon: Medical and Public Health Management," *JAMA*, 281, no. 18, (May 12, 1999), pp. 1735–1745, 1736–1737; U.S. Army Center for Health Promotion and Preventive Medicine (USACHPPM), *The Medical NBC Battlebook*, USACHPPM Technical Guide 244, p. 4-31.

39. USACHPPM, *The Medical NBC Battlebook*, p. 4-31.

40. Inglesby et al., "Anthrax as a Biological Weapon," pp. 1735–1745, 1736–1737.

41. Inglesby et al., "Anthrax as a Biological Weapon," pp. 1735–1745, 1736–1737; USACHPPM, *The Medical NBC Battlebook*, p. 4-31.

42. Ken Alibek, *Biohazard* (New York, Random House, 1999_, pp. 111–114, 261, 264.

43. *Washington Post*, August 24, 2000, p. E-1.

44. Immunity develops rapidly after vaccination against smallpox, so that even postexposure vaccination can prevent or ameliorate the disease so long as it is done within approximately four days after exposure and before rash appears.

45. USACHPPM, *The Medical NBC Battlebook*, p. 4-31.

46. Donald A. Henderson et al., "Smallpox as a Biological Weapon: Medical and Public Health Management," *JAMA*, 281, no. 18 (June 9, 1999), pp. 2127–2137.

47. Henderson et al., "Smallpox as a Biological Weapon," 2127–2137; USACHPPM, *The Medical NBC Battlebook*, p. 4-37.

48. CIA, "Terrorist CBRN: Materials and Effects," CTC 2003-4005B, May 2003.

49. Ibid. Some U.S. Army experts believe that it takes at least 35 times more botulinum to create a lethal dose than the U.S. estimates in much of its published lethality data. This uncertainty is of some interest because Iraq produced tons of botulism toxin. (*The Medical NBC Battlebook* does not give a lethal dose, but states that the infective dose is 0.001 μg/kilogram (type A). There is virtually no empirical data in normal medicine with aerosolized botulinum toxin, but it is expected to produce symptoms normal to the food-borne version. Symptoms could begin anywhere from 24 hours to several days after exposure. The initial symptoms would be those of the flu or cold until more characteristic motor symptoms appeared. The U.S. Army is still investigating a vaccine that counters five of the seven neurotoxins in the disease and seems to leave significant antibodies for more than year, and the CDC has a vaccine that deals with three out of the seven neurotoxins. A higher risk heptavalent antitoxin for neurotoxins A–G is available from the USAMIRID, but requires a protocol with informed consent. See USACHPPM, *The Medical NBC Battlebook*, pp. 4-31 to 4-32.

50. Department of Homeland Security, Planning Scenarios, Homeland Security Council, July 2004; Associated Press, March 16, 2005, Lara Jakes Jordan, "Federal Officials Catalogue Possible Terror Attacks." The details of the scenarios are summarized as follows:

Scenario: Biological Attack—Aerosol Anthrax
* *Casualties: 13,000 fatalities and injuries*
* Infrastructure Damage: Minimal, other than contamination
* **Evacuations/Displaced Persons: Possibly**
* Contamination: Extensive
* Economic Impact: Billions of dollars
* **Potential for Multiple Events: Yes**
* **Recovery Timeline: Months**

General Description: Anthrax spores delivered by aerosol delivery results in inhalation anthrax, which develops when the bacterial organism, Bacillus anthracis, is inhaled into the lungs. A progressive infection follows. This scenario describes a single aerosol anthrax attack in one city delivered by a truck using a concealed improvised spraying device in a densely populated urban city with a significant commuter workforce. It does not, however, exclude the possibility of multiple attacks in disparate cities or time-phased attacks (i.e., "reload"). For federal planning purposes, it will be assumed that the Universal Adversary (UA) will attack five separate metropolitan areas in a sequential manner. Three cities will be attacked initially, followed by two additional cities 2 weeks later.

Timeline/Event Dynamics—It is possible that a Bio-Watch signal would be received and processed, but this is not likely to occur until the day after the release. The first cases of anthrax would begin to present to Emergency Rooms (ERs) approximately 36 hours post-release, with rapid progression of symptoms and fatalities in untreated (or inappropriately treated) patients.

The situation in the hospitals will be complicated by the following facts: The release has occurred at the beginning of an unusually early influenza season and the prodromal symptoms of inhalation anthrax are relatively non-specific. Physician uncertainty will result in low thresholds for admission and administration of available countermeasures (e.g., antibiotics), producing severe strains on commercially available supplies of such medications as ciprofloxacin and doxycycline, and exacerbating the surge capacity problem.

Secondary Hazards/Events—Social order questions will arise. The public will want to know very quickly if it is safe to remain in the affected city and surrounding regions. Many persons will flee regardless of the public health guidance that is provided. Pressure may be placed directly on pharmacies to dispense medical countermeasures directly, and it will be necessary to provide public health guidance in more than a dozen languages.

Key Implications: This attack results in 328,484 exposures; 13,208 untreated fatalities; and 13,342 total casualties. Although property damage will be minimal, city services will be hampered by safety concerns. There is the potential for a huge sell-off in the economic markets; moreover, the stock exchange and large businesses may be directly affected by the attack. There may also be a decline in consumer spending and a loss of revenue for the metropolitan area. An overall national economic downturn is possible in the wake of the attack due to loss of consumer confidence. The costs of the closure of a large section of the city and the decrease in revenue from tourism for an indeterminate period would be enormous, as would the costs of remediation and decontamination.

Mission Areas Activated: Prevention/Deterrence/Protection—This area requires knowledge of those with the ability to grow and aerosolize anthrax, reconnaissance of equipment and laboratories, and public health protection measures.

Emergency Assessment/Diagnosis—It will be necessary to monitor attack impact, determine resource needs, classify the type of event, and identify other events (if any). Environmental sampling for exposure risk assessment, identification of anthrax strain, and determination of any drug resistance will also be required.

Emergency Management/Response—Management and response will require public alerts, mobilization of the Strategic National Stockpile, activation of treatment sites, traffic/access control, special population protection, protective measures (e.g., shelter-in-place), requests for resources and assistance, and public information activities.

Incident/Hazard Mitigation—Mitigation will require PEP and PPE provision, environmental testing/decontamination, care of ill persons, victim treatment, site remediation and monitoring, notification of airlines/transport providers, public information provision, and coordination with public health agencies.

Public Protection—In order to protect the public, it will be necessary to provide symptom/exposure information, warnings, and shelter-in place evacuation notification, as well as to manage traffic/access flow and mobilize the Strategic National Stockpile.

Victim Care—Care to the ill must be provided and should include disbursing PEP/vaccinations and establishing treatment/distribution centers.

Investigation/Apprehension—Law enforcement will investigate the attack in collaboration with public health officials working to identify populations at risk of disease. This also requires epidemiological trace-back of victims, parallel criminal investigations, and laboratory analyses.

Recovery/Remediation—The Environmental Protection Agency (EPA) and the CDC will coordinate this area. Extensive decontamination and cleanup will be required (anthrax is long-lived in the environment) costing billions of dollars. Remediation will also require environmental testing, highly contaminated area closures, and public information provision.

Scenario: Biological Attack—Plague
- Casualties: 2,500 fatalities; 7,000 injuries
- *Infrastructure Damage: None*
- *Evacuations/Displaced Persons: Possibly*
- Contamination: Lasts for hours
- Economic Impact: Millions of dollars
- *Potential for Multiple Events: Yes*
- *Recovery Timeline: Weeks*

Scenario Overview: Plague is a bacterium that causes high mortality in untreated cases and has epidemic potential. It is best known as the cause of Justinian's Plague (in the middle sixth century) and the Black Death (in the middle fourteenth century), two pandemics that killed millions. In this scenario, members of the Universal Adversary (UA) release pneumonic plague into three main areas of a major metropolitan city—in the bathrooms of the city's major airport, at the city's main sport arena, and at the city's major train station.

Timeline/Event Dynamics—Plague cases rapidly occur in the United States and Canada. As a result of foreign and domestic travel, rapid dissemination to distant locations occurs. By Day 3, the plague spreads across both the Pacific and Atlantic oceans and by Day 4, the plague is confirmed in eleven countries other than the United States and Canada.

Secondary Hazards/Events—As the financial world in Major City and elsewhere begins to realize the likelihood of an epidemic, a huge sell-off occurs in the markets. There is a high absentee rate at banks, other financial institutions, and major corporations. Adding to these complications is the fact that bank and other financial customers may be staying home. As a result, the phone systems at financial institutions may become completely tied up, with far fewer transactions than normal occurring. The fear of plague has raised memories of the anthrax incidents of 2001, which may cause many citizens to be afraid to open their mail.

Key Implications: Although the specific assumptions that underlie these totals are not generally available, nor can they be reliably recreated, the parameters affecting these figures include length of incubation period following primary exposure, rate of secondary transmission, incubation period following secondary exposure, and timing and effectiveness of the intervention.

Illnesses and Fatalities by Country:
- United States 7,348/2,287
- Canada 787/246
- Other Countries 33/10
- Total 8,168/2,543

Although the actual physical damage to property will be negligible, there will be an associated negative impact of buildings and areas that were or could have been contaminated. Service disruption will be significant for call centers, pharmacies, and hospitals due to overwhelming casualty needs. It will be necessary to close or restrict certain transportation modes. The threat of reduced food supply will cause food prices to rise. A huge sell-off in the economic markets is possible, and loss of life will result in a decline in consumer spending and subsequent loss of revenue in the metropolitan area. An overall national economic downturn is possible in the wake of the attack due to loss of consumer confidence.

Many people will be killed, permanently disabled, or sick as a result of the plague. The primary illness will be pneumonia, although the plague can also cause septicemia, circulator complications, and other manifestations. The long-term effects of antimicrobial prophylaxis in large numbers will require follow-up study. The associated mental health issues relating to mass trauma and terrorism events will also require assessment.

Mission Areas Activated:

Prevention/Deterrence/Protection—This area requires knowledge of persons with the skills to grow and aerosolize plague, reconnaissance of supplies and laboratories, and public health protection measures.

Emergency Assessment/Diagnosis—Although health professionals should rapidly recognize the seriousness of the incident, diagnosis of the plague may be delayed. Detection of the plague should initiate laboratory identification of the strain and a determination of the potentially known antimicrobial drug resistance. Origin of the initial contaminant should be traced back to the source.

Emergency Management/Response—Identification of drug-resistant plague strains would require full utilization of personal protective equipment (PPE) and quarantine measures. Response will require provision of public alerts mobilization of the National Strategic Stockpile, activation of treatment sites, traffic and access control, protection of special populations, potential quarantine measures including shelter-in-place recommendations, requests for resources and assistance, and public information activities. Effective communication between U.S. and Canadian governments is vital.

Incident/Hazard Mitigation—Victims must receive antibiotic therapy within 24 hours to prevent fatality. Exposed victims must be isolated and minimizing disease spread will require epidemiological assessments, including contact investigation and notification.

Public Protection—Victims must be evacuated and treated (and/or self-quarantined), and antimicrobial prophylaxis will be necessary for exposed persons, responders, and pertinent health care workers. Mobilization of the Strategic National Stockpile for additional critical supplies and antibiotics will be necessary. The public should be informed of signs and symptoms of plague.

Victim Care—Victims will require treatment or prophylaxis with ventilators and antibiotics, as well as information measures for preventing spread of the disease. Advanced hospital care will be required for those with pneumonia. The U.S. Department of State's Bureau of Consular Affairs will need to be involved in order to assist foreign populations residing in the United States, or U.S. citizens exposed or ill abroad.

Investigation/Apprehension—Point-of-source exposures and plague strain must be determined using victim trace-back, criminal investigation, and laboratory analyses.

Recovery/Remediation—Extensive decontamination and cleanup will not be necessary because plague cannot live long in the environment and is viable to heat and sunlight exposure. However, some efforts should be undertaken to support political/public confidence.

Biological Attack—Food Contamination

- Casualties: 300 fatalities; 400 hospitalizations
- *Infrastructure Damage: None*
- *Evacuations/Displaced Persons: None*
- Contamination: Sites where contamination was dispersed
- Economic Impact: Millions of dollars
- *Potential for Multiple Events: Yes*
- *Recovery Timeline: Weeks*

Scenario Overview: The U.S. food industry has significantly increased its physical and personnel security since 2001. A successful attack could only occur following the illegal acquisition of sensitive information revealing detailed vulnerabilities of a specific

production site. However, in this scenario the Universal Adversary (UA) is able to acquire these restricted documents due to a security lapse. The UA uses these sensitive documents and a high degree of careful planning to avoid apprehension and conduct a serious attack. The UA delivers liquid anthrax bacteria to pre-selected plant workers. At a beef plant in a west coast state, two batches of ground beef are contaminated with anthrax, with distribution to a city on the west coast, a southwest state, and a state in the northwest. At an orange juice plant in a southwestern state, three batches of orange juice are contaminated with anthrax, with distribution to a west coast city, a southwest city, and a northwest city.

Timeline/Event Dynamics—
- November: The biological agent is delivered to terrorists (plant workers).
- December 3: The biological agent is inserted into ground beef and orange juice at production facilities, and the packages are shipped to affected cities.
- December 5: The first signs of patients with unknown illness appear.
- December 5–15: There is a significant influx of affected individuals into hospitals with 1,200 sick, 300 dead, and 400 hospitalized in ICU.
- December 8: Health departments, the CDC, the FDA, and the USDA begin pursuing epidemiological investigations.
- December 30: A contaminated product trace is made to ground beef and orange juice production plants. Decontamination of plants commences.
- January 5: No new cases of illness are reported.

Secondary Hazards/Events—
As a result of news of the contaminated food products, there is general public concern regarding food safety, and the "worried well" are taxing medical and laboratory facilities. The public floods into medical facilities seeking prescription drugs to prevent or recover from sickness. In addition, ground beef and orange juice sales plummet, and unemployment in these two industries rises dramatically.

Key Implications:
The attack results in 300 fatalities, 400 hospitalizations, and 1,200 illnesses. Overall property damage is moderate, and due only to decontamination of affected facilities. However, property and facility disruption (downtime) are significant due to decontamination of affected facilities. Service disruption is significant in ground beef and orange juice industries, and some moderate disruption occurs in other food industries due to the public's concern about food safety in general. Although direct financial impact is significant, initial economic impact on the general economy is relatively low. However, the long-term financial impact on the beef and orange juice marketplace and associated businesses could be significant, and other food industries' income is likely to be negatively affected by the public's overall perception of unsafe food. The societal impact of attacks on the food supply generates demands for increased, costly, federally directed food security programs and other measures to reduce the possibility of future attacks. Anthrax may result in fatality and serious long-term illness.

Mission Areas Activated:
Prevention/Deterrence/Protection—Avoiding the attack is contingent on the prevention of infiltration of two different food production systems. Deterrence and protection require rapid disease diagnosis, and protective measures to assure food safety.

Emergency Assessment/Diagnosis—Determining cause of illness and tracking the contaminated source is critical.

Emergency Management/Response—Disease outbreaks in three cities spread throughout the country, which tests coordination of resources.

Incident/Hazard Mitigation—Once disease outbreak occurs, decisions must be made regarding meat and juice supplies and production.

Public Protection—Public protection will require testing alert and warning mechanisms, providing public information and education, and coordinating human and veterinary services.

Victim Care—Victim care will require diagnosis and treatment of affected population and distribution of prophylaxis for potentially exposed populations.

Investigation/Apprehension—Epidemiology will be critical to trace the source of contamination. Investigation of crime and apprehension of suspects will be needed.

Recovery/Remediation—Contaminated foodstuffs require disposal. Plants and sites where anthrax was dispersed may need to be decontaminated.

51. WHO, Deliberate Epidemics Annex 3: Biological Agents, http://www.who.int/csr/delibepidemics/biochemguide/en/index.html (accessed March 18, 2005). For similar studies and conclusions, see Report of the Advisory Panel to Assess Domestic Response Capabilities for Terrorism Involving Weapons of Mass Destruction, Assessing the Threat, December 15, 1999, http://www.rand.org/organisation/nsrd/terrpanel, pp. 73–88; and GAO/NSIAD-99-163, "Combating Terrorism: Need for Comprehensive Threat and Risk Assessments of Chemical and Biological Attacks," p. 12.

52. http://www.defenselink.mil/pubs/prolif/accesstech.html.

53. Ibid.

54. Chris Bullock, "Biological Terrorism," transcript of a program on biological warfare chaired by Professor D. A. Henderson, Director of the Johns Hopkins Center for Biodefense Studies, August 29, 1999, http://www.abc.net.au/rn/talks/bbing/stories/s48674.htm (accessed September 16, 1999).

55. National Intelligence Council, Mapping the Global Future, Report of the National Intelligence Council's 2020 Project, NIC-2004-13, December 2004, p. 101.

56. For a good technical summary of the issues involved in making such weapons, see Office of Technology Assessment, "Background Paper: Technologies Underlying Weapons of Mass Destruction," Washington, D.C., U.S. Congress, OT A-BP-ISC-115, December 1993.

57. Briefing on the JASON 1997 Summer Study, Steven M. Block, "Living Nightmares: Biological Warfare Threats Enabled by Molecular Biology"; Dando, "The Impact of Biotechnology," pp. 193–206.

58. Briefing on the JASON 1997 Summer Study, Block, "Living Nightmares."

59. Assessments of problems, and possible alternative delivery methods, posed by the weaponization process of biological agents adapted from multiple sources including NTI, Jane's: Iran's Chem-Bio Programmes, and http://www.csis-scrs.gc.ca/pblctns/prspctvs/200005-eng.asp.

CHAPTER 7

1. Figure 7.1 was adapted from multiple sources including but not limited to NTI, GlobalSecurity.org, IAEA reporting, UNSC reporting, ISIS, various intelligence agencies, and various news sources.

2. Jean du Preez and Insook Kim, "Mohamed ElBaradei Calls for a New Global Security Landscape," Center for Nonproliferation Studies, June 2, 2006, http://cns.miis.edu/cns/media/pr060531.htm.

3. "Press Conference on Iran," Secretary Condoleezza Rice, Benjamin Franklin Room, Washington, D.C., May 31, 2006, http://merln.ndu.edu/archivepdf/iran/State/67103.pdf.

4. "Security Council Demands Iran Suspend Uranium Enrichment by 31 August, or Face Possible Economic, Diplomatic Sanctions," Resolution 1696 (2006), UN Security Council SC/8792, July 31, 2006, http://www.un.org/News/Press/docs/2006/sc8792.doc.htm.

5. Michael Slackman, "Iran Defiant on Nuclear Program as Deadline Approaches," *New York Times*, August 22, 2006.

6. Glenn Kessler and Dafna Linzer, "Brief Nuclear Halt May Lead to Talks with Iran," *Washington Post*, September 12, 2006.

7. "Timeline of Iran Nuclear Stand-off." *Agence France-Presse*, June 23, 2008, http://w3 .nexis.com/new/auth/checkbrowser.do?t=1214323132418&bhcp=1.

8. "ElBaradei Calls for Timeout on Iran Nuclear Program," CNN Interview with Mohamed ElBaradei, January, 27, 2007, http://www.iaea.org/NewsCenter/Transcripts/2007/cnn270107.html.

9. Daniel Dombey, "FT-Interview: Mohamed El-Baradei," *Financial Times*, February 19, 2007.

10. Agence France-Presse, Tehran, April 5, 2007.

11. "Iran Says It Can Enrich Uranium on a Large Scale," *New York Times*, April 10, 2007, http://www.nytimes.com/2007/04/10/world/middleeast/10iran.html.

12. David E. Sanger, "Atomic Agency Concludes Iran Is Stepping Up Nuclear Work," *New York Times*, May 14, 2007; David E. Sanger, "Inspectors Cite Big Gain by Iran on Nuclear Fuel," *New York Times*, May 14, 2007.

13. "Iran's Nuclear Negotiator Resigns." *BBC News*, October 20, 2007, http://news .bbc.co.uk/2/hi/middle_east/7053963.stm.

14. "Statements of the Director General." IAEA News Centre, November 22, 2007, http://www.iaea.org/NewsCenter/Statements/2007/ebsp2007n019.html.

15. "Timeline of Iran Nuclear Stand-off," *Agence France-Presse*, June 23, 2008, http://w3 .nexis.com/new/auth/checkbrowser.do?t=1214323132418&bhcp=1.

16. David Gollust, "Major Powers Agree on Contents of New Iran UN Resolution," *Voice of America*, January 22, 2008, http://www.voanews.com/english/archive/2008-01/2008-01-22-voa72.cfm.

17. "Latest Iran Safeguards Report Circulated to IAEA Board," *IAEA News Centre*, February 22, 2008, http://www.iaea.org/NewsCenter/News/2008/iranreport0208.html.

18. "Security Council Authorizes More Sanctions against Iran over Nuclear Issue." *UN News Centre*, March 3, 2008, http://www.un.org/apps/news/story.asp?NewsID=25835 &Cr=iran&Cr1.

19. "3 164-Machine Sets from 2nd Series of 3,000 Centrifuges in Motion—Source," IRNA, April 11, 2008, http://www2.irna.ir/en/news/view/line-17/0804112108181137.htm.

20. Elaine Sciolino, "Nuclear Agency Accuses Iran of Willful Lack of Cooperation," *New York Times*, May 27, 2008.

21. Tobias Buck and Daniel Dombey, "Israel May Strike Iran, Deputy PM Says," *Financial Times*, June 7, 2008.

22. "Mofaz Criticised over Iran Threat," *BBC News*, June 8, 2008, http://news.bbc.co.uk/2/hi/middle_east/7442471.stm.

23. IAEA Information Circular (INFCIRC/730), IAEA News Centre, July 1, 2008, http://www.iaea.org/Publications/Documents/Infcircs/2008/infcirc730.pdf.

24. "Tehran Gets Last Chance of Deal on Nuclear Power," *London Times*, June 14, 2008.

25. David E. Sanger and William J. Broad, "Officials Fear Bomb Design Went to Others," *New York Times*, June 16, 2008.

26. David Albright, "Swiss Smugglers Had Advanced Nuclear Weapons Designs," ISIS, June 16, 2008, http://www.isis-online.org/publications/expcontrol/Advanced_Bomb_16June2008.pdf.

27. IAEA Information Circular (INFCIRC/729), IAEA News Centre, June 12, 2008, http://www.iaea.org/Publications/Documents/Infcircs/2008/infcirc729.pdf.

28. "IAEA Director-General Dr. Muhammad ElBaradei: Iran Can Produce Enough Enriched Uranium for a Nuclear Bomb in Six Months to a Year," The Middle East Media Research Institute, Clip No. 1797, June 20, 2008, http://www.memritv.org/clip_transcript/en/1797.htm.

29. Michael R. Gordon and Eric Schmitt, "U.S. Says Exercise by Israel Seemed Directed at Iran," *New York Times*, June 20, 2008.

30. "Iran: European Sanctions Condemned," *New York Times*, June 25, 2008.

31. Ian Black, "Syria Planned to Supply Iran with Nuclear Fuel, Israel Says," *Guardian* (Manchester), June 25, 2008, http://www.guardian.co.uk/world/2008/jun/25/syria.iran.

32. Herb Keinon, "Times: Iran Targeting Dimona Reactor," *Jerusalem Post*, June 28, 2008.

33. Carolynne Wheeler and Tim Shipman, "Israel Has a Year to Stop Iran Bomb, Warns Ex-Spy," *London Sunday Telegraph*, June 29, 2008.

34. "Iran Threatens to Shut Down Persian Gulf Oil Lanes if Attacked," *Los Angeles Times*, June 29, 2008.

35. Sara Sorcher, "Will Israel Attack Iran? Israeli Analysts Reflect on U.S. Reports of a Possible Israeli Attack on Iran," *NBC News*, July 1, 2008, http://abcnews.go.com/International/Story?id=5284361&page=1.

36. "Russia and Iran's Marriage of Convenience," *Jane's Foreign Report*, July 3, 2008.

37. Anthony Capaccio, "Iran May Get First Russian Missiles in December, Pentagon Says," *Bloomberg.com*, July 9, 2008, http://www.bloomberg.com/apps/news?pid=news archive&sid=aQFCIm6IdP0c.

38. "Broadcast News Coverage of Admiral Mullen Briefing," *CNN*, The Situation Room, July 2, 2008.

39. Robin Wright, "Iran Appears to Warm to Diplomacy," *Washington Post*, July 2, 2008.

40. Elaine Sciolino, "Iran Responds Obliquely to Nuclear Plan," *New York Times*, July 5, 2008.

41. Elaine Sciolino, "Iran Says Its Nuclear Policy Has Not Changed," *New York Times* July 6, 2008.

42. Con Coughlin, "Iran Has Resumed A-Bomb Project, Says West," *London Daily Telegraph*, July 7, 2008.

43. "U.S., Allies Hold Gulf Exercises," *Washington Times*, July 9, 2008.

44. "U.S. Seeks Sanctions for Nuclear Work," *Washington Post*, July 9, 2008.

45. Lauren Gelfand, "Iran Bolsters Retaliation Warning with Missile Tests," *Jane's Defence Weekly*, July 9, 2008, http://www8.janes.com/Search/documentView.do?docId=/content1/janesdata/mags/jdw/history/jdw2008/jdw37161.htm@current&pageSelected=allJanes&keyword=&Prod_Name=JDW&backPath=http://search.janes.com/Search.

46. Glenn Kessler, "Iran Launches Nine Test Missles, Says More Are Ready," *Washington Post*, July 10, 2008.

47. Alex Watanka, "Iran Launches Dual-Purpose Missiles," *Jane's Intelligence Review*, July 18, 2008, http://www4.janes.com/subscribe/jir/doc_view.jsp?K2DocKey=/content1/janesdata/mags/jir/history/jir2008/jir10447.htm@current&Prod_Name=JIR&QueryText=.

48. Alan Cowell and William J. Broad, "Iran Reports Missile Test, Drawing Rebuke," *New York Times*, July 10, 2008.

49. Pamela Hess, "Test Exhibits No-Long Range Rocket," *Washington Times*, July 12, 2008.

50. Elaine Sciolino, "U.S. Is Present, But Iran Nuclear Talks End in Stalemate," *International Herald Tribune*, July 20, 2008, http://www.iht.com/articles/2008/07/20/africa/20nuke.php.

51. Dan Eggen, "U.S. Talks with Iran Exemplify Bush's New Approaches," *Washington Post*, July 20, 2008, http://www.washingtonpost.com/wp-dyn/content/article/2008/07/19/AR2008071901597.html.

52. Elaine Sciolino, "Iran Offers 2 Pages and No Ground in Nuclear Talks," *New York Times*, July 22, 2008, http://www.nytimes.com/2008/07/22/world/22iran.html?_r=1&oref=slogin.

53. Robin Millard, "British PM Warns Iran in Landmark Israel Speech," *France 24*, July 21, 2008, http://www.france24.com/en/20080721-british-pm-warns-iran-landmark-israel-speech.

54. "Iran Vows no Nuclear Concessions," *BBC News*, July 23, 2008, http://news.bbc.co.uk/2/hi/middle_east/7520854.stm.

55. George Jahn, "Iran Ends Cooperation with UN Nuclear Arms Probe," *USA Today*, July 23, 2008, http://www.usatoday.com/news/topstories/2008-07-24-483908543_x.htm.

56. "Report: Iran Now Possesses 6,000 Centrifuges," *USA Today* from the *Associated Press*, July 26, 2008, http://www.usatoday.com/news/world/2008-07-26-iran-nuclear_N.htm.

57. "If US Has New Approach, Iran Will Respond: Ahmadinejad," *Agence France-Presse*, July 28, 2008, http://afp.google.com/article/ALeqM5hGxbTykDNZA2f4Bsa7wRqvqBbtpA.

58. Robin Stringer, "Iran Not Building Nuclear Bomb, Ahmadinejad Tells NBC (Update2)," *Bloomberg.com*, July 28, 2008, http://www.bloomberg.com/apps/news?pid=20601087&sid=agN336SOksKw&refer=home.

59. "U.S. Officials: Iran Rebuffed on Nuclear Support," *Associated Press*, August 2, 2008.

60. "New Sanctions Sought for Iran on Nuke Works," *Newsday*, August 4, 2008, "Iran Issues New Warning after Defying Deadline," *New York Times*, August 5, 2008.

61. William J. Broad, "Iran Reports Test of Craft Able to Carry a Satellite," *New York Times*, August 17, 2008, http://www.nytimes.com/2008/08/18/world/middleeast/18iran.html.

62. "Syria and Iran Warm to Russia as U.S. Tensions Grow," *International Herald Tribune* from the *Associated Press*, August 27, 2008, http://www.iht.com/articles/ap/2008/08/27/africa/ME-Mideast-Russia-Fallout.php.

63. "Iran Offers Nuclear Technology to Nigeria," *Voice of America News*, August 29, 2008; "Iran, Nigeria Announce Peaceful Nuclear Deal," *Mobile Register*, August 29, 2008.

64. "Iran Reports 4,000 Centrifuges in Nuclear Program," *New York Times* from the *Associated Press*, http://www.nytimes.com/aponline/world/AP-Iran-Nuclear.html?partner=rssnyt&emc=rss.

65. "Ahmadinejad Threatens West with Sanctions," *GlobalSecurity.org*, September 5, 2008, http://www.globalsecurity.org/wmd/library/news/iran/2008/iran-080829-irna01.htm.

66. Edward Wong, "China Calls for Peaceful Resolution of Nuclear Standoff," *New York Times*, September 6, 2008.

67. Mark Franchetti, "Vladimir Putin Set to Bait US with Nuclear Aid for Tehran," *Sunday Times* (London), September 7, 2008, http://www.timesonline.co.uk/tol/news/world/europe/article4692237.ece.

68. "Iran Nuclear Reactor Launch 'Irreversible' by February: Report," *Agence France-Presse*, September 8, 2008.

69. "US Sanctions Target Iran Carrier," *BBC News*, September 10, 2008, http://news.bbc.co.uk/2/hi/middle_east/7609150.stm.

70. "Experts Say Iran Resumed Nuke Weapons Plan," *UPI.com*, September 12 2008, http://www.upi.com/Top_News/2008/09/12/Experts_say_Iran_resumed_nuke_weapons_plan/UPI-12581221221568/.

71. "UN Nuclear Agency Criticises Iran," *BBC News*, September 15, 2008, http://news.bbc.co.uk/2/hi/middle_east/7616744.stm.

72. David Albright, Jacqueline Shire, and Paul Brannan, "IAEA Report on Iran: Centrifuge Operation Significantly Improving; Gridlock on Alleged Weaponization Issues," ISIS Report, September 15, 2008.

73. Mark Heinrich, "IAEA Shows Photos Alleging Iran Nuclear Missile Work," *Reuters*, September 17, 2008, http://www.iranfocus.com/en/nuclear/iaea-shows-photos-alleging-iran-nuclear-missile-work.html.

74. "Iran against Broader Cooperation with IAEA," *Agence France-Presse*, September 17, 2008, http://afp.google.com/article/ALeqM5iDAY5VRkOxsYMAUUTSVPPXLUD93g.

75. "Russia against New U.N. Measures on Iran," *Reuters*, September 20, 2008, http://www.reuters.com/article/worldNews/idUSLK12187420080920.

76. Iranian President Mahmoud Ahmadinejad addresses the United Nations General Assembly 63rd Session in New York, September 23, 2008. For his statement, see http://www.un.org/ga/63/generaldebate/iran.shtml.

77. Steven Lee Myers, "Russia Won't Meet with U.S. on Iranian Nuclear Program," *New York Times*, September 23, 2008.

78. Jonathan Steele, "Israel Asked US for Green Light to Bomb Nuclear Sites in Iran," *guardian.co.uk*, September 25, 2008, http://www.guardian.co.uk/world/2008/sep/25/iran.israelandthepalestinians1.

79. "U.S., Russia Reach Deal on New UN Iran Resolution," *Associated Press*, September 26, 2008; "UN Set to Reaffirm Iran Sanctions," *BBC News*, September 26, 2008.

80. "Iran: We Won't Halt Enrichment Even if Nuclear Fuel Supply Guaranteed," *Associated Press*, October 5, 2008; "Iran Refuses to Halt Enrichment for Fuel Guarantees," *Global Security Newswire*, October 6, 2008.

81. Elaine Sciolino, "Nuclear Aid by Russian to Iranians Suspected," *New York Times*, October 9, 2008; "Russian Aided Iranian Nuke Research, IAEA Suspects," *Global Security Newswire*, October 10, 2008.

82. Daniel Bombay and James Blitz, "Go-It-Alone Plan on Iran Sanctions," *The Financial Times*, October 12, 2008; "Western Nations Consider Independent Iran Sanctions," *Global Security Newswire*, October 14, 2008.

83. "Iranian Engineers Ready to Work on Nuclear Plant," *Associated Press*, October 14, 2008; "Western Nations Consider Independent Iran Sanctions," *Global Security Newswire*, October 14, 2008.

84. "Iran: Russia to Ship Nuke Plant Supplies," *United Press International*, October 17, 2008; "Russia Plans Major Supply Shipment to Iran," *Global Security Newswire*, October 20, 2008.

85. "Foreign Firms Interested to Build Darkhovin Nuclear Plant: Official," *Tehran Times*, October 20, 2008.

86. "IAEA Chief: Iran not Close to Developing Nuclear Weapons," *Haaretz*, October 21, 2008; "Iran Far from Nuke Capability, IAEA Chief Says," *Global Security Newswire*, October 21, 2008.

87. George Jahn, "Intel Says Iran Plans Secret Nuclear Experiments," *Associated Press*, October 30, 2008; "Iran Mulling Fuel Reprocessing Study, Report Says," *Global Security Newswire*, October 31, 2008.

88. "Russia Minister Says Moscow against New Iran Sanctions," *Agence France-Presse*, November 14, 2008; "Russia Opposes New Iran Sanctions," *Global Security Newswire*, November 17, 2008.

89. "Iran Says Preparations for Bushehr Nuclear Plant Inauguration Started," *Islamic Republic News Agency*, November 18, 2008.

90. "Implementation of the NPT Safeguards Agreement and Relevant Provisions of the Security Council Resolutions 1737 (2006), 1747 (2007), 1803 (2008) and 1835 (2008) in the Islamic Republic of Iran," International Atomic Energy Agency, November 19, 2008; Daniel Dombey and James Blitz, "Iran Increases Stockpile of Uranium," *The Financial Times*, November 19, 2008; "Iran Makes Nuclear Headway, IAEA Says," *Global Security Newswire*, November 19, 2008.

91. William J. Broad and David E. Sanger, "Iran Said to Have Nuclear Fuel for One Weapon," *New York Times*, November 20, 2008; "Iran Has Enough for A-Bomb: Agency," *The West Australian*, November 21, 2008; "Iran Rejects U.S. Reports It Has Basis for Atom Bomb," *Reuters*, November 21, 2008.

92. "Iran Says It Now Runs More than 5,000 Centrifuges," *Associated Press*, November 26, 2008; Nazila Fathi, "Iran: More Centrifuges Reported," *New York Times*, November 27, 2008.

93. Iran to Build New Nuclear Plants Instead of Second Unit at Bushehr," *RIA Novosti*, December 1, 2008; "Iran to Build Two More Nuclear Reactors," *Iranian Press TV*, December 2, 2008.

94. David Albright and Jacqueline Shire, "IAEA Report on Iran Nuclear Weapons Breakout Capability Achieved; Centrifuge Numbers and Low Enriched Uranium Output Steady; No Progress on Other Safeguards Issues," ISIS Report, February 19, 2009, http://isis-online.org/publications/iran/IAEA_Report_Analysis.pdf; the IAEA report by the Director General reported to the Board of Governors on the implementation of the NPT Safeguards Agreement and relevant provisions of Security Council resolutions 1737 (2006), 1747 (2007), 1803 (2008), and 1835 (2008) in the Islamic Republic of Iran (Iran) (GOV/2008/59) dated February 19, 2009.

95. Edward Yeranian, "Iranian, Russian Technicians Test Bushehr Nuclear Plant," *Voice of America*, February 25, 2009, http://www.voanews.com/english/2009-02-25-voa25.cfm; Tony Halpin, "Tehran Begins Test Run of Nuclear Plant Despite Weapons Fear," *The Times*, February 25, 2009, http://www.timesonline.co.uk/tol/news/world/middle_east/article5799150.ece; "Iran Says Nuclear Plant Could Start in Months," *Agence France-Presse*, February 25, 2009, http://www.google.com/hostednews/afp/article/ALeqM5hNu-qgB9EahpGMPQPyztR4NrkBXg.

96. Nasser Karimi, "Iran Says It Now Runs More than 6,000 Centrifuges, *Associated Press*, February 25, 2009, http://www.google.com/hostednews/ap/article/ALeqM5jG7bnyWW JfgaYD-JwcqmImlpRujwD96IKKTO0.

97. David Albright and Jacqueline Shire, "IAEA Report on Iran: Centrifuge and LEU Increases; Access to Arak Reactor Denied; No Progress on Outstanding Issues," ISIS Report, June 5, 2009, http://isis-online.org/publications/iran/Iran_IAEA_Report_Analysis _5June2009.pdf.

98. Jose Goldemberg, "Looking Back: Lessons from the Denuclearization of Brazil and Argentina," *Arms Control Today*, April 2006, http://www.armscontrol.org/act/2006_04/ LookingBack.

99. Earlier unclassified CIA reports on problems such as the ballistic missile threat often projected alternative levels of current and future capability. The qualifications and possible futures are far less well defined in more recent reports. For example, see CIA, "Unclassified Summary of a National Intelligence Estimate, Foreign Missile Developments and the Ballistic Missile Threat Through 2015," National Intelligence Council, December 2001, http:// www.cia.gov/nic/pubs/other_products/Unclassifiedballisticmissilefinal.htm.

100. There is no way to determine just how much the Special Plans Office team set up within the office of the Secretary of Defense to analyze the threat in Iraq was designed to produce a given conclusion or politicized intelligence. The Department has denied this and stated that the team created within its policy office was not working Iraqi per se, but on global terrorist interconnections. It also stated that the Special Plans Office was never tied to the Intelligence Collection Program—a program to debrief Iraqi defectors—and relied on CIA inputs for its analysis. It states that it simply conducted a review, presented its findings in August 2002, and its members returned to other duties. See Jim Garamone, "Policy Chief Seeks to Clear Intelligence Record," American Forces Information Service, June 3, 2003; and Briefing on Policy and Intelligence Matters, Douglas J. Feith, Under Secretary of Defense for Policy, and William J. Luti, Deputy Under Secretary of Defense for Special Plans and Near East and South Asian affairs, June 4, 2003, http://www.defenselink.mil/transcripts/2003/ tr20030604-0248.html.

Some intelligence experts dispute this view, however, and claim the team's effort was used to put press on the intelligence community. Such "B-teams" also have a mixed history. They did help identify an intelligence community tendency to underestimate Soviet strategic nuclear efforts during the Cold War. The threat analysis of missile threats posed to the United States by the "Rumsfeld Commission," however, was a heavily one-sided assessment designed to justify national missile defense. Also see Greg Miller, "Pentagon Defends Role of Intelligence Unit on Iraq," *Los Angeles Times*, June 5, 2003; and David S. Cloud, "The Case for War Relied on Selective Intelligence," *Wall Street Journal*, June 5, 2003.

101. Some press sources cite what they claim is a deliberate effort to ignore a September 2002 DIA report on Iraqi chemical weapons capabilities called "Iraq-Key WMD Facilities-An Operational Support Study." See James Risen, "Word that n Be a Weapon; by consistently finding an alternative explanation for all its actions, including concealment and actions that are limited violations of heres. (The 15-page document in fact, the unclassified excerpts from the DIA report, shows that the DIA was not stating that Iraqi did not have chemical weapons, but rather that it had, "No reliable information on whether Iraq is producing and stockpiling chemical weapons, or where Iraq has—or will—establish its chemical weapons facilities." The report went on to say that "although we lack any direct information, Iraq probably possesses CW agent in chemical munitions, possibly including artillery rockets, artillery shells, aerial

bombs, and ballistic missile warheads. Baghdad also probably possesses bulk chemical stock-piles, primarily containing precursors, but that also could consist of some mustard agent of stabilized VX."

If anything, the report is a classic example of what happens when intelligence reports do state uncertainty and of how the user misreads or misuses the result.

102. Alireza Jafarzadeh, "Iranian Regime's Plan and Attempts to Start Uranium Enrich-ment at Natanz Site," statement at the National Press Club, Washington, D.C., January 10, 2006.

103. "Iran Says It Will Resume Uranium Conversion Today," *Global Security Newswire*, August 11, 2005, http://www.nti.org/d_newswire/issues/2005/8/1/6860ebe5-d0a1-428e-829d-6005c7b26698.html.

104. Dafna Linzer, "Powell Says Iran Is Pursuing Bomb," *Washington Post*, November 18, 2004, p. A01.

105. "UN Atomic Agency Seeks to Visit Key Iranian Defense Site: Diplomats," *Agence France-Presse*, September 10, 2004.

106. Dafna Linzer, "Nuclear Disclosure on Iran Unverified," *Washington Post*, November 19, 2004, p. A01.

107. Dafna Linzer, "Powell Says Iran Is Pursuing Bomb," *Washington Post*, November 18, 2004, p. A01.

108. Linzer, "Nuclear Disclosure on Iran Unverified," p. A01.

109. Sonni Efron, Tyler Marshall, and Bob Drogin, "Powell's Talk of Arms Has Fallout," *Los Angeles Times*, November 19, 2004.

110. Carla Anne Robbins, "As Evidence Grows of Iran's Program, U.S. Hits Quandary," *Wall Street Journal*, March 18, 2005, p. 1.

111. IAEA, "Implementation of the NPT Safeguards Agreement in the Islamic Republic of Iran: Report by the Director General," November 15, 2004, p. 18, http://www.iaea.org/Pub-lications/Documents/Board/2004/gov2004-83_derestrict.pdf.

112. John R. Bolton, "Preventing Iran from Acquiring Nuclear Weapons," remarks to the Hudson Institute, Washington, D.C., August 17, 2004.

113. Information for chronology of key milestones in Iran's nuclear programs drawn from numerous open sources including multiple media outlets, www.nti.org, http://www.global securitynewswire.org/gsn/, www.globalsecurity.org, http://www.oxfordresearchgroup.org.uk/work/middle_east/iranchronology.php, www.iranwatch.org, IAEA reporting, http://www.wisconsinproject.org/countries/iran/nuke-miles.htm, http://www.isis-online.org/, etc.

114. "The Shah Meets the Press," *Kayhan International*, October 5, 1974.

115. "Moscow, Iran Sign Economic Pacts, Hint Future Arms Deals," *Los Angeles Times*, June 22, 1989.

116. "Iran Timeline: Key Events in the Lead Up to and Aftermath of the Iraq War," Wis-consin Project on Nuclear Arms Control, http://www.wisconsinproject.org/countries/iran/timeline.htm.

117. Daniel Dombey, "FT-Interview: Mohamed El-Baradei," *Financial Times*, February 19, 2007.

118. "Iran Says It Can Enrich Uranium on a Large Scale," *New York Times*, April 10, 2007, http://www.nytimes.com/2007/04/10/world/middleeast/10iran.html.

119. David E. Sanger, "Atomic Agency Concludes Iran Is Stepping Up Nuclear Work," *New York Times*, May 14, 2007; David E. Sanger, "Inspectors Cite Big Gain by Iran on Nuclear Fuel," *New York Times*, May 14, 2007.

120. "3 164-Machine Sets from 2nd Series of 3,000 Centrifuges in Motion—Source," IRNA, April 11, 2008, http://www2.irna.ir/en/news/view/line-17/0804112108181137.htm.

121. Con Coughlin, "Iran Has Resumed A-Bomb Project, Says West," *London Daily Telegraph*, July 7, 2008.

122. "UN Nuclear Agency Criticises Iran," *BBC News*, September 15, 2008, http://news.bbc.co.uk/2/hi/middle_east/7616744.stm.

123. David Albright, Jacqueline Shire, and Paul Brannan, "IAEA Report on Iran: Centrifuge Operation Significantly Improving; Gridlock on Alleged Weaponization Issues," ISIS Report, September 15, 2008.

124. Ibid.

125. Mark Heinrich, "IAEA Shows Photos Alleging Iran Nuclear Missile Work," *Reuters*, September 17, 2008, http://www.iranfocus.com/en/nuclear/iaea-shows-photos-alleging-iran-nuclear-missile-work.html.

126. "Iranian Engineers Ready to Work on Nuclear Plant," *Associated Press*, October 14, 2008; "Western Nations Consider Independent Iran Sanctions," *Global Security Newswire*, October 14, 2008.

127. "Iran: Russia to Ship Nuke Plant Supplies," *United Press International*, October 17, 2008; "Russia Plans Major Supply Shipment to Iran," *Global Security Newswire*, October 20, 2008.

128. "Foreign Firms Interested to Build Darkhovin Nuclear Plant: Official," *Tehran Times*, October 20, 2008.

129. "Implementation of the NPT Safeguards Agreement and Relevant Provisions of the Security Council Resolutions 1737 (2006), 1747 (2007), 1803 (2008) and 1835 (2008) in the Islamic Republic of Iran," International Atomic Energy Agency, November 19, 2008; Daniel Dombey and James Blitz, "Iran Increases Stockpile of Uranium," *The Financial Times*, November 19, 2008; "Iran Makes Nuclear Headway, IAEA Says," *Global Security Newswire*, November 19, 2008.

130. William J. Broad and David E. Sanger, "Iran Said to Have Nuclear Fuel for One Weapon," *New York Times*, November 20, 2008; "Iran Has Enough for A-Bomb: Agency," *The West Australian*, November 21, 2008.

131. "Iran Says It Now Runs More than 5,000 Centrifuges," *Associated Press*, November 26, 2008; Nazila Fathi, "Iran: More Centrifuges Reported," *New York Times*, November 27, 2008.

132. David Albright and Jacqueline Shire, "IAEA Report on Iran Nuclear Weapons Breakout Capability Achieved; Centrifuge Numbers and Low Enriched Uranium Output Steady; No Progress on Other Safeguards Issues," ISIS Report, February 19, 2009, http://isis-online.org/publications/iran/IAEA_Report_Analysis.pdf; the IAEA report by the Director General reported to the Board of Governors on the implementation of the NPT Safeguards Agreement and relevant provisions of Security Council resolutions 1737 (2006), 1747 (2007), 1803 (2008), and 1835 (2008) in the Islamic Republic of Iran (Iran) (GOV/2008/59), dated February 19, 2009.

133. Edward Yeranian, "Iranian, Russian Technicians Test Bushehr Nuclear Plant," *Voice of America*, February 25, 2009, http://www.voanews.com/english/2009-02-25-voa25.cfm; Tony Halpin, "Tehran Begins Test Run of Nuclear Plant Despite Weapons Fear," *The Times*, February 25, 2009, http://www.timesonline.co.uk/tol/news/world/middle_east/article5799150.ece; "Iran Says Nuclear Plant Could Start in Months."

134. Nasser Karimi, "Iran Says It Now Runs More than 6,000 Centrifuges, *Associated Press*, February 25, 2009, http://www.google.com/hostednews/ap/article/ALeqM5jG7bnyWW JfgaYD-JwcqmImlpRujwD96IKKTO0.

135. David Albright and Jacqueline Shire, "IAEA Report on Iran: Centrifuge and LEU Increases; Access to Arak Reactor Denied; No Progress on Outstanding Issues," ISIS Report, June 5, 2009, http://isis-online.org/publications/iran/Iran_IAEA_Report_Analysis _5June2009.pdf.

136. Information for Iran's key nuclear facilities drawn from numerous open sources including multiple media outlets, www.fas.org, www.nti.org, http://www.globalsecurity newswire.org/gsn/, www.globalsecurity.org, www.iranwatch.org, IAEA reporting, http:// www.wisconsinproject.org/countries/iran/nuke-miles.htm, http://www.isis-online.org/, etc.

137. "Metallurgical Engineering and Fuel Department," AEOI, http://www.aeoi.org.ir /NewWeb/department.asp?id=59.

138. "Implementation of the NPT Safeguards Agreement in the Islamic Republic of Iran," Director General IAEA, August 23, 2003, http://www.iaea.org/Publications/Documents/ Board/2003/gov2003-63.pdf.

139. Nasser Karimi, "Engineers Test-Run Nuclear Power Plant," *Washington Times*, February 26, 2009, http://www.washingtontimes.com/news/2009/feb/26/engineers-test-run-nuclear-power-plant/.

140. "Iranian Engineers Ready to Work on Nuclear Plant," *Associated Press*, October 14, 2008; "Western Nations Consider Independent Iran Sanctions," *Global Security Newswire*, October 14, 2008.

141. "Iran: Russia to Ship Nuke Plant Supplies," *United Press International*, October 17, 2008; "Russia Plans Major Supply Shipment to Iran," *Global Security Newswire*, October 20, 2008.

142. Karimi, "Engineers Test-Run Nuclear Power Plant."

143. The IAEA report by the Director General reported to the Board of Governors on the "Implementation of the NPT Safeguards Agreement and Relevant Provisions of Security Council Resolutions 1737 (2006), 1747 (2007), 1803 (2008) and 1835 (2008) in the Islamic Republic of Iran" (GOV/2009/33), June 5, 2009, http://isis-online.org/publications/iran/ IAEA_Iran_Report_5June2009.pdf.

144. David Albright and Corey Hinderstein, "Iran, Player or Rogue? The deadline Is Now. Will Iran Come Clean about Its Nuclear Doings?" *Bulletin of the Atomic Scientists*, 59, no. 5 (September/October 2003).

145. Rowan Scarborough, "U.S. Military Sees Iran's Nuke Bomb 5 Years Away", *Washington Post*, August 31, 2006.

146. Dafna Linzer, "Strong Leads and Dead Ends in Nuclear Case against Iran," *Washington Post*, February 8, 2006, p. A01.

147. Dnna Abu Nasr, "UN Nuke Chief: Iran's Program Limited," *Washington Post*, April 12, 2007; Dafna Linzer, "Boost In Iran's Capacity to Enrich Uranium Noted," *Washington Post*, April 19, 2007, p. 23; ISIS, "IAEA Letter to Iran's Representative," April 18, 2007, 5:38:23, isis@isis-online.org.

148. Frank Barnaby, "World Air Strikes Work?," Oxford Research Group, March 2007, p. 7.

149. David Albright, Jacqueline Shire, and Paul Brannan, "IAEA Report on Iran: Centrifuge Operation Significantly Improving; Gridlock on Alleged Weaponization Issues," ISIS Report, September 15, 2008.

150. David E. Sanger, "Atomic Agency Concludes Iran Is Stepping Up Nuclear Work," *New York Times*, May 14, 2007; David E. Sanger, "Inspectors Cite Big Gain by Iran on Nuclear Fuel," *New York Times*, May 14, 2007.

151. "IAEA Chief: Iran not Close to Developing Nuclear Weapons," *Haaretz*, October 21, 2008; "Iran Far from Nuke Capability, IAEA Chief Says," *Global Security Newswire*, October 21, 2008.

152. John Heilprin, "UN Nuclear Chief Says Iran Blocking Progress," *Associated Press*, October 28, 2008, http://www.iranfocus.com/en/nuclear/un-nuclear-chief-says-iran-blocking-progress-16575.html.

153. Albright and Shire, "IAEA Report on Iran Nuclear Weapons Breakout Capability Achieved"; the IAEA report by the Director General reported to the Board of Governors on the "Implementation of the NPT Safeguards Agreement and relevant provisions of Security Council resolutions 1737 (2006), 1747 (2007), 1803 (2008) and 1835 (2008) in the Islamic Republic of Iran" (GOV/2008/59) dated February 19, 2009.

154. Albright and Shire, "IAEA Report on Iran Nuclear Weapons Breakout Capability Achieved"; Israeli and other experts feel that Iran will get enough stocks of low-enriched material for a number of weapons—10–12 before it decides to convert it to weapons-grade uranium and this "breakout capability" would still require proof of ability to enrich to weapons-grade unranium.

155. Edward Yeranian, "Iranian, Russian Technicians Test Bushehr Nuclear Plant," *Voice of America*, February 25, 2009, http://www.voanews.com/english/2009-02-25-voa25.cfm; Tony Halpin, "Tehran Begins Test Run of Nuclear Plant Despite Weapons Fear," *The Times*, February 25, 2009, http://www.timesonline.co.uk/tol/news/world/middle_east/article5799150.ece; "Iran Says Nuclear Plant Could Start in Months."

156. Karimi, "Iran Says It Now Runs More than 6,000 Centrifuges."

157. David Albright and Jacqueline Shire, "IAEA Report on Iran: Centrifuge and LEU Increases; Access to Arak Reactor Denied; No Progress on Outstanding Issues," ISIS Report, June 5, 2009, http://isis-online.org/publications/iran/Iran_IAEA_Report_Analysis_5June2009.pdf.

158. Borzou Daragahi, "Iran Nuclear Program Advancing, U.N. Agency Says," *Los Angeles Times*, June 6, 2009, http://www.latimes.com/news/nationworld/world/la-fg-iran-nuclear6-2009jun06,0,515299.story.

159. Assessments from NIE report, "Iran: Nuclear Intentions and Capabilities," November 2007.

160. John R. Bolton, "Preventing Iran from Acquiring Nuclear Weapons," Remarks to the Hudson Institute, Washington, D.C., August 17, 2004.

161. Paul Kerr, "Russia, Iran Sign Deal to Fuel Bushehr Reactor," *Arms Control Today*, November 2006, http://www.armscontrol.org/act/2006_11/RussiaIran.asp.

162. Bolton, "Preventing Iran from Acquiring Nuclear Weapons."

163. Frank Barnaby, "World Air Strikes Work?," Oxford Research Group, March 2007, p. 7.

164. IAEA, "Implementation of the NPT Safeguards Agreement in the Islamic Republic of Iran: Report by the Director General," September 2, 2005, Annex 1, p. 14, http://www.iaea.org/Publications/Documents/Board/2005/gov2005-67.pdf.

165. Ian Black, "Syria Planned to Supply Iran with Nuclear Fuel, Israel Says," *Guardian* (London), June 25, 2008, http://www.guardian.co.uk/world/2008/jun/25/syria.iran.

166. IAEA, "Implementation of the NPT Safeguards Agreement in the Islamic Republic of Iran: Report by the Director General," p. 7.

167. "Iran Far from Nuclear Bomb-Making Capacity: Ex-UN Weapons Chief Blix," *Agence France-Presse*, June 23, 2005.

168. Frank Barnaby, "World Air Strikes Work?," Oxford Research Group, March 2007, p. 8.

169. Revati Prasad and Jill Marie Parillo, "Iran's Programs to Produce Plutonium and Enrichment Uranium," *Carnegie Fact Sheet*, February 2006.

170. Ali Akbar Dareini, "Iran to Move to Large Scale Enrichment," *Associated Press*, April 12, 2006.

171. "Iran Says to Go Ahead with Fuel Work," *Reuters*, August 27, 2006.

172. Ali Akbar, "Iran Hits Milestone in Nuclear Technology," *Associated Press*, April 11, 2006.

173. According to the "Iran Nuclear Timetable," *IranWatch.org*, University of Wisconsin Project on Nuclear Arms Control, updated February 2, 2009, based on IAEA reporting, Iran introduced 9,750 kg of UF_6 into centrifuges at Natanz from the beginning of operations in February 2007, to November 7, 2008 (http://www.iranwatch.org/international/IAEA/documents/iaea-iranreport-111908.pdf). The IAEA report by the Director General reported to the Board of Governors on the "Implementation of the NPT Safeguards Agreement and Relevant Provisions of Security Council Resolutions 1737 (2006), 1747 (2007), 1803 (2008) and 1835 (2008) in the Islamic Republic of Iran (Iran) (GOV/2008/59) dated February 19, 2009. David Albright and Jacqueline Shire "IAEA Report on Iran Nuclear Weapons Breakout Capability Achieved."

174. David Albright and Jacqueline Shire, "IAEA Report on Iran: Centrifuge and LEU Increases; Access to Arak Reactor Denied; No Progress on Outstanding Issues," ISIS Report, June 5, 2009, http://isis-online.org/publications/iran/Iran_IAEA_Report_Analysis_5June2009.pdf.

175. John R. Bolton, "Preventing Iran from Acquiring Nuclear Weapons," remarks to the Hudson Institute, Washington, D.C., August 17, 2004.

176. Revati Prasad and Jill Marie Parillo, "Iran's Programs to Produce Plutonium and Enriched Uranium," *Carnegie Fact Sheet*, February 2006.

177. IAEA, "Implementation of the NPT Safeguards Agreement in the Islamic Republic of Iran: Report by the Director General," November 15, 2004, http://www.iaea.org/Publications/Documents/Board/2004/gov2004-83_derestrict.pdf.

178. IAEA, "Implementation of the NPT Safeguards Agreement in the Islamic Republic of Iran: Report by the Director General," September 2, 2005, http://www.iaea.org/Publications/Documents/Board/2005/gov2005-67.pdf.

179. Ibid.

180. Prasad and Parillo, "Iran's Programs to Produce Plutonium and Enrichment Uranium."

181. IAEA, "Implementation of the NPT Safeguards Agreement in the Islamic Republic of Iran: Report by the Director General," September 2, 2005.

182. Prasad and Parillo, "Iran's Programs to Produce Plutonium and Enrichment Uranium."

183. "Iran Is Reported to Test New Centrifuge," *New York Times*, February 8, 2008; "Iran Testing New Centrifuges to Make Fuel," *The Weekend Australian*, February 9, 2008; David Albright and Jacqueline Shire, "Iran Installing More Advanced Centrifuge at Natanz Pilot

Enrichment Plant: Factsheet on the P-2/IR-2 Centrifuge," The Institute for Science and International Security, February 7, 2008.

184. Nazila Fathi and Christine Hauser, "Iran Marks Step in Nuclear Development," *New York Times,* April 11, 2006.

185. David Albright and Corey Hinderstein, "Iran's Next Steps: Final Tests and the Construction of a Uranium Enrichment Plant," Institute for Science and International Security, Issue Brief, January 12, 2006, http://www.isis-online.org/publications/iran/irancascade.pdf.

186. Prasad and Parillo, "Iran's Programs to Produce Plutonium and Enrichment Uranium."

187. IAEA, "Implementation of the NPT Safeguards Agreement and Relevant Provisions of Security Council Resolution 1737 (2006) in the Islamic, Republic of Iran, Report by the Director General" (Gov/2007/8), February 22, 2007.

188. David Albright and Jacqueline Shire, "Latest IAEA Report on Iran: Continued Progress on Cascade Operations, No New Cooperation with IAEA," Institute for Science and International Security, November 14, 2006.

189. Jacqueline Shire and David Albright, "Iran's Centrifuges: How Well Are They Working?," Institute for Science and International Security, March 15, 2007.

190. Ibid.

191. David Albright, "Iran's Nuclear Program: Status and Uncertainties," prepared testimony by David Albright, President, Institute for Science and International Security (ISIS), before the House Committee on Foreign Affairs, Subcommittee on Terrorism, Nonproliferation, and Trade, Subcommittee on the Middle East and Asia, March 15, 2007, p. 4.

192. Shire and Albright, "Iran's Centrifuges: How Well Are They Working?"

193. Barbara Slavin, "Iran Claims Nuclear Advance," *USA Today,* April 10, 2007, p. 1; Donna Abu Nasr, "UN Nuke Chief: Iran's Program Limited," *Washington Post,* April 12, 2007; Dafna Linzer, "Boost in Iran's Capacity to Enrich Uranium Noted," *Washington Post,* April 19, 2007, p. 23; ISIS, "IAEA Letter to Iran's Representative," April 18, 2007, 5:38:23, isis@isis-online.org; IAEA, "Communication Dated 18 April 2007 from the Secretariat to the Resident Representative of the Islamic Republic of Iran," IAEA GOV/Inf/2007/10, April 18, 2007.

194. Dr. Frank Barnaby, "Iran's Nuclear Activities," Oxford Research Group, February 2006.

195. IAEA, "Implementation of the NPT Safeguards Agreement in the Islamic Republic of Iran: Report by the Director General," September 15, 2008.

196. David Albright, Jacqueline Shire, and Paul Brannan, "IAEA Report on Iran: Centrifuge Operation Significantly Improving; Gridlock on Alleged Weaponization Issues," ISIS Report, September 15, 2008. Based on Iran's stated feed rates of 70 grams per hour per cascade, one would expect that a single cascade would consume 50 kg per month, with 18 cascades consuming 900 kg. Between May 7, 2008, and August 30, 2008, we calculate that 21 cascades were operating on average, with a potential maximum feed of 4,200 kg. Iran introduced 3,630 kg during this period, indicating that the cascades were operating at approximately 85-percent capacity. This is a significant increase over the 50-percent capacity indicated by the last IAEA report.

197. Albright, Shire, and Brannan, "IAEA Report on Iran: Centrifuge Operation Significantly Improving."

198. David Albright and Jacqueline Shire, "IAEA Report on Iran: Centrifuge and LEU Increases."

199. Albright, Shire, and Brannan, "IAEA Report on Iran: Centrifuge Operation Significantly Improving."

200. Figure 7.5 is adapted from the "Iran Nuclear Timetable," *IranWatch.org*, University of Wisconsin Project on Nuclear Arms Control, June 9, 2009, http://www.iranwatch.org/ourpubs/articles/iranucleartimetable.html. Some numbers reflect updates from the most recent IAEA report by the Director General reported to the Board of Governors on the "Implementation of the NPT Safeguards Agreement and relevant provisions of Security Council Resolutions 1737 (2006), 1747 (2007), 1803 (2008) and 1835 (2008) in the Islamic Republic of Iran" (GOV/2009/33) dated 5 June 2009 http://www.iranwatch.org/international/IAEA/iaea-iranreport-060509.pdf.

201. According to the IAEA, Iran had produced a total of 839 kg of low-enriched UF_6 as of November 17, 2008. Since then, Iran has produced approximately 500 kg of this material for a total of 1,339 kg (see note 209) (http://www.iranwatch.org/international/IAEA/iaea-iranreport-060509.pdf). Of that amount, 905 kg is uranium; 905 kg of uranium enriched to 3.5 percent contain 31.68 kg of U-235.

202. Iran is estimated to produce about 2.75 kg of low-enriched UF_6 each day (see note 210), for an average monthly production rate of 84 kg, 56 kg of which is uranium; enriched to 3.5 percent, this 56 kg contains 1.96 kg of U-235.

203. Sixteen kilograms are assumed to be sufficient for an implosion bomb. This was the amount called for in the implosion device Saddam Hussein was trying to perfect in the 1980s, and the design for such a device has circulated on the nuclear black market, to which Iran has had access. The critical mass of a sphere of U-235 metal is only 15 kg with a beryllium reflector. See Gunter Hildenbrand, "Nuclear Energy, Nuclear Exports and the Proliferation of Nuclear Weapons," AIF Conference on International Commerce and Safeguards for Civil Nuclear Power, March 1977. (For a schematic diagram of an implosion bomb, see www.wisconsinproject.org/bomb-facts/images/nw-1.jpg.)

204. Because of losses during the enrichment and weaponization processes, Iran would need about 914 kg (see note 212) of UF_6 enriched to 3.5 percent U-235, of which about 618 kg would be uranium, in order to achieve 16 kg of weapons-grade uranium. 618 kg of uranium enriched to 3.5 percent U-235 contains 21.6 kg of U-235. See the Separative Work Unit (SWU) calculator published by URENCO, a European uranium enrichment consortium: web.archive.org/web/20021226100607/www.urenco.de/trennarbeit/swucal_e.html.

205. Assuming 19.9 kg of U-235 on hand as of November 17, 2008, a requirement of 21.6 kg for a first bomb, and a production rate of 1.6 kg of U-235 each month, Iran would have had enough in December 2008.

206. Once enriched to weapons grade, this material would still need to be converted from gas to metal and then machined into a form suitable for a bomb. The IAEA estimates the conversion time for low-enriched uranium to weapons-grade uranium metal to be approximately 3–12 months (www-pub.iaea.org/MTCD/publications/PDF/nvs-3-cd/PDF/NVS3_prn.pdf). However, if it would take approximately 822 SWUs to produce 16 kg of weapons-grade uranium from a stockpile of 3.8 percent enriched uranium and if Iran is producing at least 6,000 SWUs per year, then a conversion time at the lower end of this range is probable. Therefore, Iran could have weapons-grade UF_6 within 2–3 months, even assuming a delay in processing.

207. If Iran were to add by April 1, 2009, the 1,476 centrifuges it has installed and placed under vacuum, the monthly production rate of U-235 would increase by about 37 percent to 2.2 kg per month, and if by June 2009 Iran operates all 5,904 centrifuges that are currently

either in use or being installed, and adds no additional centrifuges, the monthly production rate of U-235 would increase by about 9 percent to approximately 2.4 kg per month. These production rates would allow Iran to accumulate the requisite 21.6 kg for a second bomb by October 2009.

208. If by June 2009 Iran operates all 5,904 centrifuges that are currently either in use or being installed, and if the feed rate for these machines improves modestly, the monthly production rate of low-enriched UF_6 would be approximately 150 kg and Iran could accumulate the requisite 707 kg by November 2009.

209. According to the IAEA, Iran had an inventory of 839 kg of low-enriched UF_6 as of November 17, 2008, based on production from the beginning of operations (http://www.iranwatch.org/international/IAEA/documents/iaea-iranreport-021909.pdf); Iran has estimated that it produced 171 kg of this material from November 18, 2008, through January 31, 2009, and 329 kg between February 1, 2009, and May 31, 2009, for a total of 1,339 kg of low-enriched UF_6 (http://www.iranwatch.org/international/IAEA/iaea-iranreport-060509.pdf).

210. Iran estimates that it produced 330 kg of low-enriched UF_6 over 120 days, from February 1, 2009, to May 31, 2009, for an average daily production rate of 2.75 kg.

211. According to the IAEA, Iran produced about 150 kg of low-enriched UF_6 from September 1, 2008, to November 7, 2008; Iran had 480 kg of this material as of August 30 (www.iranwatch.org/international/IAEA/iaea-iranreport-091508.pdf) and 630 kg as of November 7 (http://www.iranwatch.org/international/IAEA/documents/iaea-iranreport-111908.pdf); thus, Iran produced 150 kg of low-enriched UF_6 over 2.1 months, or approximately 71.4 kg/month.

212. This is assuming uranium tails of 1 percent U-235, a feed assay of 3.5 percent U-235, a product assay of 93 percent U-235, a 5-percent loss of material during bomb manufacture, and that 16 kg of this product are needed for a bomb. See the SWU calculator published by URENCO.

213. The Separative Work Unit is the standard measure of the effort required to increase the concentration of the fissionable U-235 isotope. See www.urenco.com/Content/89/Glossary.aspx.

214. Based on the assumptions set forth above (see note 212), Iran would need approximately 840 SWUs to bring 914 kg of low-enriched UF_6 to weapons grade. See the SWU calculator published by URENCO.

215. According to the IAEA, Iran is operating an 18-cascade unit (A24) of 2,952 machines and 12 cascades (1.968 machines) in a second unit (A26) at the Natanz Fuel Enrichment Plant (http://www.iranwatch.org/international/IAEA/iaea-iranreport-060509.pdf).

216. Iran is operating its IR-1 centrifuges at well below their estimated capacity. For instance, between November 2008 and May 2009, during which Iran was operating an average of 4.346 machines, an estimated 500 kg of low-enriched UF_6 were produced. Assuming a product assay of 3.5 percent U-235 and tails of .4 percent U-235, this amounts to about 1,230 SWU, or nearly .3 SWU per machine.

217. Between December 2007 and November 2008, during which Iran was operating an average of 3,444 machines, 764 kg of low-enriched UF_6 were produced. Assuming a product assay of 3.5 percent U-235 and tails of .4 percent U-235, this represents about 1,880 SWUs, or just over .5 SWU per machine.

218. According to the IAEA, Iran is operating an 18-cascade unit (A24) of 2,952 machines and 12 cascades (1,968 machines) in a second unit (A26); a further six cascades (984

machines) at unit A26 and seven cascades (1,148 machines) at unit A28 are installed and under vacuum (http://www.iranwatch.org/international/IAEA/iaea-iranreport-060509.pdf).

219. Iran's IR-1 centrifuge is widely estimated to have an annual enrichment capacity of about two SWUs. Iran, however, has been achieving a much lower output (see note 216). If Iran were to increase the efficiency of its centrifuges to one SWU per machine, the machines operating at the Natanz Fuel Enrichment Plant would produce about 7,000 SWUs per year.

220. If 840 SWUs are needed to bring a bomb's worth of Iran's stockpiled low-enriched UF_6 to weapons grade, and if Iran's centrifuges produce approximately 7,000 SWUs per year, or 583 SWUs per month, then it would probably take less than two months to achieve 840 SWUs.

221. According to the "Iran Nuclear Timetable," *IranWatch.org*, University of Wisconsin Project on Nuclear Arms Control, updated March 1, 2009, based on IAEA reporting, 348 metric tons is the total amount of UF_6 produced by Iran at its Uranium Conversion Facility from the beginning of operations in March 2004 to November 7, 2008 (http://www .iranwatch.org/international/IAEA/documents/iaea-iranreport-111908.pdf).

The IAEA report by the Director General reported to the Board of Governors on the "Implementation of the NPT Safeguards Agreement and Relevant Provisions of Security Council resolutions 1737 (2006), 1747 (2007), 1803 (2008) and 1835 (2008) in the Islamic Republic of Iran (GOV/2008/59), dated February 19, 2009, states that "As of 9 February 2009, approximately 42 tonnes of uranium in the form of UF6 had been produced at the Uranium Conversion Facility (UCF) since 8 March 2008, the date of the last PIV carried out by the Agency at UCF. This brings the total amount of uranium in the form of UF6 produced at UCF since March 2004 to 357 tonnes, some of which was transferred to FEP and PFEP," http://www.isisnucleariran.org/assets/pdf/IAEA_Report_Iran_Feb_2009.pdf.

222. Natural uranium feed, a product assay of 93 percent, and tails of .4 percent, 357 metric tons of UF_6 would yield approximately 800 kg of uranium enriched to 93 percent U-235; if 16 kg of 93-percent material are required to fuel one first-generation implosion device, then this 800 kg of uranium would be enough to fuel 45–50 such weapons.

223. According to the "Iran Nuclear Timetable," *IranWatch.org*, University of Wisconsin Project on Nuclear Arms Control, updated February 2, 2009, based on IAEA reporting, Iran introduced 9,750 kg of UF_6 into centrifuges at Natanz from the beginning of operations in February 2007, to November 7, 2008 (http://www.iranwatch.org/international/IAEA/docu-ments/iaea-iranreport-111908.pdf).

The IAEA report by the Director General reported to the Board of Governors on the "Implementation of the NPT Safeguards Agreement and relevant provisions of Security Council resolutions 1737 (2006), 1747 (2007), 1803 (2008) and 1835 (2008) in the Islamic Republic of Iran" (GOV/2008/59), dated February 19, 2009, states that "the Agency has verified that, as of 17 November 2008, 9956 kg of UF6 had been fed into the cascades since February 2007," http://www.isisnucleariran.org/assets/pdf/IAEA_Report_Iran_Feb_2009.pdf.

224. According to the IAEA, Iran fed centrifuge cascades at the Natanz Fuel Enrichment Plant with 2,150 kg of UF_6 from August 30, 2008 to November 7, 2008.

225. According to the IAEA, during this 8.5-month period, Iran fed 5,930 kg of UF_6 into operating cascades at the Natanz Fuel Enrichment Plant.

226. According to the IAEA, during this 10.5-month period, Iran fed 1,670 kg of UF_6 into operating cascades at the Natanz Fuel Enrichment Plant, yielding 75 kg of low-enriched UF_6.

227. According to the IAEA, during this 8.5-month period, Iran fed 5,930 kg of UF_6 into operating cascades at the Natanz Fuel Enrichment Plant, yielding 405 kg of low-enriched UF_6.

228. Figure 7.6 is adapted from the "Iran Nuclear Timetable," *IranWatch.org*, University of Wisconsin Project on Nuclear Arms Control, June 1, 2009, http://www.iranwatch.org/our-pubs/articles/iranucleartimetable.html. Some numbers reflect updates from the most recent IAEA report by the Director General reported to the Board of Governors on the "Implementation of the NPT Safeguards Agreement and relevant provisions of Security Council resolutions 1737 (2006), 1747 (2007), 1803 (2008) and 1835 (2008) in the Islamic Republic of Iran" (GOV/2009/35), dated June 5, 2009, http://isis-online.org/publications/iran/IAEA _Iran_Report_5June2009.pdf.

229. IAEA, "Implementation of the NPT Safeguards Agreement in the Islamic Republic of Iran: Report by the Director General," September 1, 2004, Annex, p. 7, http://www.iaea.org/ Publications/Documents/Board/2004/gov2004-60.pdf.

230. Ibid.

231. Ibid.

232. Ibid.

233. IAEA, "Implementation of the NPT Safeguards Agreement in the Islamic Republic of Iran: Report by the Director General," September 1, 2004, p. 7, http://www.iaea.org/ Publications/Documents/Board/2004/gov2004-60.pdf.

234. Dr. Frank Barnaby, "Iran's Nuclear Activities," Oxford Research Group, February 2006.

235. Ali Akbar, "Iran Confirms Uranium-to-Gas Conversion," *Associated Press,* May 9, 2005.

236. Elaine Sciolino and William J. Broad, "Atomic Agency Sees Possible Link of Military to Iran Nuclear Work," *New York Times*, February 1, 2006, p. 1.

237. Linzer, "Strong Leads and Dead Ends in Nuclear Case against Iran," *Washington Post,* p. A01.

238. IAEA, "Implementation of the NPT Safeguards Agreement in the Islamic Republic of Iran: Resolution Adopted on 4 February 2006, February 4, 2006, http://www.iaea.org/ Publications/Documents/Board/2006/gov2006-14.pdf.

239. IAEA, "Implementation of the NPT Safeguards Agreement in the Islamic Republic of Iran: Report by the Director General," November 18, 2005, p. 11, http://www.iaea.org/ Publications/Documents/Board/2005/gov2005-87.pdf.

240. Ian Traynor, "Papers Found in Iran Are Evidence of Plans for Nuclear Weapon Manufacture, Says UK," *Guardian* (Manchester), November 25, 2005, http://www.guardian .co.uk/iran/story/0,,1650423,00.html.

241. "Iran Hands over Suspected Atom Bomb Blueprint: IAEA," *Agence France-Presse*, November 18, 2005.

242. David Albright and Corey Hinderstein, "The Clock Is Ticking, But How Fast?," Institute for Science and International Security, Issue Brief, March 27, 2006, http://www .isis-online.org/publications/iran/clockticking.pdf.

243. "Iran Hands over Suspected Atom Bomb Blueprint."

244. "Iran Far from Nuclear Bomb-Making Capacity: Ex-UN Weapons Chief Blix," *Agence France-Presse*, June 23, 2005.

245. Kelly Hearn, "Iranian Pact with Venezuela Stokes Fears of Uranium Sales," *Washington Times*, March 13, 2006, p. 1.

246. The document is available at http://www.dni.gov/press_releases/20071203 _release.pdf.

247. Director of National Intelligence, "Iran: Nuclear Intentions and Capabilities," National Intelligence Estimate, November 2007, http://www.dni.gov/press_releases/20071203_release.pdf.

248. Extract from J. Michael McConnell, Director of National Intelligence, "Annual Threat Assessment of the Intelligence Community for the Senate Armed Services Committee," February 27, 2008.

249. Dennis C. Blair, Director of National Intelligence, "Annual Threat Assessment of the Intelligence Community for the Senate Select Committee on Intelligence, Office of the Director of National Intelligence," February 12, 2009, pp. 19–20.

250. Drawn from quotes assembled by Y Mansharof of MEMRI, *Inquiry and Analysis-Iran*, No. 342, www.themeriblog.org.

251. IRNA, Keyan, April 10, 2007.

252. IRNA, (Iran) April 10, 2007.

253. IRNA (Iran) and Keyhan, April 10, 2007.

254. Keyhan editorial, "The West Must Expect a Shock from Iran at Any Moment, April 10, 2007.

255. Keyhan editorial, "Duel with an Unloaded Gun," April 11, 2007.

256. "Iran: We Won't Halt Enrichment Even if Nuclear Fuel Supply Guaranteed," *Associated Press*, October 5, 2008; "Iran Refuses to Halt Enrichment for Fuel Guarantees," *Global Security Newswire*, October 6, 2008.

257. "Iranian Engineers Ready to Work on Nuclear Plant," *Associated Press*, October 14, 2008; "Western Nations Consider Independent Iran Sanctions," *Global Security Newswire*, October 14, 2008; "Iran: Russia to Ship Nuke Plant Supplies," *United Press International*, October 17, 2008; "Russia Plans Major Supply Shipment to Iran," *Global Security Newswire*, October 20, 2008.

258. Nasser Karimi, "Engineers Test-Run Nuclear Power Plant," *Washington Times*, February 26, 2009, http://www.washingtontimes.com/news/2009/feb/26/engineers-test-run-nuclear-power-plant/.

259. IAEA, "Implementation of the NPT Safeguards Agreement and Relevant Provisions of Security Council Resolutions 1737 (2006), 1747 (2007), 1803 (2008) and 1835 (2008) in the Islamic Republic of Iran," June 5, 2009, http://isis-online.org/publications/iran/IAEA_Iran_Report_5June2009.pdf.

260. Elaine Sciolino and William J. Broad, "Atomic Agency Sees Possible Link of Military to Iran Nuclear Work," *New York Times*, February 1, 2006, p. 1.

261. Dafna Linzer, "Powell Says Iran Is Pursuing Bomb," *Washington Post*, November 18, 2004, p. A01.

262. Linzer, "Strong Leads and Dead Ends in Nuclear Case against Iran," p. A01.

263. Ibid.

264. IAEA, "Implementation of the NPT Safeguards Agreement in the Islamic Republic of Iran: Resolution Adopted on 4 February 2006."

265. Linzer, "Strong Leads and Dead Ends in Nuclear Case against Iran," p. A01.

266. David Albright, Jacqueline Shire, and Paul Brannan, "IAEA Report on Iran: Centrifuge Operation Significantly Improving; Gridlock on Alleged Weaponization Issues," ISIS Report, September 15, 2008.

267. Mark Heinrich, "IAEA Shows Photos Alleging Iran Nuclear Missile Work," *Reuters*, September 17, 2008, http://www.iranfocus.com/en/nuclear/iaea-shows-photos-alleging-iran-nuclear-missile-work.html.

268. IAEA Director General Dr. Mohamed ElBaradei, Statement to the Sixty-Third Regular Session of the United Nations General Assembly, UN General Assembly New York, October 28, 2008, http://www.iaea.org/NewsCenter/Statements/2008/ebsp2008n010.html.

CHAPTER 8

1. This explanation is adapted from "Nuclear Weapons Design," Wikipedia, http://en.wikipedia.org/wiki/Nuclear_weapon_design. All nuclear weapons design data in this chapter are deliberately chosen to be nominal and available in open-source material. The concepts presented are broadly correct, but a deliberate effort had been made to avoid any "how to" level of accuracy.

2. Ibid.

3. Energy Information Agency (EIA), *International Energy Outlook, 2008*, Washington, Department of Energy, June 2008, p. 207.

4. The key problems are dispersion and the lethality of the dispersed material. For further details, see Anthony H. Cordesman, "Radiological Weapons as a Means of Attack," CSIS Burke Chair, November 8, 2001, http://www.csis.org/index.php?option=com_csis_pubs &task=view&id=1288; Centers for Disease Control and Prevention, "Frequently Asked Questions About Dirty Bombs," http://www.bt.cdc.gov/radiation/dirtybombs.asp; Nuclear Regulatory Commission, "Fact Sheet on Dirty Bombs, http://www.nrc.gov/reading-rm/doc-collections/fact-sheets/dirty-bombs.html. A model of potential "worst-case" attacks is summarized in the testimony of Dr. Henry Kelly, President of the Federation of American Scientists, before the Senate Committee on Foreign Relations, March 6, 2002, http://www.fas.org/ssp/docs/030602-kellytestimony.htm.

5. The Report of the Commission on the Prevention of WMD Proliferation and Terrorism, World at Risk, New York, Vintage Books, December, 2008, documents.scribd.com/docs/2avb51ejt0uadzxm2wpt.pdf or www.globalsecurity.org/wmd/library/report/2008/wmd-prolif-terror-commission.htm, pp. xvi, xvii, 11–13.

6. Daniel Dombey and Stephanie Kirchgaessner, "Fresh Ways of Turning the Screw on Iran," *Financial Times*, October 22, 2007.

7. Gareth Smyth, "Sanctions Fail to Fuel Dissent on Iran's Streets," *Financial Times*, July 24, 2007.

8. Danielle Pletka, "Congress's Ill-Timed Iran Bills," *Washington Post*, August 28, 2007.

9. Bertrand Benoit, "Berlin Hardens Trade Stance with Iran," *Financial Times*, February 11, 2008.

10. See Keith Crane, Rollie Lal, and Jeffrey Martini, *Iran's Political, Demographic, and Economic Vulnerabilities*, (Santa Monica, CA: RAND, 2008), www.rand.org/pubs/monographs/2008/RAND_MG693.sum.pdf; Borzou Daragahi and Ramin Mostaghim, "Iran Mulls Financial Bailout as Stock Market Falls," *Los Angeles Times*, December 19, 2008; Omid Memarian, "Economy Iran: From Bad to Worse," IPS, December 22, 2008, http://ipsnews.net/news.asp?idnews=45184; CIA, "Iran," *World Factbook, 2008*, https://www.cia.gov/library/publications/the-world-factbook/geos/ir.html; Greg Bruno, "With Oil Down, Will Iran Follow?," Council on Foreign Relations, Daily Analysis, October 28, 2008, http://www.cfr.org/publication/17626/with_oil_down_will_iran_follow.html.

11. CIA, "Iran," *World Factbook, 2008*.

12. EIA, "Iran, A Country Analysis," October 2007, http://www.eia.doe.gov/emeu/cabs/Iran/Background.html.

13. EIA, OPEC Oil Revenues Fact Sheet, December 2008, http://www.eia.doe.gov/cabs/OPEC_Revenues/Factsheet.html.

14. Memarian, "Economy Iran: From Bad to Worse"; Bruno, "With Oil Down, Will Iran Follow?".

15. "Iran Transactions Regulations", U.S. Department of Treasury's Office of Foreign Assets Control (OFAC), 26 November 26, 2008, http://www.treas.gov/offices/enforcement/ofac/programs/iran/iran.shtml.

16. IEA, World Energy Outlook 2005, Middle East and North Africa Insights, OECD/IEA, Paris, 2005, p. 361.

17. The EIA reports that Iran has a combined capacity of 1.64 MMBD according to Oil and Gas Journal. Major refineries include: Abadan (400,000-bbl/d capacity); Isfahan (265,000 bbl/d); Bandar Abbas (232,000 bbl/d); Tehran (225,000 bbl/d); Arak (150,000 bbl/d); and Tabriz (112,000 bbl/d). Gasoline demand is forcast to be growing at around 11.4 percent per year. Iran plans to increase its refining capacity to 2.54 million bbl/d by 2010. One goal of this expansion is to allow Iran's refineries to process a heavier crude slate, while decreasing the fuel oil cut. Currently, Iran's refineries produce around 30 percent heavy fuel oil and just 16 percent gasoline. In addition, diesel sulfur levels are slated for a major reduction from 500 parts per million (ppm) to 50 ppm by 2010, requiring significant additional hydrotreating capacity.

The National Iranian Oil Refining and Distribution Company (NIORDC) plans to begin construction work as early as September 2006 on three units aimed at increasing gasoline production from the Isfahan refinery. Currently, technical proposals are being reviewed for the construction of three units: a 32,000 bbl/d continuous catalytic reformer (CCR) unit; a 27,000 bbl/d isomerization unit; and a 62,000 bbl/d hydrotreater. Construction is expected to cost $300 million. NIORDC is negotiating with bidders to reduce construction time from 36 months to 30 months.

In June 2004, Japan's JGC reached an agreement with Iran to expand Arak to 250,000 bbl/d by 2009. In addition, in 2005 it was announced that a new 180,000-bbl/d-capacity refinery is being planned for Abadan. Bandar Abbas is being expanded in several phases and is on schedule to meet goals of adding around 250,000 bbl/d of capacity by 2010. Two planned grassroots refineries include a 225,000-bbl/d plant at Shah Bahar and a 120,000-bbl/d unit on Qeshm Island. Under Iranian law, foreign companies are permitted to own no more than 49 percent of Iranian oil refining assets.

Iran plans to boost capacity at its northern refineries at Arak, Tebriz, and Tehran in order to process additional Caspian oil. In August 2003, a $500 million tender was issued to upgrade the Tehran and Tabriz refineries in order to handle 370,000 bbl/d of high sulfur Caspian crude. This follows a $330 million project, completed by a Sinopec-led consortium in late 2003, to expand storage at Neka and to upgrade the Tehran and Tabriz refineries. (EIA, "Iran," *Country Analysis Briefs*, January 2006, http://www.eia.doe.gov/emeu/cabs/Iran/pdf.pdf.)

18. EIA, "Iran, A Country Analysis," October 2007, http://www.eia.doe.gov/emeu/cabs/Iran/Full.html.

19. Aussenwirtschaft Österreich, Iran—*Newsletter Nr. 15*, November 2005.

20. Bhushann Bahree and Marc Champion, "In Iran Nuclear Standoff, Scant Leverage for West," *Wall Street Journal*, August 21, 2006.

21. EIA, "Oil Market Report," December 11, 2008, http://omrpublic.iea.org/currentissues/full.pdf; Hashem Kalantari, "Iran Could Cope with Oil as Low as $5—Ahmadinejad,"

Reuters, November 23, 2008, http://www.iranfocus.com/en/iran-general-/iran-could-cope-with-oil-as-low-as-5-ahmadinejad-16732.html; Ian King, "Iran and Venezuela to Link up at OPEC Talks in Drive to Push Oil Price Back to $100 a Barrel," *The Times*, November 28, 2008, http://www.iranfocus.com/en/iran-general-/iran-and-venezuela-to-link-up-at-opec-talks-in-drive-to-push-oil-price-back-to-100-a-barrel-16771.html.

22. Jeffrey J. Schott, "Economic Sanctions, Oil, and Iran," statement by Jeffrey J. Schott before the Joint Economic Committee, United States Congress Hearing on "Energy and the Iranian Economy," July 25, 2006.

23. Bhushann Bahree and Marc Champion, "In Iran Nuclear Standoff, Scant Leverage for West," *Wall Street Journal*, August 21, 2006.

24. EIA, "Iran," *Country Analysis Briefs*, October 2007, http://www.eia.doe.gov/emeu/cabs/Iran/pdf.pdf.

25. EIA, "Iran Country Analysis Webpage," updated January 2009, http://www.iea.org/Textbase/country/n_country.asp?COUNTRY_CODE=IR#bottom; and EIA, "World Energy Outlook 2008," December 8, 2008, http://www.iea.org/Textbase/speech/2008/Tanaka/cop_weosideeven.pdf.

26. NZZ, Wie resistent ist Irans Wirtschaft gegen Sanktionen?, March 1, 2007.

27. EIA, "Iran," *Country Analysis Briefs*, January 2006, http://www.eia.doe.gov/emeu/cabs/Iran/pdf.pdf.

28. EIA, "Iran Energy Profile," updated December 17, 2008, http://tonto.eia.doe.gov/country/country_energy_data.cfm?fips=IR.

29. Gareth Smyth, "Expenditure to Rise 20% under Iranian Budget Proposals," *Financial Times*, January 22, 2007.

30. Aussenwirtschaft Österreich, Iran—*Newsletter Nr. 12*, December 2005, p. 3; Daniel Altman, "Quandary over Iran Sanctions," *The International Herald Tribune*, January 24, 2006.

31. NZZ, Wie resistent ist Irans Wirtschaft gegen Sanktionen?, March 1, 2007.

32. IEA, World Energy Outlook 2005, Middle East and North Africa Insights, OECD/IEA, Paris, 2005, p. 568.

33. Gareth Smyth, "Iranians to Lose Access to Unlimited Cheap Fuel," *Financial Times*, March 9, 2007.

34. Daniel Glaser, testimony before the House Committee on Foreign Affairs Subcommittee on the Middle East and South Asia and the Subcommittee on Terrorism, Nonproliferation, and Trade, April 17, 2008, HP-933.

35. Examples compiled from CRS Report for Congress (RL34525) on Iran's Economy dated 22 August 2008 by Shayerah Ilias Analyst in International Trade and Finance Foreign Affairs, Defense, and Trade Division.

36. E.O. 13224, "Blocking Property and Prohibiting Transactions with Persons Who Commit, Threaten to Commit, or Support Terrorism," September 23, 2001; IMF, "Islamic Republic of Iran: 2006 Article IV Consultation," IMF Country Report No. 07/100, March 2007, p. 17.

37. E.O. 13382, "Blocking Property of Weapons of Mass Destruction Proliferators and Their Supporters," June 28, 2005; Treasury press release, "Iran's Bank Sepah Designated by Treasury," January 9, 2007, http://www.treas.gov/press/releases/hp219.htm.

38. Treasury press release, "Statement by Secretary Paulson on Iran Designations," October 25, 2007, http://www.treas.gov/press/releases/hp645.htm. Treasury press release, "Factsheet: Designation of Iranian Entities and Individuals for Proliferation Activities and Support for Terrorism," October 25, 2007, http://www.treas.gov/press/releases/hp644.htm.

39. Ibid.

40. Treasury press release, "Treasury Designates Iran-Controlled Bank for Proliferation: Future Bank Controlled by Iran's Bank Melli," March 12, 2008, http://www.treas.gov/press/releases/hp869.htm.

41. "Iran: Iran Dismisses US Allegations against Banks as Ridiculous," *Thai News Service*, August 18, 2008.

42. Samuel Ciszuk, "UN Security Council Tightens Iran Sanctions, Complicating Oil and Gas Developments and Trade," *Global Insight Daily Analysis*, March 4, 2008.

43. Christian Oliver and Alireza Ronaghi, "Iran's Powerful Bazaar Braced for Atomic Storm," *Reuters*, February 7, 2006.

44. Christian Oliver, "Iran Bravado on UN Sanctions May Ring Hallow," *Reuters*, February 1, 2006.

45. CRS Report to Congress (RL34525) on Iran's Economy, June 12, 2008, by Shayerah Ilias Analyst in International Trade and Finance Foreign Affairs, Defense, and Trade Division.

46. CIA, "Iran," *The World Fact Book*, 2008, https://www.cia.gov/cia/publications/factbook/geos/ir.html.

47. Nazila Fathi and Andrew E. Kramer, "With Threat of Sanctions, Iran Protects Some Assets," *New York Times*, January 21, 2006, p. 5.

48. "Iran Denies Shifting Assets in Europe," *Gulf Daily News*, January 20, 2006, http://www.gulf-daily-news.com/Story.asp?Article=133050&Sn=BesueID=28306.

49. Aussenwirtscd vereft Österreich, Iran—*Newsletter Nr. 12*, p. 4.

50. "Iran," World Bank, http://web.worldbank.org/WBSITE/EXTERNAL/COUNTRIES/MENAEXT/IRANEXTN/0,,menuPK:312962~pagePK:141159~piPK:141110~theSitePK:312943,00.html.

51. Anna Fifield, "No Problem," *Financial Times*, April 14, 2008. CRS Report to Congress (RL34525) on Iran's Economy, June 12, 2008, by Shayerah Ilias Analyst in International Trade and Finance Foreign Affairs, Defense, and Trade Division.

52. David Albright, Paul Brannan, and Andrea Scheel, "Iranian Entities' Illicit Military Procurement Networks," ISIS, January 12, 2009, http://isis-online.org/publications/expcontrol/IranMilitaryProcurement.pdf.

53. The package is formally outlined in Annex I to U.N. Resolution 1747.

54. Annex I to U.N. Resolution 1747 as summarized in: CRS Report to Congress (RL32048) "Iran: U.S. Concerns and Policy Response," November 24, 2008, by Kenneth Katzman Specialist in Middle Eastern Affairs Foreign Affairs, Defense, and Trade Division.

55. CRS Report to Congress (RL32048) "Iran: U.S. Concerns and Policy Response," November 24, 2008, by Kenneth Katzman Specialist in Middle Eastern Affairs Foreign Affairs, Defense, and Trade Division.

56. Ibid.

57. Ibid.

58. Ibid.

59. Ibid.

60. The list of such groups keeps changing. For a summary list current in 2008, and a description of many of the groups involved, see Global Security, "Iran Opposition Groups," http://www.globalsecurity.org/intell/world/iran/links.htm.

61. See note 42, Chapter 2. For a good summary description, see Holly Fletcher, *Mujahadeen-e-Khalq (MEK) (aka People's Mujahedin of Iran or PMOI)*, Backgrounder, New York, Council on Foreign Relations, April 18, 2008.

62. Ernesto Londoño, "Iraq Threatens to Expel Iranian Rebels," *Washington Post*, December 22, 2008, page A15.

63. David E Sanger, "U.S. Rejected Aid for Israeli Raid on Iranian Nuclear Site," *New York Times*, January 11, 2009.

64. For a sample of unclassified satellite imagery, see David Albright, Paul Brannan, and Jacqueline Shire, "Can Military Strikes Destroy Iran's Gas Centrifuge Program? Probably not," Institute for Science and International Security (ISIS), August 7, 2008, http://www.isis-online.org/. ISIS has other publications at the same location showing a wider range of satellite pictures.

65. Information for Iran's key nuclear facilities is drawn from numerous open sources including (but not limited to) multiple media outlets; www.fas.org; www.nti.org; http://www.globalsecuritynewswire.org/gsn/; www.globalsecurity.org/GlobalSecurity.org; http://www.globalsecurity.org/wmd/world/iran/nuke-fac.htm; www.iranwatch.org; IAEA reporting; , http://www.isis-online.org/: Frank Barnaby, "World Air Strikes Work?, " Oxford Research Group, March 2007, pp. 9 and 1.

66. Figures 8.5–8.8 were made available for this publication courtesy of the Nuclear Threat Initiative and are available at www.nti.org.

67. Robin Hughes, "Iranian Nuclear Facilities Digging in with 10,000 m2 of Reinforced Concrete Tunnels: Tehran Takes Steps to Protect Nuclear Facilities, *Jane's Defence Weekly*, January 25, 2006.

68. Ibid.

69. Ibid.

70. "Iran Will Destroy Israeli Nuke Facilities if Attacked," *Agence France-Presse*, August 2004, http://www.rense.com/general56/kjune.htm; T. Orszaq-Land, "Iran Threatens to Abandon the NPT," Jane's Islamic Affairs Analyst, October 1, 2004.

71. David E. Sanger, "Cheney Says Israel Might 'Act First' on Iran," *New York Times*, January 21, 2005, http://www.nytimes.com/2005/01/21/politics/21cheney.html.

72. Target Iran—Air Strikes—2004 Developments, *GlobalSecurity.org*, http://www.globalsecurity.org/military/ops/iran-strikes-2004.htm.

73. "Iran Report," RFE/RL, 9, no. 2, January 23, 2006.

74. "Israel Said to Be Studying Iran Attack," *UPI*, December 4, 2008; "Israel 'Prepared to Attack' Iran Nuclear Plants," *Times online*, December 4, 2008; Tim Butcher, "Israel Willing to Go It Alone on Iran Attack," *The Telegraph*, December 4, 2008; Yaakov Katz, "IDF Preparing Options for Iran Strike," *Jerusalem Post*, December 4, 2008;

75. David E Sanger, "U.S. Rejected Aid for Israeli Raid on Iranian Nuclear Site," *New York Times*, January 11, 2009.

76. Barbara Opall-Rome, "Why Israel Won't Strike Iran's Nuclear Facilities Alone," *Defense News*, May 2, 2005.

77. Con Coughlin, "Israel Seeks All Clear for Iran Strike," *Daily Telegraph*, February 24, 2007.

78. Shlomo Brom, "Is the Begin Doctrine Still a Viable Option for Israel?" in *Getting Ready for A Nuclear Iran*, ed. Henry Sokolski and Patrick Clawson (Washington, DC: Strategic Studies Institute, October 2005).

79. http://www.globalsecurity.org/military/world/israel/f-15i-specs.htm.

80. Photos at http://www.fas.org/man/dod-101/sys/smart/gbu-28.htm.

81. Federaton of American Scientists, "Guided Bomb Unit-28 (GBU-28) BLU-113 Penetrator," http://www.fas.org/man/dod-101/sys/smart/gbu-28.htm.

82. Kenneth R. Timmerman, "War within Range," *FrontPageMagazine.com*, January 5, 2006, http://www.frontpagemag.com/Articles/Read.aspx?GUID=920D7D04-E360-48BB-AEDC-004767D4600D; and "Timmerman on Iran," *MissileThreat.com*, January 9, 2006, http://www.missilethreat.com/archives/id.577/detail.asp.

83. World Tribune, "U.S. Rushing Bunker-Busters to Israel," July 24, 2006, http://www.worldtribune.com/worldtribune/06/front2453941.072222222.html; The Hashmonean, "Special Delivery Please: Israel Requests 'Iran Busters,'" July 22, 2006, http://hashmonean.com/2006/07/22/special-delivery-please-israel-requests-iran-busters/. Other reports indicate that the weapon has a casing made out of an approximately 16-foot (5-meter) section of artillery barrel that is 14.5 inches (37 cm) in diameter. These barrels are made of extremely strong hardened steel to withstand the repeated blasts of artillery shells. There are nearly 650 pounds (295 kg) of tritonal explosive inside this casing. Tritonal is a mix of TNT (80 percent) and aluminum powder (20 percent). The aluminum improves the brisance of the TNT—the speed at which the explosive develops its maximum pressure. The addition of aluminum makes tritonal about 18 percent more powerful than TNT alone. A laser-guidance assembly is attached to the front of the barrel; the bomb homes in on the illuminated spot. The guidance assembly steers the bomb with fins that are part of the assembly. (See GBU-28 at howstuffworks.com.)

84. Associated Press, "US Agrees to Sell Israel Bunker-Busters," *International Herald Tribune*, September 15, 2008.

85. The 113-kg bomb is reported to have the same penetration capabilities as a normal 900-kg bomb, but only has 22.7 kg of explosives. It is 1.75 meters long. According to the *Jerusalem Post*, U.S. tests showed the bomb was capable of penetrating at least 90 cm of steel-reinforced concrete. The GBU-39 can be used in adverse weather conditions and has a stand-off range of more than 110 km due to pop-out wings.

86. Peter Brookes, "Iran-Israel Confrontation Brewing?" Heritage Foundation, *Military.com*, September 29, 2004, http://www.military.com/Opinions/0,,Brookes_092904,00.html.

87. Uzi Mahnami and Sarah Baxter, "Revealed: Israel Plans Nuclear Strike on Iran," *The Sunday Times*, January 7, 2007.

88. "Iran Says Russia Delivering S-300 Air Defense Systems," *Moscow Times*, December 22, 2008, http://www.themoscowtimes.com/article/1009/42/373338.htm; Saed Bannoura, "Russia to Sell Iran S-300 Surface-to-Air Missile System," IMEMC & Agencies, December 22, 2008, http://www.imemc.org/article/58108.

89. Ibid.

90. "Iran Takes Russian Air Defense System," *BBC*, December 22, 2008, http://www.military.com/news/article/iran-takes-russian-air-defense-system.html.

91. "Iran: Air Force," Global Security, October 7, 2008, http://www.globalsecurity.org/military/world/iran/airforce.htm; "Tomcat in Service with Iran," December 28, 2007, http://home.att.net/~jbaugher1/f14_6.html.

92. Ewen MacAskill and Simon Tisdall, "Iran's Message to the West: Back Off or We Retaliate," *Guardian* (London), February 2, 2006, http://www.guardian.co.uk/world/2006/feb/02/iran.nuclear.

93. "IAEA Chief Says Israeli Strike on Iran Would Be 'Insane,'" *Khaleej Times*, May 17, 2009.

94. http://www.globalsecurity.org/military/systems/munitions/blu-109-specs.htm.

95. http://www.globalsecurity.org/military/systems/munitions/jdam.htm.

96. http://www.globalsecurity.org/military/systems/munitions/blu-116.htm.

97. http://www.globalsecurity.org/military/systems/munitions/agm-130.htm.

98. NewsMax.com Wires, "U.S. Outfitting B-2's with Monster Bunker Buster Bombs—Iran May Be Target," July 27, 2007; Lisa Burgess, "New Bunker-Buster Fitted Aboard Stealth B-2 Bomber," *Mideast Stars and Stripes*, January 5, 2008, http://www.military-quotes.com/forum/new-bunker-buster-fitted-aboard-t51220.html. The United States experimented with the use of nuclear weapons to penetrate buried targets as early as 1998 and dropped B61-11 bomb casings that penetrated 15-25 feet before the point it would detonate. See Senior Airman Adam Stump. "B-2 Successfully Drops improved Bunker Buster Bomb," 354th Fighter Wing Public Affairs, Eielson Air Force Base, March 26, 1998, http://www.fas.org/nuke/guide/usa/bomber/n19980326_980417.html.

99. Robin Huges, "Tehran Takes Steps to Protect Nuclear Facilities," *Jane's Defence Weekly*, January 25, 2006.

100. December 20, 2002, edition of Fox News, The Big Story with John Gibson; April 12 edition of Fox News, *The O'Reilly Factor*, http://mediamatters.org/items/200604140006.

101. Jahangir Arasli, "Obsolete Weapons, Unconventional Tactics, and Martyrdom Zeal: How Iran Would Apply Its Asymmetric Warfare Doctrine in a Future Conflict," George C. Marshall European Center For Security Studies, Occasional Paper Series No. 10, April 2007.

102. Just how much over time is unclear. See Roger Stern, "The Iranian Petroleum Crisis and United States National Security," PNAS, PNAS 2007; 104,377-382, *PNAS.org*. Originally published on December 26, 2006, and updated to March 2007.

103. There are no reliable sources on Israeli forces. For good unclassified analysis, see the FAS, "Israel: Special Weapons Guided," http://www.fas.org/nuke/guide/israel/index.html; CDI, "Nuclear Weapons Database: Israeli Nuclear Delivery System," http://www.cdi.org/issues/nukef&f/database/isnukes.html; SPRI, "Israeli Nuclear Forces, 2006," www.sipri.org/contents/expcon/Israel.pdf, and NTI, "Country Overviews: Israel: Profile and NTI: Issue Brief: WMD in the Middle East" (www.nti.org/e_research/profiles/israel/index.html). There are also far more speculative reports such as Michael Carmichael, "Israel's Plans to Wage Nuclear War on Iran: History of Israel's Nuclear Arsenal, Hundreds of Nuclear Warheads under the Control of Israel's Defense Establishment," *Global Research*, January 15, 2007, http://www.globalresearch.ca/index.php?context=viewArticle&code=CAR20070115&articleId=4477; and PMA, "Israel Has Sub-Based Atomic Arms Capability," June 15, 2002, www.converge.org.nz/pma/cra0532.htm.

104. "WarGames" was released in June 1983, was directed by John Badham, and starred Matthew Brodrick, Danby Coleman, John Wood, and Ally Sheedy. The plot revolves around a U.S. decision to turn nuclear retaliation over to a computer that cannot distinguish between the exchange it can trigger and the reality of nuclear war, comparing such an exchange to a game of tic-tac-toe of which no one can win.

About the Authors

ANTHONY H. CORDESMAN holds the Arleigh A. Burke Chair in Strategy at the Center for Strategic and International Studies and is an analyst and commentator for ABC News. He has written extensively on energy and Middle Eastern politics, economics, demographics, and security. He has served in a number of senior positions in the U.S. government, including the Department of Energy, and several assignments in the Middle East.

ADAM C. SEITZ is research associate at the Center for Strategic and International Studies Burke Chair in Strategy where his research focus has been Middle East and South Asia security studies, weapons of mass destruction, weapons proliferation, terrorism, and asymmetric warfare. He has published a number of papers on these subjects, available at the CSIS Burke Chair Web site. Seitz served in the U.S. Army as an Intelligence Analyst and is an Operation Iraqi Freedom Veteran. He earned his B.A. in International Affairs from the University of Colorado.

Recent Titles by Anthony H. Cordesman